Advances in Spatial Science

Editorial Board

Manfred M. Fischer
Geoffrey J.D. Hewings
Anna Nagurney
Peter Nijkamp
Folke Snickars (Coordinating Editor)

For further volumes:
http://www.springer.com/series/3302

Johan Klaesson • Börje Johansson •
Charlie Karlsson
Editors

Metropolitan Regions

Knowledge Infrastructures
of the Global Economy

Editor
Assoc. Prof. Johan Klaesson
Prof. Dr. Börje Johansson
Prof. Dr. Charlie Karlsson

Department of Economics, Finance and Statistics
Jönköping International Business School
Jönköping University
Jönköping, Sweden

The Editors gratefully acknowledge financial support from the Swedish Agency for Economic and Regional Growth

ISSN 1430-9602
ISBN 978-3-642-32140-5   ISBN 978-3-642-32141-2 (eBook)
DOI 10.1007/978-3-642-32141-2
Springer Heidelberg New York Dordrecht London

Library of Congress Control Number: 2013931185

© Springer-Verlag Berlin Heidelberg 2013
This work is subject to copyright. All rights are reserved by the Publisher, whether the whole or part of the material is concerned, specifically the rights of translation, reprinting, reuse of illustrations, recitation, broadcasting, reproduction on microfilms or in any other physical way, and transmission or information storage and retrieval, electronic adaptation, computer software, or by similar or dissimilar methodology now known or hereafter developed. Exempted from this legal reservation are brief excerpts in connection with reviews or scholarly analysis or material supplied specifically for the purpose of being entered and executed on a computer system, for exclusive use by the purchaser of the work. Duplication of this publication or parts thereof is permitted only under the provisions of the Copyright Law of the Publisher's location, in its current version, and permission for use must always be obtained from Springer. Permissions for use may be obtained through RightsLink at the Copyright Clearance Center. Violations are liable to prosecution under the respective Copyright Law.
The use of general descriptive names, registered names, trademarks, service marks, etc. in this publication does not imply, even in the absence of a specific statement, that such names are exempt from the relevant protective laws and regulations and therefore free for general use.
While the advice and information in this book are believed to be true and accurate at the date of publication, neither the authors nor the editors nor the publisher can accept any legal responsibility for any errors or omissions that may be made. The publisher makes no warranty, express or implied, with respect to the material contained herein.

Printed on acid-free paper

Springer is part of Springer Science+Business Media (www.springer.com)

Contents

1 Introduction 1
Johan Klaesson, Börje johansson, and Charlie Karlsson

Part I Theory of Urban Growth

2 Agglomeration, Regional Growth, and Economic Development . . . 29
John M. Quigley

3 Urban Growth 47
Johan Klaesson and Börje Johansson

4 Knowledge Accessibility, Economic Growth and the Haavelmo Paradox 73
Åke E. Andersson

5 Urban Growth Policies: The Need to Set Realistic Expectations . . . 91
Paul C. Cheshire

6 Regional Economic Concentration and Growth 117
Scott R. Hacker, Johan Klaesson, Lars Pettersson, and Pär Sjölander

7 Metropolitan Labor Productivity and Urban Spatial Structure . . . 141
Evert J. Meijers

8 Wages, Productivity and Industry Composition 167
Johan Klaesson and Hanna Larsson

Part II Policies and Institutions of Urban Change

9 Scenarios for European Metropolitan Regions: Winners and Losers in a Globalized World 195
Roberta Capello and Ugo Fratesi

10 Metropolitan Regions and Export Renewal 235
Lina Bjerke and Charlie Karlsson

11 Market-Size and Employment 261
Martin Andersson and Johan Klaesson

12 Do Planning Policies Limit the Expansion of Cities? 275
Stephen Sheppard

13 The Importance of ICT for Cities: e-Governance and Cyber Perceptions 295
Peter Nijkamp and Galit Cohen-Blankshtain

14 Interlocking Firm Networks and Emerging Mega-City Regions in the Knowledge Economy 309
Alain Thierstein and Stefan Lüthi

Part III Case Studies of Urban Growth

15 Polycentric Urban Trajectories and Urban Cultural Economy 339
Michaël Deinema and Robert Kloosterman

16 Analysing the Competitive Advantage of Cities in the Dutch Randstad by Urban Market Overlap 375
Martijn J. Burger, Frank G. van Oort, Ronald S. Wall, and Mark J.P.M. Thissen

17 Capitalising on Institutional Diversity and Complementary Resources in Cross-Border Metropolitan Regions: The Case of Electronics Firms in Hong Kong and the Pearl River Delta 393
Javier Revilla Diez, Daniel Schiller, and Susanne Meyer

18 Impacts of Transport Infrastructure Policies in Population-Declining Metropolitan Area 425
Kiyoshi Yamasaki, Takayuki Ueda, and Shinichi Muto

19 Innovation and Knowledge Links in Metropolitan Regions: The Case of Vienna 451
Franz Tödtling and Michaela Trippl

20 Immigrant Location Patterns in a Southern European Metropolis: The Case of Athens 473
Paschalis A. Arvanitidis, George Petrakos, and Dimitrios Skouras

Contributors

Åke E. Andersson Jönköping International Business School, Jönköping, Sweden

Martin Andersson Economics, Jönköping International Business School (JIBS), Jönköping, Sweden; Jönköping and Royal Institute of Technology, Stockholm, Sweden

Paschalis A. Arvanitidis Department of Economics, University of Thessaly, Volos, Greece

Lina Bjerke Jönköping International Business School, Jönköping, Sweden

Martijn J. Burger Erasmus University Rotterdam and ERIM, Rotterdam, The Netherlands

Roberta Capello Department of Building, Environment, Science and Technology (BEST), Politecnico di Milano, Milan, Italy

Paul C. Cheshire Department of Geography and Environment, London School of Economics, London, UK

Galit Cohen-Blankshtain Department of Geography and School of Public Policy, Hebrew University, Jerusalem, Israel

Michaël Deinema University of Amsterdam, Amsterdam, The Netherlands

Javier Revilla Diez University of Hannover, Hannover, Germany

Ugo Fratesi Department of Building, Environment, Science and Technology (BEST), Politecnico di Milano, Milan, Italy

Scott R. Hacker Jönköping International Business School, Jönköping, Sweden

Börje Johansson Jönköping International Business School, Jönköping, Sweden Jönköping and Royal Institute of Technology, Stockholm, Sweden

Charlie Karlsson Jönköping International Business School, Jönköping, Sweden Jönköping and Royal Institute of Technology Stockholm, Sweden

Johan Klaesson Jönköping International Business School (JIBS), Jönköping, Sweden

Robert C. Kloosterman Amsterdam Institute of Metropolitan and International Development Studies (AMIDSt) and University of Amsterdam, Amsterdam, The Netherlands

Hanna Larsson Jönköping International Business School, Jönköping University, Jönköping, Sweden

Stefan Lüthi Chair for Territorial and Spatial Development, Munich University of Technology, Munich, Germany

Evert J. Meijers OTB Research Institute for the Built Environment, Delft University of Technology, Delft, The Netherlands

Susanne Meyer Yamanashi University, Yamanashi, Japan

Shinichi Muto Department of Civil and Environmental Planning, Yamanashi University, Yamanashi, Takeda, Kofu, Japan

Peter Nijkamp Department of Spatial Economics, VU University, Amsterdam, The Netherlands

Frank G. van Oort University Utrecht, The Netherlands

George Petrakos Department of Planning and Regional Development, University of Thessaly, Volos, Greece

Lars Pettersson Jönköping International Business School, Jönköping, Sweden; The Swedish Board of Agriculture, Jönköping, Sweden

John M. Quigley University of California, Berkeley, CA, USA

Daniel Schiller University of Hannover, Hannover, Germany

Stephen C. Sheppard Department of Economics, Williams College, Williamstown, MA, USA

Pär Sjölander Jönköping International Business School, Jönköping, Sweden; The Swedish Board of Agriculture, Jönköping, Sweden

Dimitrios Skouras Hellenic Army Aviation Corps. & Department of Planning and Regional Development, University of Thessaly, Volos, Greece

Alain Thierstein Chair for Territorial and Spatial Development, Munich University of Technology, Munich, Germany

Mark J.P.M. Thissen Netherlands Environmental Assessment Agency (PBL), The Netherlands

Franz Tödtling Institute for the Environment and Regional Development, Vienna University of Economics and Business, Vienna, Austria

Michaela Trippl Institute for the Environment and Regional Development, Vienna University of Economics and Business, Vienna, Austria

Takayuki Ueda School of Engineering, The University of Tokyo, Tokyo, Takeda, Kofu, Japan

Ronald S. Wall Erasmus University Rotterdam, Rotterdam, The Netherlands

Kiyoshi Yamasaki Value Management Institute, Tokyo, Takeda, Kofu, Japan

Chapter 1
Introduction

Johan Klaesson, Börje Johansson, and Charlie Karlsson

Metropolitan growth has been dramatic in the industrialized countries since the Second World War. Today, metropolitan regions are increasingly recognized as the national growth and development engines in a globalizing world (Jacobs 1984; Huggins 1997), and in particular as the driving forces in national as well as global innovation processes (Shefer and Frenkel 1998). In the industrialized countries, the metropolitan regions play a critical role not only as major generators of value added but also as major nodes for creativity, innovation and entrepreneurship as well as for communication and transportation. In line with Duranton and Puga (2005), one could claim that metropolitan regions are functionally specialized in the invention and creation on new products, i.e. innovation. Thus, since they are highly diversified and contain a broad range of different types of industries, local business services and firm sizes, they function as "incubator cities" (Chinitz 1961) or "nursery cities" (Duranton and Puga 2001), i.e. as superior 'incubators' for the development of innovations and for the development and growth of both new and small firms.

Traditionally, regional science research has shown that metropolitan regions provide agglomeration economies in the form of localization and urbanization economies to their economic actors. More recently, it has been stressed that they function as gateways to other regions, thus linking the economic actors in the region with economic actors in other regions nationally and abroad (Andersson and Andersson 2000, Eds.). These two aspects are critical not least for the innovative potential of metropolitan regions (Revilla Diez 2002). The innovative capacity of economic actors is not determined by their own R&D investments and capabilities only. Also the context matters, which implies that a region's innovative capacity is

---

J. Klaesson (✉)
Jönköping International Business School (JIBS), Jönköping, Sweden

B. Johansson • C. Karlsson
Jönköping International Business School (JIBS), Jönköping, Sweden and Royal Institute of Technology, Stockholm, Sweden

J. Klaesson et al. (eds.), *Metropolitan Regions*, Advances in Spatial Science,
DOI 10.1007/978-3-642-32141-2_1, © Springer-Verlag Berlin Heidelberg 2013

determined by region-specific location factors (Falck and Heblich 2008; Glaeser and Kerr 2009). The options for cooperation during innovation processes with regional partners as well as with partners in other regions are important location factors that reduce risks and uncertainties and offer opportunities for collective learning within clusters (De Bresson and Amesse 1991; Lakshmanan and Okumura 1995; Malecki and Oinas 1998; Ejermo and Karlsson 2006). The relevant partners include demanding customers, qualified suppliers, producer service companies, and competitors as well as research universities, and research institutes. Generally, innovation takes place in regions rich with knowledge-based location factors (Audretsch and Feldman 1996) and metropolitan regions are rich with such factors.

Due to their size, metropolitan regions offer a great variety and diversity of partners for innovative economic agents with a potential to ensure synergies in innovation processes. It should in this connection be observed that metropolitan regions are characterized by a high degree of openness. They are the major nodes in national and international transport and communication networks and as such they function, in particular, as import nodes for new ideas, new knowledge, and innovations (Jacobs 1969, 1984; Braudel 1979). They also host the majority of the economic actors that in particular benefit from this openness, namely the multi-national companies, domestic as well as foreign, which operate ownership, innovation, input, production, and delivery networks that include many countries and regions including other metropolitan regions and sometimes are of global proportions. Multinational companies increasingly tend to use several home bases in different metropolitan regions instead of being confined to one headquarter location in one specific metropolitan region in order to exploit resources across a wider geographical extent (Michie 2003).

Empirical studies in various countries during the last 15 years of the spatial distribution of innovative activities have convincingly shown that metropolitan regions have a high innovation potential (Anselin et al. 1997; Varga 1998; Brouwer et al. 1999; Beise and Stahl 1999; Andersson et al. 2008). Metropolitan regions have been found to be the most important locations for innovations generating 96 % of all registered product innovations in the US (Audretsch and Feldman 1999). The empirical results also indicate that diversity as suggested by Jacobs (1969) stimulates innovation. Sectoral specialization on a small number of industries generally seems to have a negative effect on the regional innovation output level.[1] Metropolitan regions are generally characterized by a more diverse economic structure than other regions, which tend to generate proportionally higher innovation outputs (Audretsch and Feldman 1999). Thus, metropolitan regions tend to offer favorable conditions for innovative economic agents. Here, these economic agents normally find a diversified economic structure, a qualified labor force, qualified and competent co-operation partners in the form customers, suppliers, competitors, producer service firms, research institutes, research universities, etc. (Ewers and Wettman 1980; Howells 1983; Suarez-Villa and Fischer 1995).

---

[1] However, there are a few studies indicating that specialization fosters innovation (Acs et al. 2002).

1 Introduction 3

Given the importance of metropolitan regions not least for innovation and growth it is critical to increase the understanding of

- How metropolitan regions function in terms of the simultaneous interactions between different metropolitan subsystems such as population, labor supply, housing, services, infrastructure, economy, workplaces, and metropolitan management, to provide a frugal seedbed for innovation,
- How the life cycles of metropolitan regions evolve over time,
- How metropolitan regions interact and compete with each other,
- How metropolitan regions interact with non-metropolitan regions,
- The factors determining differences among metropolitan regions in their capacity to nurture innovation and growth, and
- How metropolitan policies must be designed to secure the long-term vitality of metropolitan regions.

The purpose with this book is to contribute to an increased understanding of these three issues and the purpose of this introductory chapter is to lay a foundation to the contributions presented in this book.

1 Metropolitan Regions as Nodes in National and International Networks

Metropolitan regions may be perceived as large production and consumption systems based upon extensive information and knowledge processing. They are characterized by their agglomeration of economic activities and by their intra-regional transport infrastructure, facilitating very large movements of people, inputs and products within their interaction borders. One fundamental characteristic of a metropolitan region is the large integrated labor market with a much more intensive commuting as well as job search and search for labor within the region than between regions (Johansson 1997). The border of the integrated labor market region is a good approximation of the borders of a metropolitan region.[2]

In all industrialized countries the metropolitan regions are responsible for a major share of the economic activities. They are the major nodes in each country's inter-regional transport, communication and interaction networks and together they make up the major nodes in the same international networks. The role of metropolitan regions play in these networks has changed over time. When they started to develop they were normally locations for large scale industrial production. Today they are normally centers for decision making in business and government, negotiations, knowledge creation and other activities dependent upon face-to-face interaction but also for consumption and tourism.

---

[2] Fujita (1989) identifies an urban region by deriving increasing commuting costs from increasing distance to the city centre, which hosts the majority of all workplaces.

Metropolitan regions have developed out of smaller towns and cities that for extended periods have grown more rapidly than other towns and cities. However, their long term development not only include stages of fast growth but also stages of maturity, and in some cases stages of obsolescence and also decline (Jacobs 1961). Over time they have often developed specialized roles in the national and international systems (Noyelle and Stanback 1984) but at the same time they exhibit a degree of diversity not found in non-metropolitan regions. With technological and structural changes in the world economy the specialization of metropolitan regions may become obsolescent (Jacobs 1969) and rigidities develop due to that the specialization may delay the rejuvenation of their economies for extended periods. Some metropolitan regions may never be able to regain their previous position in the national and international systems since they lack locational attraction for expanding sectors in the international economy.

Urban regions develop at different speeds and in different directions in processes, which are interrelated with demographic processes. Migration and intra-urban relocation of households are not only reactions to the economic development of nations and urban regions but have their own dynamics due to different population cycles. Some of these phenomena are not only partly universal but also parallel among different industrialized nations and thus common to many urban and metropolitan regions, which may differ in many other aspects.

Urban and metropolitan regions are in many respects related. The development from a non-metropolitan to a metropolitan region is characterized by the expansion of population and economic activities and the construction of physical elements such as housing, industrial sites, office buildings, infrastructure and transportation facilities. Many attributes of these physical elements are shared by different metropolitan regions. The growth and expansion process of metropolitan regions has certain general effects, which are common for all metropolitan regions, such as more and more space becoming occupied by buildings, facilities, and other durable infrastructures and an increased density of economic activities in central locations.

Over time different rigidities are built into the metropolitan structure and the location of new economic activities becomes more demanding in terms of investments and relocation of more mature activities. Every metropolitan region develops from a young to an old structure, which may be very durable. However, the vitality may be preserved if enough resources are invested in renewal processes.

2 Market Potential and Metropolitan Regions

The concept of market potential can be used as a means to describe the economic concentration to and the opportunities of making contacts within and between metropolitan regions (Lakshmanan and Hansen 1965). There are strong reasons for making a precise distinction between the internal and the external market potentials of metropolitan regions. The geographic delineation of a metropolitan region is in a fundamental way related to the identification of its internal market

1 Introduction 5

potentials. The internal market potentials are measures of the existing opportunities in various markets inside the borders of a metropolitan region.

Goods and services vary with respect the contact- and/or interaction-intensity associated with their input and/or output transactions (von Thünen 1826; Lösch 1943; Hirsch 1967). Little or no direct contact between buyer and seller is necessary for goods and services with standardized and routine transaction procedures. Moreover, when a pair of suppliers and customers repeats the delivery of a certain good or service, the interaction between these two actors can normally be routinised, and hence the contact intensity decreases and the transaction costs decline. On the other hand, many goods and services are traded under complex and contact-intensive conditions, which often involve transaction phenomena such as inspection, negotiations and contract discussions, technical and legal consultation, and documentation of agreements. Such goods and services may themselves be complex and have a rich set of attributes. However, the basic thing is that, from a transaction point of view, they are not standardized, and the interaction procedures are not routine. A special case of a contact-intensive transaction is when a good or a service is customized and designed according to specifications made by the customer during an often time-consuming process of supplier-customer interaction.

Interaction costs are normally much lower for transactions within a metropolitan region than between regions. This implies that contact-intensive goods and services have distance-sensitive transaction costs and that these geographic transaction costs rise sharply when transactions are made between regions (Johansson and Karlsson 2001). Of course, goods and services can also be distance-sensitive with respect to input transactions. As a result, the interaction-frequency associated with distance-sensitive goods and services supplied in a given metropolitan region can be assumed to decrease with increasing time distance from the centre of the region (Holmberg et al. 2003).[3]

For each type of good or service in any region it is possible to divide the total market potential into the internal (intraregional) and the external (interregional) market potential. Companies who want to supply distance-sensitive goods or services must find a sufficiently large demand for their sales within their location region. Since internal economies of scale normally prevail, the internal market potential must exceed a certain threshold if companies producing distance-sensitive goods and services shall be able to make a profit. This implies that "economic density" matters (Ciccone and Hall 1996; Karlsson and Pettersson 2005), which gives metropolitan regions special advantages when it comes to supplying distance-intensive goods and services.

The size of the internal market potential in a metropolitan region is among other things a function of the capacity and quality of its interaction infrastructure. Such infrastructure has the role of offering high density combined with low transaction costs, i.e. a high intraregional accessibility (Johansson 1996). A high intraregional

---

[3] It is a general result from spatial interaction theory that the interaction intensity is a decreasing function of the time distance between origin and destination (Sen and Smith 1995).

accessibility implies that suppliers of distance-sensitive goods and services can reach a large number of potential customers and that producers can be reached by many suppliers offering distance-sensitive inputs as well as by many households supplying specialized labor inputs.

A rich infrastructure for interaction is a special characteristic of metropolitan regions. This infrastructure, which reduces interaction costs, primarily consists of the entire built environment with its various networks for transportation and communication and its many different arenas for meetings, negotiations, education, and so on (Batten et al. 1989; Kobayashi 1995). However, it also includes the links connecting the metropolitan region with other regions and the associated external market potential. The intra- and inter-regional infrastructure has two fundamental roles (Lakshmanan 1989): (1) it influences the consumption, production and innovation possibilities of regions, and (2) it is intrinsically a collective good in the sense that it is common to all economic agents in a region, households as well as companies. Thus, the infrastructure in a basic way will influence the internal and external market potential of a metropolitan region by (1) extending its spatial interaction links, and (2) determining the intra- and interregional accessibility of the region. Infrastructure also extends over time through its durability, which creates sustainable conditions for innovation, production and consumption for extended time periods.

The intra-regional infrastructure makes it possible to combine a high economic density with low interaction costs for all markets. High density and low geographic transaction costs in metropolitan regions imply 'thick' markets with large demand, many customers and suppliers and frequent transactions. Moreover, investments in the interaction infrastructure may also enlarge the markets of metropolitan regions in a complementary way by including more and more of surrounding geographic domains. In this case, extensions and/or improvements of transport infrastructure integrate new geographical areas with the metropolitan region by reducing the travel time distances to these areas. This form of enlargement also implies that the internal market potential of the metropolitan region grows.

3 Metropolitan Regions as Nodes of Knowledge Generation and Innovation

Earlier work have investigated metropolitan regions as innovation systems. Innovation systems consist of a number of actors that interact in generating, diffusing and using new knowledge. Such actors can be firms, organizations and institutions. Metropolitan (regional) innovation systems have been proposed to be more important than the national systems of innovation that where studied in the 1990s. (Fischer et al. 2001)

Metropolitan regions function as birth places for new technologies and innovations in the form of new products and/or new production methods. This implies that they attract economic agents specialized in innovation based upon specific external economies of scale, which arise at the regional level (Marshall 1920). There are two major groups of external economies: pecuniary externalities and knowledge externalities (Krugman 1991; Ellison and Glaeser 1997). Pecuniary externalities emanate from natural regional advantages such as natural and/or man-made resource endowments, advantageous location and/or comparatively low labor costs (Ellison and Glaeser 1999).

Knowledge externalities, on the other hand, need not be related to natural regional advantages but to a milieu that attracts highly skilled people, whose knowledge and experiences, knowledge exchange and knowledge creation contribute to increase the regional knowledge stock. Even if we assume that this knowledge is non-rival, it doesn't imply that it is freely accessible to everyone. In particular, new knowledge is not only highly specialized but also "sticky" (von Hippel 1994), i.e. highly contextual and uncertain. This implies the persons who should evaluate and apply it must have the relevant training but also opportunities for frequent face-to-face interaction to fully interpret it. Obviously, metropolitan regions have large advantages here since they offer both a large and varied supply of highly skilled people and a well-developed intra-regional transportation infrastructure together with a large variety of different meeting places suitable for intense face-to-face communication. Metropolitan regions offer comparative advantages in the production of new knowledge (Henderson 2005), and the costs of innovation tend to be lower in such regions (Feldman 1994). Thus, the formative, innovative stages of product development are more likely to be located in regions with diverse economies and corresponding spillovers, both of which is conducive to the creation of new products (Duranton and Puga 2001). Empirical evidences also clearly indicate that newly developed knowledge codified in the form of patents, in particular, stimulate the development of further knowledge within the same region (Jaffe et al. 1993). This implies that there is a distance-decay in the diffusion of knowledge, since the critical knowledge tends to be tacit, i.e. embodied in people and thus at least in the short-run stuck to the region of origin (Audretsch and Feldman 1996).

Innovations, which are yet un-standardized goods and services, tend to a high extent to be brought into the market via the entry of new companies (Aghion et al. 2009). The driving force behind innovation and thus entry originates often outside the set of incumbent companies, i.e. from companies and/or basic research laboratories in technology-related industries (Winter 1984). As the knowledge generated in private as well as public R&D laboratories is likely to spill out, metropolitan regions offer an atmosphere consisting of a variety of intellectual externalities waiting to be absorbed by entrepreneurs consistent with the idea of inter-industry spillovers resulting from the diversity in metropolitan regions advanced by Jacobs (1969). Metropolitan regions also offer a large enough internal market potential to make the launching of innovations profitable as well as the low internal geographical transaction costs, which are critical for reducing the interaction costs for the companies developing innovations.

Entrepreneurs in metropolitan regions are likely to have lived in the region all their life or at least to have lived and worked there for many years (Keeble and Walker 1994; Saxenian 1999; Greene et al. 2008). This implies that these entrepreneurs have had time to create dense social networks based upon past experience and frequent social interactions in the region that provide access to information and knowledge but also facilitate the process of resource generation (Stuart and Sorensen 2005; Michelacci and Silva 2007). Thus, entrepreneurship should be looked upon as a regional phenomenon (Feldman 2001; Stam 2007) stimulated by the entrepreneurial opportunities, which emerge from the regional economic milieu. In metropolitan regions it is in particular various diverse knowledge externalities, which stimulate various kinds of innovation-driven entrepreneurship.

Knowledge-intensive and high-tech industries tend to locate in new spatial patterns with a preference for larger metropolitan regions with a rich and varied supply of higher education, research, and cultural and other amenities. This implies for smaller metropolitan regions that the adjustment to technological and structural changes in the world economy and shifts in the international division of labor is of special importance. If they fail to adjust their way of functioning to the changes in the world economy and the reorientation and expansion of R&D activities they may become the losers in the international competition between metropolitan regions. Thus, for these regions the renewal of the internal structure and revitalization of their international contact patterns is critical.

4 Internal Dynamics of Metropolitan Regions and Metropolitan Management

Over time, a metropolitan region must adjust its internal structure in response to external technological, economic and demographic changes to preserve its vitality and competitiveness. The changes include short term economic fluctuations as well as slowly changing conditions as regards the metropolitan region's interaction and exchange with other regional economies nationally and internationally. The foundation of this theory of nested dynamics of metropolitan processes and policies originated from the work of the IIASA regional development group in the early 1980s. One slow internal process, which functions as an almost exogenous driving force is the time-dependent change in the age composition of the region's population.

The internal processes of metropolitan change include complex dynamics of spatial relocation of firms and households, the entry, growth and exit of firms, goods and services, household formation, which are influenced by prevailing in-congruencies between the supply of and the demand for capacities in the transportation, facility, housing, and service systems. To influence these processes and to support metropolitan development there exist a number of instruments for the management of metropolitan regions including land use planning, regulation and taxation, investments in infrastructure, operation of public facilities and services, migration and labor market policies, housing market control, and policies aiming at stimulating innovation and entrepreneurship.

Seen from a long-term perspective, the instruments for metropolitan management may affect the attractiveness and development potential of the metropolitan region. In this context, the metropolitan policies may try to influence the location

1 Introduction

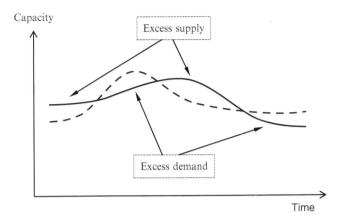

Fig. 1.1 Tension signals (Source: Johansson 1985, p. 117)

of (1) public and private R&D activities and institutions of higher education, (2) infrastructure and communication networks, (3) labor with different education, skill and competence profiles, and (4) manufacturing and service firms.

A major part of the metropolitan management takes the form of adjustments and responses to signals of malfunctioning and tensions in the various metropolitan systems. However, such signals may be misleading seen from a longer time perspective, if the dynamics of the actual system are only vaguely understood. Figure 1.1 highlights a case in which both the demand and the supply of capacity develops in a smooth way. In spite of this the tension signals do fluctuate. The "capacity" in the figure may refer to any metropolitan system, such as the labor market, the land market, the market for office space, the housing market or the market for metropolitan transport.

Although the two developments paths in Fig. 1.1 follow each other fairly closely, the sign of the capacity tension fluctuates. Quick responses to this type of signals risk aggravating the short-term mismatching, and causing new oscillations in the supply and demand paths, and thereby produce confusing signals of tension. Actually, the possible overshooting in the response pattern may be obtained through both (1) planning and public interventions, and (2) market reactions. In many cases the market and public metropolitan management may stimulate each other to an "over-reactive" behavior. When the speed of change is fast in a certain dimension, the imbalances in some metropolitan systems may be substantial. In highly attractive metropolitan regions, local inflation in the housing market and related service sectors and congestion in the transportation networks are typical indicators of disequilibria.

Metropolitan management and market behavior associated with the change processes of the type described above concerns to large extent extremely durable structures. Construction and location of infrastructure, housing areas, service and manufacturing sites, and commercial centers usually affects the life of metropolitan regions many decades into the future. A lot of metropolitan structures were determined many decades and even centuries ago. In particular, the process of capital formation determines the anatomy of the whole metropolitan region.

5 Speed of Adjustment: Fast and Slow Processes

A common element of the change processes in most metropolitan regions is the inertia in the inter-process adjustment mechanisms. As housing is constructed in peripheral rings to accommodate an increasing population, the pressure on the land in the down-town business district may accelerate. A relocation of households and workplaces between different zones in a metropolitan region may bring about multi-faceted tensions in the sense that both the land market and the transport system are affected. The tensions and their signals of manifestation give rise to adjustments on different time scales. Capital stock inertia and differentials in household and sector mobility may thereby give different zones traits, which are typical for their vintage of construction.

Figure 1.2 is an attempt to provide a schematic illustration of generic types of adjustment processes in metropolitan regions. The interaction between the production system and the given infrastructure comprises adjustments, which are close to be instantaneous, given the capacity constraints that prevail at each point in time and space. Changes in the capacity constraints and relocations must be filtered through time-consuming decision and investment processes. Thus, investment and relocation decisions are delayed in relation to the observed tension signals of under- or over-utilization of existing capacities (in the form of congestion, queuing, local inflation, etc.).

Investment processes bring about new capacities at a slower pace than the B-type interactions (capacity use). The resource consumption in the investment activities contains fast adjustments. The capacity change in individual locations within metropolitan regions occur with sudden jumps, but the overall change of capacities in the production, housing and transportation systems is a much slower process than the adjustments of B-type. Investments in the built structure in a metropolitan region, for example, seldom reach more than a few percent of the value of existing structures. Spatial relocation of households and production units of various kinds represents a medium-speed type of adjustments.

The classification in Fig. 1.2 can be used to shed light on the possibilities to explain, model and forecast metropolitan dynamics. If a model is applied to analyze the fast adjustments, the slower processes will appear disguised in the form of parameters in the model. Similarly, a model of the slow adjustments will contain parameters, which are explicitly or implicitly affected by the fast adjustment mechanisms. In both cases, the parameters are not actually constants but may instead change slowly over time. Nonlinear models will in this case generate sudden shifts, i.e. catastrophes, based upon bifurcations or singularities in the model behavior for certain parameter values (Varaiya and Wiseman 1984).

The problem of the relationship between fast and slow processes in metropolitan development may also be studied from a slightly different perspective. If the system illustrated in Fig. 1.2 develops in such a manner that new capacities are created at the same speed as the demand for new capacities, there will be no imbalances or tensions. Such change processes develop along trajectories, which may be looked upon as equilibrium paths. In a sense such a path represents a balanced rate of change for the

1 Introduction

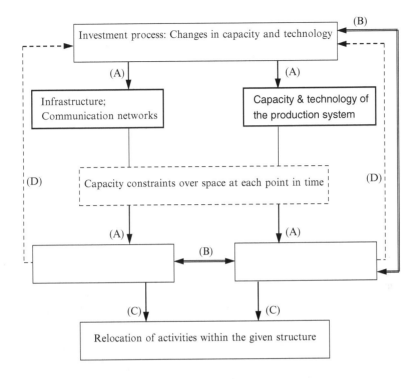

(A) Delayed adjustments that affect specific capacities in specific locations with sudden jumps; the overall change of capacities is usually slow
(B) Fast adjustments
(C) Delayed, medium speed adjustments
(D) Investment decisions which generally involve considerable time lags

Fig. 1.2 Variations in speed of adjustment (Source: Johansson 1985)

system as a whole. However, a system following such a steady path may suddenly be influenced by strong exogenous changes, e.g. a fall in the demand for certain of the metropolitan region's export products or a shift in migration or fertility rates. Such exogenous changes will bring about a faster speed of change in some parts of the system.

A third type of change is the catastrophes mentioned above. In this case, it is usually possible to pick out a specific subset from a large dynamic process in such a way that the smaller system describes the mechanisms that give rise to catastrophic shifts in the speed of change (Casti 1985). Figure 1.3 illustrates a case in which shifts occur repetitively (cyclically), possibly with a long duration for the slow phases. The figure may for example describe the relation between land values and activity density in a given zone in a metropolitan region. The centre point of the figure represents an unstable equilibrium of the change process. The system illustrated will develop in cycles around the equilibrium point with longer periods of slow change broken by short periods of fast change.

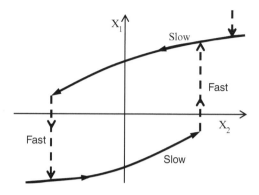

Fig. 1.3 Oscillations of fast and slow time scales (Source: Johansson 1985)

6 Market Potential and the Development of Metropolitan Regions

The input and output market potentials of metropolitan regions represent factors that adjust on a slow time scale, which implies that the growth (and decline) of metropolitan regions is a gradual process. This in turn implies that these market potentials, as well as their specific components, play the same role as metropolitan infrastructure. The input and output market potentials of a metropolitan region provide arenas for processes that adjust on a fast or medium-speed time scale. It should in this connection be observed that the input market potential comprise, among other things, the supply of capital, labor (with different education, experiences and skills), and built environment of the metropolitan region, which are all factors emphasized in resource-based models of regional economic development.

Metropolitan regions are among other things characterized by a knowledge-intensive labor force, which raises questions about the factors attracting such labor to metropolitan regions. Many empirical studies support the assumption that households whose members have a university education and other specific skill attributes, such as entrepreneurial skills, are attracted to migrate to and stay in regions that offer an attractive regional household milieu (Glaeser et al. 2001; Clark et al. 2002; Florida 2002). The regional household milieu consists of, on the one hand, natural amenities including climate conditions in the region, and, on the other hand, the household infrastructure in the region. The regional household infrastructure comprises the region's housing market potential and the accessibility it offers from housing areas to other market potentials in the form of different kinds of (1) household services, (2) amenities, (3) institutions of higher education, and (4) job opportunities in different workplace areas. Regions with an attractive household milieu are among other things characterized by large and varied household market potentials, which is one of the characteristics of metropolitan regions.

The perspective presented here implies that a metropolitan region's household milieu is a partly independent attractor (repellent) of household location and regional labor supply. However, it also implies that regional labor markets adjust by means of a process where companies follow the location of the labor supply, rather than the opposite (Quigley 1990; Maclellan 1990). This form of causation is associated with

1 Introduction

the "knowledge society" in which the growing economic sectors have a high demand for knowledge-intensive labor, primarily with a university education. Under these conditions, knowledge-intensive households chose residential location in regions with an attractive household milieu, which to a high extent tend to be metropolitan regions. As a result, companies with a large demand for knowledge-intensive labor have to adjust their location accordingly. Thus, the supply of knowledge-intensive labor is one of the factors driving the growth of metropolitan regions.

The overall market potential of a metropolitan region, i.e. its size and density, is an infrastructure phenomenon in itself. It changes in a process of very slow adjustments and offers collective market opportunities that benefit both households and companies. In growing metropolitan regions, the location of households and firms form a self-reinforcing dynamic process, i.e. a cumulative causation process with positive feed-backs (Myrdal 1957). These positive feed-backs are in general constrained, on the one hand, by the development of the demand in the metropolitan region and in its external markets, and, on the other hand by the existing capacities in the form of built environment, the accessibility offered by the transport system, production capacities, and labor supply. For the expansion of certain activities these constraints may not be binding, whereas the expansion of other activities requires adjustments of durable capacities. The market potential can be assumed to adjust on a faster time scale than the durable capacities. In the longer time perspective, regional capacities and the regional economic and household milieu will adjust through a system of coupled feed-backs.

Over time, the (slow) formation of regional infrastructure affects the household and company location processes by gradually building up the basic conditions for the household milieu and the economic milieu of companies. Naturally, the economic milieu is partly determined by the household and company location processes. However, it is natural to assume that the household milieu and the economic milieu, respectively, as a whole changes at a much slower pace than the location of households and companies. Hence, in a limited time perspective it is possible to treat the milieu characteristics as approximately invariant. The regional change process described here has the form of interdependent dynamics such that companies and households mutually adjust to each other.

7 Organization and Content of the Book

7.1 Part 1 Theory of Urban Growth

7.1.1 Chapter 2. John M. Quigley

Agglomeration, Urbanization, and the Growth of Metropolitan Regions
The United Nations Population Fund released a report declaring that for the first time in recorded history, more than half the world's population resided in urban – not rural – areas. Another report from the United Nation argued that in

many cases the economic circumstances of urban migrants are worse than those of rural peasants. How bad can urbanization be for the development process? Urbanization simply cannot be all that bad for those who live in cities in developing countries – after all, in most instances migrants to cities and urban areas could simply return to rural life if such moves improved their economic circumstances.

In this essay, we consider the evidence about the mechanisms increasing economic efficiency in metropolitan regions and the record of cities in facilitating economic output and improving the consumption opportunities available to workers. Much of this evidence is based on observations on highly-developed countries, but a growing body of evidence is based upon analyses of developing economies and low-income countries. This evidence clearly supports the conclusion that cities and metropolitan conurbations are important in facilitating economic growth, increasing worker productivity and augmenting incomes in poor and rich nations alike. Policies to facilitate, not inhibit, urbanization will improve economic conditions in developing countries. The analysis suggests a variety of broad polices – predispositions for policy – that would improve resource allocation and increase incomes in poorer countries.

7.1.2 Chapter 3. Börje Johansson and Johan Klaesson

Urban Growth: Co-evolution of Producer Services and Other Sectors.
A major characteristic of the economic development in Sweden during the past 10–15 years is a fast expansion of the producer-service sector. To analyse this process, the present paper employs an approach to identify the spatial pattern of local, regional and extra-regional demand for producer services. In the associated theoretical model producer-service firms grow in locations with large market access. The estimated model predicts that the supply of producer services grows in urban areas with large market access, whereas the rest of the economy shrinks in the same areas and expands in other parts of the urban region. The change process is interpreted as an effect of firms' outsourcing of service activities when they can rely on accessibility to service suppliers. As a result service suppliers agglomerate in central parts of the urban region, where they obtain high accessibility to their customers. The estimated change process comprises a non-linear response mechanism.

7.1.3 Chapter 4. Åke E. Andersson

Knowledge Accessibility, Economic Growth and the Haavelmo Paradox
Economic growth has conventionally been modelled for space-less economies. Econometrically, growth models have mostly been estimated on time series of national economies with minimal distinctions between economies as large as Japan or the USA and as small as the smallest economies of Asia and Europe. This approach to the analysis of economic growth is especially dangerous when the impact of scientific and technological knowledge is important for the process of growth. Creative activities and the formation of knowledge is highly clustered

in space. Thus, the spatial distribution of accessibility to knowledge capital and investments determines economic growth of nations and other spatial aggregates.

The Haavelmo paradox contrasts chaos as the generic property of non-linear dynamic models with the fact that most statistics on macroeconomic growth processes tend towards persistent constant positive rates of growth. The paradox can be resolved if the non-linear dynamic model is subdivided into fast, private variables and very slow, public variables. Modelling spatial accessibility of knowledge as a slow, public variable and machinery and similar material capital as a relatively faster, private variable ensures stable growth, at least in the short and medium terms of the economic growth processes.

7.1.4   Chapter 5. Paul C. Cheshire

Urban Growth Policies: The Need to Set Realistic Expectations
This paper reviews local growth promotion policies in the light of an analysis of the drivers of differential urban growth. It starts by arguing that major shifts in urban functions interacting with European integration and the wider process of internationalisation, have produced incentives to create local growth promotion agencies. The supporters of such agencies and the agencies themselves naturally have to make claims both as to their necessity and their likely success. An analysis of growth drivers, however, shows that there is only a restricted scope for local – indeed any – policy to influence city growth. Moreover, some existing policies work directly against urban economic growth. The most successful policies are likely to be the efficient execution of well known functions, including policies to reduce the costs of city size and efficient public administration. There is a danger, therefore, not only of raising expectations with respect to the potential contribution of local growth promotion agencies but of such agencies concentrating on inappropriate actions which are more visible but likely to be less effective.

7.1.5   Chapter 6. Scott R. Hacker, Johan Klaesson, Lars Pettersson and Pär Sjölander

Regional Economic Concentration and Growth. The Effects of Agglomeration in Different Types of Regions.
The regional relationships between agglomeration and economic growth are expected to be different in different types of regions. In the literature of the new economic geography it is common to stress the importance of access to cities with agglomeration of economic activities in the form of firms and households in order to be able to explain regional growth. However, it is also well known that many rural areas are performing fairly well in terms of employment and economic opportunities.

The purpose of the present research is to analyze if concentration of population drives economic growth or if it is the other way around. A second question is if this

16   J. Klaesson et al.

relationship between concentration of population and growth is different in different types of regions.

In order to shed light on these two questions the economic performance of three types of Swedish regions (metropolitan-, cities- and rural regions) is related to changes in population densities.

In the empirical analysis the Shannon index is used in the measurement of regional concentration. By considering the effect of previous levels of the Shannon index on average wages we extract information on how regional concentration affects regional economic growth (expressed as growth in average wages). In the empirical analysis we employ a VAR Granger causality approach on regional Swedish yearly data from 1987 to 2006. From this analysis we are able to conclude that there are strong empirical indications that geographic agglomeration of population unidirectionally drives economic growth in metropolitan- and city regions. Concerning the rural regions no such indication is found in either direction. This is a fairly strong indication that urban regions are more dependent on economies of agglomeration compared to rural areas.

7.1.6 Chapter 7. Evert J. Meijers

Metropolitan Labor Productivity and Urban Spatial Structure. A comparison of U.S. Monocentric and Polycentric Metropolitan Regions

This paper questions the extent to which agglomeration economies can develop in a cluster of close-by cities, so-called polycentric metropolitan regions or polycentric urban regions (PURs). Theory suggests that agglomeration economies are also increasingly associated with more dispersed spatial structures. Are polycentric metropolitan regions, despite their polycentric spatial layout, able to reap the advantages of urban size to a similar extent as monocentric metropolitan regions? By means of a novel method, the most monocentric metropolitan regions (a MSA or CSA dominated by a single city) and most polycentric metropolitan regions (MSAs or CSAs in which several cities of rather equal size are located close-by) are identified. Polycentric metropolitan regions are furthermore divided into conurbations and polycentric metropolitan regions proper, which is based on the question of whether the cities in a polycentric metropolitan region are part of a contiguous urban area (conurbation) or not. Labour productivity serves as a proxy for agglomeration economies. Using 2006 data, strong evidence was found for metropolitan labour productivity, and hence agglomeration economies, being higher in polycentric metropolitan regions compared to monocentric ones. Referring to Alonso, this means that in polycentric metropolitan regions, cities are able to 'borrow size' from each other. The findings suggest that the location of a city nearby other relatively similar-sized cities results in a 'borrowed size' effect of 11 % in polycentric metropolitan regions. This borrowed size effects suggests that polycentric metropolitan regions on average outperform monocentric, single cities, controlling for the size of the urban population, urban density, human capital and the structure of the metropolitan economy. A similar result is found when explaining mean annual wages, though the elasticity of urban spatial structure is 5.7 %. Polycentric conurbations resemble monocentric metropolitan regions more. Furthermore, it is demonstrated that while many sectors of economic activity have a stronger presence in monocentric metropolitan regions, productivity in many sectors tends to be higher in polycentric metropolitan regions. One explanation is that the spatial range of agglomeration advantages has been regionalized, while agglomeration diseconomies remain relatively more limited to the local level.

7.1.7 Chapter 8. Johan Klaesson and Hanna Larsson

Wages, Productivity and Industry Composition: Agglomeration Economies in Swedish Regions

It is a well known fact that wages have a tendency to be higher in larger regions. The source of the regional difference in wages between larger and smaller areas can be broadly divided into two parts. The first part can be attributed to the fact that regions have different industrial compositions. The second part is due to the fact that average regional productivity differs between regions. Using a decomposition method, akin to shift-share, we are able to separate regional wage disparities into an industrial composition component and productivity component. According to theory it is expected that productivity is higher in larger regions due to different kinds of economies of agglomeration. Also, larger regions are able to host a wider array of sectors compared to smaller regions. Output from sectors demanding a large local or regional market can only locate in larger regions. Examples of such sectors are e.g. various types of advanced services with high average wages. The purpose of the paper is to explain regional differences in wages and the productivity and composition components, respectively.

The paper tests the dependence of wages, productivity and industrial composition effects on regional size (using a market potential measure). In the estimation we control for regional differences in education, employment shares, average firm size and self-employment. Swedish regional data from 2004 are used. The results verify that larger regions on average have higher wages, originating from higher productivity and more favourable industry composition.

7.2 Part 2 Institutions and Policies of Urban Change

7.2.1 Chapter 9. Roberta Capello and Ugo Fratesi

Scenarios for European Metropolitan Regions: Winners and Losers in a Globalized World

Cities are highlighted in traditional theories to be the most efficient drivers of economic growth; they pro-act, and react, to economic volatility, by anticipating expectations on future economic trends and by absorbing the economic effects once they take place. This is true for both virtuous as well as declining cycles of development. The reasons for their static and dynamic efficiency lie in three main elements: the physical size, source of economies of scale; the functional specialisation in advanced value-added functions, source of creativity, learning, and knowledge; the urban system (or the network of cities) in which cities lie, where advantages of scale can easily be exploited avoiding hyper-concentration of production and residential activities. In the age of globalisation like the one we are going through nowadays, cities are areas able to grasp advantages of international competition from outside Europe, and they are expected to be the drivers of growth. In this paper, the aim is to analyse – with a prospective approach – the economic performance that European cities will manifest under different assumptions on the globalisation patterns that may develop in the future. With respect to the present literature, this paper contributes in two new directions: firstly, the aim is to highlight empirically the different actions and reactions that cities of different size, different functional specialisation and located in regions with different settlement structures have in front of a world economic integration; secondly, the aim is to analyse how cities act and react to alternative globalisation patterns, to different quality of competition from outside Europe, which may be sources of different opportunities and threats for different urban areas.

7.2.2 Chapter 10. Lina Bjerke and Charlie Karlsson

Metropolitan Regions and Export Renewal

In smaller countries, the non-metropolitan regions are to a substantial degree linked together with the metropolitan regions through various networks. The national infrastructure and transport networks are often organised with the metropolitan region as the central hub. This creates a number of dependencies between the metropolitan region and the non-metropolitan regions in a small country. In this paper we focus on the role that metropolitan regions play for the renewal of the export base in the non-metropolitan regions in a small country. The analytical part can be divided into three main parts: (1) the role of the Stockholm metropolitan region for the renewal of the export base in the rest of Sweden between 1997 and 2003; (2) which non-metropolitan regions gain renewal of their export base; and (3) what factors can explain the spatial distribution of these gains. The results show that distance has little to do with the potential success of an export products diffused from Stockholm. Instead, regional characteristics such as a large manufacturing sector, educational level, size of public and/or agricultural sector, and access to producer services have a larger influential potential.

7.2.3 Chapter 11. Martin Andersson and Johan Klaesson

Market-Size and Employment: Separating Scale and Diversity Effects.

What drives the relation between market-size and employment? There is a relationship between the size of an agglomeration and its diversity; in terms of number of sectors present and in terms of number of firms within each sector. There is also a relationship between the size of different agglomerations and the average size of firms located in them. Total employment in a region may be expressed as the product of number of sectors, number of firms in each sector and average firm size in each sector.

In the literature it is emphasized that diversity may be important for aggregate productivity and growth. The scale of operations in individual firms may also be important for productivity. Thus, the productivity in a region depends on both external and internal economies of scale. Looking at the relationship between regional size and employment it is possible to reveal the relative importance of each of the three factors.

The applied technique allows us to untangle the overall elasticity of employment with respect to market-size and estimate the contribution of each component to the overall elasticity. Using data on Swedish regions over the time period 1990–2004 we show that there are marked differences between manufacturing and service sectors in terms of the contribution of the different components to the overall elasticity. The contribution of the respective component is also different for regional and extra-regional market-size.

7.2.4 Chapter 12. Stephen Sheppard

Do Planning Policies Limit the Expansion of Cities?

> ... it is essential ... that the town should be planned as a whole, and not left to grow up in a chaotic manner as has been the case with all English towns, and more or less with the towns of all countries. A town, like a flower, or a tree, or an animal, should, at each stage of its growth, possess unity, symmetry, completeness, and the effect of growth should never be to destroy that unity, but to give it greater purpose. ... (Ebenezer Howard, Garden Cities of Tomorrow 1898)

This paper considers whether planning policies, as practiced in the world's cities, have the potential for controlling or limiting the expansion of urban land use. The question is certainly relevant for design of policies to respond to urban sprawl. The analysis does not establish that these constraints are necessarily desirable, but does find some evidence that some aspects of planning regulations can be effective in limiting urban expansion.

7.2.5 Chapter 13. Peter Nijkamp and Galit Cohen-Blankshtain

The Importance of ICT for Cities: e-Governance and Cyber Perceptions

This paper offers a critical review of current debates on the importance and the potential of ICT for modern cities. Much attention is given to the opportunities offered by local e-governance, as a systematic strategy to exploit the potential of ICT for the public domain in European cities. Since the views of many experts and elected policy-makers in cities (so-called 'urban frontliners') is coloured by subjective expectations and perceptions, we examine in particular the extent to which the expected influences of ICT, as perceived by urban frontliners, affect their perceptions of the relevance of ICT to mitigate contemporary urban challenges. The final (empirical) part of the paper addresses the issue of the systematic study of cyber perceptions of cities in Europe.

20 J. Klaesson et al.

7.2.6 Chapter 14. Alain Thierstein and Stefan Lüthi

Interlocking Firm Networks and Emerging Mega-City Regions in the Knowledge Economy

Globalisation has entailed a reorganisation of spatial development processes on a global, European, national and regional scale. Cities cannot be separated from their regional hinterlands as they often compose a functional division of labour in terms of different kinds of services and value chains among firms. A process of selective decentralisation of particular urban functions has led to the emergence of polycentric Mega-City Regions. The main objective of this contribution lies in the exploration of the Mega-City Region hypothesis. One section focuses on the theoretical building blocks of the Mega-City Region concept. Based on these findings, the next section explains the Mega-City Region hypothesis that identifies polycentric Mega-City Regions as an emerging spatial phenomenon based on re-scaling processes of agglomeration and network economies. Mega-City Regions is the result of two interdependent processes: agglomeration economies as well as network economies. Agglomeration economies result from the clustering of knowledge-intensive firms in certain areas enabling them to benefit from spatial proximity. Network economies, however, result from global sourcing strategies of knowledge-intensive firms leading to relational proximity and international knowledge exchange.

7.3 Part 3 Case Studies of Urban Growth

7.3.1 Chapter 15. Michaël Deinema and Robert Kloosterman

Polycentric Urban Trajectories and Urban Cultural Economy: Cultural Industries in Dutch Cities Since 1900.

This chapter traces the urban employment trends in cultural industries in the Netherlands from 1899 onwards and argues that a historical approach is necessary to understand economic geographical patterns in this post-industrial growth sector. Longitudinal employment data for the country's four main cities and case-study information on the spatial and institutional development of separate cultural industries in the Netherlands reveal long-term intercity hierarchies of performance and historically-rooted local specializations in different forms of cultural production. The effects of historical local trajectories on the present-day distribution of cultural industry activities between the major Dutch cities are tentatively weighed against more volatile factors such as creative class densities. Implications for the general outlook and development of these post-industrial urban economies are then explored, whereby the connectivity of the cities in international and regional networks is taken into account. The chapter concludes with identifying the evolutionary mechanisms at work in Dutch cultural industries and the value of a historical perspective vis-à-vis other geographical approaches to the urban

1 Introduction

cultural economy. As the four cities are all part of the Randstad megacity region, the dynamic Dutch urban cultural economy represents an unlikely case for stable inequalities between cities based on local trajectories, so that strong implications may be inferred for cultural industry dynamic in other contexts.

7.3.2 Chapter 16. Martijn J. Burger, Frank G. van Oort, Ronald S. Wall and Mark J.P.M. Thissen

Analysing the Competitive Advantage of Cities in the Dutch Randstad by Urban Market Overlap

At the present day and age, it has become widely acknowledged in urban studies and the planning literature that cities compete over product markets, inward investments, firm establishments, tourists, hallmark events and government funding and that this competition takes place at a local, regional, national, and even continental and global scales. In order to maintain their position within the urban system, cities have to work on their competitiveness, or their ability to successfully compete with other cities. In order to keep and attract firms, workers and tourists one should not only think of cost reductions such as tax credits and project financing, but also of investments in amenities, physical infrastructure, and public transportation networks.

In this chapter we focus on the measurement of revealed competition between cities. We calculate the relative amount of market overlap that a certain city has with any other city within an urban system, identify clusters of competitive cities, and the determinants of this competition. We thus measure the intensity of competition between cities in the Dutch Randstad on the basis of the functional linkages that these cities have with other cities. Cities are in competition to the extent that they serve the same market area for the same urban functions. We will focus on economic competition between cities in terms of providing similar products to the same market areas. In particular, attention is paid to firms in basic sectors, which have a non-local export market and are according to Economic Base Theory.

Our main conclusion is that in the Dutch Randstad region, urban competition is more the rule than the much-anticipated urban complementarities, as urban functional influences – especially of the four largest cities – spatially overlap. The prosperous co-evolution of the Randstad economy with growing urban competition even suggests a positive relationship that better should not be battled by policy.

7.3.3 Chapter 17. Javier Revilla Diez, Daniel Schiller and Susanne Meyer

Capitalising on Institutional Diversity and Complementary Resources in Cross-Border Metropolitan Regions: The Case of Electronics Firms in Hong Kong and the Pearl River Delta

The opening of China during the last 30 years has resulted in tremendous cross-border economic activities of Hong Kong manufacturers in the Pearl River Delta (PRD). More recently, the competitiveness of the business model has been put under strain by forceful challenges that change the business environment in the PRD: rising production costs, upgrading pressures, new regulations for export processing businesses, labour shortages, a more employee-friendly labour law, and environmental issues. Against this background, it is the purpose of this paper to present and discuss findings from two surveys of electronics firms in HK and the PRD conducted in 2007 and 2008. The research question is based on the agility hypothesis, that supposes that business in highly competitive environments depends on competencies and resources of firms to capitalise on formal and informal business practices alike to gain flexibility. The results of our analysis may help to better understand how the HK-PRD business model did develop and eventually may sustain its competitiveness in the face of new challenges.

The chapter is based on the assumption that cost- and time-sensitive production in the Greater Pearl River Delta (GPRD) is embedded within fragmented global value chains and therefore largely benefits from informal dynamics.

7.3.4 Chapter 18. Kiyoshi Yamasaki, Takayuki Ueda and Shinichi Muto

Impacts of Transport Infrastructure Policies in Population-Declining Metropolitan Area: Business Productivity and Quality of Urban Life in Tokyo

In Tokyo metropolitan area, the population growth and the economic growth have caused the serious urban problems like sprawl at urban fringe, heavy congestion not only in road network but also in rail network, environmental emission and so on. Although there still now remain the difficult problems for us to tackle with, the transport infrastructure policies until today have succeeded in sustaining the high business productivity and quality of urban life in the population-growing trend. The spatial agglomeration in Tokyo metropolitan area has been functioning effectively with the transport infrastructures.

Japan is however now at the down-slope of the population trend curve and Tokyo is predicted to soon lose its population in a decade. The significant population decline in Tokyo metropolitan area is an inexperienced situation for the people and policy makers. They may be afraid that the population decline would reduce the great merit of spatial agglomeration in Tokyo. The question at the heart of policy discussion is how we can sustain the high level of business productivity and quality of urban life in the Tokyo metropolitan area by spatial restructuring. This paper has developed the Computable Urban Economic Model, which re-formalizes the conventional landuse-transport interaction model on the basis of microeconomic foundation, so as to answer the above question.

As a result, we found that the central Tokyo remains as the center of the economy in 2050 with high spatial agglomeration since the agglomeration is accelerated by the scale economy. On the other hand, population which is not affected by agglomeration, is decreasing at each zone with the same level.

The investment to the 3 Ring Roads is expected to contribute to developing more dispersive urban structure since the 3 Ring Roads increase the transportation convenience at the suburb and it induces to the entry of the firms and population as well. This does not, however, the central Tokyo loses its competitiveness but they still remain strong in terms of the spatial distribution of the firms. The reduction of population mitigates the congestion of the road network. It enables us to increase our convenience in terms of the trip by car. It induces to more trips to the households and business people, which bring about more communication, that is one of the keys for the productivity growth and the enhancement of households' utility. During this period, motorization advances due to the enhancement of the transport convenience by car.

7.3.5 Chapter 19. Franz Tödtling and Michaela Trippl

Innovation and Knowledge Links in Metropolitan Regions: The Case of Vienna

Given the high density and large variety of knowledge generating organizations present in metropolitan regions and the good availability of expertise and skills, these areas are acknowledged to be important nodes in the knowledge-based economy. There is, however, also empirical evidence showing that the positive relation between metropolitan regions and innovation may not be as clear as it seems to be at the first glance. In fact, many metropolitan regions suffer from various kinds of innovation. (1) Metropolitan regions might lack particular elements of a regional innovation system (RIS). (2) There might be a lack of networking between firms in the RIS and in relevant clusters. In the literature such a constellation is referred to as "fragmented" innovation system. (3) For historic reasons there might also be a specialization in low tech or non-innovative industries. (4) There might be a lack of innovation culture in a particular region.

Vienna has suffered to some extent from the weaknesses of Austria's national innovation system, which has been characterized by a low R&D quota, weak patenting activities and a poor availability of venture capital. The central purpose of this chapter is to examine whether or not the key deficiency of Vienna's RIS in the past, i.e. fragmentation is also a characteristic feature of new knowledge intensive industries, which have emerged and grown in the last few years in the region under investigation. Such sectors are regarded to be vital for the competitiveness of metropolitan regions.

7.3.6 Chapter 20. Paschalis A. Arvanitidis George Petrakos and Dimitrios Skouras

Immigrant Location Patterns in a Southern European Metropolis: The Case of Athens.

Over the last two decades, Greece has seen a substantial influx of economic immigrants giving rise to a number of studies examining the social, economic and spatial implications immigration has for the country. In terms of the spatial impact, the observed tendency is immigrants to move primarily into metropolitan areas, which offer employment opportunities and anonymity. However, very little is known with regard to the specific, intra-urban, locations immigrants choose for their residence and the factors that affect such decisions. The current study attempts to shed light on the above issues, analysing the spatial distribution of economic immigrants within the metropolitan area of Athens, their mobility patterns and the resultant metropolitan structure. Our findings indicate a slight preference for central areas, but, over the time, the general dispersion of such immigrants to peripheral locations. On these grounds, spatial segregation, to the formation of clear ethnic enclaves, seems less plausible.

References

Acs ZJ, FitzRoy FR, Smith I (2002) High technology employment and R&D in cities: heterogeneity vs specialization. Ann Reg Sci 36:373–386

Aghion P et al (2009) The effects of entry on incumbent innovation and productivity. Rev Econ Stat 91:20–32

Andersson ÅE, Andersson DE (eds) (2000) Gateways to the global economy. Edward Elgar, Cheltenham

Andersson M, Gråsjö U, Karlsson C (2008) University and industry R&D accessibility and regional economic growth. Ital J Reg Sci 7:97–117

Anselin L, Varga A, Acs Z (1997) Local geographic spillovers between university research and high technology innovations. J Urban Econ 42:422–448

Audretsch DP, Feldman MP (1996) Innovative clusters and the industry life-cycle. Rev Ind Organ 11:253–273

Audretsch DB, Feldman MP (1999) Innovation in cities: science-based diversity, specialization and localized competition. Eur Econ Rev 43:409–429

Batten DF, Kobayashi K, Andersson ÅE (1989) Knowledge, nodes and networks: an analytical perspective. In: Andersson ÅE, Batten DF, Karlsson C (eds) Knowledge and industrial organization. Springer Verlag, Berlin, pp 31–46

Beise M, Stahl H (1999) Public research and industrial innovations in Germany. Res Policy 28:397–422

Braudel F (1979) Le Temps du Monde. Librarie Armand Colin, Paris

Brouwer E, Budil-Nadvornicova H, Kleinknecht A (1999) Are urban agglomerations a better breeding place for product innovation? An analysis of new product announcements. Reg Stud 33:541–549

Casti J (1985) Simple models, catastrophes and cycles. Research report RR-85-2. IIASA, Laxenburg

Chinitz B (1961) Contrasts in agglomeration: New York and Pittsburgh. Am Econ Rev 51:279–289

Ciccone A, Hall RE (1996) Productivity and the density of economic activity. Am Econ Rev 86:54–70

Clark TN et al (2002) Amenities drive urban growth. J Urban Aff 25:493–515

De Bresson C, Amesse F (1991) Networks of innovators: a review and introduction to the issue. Res Policy 20:363–379

Duranton G, Puga D (2001) Nursery cities: urban diversity, process innovation and the life cycle of products. Am Econ Rev 91:1454–1477

Duranton G, Puga D (2005) From sectoral to functional urban specialization. J Urban Econ 57:343–370

Ejermo O, Karlsson C (2006) Interregional inventor networks as studied by patent coinventorships. Res Policy 35:412–430

1 Introduction

Ellison G, Glaeser EL (1997) Geographic concentration in U.S. manufacturing industries: a dartboard approach. J Polit Econ 105:889–927

Ellison G, Glaeser EL (1999) The geographic concentration of industry: does natural advantage explain agglomeration? Am Econ Rev 89:311–316

Ewers HJ, Wettman R (1980) Innovation-oriented regional policy. Reg Stud 14:161–179

Falck O, Heblich S (2008) Modern location factors in dynamic regions. Eur Plann Stud 16:1385–1403

Feldman MP (1994) The geography of innovation. Kluwer, Boston

Feldman MP (2001) The entrepreneurial event revisited: firm formation in a regional context. Ind Corp Change 10:861–891

Fischer MM, Deiz JR, Snickars F (2001) Metropolitan innovation systems – theory and evidence from three metropolitan regions in Europe. Springer Verlag, Berlin

Florida R (2002) The economic geography of talent. Ann Assoc Am Geogr 92:743–755

Fujita M (1989) Urban economic theory. Cambridge University Press, Cambridge

Glaeser EL, Kerr WR (2009) Local industrial conditions and entrepreneurship: how much of the spatial distribution can we explain? J Econ Manage Strategy 18(3):623–663

Glaeser EL, Kolko J, Saiz A (2001) Consumer city. J Econ Geogr 1:27–50

Greene F, Mole K, Storey DJ (2008) Three decades of enterprise culture. Palgrave, London

Henderson JV (2005) Urbanization and growth. In: Aghion P, Durlauf S (eds) Handbook of economic growth. Elsevier, Amsterdam, pp 1543–1591

Hirsch S (1967) Location of industry and international competitiveness. Oxford University Press, Oxford

Holmberg I, Johansson B, Strömquist U (2003) A simultaneous model of long-term job and population changes. In: Andersson ÅE, Johansson B, Anderson WP (eds) The economics of disappearing distance. Ashgate, Aldershot, pp 161–189

Howard E (1898) Garden cities of tomorrow. Reprinted in 1902, Faber and Faber, London

Howells J (1983) Filter-down theory: location and technology in the UK pharmaceutical industry. Environ Plann A 15:147–164

Huggins R (1997) Competitiveness and the global region: the role of networking. In: Simmie JM (ed) Innovation, networks and learning regions. Jessica Kingsley, London, pp 101–123

Jacobs J (1961) The death and life of great American cities. Random House, New York

Jacobs J (1969) The economy of cities. Random House, New York

Jacobs J (1984) Cities and the wealth of nations. Camden Press, New York

Jaffe A, Trajtenberg M, Henderson R (1993) Geographic localization of knowledge spillovers as evidenced by patent citations. Quart J Econ 63:411–427

Johansson B (1985) Dynamics of metropolitan processes and policies. Scand Hous Plan Res 2:115–123

Johansson B (1996) Location attributes and dynamics of job location. J Infrastruct Plann Manage 530:1–15

Johansson B (1997) Infrastructure, market potential and endogenous economic growth. Paper presented at the Kyoto workshop 1997. Department of Civil Engineering, Kyoto University, Kyoto

Johansson B, Karlsson C (2001) Geographic transaction costs and specialization opportunities of small and medium-sized regions: scale economies and market extension. In: Johansson B, Karlsson C, Stough RR (eds) Theories of endogenous regional growth – lessons for regional policies. Springer, Berlin, pp 150–180

Karlsson C, Pettersson L (2005) Regional productivity and accessibility to knowledge and dense markets. CESIS working paper 32. The Royal Institute of Technology, Stockholm

Keeble D, Walker S (1994) New firms, small firms and dead firms: spatial patterns and determinants in the United Kingdom. Reg Stud 28:411–427

Kobayashi K (1995) Knowledge network and market structure: an analytic perspective. In: Batten DF, Casti J, Thord R (eds) Networks in action. Communication, economics and human knowledge. Springer, Berlin, pp 127–158

Krugman P (1991) Geography and trade. MIT Press, Cambridge, MA

Lakshmanan TR (1989) Infrastructure and economic transformation. In: Andersson ÅE, Batten DF, Johansson B (eds) Advances in spatial theory and dynamics. North-Holland, Amsterdam, pp 241–262

Lakshmanan TR, Hansen WG (1965) A retail market potential model. J Am Inst Plann 31:134–143

Lakshmanan TR, Okumura M (1995) The nature and evolution of knowledge networks in Japanese manufacturing. Pap Reg Sci 74:63–86

Lösch A (1943) Die raumliche Ordnung der Wirtschaft. Gustav Fischer, Stuttgart

Maclellan D (1990) Urban change through environmental instruments. In: Urban challenges. Allmänna Förlaget, Stockholm, pp 51–76

Malecki E, Oinas P (1998) Making connections – technological linking and regional economic change. Ashgate, Aldershot

Marshall A (1920) Principles of economics, 8th edn. Macmillan, London

Michelacci C, Silva O (2007) Why so many local entrepreneurs. Rev Econ Stat 89:615–633

Michie J (2003) The handbook of globalization. Edward Elgar, Cheltenham

Myrdal G (1957) Economic theory and under-developed regions. Ducksworth, London

Noyelle TJ, Stanback JTM (1984) The economic transformation of American cities. Rowman & Allanhead, Totowa

Quigley J (1990) The quality of housing. In: Urban challenges. Allmänna Förlaget, Stockholm, pp 39–50

Revilla Diez J (2002) Metropolitan innovation systems: a comparison between Barcelona, Stockholm, and Vienna. Int Reg Sci Rev 25:63–85

Saxenian A (1999) Silicon valley's new immigrant entrepreneurs. Public Policy Institute of California, San Francisco

Sen A, Smith T (1995) Gravity models of spatial interaction behavior. Springer, Berlin

Shefer D, Frenkel A (1998) Local milieu and innovations: some empirical results. Ann Reg Sci 32:185–200

Stam E (2007) Why butterflies don't leave. Locational behavior of entrepreneurial firms. Econ Geogr 83:27–50

Stuart TE, Sorensen O (2005) Social networks and entrepreneurship. In: Alvarez S, Agarwal R, Sorensen O (eds) Handbook of entrepreneurship: disciplinary perspectives. Springer, Berlin, pp 211–228

Suarez-Villa L, Fischer MM (1995) Technology, organization and export-driven research and development in Austria's electronics industry. Reg Stud 29:19–42

Varaiya P, Wiseman M (1984) Bifurcation models of urban development. In: Andersson ÅE, Isard W, Puu T (eds) Regional and industrial development theories, models and empirical evidence. North-Holland, Amsterdam, pp 61–68

Varga A (1998) University research and regional innovation: a spatial econometric analysis of academic technology transfer. Kluwer, Boston

von Hippel E (1994) Sticky information and the locus of problem solving: implications for innovation. Manage Sci 40:429–439

von Thünen JH (1826) Der isolierte Staat in Beziehung auf nationale Ökonomie und Landwirtschaft. Gustav Fischer, Stuttgart

Winter S (1984) Schumpeterian competition in alternative technological regimes. J Econ Behav Organ 5:287–320

Part I
Theory of Urban Growth

Chapter 2
Agglomeration, Regional Growth, and Economic Development

John M. Quigley

Abstract In the summer of 2007, the United Nations Population Fund released a report forecasting greatly increased levels of urbanization during the next two decades, especially in the developing world (United Nations 2007a). The report declared that for the first time in recorded history, more than half the world's population resided in urban – not rural – areas. At roughly the same time, another agency of the United Nations (UN-Habitat) issued a report highlighting the slums and deplorable living conditions in cities in developing countries and estimating that at the end of 2007 there were more than a billion slum dwellers, largely in developing countries (United Nations 2007b). This latter report argued that in many cases the economic circumstances of urban migrants are worse than those of rural peasants. Four years earlier, it had been reported, also by the UN (United Nations 2003), that surveys of member governments eliciting their attitudes towards urbanization found that the "vast majority" of these governments would wish to shift populations back to rural areas and stem the tide of urbanization that has been experienced around the world.

Keywords Agglomeration • Regional growth • Economic development

---

Previous revisions of this paper were presented at the Metropolitan Regions Workshop sponsored by Jonkoping University, Linkoping, Sweden, April 2008, and at the Dialogue on Urbanization and National Growth Strategies, Washington, DC, April 2008. I am grateful for the comments of conference participants and also for the comments of Patricia Annez and Robert Buckley. Portions of this draft have benefited from conversations with Vernon Henderson and Stephen Malpezzi.

J.M. Quigley (✉)
University of California, Berkeley, CA, USA
e-mail: quigley@econ.berkeley.edu

J. Klaesson et al. (eds.), *Metropolitan Regions*, Advances in Spatial Science,
DOI 10.1007/978-3-642-32141-2_2, © Springer-Verlag Berlin Heidelberg 2013

1 Introduction

In the summer of 2007, the United Nations Population Fund released a report forecasting greatly increased levels of urbanization during the next two decades, especially in the developing world (United Nations 2007a). The report declared that for the first time in recorded history, more than half the world's population resided in urban – not rural – areas. At roughly the same time, another agency of the United Nations (UN-Habitat) issued a report highlighting the slums and deplorable living conditions in cities in developing countries and estimating that at the end of 2007 there were more than a billion slum dwellers, largely in developing countries (United Nations 2007b). This latter report argued (p. 12) that in many cases the economic circumstances of urban migrants are worse than those of rural peasants. Four years earlier, it had been reported, also by the UN (United Nations 2003), that surveys of member governments eliciting their attitudes towards urbanization found that the "vast majority" of these governments would wish to shift populations back to rural areas and stem the tide of urbanization that has been experienced around the world.

How bad can urbanization be for the development process? Urbanization simply cannot be all that bad for those who live in cities in developing countries – after all, in most instances migrants to cities and urban areas could simply return to rural life if such moves improved their economic circumstances. Why all the fuss about urbanization and development?

In this essay, we consider the evidence about the mechanisms increasing economic efficiency in metropolitan regions and the record of cities in facilitating economic output and improving the consumption opportunities available to workers. Much of this evidence is based on observations on highly-developed countries, but a growing body of evidence is based upon analyses of developing economies and low-income countries. This evidence clearly supports the conclusion that cities and metropolitan conurbations are important in facilitating economic growth, increasing worker productivity and augmenting incomes in poor and rich nations alike. Policies to facilitate, not inhibit, urbanization will improve economic conditions in developing countries.

The analysis suggests a variety of broad polices – predispositions for policy – that would improve resource allocation and increase incomes in poorer countries.

2 Why Metropolitan Development?

A simple but useful point of departure for investigating the link between cities and economic development is consideration of the threshold question: why do people and firms choose to locate in the close proximity characterized by developed metropolitan regions? Clearly autarchy, a uniform distribution of populations over space, would reduce competition for locations, thus the rents paid by households and firms, making them both better off (Starrett 1974).

The answer to this question starts to provide a rationale for the existence of cities and for the development to new metropolitan regions. Clearly there must be compensating benefits of urban location, either in terms of cost reduction, output enhancement, or else utility gains, to make dense location and the payment of location rent sensible choices for households and firms.

The putative utility gains from urbanization have been the subject of much speculation and analysis by non-economists. The once-popular refrain "How're ya gonna keep them down on the farm...?" trivializes the principal insight. However, the vivid prose of Jane Jacobs (1969) argues seriously that the potential for variety in consumption is itself valuable to consumers. As long as the higher density of cities is associated with greater variety – in people, in goods, in services – there are some utility gains to those who value diversity. These gains compensate consumers for some or all of the increased location rents in cities. It is not hard to incorporate a taste for variety into economists' models of consumer preferences. (Quigley 2001 explores some of these models.)

In contrast, the productivity gains, cost reductions, or output enhancements associated with collocation have been the subject of extensive analysis by professional economists. The historical reasons for city formation and the rationalization for the payment of location rents emphasize transport costs and internal economies of scale to the exclusion of other factors. (See, for example, Hoover 1975.) Transport costs refer to those incurred in delivering inputs – raw materials and labor – to an industrial site as well as the costs of delivering outputs – finished products – to local, national and world markets. From this perspective, it is no accident that many of the large cities of the world developed along waterways Rappaport and Sacks (2003), where ocean vessels facilitated lower-cost shipment of products to far-flung markets, or along trade routes, at entrepots where the transshipment of products had already been established.

After the industrial revolution, the internal scale economies arising from factories and production facilities provided a new rationale for urbanization. The factory system replaced cottage industry, and the new division of labor required larger facilities and more workers at these facilities for the production of commodities. The economies of scale in the woolen industry dictated large mills near cheap water power, and the residences of workers came to be concentrated nearby. The development of denser settlements – industrial plants and tenements – allowed firms to operate at scales where average costs could be reduced. Aggregate rents and the higher wages paid by firms to workers were more than offset by the value of increased output. The growth of many large cities in the developed world in the nineteenth and early twentieth century (e.g., Pittsburgh, Manchester, Detroit) reflects the importance of internal economies of scale.

3 Growth and Metropolitan Development

If transport costs and internal scale economies were the only economic rationale for cities, the effects of urbanization upon economic growth more generally would be quite limited. The economic importance of cities would be strictly determined by the technologies available for transport and production. And the secular reductions during the past century in both travel cost and in the scale of the "best practice" manufacturing plant surely would have made cities less important to the health of national economies. But the importance of metropolitan regions to the modern economy hardly emphasizes internal scale economies at all, but rather external effects, spillovers, and external economies of scale. And these factors have become more important with increased industrialization, technical progress, and with economic development.

These external effects can be characterized along a variety of dimensions, and there are many taxonomies. One useful taxonomy distinguishes among productivity gains arising from specialization, those arising from transactions costs and complementarities in production, more generally from education, knowledge and mimicking, and those arising simply from the proximity to large numbers of other economic actors.

3.1 Specialized Services and Intermediate Goods

The gains from specialization arise because denser conurbations with a larger number of firms producing in proximity can support firms which are more specialized in producing intermediate products. Specialization can lead to enhanced opportunities for cost reduction in goods production – for example, when the components of intermediate goods can be routinized in production, or when the components of final products can be mechanized or automated. But the gains from specialization extend to the production of services as well. For example, specialized legal services may be provided more efficiently by firms large enough to support concentrations in taxation, copyright law, secured transactions, and so forth. In both intermediate goods and in services, specialization increases the opportunities for cost reduction.

The potential gains from specialization are further enhanced by the opportunities for sharing inputs among firms, and these are facilitated by larger and more dense urban areas. Specialized services – for example, repair, printing, advertising, and communications – can be provided to a wide spectrum of goods producers if the density of establishments is high enough.

These external gains from specialization may arise because firms producing for final demand are themselves more spatially concentrated by industry or product, giving rise to localization economies. But these gains may also arise because firms producing diverse goods for final demand are more densely packed in space, giving rise to urbanization economies. In either case, the environment permits more specialization among firms producing intermediate goods and services. This specialization, in turn, leads to cost reductions.

3.2 Transactions Costs and Complementarities

Externalities from transactions costs and complementarities in production can arise because a larger urban scale can facilitate better matches between worker skills and job requirements or between intermediate goods and the production requirements for final output. In the labor market, for example, the opportunity for better skill matches reduces the search costs of workers with differentiated skills and the search costs of employers with differentiated demands for labor. Complementarities in production between physical and human capital suggest that, when the pool of urban workers has a greater stock of human capital, firms that expect to employ these workers will invest more in physical capital. With costly search and imperfect matching in urban labor markets, some workers of lower skill will end up working with more physical capital; they will be more productive and earn higher incomes. The return on workers' human capital and on employers' physical capital thus rises with the stock of human capital in the city – even when production at each worksite is undertaken with constant returns to scale.

The same principle – externalities arising from better matches in larger urban environments – applies to specialized machines in production and to entrepreneurs in firms. Better matches can also reduce the potential losses from business failures and bankruptcy by rendering equipment more useful in resale markets.

3.3 Education, Knowledge Mimicking

The notion of complementarities in labor market matching can be distinguished from externalities arising from the collocation of workers of similar education and skills in dense urban areas. The effects of aggregate levels of schooling in urban areas upon aggregate output may be distinguished form the effects of an individual's schooling on her individual earnings. Productivity spillovers – educated or skilled workers increasing the productivity of other workers – may arise in denser spatial environments regardless of whether the urban industrial structure is diversified or specialized. The diffusion of technique among firms, the copying and innovation in style, and the genealogy of patents among firms are all examples of local externalities in production which are encouraged by urban density and concentrations of skilled workers near to each other. These economies may arise with spatial concentration by industry (localization economies) or with higher densities of diverse industries (urbanization economies).

3.4 The Law of Large Numbers

Finally, considerable cost savings may arise simply from the presence of large numbers of economic actors in close proximity. For example, to the extent that fluctuations in demand are imperfectly correlated across firms in an urban labor market, employment can be stabilized – since some firms will be hiring workers while other firms will be contracting. To the extent that fluctuations in demand for products are uncorrelated across buyers, firms need carry less inventory, since some consumers are buying while others are not. The decisions of large numbers of imperfectly correlated economic actors in close proximity can dampen cyclical fluctuations and provide a form of natural insurance.

The basic insight from the law of large numbers is straightforward; it is possible to get a better estimate of the moments of a distribution with a larger sample size. This allows all economic actors to make decisions based upon better information. This is true on the buying and selling sides of markets for purchasing inputs, storing intermediate products, and selling outputs.

3.5 Beyond Productivity Gains

As noted previously, the benefits of urbanization are not limited to productivity enhancements. Increased density and reduced transport costs augment consumer welfare by increasing consumption opportunities for residents. This increased diversity is manifest, not only in the diversity of purchased goods and services, but also in the diversity of neighborhoods and neighborhood types, of available social interactions, and of the packages of public services available for consumption.

4 Limitations on City Sizes

The external effects of the urban environment on productivity described above all point to larger and more dense accommodations and indicate that there is a strong positive relationship between urbanization and economic development. What are the limits, if any, to the extent of urbanization and thus the efficient sizes of cities? There are at least three sources limiting the sizes of cities and affecting the efficiency of city sizes: land and transport costs; unpriced externalities of urban life and higher densities; and explicit public policies affecting the gains from urbanization.

4.1 Land and Transport Costs

Important factors limiting city sizes arise from the same technological considerations that spawn cities in the first place. Increased housing and land prices mean that the attractiveness of larger cities for residents declines, holding the wages offered constant. (Any decline in the attractiveness of cities will, of course, be less pronounced if the consumption externalities of cities are large.)

Alternatively, the wages offered as cities expand must increase enough to offset the higher costs that workers must bear if they choose to live and work in these locations. The efficiency gains in production from higher densities must be at least as large as the increased wage payments required. The operation of these factors, housing and land prices, together with wages and output prices, limit the efficient sizes of cities.

4.2 Unpriced Externalities of Urban Density

The increased transport costs and higher densities of cities may bring their own externalities, and if these are large enough they will limit the extent of urbanization. Of course, if these externalities are unpriced, they will not limit urbanization sufficiently. In higher income countries, air pollution from vehicles is typically underpriced, and until recently congestion in cities was hardly ever priced. Externalities from vehicle accidents are seldom compensated. In low-income countries, there may be additional external costs of higher-density living in the form of potential disease, epidemic, or conflagration. These external effects are certainly unpriced. To the extent that these external effects are underpriced in cities, potential rural migrants do not face the marginal costs of urban life. Hence migration will be in excess, and cities will be larger than their efficient sizes.

4.3 Explicit Policies

Finally, explicit governmental policies, especially in developing countries, may provide strong indirect incentives affecting the extent and distribution of urbanization. For example, it was widely thought that governments in developing countries favor producers and consumers in urban areas at the expense of rural and agricultural workers, for example, by imposing below-market prices for agricultural output and above-market prices for urban products. Structural adjustment policies, widely adopted from the 1980s onwards, have greatly reduced the scope for this urban bias and the distorted migration signals inherent in these subsidies. But a continuing form of central government bias may be a set of policies favoring particular cities, for example, the national capital. Policies favoring the locations which benefit elites and bureaucrats may be enacted as a result of rent-seeking behavior or as a consequence of corruption by elites. Questionable policies may include direct public investments in plant and equipment, or in infrastructure, capital controls on investment across cities, differences in rules imposed on cities for access to capital markets, or for obtaining licenses and permissions. In some countries, these restrictions have included explicit limitations on labor mobility as well.

4.4 Summary

All of the factors suggest reasons why productivity is higher in larger cities than in smaller cities. Larger cities permit greater specialization and admit more complementarities in production. They facilitate spillovers and learning within industries and across industries. And they facilitate sharing and risk-pooling by their very size.

Even recognizing the potential negative externalities of larger cities, these factors still suggest that real wages in larger cities in developed and developing countries will exceed those in smaller cities. In the development context, it is hardly necessary to stress that urban productivity will be higher than rural productivity and that this differential will facilitate migration from the labor surplus hinterland to the more productive urban areas.

Early models of rural–urban migration, beginning with Kuznets, recognized the free flow of labor from unproductive agriculture to urban employment, tending to equalize wages, as a vital part of the development process. In the 1970s analysts emphasized the importance of minimum wage rules in cities and the tendency towards equalization of expected wages across sectors. These models, beginning with those of Harris and Todaro in 1970, reconciled high levels of wages and worker productivity with unemployment in cities in developing countries. Inexplicably, the reasoning behind these models has been used by some to "justify" actions by governments in developing countries to limit mobility to the productive cities rather than to remove barriers to competition in the labor market. Indeed, comparing high levels of official unemployment in cities with equally "official" statistics from rural areas, which ignore disguised rural unemployment, often seems to be deployed by agrarian romantics indulging an anti-urban bias. (See Lall et al. 2006, for a more balanced discussion of these issues – but one which reaches a similar conclusion, e.g., pp. 47–48.)

5 Empirical Evidence: Productivity Gains

5.1 Basic Findings

Despite the attention paid to agglomeration economies – going back to observations by Alfred Marshall in the 1890s – verification of efficiency gains by direct observation proved difficult at first, even using data from advanced industrial economies. A number of early studies estimating aggregate production functions are suggestive, but most of these efforts lacked critical data (for example, measures of capital stock), making inferences about the importance of external effects problematic. These issues are reviewed by Rosenthal and Strange (2004).

More recent work using micro data sets on firms and establishments for the U.S. has overcome most of these measurement problems. For example, Henderson's (2003b) careful analyses of machinery and high tech industries tested directly for the presence of localization economies (agglomeration within an industry) and urbanization economies (agglomeration across industries), by estimating plant-level production functions. A panel of plants across counties and metropolitan areas makes it much easier to test for the importance of local conditions upon the productivity of plants and their levels of output. Henderson's results verify that productivity in single establishment firms is higher as a result of localization economies.

Even with appropriate micro data, however, simple statistical models may lead to misleading inferences. If agglomeration economies do enhance firm

2 Agglomeration, Regional Growth, and Economic Development

productivity, then more talented entrepreneurs will certainly seek out these more productive locations. To account for this simultaneity, more sophisticated statistical methods are necessary. Henderson certainly recognizes this in applying more appropriate statistical methods of estimation in his study of high tech and machinery industries, but the instruments he relies upon (i.e., measures of the local environment) are weak, rendering the statistical results problematic.

A recent unpublished paper by Greenstone et al. (2007) solves this identification problem. The authors study the effects of the opening of large-scale plants ("million dollar plants") on the productivity of pre-existing plants nearby, using a panel of establishments from the same data source relied upon by Henderson. For each of the million dollar plants, the authors have information on the county chosen for investment and also on the county which was not ultimately selected – but which was under final consideration by the parent firm for the location of the new plant. This permits a direct side-by-side comparison of the course of productivity in plants located in the counties chosen for exogenous investment with the course of productivity in plants located in the "runner up" counties. The authors found clear evidence of a discontinuity in total factor productivity in plants after the opening of a large plant nearby. Total factor productivity was enhanced in those pre-existing plants located in the "winning" counties, but not in the losing counties, confirming the existence of urbanization economies. This is important evidence.

A variety of less direct approaches have been employed to make inferences about agglomeration. Rosenthal and Strange (2003), among others, have studied the locations of firm births. Problematic data on factor inputs (e.g., the legacy of sunk capital) are not necessary for inquiries about new firms, and new establishments may plausibly take the existing economic geography of regions as exogenous. This empirical work suggests that births are substantially more likely to occur where there is an existing concentration of firms in the same industry. (See also earlier work done by Carlton 1983.) To the extent that profit-seeking entrepreneurs are drawn to more productive locations, this emphasizes the importance of localization economies.

Alternatively, the study of the spatial distribution of wages and rents may provide indirect evidence about economies of agglomeration. In more productive regions, the marginal product of labor will be higher, and wages will be higher. Analogously, locations where industrial rents are higher are those possessed of compensating differentials in productivity. Investigations using U.S. data on wages are reported by Wheaton and Lewis (2002) and using U.S. data on rents by Gabriel and Rosenthal (2004). An analogous investigation using rent data from Japanese prefectures to make inferences about agglomeration has also been undertaken by Dekle and Eaton (1999). All of these investigations document agglomerative economies.

Finally, patterns of employment growth may provide indirect evidence on the importance of agglomeration. If agglomeration economies enhance productivity, then more productive regions will grow more rapidly. An important paper by Glaeser et al. (1992) used aggregate employment data from U.S. metropolitan areas to confirm these effects. Henderson et al. (1995) conducted a more precise test using employment in manufacturing.

The specific mechanisms transmitting these urbanization and localization efficiencies have been studied by economists. Perhaps the clearest evidence of external effects in local labor markets comes from education and training. Early studies by Rauch (1993), predating the Lucas (1998) hypothesis, identified the external effects of schooling upon wages in cross-sectional models of wage determination, using U.S. cities as units of observation. Recent work by Moretti (2004) extends this analysis to explain longitudinal as well as cross-sectional variation in wages across labor markets.

Perhaps the most persuasive evidence of the importance of educational externalities comes from Moretti's (2004) analysis of educational spillovers and productivity in the United States. This research is based upon the estimation of total factor productivity and the effects of education at the level of the individual plant or establishment.

These productivity findings are confirmed, at least roughly, in a recent study of the service sector. Arzaghi and Henderson (2006) analyzed advertising firms in Manhattan, documenting the substantial increases in productivity attributable to the networking opportunities arising from the nearby location of similar firms.

Beyond these direct inquiries into the production of goods and services, it has been widely reported that incomes have grown more rapidly in U.S. cities with high initial levels of human capital (e.g., Glaeser et al. 1995), consistent with skill acquisition and diffusion through the interaction of workers in more dense urban areas (Glaeser and Mare 2001; Duranton and Puga 2004).

Lacking direct observations on workers' interactions, economists have evaluated one important "paper trail" of these interactions, namely data on patent applications and awards. Patent applications list the addresses of the holders of antecedent patents as well as the addresses of patent applicants. This makes possible the study of the localization of patents and the analysis of the spatial decay of patent citations with distances between firms and between inventors (Jaffee et al. 1993). This work has provided explicit confirmation of the importance of geographic spillovers in the development of new knowledge.

Of course, there has been direct anthropological study by sociologists and others, observing worker interactions in dense locations, most authoritatively (Saxenian 1994) among highly educated workers in Santa Clara County, California ("Silicon Valley") and along the technical corridor ("Route 128") outside Boston. These investigations are broadly consistent with the results of quantitative investigation by economists.

5.2 Corroboration from Developing Countries

Many of the models reported in the previous section have been adapted, extended and applied using data from low-income and developing countries. Much of this work has been pioneered by Vernon Henderson and his collaborators. Henderson's 1998 book includes a detailed chapter estimating the extent and importance of agglomeration economies in Brazil using detailed industrial census data. Henderson found clear evidence of external economies of scale, localization economies for two-digit industries. (Unfortunately, for at least some cities analyzed by Henderson, a single industry was dominant, meaning that factor prices and populations are endogenously determined. This is a major limitation.) This work on Brazil is similar to (but much more primitive than) the work reported by Henderson (1993b) and by Greenstone, Moretti, and Hornbeck (2007) using U.S. data. In a more recent analysis of city growth in Brazil, Henderson and his and his collaborators analyzed aggregate data for 123 cities observed during three decades beginning in 1970 (da Mata et al. 2007). The authors laid out an ambitious model of the structure of supply and demand for output at the municipal level, and they estimated relationships describing the evolution of city sizes in Brazil and their decennial growth. The empirical results indicate that increases in the sizes of local markets and their access to domestic markets have very strong effects upon the growth rates of cities. Improvements in labor force quality and in the initial levels of educational attainment matter significantly and importantly for economic growth. In these respects, recent work on Brazil confirms and extends the conclusions of Glaeser et al. (1992) in their earlier study of American cities.

Other direct investigations of agglomeration and productivity have been undertaken in Korea, Indonesia, China, and in India as well.

Evidence of localization economies was reported for Korean industry, including transport and traditional industry, by Henderson et al. (2001). The authors analyze metropolitan level data for 23 Korean industries in five major groups at the metropolitan level during the 1983–1993 period, a time of rapid deconcentration of economic activity from the capital Seoul to smaller metropolitan areas. The authors estimate aggregate production functions, relying upon census estimates of capital stock and labor, testing for the importance of the potential urbanization and localization economies provided in the sample of Korean cities. The results confirm the clear importance of localization economies in Korean industry, most importantly in heavy industry and transportation. Significant localization economies were also found in machinery and high-tech industries, and to a lesser extent in "traditional manufacturing."

These results are confirmed by the contemporaneous work of Lee and Zang (1998) applying somewhat different statistical models to the same basic source of data from the Korean Census of Manufacturing.

Related empirical work for Indonesia, by Henderson and Kuncoro (1996), reports substantial localization economies for many industries and less pronounced urbanization economies. Henderson and Kuncoro estimate models of the choice of location for plants and establishments of small and medium-sized firms in Java. Their results indicate that manufacturing plants are much more likely to choose locations that already include mature establishments and plants in the same or related industries. These results are consistent with the work on firm births in the U.S, by Rosenthal and Strange (2001), and they suggest that entrepreneurs actively seek out localization and agglomeration to improve productivity and profits.

A more recent and quite ambitious paper by Deichmann et al. (2005) extends these results for Indonesia, analyzing a large sample of plant locations for the entire country. Their statistical analysis documents the importance of localization economies and the influence of existing firms in the same industry in affecting location choice. The econometric results also suggest the importance of existing backward linkages to suppliers in affecting location choice. Urbanization economies, *per se*, seemed much less important.

Simulations based upon these statistical results illustrate the difficulties faced by lagging regions in attracting new economic activity.

Au and Henderson (2006) used aggregate data on some 285 Chinese cities to estimate the effects of urban agglomeration on productivity. This analysis was facilitated by detailed data reporting GDP by Chinese metropolitan area in three categories. The aggregate productivity relationship exhibits an inverted U shape in metropolitan size and scale, as expected. The estimated urban agglomeration benefits are quite high, and it appears that a large fraction of cities in China are under-sized due to migration controls imposed at the national level. These results are consistent with earlier and less complete work by Chen (1996). Some of the policy implications of this line of research are discussed in CERAP (2007).

The evidence from India includes an analysis of the relationship between urban populations and total factor productivity by state and industry over a 16-year period (Mitra 2000). Of more significance, perhaps, is the analysis of plant-level data undertaken by Lall et al. (2003). Lall and his collaborators use these micro data on establishments, from the Indian Survey of Industries in 1998, to estimate the parameters of a translog cost function. The authors provide direct estimates of the elasticity of costs with respect to four different measures of agglomeration, separately for eight industrial groupings and three size classes of plants. The results provide rather strong support for the importance of urbanization economies in reducing costs per unit of output. This finding is consistent across all industries and size classes of Indian plants. This paper provides important evidence on urbanization economies in India, and perhaps in other developing economies as well.

5.3 Summary

The scientific quality of the evidence from developing countries cited above is probably lower than that obtained from more advanced countries – if only because more reliable data on economic activity are available for a larger period for developed countries. Nevertheless, the quantitative results obtained from low-income and developing countries in Asia and Latin America is remarkably consistent with that obtained from more advanced economies. Comparable evidence from low-income countries in Africa is conspicuously absent (Collier 2007).

Urbanization and localization do support increases in productivity. Of course, it may well be that the economic return to mimicking successful ideas or investments is especially high in developing countries where mimicking could result in too little entrepreneurial activity in low-income countries. (This allegation is made by Hausmann and Rodrik 2002, 2006.) But there is no systematic evidence that the potential returns to mimicking are greater in poorer countries than in richer ones.

2 Agglomeration, Regional Growth, and Economic Development 41

And, as the evidence on patent citations suggests, denser and more specialized local economies may simply generate a larger stock of entrepreneurial capital to be copied.

Of course, none of this really proves a tight causal link between urbanization and economic development. (See Henderson 2003, for a balanced discussion.) And there is evidence from elsewhere that urbanization is certainly not a sufficient condition for economic development to occur (Fay and Opal 2000). Nevertheless, it seems quite clear that productivity is enhanced by the localization and urbanization features of cities, in developing economies as well as industrialized countries. The cumulative evidence is overwhelming.

6 Efficient City Sizes

Given the productivity advantages of larger cities in developing countries documented in the previous section, we should expect urbanization to be a natural concomitant of increased output and well-being in low-income countries. City sizes are determined by the tradeoff between the increased productivity and incomes in larger conurbations and the increased rent and transport costs consumers confront in larger cities. To the extent that congestion, pollution, and the risk of epidemic are not considered appropriately by rural workers contemplating moves to cities, the cities will be "too large," but not by much. Some of these externalities can be eliminated by improved technology; others by investments in public health.

It is quite surprising that there does not seem to be a coherent literature – or much economic literature at all – relating these externalities to levels of urbanization in low-income countries. There are case studies of the linkage between traffic fatalities and economic growth (e.g., Kopits and Cropper 2005), but not between traffic fatalities and urbanization, much less studies of the linkage between externalities from traffic fatalities and levels of urbanization. It is relatively straightforward to estimate the correlation between the incidence of some communicable diseases (e.g., diarrhea, tuberculosis) and urbanization at the country level and to estimate the correlation between access to water and sanitation, on the one hand, and urbanization, on the other hand. Indeed, many of these correlations may be investigated on line (for example, by relying upon "WDI Online"), and it is reported that infant mortality is higher in urban slums in developing countries. (See Evans 2007.) But these correlations are barely hints about the causal mechanisms at work. Nevertheless, these results are widely interpreted as if there were some causal mechanism.

At this point, we can only conclude that unpriced externalities are probably a bit more important in distorting migration flow to cities in developing countries than in developed countries. But in both cases, these distortions can be reduced by direct pricing or by indirect levies such as urban property taxes.

What about the explicit policies of governments?

As noted above, there has been widespread belief that explicit policies of developing countries have inappropriately favored cities at the expense of agriculture, and this has interfered with economic development. The most direct accusation of an "urban bias" is due to Lipton three decades ago (1976), but see also Lipton 1993. If macroeconomic and national trade policies distort price signals, by raising the value added in the urban sector, when value added is computed using local prices, this provides incentives for inefficiently high levels of urbanization. And if urban products are valued at inflated prices while rural products are valued at deflated prices, productivity advantages attributed to cities may be simply illusory.

It is not clear how these price distortions can be measured (See Becker and Morrison 1999), or how the implications of this bias could be tested directly. But after two decades of structural adjustment policies advocated by the international organizations, it is quite clear that in most developing countries price liberalization has caused local relative prices to converge closer to world prices reflecting economic scarcity. Indeed, the World Bank's 15-year old treatise on urban policy (1991), "an agenda for the 1990s," documents the contemporaneous effects of structural adjustment policies in removing any artificial price advantages of cities (and in reducing the economic circumstances of the poor in cities in low-income countries). The controversy over policies to undo distortions in relative prices seems somehow dated.

But certain limited aspects of "bias" in development policies may be well taken, and they may be a continuing concern. Of particular concern are government policies that favor particular cities or regions for political or ideological reasons.

A remarkable regularity observed across systems of cities is the rank-size rule, namely that the product of the city rank in the size distribution and the city population is roughly constant (and thus the second ranking city in a country is half the size of the first, and so forth). This relationship (more generally, a power relation) has proved robust across time periods for the U.S. (Dobkins and Ioannides 1998) and other countries, and across countries as well (Rosen and Resnick 1980; Soo 2005). Many explanations for the general findings are purely mechanical. Fujita et al. (1999) describe "nihilistic and simplistic" models that generate this pattern; Gabaix (1999) shows that if, over some range if city sizes, the expected growth rate of population and its variance are independent of size, the distribution of city sizes follows a simple power relation. Puga (1998) has hypothesized that the higher costs of spatial interaction and the less elastic labor supply in the nineteenth century help explain why a smaller share of national population lives in large old European cities than in large cities in developing countries. As Puga stresses, the nature of increasing and decreasing returns to city size govern the size distribution of cities in the long run. For example, there will be a more uneven distribution of city sizes if there are stronger external economies of scale in cities. But the exact relationships are elusive Fujita et al. (1999).

Despite this uncertainty about the economic process governing the rank-size relationship, considerable evidence suggests that political variables affect the distribution of city sizes. For example, Soo's analysis (2005) of the size distribution of cities across 73 countries suggests that political measures – dictatorial government, measures of political rights and liberties, and the length of time a nation has been independent – are more important than economic variables in explaining deviations from a common exponential relationship relating city rank and city sizes.

2 Agglomeration, Regional Growth, and Economic Development

These results generalize the more primitive analysis by Ades and Glaeser (1995) of the primacy of a single city in national economic life. Ades and Glaeser analyzed variations in the national population residing in the largest city for a sample of 85 cities over 15 years. Their empirical analysis suggests that countries currently governed by dictatorships have principal cities that are about 45 % larger than the principal cities found in democracies, and democratically-governed countries have principal cities about 40 % larger if they were governed by dictators in the past. These and similar results survive a variety of tests for causality.

Most of the discussion of "excessive" concentration in cities by economists is framed in terms of the extreme primacy of one or a few cities in many developing countries. (See Henderson 1999, and the references therein.) Little or none of the criticism of "excessive" concentration is based upon the empirical evaluation of externalities in developing countries. This is surprising.

Clearly excessive concentration may be abetted by government policy. The mechanisms by which authoritative governments are able to favor particular cities or regions are not hard to visualize, but they may be quite hard to document. These mechanisms may be quite indirect, ranging from weaker benefit-cost tests imposed on infrastructure investment to a relaxation of licensing rules in favored cities, to explicit allocation of credit to favored regions, to decisions favoring investments by public officials and cronies in national capitals.

In this sense, there may be an "urban bias" in government policy, and it may result in discrimination against rural development. But this bias also discriminates against most of the small and medium-sized cities in developing countries as well as rural areas.

7 Some Conclusions

This review documents the strong relationship between urbanization, on the one hand, and economic productivity and development, on the other hand. This documentation is based upon extensive analyses of data from the U.S. and high-income countries and less-extensive analyses of data from developing countries. It suggests that the effects upon productivity can arise from specific mechanisms fostered by the urbanization and localization of industry. The available evidence does not conclude that urbanization is necessary for the development process, nor is urbanization sufficient to increase output and well-being in low-income countries. But the case is strong, and the causal relationship is nevertheless clear.

Despite equivocation, it is clear that urbanization and economic development are intimately related, and the concentration of resources – labor and capital – in cities is a part of this process. To the extent that these movements are the sensible response to market signals about scarcity, there is no reason for concern about the size of any city or the size distribution of cities in general. To the extent that external effects – pollution and congestion, for example – are unpriced in cities, conurbations will be too large, but not by a lot. Public concerns about pricing scarce roadways and about water supply and public health investments to decrease the chances of epidemic are well-placed; aggressive action may be justified to price urban externalities. But from this perspective, the concern with urban slums *per se* is less important. Urban poverty is not an excuse for policies limiting the extent of urbanization in low-income countries.

It is hard to know how important corruption and anti-democratic policies are in inhibiting or directing flows of factors to and among cities. Their existence in developed as well as underdeveloped countries provides strong argument to allow natural market forces to determine the spatial distribution of labor and capital. Urbanization and Economic development will be increased, and the level of urbanization will also increase.

Increased urbanization certainly facilitates the development process, and explicit policies to discourage urbanization are surely misguided.

References

Ades A, Glaeser E (1995) Trade and circuses: explaining urban giants. Q J Econ 110(1):195–228
Arzaghi M, Henderson JV (2006) Networking off Madison Avenue (unpublished paper)
Au C-C, Henderson JV (2006) Are Chinese cities too small? Rev Econ Stud 73(3):549–576
Becker CM, Morrison AR (1999) Chapter 43. Urbanization in transforming economies. In: Paul C, Edwin SM (eds) Handbook of regional and urban economics. Elsevier, Amsterdam
Carlton DW (1983) The location and employment choices of new firms: an econometric model with discrete and continuous endogenous variables. Rev Econ Stat 65(3):440–449
CERAP (China Economic Research and Advisory Programme) (2007) Urbanization in China. Professional report #P07-001, Institute of Business and Economic Research. University of California, Berkeley
Chen Y (1996) Impact of regional factors on productivity in China. J Reg Sci 36(3):417–436
Collier P (2007) The bottom billion: why the poorest countries are failing and what can be done about it. Oxford University Press, London
Da Mata D, Deichmann U, Henderson JV, Lall SV, Wang HG (2007) Determinants of city growth in Brazil. J Urban Econ 62(2):252–272
Deichmann U, Kaiser K, Lall SV, Shalizi Z (2005) Agglomeration, transport, and regional development in Indonesia. World Bank Policy Research Working Paper No. 3477
Dekle R, Eaton J (1999) Agglomeration and land rents: evidence from the prefectures. J Urban Econ 46(2):200–214
Dobkins L, Ioannides Y (1998) Dynamic evolution of the U.S. city size distribution. In: Huriot J-M, Thisse J-F (eds) The economics of cities. Cambridge University Press, New York
Duranton G, Puga D (2004) Microfoundations of urban agglomeration economies. In: Henderson JV, Thisse J-F (eds) Handbook of regional and urban economics, vol 4. Elsevier, Amsterdam
Evans T (2007) Research for urban health: towards a global agenda. World Health Organization Global Summit, Bellagio
Fay M, Opal C (2000) Urbanization without growth: a not-so-uncommon phenomenon. World bank policy research working paper #2412. World Bank, Washington, DC
Fujita M, Krugman P, Venables A (1999) The spatial economy. MIT Press, Cambridge
Gabaix X (1999) Zipf's law for cities: an explanation. Q J Econ 114(3):739–767
Gabriel SA, Rosenthal SS (2004) Quality of the business environment versus quality of life: do firms and households like the same cities? Rev Econ Stat 86(1):438–444
Glaeser EL, Mare DC (2001) Cities and skills. J Labor Econ 19(21):316–342

Glaeser EL, Scheinkman J, Shleifer A (1995) Economic growth in a cross-section of cities. J Monetary Econ 36:117–143

Glaeser E, Kallal H, Scheinkman J, Schleifer A (1992) Growth in cities. J Polit Econ 100(6):1126–1152

Greenstone M, Moretti E, Hornbeck R (2007) Identifying agglomeration spillovers: evidence from million dollar plants (unpublished paper)

Hausmann R, Rodrik D (2002) Economic development as self discovery. NBER working paper #8952, May 2002

Hausmann R, Rodrik D (2006) Doomed to choose: industrial policy as predicament, John F. Kennedy School of Government (unpublished paper)

Henderson JV (2003b) Marshall's scale economies. J Urban Econ 53(1):1–28

Henderson JV, Kuncoro A (1996) Industrial centralization in Indonesia. World Bank Econ Rev 10(3):513–540

Henderson J, Vernon AK, Turner M (1995) Industrial development in cities. J Polit Econ 103(5):1067–1085

Henderson J, Vernon TL, Lee JY (2001) Scale externalities in Korea. J Urban Econ 49(3):479–504

Hoover EM (1975) An introduction to regional economics, 2nd edn. Alfred A. Knopf, New York

Jacobs J (1969) The economy of cities. Random House, New York

Jaffe AB, Trajtenberg M, Henderson R (1993) Geographic localization of knowledge spillovers as evidenced by patent citations. Quart J Econ 108:577–598

Kopits E, Cropper M (2005) Traffic fatalities and economic growth. Accid Anal Prev 37(1):169–178

Lall SV, Koo J, Chakravorty S (2003) Diversity matters: the economic geography of industry location in India. World Bank policy research working paper #3072. World Bank, Washington, DC

Lall SV, Selod H, Shalizi Z (2006) Rural urban migration in developing countries: a survey of theoretical predictions and empirical findings. World Bank policy research working paper #3915. World Bank, Washington, DC

Lee YJ, Zang H (1998) Urbanization and regional productivity in Korean manufacturing. Urban Stud 35(11):2085–2099

Lipton M (1976) Why poor people stay poor: urban bias in world development. Harvard University Press, Cambridge

Lipton M (1993) Urban bias: of consequences, classes and causality. J Dev Stud 29(4):229–258

Lucas RE (1988a) On the mechanics of economic development. J Monetary Econ 22:3–42

Mitra A (2000) Total factor productivity growth and urbanization economies: a case of Indian industries. Rev Urban Reg Dev Stud 12(2):97–108

Moretti E (2004) Estimating the social return to higher education: evidence from longitudinal and repeated cross-sectional data. J Econometrics 121:175–212

Puga D (1998) Urbanization patterns: European versus less developed countries. J Reg Sci 38(2):231–252

Quigley JM (2001) The renaissance in regional research. Ann Reg Sci 35(2):167–178

Rappaport J, Sacks J (2003) The United States as a coastal nation. J Econ Growth 8(1):5–46

Rauch J (1993) Productivity gains from geographic concentration of human capital: evidence from the cities. J Urban Econ 34:380–400

Rosen K, Resnick M (1980) The size distribution of cities: an examination of the Pareto law and primacy. J Urban Econ 8(2):165–186

Rosenthal SS, Strange WC (2001) The determinants of agglomeration. J Urban Econ 50(2):191–229

Rosenthal SS, Strange WC (2003) Geography, industrial organization, and agglomeration. Rev Econ Stat 85(2):377–393

Rosenthal S, Strange WC (2004) Evidence on the nature and sources of agglomeration economies. In: Henderson JV, Thisse J-F (eds) Handbook of urban and regional economics, vol 4 of the series Cities and geography. North Holland, Amsterdam

Saxenian A (1994) Regional advantage: culture and competition in silicon valley and route 128. Harvard University Press, Cambridge, MA

Soo KT (2005) Zipf's law for cities: a cross-country investigation. Reg Sci Urban Econ 35:239–263

Starrett DA (1974) Principles of optimal location in a large homogeneous area. J Econ Theory 9(4):418–448

United Nations (2003) World population policies. United Nations, New York

United Nations, UN Population Fund (2007) State of world population 2007: unleashing the potential of urban growth. United Nations, New York

United Nations, UN-Habitat (2007) The state of the world's cities report 2006/2007. Earthscan, London

Henderson JV (1999) How urban concentration affects economic growth. World Bank policy research working paper #2326. World Bank, Washington, DC

Wheaton WC, Lewis MJ (2002) Urban wages and labor market agglomeration. J Urban Econ 51(3):542–562

World Bank (1991) Urban policy and economic development: an agenda for the 1990s. The World Bank, Washington

Chapter 3
Urban Growth

Co-evolution of Producer Services and Other Sectors

Johan Klaesson and Börje Johansson

Abstract A major characteristic of the economic development in Sweden during the past 10–15 years is a fast expansion of the producer-service sector. To analyse this process, the present paper employs an approach to identify the spatial pattern of local, regional and extra-regional demand for producer services. In the associated theoretical model producer-service firms grow in locations with large market access. The estimated model predicts that the supply of producer services grows in urban areas with large market access, whereas the rest of the economy shrinks in the same areas and expands in other parts of the urban region. The change process is interpreted as an effect of firms' outsourcing of service activities when they can rely on accessibility to service suppliers. As a result service suppliers agglomerate in central parts of the urban region, where they obtain high accessibility to their customers. The estimated change process comprises a non-linear response mechanism.

Keywords Agglomeration • Producer services • Regions • Accessibility

---

J. Klaesson (✉)
Jönköping International Business School (JIBS), Gjuterigatan 5, Box 1026, Jönköping
551 11, Sweden
e-mail: jobo@jibs.hj.se

B. Johansson
Centre of Excellence for Science and Innovation Studies, Royal Institute of
Technology (KTH), Stockholm 100 44, Sweden
e-mail: borje.johansson@jibs.hj.se

J. Klaesson et al. (eds.), *Metropolitan Regions*, Advances in Spatial Science,
DOI 10.1007/978-3-642-32141-2_3, © Springer-Verlag Berlin Heidelberg 2013

1 Introduction

1.1 Agglomeration, Producer Services and Growth

Economic as well as population growth take place in a spatially selective manner, and technological, social and life-style innovations are clustered in space, bringing about geographic concentrations of economic renewal. Moreover, the diffusion of novelties is spatially differentiated such that novelties reach large urban regions faster than other places. This implies that economic change is driven by processes in metropolitan and other large urban regions, in a context where the individual city region can be characterised as a major social institution for technological, commercial and social innovations (Fujita and Thisse 2002).

Hohenberg and Lees (1985) argue convincingly that cities have remained the prime operators of economic change through centuries. In the contemporary global economy, urban regions function as independent and dynamic market places which stimulate each other via knowledge and commodity flows. Each such region has its own base of scientific, technological and entrepreneurial knowledge, represented by knowledge assets of localised firms and the human and social capital associated with the region's population.

Following Karlsson and Johansson (2006), we can observe a global transformation of large urban regions from predominantly industrial economies to knowledge economies, changing the composition of industries, the location of production, the occupational structure, the education level, the variety of goods and services and the R&D intensity. In this process, outsourcing of producer services plays a major role, allowing producers of both goods and services to decompose their production into sub-processes, which can be outsourced to new and separated suppliers of producer services. In large and dense urban environments the demand is large enough to make it profitable for an expanding number of specialised suppliers of diversified services to emerge (Camacho and Rodriguez 2005).

In view of the described structural change of the contemporary economy, this paper will examine urban growth in Sweden with a focus on the role of producer services and, in particular, knowledge-intensive producer services. We will examine which urban regions grow and which decline, and identify the characteristics that determine the growth process of urban regions. The overall picture tells us that producer services grow faster in large regions and particularly in metropolitan regions. These regions constitute the urban environments that foster R&D activities and the presence of knowledge-intensive producer services and knowledge intensive labour in general. Our findings support the idea that the size and the diversity of urban regions stimulate the growth of jobs in knowledge-intensive producer services, which increases productivity according to models by e.g. Rivera-Batiz (1988) and Abdel-Rahman and Fujita (1990).

Fujita and Thisse (2002) present a model which illustrates the relation between agglomeration and growth, with reference to Martin and Ottaviano (2001), Baldwin et al (2001) on the one hand, and Romer (1990) and Grossman and Helpman (1991) on the other. This theoretical setting recognises how urban knowledge-flows provide a milieu for productivity enhancing R&D as assumed in endogenous growth theory.

3 Urban Growth

This is combined with a dynamic process in which knowledge-intensive labour is attracted to migrate into urban agglomerations with a demand for such labour. The described inflow of labour stimulates the urban region to grow and thereby increases the demand for an augmenting number of consumption varieties, which are sensitive to distance and this favours local supply. In this setting, economic growth is influenced positively by agglomeration, while economic growth brings about further agglomeration. This evolution is recognized as endogenous economic growth in Black and Henderson (1999).

Empirical studies of "endogenous" urban growth focus on size, amenity factors, and human capital, where size reflects the "home market effect", where amenities are attractors for knowledge intensive labour, and where the latter is a precondition for creativity and R&D (e.g. Martin and Ottaviano 1999; Glaeser 2000; Cheshire and Malecki 2004). Earlier contributions include Henderson (1988) and date back to Hoover (1937) and Ohlin (1933). Cheshire and Magrini (2005) present a study of urban growth with reference to endogenous growth theory by including R&D and human capital among the set of explanatory variables, based on a framework in Magrini (1998), while recognising the spillover of knowledge between adjacent regions. In this context, Florida (2002) emphasises the location of creative occupations and talent as an urban growth factor.

The present study adds to the existing literature by modelling the spatial structure of city regions as well as smaller urban regions by identifying the size of opportunities for economic interaction in the different locations of a region. Using information about location concentrations and time distances between locations, we map the spatial structure in order to reflect opportunities for interaction. In this way we obtain models reflecting how the spatial economic structure influences growth and decline across urban regions. Where growth is present, the development of diversified producer services play a core role in the evolution, with a fast growth of knowledge intensive as well as ordinary producer services. The central aspect in this context is that producer services in general are contact intensive and hence distance sensitive, and because of this service suppliers have an incentive to find locations with good accessibility to many customer firms Storper and Venables (2004). When such opportunities are present, customer firms get a motive to outsource parts of their in-house service activities (compare (Feenstra and Hanson 1999).

1.2   Distance-Sensitive Transactions and Market Access

In the framework for the subsequent analysis we use the label product to refer to both goods and services. Regarding transactions, the prime characteristic is the distance sensitivity of a transaction. The faster transaction costs (including associated displacement costs) increase with distance, the higher the distance sensitivity. In particular, distance sensitivity increases when the frequency of contacts between buyer and seller increases. To the extent that transaction techniques are product specific, we can also classify products on a scale of varying distance sensitivity. A basic assumption is that producer service deliveries are distance sensitive.

The study concentrates on producer services, divided into knowledge-intensive and ordinary producer services. The first category expands because firms demand for knowledge inputs increase in a knowledge economy. The second category expands as a consequence of outsourcing decisions by firms in all sectors. Both categories are contact intensive, including meetings between seller and buyer and deliveries where the supplier has to visit the customer.

With the distinctions made, the rationale for the existence of urban areas and cities is to function as (a) a market place for distance sensitive transactions and (b) an arena for communication and related interaction. In this sense, an urban environment can be thought of as an important institution for the generation of novelties in economic and social life. The leading suggestion is that new ideas and solutions spring from face-to-face (FTF) interaction and related communication. In this context the urban environment stimulates proximity externalities associated with firms' development activities (Johansson and Forslund 2008).

Time distances between buyer and seller are evaluated in a geography of an urban region, where each region consists of urban areas, which in turn consists of zones. Thus, to establish the distance between a service supplier in a specific zone and a customer in another zone we consider the time it takes to travel from one zone to the other zone when travelling by car.

Historically, labour market commuting has remained a basic distance-sensitive activity together with consumers' purchase of household services. Knowledge creation and business development are activities that relate to urban communication externalities as discussed by Fujita and Thisse (2002). Product development and other R&D activities of a firm benefit from distance-sensitive FTF-interaction with suppliers of knowledge-intensive producer services (KP-services). Just like other services, KP-services include direct contacts between buyer and seller as well as between collaborators. As the contemporary knowledge economy develops, the KP-services can be expected to develop into a dominating part of urban economic life. The customers of KP-services comprise manufacturing firms, household service as well as producer service firms. Ordinary producer services (OP-services) also have customers in the entire set of industries and public sector activities. Every firm is a buyer of producer services.

1.3 Producer Services are Distance Sensitive

This paper focuses on suppliers of producer services and the local, regional and extra regional accessibility that a producer-service firm has to its customers. Proximity to many other firms which are potential customers increases the market opportunities of a producer-service supplier. In this way the market size of each producer-service firm can be determined as the distance-discounted value of other firms' economic activity (purchasing power), assuming that firms' demand for producer services on average is proportional to their output value (or their variable costs).

An urban region can function as an arena for distance-sensitive interaction between buyer and seller by combining size, density and short time distances for the pertinent interaction. In order to characterise these properties of an urban region, this study employs three accessibility measures. In this way we can describe for each urban area the size of (a) intra-urban, (b) intra-regional, and (c) extra-regional interaction opportunities Johansson et al. (2003). With this information we can focus on a producer-service supplier in a given urban area and depict this supplier's access to demand in (a) the own urban area, (b) other areas in the same urban region, and (c) other urban regions. This means that each location in an urban region has a specific market access. Because of this, we should expect that the growth of producer-service supply will be differentiated for alternative locations in the urban region.

The variables depicting intra-urban, intra-regional and extra-regional sales opportunities are used in a model to depict and explain the change of jobs in (a) KP-sectors, OP-sectors and O-sectors, where the latter comprise the rest of the economy. Based on these regressions it is also possible to predict the total change of jobs in the economy as a whole (of an urban area) by summing up the changes of the economy's three sectors.

Local, intra-regional and extra-regional accessibility measures have previously been used as explanatory variables in the analysis of location and location dynamics in Klaesson and Pettersson (2006), Andersson and Klaesson (2006) and Johansson and Klaesson (2007). In all these three cases the accessibility variables express the size of local, intra-regional and extra-regional interaction opportunities. These opportunities are created by a combination of (a) number or size of opportunities and (b) proximity to opportunities. In this sense the accessibility measures a kind of opportunity density.

By studying the dynamics of three exhaustive groups of economic sectors, the estimated models also inform about sector substitution in urban areas. Such substitution phenomena in urban regions are analysed in Forslund-J (1988) and Forslund-J and Johansson (2000) in models describing how knowledge-oriented activities increase their share of the economic life of a city region, while routine-based activities decrease their share, in a model framework which makes explicit how expanding activities compete with declining activities for location space. In the present study the share of KP-sectors, OP-sectors and O-sectors compete for location and labour resources in each urban region in a dynamic substitution process. In this framework, the accessibility to customers' demand for producer services changes on a slow time scale, whereas the supply from KP-firms and OP-firms changes more rapidly.

1.4 Outline of the Presentation

Section 2 of the chapter presents a theoretical framework which illuminates the role of producer services in an urban economy. This framework is applied in the presentation of descriptive statistics that provides an overview of urban development in Sweden. Section 3 introduces the reader to how the spatial organisation of an urban region is modelled and how market access of producer-service firms is measured, and how this measurement can be associated with a random choice model of producer-service firms' location preferences. Section 4 presents regression equations and estimation results, emphasising that accessibility vectors drive the change process in a non-linear way. In Sect. 5 the results are assessed from a broader perspective, and new model alternatives are discussed.

2 Producer Services: Theory and Empirical Observations

2.1 Producer Service Supply

Our starting point is an urban region, R, in which we focus on the urban area r. A producer service supplier in area r faces three sources of demand, generated by customers (a) in area r, (b) in other urban areas in region R, denoted by $R(r)$, and in urban areas outside region R, denoted by $E(r)$. For a firm in urban area r, we let A_{rr} signify the market access to potential demand in urban area r, $A_{R(r)}$ signify the market access to potential demand in the rest of region R, and $A_{E(r)}$ signify the market access to potential demand in areas outside region R. With this background we introduce the following market-access vector:

$$A_r = [A_{rr}, A_{R(r)}, A_{E(r)}] \tag{3.1}$$

Market access to customers in each of the three regional demand sources is assumed to increase with the value of economic activities of firms in r, $R(r)$ and $E(r)$, and to decrease with the time distance to the same economic activities. Having reached this far: why does the size of market access, as expressed by the A_r-vector matter? In view of results from models of the economics of cities and agglomeration (Fujita and Thisse 2002), the size of the accessible market determines whether a certain location is feasible for a firm that supplies a differentiated, distance-sensitive product under conditions of (a) monopolistic competition, and (b) fixed costs. A simple model of this type is presented in Johansson and Forslund (2008) and Andersson and Johansson (2008). Such a model is specified in this subsection to illustrate the basic factors that determine the location of firms supplying services to other firms. In this endeavour we specify a demand function, an optimal pricing policy and a location feasibility criterion.

We assume that each service variety i has a negatively sloping demand function, showing how the sales of variety i, x_{ir}, depends on the price p_i and the market access vector A_r when the location of supply is in r:

$$x_{ir} = \delta_i G_i (A_r) p_i^{-\theta_i} \tag{3.2}$$

3 Urban Growth

where $G_i(A_r)$ is market size function which increases in the components of the A_r-vector, $\theta_i > 1$ is the price elasticity of demand, δ_i is a market share coefficient that shrinks as the number of competing varieties increases (Andersson and Johansson 2008).

In the standard model of monopolistic competition each firm supplies one variety. However, in the present formulation the competition will prevent that two firms supply the same variety, whereas one firm may offer its customers several varieties. However, each variety has its own demand schedule, and hence there is an optimal price for each variety, as specified in formula (3.3):

$$p_i = [\theta_i/(\theta_i - 1)]v_i \qquad (3.3)$$

where v_i denotes variable cost and where $\theta_i/(\theta_i - 1) > 1$ represents the mark-up coefficient. With a positive mark-up and a sufficiently large supply, x_{ir}, a firm can cover the fixed costs, F_i associated with variety i. Given that firms select their respective price according to (3.3), the feasibility condition for a location in r becomes

$$p_i \geq v_i + F_i/x_{ir} \qquad (3.4)$$

where we observe that price, variable cost and fixed cost are not location-dependent variables, only the size of output is. The model outlined in (3.2), (3.3), and (3.4) predicts an adjustment process, which is summarised in Table 3.1. According to the table, new producer-service varieties are introduced as $G_i(A_r)$ grows, implying that $x_{ir} = \delta_i G_i(A_r)p_i^{-\theta_i}$ expands, which generates short-term market solutions where $p_i > v_i + F_i/x_{ir}$, which in turn provides incentives for firms to introduce new varieties. In complementing models presented by Rivera-Batiz (1988) and Abdel-Rahman and Fujita (1990), a richer variety of producer services generates increasing productivity of urban-region economies. When this happens new service varieties will induce urban growth and augmented demand for additional producer services.

The model outlined in (3.2), (3.3), and (3.4) has an important extension, which obtains if we recognise the land rent, ρ_r, of each location r, which can be assumed to increase as $G_i(A_r)$ increases. This implies that land rents work as a counteracting factor that reduces growth as $G_i(A_r)$ expands, and the location-feasibility criterion in (3.4) changes to

$$p_i \geq v_i + F_i/x_{ir} + \rho(G_i(A_r)) \qquad (3.5)$$

Given the adjustment process illustrated in Table 3.1, we should expect (a) that large urban agglomerations have a larger share of producer services, (b) that urban regions with a larger share of producer services grow faster than other urban regions. These suggestions are investigated in the rest of this section. In Sect. 3 the focus is on how to identify the function $G_i(A_r)$ and to measure the value of

54   J. Klaesson and B. Johansson

Table 3.1 Dynamic adjustments of demand for and supply of producer services

Change	Consequence
As an urban region grows and/or gets more connected, the A_r-vector will grow	Growth of A_r stimulates $x_{ir} = \delta_i G_i (A_r) p_i^{-\theta_i}$ to expand. This expansion will generate positive net profits which remain as long as new varieties are not invented and introduced
Growing sales such that $x_{ir} = \delta_i G_i (A_r) p_i^{-\theta_i}$ expands will make F_i/x_{ir} smaller	As F_i/x_{ir} falls in value, profit per delivered variety becomes larger so that $p_i > v_i + F_i/x_{ir}$, which provides incentive for new varieties to enter
As new varieties are introduced more people are employed in the producer-service sector	As the producer-service sector grows, the entire urban-region economy is stimulated to grow, leading to an increasing A_r-vector, implying a case of cumulative growth
As $G_i(A_r)$ expands the competition for land increases	Growing competition for land leads to increasing values of $\rho_r = \rho(G_i(A_r))$, and hence the feasible-location criterion changes to $p_i \geq v_i + F_i/x_{ir} + \rho(G_i(A_r))$

$G_i(A_r)$ at different points in time for all urban regions in Sweden. This is followed up by empirical estimations in Sect. 4.

The reader should also observe that the initial text in Table 3.1 is "As an urban region grows and/or gets more connected, the A_r-vector will grow." If this statement is reversed, the self-reinforcing adjustments in the table will predict decline, and in the empirical part of the paper such negative spirals (when the A_r-vector is "too small") will be identified.

2.2   *Urban Growth in Sweden*

The following question is asked in this subsection: do the largest urban agglomerations grow faster than other regions in Sweden? The growth process is examined in a long time perspective, from 1950 to 2005. The presentation separates urban regions into the following four types of regions: (a) the three metropolitan regions Stockholm, Göteborg and Malmö, (b) the two integrating regions Norrköping and Linköping, (c) medium-sized urban regions, and (d) small regions with less than 100,000 inhabitants.

Two major features characterise the development of urban regions in Sweden during the last 55 years. The first is an urbanisation process, implying that the share of population living in urban areas has grown during the decades. The second feature is a steady region enlargement, such that the number of urban regions has declined in a monotonic way, based on improved transport conditions which have reduced the time distance between urban areas and thereby brought about an integration of initially separated urban areas into urban regions with increasingly larger geographical territories.

3 Urban Growth

Table 3.2 Long-term population change for urban regions with constant delineation

Urban region	1950–2005 (%)	1990–2000 (%)	2000–2005 (%)	Population 2005
Stockholm	72.4	10.8	3.6	2,250,310
Göteborg	61.3	8.0	3.8	1,016,661
Malmö	43.6	6.8	3.9	1,005,712
Norrköping-Linköping	16.1	2.1	−1.2	412,437
Medium-sized regions	17.9	0.4	1.0	3,119,994
Small regions	−12.4	−5.4	−2.1	1,242,638
The whole country	28.4	3.4	1.8	9,047,752

Source: Elaboration of data from statistics Sweden
Remark: Fixed regional boundaries of 72 FA-regions

Table 3.2 provides an overview of the population development for urban regions with functional boundaries defined according to the situation in 2005. These regions were not functional regions in 1950, which means that the present structure guides how we trace the realised history in the spirit of "backward induction." Four regions are considered individually, consisting of the three metropolitan regions Stockholm, Göteborg and Malmö, plus the "twin-city region" Norrköping-Linköping. In addition the table shows the development of the groups of medium-sized regions and small regions.

As described in Table 3.2, the metropolitan regions have grown faster than medium-sized and small regions, where many small regions display a path with shrinking populations. In particular, we note that for the period 1950–2005, the growth of the Stockholm region is 2.5 times as fast as for the country average. The corresponding values for Göteborg and Malmö are 2.2 and 1.5, respectively. The overall finding in Table 3.2 is that the three metropolitan regions grow, the medium-sized regions change very little and the small regions decline.

The picture of urban region change in the table can also be described in terms of different regions' share of the total population in the country. Table 3.3 illustrates how the population share of the Stockholm region has increased from just above 18 % in 1950 to almost 25 % in 2005. During the same period the three metropolitan regions increased their population share from 37 % to 47 %. This observation puts the three metropolitan regions into a special category: they have – as a group – increased their share of the total population, whereas Norrköping-Linköping, the group of medium-sized as well as the group of small urban regions had a larger population share in 1950 than in 2005.

Altogether, this illustrates a slow but steady concentration in metropolitan-like regions, which constitute a milieu for producer and household services. As shown in Johansson et al. 2010) a similar process can be identified for urban regions across the European Union. In the Swedish context, much of this change is a substitution process, in which producer services play a fundamental role, having manufacturing, household and producer service firms as customers.

The information in Table 3.3 could also be formulated in terms of GDP or total wage sum for each region, although the necessary information would have to be estimated with less accuracy than population figures for the years 1950 and 1970. In the following subsection, we describe the development of the wage sum over a much more recent period.

Table 3.3 Share of metropolitan population 1950–2005. Percent

Urban region	1950	1970	1990	2005
Stockholm	21.4	22.8	24.4	24.9
Göteborg	10.1	10.6	11.0	11.2
Malmö	10.3	10.5	10.9	11.1
Norrköping-Linköping	4.7	4.6	4.6	4.6
Medium-sized regions	36.4	35.8	34.8	34.5
Small regions	17.1	15.6	14.3	13.7

Source: Elaboration of data from statistics Sweden
Remark: Fixed regional boundaries of 72 FA-regions

2.3 Growth of Producer Services

All sectors of an urban economy consists of firms which are customers to suppliers of producer services. The purchasing power of those customers can be proxied by the wage sum in each urban region. When doing this, we assume that on average each firm's wage sum is proportional to its output as well as its total costs. Therefore, the wage sum of firms (as a group) in an urban region will be approximately proportional to the total demand for producer services in each urban area as well as in each urban region. Moreover, as a rule the wage sum in an urban region will exceed 70 % of value added.

Table 3.4 is thus our first rough indicator of how the potential demand for producer services has increased in different regions during the period 1999–2006. The overall message is that the wage sum has increased faster in the three metropolitan regions than elsewhere in the country.

A background for the present analysis is that the number of person employed in producer-service sector has increased faster than employment in other sectors, and that this increase has been faster in large urban agglomerations than elsewhere in the economy. To shed light on this phenomenon, Table 3.5 provides information about the employment growth in producer services and the rest of the economy. The table distinguishes between knowledge-intensive producer services (KP-sectors), ordinary producer services (OP-sectors, and the rest of the economy (O-sectors). The message from the table is that KP-services have grown much faster than the total wage sum in the three metropolitan regions and in the Norrköping-Linköping region. Moreover, in the metropolitan and medium-sized regions OP-services have grown at a similar pace as the wage sum in the same regions. In the small regions the OP-services have grown slower than the wage sum in these regions.

Taken together, the producer services have grown faster than the entire economy of each region. As a consequence, the growth in the rest of the economy has been slower than the growth in the economy as a whole (all sectors). Thus we can conclude across regions (a) that KP-services grow much faster than the entire economy, (b) that OP-services grow at a pace above that of the entire economy, and (c) that the rest of the economy grows at a slower pace.

The Swedish observation that producer-service employment increases its share of urban-region employment has also been documented as a pattern that prevails in other OECD countries in Kox and Rubalcaba (2007), Kolko (2009), and Camacho

3 Urban Growth

Table 3.4 The wage sum (W) in Swedish urban regions 1999 and 2006

Urban region	1999 (billion SEK)	2006 (billion SEK)	Percentage growth
Stockholm	243	300	23
Göteborg	90	117	30
Malmö	80	101	26
Norrköping-Linköping	34	41	21
Medium-sized regions	259	310	20
Small regions	99	116	17

Remark: The regions consists of 72 FA-regions and the source is statistics Sweden

Table 3.5 Growth of employment in sectors 1999 – 2006 in percent

Urban region	KP-services	OP-services	Other sectors	All sectors
Stockholm	39.89	19.71	−1.14	8.11
Göteborg	41.15	27.13	7.52	14.04
Malmö	65.81	34.16	3.58	12.83
Norrköping and Linköping	60.19	24.84	−0.58	5.50
Medium-sized regions	24.65	19.94	5.68	8.53
Small regions	17.75	11.00	3.12	4.44

Source: AST-information from statistics Sweden

and Rodriguez (2005). The increasing share of KP-services is documented for individual European countries in Muller and Doloreux (2007), Wood (2002, 2006) with regard to the UK, Koch and Stahlecker (2006) with regard to German metropolitan regions, and Kox and Rubalcaba (2007) in an EU-wide context.

To provide a sharper picture of the information provided this far, Table 3.6 presents the development of the economy's sectors as employment shares for the first and last year of the period 1999–2006. The table tells us that the share of producer services is growing between 1999 and 2006. The growth of KP-services is much faster in the four largest urban regions than in either medium-sized or small regions. The growth rate for OP-services is more evenly spread across medium-sized and larger regions. At the same time the growth rate is about half as high for the small regions.

In 2006, the employment share for the entire set of producer services is more than 40 % in the Stockholm region and more than 30 % in the other two metropolitan regions. In medium-sized and small regions the share is 15–20 %. We have argued that the increasing share of producer services reflects that the texture of the economy is becoming finer with an extended "division of labour" and diversified specialisation, caused by outsourcing service activities from seemingly all types of firms. The intensity of this structural change in the metropolitan regions is double that in medium-sized regions, implying a profound difference between metropolitan and non-metropolitan.

The three measures of market access are such that their values increase with the size of an urban region. In particular for small urban areas in large regions, the $A_{R(r)}$ – measure co-varies strongly with total employment of the pertinent region.

Table 3.6 Share of producer services in urban regions 1999 and 2006

Urban region	KP-services 1999 (%)	KP-services 2006 (%)	OP-services 1999 (%)	OP-services 2006 (%)
Stockholm	8.56	11.07	27.51	30.46
Göteborg	6.82	8.45	21.56	24.03
Malmö	5.46	8.02	19.15	22.77
Norrköping and Linköping	3.53	8.92	15.48	18.31
Medium-sized regions	3.76	4.32	14.97	16.55
Small regions	2.42	2.73	12.19	12.96

Remark: Share of persons employed in producer service sectors to total employment

Moreover, the A_{rr}-measure of the largest urban area in a region increases in concordance with the absolute size of the region. As a consequence, we should expect exactly the pattern which is presented in Table 3.6. There we can see that the share of KP-service jobs attains the highest value in the largest urban region (Stockholm), the second highest in the second largest region (Göteborg), and it continues to fall with the size of each urban region. The smallest share (in small regions) is less than one third of that in the Stockholm region for the year 2006. This pattern holds both for KP-services and OP-services. The strong service concentration in the Stockholm region has been stressed by Hermelin (2007)

3 Formation of Demand for Producer Services

3.1 Spatial Organisation

A basic feature of the spatial economy is a set of nodes where activities are concentrated and a corresponding set of links, which form a network, connecting the nodes. We shall consider three different layers of nodes. The medium layer consists of urban areas, which can be towns and cities, depending on the size. The lower layer consists of zones within an urban area, and the upper layer consists of functional urban regions, frequently referred to as just urban regions. An urban region usually consists of a set of urban areas, between which the interaction is more intense than it is between two urban areas belonging to two different urban regions.

Each link connecting two urban areas, r and s, is characterised by the time distance, t_{rs}, between the two areas. For an individual urban area we can also identify the average time distance, t_{rr}, between any pair of zones within the area. Consider now a model formulation, where each urban area in a region is defined as a node in the region. The spatial organisation of the region can then be described by (a) the location of activities in each node and (b) the time distance between the nodes. In an aggregate sense, the models in the present paper consider two types of activity measures. The first is designed to reflect the size of economic activities,

3 Urban Growth 59

Table 3.7 Organisation of urban space

Nodal layers	Time distances	Notation
Zone in an urban area	The time distance for interaction is considered negligible	
Urban area (municipality with a local government)	The urban area is a city or a town, consisting of zones, between which the average time distance, t_{rr}, varies around 10 min by car	An urban area is denote by r and s
Functional urban region (FUR)	The FUR consists of urban areas, between which the time distances by car vary between 15 and 50 min	$R(r)$ denotes all areas belonging to the same urban region as r, except r itself
Extra-regional territory	Urban areas belonging to other regions. The average time distance between urban areas in two different regions exceeds 60 min by car	$E(r)$ denotes all areas belonging to other regions than region R to which r itself belongs

Source: Johansson and Klaesson (2007)

W_r, in area r, measured by the sum of all wages generated by firms in the area. The second reflects the size of employment (number of jobs) in different sectors in each urban area r, where L_r denotes the total number of jobs in r.

The focus of the analysis is the location of producer services in each urban area, and the associated location advantage in each area. The advantage of a location will be measured by the access to customers' potential demand facing suppliers in a given urban area. Once such a measure is established, we assume that the supply of producer services in an urban area is stimulated to expand in response to the size of the accessible demand for the output from suppliers located in that area. When the stimulation is low, expansion turns into contraction. In this way we can formulate equations for the location dynamics across urban areas.

We will assume that the potential demand in urban area r for producer services is a function of the size of economic activities in area r as measured by the wage sum, W_r. Consider now a supplier who is located in a particular zone in the urban area r. As outlined in Table 3.7, the selected supplier firm perceives that it has the same average time distance, t_{rr}, to all zones in the given area r. A supply firm in r has potential customers in its own urban area r, in other intra-regional areas $s \in R(r)$, and in extra-regional areas $k \in E(r)$.

3.2 Market Access of Producer-Service Suppliers

As described in formula (3.1), the market of suppliers of producer services is divided into three categories: intra-urban customers, intra-regional customers, extra-regional customers, where the latter are located in other regions. We shall consider a measures of a supplier's access to customer demand based on the assumption that producer-service suppliers make the effort to contact their customers.

First, consider a typical supplier in urban area r, who wants to assess the possibilities to find customers in different areas. We assume that the supplier has a random-choice preference function $\tilde{V}_{rs} = V_{rs} + \varepsilon_{rs}$, which consists of a systematic part V_{rs} and an extreme-value distributed random part, denoted by ε_{rs}. The systematic part is specified as follows:

$$V_{rs} = \phi_{rs} - \lambda_{rs}t_{rs} \tag{3.6}$$

As shown in the Appendix, the location-preference function in (3.6) can be applied to define three market access measures, ordered in the vector $A_r = [A_{rr}, A_{R(r)}, A_{E(r)}]$, where

$$A_{rr} = W_r \exp\{-\lambda_1 t_{rr}\} \text{ is the access to demand inside urban area } r \tag{3.7a}$$

$$A_{R(r)} = \sum_{s \in R(r)} W_s \exp\{-\lambda_2 t_{rs}\} \text{ is the access to demand in the rest of the}$$

$$\text{region associated with urban area } r \tag{3.7b}$$

$$A_{E(r)} = \sum_{k \in E(r)} W_k \exp\{-\lambda_3 t_{rk}\} \text{ is the access to demand outside the region}$$

$$\text{associated with urban area } r. \tag{3.7c}$$

The wage-sum variable W_s in each urban area s reflects the size of activities of firms in the area, whereas $\exp\{-\lambda_i t_{rs}\}$ discounts the value of W_s, where t_{rs} is the time distance between area r and s, and where λ_i is the time sensitivity that takes the value λ_1 when $r = s$, λ_2 when $s \in R(r)$ which means that s and r belong to the same region, and λ_3 when $s \in E(r)$ which means that s and r belong to different regions. Time distances follow a pattern such that (a) $t_{rk} > t_{rs}$ when $s \in R(r)$ and $k \in E(r)$, and (b) $t_{rs} > t_{rr}$ when $s \in R(r)$.

The definitions of the three market access measures imply that the market access increases as the wage sums increase, and as the time distances decrease. As a consequence, improvements of transport conditions in an urban region increases the market access, if other factors are kept constant. Moreover, when urban growth generates congestion, time distances will increase and hence market access may be reduced.

3.3 Sectors of the Urban Region Economies

Consider the basic conditions of a firm. On the one hand the firm makes use of markets for buying inputs, and on the other it makes use of markets for selling its output. In both cases the firm's entire market is decomposed into local, regional and extra-regional market demand. Suppliers of distance-sensitive

3 Urban Growth

producer services benefit from large values of A_{rr} and $A_{R(r)}$, as formally outlined in subsection 2.1. The mirror case comprises firms with distance-sensitive service inputs. Also these firms benefit from accessibility to their service suppliers. This latter externality is not measured directly. However, locations where service suppliers have large market access (large values of A_{rr} and $A_{R(r)}$) are also locations where service customers have favourable accessibility to service suppliers. In summary we may observe the following:

> A firm which is a seller of distance-sensitive producer services benefit from high market access values, and thus has an incentive to chose a location with favourable market access.
>
> As a buyer of distance-sensitive producer services any firm will benefit from favourable accessibility to service suppliers. Such favourable accessibility, from a location r, is indirectly captured by high values of A_{rr} and $A_{R(r)}$.

In the discussion above we have avoided to include the third market access measure, namely $A_{E(r)}$. The reason for that is twofold. First, in the empirical part of the paper that follows we can observe that the extra-regional market access influences location decisions in a weaker and in a more ambiguous way. Second, high extra-regional market access corresponds to a situation where the individual firm may contemplate to locate outside the region. With an alternative formulation, high values of $A_{E(r)}$ is a signal of inter-regional competition.

So far the arguments put forward are limited to assessment of location decisions in a static perspective, focussing on the question whether an individual firm has any incentive to change location. In the following analysis we extend this idea by assuming that the growth of producer services in a region is influenced by the market access vector $A_r = (A_{rr}, A_{R(r)}, A_{E(r)})$, which corresponds to the idea that firms adjust their location and the size of their supply from a given location in response to the A_r-vector, and while doing that they also influence the A_r-vector in a cumulative way.

We limit the analysis to examine the structure of urban economies, by decomposing them into two major sectors: (a) producer services and (b) all other sectors of the economy. Moreover, producer services are subdivided into knowledge intensive and other (ordinary) producer services. Thus, the economy consists of the KP-sector supplying knowledge-intensive producer services, the OP-sector supplying ordinary producer services, and the O-sector supplying all other goods and services. In this way the total employment in urban area r, L_r, is divided in the following way:

$$L_r = L_r^{KP} + L_r^{OP} + L_r^{O} \tag{3.8}$$

L_r^{KP} = Employment in the KP-sector in urban area r
L_r^{OP} = Employment in the OP-sector in urban area r
L_r^{O} = Employment in the O-sector in urban area r

The entire focus is on urban growth decomposed into change of employment in each of the three sectors. The change process will be examined during the period 1999–2006, by making panel-data regressions of change for a sequence of three

5-year periods. In earlier studies 8-year periods have been applied to take into account that firms' location response to market access patterns is a fairly slow process. In this study the time period has been shortened due to limited availability of data.

For the chosen period, we observe three changes, denoted by $\Delta L_r^{KP}, \Delta L_r^{OP}$, and ΔL_r^O, which describe the change in urban area r with regard to (a) knowledge-intensive producer services, (b) other producer services and (c) the aggregate of all other sectors of the economy. These change variables will first be regressed against the three market access variables $A_{rr}, A_{R(r)}, A_{E(r)}$, contained in the vector $[A_{rr}, A_{R(r)}, A_{E(r)}]$. This regression is referred to as the *linear adjustment model*.

In a second step we apply a regression o six variables, collected from the vector $[A_{rr}, A_{R(r)}, A_{E(r)}]$ and from the associated vector $[(A_{rr})^2, (A_{R(r)})^2 (A_{E(r)})^2]$, where the latter components are included to reflect non-linearities. Thus, the latter type of regression is referred to as the *non-linear (quadratic) adjustment model*.

From the empirical exposition in previous subsections we can conjecture that the change in the two producer services will adjust in a similar way, such that ΔL_r^{KP} responds to the market access structure in a similar way as ΔL_r^{OP} responds. These two change variables are assumed to react positively to large values of A_{rr} and $A_{R(r)}$. Having said this, we observe that when these values grow, the location costs increase, because land rents grow. For the O-sector of the economy, the willingness to pay for accessibility is assumed to be lower on average, reflecting that pertinent firms supply less contact-depending goods and services, and have less to gain from locations with high accessibility. Thus, we expect to find results that imply that ΔL_r^O responds to market access with a different sign than what applies to ΔL_r^{KP} and ΔL_r^{OP}.

4 Estimating the Change Processes

4.1 Accessibility Vectors Drive the Growth of Supply

In Appendix three time-sensitivity parameters are specified in (***A.5) and in the text. In our analysis we assume that these parameters are the same for KP-services, OP-services and the O-sector. However, the proximity parameters for intra-area preferences, ϕ_1, intra-region preferences, ϕ_2, and extra-region preferences, ϕ_3, are not included in our market access measures. These preference parameters will instead be embedded in the estimation of the response parameters α_i and β_i, as given by formulas (3.9) and (3.10).

The intention with the econometric analyses is to estimate two types of change equations, specified as follows for an urban area r:

$$\Delta L_r^j = \alpha_0 + \alpha_1 A_r + \alpha_2 A_{R(r)} + \alpha_3 A_{E(r)})$$

(3.9)

3 Urban Growth

$$\Delta L_r^j = \alpha_0 + \alpha_1 A_r + \alpha_2 A_{R(r)} + \alpha_3 A_{E(r)} + \beta_1 (A_r)^2 + \beta_2 (A_{R(r)})^2 + \beta_3 (A_{E(r)})^2 \quad (3.10)$$

where the top index of ΔL_r^j satisfies $j = $ KP, OP and O, which means that it refers to knowledge intensive and ordinary producer services, and to other sectors of the economy. The first equation (3.9) represents the linear adjustment model, in which the market access variables influence the change of employment in each of the three sectors. In particular we may note that when the parameter α_0 is negative, then this reveals that there is a threshold value of $\alpha_1 A_r + \alpha_2 A_{R(r)} + \alpha_3 A_{E(r)}$, below which the change will be a reduction in employment

The second equation in (3.10) extends the first equation by including the squared values of the three market access variables, which allows for non-linear adjustments. Consider for example that $\alpha_1 > 0$ and $\beta_1 < 0$. Then this reflects a relationship such that the response to the intra-urban market access is concave, which means that below a certain level the market access has a positive growth impact, whereas for larger values, the impact will reduce and ultimately become negative. Analogously, if $\alpha_2 < 0$ and $\beta_2 > 0$, this will reflect an exponential growth impact where values of $A_{R(r)}$ above a critical level will bring about increasing stimulus to growth.

The approach specified in (3.9) and (3.10) is illustrated by Fig. 3.1 which emphasises the idea that the two market access vectors $[A_{rr}, A_{R(r)}, A_{E(r)}]$ and $[(A_{rr})^2, (A_{R(r)})^2 (A_{E(r)})^2]$ are modelled as the sole driving forces for each of the three sectors. It should then be observed that over time the changes represented by ΔL_r^{KP}, ΔL_r^{OP} and ΔL_r^O will affect the values of the components in the two vectors: This phenomenon represents cumulative change, comprising both self-reinforcing growth and decline in the set of urban areas.

Figure 3.1 illustrates a major aspect of the research issue in this paper. The issue is two pronged. First, is there empirical evidence in favour of the hypothesis that market access variables influence the change of producer services as stated in Sects. 2 and 3? Second, can the influence be correctly depicted by the linear adjustment model in formula (3.9) or does the specification have to be extended to the non-linear adjustment model in formula (3.10)? The econometric results in Sects. 4.2 and 4.3 will shed some light on these questions, while at the same time allow additional insights about sectoral differences presented in Sect. 4.4.

The data for the econometric analysis are based on annual (a) wage sum values for each urban area (municipality) and (b) sector employment for each sector and urban area over the period 1999–2006, collected from Statistics Sweden. In addition the analysis makes use of a matrix of time distances between all zones across the set of urban areas, based on information from the Swedish National Road Administration. The data have been arranged in three periods, each 5 years long. Using $t = 1$ for 1999 and $t = 8$ for 2006, we feed the econometric procedure with the following information for each of the three periods:

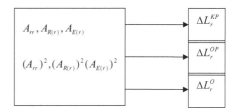

Fig. 3.1 Impact on sector change of the market access pattern

$$\Delta L_r^j(6) = L_r^j(6) - L_r^j(1) \text{ and } [A_{rr}(1), A_{R(r)}(1), A_{E(r)}(1)]$$
$$\Delta L_r^j(7) = L_r^j(7) - L_r^j(2) \text{ and } [A_{rr}(2), A_{R(r)}(2), A_{E(r)}(2)]$$
$$\Delta L_r^j(8) = L_r^j(8) - L_r^j(3) \text{ and } [A_{rr}(3), A_{R(r)}(3), A_{E(r)}(3)]$$

The described scheme means that the market access vector of each urban region for a given year, is used as a predictor of employment change in sector j 5 years ahead. In this way the procedure attempts to reveal a causal relation between slowly changing market access values and the more rapidly changing pattern of jobs in the examined sectors.

4.2 The Linear Adjustment Model

Section 4.1 contains a discussion of how producer-service sectors in an urban area change over time in response to the area's intra-urban, intra-regional and extra-regional market access. In this subsection we use the regression equation in (3.9), which corresponds to the linear adjustment model to find out how far it takes the analysis. With regard to the linear adjustment equation, $\Delta L_r^j = \alpha_0 + \alpha_1 A_r + \alpha_2 A_{R(r)} + \alpha_3 A_{E(r)}$, we observe the following properties:

- $\alpha_0 < 0$ reflects the presence of a threshold value, above which positive growth of sector j will obtain.
- Positive stimuli from intra-urban and intra-regional market access require that $\alpha_1 > 0$ and $\alpha_2 > 0$.

Table 3.8 presents results, where producer-service jobs respond positively and with significant parameters to the size of intra-urban and intra-regional market access. For KP-services, the response to extra-regional market access is significantly negative. Our interpretation of this is that when a given urban area is close to one or several large extra-regional markets, then this implies that jobs will rather grow in these extra-regional locations. This may labelled as an inter-regional competition effect.

The results in Table 3.8 can be evaluated in view of our hypotheses. The first of these concerns the presence of a size threshold, recognised as a negative value of the intercept. This is satisfied for the two producer-service sectors KP and OP, but not for the O-sector, which contains manufacturing and household services as the main components. However, as will be shown in the subsequent subsection, the O-sector has a threshold value in the non-linear adjustment model.

3 Urban Growth

Table 3.8 Linear adjustment model. Sequence of three 5-year periods, 1999–2006

Regressand			ΔKP	ΔOP	ΔO
Intercept		(α_0)	$-160.31\ (5.49)^{***}$	$-187.47\ (5.39)^{***}$	$493.45\ (3.23)^{***}$
Intra-urban	A_{rr}	(α_1)	$673.63\ (63.72)^{***}$	$867.92\ (68.97)^{***}$	$-1011.84\ (18.32)^{***}$
Intra-regional	$A_{R(r)}$	(α_2)	$3.23\ (0.76)$	$13.18\ (2.60)^{***}$	$18.830\ (0.85)$
Extra-regional	$A_{E(r)}$	(α_3)	$-179.68\ (3.20)^{***}$	$-115.00\ (1.72)^{*}$	$427.74\ (1.46)$
R-sq. (overall)			0.90	0.92	0.52

Between effects estimation. Absolute value of t statistics in *parentheses*. * significant at 10 %; ** significant at 5 %; *** significant at 1 %

As a second hypothesis, the intra-urban market access parameter α_1 is expected to be positive and significant for producer services, and this is satisfied for both KP and OP. This provides arguments in favour of the view that suppliers of producer services adjust so as to have a close proximity to customers, which are firms in all sectors.

Our third observation is that intra-urban access is negatively related to the change of the O-sector. The effect is significant, but we may ask: is the repelling force from intra-urban market access present both for small and large urban areas? Again, we may look for an answer in the subsequent subsection.

4.3 The Non-linear Adjustment Model

In the non-linear adjustment model presented in formula (3.10) each market access value appears twice, first in normal form and then as a squared value. In view of the O-sector this specification allows for a result where $\alpha_1 > 0$ combined with $\beta_1 < 0$. Such a result would correspond to an adjustment pattern where O-sector activities are stimulated to grow when the intra-urban value, A_{rr}, is low, while larger values will make $\beta_1 A_{rr}$ larger than $\alpha_1 A_{rr}$ so that the O-sector starts to lose employment in urban area r when the intra-urban market access gets large enough.

Table 3.9 presents the estimated parameters with the non-linear adjustment model. Not surprisingly the overall R-square increases, and this effect appears especially for the O-sector. The first observation is that extra-regional market access has almost exclusively insignificant parameters, except for knowledge-intensive producer services, represented by ΔKP. A second clear-cut observation is that in the non-linear adjustment model there is a threshold for each sector, presented by $\alpha_0 < 0$.

For the two producer-service sectors, the result is strongly in favour of the basic hypothesis, which states that these sectors are stimulated by intra-urban market access. This follows from the result with both α_1 and β_1 significant and positive. Thus, intra-urban market access stimulates the growth of producer services, and the influence is exponential in the estimation.

Intra-regional market access has a more complex structure. The α_2 parameter is negative for both producer-service sectors, whereas the β_2 is positive and significant in both cases. This result indicates the demand arising in the rest of the region has a negative or insignificant effect as long as the intra-regional market access is

Table 3.9 Non-linear growth model. Sequence of three 5-year periods, 1999–2006

Regressand			ΔOP	ΔOP	ΔKP	ΔOP	ΔO
Intercept		(α_0)			-34.394 (1.24)	-111.070 (2.55)**	-180.537 (1.69)*
Intra-urban	A_{rr}	(α_1)			392.583 (19.62)***	802.878 (25.49)***	825.279 (10.68)***
	$(A_{rr})^2$	(β_1)			15.325 (15.31)***	3.791 (2.41)**	-100.114 (25.91)***
Intra-regional	$A_{R(r)}$	(α_2)			-9.070 (1.00)	-32.396 (2.27)**	85.074 (2.43)**
	$(A_{R(r)})^2$	(β_2)			1.132 (2.29)**	2.739 (3.52)***	-6.727 (3.53)***
Extra-regional	$A_{E(r)}$	(α_3)			-216.322 (2.63)***	-154.495 (1.19)	-5.847 (0.02)
	$(A_{E(r)})^2$	(β_3)			56.262 (1.24)	24.625 (0.35)	60.239 (0.35)
R-sq. (overall)					0.93	0.92	0.82

Between effects estimation. Absolute value of t statistics in *parentheses* * significant at 10 %; ** significant at 5 %; *** significant at 1 %

small. However, as the access to demand in the rest of the region becomes larger, the same demand will stimulate the employment in producer-service sectors to grow. This pattern is present as an advantage for small urban areas that belong to a large urban region.

The results in Table 3.9 shed light on the O-sector. First, we can observe a negative threshold parameter also for this sector. Second, the sector is positively stimulated to grow by the intra-urban market access, revealed by $\alpha_1 > 0$. However, $\beta_1 < 0$, which implies that when the intra-urban market access gets larger, then the firms of the sector are stimulated to grow in other parts of the region, while the intra-urban employment shrinks. This process may be described as a substitution phenomenon, where producer-service activities squeeze out the O-sector activities. In other words, those sectors in which firms are willing to pay higher land rents in order to achieve a better market access drive out those firms which cannot afford higher land rents.

4.4 Differences Between Producer Services and the Rest of the Economy

The separation of the economy into producer-service sectors and other sectors of the economy is a coarse demarcation. In spite of this it captures basic phenomena associated with urban regions that either grow or decline. The first observation is that for small urban areas, all economic activities are positively stimulated by the size of intra-urban market access. However, as the size of the intra-urban market grows, at some stage the O-sector activities start to be negatively stimulated by the size of the intra-urban market access, whereas the producer-service sectors continue to respond with positive growth to the size of market access. The interpretation of this phenomenon is as follows:

All sectors benefit from a location with proximity to customers. However, producer-service sectors benefit more than O-sectors and hence producer-service firms are prepared to pay higher land rents as central locations become more crowded, which is exactly what happens when intra-urban market access increases.

Producer-service firms pay higher land rents for a location in an area r as A_{rr} gets larger, which gradually forces firms in the O-sector to expand in other locations.

For firms located in urban area r, the inter-regional market access, $A_{R(r)}$ does not stimulate producer-service firms to grow when $A_{R(r)}$ is small, whereas it stimulates the growth of firms in the O-sector for small market access values. As these values increase, the employment in the O-sector is stimulated to decrease whereas the opposite applies to KP-firms and OP-firms. Also in this case we may observe that when $A_{R(r)}$ gets larger, the land rents in urban area r will increase. Higher intra-regional market access bring stronger benefits to producer-service firms than to O-sector firms. Hence the former firms will be more willing to pay growing land rents in area r. As a consequence the employment in the producer-service sectors will expand in area r and replace employment in the O-sector.

5 Discussion and Summary

As a theoretical background to the analyses of change processes, the present paper refers to the market access measure $B_{rs} = W_s \exp\{V_{rs}\}$ as the potential demand in location s that is accessible to a firm in location r, as discussed in the Appendix. In this measure W_s represents the "purchasing power" available in location s, and $V_{rs} = \phi_{rs} - \lambda_{rs}t_{rs}$. Thus,

$$B_{rs} = \exp\{\phi_i\}W_s \exp\{-\lambda_{rs}t_{rs}\}$$

represents information about how the purchasing power in location s adds to value associated with a supply location in r.

Consider now that $s \in R(r)$. Then our dynamic adjustment equations are specified as dependent on $\hat{\alpha}_1 B_{rs}$ and $\hat{\beta}_1 (B_{rs})^2$, where

$$\hat{\alpha}_1 B_{rs} = \alpha_1 W_s \exp\{-\lambda_{rs}t_{rs}\} \text{ and } \hat{\beta}_1 (B_{rs})^2 = \beta_1 [W_s \exp\{-\lambda_{rs}t_{rs}\}]^2$$

The two parameters α_1 and β_1 may seem to replace the ϕ_1 parameter. However, together α_1 and β_1 reflect properties of a change process where increased density and growing land values play a fundamental role. In view of this, it is important to see that the dynamic process has $W_s \exp\{-\lambda_{rs}t_{rs}\}$ as the basic attraction variable, and this variable affects the change process in a non-linear way.

Focusing on the non-linear adjustment model, we may conclude that both types of producer-service firms respond in their change pattern to market access in a similar way. In this sense the presented analysis indicates that producer services differ compared to all other sectors of urban economies by having all firms in the economy as customers. Because of this, market access influences the change process of producer-service firms in a particular way that separates them from other firms. These findings can be summarised for the following types of urban areas:

1. The central (largest) urban area of a metropolitan region has large values of both A_{rr} and $A_{R(r)}$, and this stimulates growth in these urban areas with special strength
2. The small urban areas in metropolitan regions have a small value of A_{rr} and a large value of $A_{R(r)}$, and this gives these smaller urban areas a stronger expansion of the producer-service sector than other small urban areas.
3. The central urban area of each medium-sized urban region has a value of A_{rr} which is sufficiently large to make producer-service supply grow in area r, whereas the value of $A_{R(r)}$ tends to be low, and hence the intra-regional market access does not add much to the growth.
4. In small urban regions all urban areas are small, and hence the growth of producer-service activities expand more moderately.

The pattern of growth responses presented above also imply that the Swedish metropolitan are superior in the sense that many non-central urban areas have higher market access than the central urban area in most medium-sized regions.

3 Urban Growth

Because of this the options for outsourcing services are much greater in the metropolitan regions. It remains to show that this feature bring productivity advantages to the metropolitan regions. It also remains to clarify the expansion of producer-service supply on a finer level of sector decomposition.

Appendix

For a service-supplying firm located in r, the undiscounted purchasing power in area r is W_r. In area $s \in R(r)$ the purchasing power is W_s, and area $k \in E(r)$ it is W_k. The time distances to customers in each of these three areas are t_{rr}, t_{rs} and t_{rk}, respectively. Now, let λ_1 denote the time sensitivity inside an urban area, λ_2 denote the time sensitivity inside an urban region, and λ_3 the time sensitivity for contacts outside a region. Then we can define the market access to customers in locations r, s, and k as $A_{rr} = W_r \exp\{-\lambda_1 t_{rr}\}$, $A_{rs} = W_s \exp\{-\lambda_2 t_{rs}\}$, and $A_{rk} = W_k \exp\{-\lambda_3 t_{rk}\}$, respectively. From this we can define:

$$A_{rr} = W_r \exp\{-\lambda_1 t_{rr}\} = \text{Intra} - \text{urban market access} \tag{3.11}$$

$$A_{R(r)} = \sum_{s \in R(r)} A_{rs} = \sum_{s \in R(r)} W_s \exp\{-\lambda_2 t_{rs}\} = \text{Intra} - \text{regional market access}$$
$$\tag{3.12}$$

$$A_{E(r)} = \sum_{k \in E(r)} A_{rk} = \sum_{k \in E(r)} W_k \exp\{-\lambda_3 t_{rk}\} = \text{Extra} - \text{regional market access}$$
$$\tag{3.13}$$

These market access measures can be derived from a model where each firm has a random-choice, location-preference function $\tilde{V}_{rs} = V_{rs} + \varepsilon_{rs}$, which consists of a systematic part V_{rs} and extreme-value distributed random part, denoted by ε_{rs}, where $\tilde{V}_{rs}$ represents the value of locating in r for serving customers in s. The systematic part is specified as follows:

$$V_{rs} = \phi_{rs} - \lambda_{rs} t_{rs} \tag{3.14}$$

where t_{rs} is the time distance between r and s, ϕ_{rs} reflects spatial preferences of customers in area r with regard to area s, and λ_{rs} is a time-sensitivity coefficient, where the parameters are specified in (3.15).

$$\phi_{rs} = \begin{cases} \hat{\phi}_1 & \text{as } r = s \\ \hat{\phi}_2 & \text{as } r \in R(s) \\ \hat{\phi}_3 & \text{as } r \in E(s). \end{cases} \quad \lambda_{rs} = \begin{cases} \lambda_1 & \text{as } r = s \\ \lambda_2 & \text{as } r \in R(s) \\ \lambda_3 & \text{as } r \in E(s). \end{cases} \tag{3.15}$$

where $V_{rr} = \phi_1 - \lambda_1 t_{rr}$, $V_{rs} = \phi_2 - \lambda_2 t_{rs}$ for $s \in R(r)$, and $V_{rs} = \phi_3 - \lambda_3 t_{rs}$ for $s \in E(r)$. According to estimations in Johansson and Klaesson (2007), the time sensitivity as expressed by λ satisfy the condition $\lambda_2 > \lambda_3 > \lambda_1$, which implies that the spatial discounting is especially strong for the intra-regional accessibility. At the same time there is a preference ordering with regard to intra-urban, intra-regional and extra-regional contact such that $\phi_1 > \phi_2 > \phi_3 \geq 0$. The latter condition implies that for given time distances, the access to intra-urban demand is especially high, while the access to extra-regional demand is especially low.

Established results for a random-choice model of the type introduced here tell us that the probability, P_{rs}, of suppliers in area r to contact customers in area s equals (Mattsson 1984):

$$P_{rs} = W_s \exp\{V_{rs}\} \bigg/ \sum_s W_s \exp\{V_{rs}\} \tag{3.16}$$

where W_s is the total wage sum in urban area s, which represents the total purchasing capacity in area s, which we assume is positively related to the demand for producer services. The variable P_{rs} reflects the share of demand from customers in s. In view of this, the denominator of (3.16) can be used as an indicator of the potential demand for services supplied by firms located in urban area r. Because of this, the expression is interpreted as area r's accessibility to demand, signified by $\sum_s W_s \exp\{V_{rs}\} = A_{rr} \exp\{\phi_1\} + A_{R(r)} \exp\{\phi_2\} + A_{E(r)} \exp\{\phi_3\}$, in accordance with the specification in (3.11), (3.12), (3.13). In this way the random-choice approach leads us to a measure for market access pattern, given by $A_r = (A_{rr}, A_{R(r)}, A_{E(r)})$.

Formally, $A_{rr} \exp\{\phi_1\}$ denotes local (intra-urban) accessibility to demand, $A_{R(r)} \exp\{\phi_2\}$ denotes regional (intra-regional) accessibility to demand, and $A_{E(r)} \exp\{\phi_3\}$ denotes extra-regional accessibility to demand. These accessibility measures are related to market access as given by $A_r = (A_{rr}, A_{R(r)}, A_{E(r)})$ by the coefficients $\exp\{\phi_1\}$, $\exp\{\phi_2\}$, and $\exp\{\phi_3\}$, respectively. In our regressions we obtain new coefficients that replace those three coefficients. This approach is feasible, since we have the following pattern of proportionality:

$$A_{rr} \exp\{\phi_1\}/A_{ss} \exp\{\phi_1\} = A_{rr}/A_{ss} \tag{3.17}$$

$$A_{R(r)} \exp\{\phi_2\}/A_{R(s)} \exp\{\phi_2\} = A_{R(r)}/A_{R(s)} \tag{3.18}$$

$$A_{E(r)} \exp\{\phi_3\}/A_{E(s)} \exp\{\phi_3\} = A_{E(r)}/A_{E(s)} \tag{3.19}$$

References

Abdel-Rahman H, Fujita M (1990) Product variety, Marshallian externalities, and city sizes. J Reg Sci 30(2):165–183

Andersson M, Johansson B (2008) Innovation ideas and regional characteristics: product innovations and export entrepreneurship by firms in Swedish regions. Growth Change 39:193–224

Andersson M, Klaesson J (2006) Growth dynamics in a market-accessibility hierarchy – does the ICT service sectors follow the overall pattern. In: Johansson B, Karlsson C, Stough RR (eds) The emerging digital economy: entrepreneurship, clusters and policy. Springer Verlag, Berlin

Baldwin RE, Martin P, Ottaviano G (2001) Global income divergence, trade and industrialization: the geography of growth take-offs. J Econ Growth 6:5–37

Black D, Henderson V (1999) A theory of urban growth. J Polit Econ 107:252–284

Camacho JA, Rodriguez M (2005) Services and regional development: an analysis of their role as human capital drivers in the Spanish regions. Serv Ind J 25:563–577

Cheshire P, Magrini S (2005) Regional demographic or economic dynamism? Different causes, different consequences. Paper for JIBS workshop, June 2005, Jönköping International Business School

Cheshire P, Malecki E (2004) Growth, development and innovation: a look backward and forward. Pap Reg Sci 83:249–268

Feenstra RC, Hanson GH (1999) The impact of outsourcing and high-technology capital on wages: estimates for the United States. Q J Econ 114:907–940

Florida R (2002) The rise of the creative class. Basic Books, New York

Forslund-J UM (1988) Education intensity and interregional location dynamics. In: Reggiani A (ed) Accessibility trade and location behaviour. Ashgate, Aldershot, pp 97–120

Forslund-J UM, Johansson B (2000) Product vintages and specialisation dynamics in a hierarchical urban system. In: Batten DF, Bertuglia CS, Martellato D, Occeli S (eds) Learning innovation and urban evolution. Kluwer, Boston, pp 165–196

Fujita M, Thisse J-F (2002) Economics of agglomeration: cities, industrial location, and regional growth. Cambridge University Press, Cambridge

Glaeser EL (2000) The new economics of urban and regional growth. In: Gordon C, Meric G, Feldman M (eds) The oxford handbook of economic geography. Oxford University Press, Oxford, pp 83–98

Grossman G, Helpman E (1991) Innovation and growth in the world economy. The MIT Press, Cambridge, MA

Henderson JV (1988) Urban development theory, fact and illusion. Oxford University Press, Oxford

Hermelin B (2007) The urbanization and suburbanization of the service economy: producer services and specialization in Stockholm. Geogr Ann 89B:59–74

Hohenberg P, Lees LH (1985) The making of urban Europe (1000–1950). Harvard Univ Press, Cambridge

Hoover EM (1937) Spatial price discrimination. Rev Econ Stud 4:182–191

Johansson B, Forslund UM (2008) The analysis of location, co-location and urbanization economies. In: Karlsson C (ed) Handbook of research on cluster theory. Edward Elgar, Cheltenham, pp 39–66

Johansson B, Klaesson J (2007) Infrastructure, labour market accessibility and economic development. In: Karlsson C, Andersson WP, Johansson B, Kobayashi K (eds) The management and measurement of infrastructure – performance, efficiency and innovation. Edward Elgar, Cheltenham, pp 69–98

Johansson B, Klaesson J, Olsson M (2003) Commuters' non-linear response to time distances. J Geogr Syst 5:315–329

Johansson B, Ryder-Olsson A, Lööf H (2010) Firm location, corporate structure and innovation. In: Karlsson C, Johansson B, Stough RR (eds) Entrepreneurship and innovations in functional regions. Edward Elgar, Cheltenham

Karlsson C, Johansson B (2006) Dynamics and entrepreneurship in a knowledge-based economy. In: Karlsson C, Johansson B, Stough RR (eds) Entrepreneurship and dynamics in the knowledge economy. Routledge, New York/London, pp 12–46

Klaesson J, Pettersson L (2006) Interdependent urban–rural development in Sweden. In: Karlsson C, Stough R, Cheshire P, Andersson Å (eds) Contributions to spatial science. Springer Verlag, New York

Koch A, Stahlecker T (2006) Regional innovation systems and the foundation of knowledge intensive business services. A comparative study in Bremen, Munich and Stuttgart, Germany. Eur Plann Stud 14:123–145

Kolko J (2009) Urbanization, agglomeration and co-agglomeration of service industries. Public Policy Institute of California

Kox H, Rubalcaba L (2007) Business services and the changing structure of European economic growth. MPRA paper No 3750, Munich personal RePEc archive, University of Munich

Magrini S (1998) Modelling regional economic growth: the role of human capital and innovation. Ph.D. thesis, London school of economics

Martin P, Ottaviano G (1999) Growing locations: industry location in a model of endogenous growth. Eur Econ Rev 43:281–302

Martin P, Ottaviano G (2001) Growth and agglomeration. Int Econ Rev 42:947–968

Mattsson L-G (1984) Some applications of welfare maximization approaches to residential location. Pap Reg Sci 55:103–120

Muller E, Doloreux D (2007) The key dimensions of Knowledge-Intensive Business Services (KIBS) analysis. Working papers firms and regions U1/2007, Frauenhofer ISI, Karlsuhe

Ohlin B (1933) Interregional and international trade. Harvard University Press, Cambridge

Rivera-Batiz FL (1988) Increasing returns, monopolistic competition, and agglomeration economies in consumption and production. Reg Sci Urban Econ 18:125–153

Romer P (1990) Endogenous technological change. J Polit Econ 98:71–102

Storper M, Venables AJ (2004) Buzz: face-to-face contact and the urban economy. J Econ Geogr 4:351–370

Wood P (2002) Knowledge-intensive services and urban innovativeness. Urban Stud 39:993–1002

Wood P (2006) Urban development and knowledge-intensive business services: too many unanswered questions? Growth Change 37:335–361

Chapter 4
Knowledge Accessibility, Economic Growth and the Haavelmo Paradox

Åke E. Andersson

Abstract Economic growth has conventionally been modelled for space-less economies. Econometrically, growth models have mostly been estimated on time series of national economies with minimal distinctions between economies as large as Japan or the USA and as small as the smallest economies of Asia and Europe. This approach to the analysis of economic growth is especially dangerous when the impact of scientific and technological knowledge is important for the process of growth. Creative activities and the formation of knowledge are highly clustered in space. Thus, the spatial distribution of accessibility to knowledge capital and investments determines economic growth of nations and other spatial aggregates.

The Haavelmo paradox contrasts chaos as the generic property of non-linear dynamic models with the fact that most statistics on macroeconomic growth processes tend towards persistent constant positive rates of growth. The paradox can be resolved if the non-linear dynamic model is subdivided into fast, private variables and very slow, public variables. Modelling spatial accessibility of knowledge as a slow, public variable and machinery and similar material capital as a relatively faster, private variable ensures stable growth, at least in the short and medium terms of the economic growth processes.

Keywords Economic growth • Chaos • Multiple time scales • Synergetics • Adiabatic approximation

---

Å.E. Andersson (✉)
Jönköping International Business School, Jönköping, Sweden
e-mail: Ake.Andersson@jibs.hj.se

J. Klaesson et al. (eds.), *Metropolitan Regions*, Advances in Spatial Science,
DOI 10.1007/978-3-642-32141-2_4, © Springer-Verlag Berlin Heidelberg 2013

1 Background

Macroeconomic theory was traditionally focused on comparative static and business cycle analysis. The problem of economic growth was not properly addressed before 1936, when the seminal paper by John von Neumann appeared in German (von Neumann 1935–1936, 1937, 1945). In this paper, von Neumann proved the existence of a general equilibrium rate of growth, product proportions and relative prices with the growth rate equal to the equilibrium rate of interest. This growing economy was modelled with interdependencies, joint production, possibilities of substitution and constant returns to scale. The analysis was quite abstract mathematically, and was accordingly not observed by the English speaking world until 1945, when a translated and commented version of the paper was published in *Journal of Economic Theory* (von Neumann 1935–1936, 1937, 1945). The paper triggered an interest in the problem of economic growth, resulting in a flow of books and papers on the subject (most notably by Harrod (1939), Domar (1957), and Leontief (1951)).

These analysts showed that the rate of growth of a macro economy would be determined as the product of the net savings-output-ratio and the productivity of capital, under the provision of unlimited supply of labour (possibly measured as efficiency units of labour).

In two papers by Solow (1956) and Swan (1956), the assumption of unlimited growth of the supply of labour was questioned. Reformulating the theory in terms of product and capital per unit of labour and assuming constant returns to scale they concluded that the macro economy would eventually converge towards a constant capital–labour ratio, at which there would be no growth in consumption per unit of labour. The only expansion of standard of living, as reflected in income and consumption per capita, would be by an increase in the total factor productivity, defined as A in the production function $Af(K,L)$. Assuming A to shift upwards over time is then interpreted as exogenous changes of technology (or improved economic organization).

However, by the mid-1960s Uzawa (1965) and Shell (1966) suggested that the changes of A were actually endogenous and determined by investments in research and technology.

2 Knowledge Accumulation and Growth: The Accounting Approach

In the early 1960s Denison (1967) initiated an extensive discussion about the relative role of different factors of production in determining the rate of growth at different national economies. One of his starting points was the observation by Robert Solow (1956) that the long-term rate of growth of per capita income in the USA could only to a very limited extent be explained by the growth of the stock of material capital and the increases of quantitative labour supply. In an econometric estimation of the rate of growth of the national product per capita, Solow estimated

4 Knowledge Accessibility, Economic Growth and the Haavelmo Paradox

the contributions by growing capital stock and labour inputs to account for no more than one third of the total rate of growth. The remaining two thirds of the rate of growth of the USA had to be some 'residual factor', interpreted as technological change. A number of economists beside Dennison proceeded to explain the different components of the residual factor of economic growth accounting, among these Kuznets (1966) should be mentioned, especially because of his development of an outstanding data base for a large number of countries.

In important contributions by Angus Maddison (1982, 1995) the macro-economic accounting data assembled by Kuznets was extended to cover a very long historical record for a large number of industrialized nations. These data bases have increased our possibilities to understand the relative importance of the growth of different inputs contributing to the rate of growth of real national products.

If we assume that the national (or regional) product Y could be explained by the use of different inputs according to a linearly homogenous Cobb–Douglas macro production function (corresponding to the idea that the net output of the economy would be determined by a weighted geometric average of different inputs) we have the following growth accounting equation:

$$\frac{\Delta Y}{Y} = \alpha_1 \frac{\Delta R}{R} + \alpha_2 \frac{\Delta K}{K} + \alpha_3 \frac{\Delta H}{H} + \alpha_4 \frac{\Delta L}{L} + \alpha_0 \tag{4.1}$$

where
$\frac{\Delta Y}{Y}$ = rate of growth of GDP,
$\frac{\Delta R}{R}$ = rate of growth of knowledge, in which ΔR=investments in industrial research and development (R&D) and R=the stock of technological knowledge (equal to the accumulated investments in industrial R&D),
$\frac{\Delta K}{K}$ = rate of growth of the material capital stock,
$\frac{\Delta H}{H}$ = rate of growth of human capital,
$\frac{\Delta L}{L}$ = rate of growth of the number of working hours.

The parameters α could be estimated by the factor shares in GDP, if $\alpha_i > 0$ and $\Sigma\, \alpha_i = 1$, corresponding to an assumption of constant returns to scale. If material investments are constrained by savings, Eq. 4.1 could be rewritten as Eq. 4.2. Thus

$$\Delta K = S = (s_H + s_M + n + t - g)Y = s_T Y \tag{4.2}$$

where
S=savings,
s_H=household savings ratio,
s_M=firm savings ratio for material investment,
n=net import surplus ratio,
t–g=net government taxation surplus ratio,
s_T=total net savings ratio.
Further $\alpha_2 = \frac{\partial Y}{\partial K} \cdot \frac{K}{Y}$. Thus

$$\alpha_2 \frac{\Delta K}{K} = [s_H + s_M + n + (t - g)]Y \frac{\partial Y}{\partial K} \frac{K}{Y} / K. = s_T \frac{\partial Y}{\partial K} \tag{4.3}$$

where

$\frac{\partial Y}{\partial K}$ = marginal productivity of material capital,

ΔR = research and development investments

$\quad = s_R \cdot Y$

$$\alpha_1 \frac{\Delta R}{R} = s_R \frac{Y}{R} \alpha_1 = s_R \frac{Y}{R} \frac{\partial Y}{\partial R} \frac{R}{Y} = s_R \frac{\partial Y}{\partial R} \tag{4.4}$$

where $\partial Y / \partial R$ = the marginal productivity of research and development investments.

The accumulation of human capital is primarily determined by government spending and foregone earnings.

The growth of labour supply, measured in working hours, is close to zero in many advanced economies. Equation 4.1 can then be rewritten as Eq. 4.5.

The most important explanatory variables accounted for in Maddison are capital investments, knowledge accumulated by an increased number of school years and the role of international trade in the supply of material capital investments. In addition to the national supply of savings from household income and profit retention ratios of firms, the economy can also support a high rate of capital accumulation by an import surplus (equalling international credits). This is reflected by Eq. 4.5.

$$\frac{\Delta Y}{Y} = s_R \frac{\partial Y}{\partial R} + s_T \frac{\partial Y}{\partial K} + \alpha_3 \frac{\Delta H}{H} + \alpha_4 \frac{\Delta L}{L} + \alpha_5 \tag{4.5}$$

Assume s_R to be in the range of 3%, $\partial Y / \partial R$ to be in the order of 0.25, s_T to be in the order of 0.20, $\partial Y / \partial K$ equal to 0.10, K_3 equal to 0.3, $\Delta H / H$ equal to 0.015 and α_S and $\Delta L / L$ to be zero. Then the rate of growth of the economy would be in the order of 3.0% per year, which would also be the rate of growth of income per working hour.

As the rate of national growth of labour supply is often close to zero in mature economies the main factors determining growth are:

- Marginal productivities of material and knowledge capital,
- Propensity to save of households, firms and government,
- Rate of growth of industrial knowledge capital, and
- Rate of growth of human capital by investments in education.

The marginal productivities of material and knowledge capital are to a large extent determined by the spatial allocation. It is well known that the public nature of ideas and other knowledge capital tends to be more clustered in space than material capital and other mainly private resources. It is one intention of this chapter to show that the dynamics of such clustering can be endogenously determined in the long term economic growth process.

4 Knowledge Accessibility, Economic Growth and the Haavelmo Paradox

Table 4.1 Annual hours of work per capita of the labour force in different OECD countries 1870–1979

	1870	1900	1929	1950	1979
Australia	2,945	2,688	2,139	1,838	1,619
Belgium	2,964	2,707	2,272	2,283	1,747
Canada	2,964	2,789	2,399	1,967	1,730
Denmark	2,945	2,688	2,279	2,283	1,721
France	2,945	2,688	2,297	1,989	1,727
Germany	2,941	2,684	2,284	2,316	1,719
Netherlands	2,964	2,707	2,260	2,208	1,679
Norway	2,945	2,688	2,283	2,101	1,559
Sweden	2,945	2,688	2,283	1,951	1,461
United Kingdom	2,984	2,725	2,286	1,958	1,617
United States	2,964	2,707	2,342	1,867	1,607

Sources: different sources as given in Maddison (1982)

The growth of human capital by education has been substantial in all of the industrialized economies. According to Maddison (1982) the average level of education of the labour force of most OECD countries was close to 3 years of formal education around 1900. Currently the average level of formal education of the labour forces of Europe, USA and Japan is close to 12 years. This corresponds to an average increase of the supply of educational capital per capita of 1.5% per year since 1900.

The contribution to the growth of the national product from material capital is determined by the product of the savings rate (as influenced by national savings and import surpluses) and the marginal productivity of investments. The marginal productivity of investments can essentially be influenced by two factors only. The first factor is the capacity to reallocate capital from inefficient to efficient firms or regions, and the second factor is the capacity to develop and use new technologies of production. The development of new technologies of production is closely related to the accumulation of knowledge by research and development investments.

The data on the long-term growth of the supply of labour as provided by Maddison show that the total number of working hours per unit of labour is steadily decreasing with the rate of growth of income per capita. This indicates that leisure time is a complement to consumption of goods. Table 4.1 summarizes the development of the per capita working hours.

Estimating the dependence on working hours upon real income indicates an income elasticity of working hours per capita of approximately −0.2 to −0.3 for the different OECD countries.

The effect of increasing number of persons employed and the decline of working hours per employed has implied a fairly constant supply of labour in most developed market economies. This implies that growth is primarily dependent upon *three forms of capital accumulation*:

1. In material capital,
2. In human capital by education investments and
3. In other knowledge capital by research and development investments,
4. And the productivity of such investments

3 The Productivity and Returns of Educational Knowledge Capital

Education is primarily a private capital and measurement of the returns to investment in education ranges from 5 % to 10 % for advanced economies, when measured with the Mincer–Becker estimation equation. This type of measurement separates the effect of years of education and years of work experience into account, but abstains from analysing the effects of occupational and regional mobility. Such mobility is in fact decided upon as part of the decision to take on some education.

A large number of studies of the empirical relation between education and income have been performed, all supporting a strong positive relation between personal income and the level of education (ceteris paribus). Relating the gender, age and years of education with income gives the following estimate for Sweden, 1990. The estimation is based on census data after grouping. The result of the regression is given by the following table.

There is no self-evident way of deciding on a best functional form and therefore a number of different forms have been tested, including the log-linear form proposed by Becker and Mincer. The advantage of the equation estimated as in Table 4.2 is the non-linearity of returns to years of education. In this equation the rate of return declines from around 10 % at the level of junior high school towards approximately 5 % return on post-graduate university education. These levels of rates of return are quite low, especially when compared to the USA, where returns to higher education tend to be as high as 10 %. Some reasons for this discrepancy are presumably the difference in the size of the labour market, the much larger mobility of the Americans and the government subsidies of higher education in Sweden.

Much of the advantages of education can only be realized after a proper relocation of the household. In Sweden and most other European countries young people tend to either relocate to a region with long-run growth potential before they embark upon a higher education or immediately after graduation. After the formation of a family most tend to stay in the region chosen earlier.

The human (or educational) capital thus tends to be clustered in certain regions as is illustrated by the following map of Sweden (Fig. 4.1).

The university graduates tend to finally locate in the southern metropolitan commuting regions of Stockholm, Göteborg and Malmö or close to university towns elsewhere. Concentration of human capital tends to reinforce and be reinforced by the concentration in space of scientific and industrial knowledge capital.

Table 4.2 The econometric cross-section relation between the logarithm of personal income, age, and years of education in Sweden 1990 with gender as a dummy variable

Variable	Coefficient	Standard error of estimate	t-value
Intercept	2.31		
Gender (female = 1, male = 0)	−0.25	0.026	9.6
ln of age (experience)	0.32	0.05	6.4
ln of years of education	0.73	0.05	14.7

Source: Swedish central bureau of statistics, census 1990

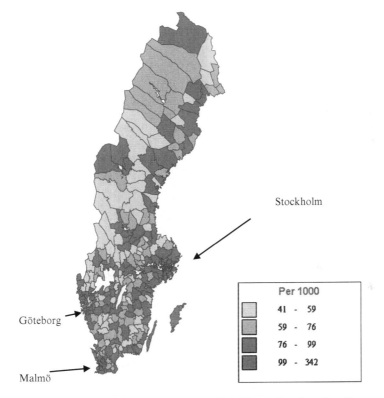

Fig. 4.1 Location of university graduates per 1,000 of inhabitants of regions. Locality quartiles

4 Knowledge as Public Goods and Spatial Discounting of Knowledge Value

Knowledge in the form of research findings is different from educational capital. Education is clearly private in terms of effects, while research findings are at least potentially public. Early measurements by Mansfield clearly show that the industry wide returns to investment in industrial R&D can be as large as three times the level of private returns. From such micro-economic studies of knowledge as a public good some macroeconomists (e.g. Romer (1986, 1990)) have concluded that total research capital would exhibit increasing returns to scale at the level of national macroeconomies.

However, econometric studies have shown that such claims are unwarranted (see e.g. Braconier 1998). The spillovers are within segments of the economy, where the segments could be product groups, occupations or regions.

Affinity of or distance between scientists is thus of importance in determining spillovers.

Knowledge available at distances is less valuable as an input than knowledge within certain borders (of the firm, occupation or region). The problem of assessing the value of public knowledge available elsewhere is analogous to assessment of returns accruing at distant instances of time. To resolve the issue of valuing over time economists use discounting of future returns. A similar procedure can be used in spatial discounting. The idea is then to estimate the value of knowledge available in different locations in the following way:

$$V_i = \sum_j \exp\left(-\beta d_{ij}\right) R_j \tag{4.6}$$

where
V = knowledge value
d = distance
R = stock of knowledge
i,j = locations
β = constant rate of spatial discounting

The advantage of spatial exponential discounting is the unit upper bound, which indicates that the full value of knowledge can only occur in the 'home' location, while the value of knowledge as an input approaches zero at infinite distance (in geographical, occupational or industrial space). The value equation is conventionally called *accessibility of knowledge*.

5 The Haavelmo Paradox and the Fast and Slow Processes of Economic Development

In a conversation with the Nobel laureate T. Haavelmo, I asked him how he reacted to the new mathematics of complex dynamic systems. According to the theorems of complex dynamic systems the mathematically most probable outcome is chaos or total un-predictability. He then reacted in a way that I would call the Haavelmo Paradox.

> **The Haavelmo Paradox**: It is true that in non-linear economic dynamics outcomes are generically unpredictable if models are general. Realistic models obviously tend to be non-linear. However, national statistical yearbooks report similar relative economic data, year by year indicating surprisingly persistent, stable equilibrium growth.

4   Knowledge Accessibility, Economic Growth and the Haavelmo Paradox

Evidently, some mechanisms are there to generate conditions leading to the mathematically improbable stable equilibrium results (at least in the short and medium run).

Synergetics has been proposed by Haken (1978, 1982) which could provide a method to resolve the Haavelmo paradox.

The synergetics modelling strategy implies primarily a subdivision of variables, according to relevant time scales.

It has e.g. been successfully applied to experiment oriented modelling of:

- Lasers
- Cognition and pattern formation.
- Biochemical processes.
- Neural nets.
- Physiological phenomena.

Applying the synergetic approach to modelling of non-linear interdependencies in economic growth and development requires:

1. Careful separation of time scales.
2. Careful separation of variables according to their individual (or private) versus collective (or public) effects.

The following table shows such a subdivision of the different goods for a synergetic analysis of the dynamic economic system (Fig. 4.2).

Each group of goods should, according to the principles of synergetics, be modelled so as to represent the differences in time scales and degree of collectivity of impacts.

Individual goods would then be represented by the following equation:

$$dp/dt = \mathrm{f}(p, k, y, A) \qquad (4.7)$$

where p is a vector of prices of ordinary market goods (including factor services), $k=$a vector of capital or investment goods, $y=$information, and $A=$infrastructure as represented by accessibility.

Investment or capital accumulation would be represented by the following equation:

$$s(k)dk/dt = \mathrm{g}(p, k, y, A) \qquad (4.8)$$

where $s(k)=$a constant representing the time scale conversion between ordinary market goods and capital goods, i.e. $s(k)=t/T(k)$. If t is equal to 1 year and $T(k)$ is equal to 10 years we would have $s(k)=0.1$.

Information is modelled as:

$$s(y)dy/dt = \mathrm{h}(p, k, y, A) \qquad (4.9)$$

where $s(y)$ is larger than or equal to 1, signifying a rapid time scale.

EFFECTS\Rate of change	Fast	Slow
INDIVIDUAL (PRIVATE)	*ORDINARY MARKET GOODS*	*INVESTMENT GOODS*
COLLECTIVE (PUBLIC)	*INFORMATION*	*INFRASTRUCTURE*

Fig. 4.2 Different goods, classified by rate of change and scope of effects

Finally, the development of infrastructure (as represented by accessibility to fundamental knowledge) can be represented by the equation:

$$s(A)dA/dt = \mathrm{m}(p, k, y, A) \qquad (4.10)$$

where $s(A) = t/T(A)$. $T(A)$ is a very slow (although positive) time scale, indicating that $s(A)$ is a very small, positive number, possibly in the order of 0.01 or lower. This implies that in the time frame of the other variables of this system dA/dt can be set approximately equal to zero, most of the time.

We thus have a dynamic system:

$$dp/dt = \mathrm{f}(p, k, y, A^*)$$

$$s(y)dy/dt = \mathrm{h}(p, k, y, A^*) \qquad (4.11)$$

$$s(k)dk/dt = \mathrm{g}(p, k, y, A^*)$$

to be solved subject to the constraint:

$$\mathrm{m}(p, k, y, A^*) = 0 \qquad (4.12)$$

For systems of this kind we can apply Tikhonov's theorem (Sugakov 1998):

Assume a dynamic system of N ordinary differential equations, which can be divided into two groups of equations. The first group consists of m fast equations, the second group consists of $m+1, \ldots, N$ slow equations. Tikhonov's theorem states that the system

$$dx_i/dt = \mathrm{f}_i(x, g); \quad i = 1, \ldots, m \text{ (fast equations)}$$

$$\mathrm{f}_j(x, g) = 0; \quad j = m + 1, \ldots, N \text{ (slow equations)}$$

4 Knowledge Accessibility, Economic Growth and the Haavelmo Paradox

has a solution if the following conditions are satisfied:

1. The values x_j are isolated roots,
2. The solutions x_j constitute a stable stationary point of the system of $f_j = 0$ for any x_i and the initial conditions are in the domain of attraction of this point.

For each position of the slow subsystem the fast subsystem has plenty of time to stabilize. Such an approximation is called adiabatic (Sugakov 1998).

In the very short run, a market equilibrium could be established as the fixed point solution of the first two Eqs. (4.7) and (4.8), i.e. $f^*(p,y)=0$ and $h^*(p,y)=0$, keeping the approximate values of $dk/dt=0$ and $dA/dt=0$. This solution corresponds to a conventional 'general equilibrium' of the Walras type.

In the medium term we would have an expansion of capital, implying that $s(k)dk/dt=h^{**}(k)$, where the double star indicates that A is approximately constant, and x and y are kept at their equilibrium values (mutatis mutandis).

The solution is thus a fixed point solution of $dk/dt/k=g$, where g is the balanced rate of growth, which is ensured to exist as long as $h^{**}(k)$ fulfils the requirements of the Nikaido theorem, given below. This solution could either correspond to Solowian or von Neumann steady state solutions.

In the very long run dA/dt cannot be assumed to be zero and the system as a whole would then cease to be as well behaved as in the short and medium terms of dynamics. The system would in the very long term have all the bifurcation properties, typical of non-linear, interactive dynamic systems. Between periods of change of the economic structure, there would be periods of stable growth equilibrium.

We can thus conclude that the Haavelmo paradox can be resolved if we admit the possibility of separation of time scales and degree of collectivity (publicness) of different economically important variables. This implies that general equilibrium theory as conventionally formulated by Arrow, Debreu and others are not general enough to be expandable into dynamic systems (or combined spatial and dynamic systems).

The representation of the economy along these lines is not unknown in economics although the mathematics needed for dynamic modelling has not been available to these theoretical economists.

Important examples are:

- Classical population–economy interaction theory (Wicksell 1901; Hotelling in Puu 1997).
- Theories of interactions between transport infrastructure and economic development (von Thünen 1875; Pirenne 1939; Braudel 1982).
- Theories of interactions between institutions and economic development (Adam Smith 1776, 2001; Eli F. Heckscher 1955; Douglass North 1991).
- Theories of cultural and economic interactive development (Weber 1930; Morishima 1982).
- Schumpeterian theories of interaction between knowledge, entrepreneurial activity, political processes and economic development (Schumpeter 1912; Zhang 1991).

- Recent modelling of interactions between networks, knowledge and economic development (Andersson and Beckmann 2009).
- Emerging theories of dynamic ecology–economy interaction (Rosser 2008).

6 Modeling Accessibility to Knowledge Resources and Economic Growth

I now assume that scientific knowledge is measured in accumulated units of research output. For simplicity, we will assume that in each point of space there will be an aggregate of such knowledge capital, called R_i. We will further assume that the productivity of the knowledge capital, available elsewhere is declining monotonously with an increasing distance, from a user of knowledge j to a holder of knowledge. The maximal productivity is reached if $i=j$. As argued above, a reasonable and yet simple candidate of an accessibility function of i with respect to j is the spatial discounting function:

$$A_{ia} = \sum e^{-d_{ij}} R_j \tag{4.13}$$

where A=accessibility and R=scientific knowledge capital. The production function of each node i of the network can be formulated as:

$$Q_i = F(K_i, A_i, M_i) \tag{4.14}$$

where
Q_i=production in node i
A_i=accessibility of scientific knowledge capital
M_i=economically useful area of node i
K_i=private capital, available in node i
Accumulation of knowledge capital of node i is determined by the equation:

$$s(R)dR_i/dt = H(Q_i, A_i, M_i) \tag{4.15}$$

$$s(A)dA_i/dt = L(Q, A), \tag{4.16}$$

where Q and A are vectors giving the production and accessibility of every node. $s(R)$ and $s(A)$ are both assumed to be positive, very small numbers representing the speed of adjustment.

In order to illustrate some possible properties of such a differential equation assume that the production function can be decomposed into three factors: (1) local impact of capital, (2) spatial congestion, and (3) accessibility of knowledge.

4 Knowledge Accessibility, Economic Growth and the Haavelmo Paradox

$$\dot{K}_i = s_i K_i^{\alpha} \left(\frac{\bar{M}_i}{K_i}\right)^{\beta} \left[\sum_{i \neq j} e^{-\gamma d_{ij}} R_j\right]^{\lambda} \tag{4.17}$$

$$\dot{K}_i = s_i K_i^{\alpha-\beta} \bar{M}_i^{\beta} \left[\sum_{i \neq j} e^{-\gamma d_{ij}} R_j\right]^{\lambda}$$

Because of the slow speed of change of scientific knowledge and transport capacities Eqs. 4.9 and 4.10 are approximately equal to zero. Thus, the equation system (4.11) will be solved for an equilibrium rate of growth, subject to Eqs. 4.9 and 4.10.

The following theorem (Nikaido 1968) ensures the existence of a growth equilibrium:

$$\dot{x}_i = M(x) = \lambda x_i; \; i = 1, \ldots, n \tag{4.18}$$

where $M(x)$ is a semi-positive mapping from x to $\dot{x}$. For such a system a theorem by Nikaido (1968) can be applied.

Assumptions.

(a) $M(x) = [M_i(x)]$ is defined for all $x \geq 0$.
(b) $M(x)$ is continuous as a mapping $M: R_+^n \to R_+^n$, except possibly at $x=0$.
(c) $M(x)$ is positively homogenous of order m, $0 \leq m \leq 1$ in the sense that $M(x) \geq 0$ and $x \geq 0$.

Theorem.

$$\text{Let } \Lambda = \{M(x) = \lambda x\} \text{ for } x \in p_n$$

where

$$p_n = \left\{ x \middle| x \geq 0, \sum_{i=1}^{n} x_i = 1 \right\}$$

is the standard simplex. Then $M(x)$ contains a maximum characteristic value which is denoted $\lambda(M)$. Furthermore, if $M(x)$ is homogenous of degree 1, i.e. if $m=1$ as a special case of assumption (c) then $\lambda(M)$ is the largest of all the eigen-values of $M(x)$.

Proof. Nikaido (1968).

In the vicinity of an equilibrium $\lambda(M)$ can be locally linearized as $M[x(t)]=M(x^*)$, where x^* is x on the equilibrium trajectory. We then have the eigen-equation

$$\gamma z = M(x^*) z \tag{4.19}$$

with the equilibrium growth rate γ^* $[M(x^*)]$.

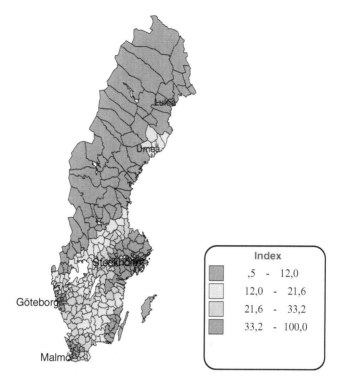

Fig. 4.3 Accessibility of university based research in Sweden 2001, local quartiles

7 Accessibility of Knowledge and Regional Economic Growth: An Empirical Example

The accessibility of fundamental knowledge varies systematically in all countries with peaks in the vicinity of university high-tech-industry locations. A typical empirical example is the knowledge accessibility landscape of Sweden as pictured in the following maps.

As can be seen from the map in Fig. 4.3, Sweden has a spatially very uneven distribution of accessibility to university based research activities and thus presumably also to scientific knowledge inputs.

The map in Fig. 4.4 illustrates the spatial distribution of accessibility of industrial research and development. There is a remarkable similarity between the scientific and industrial research maps.

The most accessible regions will in the long run be regions of relative growth of material and human capital as well as real income.

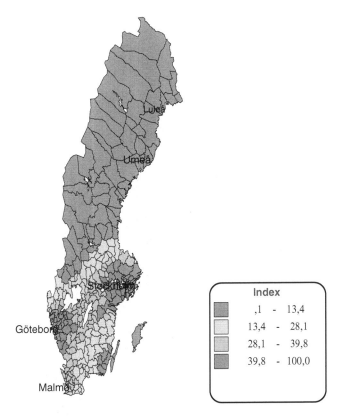

Fig. 4.4 Industrial R&D accessibility in Sweden 2001, local quartiles

There are substantial differences in growth rates of Swedish localities, as given by the Sharpe-ratios (defined as the average growth rates divided by the standard deviations of the growth rates).

The map in Fig. 4.5 clearly shows that the regional movements of people, which essentially mirror the movements of human capital, are towards the areas of superior scientific and technological accessibility of knowledge as indicated by the maps in Figs. 4.3, 4.4, and 4.5.

In post-industrial, knowledge oriented economies like the Swedish, we should expect a long run, almost complete, exodus from the regions of low accessibility to knowledge and a corresponding growth of population, human capital and income per capita in regions of high knowledge accessibility.

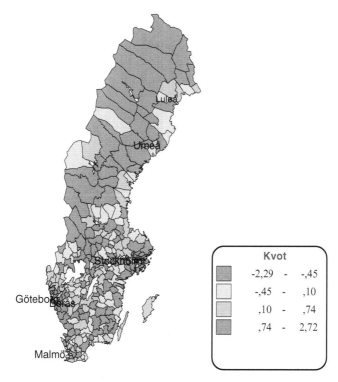

Fig. 4.5 Sharpe-ratios of persistent regional population growth patterns in Sweden, locality quartiles

8 Conclusions

The theory of economic growth was originally developed for a non-spatial macroeconomy. This was a reasonable approach as long as linearity (including log-linearity) could be assumed. However, as soon as public goods are introduced, non-linearity is a necessary aspect of the dynamic economy. Knowledge is the most important public good of a growing economic system. With the growing importance of scientific and industrial research and technological development it has become necessary to formulate the dynamic economic theory with an explicit inclusion of knowledge as an endogenous variable. This was done already in the 1960s by Uzawa and Shell, assuming constant returns and employing optimal control theory to achieve closed form solutions to their problem formulation.

In the 1970s and 1980s some important steps were taken to include publicness of knowledge into the growth models. Unfortunately, these approaches implied increasing returns and other non-linear features of the models proposed. Examples are the growth models by Paul Romer, featuring increasing returns at the level of the macro-economy. It can easily be shown (see Andersson and Beckmann 2009) that such a model diverges rapidly. Thus, such economies are not feasible.

Empirical studies have shown that the diffusion of knowledge tends to be constrained by space, industrial and occupational affinities. Macro models featuring whole economies are thus not suitable representations of endogenous growth processes. Accessibility of knowledge, based on spatial discounting is a reasonable way to represent the variable degree of publicness of knowledge. However, knowledge accessibility implies non-linearity of the growth models with severe consequences for the predictability of the dynamic trajectories of the model variables.

Subdivision of the different variables can provide a means to achieve predictability of the non-linear growth models. Such a synergetic procedure is chosen in this study. In the model proposed above, accessibility and knowledge are assumed to be on a slow time scale, allowing for an adiabatic approximation. This implies that in the faster time scales of ordinary, private goods (including private material capital) the solutions can be determined, subject to approximate constancy of accessibility of knowledge.

The Swedish regional economy fits such a theoretical approach. The accessibility of knowledge is relatively concentrated and stable. The pattern of growth of the regional economies is also quite stable and follows the pattern of accessibility of knowledge from the 1980s when the transformation into the postindustrial knowledge economy started.

References

Andersson ÅE, Beckmann MB (2009) Economics of knowledge – theory, models and measurements. Edward Elgar, Cheltenham/Northampton

Braconier H (1998) Essays on R&D and growth, vol 72, Lund economic studies. Department of Economics, Lund University, Lund

Braudel F (1982) The wheels of commerce civilization and capitalism 15th–18th century, vol II. Harper and Row, New York

Denison EF (1967) Why growth rates differ. The Brookings Institution, Washington

Domar ED (1957) Essays in the theory of economic growth. Oxford University Press, New York

Haken H (1978) Synergetics: an introduction. Nonequilibrium phase transitions and self-organization in physics chemistry and biology. Springer, Berlin

Haken H (1982) Synergetics: an introduction. Nonequilibrium phase transitions and self-organization in physics chemistry and biology. Springer, Berlin

Harrod RF (1939) An essay in dynamic theory. Econ J 49:14–33

Heckscher EF (1955) Mercantilism, 2 vols. Allen and Unwin, London

Kuznets S (1966) Modern economic growth: rate, structure and spread. Yale University Press, New Haven

Leontief WW (1951) Studies in the structure of the American economy 1919–1939. Oxford University Press, New York

Maddison A (1982) Phases of capitalist development. Oxford University Press, Oxford

Maddison A (1995) Monitoring the world economy: 1820–1992. Organization for Economic Cooperation and Development, Paris

Morishima M (1982) Why has Japan succeeded? Cambridge University Press, Cambridge

Nikaido H (1968) Convex structures and economic theory. Academic, New York

North D (1991) Institutions, institutional change and economic performance. Cambridge University Press, Cambridge

Pirenne H (1939) Medieval cities: their origins and the revival of trade. Princeton University Press, Princeton

Puu T (1997) Nonlinear economic dynamics, 4th edn. Springer, Berlin

Romer PM (1986a) Increasing returns and long-run growth. J Pol Econ 94:1002–1037

Romer PM (1990) Endogenous technological change. J Pol Econ 98:71–102

Rosser JB Jr (2008) Dynamic discontinuities in ecologic-economic systems. In: Allen CR, Holling CS (eds) Discontinuity theory in ecosystems and other complex systems. Columbia University Press, New York

Schumpeter JA (1912) Theorie der wirtschaftlichen Entwicklung. Duncker und Humblot, Berlin

Shell K (1966) Toward a theory of inventive activity and capital accumulation. Am Econ Rev 56(2):62–68

Smith A (1776, 2001) An inquiry into the nature and causes of the wealth of nations, Edinburgh (1776), edited and prefaced by Dr. Eamonn Butler. The Adam Smith Institute, London

Solow RM (1956) A contribution to the theory of economic growth. Quart J Econ 70:65–94

Sugakov VI (1998) Lectures in synergetics. World Scientific, Singapore

Swan W (1956) Economic growth and capital accumulation. Econ Record 32:334–361

Uzawa H (1965) Optimum technical change in an aggregative model of economic growth. Int Econ Rev 6:18–31

von Neumann (1935–1936, 1937, 1945) Uber ein ökonomisches Gleichungssystem und eine Verallgemeinerung des Brouwerschen Fixpunktsatzes. In: Ergebnisse eines Mathematischen Kolloquiums, 8, 1935–1936. Franz–Deuticke, pp. 73–83. (Translated: A model of general economic equilibrium. Rev Econ Stud 13:1–9, 1945)

von Thünen J-H (1875) Der isolierte Staat in Beziehung auf Landwirtschaft und Nationaloekonomie. Wiegandt, Hempel & Parey, Berlin

Weber M (1930) The protestant ethic and the spirit of capitalism. Allen and Unwin, London

Wicksell K (1901) Föreläsningar i nationalekonomi, första delen: Teoretisk nationalekonomi, Lund. Translated as lectures on political economy. vol 1. General theory. Routledge, London (1935). Reprint (1978), Kelley, New York

Zhang W-B (1991) Synergetic economics: time and change in non-linear economics. Springer Verlag, New York/Berlin

Chapter 5
Urban Growth Policies: The Need to Set Realistic Expectations

Paul C. Cheshire

Abstract This paper reviews local growth promotion policies in the light of an analysis of the drivers of differential urban growth. It starts by arguing that major shifts in urban functions interacting with European integration and the wider process of internationalisation, have produced incentives to create local growth promotion agencies. The supporters of such agencies and the agencies themselves naturally have to make claims both as to their necessity and their likely success. An analysis of growth drivers, however, shows that there is only a restricted scope for local – indeed any – policy to influence city growth. Moreover, some existing policies work directly against urban economic growth. The most successful policies are likely to be the efficient execution of well known functions, including policies to reduce the costs of city size and efficient public administration. There is a danger, therefore, not only of raising expectations with respect to the potential contribution of local growth promotion agencies but of such agencies concentrating on inappropriate actions which are more visible but likely to be less effective.

Keywords Urban growth • Urban policy • Agglomeration economies

---

Paper prepared for **METROPOLITAN REGIONS:** Preconditions and strategies for growth and development in the global economy **LINKÖPING, Sweden, 24 to 26 April 2008, Jönköping International Business School**.

P.C. Cheshire (✉)
Department of Geography & Environment, London School of Economics,
Houghton St, London WC2A 2AE, UK
e-mail: p.cheshire@lse.ac.uk

J. Klaesson et al. (eds.), *Metropolitan Regions*, Advances in Spatial Science,
DOI 10.1007/978-3-642-32141-2_5, © Springer-Verlag Berlin Heidelberg 2013

1 Introduction

There are reasons why 'competition' between places is seen to be increasing and city growth promotion agencies are proliferating. There are fundamental forces generating radical urban change and these forces themselves increase the incentives for 'city growth policies'.

The function of cities throughout the world is being transformed. In the poorer countries, and those that are newly industrialising, a process is in train akin to that which occurred in Europe during the late eighteenth and first half of the nineteenth Centuries. A peasant and rural subsistence population is flocking to the cities which no longer serve as administrative and commercial centres for a dominant rural population but have become the focus of industrial production and now outsourcing of routine services. In OECD countries, the problem that was seen as de-industrialisation is now seen as transformation: a transformation as radical as that associated with the Industrial Revolution. People could have thought of the Industrial Revolution as being a process of 'de-agriculturalisation'. Indeed, to some extent, people did and regretted the passing of the era of the peasant and a romanticised idyll of rural life. The reality was more that low productivity peasant agriculture chained the mass of the population to the countryside. Most of those who regretted the passing of the feudal age were those who were privileged by it.

In rich countries cities are no longer centres where physical things are produced; or even distributed in bulk. Factories have moved to the Newly Industrialising Counties or to low density green environments and so has wholesale distribution, borne on highways, lorries and containerisation. Cities have become again, as they were before the Industrial Revolution, places where commerce is located, people organise trade, education and business services: centres of culture and tourism, of government and, of course, places to choose to live. Higher education and health care now contribute more to the London economy than manufacturing.

Central to the success of cities are agglomeration economies: firms are more productive because they are located more closely to other firms, to households and to specialist labour. At the same time labour markets are more efficient if there are more opportunities within a given travel time/cost. The paradox is that the great majority of research until Ciccone and Hall (1996) which tried to quantify agglomeration economies looked at them narrowly as enhanced factor productivity in manufacturing. Ciccone and Hall point out the likely driver of agglomeration economies is density of economic activity (more properly 'effective density' to include a measure of the cost of contacts between economic agents as well as the number of economic agents within a given area) rather than just city size, although the two are positively correlated, and the service sector is a significant driver of agglomeration economies. Their conclusion, for the US, was that doubling density of economic activity increased labour productivity by 6 % all else equal.

In addition to agglomeration economies in production there are likely to be welfare, or consumption, agglomeration economies, too. Households benefit from greater variety in consumption, greater choice of neighbourhood types and opportunities for social interactions, as city size and density increase. This consumption advantage of cities is, indeed, what Joshua and Glaeser (2006) claim is the more important driver of the recent urban revival in the US. The key evidence they cite is the rising real price of housing in cities implying that even if urban productivity and wages have been rising relative to rural areas, people are differentially choosing to live in cites causing urban house prices to rise faster than urban productivity. On the other hand, there are costs which rise with density and city size also: notably the price of space and congestion.

Interacting with this change in the functions of cities and the increasing salience of agglomeration economies has been a double process of integration. In Europe, we have deliberately promoted integration by reducing the costs and barriers to trade, investing in trans-European transport links (most obviously the Channel Tunnel and the Øresundsbron link) and reducing the barriers to labour mobility. This has reinforced an international process of 'globalisation' or internationalisation, brought about both by conscious policies to reduce trade barriers and impediments to international capital movements but also by radical technical changes in transport and communications.

In combination these changes have led to economic activity becoming very much more spatially mobile but they have also conferred advantages and disadvantages on particular types of cities. In Western Europe and North America those specialising in old, resource based activities and in manufacturing, have suffered. Larger cities, and especially those with more skilled and flexible labour, strong international connections and with a diverse range of economic activities, have gained. But the scope for economic change at the city level and the perception that economic success is more dependent on city and regional capacities has created strong incentives for local policy makers to try to influence outcomes, to develop 'growth promotion' policies.

Systematic analysis of the drivers of urban economic growth, however, show that there is only a restricted impact even the most successful local policies can have on the growth trajectory of any urban area and that most of the factors influencing differential rates of growth are outside the control of any policy maker at the local or national level. There are, however, systematic factors relating to systems of urban government arrangements and how these map onto the functional reality of urban regions that appear to condition the potential contribution – restricted though that may be – of local policy. There is thus a problem facing local policy makers and the agencies they represent. On the one had they need to promote themselves and talk up their ability to influence local economic performance. If they do not they cannot secure the resources necessary to perform their roles. Moreover given the perception of footloose activity and growth up for grabs, they may seem to be failing in their responsibilities if they do not promote their cities as locations for growth. On the other hand, since their real ability to influence outcomes is restricted, there is a serious danger that they will set unrealistic expectations and lose credibility.

The purpose of the present paper is to try to chart a course between these two dangers and define more clearly the set of growth drivers which policy makers may hope to influence and the factors which condition their ability to successfully promote growth. In the process I hope to identify some of the actions which are potentially at least likely to be more effective and offer a better return. The conclusion here is that the most effective functions of policy are still those derived from classic local public finance analysis. Policy is most effective at promoting growth when it is inconspicuous and facilitates actions by private actors, supplies local public goods and focuses on resolving problems of local market failure.

2 Why the Pressure for Local Growth Promotion?

The main factors generating increased pressure for local growth promotion were outlined in the introduction. In this section I elaborate a little on them and the influence they have been exerting on patterns of urban development. As was suggested above, European integration is really just a local, policy driven, additional element in the process of economic internationalisation affecting all trading economies. A particular feature of European integration is that not only have we encouraged trade in goods and services by reducing tariffs and non-tariff barriers but we have strongly encouraged the mobility of capital and labour. De facto labour and capital is more mobile throughout the world but this is a particular feature of integration within the European Union.

Given the increasing freedom to trade both within and beyond Europe this has led to an increasing footlooseness of economic activity. Not only the whole European market can be served from any point within Europe but a multinational can trade beyond the European Union as well. A Japanese car plant in Britain can ship its output to Russia as well as Poland: an American pharmaceuticals company can sell its French manufactured drugs in North Africa.

There are net gains from free trade and factor mobility but these gains can only be realised if there are losers as well as winners. The Cecchini Report (CEC 1988) and associated studies such as Buigues et al. 1990, for example, identified four sources of gain from European integration. These were:

1. The ability to exploit economies of scale more fully;
2. Increased competition leading to industrial rationalisation and re-organisation;
3. A greater exploitation of comparative advantage;
4. Dynamic effects from additional investment flowing from the exploitation of the above listed sources of gain.

The most cursory analysis of these sources of gain tells one immediately that there will not only be losers as well as winners but that the process of extracting the benefits will necessarily entail an uneven spatial distribution of them. If there are not, there can be no gains from integration. Exploiting economies of scale more fully and more efficient industrial organisation, imply closing smaller and less efficient plants/establishments. Exploiting comparative advantage means activities which lack comparative advantage have to close as the local market is supplied by more efficient producers elsewhere. If there are dynamic gains because of induced investment and growth, these gains, too, will be differentially located in gaining firms, plants, establishments and sectors, and the locations where these

5 Urban Growth Policies: The Need to Set Realistic Expectations

are concentrated. That there are losers as well as winners does not mean that there is not a potential Pareto gain from the whole process; just that the winners cannot win unless in the process they are taking market share from the losers. Since firms and establishments have specific locations, and some locations will be more specialised in 'winning' activities and some in 'losing' ones, there will also be an uneven spatial distribution of the gains (and losses) from integration. There will be losing places/regions as well as winning ones.

At the same time integration within Europe reduced the incentive for national governments to control the activities of 'place promotion' agencies. If activity is more mobile, the locational choice of a firm serving the British and European market is no longer restricted to, say, either London or Manchester, any more than is that of a firm aiming to serve the Swedish and European markets confined to say Linköping or Jönköping. Firms become increasingly able to choose any comparable city-region in the EU offering a competitive location for their particular markets. So by restricting the activities of growth promotion agencies in, say, London or Jönköping, national governments had increasingly little reason to believe they would be benefiting their regions which national policy might in principle favour. Indeed this may partly explain the increasing tendency of national governments to force re-location of national agencies to such target regions: for example, the British government's requirement that the National Statistical Office move to South Wales or significant parts of the BBC move to Manchester.[1]

Two examples illustrate the way in which large companies exploited the opportunities created by this dual process of European integration and internationalisation. Tambrands is the dominant seller of tampons in OECD countries. Up to 1989 it served the markets of Western Europe via four national companies marketing between them 220 separate packages. It re-organised post 1990 into one EU-wide company with its HQ in London, its marketing based in Paris and selling only two basic, multilingual packages to the whole of Western Europe. By 1992 its European sales had increased 48 % and its sales per employee by 21 %.

Curzon Global Partners represents a different type of exploitation of the opportunities arising from European economic integration and internationalisation. It was a specialist US financial services company originating in Boston. Taking advantage of financial products and expertise developed in the large, integrated US market and anticipating the effects of the creation of the Euro and the freeing up of competition within the EU in financial services, it established itself with a

---

[1] Interestingly a policy increasingly criticised as being contrary to the long term growth prospects of the poorer regions to which the agency is re-located on the grounds that the main advantage of the poorer regions is lower wage costs and government agencies typically have national wage agreements (and, even more typically, when moving, agree to do so without reduction in wages to workers who move). It is argued that the longer term result is to crowd out private sector employment in such regions and allow the public agencies to attract the most skilled labour. This is quite apart from any possibility that such activities as National Statistics or broadcasting might be subject to agglomeration economies not only affecting their own costs but affecting the costs of private sector firms in the prosperous regions.

joint venture based in London in 1997. In that year it had four European employees and no funds under management. By 2004 the company had evolved into an independent venture, still based in London, but with 100 offices across the EU, 210 employees, €10.6 bn of managed funds and €60 mn annual revenues.

In this process of integration the winning and losing regions have not been randomly distributed. Particular types of places have had specific advantages and disadvantages. Partly this reflected the sectors most affected by an increased ability to trade and re-structure. Older manufacturing sectors had had only minor barriers to trade, especially within Europe, since the 1960s but the Single European Market and liberalisation since about 1990, have particularly affected tradable services and previously protected sectors such as telecommunications, pharmaceuticals or defence related industries. These advanced sectors had a particular dependence on very highly skilled labour and because they tended to have high value to weight ratios for their products (or rely, like financial services or the media, on business travel of highly paid personnel) on accessibility to major international airports. It is not chance that industrial premises close to Heathrow airport are the most expensive per square metre of any in the world (KingSturge 2008)[2]. In addition, functions within sectors are differentially affected. As the example of Tambrands illustrates, HQs tended to concentrate, and concentrate in the largest cities with good international communications. London appears to have a comparative advantage in HQs of multinational enterprises. In 1990 28 % of the HQs of major European companies were in London (Rozenblat and Pumain 1993): between 1997 and 2002 35 % of new multinational HQ projects were in the London region and moreover, projects in London were weighted towards those of the biggest companies (Ernst and Young 2003). As Duranton and Puga (2005) show, functional specialisation between cities is a widespread phenomenon.

Together these changes increasing the mobility of economic activity, reducing the incentives for national governments to restrict the activities of local growth promotion agencies and the perception, based on fact, that the gains of European integration and internationalisation were up for grabs but tended to favour particular kinds of city regions at the expense of others substantially increased incentives to create local development – or 'growth promotion' – agencies.

Before moving on to analyse the role and potential contribution of 'growth promotion' there is one more aspect of urban change that should be considered: the apparently increasing importance of agglomeration economies.

Cities impose costs – of pollution, waste disposal, congestion, crime, and most systematically, of increased land/space prices. These costs all rise with city size. The fear of 'grid-lock' is at least 2000 years old – as old as ancient Rome. The city authorities of ancient Rome imposed their own special form of 'congestion charge':

---

[2] A combination of the particularly restrictive British system of land use regulation which constricts the supply of all types of space and the strong demand for access to Heathrow by producers and distributors of high value goods and goods the value of which is significantly determined by speed and reliability of delivery (such as parts for complex machine tools, aircraft or medical equipment).

heavy wagons were only allowed to enter the city during restricted hours in the night when other traffic was lighter.

Yet despite these costs of city size large cities exist and, as we shall see below, there is evidence that larger cities have been systematically outperforming smaller ones over the past 20 years or so. So cities must 'produce' something. There must be a trade-off between the costs and benefits of increasing city size. The benefits are significantly in the form of agglomeration economies, external to individual agents and benefiting both the costs of producing and the incomes and welfare of individual households and people.

The precise mechanisms producing agglomeration economies are still imperfectly understood but there is increasingly sophisticated and persuasive research estimating their net impacts. For example Rosenthal and Strange (2004) suggest credible estimates of the impact of increasing city size on total factor productivity range from about 3–8 % for every doubling of city size. More recently a number of authors, such as Graham and Kim (2008), have produced evidence showing wide variation in the incidence of agglomeration economies between sectors, with the highest values being found in several traded services and the lowest in manufacturing and construction. It is likely that it is agglomeration economies, coupled with decreased costs of communication, that have accelerated the functional specialisation between cities noted by Duranton and Puga (2005).

But as was remarked in the introduction, larger city size does not just confer advantages on producers and factor productivity, but it also provides advantages to individuals both via the effect of city size on labour market matching, allowing for higher expected lifetime earnings (Costa and Kahn 2000), and directly on welfare. This latter effect arises through the greater choices in consumption and competition between sellers larger cities facilitate: and not just consumption of market goods and services but of more intangible 'goods' such as social interactions and the ability to choose to live in congenial neighbourhoods.

Variations in the incidence of agglomeration economies between firms and activities and the costs of city size (more expensive space is a more significant cost for a family with many dependent children or space intensive activities such as manufacturing) mean that different activities and households are likely to sort between city sizes. If preferences also vary between households in their taste for consuming 'urban' as opposed to low-density amenities and lifestyles, this would reinforce the sorting effect between sizes of cities. There is categorically no single, optimal, city-size. Because of externalities, in the absence of intervention, there may, however, be a tendency for each city to grow beyond its optimal size. If we consider a city open to inward movement then people would tend to move to the city until the marginal private benefit was equal to the marginal private cost; but since each new arrival would impose costs on existing inhabitants in the form of congestion and space prices, each city would tend to grow beyond its optimal size. This is likely to be a purely theoretical case, however, since – particularly in Europe – we impose very stringent growth controls on cities. These partly take the form of land us controls, especially the widespread application of growth boundaries (in the UK, policies of 'urban containment') and densification.

But another de facto restriction on urban growth is the effect of policies to reduce spatial disparities – universal in the EU. These reduce the growth of the largest (and most prosperous) cities in favour of smaller and more peripheral ones. This is regardless of the fact that since one feature of urban size is rising costs, higher money wages in larger cities are partly compensation for higher housing and other costs, reflecting also the agglomeration economies making labour more productive in larger cities. The differential in real wages between larger and smaller cities may be far smaller than those in money wages.

3   Growth Promotion as an Economic Activity

If we suspend our disbelief and assume that policy agencies promoting local growth can generate growth, then it is apparent that local growth promotion is the production of a *local public good*[3]. Any extra growth generated is non-rival in consumption: if one person's employment prospects improve that does not reduce those of another. And it is non-excludable. If the effects of local growth spill over to improve the prospects of neighbouring jurisdictions there is nothing the community which had expended the effort to promote local growth can do about it.

This immediately raises the question: how will growth promotion policies be provided? We need to view them as form of investment: there are costs now but returns (growth dividends) are expected in the future. So we can analyse the incentives facing jurisdictions conditioning their probability of engaging in effective growth promotion. Other things being equal a local community will be more likely to engage seriously in growth promotion the lower are the costs to them of engaging and the greater are the expected gains to participating agents.

At least in Europe, one factor determining the expected growth dividends will be the extent to which a location is exposed to potential integration effects – either because of the industrial structure of the local economy or because of its location: or a mix of both. A second, more political economy type factor, will influence the probability of forming a local growth promotion coalition. That is the extent to which local political control is influenced by representatives of agents gaining most from local growth. These will be 'rent' earners – not just local property earners but those earning quasi-rents as well, such as those who possess locally applicable but scarce skills. In addition, economic agents the revenues of which derive from the existing local economic structure will have a greater incentive to promote local growth: agents such as utilities, business service providers or dominant locally based firms. An inspection of the business supporters of almost any local growth promotion agency will provide evidence of the power of economic rents and self-interest in driving political action. The agency for London, London First, for example includes the most prominent representatives of all those sectors

---

[3] This section draws on Cheshire and Gordon 1996.

identified above as well as some representatives of the near market sector including the London School of Economics.

The third factor, and the most important for the present analysis, is the extent of spillover losses. For a given potential expected growth dividend to the local economy, the value to any jurisdiction will be determined by the proportion of the whole local economy it represents. Take, for example, a city like Brussels. For historic and political reasons it is a bilingual enclave between the Flemish speaking north of Belgium and the French speaking south. In 1991, the population of the administrative region of Brussels – the city at the centre of the Brussels economic region, was some 960,000: but the population of its economic region, defined as the area from which workers commuted to work in the economic core of Brussels, was over 3,500,000 (IAURIF 2003). Thus any success a growth promotion agency funded by the citizens of Brussels might have would be largely lost, in the form of spillovers, to households living in other jurisdictions spread over nearly a third of Belgium.

In analysing the incentives to establish local growth promotion agencies, however, we need to consider the costs as well as the benefits. There may be some hopeless cases of regions that expect to be influenced strongly by integration and the increased mobility of economic activity but the agencies which represent them make a judgement that their location or industrial structure is so disadvantageous that no local efforts can be expected to have much impact. The incentive in such regions is therefore to lobby national governments and the EU to undertake direct redistribution: in other words, for policies at a national or European level to reduce 'spatial disparities'. For jurisdictions that judge their prospects to be better or even promising if helped by appropriate local growth promotion policies, the costs of such policies will be significantly determined by the transactions costs involved in forming an effective 'growth promotion club', typically a public private partnership led by the relevant local government or public agency. These transactions costs will increase as the number of local jurisdictions encompassing the area containing the growth dividends increases; and perhaps as there is less clearly a single, dominant, local jurisdiction to lead the others.

Together these arguments lead one to conclude that the factors which will determine the probability that any given local economic region will effectively engage in growth promotion will relate to the degree of fragmentation of the local jurisdictions within it. The larger is the leading administrative authority relative to the size of the economic region, the less will be any spillover losses from policy induced growth and the lower will be transactions costs. If we can define the area most closely approximating the 'economic region' of an urban centre, therefore, we can easily identify a variable to reflect the incentive and capacity of the city/region to form a growth promotion club or agency. If such agencies have any influence on the growth rates of the territories they represent then, in addition, this variable should be correlated with differences in growth between cities. We have a sort of 'anti-Tiebout' (Tiebout 1956) world in which local public goods (in this case extra growth) have spillover effects across jurisdictions but people are relatively immobile between jurisdictions. For a given 'economic region' more, smaller competing jurisdictions will be associated with less production of the local public good, local economic growth promotion.

4 Functional Urban Regions (FURs) Contain Growth Benefits

In the statistical results reported below we use as our units of analysis core-based urban regions – or Functional Urban Regions (FURs) – similar in concept to the Standard Metropolitan Statistical Areas (SMSAs) familiar from the US. The FURs used here were originally defined in Hall and Hay (1980) but their boundaries were slightly updatcd and revised in Cheshire and IIay (1989) where full details are available. Since then, the data set relating to these FURs has been continuously updated although their boundaries remain fixed as at 1971. The urban cores are identified on the basis of concentrations of jobs. Using the smallest spatial units in each country for which the basic data were available, all contiguous units with job densities exceeding 12.35 per hectare were amalgamated to identify the FUR 'core-city' (in the case of Brussels, an area containing 1,031,000 residents – more than in the official NUTS region of Brussels). The FUR hinterland was then identified by amalgamating all the contiguous units from which more people commuted to jobs in the given core than commuted elsewhere with a minimum cut-off of 10 %. These criteria were used for the great majority of countries but, in some, critical data were unavailable, so alternative methods had to be used. The most extreme departure was in Italy where previously defined retail areas were substituted for the FUR boundaries. Because of the difficulties of estimating comparable data for the FURs, in what follows we analyse patterns of growth only in the largest 121. These are all FURs in the former EU of 12^4 – excluding Berlin – with a total population of more than one third of a million and a core city of more than 200,000 at some date since 1951.

There are substantial advantages of using as the units of analysis functionally as opposed to the commonly used administratively defined regions. Even across a comparatively unified country such as the USA, states, counties and cities vary considerably in how they relate to patterns of behaviour or economic conditions. In Europe, the official regions (the NUTS[5]) are far more disparate since they combine within one system very different national systems. Even within one country – Germany – the regions vary from historical hangovers from the Middle Ages – such as Bremen (population 0.7 million) or Hamburg (1.7 million) – to regions such as Bavaria, with a population of 12.3 million and the size of several

---

[4] That is in the countries of Belgium, Denmark, France, Germany, Greece, Ireland, Italy, Luxembourg, The Netherlands, Portugal, Spain and the United Kingdom.

[5] Nomenclature des Unités Territoriales Statistiques (N.U.T.S.) regions. This is a nesting set of regions based on national territorial divisions. The largest are Level 1 regions; the smallest for which a reasonable range of data is available are Level 3. Historically these corresponded to Counties in the UK, Départements in France; Provincies in Italy or Kreise in Germany.

smaller European countries run together. In terms of administrative competence, Germany has 16 of the functionally very disparate Länder (NUTS Level 1 regions), each with substantial powers and constituting the elements of its Federal system; and below that the Kreise (NUTS Level 3) – 439 of them in 2003. Britain has 12 NUTS 1 regions, corresponding in mean size to the Länder, but only one of them – Scotland – has any real administrative or fiscal independence. In Britain there are only 133 of the smaller units supposedly equivalent to the Kreise. Bavaria, despite including major cities such as Munich, had a population density of only 174 people per square km compared to 4,539 in the NUTS Level 1 region of London or 2,279 in Hamburg (CEC 2004).

More significant than their heterogeneity in size and administrative powers is the fact that the official NUTS regions are economically heterogeneous, in some cases containing very different local economies within the same statistical unit (for example, Glasgow and Edinburgh in Scotland or Lille and Valenciennes in Nord-Pas-de-Calais) and in others dividing a single city-region between as many as three separate units. The functional reality of Hamburg, for example, is divided between three different Länder, Hamburg, Schleswig-Holstein and Niedersachsen. There are thus many NUTS regions with large scale and systematic cross border commuting and some contain mainly dormitory suburban areas of large cities. Others (for example, Brussels, London, Bremen or Hamburg) are effectively urban cores or only small parts of urban cores. This means that residential segregation influences the value of variables such as unemployment, health or skills if measured on the basis of the boundaries of NUTS; and measures of Gross Domestic Product or Value Added per capita, or productivity, can be grotesquely distorted since output is measured at workplaces and people are counted where they live.

These are obvious points, causing serious reservations in relation to the many published analyses of regional growth rates in Europe, using the official Eurostat data for NUTS regions. They mean official measures of so-called 'regional disparities' – showing, for example, that in 2001 the 'region' of Inner London was 2.5 times as 'rich' in per capita GDP as the mean for the EU of 15 and 3.2 times as 'rich' as the UK's poorest region, are complete nonsense. It is for these reasons that we rely on our own data for FURs.

A further advantage of using FURs is that they do not exhaust national territories. The total population of the EU of 12 in 2001, excluding Berlin, was some 340.5 million. Almost exactly half – 169.2 million – lived in its major Functional Urban Regions as defined here. This property of the FURs allows us to define an additional control variable: the rate of growth of GDP pc at PPS in the area of each country outside its major FURs. This is calculated over the same period as the dependent variable.

There is one critical, additional advantage of using data for FURs (rather than administrative regions) in the present context. FURs are as economically independent divisions of national territories as it is possible to construct. They represent concentrations of jobs and all those people who depend on those jobs – the economic spheres of influence of major cities. So any growth dividend a local growth promotion agency might generate – the benefits of additional employment or output – are as confined to those who live within them as is possible for any sub national regions. In other words FURs are a close approximation of 'economic regions' in the sense discussed above, so the ratio of the population living in the administrative jurisdiction representing the 'city' to that of the FUR as a whole should provide a quantitative measure of the relevant degree of fragmentation of city government in conditioning the incentives to generate local growth promotion policies. The larger is the size of the government unit representing the city to the size of the FUR, the lower will be spillover losses from growth promotion and the lower will be transactions costs in forming a 'growth promotion club'. We call this the 'policy incentive' variable. For further details see Cheshire and Magrini (2009), from which this and the following section, draws.

5 Some Empirical Results

Appendix Tables 5.1 defines the main variables used. The approach is first to build a 'base' model and test it for standard specification problems and for spatial dependence. In the latter tests we pay particular attention to the specification of the spatial weights matrix – choosing weights which maximise the indicated sensitivity to problems of spatial dependence while conforming to obvious economic logic. OLS is used to estimate the models except where there is a spatial lag, when we use maximum likelihood. We take care to minimise problems of endogeneity although we accept that our efforts do not necessarily entirely eliminate all such problems. Our position is that ultimately there must be some judgement and what matters is that any remaining endogeneity problems do not seriously influence the results.

The dependent variable is the FUR rate of growth of GDP pc at PPS measured from the mean of 1978–80 to the mean of 1992–94. There are some more or less standard control variables. We have consistently found that specific measures of reliance on old, resource-based industries – the coal industry, port activity and agriculture – perform better than more generalised measures such as employment in industry or unemployment at the start of the period (although the latter is included in one model and is marginally useful). Since reliance on the coal industry is measured with a geological indicator, it seems safe to assume it is exogenous. Port activity is measured very early – in 1969 – before the main transformation of the industry to modern methods and before any likely integration effects of creating the European Union would be apparent. Specialisation in agriculture is measured in the larger region containing the FUR – again well before the start of the period covered by the dependent variable.

In cross-sectional, cross-national analyses of regional growth, the conventional control for all country specific factors (notably the incidence of the national economic cycles but also institutional and policy differences between countries) has been national dummies. This would be problematic with our data set since in Denmark, Greece, Ireland and Portugal there are only one or two major FURs, so we would have to arbitrarily choose which countries to pool to construct national dummies. More interestingly, since we wish to infer causation, our underlying assumption must be that our observational units – the major FURs of Western Europe – are, in

5 Urban Growth Policies: The Need to Set Realistic Expectations

Table 5.1 Variable definitions – rate of growth of GDP pc at PPS 1978/80 to 1992/94 dependent variable

No	Variable name	Description
	Constant	
1	Population size	Population size in 1979 (natural logarithm)
2	Population density	Density of population in FUR in 1979 (1,000 inhabitants/Km^2)
3	Coalfield dummy: core	Dummy $= 1$ if the core of the FUR is located within a coalfield
4	Coalfield dummy: hinterland	Dummy $= 1$ if the hinterland of the FUR is located in a coalfield
5	Port size[a]	Volume of port trade in 1969 (100 t)
6	Agriculture[a]	Share of labour force in agriculture in surrounding NUTS 2 in 1975
7	Unemployment[a]	Unemployment rate (average rate between 1977 and 1981 – from Eurostat NUTS3 data)
8	National non-FUR growth	Growth of GDP p.c. in the territory of each country outside the FURs (annualised rate between 1978/80 and 1992/94)
9	Policy incentive[a]	Ratio of the population of the largest governmental unit associated with the FUR to that of the FUR in 1981 (see below for details)
10	Integration gain	Change in economic potential for FUR resulting from pre-Treaty of Rome EEC to post enlargement EU with reduced transport costs (estimated from Clark et al. 1969 and Keeble et al. 1988)
11	Peripherality dummy	Dummy $= 1$ if the FUR is more than 10 h away from Brussels
12	University students[a]	Ratio of university students (1977–78) to total employment (1979)
13	R&D facilities[a]	R&D laboratories of Fortune 500 companies per 1,000 inhabitants in 1980
14	Unemployment density	Sum of differences between the unemployment rate (average between 1977 and 1981) of a FUR and the rates in neighbouring FURs (within 2 h), discounted by distance (with 10 h time penalty for national borders)
15	University student density	Sum of university students per employees in neighbouring FURs (within 2.5 h), discounted by distance (with 10 h time penalty for national borders)
16	R&D facilities density	Sum of R&D laboratories per 1,000 inhabitants in neighbouring FURs (within 2.5 h), discounted by distance (with 10 h time penalty for national borders)

Source: Cheshire and Magrini 2009
[a]Denote variables tried with a quadratic specification for reasons explained in the text. Never entered as squared value alone.

statistical terms, a homogeneous population. A more elegant solution to control for national factors not explicitly included as independent variables is, therefore, to include 'non-FUR growth' as a continuous control variable.

There are two further control variables in the base models: the size of each FUR measured in 1981 and represented as the log of the population; and the density of population in 1981. As was discussed in Sect. 2, there is evidence that agglomeration economies have been becoming more important over the past 20 or 30 years in the cities of OECD countries as structural transformation of advanced economies and the evolving functions of cities favoured activities with stronger agglomeration

Table 5.2 Dependent variable annualised rate of growth of GDP p.c. @ PPS: mean 1978/80 to mean 1992/4: Model 1: base model OLS: Model 2: base model + spatial lag, max. likelihood

	Model 1		Model 2	
R^2	0.5903		0.6053	
Adjusted R^2	0.5570			
LIK	485.56		488.74	
Constant	−0.0205		−0.0240	
t-test – prob	−2.05	0.04	−2.55	0.01
Spatial lag of dep. variable			0.2648	
t-test – prob			2.61	0.01
National non-FUR growth	0.8600		0.7119	
t-test – prob	8.06	0.00	6.24	0.00
Coalfield: core	−0.0054		−0.0050	
t-test – prob	−4.25	0.00	−4.13	0.00
Coalfield: hinterland	−0.0057		−0.0054	
t-test – prob	−3.29	0.00	−3.37	0.00
Port size	−0.1364		−0.1416	
t-test – prob	−3.18	0.00	−3.56	0.00
Port size squared	0.6166		0.6550	
t-test – prob	2.28	0.02	2.61	0.01
Agriculture	0.0409		0.0254	
t-test – prob	2.55	0.01	1.67	0.10
Agriculture squared	−0.1125		−0.0737	
t-test – prob	−2.51	0.01	−1.75	0.08
Population size	0.0021		0.0019	
t-test – prob	3.16	0.00	3.11	0.00
Population density	−0.0015		−0.0015	
t-test – prob	−2.00	0.05	−2.19	0.03

Source: Cheshire and Magrini 2009

economies, such as financial and business services or media. The logic for including both size and density separately is briefly discussed below.

These control variables were chosen to reflect economic factors and, as the results reported in Table 5.2 show, they appear to work satisfactorily. The rate of growth of GDP pc outside the major FURs (Non-FUR Growth) proves significant and, as the models become more fully specified, the value of the estimated co-efficient tends to get closer to 1 (compare results in Tables 5.2 and 5.3). All variables are significant and have the expected signs although adding a spatial lag of the dependent variable reduces the significance of the concentration in agriculture in the wider region. There are indications of dynamic agglomeration economies – larger FURs grew faster, other factors controlled for – but once this was done FURs which were denser grew more slowly. The reasoning underlying the inclusion of these variables independently is that factors generating agglomeration economies are distinct from density itself. Agglomeration economies arise as a result of the number and net value of productive interactions between economic agents and these are larger in larger cities. Larger cities also tend to have denser population and, in studies of agglomeration economies, density of employment or population

5 Urban Growth Policies: The Need to Set Realistic Expectations

Table 5.3 Dependent variable annualised rate of growth of GDP p.c. Mean 1978/80–mean 1992/4 – models excluding and including 'Spatial Variables'

	Model 3		Model 4		Model 5	
R^2	0.6765		0.7413		0.7555	
Adjusted R^2	0.6372		0.6986		0.7095	
LIK	499.86		513.38		516.80	
Constant	−0.0320		−0.0233		−0.0261	
t-test – prob	−3.14	0.00	−3.52	0.01	−2.84	0.01
National non-FUR growth	0.9442		0.8975		0.9050	
t-test – prob	9.22	0.00	9.07	0.00	9.31	0.00
Coalfield: core	−0.0062		−0.0051		−0.0051	
t-test – prob	−5.18	0.00	−3.99	0.00	−4.00	0.00
Coalfield: hinterland	−0.0042		−0.0034		−0.0032	
t-test – prob	−2.61	0.01	−2.23	0.03	−2.06	0.04
Port size	−0.1474		−0.1003		−0.0932	
t-test – prob	−3.69	0.00	−2.62	0.01	−2.46	0.02
Port size squared	0.7634		0.4871		0.4669	
t-test – prob	3.04	0.00	2.02	0.05	1.97	0.05
Agriculture	0.0508		0.0384		0.0478	
t-test – prob	3.22	0.00	2.48	0.01	3.02	0.00
Agriculture squared	−0.1345		−0.1126		−0.1231	
t-test – prob	−3.21	0.00	−2.82	0.01	−3.12	0.00
Unemployment			−0.0332		−0.0312	
t-test – prob			−2.45	0.02	−2.29	0.02
Population size	0.0021		0.0016		0.0016	
t-test – prob	3.53	0.00	2.90	0.00	2.87	0.01
Population density	−0.0015		−0.0015		−0.0013	
t-test – prob	−2.25	0.03	−2.36	0.02	−2.07	0.04
Integration gain			0.0073		0.0082	
t-test – prob			3.20	0.00	3.61	0.00
University students	0.0309		0.0367		0.0303	
t-test – prob	2.67	0.01	3.62	0.00	2.87	0.01
R&D facilities	0.8079		0.8947		0.8512	
t-test – prob	2.84	0.01	3.26	0.00	3.10	0.00
Policy incentive	0.0075		0.0026		0.0086[a]	
t-test – prob	2.24	0.03	2.45	0.02	2.49	0.01
Policy incentive squared	−0.0021				−0.0027[a]	
t-test – prob	−1.32	0.19			−1.72	0.09
R&D facilities density			0.0531		0.0703	
t-test – prob			2.19	0.03	2.70	0.01
Peripherality dummy			0.0059		0.0054	
t-test – prob			4.51	0.00	4.10	0.00
University student density			−0.0025		−0.0030	
t-test – prob			−2.46	0.02	−2.93	0.00
Unemployment density					−0.0036	
t-test – prob					−1.92	0.06

Source: Cheshire and Magrini 2009
[a]Test of joint significance: $\chi^2(2) = 10.4333$ (0.01).

has often been used as the 'explanatory' variable. This is not inappropriate in unregulated conditions but in the conditions ruling in a number of EU countries in which there are very strong urban containment policies, density and size will vary to an extent independently of each other. Once size has been allowed for, higher density should be associated with higher space costs and more congestion and so is expected to be associated with less favourable conditions for economic activity.

We do not report the test statistics here but those for standard problems of heteroskedasticity, non-normality of errors, multicollinearity and functional form were all acceptable (see Cheshire and Magrini 2009). So, too, were tests for spatial dependence unless an additional time-distance penalty for national borders was included. Experimentation showed that indicated spatial dependence problems were maximised if this national border penalty was set at 600 min. Indeed, if no time distance penalty for national borders was included in the distance weights matrix, there was no sign of spatial dependence. The indicated textbook solution for spatial dependence is to include the spatially lagged dependent variable as an additional independent variable. Results of doing so are shown in the second set of columns in Table 5.2. The spatially lagged dependent variable is significant but makes little difference to the other estimated parameters.

Our preferred approach to problems of spatial dependence is to treat a significant result as indicating a problem of omitted variables: in the present case the omission of variables driving systematic spatial patterns of FUR growth. Table 5.3 shows the results of including such variables, plus additional variables designed to test specific hypotheses, especially the impact of government fragmentation on growth performance.

The idea that concentrations of highly skilled human capital should be associated with faster rates of real GDP pc growth (itself very closely related to productivity growth) is not novel. It is represented here as the ratio of university students to total employees at the very start of the period (to help reduce any possible problems of endogeneity). Equally, there is a large literature on the tendency for patents to be applied closer to their points of origin (see, for example, Audretsch 1998 or, for a recent application to a European context, Barrios et al. 2007). So we should expect FURs with greater concentrations of R&D activity at the start of the period to have grown faster. This is measured as R&D facilities of the largest firms per 1,000 inhabitants – again at the start of the period.

The third variable designed to test hypotheses about the drivers of economic growth is the 'policy incentive' variable discussed in Sects. 3 and 4. That is simply a measure of how closely each FUR's boundaries match those of the largest effective jurisdiction[6] associated with the FUR. This is defined as the ratio of jurisdiction's to FUR's population at the start of the period. The hypothesis is that the more closely these match, the greater will be the payoff to forming an effective growth promotion club or agency, other things being equal. It could be that the advantage increases as the size of the governmental unit gets bigger than the FUR itself

---

[6] Usually the jurisdiction representing the core city but in some cases – for example in Spain – a regional tier of government (for details see Cheshire and Magrini 2009).

5 Urban Growth Policies: The Need to Set Realistic Expectations

(as happens in some European countries in which there is an effective regional tier of government – Madrid might be an example) because the resources and clout of the governmental unit will be bigger. But if the governmental unit is too large, the interests of the main FUR within it may get diluted by those of outlying smaller cities and rural areas. This implies – if growth promotion agencies are able to have any impact on local economic growth – that we should expect a positive relationship between the variable we call the 'policy incentive' and GDP pc growth with perhaps a quadratic relationship, since having a regional tier of government too greatly exceeding the size of your economic region or FUR, may dilute the positive impact on growth.

Model 3 in Table 5.3 includes all these variables and we can see they are all significant and have the expected sign. Their inclusion improves the fit of the model without significantly changing the estimated parameter values of the existing variables and only the functional form of the policy incentive variable is unclear, since the quadratic term, although it has the expected sign, is not significant. Testing for spatial dependence (see Cheshire and Magrini 2009, for details), however, reveals apparent problems if the 600 min time-distance penalty is included for national borders. This suggests that variables reflecting systematic spatial patterns are omitted.

Models 4 and 5 show the impact of including variables designed to capture such spatial influences. The first is the 'Integration Gain' variable, intended to capture the spatial effect of European integration. This measures the change in economic potential for each FUR, associated with European integration and transport cost reductions, and is estimated from the work of Clark et al. 1969. Partly as a response to the perceived advantage accruing to 'core' regions from European integration, Europe – starting from the mid-1970s – has developed stronger policies aimed at redistributing economic activity to 'peripheral' regions than any other political grouping. Such policies in 1972 accounted for 4 % of spending by the European Commission but increased their share of the budget to 15 % by 1980 and to some 30 % by 1994. Although their impact has been questioned (see, Midelfart and Overman 2002; Rodriguez-Pose and Fratesi 2004) it still seems worth including a variable for 'peripherality'. To avoid subjectivity and problems of endogeneity this is arbitrarily defined as being all FURs more than 600 min time-distance from Brussels.

It is also plausible that in the more densely urbanised parts of Europe, conditions in FURs will influence each other – there will be interaction between the economic performance of neighbouring FURs. Three variables are included to try to capture this, drawing on the literature on spatial labour markets and the distance decay effect of innovations. Since there is evidence, particularly from the spatial applications of patents, that new innovations are subject to a distance decay effect and we have already seen that concentrations of R&D favour FUR growth, so, if there are concentrations of R&D in a FUR one would expect that to favour growth in other FURs close by – subject to a distance decay effect. This is reflected in the design of the 'R&D Facilities Density' variable. Equally if a concentration of highly skilled labour favours a FUR's growth, then having a higher concentration in neighbouring FURs would be expected to reduce its growth since the faster growth generated in the surrounding FURs will tend to attract highly skilled commuters away from the slower growing FUR. This is reflected in the 'University Student Density' variable. Finally, some studies suggest an initial higher level of unemployment is prejudicial to subsequent growth. Glaeser et al. 1995, for example, report that in their study.

Models 4 and 5, therefore, include both the initial level of unemployment in FUR_i and an Unemployment Density variable calculated as the distance weighted level of unemployment in all neighbouring $FURs_{j-n}$ up to 120 min between centroids. The time distance cut-off applied to calculating the R&D Facilities and University Students Density variables is rather higher – 150 min. These differential cut-offs both provide better statistical performance but are also consistent with underlying reasoning. The unemployed, who are biased towards the least skilled, are likely to have a geographically more confined influence than the most highly skilled or innovation. In all cases the 600 min time-distance penalty for national borders is applied in calculating the value of these spatial interaction variables for each FUR. Again this not only performs better statistically but is consistent with underlying logic and other empirical findings.

The results are reported in Table 5.3. We can see that all variables have the expected sign and are significant at at least the 10 % level – even the quadratic term for the policy incentive variable. Tests for joint significance provide further evidence of the fact that the underlying functional form of the policy incentive variable is quadratic (with the maximum favourable impact of the relationship between FUR and administrative boundaries coming when the administrative jurisdiction containing the FUR is about 1.5 times its size). More encouraging (reported in detail in Cheshire and Magrini 2009) is the fact that all signs of spatial dependence are eliminated. As before no conventional econometric problems are indicated.

In the context of understanding the main drivers of the rate of FUR GDP pc growth these results suggest that there is evidence of dynamic agglomeration economies but – other things equal – higher population density is bad for growth. They also suggest that while the process of European integration has, indeed, favoured 'core' regions, policies to reduce 'spatial disparities' (the official aim of European regional policies) may at least in part have offset for that. The results are certainly consistent with concentrations of highly skilled human capital and R&D favouring local growth. Perhaps more surprisingly they suggest not only that local growth promotion policies may have some positive impact but the incentives regional actors face in developing such policies are themselves influential. It helps if local jurisdictional boundaries coincide more closely with those of self-contained economic regions – FURs – because given the spillovers losses from any successful growth promotion and transactions costs in forming effective growth promotions clubs, such a coincidence of boundaries means there are greater expected gains to actors. Finally, when investigating issues of spatial dependence, we find strong evidence of the barrier national boundaries still provide to processes of spatial adjustment in Europe.

Table 5.4 shows the estimated impact of each variable on a FUR's growth rate over the period analysed by showing the percentage change in growth associated with a one Standard Deviation change in the value of the independent variable. The

5   Urban Growth Policies: The Need to Set Realistic Expectations   109

Table 5.4 Growth impact: effect on predicted growth of a change (+ or − 1 sd) of an independent variable

| | Growth impact | |
| | Model 4 | |
	+1 std (%)	−1 std (%)
Population size	1.81	−1.81
Population density	−1.34	1.34
Coalfield: core	−3.06	3.06
Coalfield: hinterland	−1.29	1.29
Port size[a]	−2.68	3.40
Agriculture[a]	3.74	−5.57
Unemployment	−1.70	1.70
National non-FUR growth	6.18	−6.18
Policy incentive[a]	2.97	−4.13
Integration gain	3.36	−3.36
Peripherality	4.16	−4.16
University students	1.92	−1.92
R&D facilities	2.24	−2.24
Unemployment density	−1.26	1.26
University students density	−2.69	2.69
R&D facilities density	2.91	−2.91

Source: Cheshire and Magrini 2009
[a]The effects of port size, agriculture and the policy incentive variables are calculated through the estimated quadratic relationship.

most obvious point here is how diffused the impact of the growth drivers is. Although the performance of the national economy outside the area of the FURs – included to control for national factors including differences in the temporal incidence of the economic cycle across countries – has substantially the largest influence on growth differentials, the influence of the others is relatively evenly distributed. Rather like the most significant factor determining the probability of someone being rich is having rich parents the most important influence in determining how fast a city's economy grew was how fast the economy of the non-urban area of the country in which it was located grew. The impact of the dummy variables (located in a coalfield or whether the FUR was classified as peripheral) is probably overstated by the measure used in Table 5.4. So the only other variables standing out at all as having greater influence were concentrations of the most highly qualified labour and R&D facilities in the FUR itself and in its neighbours, the systematic spatial impacts of integration and the policy incentive variable.

6   Main Conclusions for Urban Policies

The first and most obvious conclusion is that economic growth at the level of the city-region is a multivariate process. No individual determinant is dominant and the process is significantly path dependent because many of the fundamental drivers reflect an inheritance of industrial structure – past dependence on resource based industries such as coal or port activity being a particular and continuing disadvantage – or factors such as city location, size or density. Moreover, while it is necessarily true that better city growth contributes to national growth performance, it is too simple to assert that 'cities are the drivers of growth'. Agglomeration economies appear to be more salient than perhaps they were when the leading sectors were heavy manufacturing industry but there is a pervasive influence of national factors. These include institutional arrangements, educational systems, legal frameworks and macroeconomic policies as well, perhaps, as more intangible factors such as culture. National non-FUR economic performance is the single most influential variable explaining differences in city performance.

The findings do not suggest many obvious 'policy levers' available at the local level. Some possibilities would seem to be the provision of highly skilled – graduate – labour, R&D activity and perhaps density (in so far as higher density for given size represents a policy failure rather than topographical constraints). Even these have question marks against them. While in principle constraints on urban land availability could be relaxed it is, as policy makers in Britain have found, difficult to implement. There are strong vested interests bound up in the status quo once land use regulation has helped generate asset values and a spatial distribution of amenities. Even if there was a relaxation of land use constraints, the impact on urban density would be a long time coming since new construction is such a small proportion of the stock of buildings.

Equally it is not clear that even if city authorities or growth promotion agencies could create new universities, or expand existing ones, the impact would be the same as starting with a higher concentration of university students per employee. New universities, and the students they attracted, might differ in unobservable ways from established universities. Similarly dirigiste policies with respect to the location of private sector R&D do not have a great history of success. Forcing companies to locate their R&D facilities in particular cities might simply slow innovation in the company. Setting up new publicly assisted R&D establishments would not be equivalent to firms' own R&D activity.

The most hopeful 'policy lever' would seem to be reform of administrative structures so that the boundaries of jurisdictions responsible – at least for certain strategic functions with significant spatial spillovers such as growth promotion – closely approximated those of FURs. Even though this might seem a simple 'policy lever' still there are arguments that suggest its impact might not be symmetric. Increasing the size of the area administered by all those city jurisdictions much smaller than their FURs might not have the simple effect suggested by a direct interpretation of the results reported in Tables 5.3 and 5.4. The analysis reported in these does provide evidence that city-regions equipped with more effective government structures perform better, so indirectly it supports the claim that local development efforts on average have a favourable impact. Many local growth promoting policies, however, may displace growth from other FURs: not increase total growth. So the success of the more successful FURs, with 'effective' local government structures, may result partly from failure of the FURs with fragmented government structures. Moreover even some policies which increase the total growth in the system of cities may also have 'displacement effects'. For example, if a jurisdiction improves its infrastructure that may increase total factor productivity and so growth for existing firms within the FUR but it also may attract mobile investment which would have located in some other FUR. Equally, improved training may increase system growth but in so far as one FUR has a more skilled labour force than other(s) it may attract mobile investment. While it may be the case that a more successful London or Stockholm has positive growth spin-offs in other FURs, we cannot at present quantify these and there may be displacement effects as well.

It is probably safest to assume that local growth promotion policies – in so far as they are effective – mainly generate growth which is a mixture of displacement and system wide growth, although the balance between those two will depend on what policies are pursued. Location incentives (in so far as they have any effect) are likely largely to displace growth from other locations: effective training policies, at the other extreme, are likely mainly to be system enhancing since the trained can move elsewhere as well as apply their skills locally. And some local growth policies, such as advertising the attractions of your city, are quite likely to be pure waste in that they have no influence on the behaviour of economic agents. So even though it seems plausible that a FUR with fragmented jurisdictional boundaries could improve its chances of developing effective growth promotion policies by reforming them so those for strategic actions minimised spatial spillovers, still the gains to the FUR in question and to the system of cities as a whole, would be unlikely to be as large as a simple reading of Table 5.4 might indicate.

This is still abstracting from what types of policy are most likely to help local growth prospects. Can cities become more 'competitive'? Firms can be more competitive in a simple sense. They produce a more or less homogeneous product or set of products. They have identifiable markets and any increased competitiveness is readily judged by profitability. Moreover firms have 'entry' and 'exit' options. They can stop selling a product line or, indeed, go out of business altogether. Cities, in contrast, have no 'product' or obvious market. They have a very heterogeneous 'offer' and, in practice, no 'exit' (even entry) option. It is not even obvious how any increase in a city's 'competitiveness' could be accurately measured. While it might be an increasing relative rate of growth of total factor productivity, there is the problem of the counterfactual. Even if total factor productivity is relatively falling, it might – as a result of effective growth policies – be falling less sharply than it would otherwise have been doing.

In very general terms, policies which make a city a more attractive place to live, work or do business would seem to be those that would make it more competitive. The more attractive a city is to live in then, other things equal, the lower the effective costs of production will be. People will want to live there, so at the margin they will take lower real wages and money costs of production will be lower. However, even this may not be true in full spatial equilibrium since the greater attractiveness of the city would tend to get capitalised into housing costs so bidding up money wages.

There certainly does not seem to be a simple policy recipe for direct policy actions of a dirigiste type. All cities start with different endowments and offers, so picking winners seldom works. There are too many relevant variables determining what activity might have a fundamental comparative advantage in a given city and no knowledge of the individual quantitative effect of any given variable. It is unlikely that policy makers are omniscient. A market mechanism which weeds out the unsuccessful new efforts, plenty of new start-ups, and a system which facilitates such start-ups, is likely to be the best way of 'picking winners'. The non-winners disappear but the winners thrive.

Policy makers' efforts to predict specific future developments do not have a good track record. The city fathers of Frankfurt determined to get the new European Central Bank to locate there and made substantial efforts to achieve that aim in the early 1990s. It seemed highly plausible that doing so would assist the competitive success of Frankfurt's already successful financial and banking sectors. The Euro has proved to be successful. But as a financial sector London – which did not even join the Euro zone, let alone secure the location of the European Bank – outperformed Frankfurt as a financial centre throughout the 1990s and through to 2007. Frankfurt, which till 1994 had been economically the most successful city within the EU, has had a sluggish economic performance ever since. About the only example of a 'picking-winners' strategy that seems to have been successful is the aerospace industry in Toulouse: and that was more or less by accident. In the 1920s the French government want to establish their emerging aircraft industry as far from the German border as possible and Toulouse was the most distant city with a significant university.

There would seem to be a fundamental reason why in fact 'picking-winners' is unlikely to work. It works against the very strengths of cities. This is their diversity which tends to come with size, as well, perhaps, as their typically more highly educated population, better communications and higher intensity of interactions. The result is not only more new ideas and innovation more rapidly diffused but more commercial ideas and opportunities coming forward and resulting in business start-ups. As noted above, of these start-ups, the successful grow. But a policy of public taxes being used to back winners is likely to crowd out diversity and activities which would otherwise have started up. And some of those would have been real winners. So using public resources to pick winners endangers unknown, future successes. In general, cities are more successful if they are bigger and brighter and have policies to facilitate, rather than restrict, growth and innovation.

The best policies seem likely to be the least glamorous and activist and the most discrete. As was reported above, there is real evidence that larger cities have a competitive edge because of agglomeration economies. But larger city size brings costs: particularly higher space costs but also greater congestion and, typically, crime and pollution. One obvious set of policies to support economic growth are those, therefore, which reduce the costs of city size, especially where those costs arise at least in part because of market failure. Here the most obvious example of would be congestion. As is well known, congestion entails a problem of market failure since marginal users (whether of roads or other transport systems) only pay the marginal private costs of congestion not the social costs which result for all existing users when a marginal user joins the network. Primitive boundary fees – such as that imposed in London – hardly address the underlying problem. Charges need to reflect as closely as possible the marginal social cost imposed by an additional user at any specific place or time. Devising and imposing congestion charging which proxies this cost[7] will lead to a more efficient use of the system as a whole as well as reducing congestion for any given total of potential users. So, as well as providing for mass transit systems when the size and traffic density of a city reaches an appropriate threshold[8], by imposing well designed congestion charging city policy makers can favourably influence total factor productivity and urban economic growth.

Policies to reduce crime and pollution are widely discussed and crime reduction in US cities has been cited by Glaeser and Gottlieb (2006) amongst others, as one of the drivers of the relative resurgence of American cities. The analysis offered in this paper suggests a regional tier of government with the appropriate responsibilities (those where the spatial range of policies extends to the economic region or FUR) can help. It also suggests that policies aimed specifically at restricting the physical growth of cities will be damaging to economic growth. This seems to be a clear cut case of policy, rather than market, failure since many countries practise through their land use regulation regimes, policies of urban containment and urban densification. This will increase the costs of space in cities for any given size and so not just restrict their growth physically but also in terms of their economic mass and the agglomeration economies that come with that. Indeed, via its backing for 'sustainable cities' and 'multi-polarity' in the name of 'balanced growth' the European Commission supports restricting the growth of larger cities. There is no clear evidence that either densification or urban containment reduces energy use. By increasing congestion for a given total size and increasing the length of commuting by forcing people to move across 'Green Belts' to satellite communities, urban containment policies may well, in fact, increase energy use. On the basis of the evidence presented here, urban containment policies would seem not only to restrict the economic growth of individual cities (lost agglomeration economies and more congestion) but also restrict economic growth in the system as whole since agglomeration economies contribute most in the largest cities.

The fundamental condition for successful growth promotion however, is efficient public administration: a system which embodies transparent and effective decision making. Clear cut and well known rules for decision making and transparent routes by which actors can influence decisions, coupled with speed and consistency in decision making, all seem obvious but are sadly rare. Clarity, transparency and consistency in public decision making reduce uncertainty for private investors. The British land use planning system has been an example of a failure to obey these simple rules. The protracted delays and immense expense associated with

---

[7] An interesting solution which does not rely on universal GPS was devised (but not implemented) for the City of Cambridge in the UK. This was a smart card plus reader which charged for time spent stationary with the engine running or moving for a given period at a given (slow) speed.

[8] In general as is argued by Eddington 2006, investment in transport infrastructure should follow demand rather than try to lead it (a form of picking winners). There is scant evidence that new transport infrastructure generates growth in a lagging region but plenty that a lack of infrastructure in a growing, prosperous and congested region imposes significant costs.

major decisions about new development in Britain have been widely remarked on (see Barker 2006a, b or Eddington 2006). The decision as to whether to allow a fifth terminal at London's Heathrow airport took 12 years and the direct costs were of the order of £100 million. The indirect costs, in terms of foregone investment where that investment relied on an efficiently functioning Heathrow, are unquantifiable but likely to have been orders of magnitude greater.

Thus the recommendations for policy to assist a city's economic growth are rather low key. The most successful policies are likely to be the efficient execution of well known functions, including policies to reduce the costs of city size and efficient public administration. Efficient public administration includes a requirement to design jurisdictional boundaries which minimise inter-jurisdictional spillovers. Policy needs to off set for market failures in urban systems and provide appropriate levels of local public goods, including transport services and training. Policy needs undramatically to facilitate innovation and that includes allowing physical development. While continuing to offset for problems of market failure related to patterns of land use, still policy needs to permit city growth rather than restrict it; and above all, perhaps, it needs not to do obviously stupid things which may include highly visible and apparently pro-growth actions such as using citizens' taxes to subsidise inward investment or attempting to pick winners. There is a danger, therefore, not only of unrealistically raising expectations with respect to the potential contribution of growth promotion agencies but of such agencies concentrating on actions which are highly visible but likely to be less effective.

References

Audretsch DB (1998) Agglomeration and the location of innovative activity. Oxford Rev Econ Pol 14(2):18–29

Barker K (2006a) Barker review of land use planning; interim report – analysis. HMSO, London

Barker K (2006b) Barker review of land use planning; final report – recommendations. HMSO, London

Barrios S, Bertinelli L, Heinen A et al (2007) Exploring the link between local and global knowledge spillovers. MPRA No 6301

Buigues P, Ilkovitz F, Lebrun J-F (1990) The impact of the internal market by industrial sector: the challenge for members states. European Economy, Social Europe, special edition. Office for Official Publications of the European Communities, Luxembourg

CEC (Commission of the European Communities) (1988) The costs of non-Europe: report of the Cecchini committee. Office of Official Publications, Luxembourg

CEC (Commission of the European Communities) (2004) Third report on social and economic cohesion: main regional indicators, Luxembourg

Cheshire PC, Gordon IR (1996) Territorial competition and the predictability of collective (In) action. Int J Urban Reg Res 20:383–399

Cheshire PC, Hay DG (1989) Urban problems in Western Europe: an economic analysis. Unwin Hyman, London

Cheshire PC, Magrini S (2009) Urban growth drivers in a Europe of sticky people and implicit boundaries. J Econ Geogr 9(1):85–115

5 Urban Growth Policies: The Need to Set Realistic Expectations

Ciccone A, Hall RE (1996) Productivity and the density of economic activity. Am Econ Rev 86(1):54–70

Clark C, Wilson F, Bradley J (1969) Industrial location and economic potential in Western Europe. Reg Stud 3:197–212

Costa DL, Kahn ME (2000) Power couples: changes in the locational choice of the college educated, 1940–1990. Quart J Econ 115(4):1287–1315

Duranton G, Puga D (2005) From sectoral to functional urban specialization. J Urban Econ 57:343–370

Eddington R (2006) The Eddington transport study, her majesty's stationery office, PU138, HM Treasury. http://www.hm-treasury.gov.uk/media/39A/41/eddington_execsum11206.pdf

Enst, Young (2003) European Investment Monitor (EIM) http://www.eyeim.com/methodology. htm. Cahiers de l'Institut d'aménagement et d'urbanisme de la région d'Ile-de-France (2003) 133/134 ISSN 0153-6184 Institut d'Aménagement et d'Urbanisme de la Région d'Ile de France, Paris

Glaeser EL, Scheinkman JA, Shleifer A (1995) Economic growth in a cross-section of cities. J Monetary Econ 36:117–143

Graham DJ, Kim HY (2008) An empirical analytical framework for agglomeration economies. Ann Reg Sci 42:267–289

Hall PG, Hay DG (1980) Growth centres in the European urban system. Heinemann Educational, London

IAURIF (2003) Cahiers de l'Institut d'aménagement et d'urbanisme de la région d'Ile-de-France, 133/134 ISSN 0153-6184, Institut d'Aménagement et d'Urbanisme de la Région d'Ile de France, Paris

Joshua D, Glaeser EL (2006) Urban resurgence and the consumer city. Urban Stud 43:1275–1299

Keeble D, Offord J, Walker S (1988) Peripheral regions in a community of twelve member states. Office of Official Publications, Luxembourg

KingSturge (2008) Global industrial and office rents. KingSturge, London

Midelfart KH, Overman HG (2002) Delocation and European integration: is European structural spending justified? Econ Pol 35:321–359

Rodriguez-Pose A, Fratesi U (2004) Between development and social policies: the impact of European structural funds in objective 1 regions. Reg Stud 38(1):97–113

Rosenthal S, Strange W (2004) Evidence on the nature and sources of agglomeration economies. In: Henderson JV, Thisse J-F (eds) Handbook of regional and urban economics, vol IV. Elsevier, Amsterdam

Rozenblat C, Pumain D (1993) The location of multinational firms in the European urban system. Urban Stud 30:1691–1709

Tiebout C (1956) A pure theory of local expenditures. J Polit Econ 64:416–424

Chapter 6
Regional Economic Concentration and Growth

The Effects of Agglomeration in Different Types of Regions

Scott R. Hacker, Johan Klaesson, Lars Pettersson, and Pär Sjölander

Abstract The regional relationships between agglomeration and economic growth are expected to be different in different types of regions. In the literature of the new economic geography it is common to stress the importance of access to cities with agglomeration of economic activities in the form of firms and households in order to be able to explain regional growth. However, it is also well known that many rural areas are performing fairly well in terms of employment and economic opportunities.

The purpose of the present research is to analyze if concentration of population drives economic growth or if it is the other way around. A second question is if this relationship between concentration of population and growth is different in different types of regions.

In order to shed light on these two questions the economic performance of three types of Swedish regions (metropolitan-, cities- and rural regions) is related to changes in population densities.

In the empirical analysis the Shannon index is used in the measurement of regional concentration. By considering the effect of previous levels of the Shannon index on average wages we extract information on how regional concentration affects regional economic growth (expressed as growth in average wages). In the empirical analysis we employ a VAR Granger causality approach on regional Swedish yearly data from 1987 to 2006. From this analysis we are able to conclude that there are strong empirical indications that geographic agglomeration of population unidirectionally drives economic growth in metropolitan- and city regions. Concerning the

---

S.R. Hacker • J. Klaesson
Jönköping International Business School, P.O. Box 1026, Jönköping 551 11, Sweden

L. Pettersson • P. Sjölander (✉)
Jönköping International Business School, P.O. Box 1026, Jönköping 551 11, Sweden

The Swedish Board of Agriculture, Jönköping, Sweden
e-mail: par.sjolander@jibs.hj.se

J. Klaesson et al. (eds.), *Metropolitan Regions*, Advances in Spatial Science,
DOI 10.1007/978-3-642-32141-2_6, © Springer-Verlag Berlin Heidelberg 2013

rural regions no such indication is found in either direction. This is a fairly strong indication that urban regions are more dependent on economies of agglomeration compared to rural areas.

Keywords Agglomeration economies • Productivity • Regions • Granger causality • Sweden

1 Introduction

According to theory in the field of New Economic Geography (NEG), it is reasonable to assume that the presence of agglomeration economies in urban areas can explain economic growth performance. However, we also find that many rural areas are performing well with respect to growth performance. One interesting question is if urbanization also is of the same importance in all types of regions, or if the impact from urban agglomerations differs in terms of relative importance in different parts of the economy.

The problem we analyze in this paper is if urban agglomeration drives economic growth or if it is the other way around. We acknowledge differences with respect to urbanization in different types of areas of the Swedish economy. In the empirical analysis in this paper, the Swedish economy is divided into three different categories of geographical areas; metropolitan regions, city regions, and countryside regions. We employ the Shannon index for population concentration and local economic growth in terms of wage sums in the analysis of how urbanization causes growth, or vice versa. The study is based on Swedish yearly data from 1987 to 2006, and a VAR Granger causality approach is used in order to analyze if urbanization causes growth or vice versa in the three different categories of areas. It is concluded that there are strong empirical indications that geographic agglomeration unidirectionally drives economic growth in metropolitan and city regions, while there is no empirical support for any corresponding causal relationship between these variables in the countryside regions. Therefore, in contrast to rural areas, the urban areas seem to be more dependent on economies of agglomeration that is generated from the relative size of these cities.

2 Literature Review

Hanson (2001) reviews the empirical research on agglomeration economies and spatial economic behavior. His focus is on the estimation problems inherent in these types of studies. He finds two robust results: (1) Wage rates are positively influenced by the presence of highly educated workers in the local labor force (suggesting the existence of localized human capital externalities), (2) For some industries long-run growth is higher in regions with a wider array of industrial activities (suggesting that firms benefit from locating in diverse environments).

One of the more influential articles studying the relationship between productivity and concentration of economic activity is Ciccone and Hall (1996). In this study the authors relate labor productivity to economic density which is measured as employment per acre. They find that differences in economic density can explain more than 50 % of the regional (county) differences in labor productivity in the U.S.

Later Ciccone (2002) performed a similar study of five European countries (France, Germany, Italy, Spain and UK). He found that there are substantial agglomeration effects and that the size of the effects are not significantly different between the countries.

Polese (2005) discuss the question of causality between urbanization and economic growth. He performs a thorough literature review and present evidence for and against the Jacobs Hypothesis which states that (loosely speaking) cities are sources of economic growth. His conclusion is that the socio-economic processes that explain economic growth are best understood in a national rather than a city context.

Using a data on an industry-city level Glaeser et al. (1992) show that employment growth is positively influenced by competition and variety but negatively influenced by specialization. The results are interpreted as evidence for the importance of cross industry spillovers.

In a review article by Quigley (1998) on the relationship between diversity and economic growth the author concludes that although there are costs associated with urban agglomerations cities have been and continue to be an important source of economic growth.

In a study of growth and convergence Bosker (2007), using a panel of 208 European regions over 25 years, concludes that denser regions grow comparatively slower than other regions. Thus, agglomeration seem to have a negative impact on growth performance, suggesting some form of congestion effects. However, the results also reveal a positive growth impact from growing neighboring regions.

Varga and Schalk (2004) address the question of agglomeration and macroeconomic growth. They develop an empirical model based on Romer's (1990) endogenous growth model. At the heart of their model is a variable measuring the change in technology and they apply a growth accounting framework. Using Hungarian data they show that localized knowledge spillovers are important even when national and international spillovers are accounted for. They argue that the spatial dimension should be incorporated into the theory of macroeconomic growth.

Brulhart and Mathys (2008) estimate agglomeration economies, defined as the effect of density on labor productivity for regions in Europe. They find significant agglomeration effects and also that these effects seem to strengthen over time. The main pattern in their results is that urbanization economies are positive but that localization economies are negative with respect to growth (with the notable exception of financial services).

In the literature we found one article (Sbergami 2002) that did not corroborate the general finding that growth (or productivity) correlates with spatial concentration. In this study the result is that dispersion of economic activities is good for national economic growth. One reason for this result is probably that the economic activities studied is manufacturing industries for which it can be argued that agglomeration effects might not be so important. The author speculate that results may have turned out different if R&D activities in the sectors had been used as an alternative.

An important question in most of the studies mentioned above is the question of possible reverse causality.

In the literature the strategy for minimizing the potential problem of endogeneity bias has been that of instrumenting the explanatory variables with instruments correlated with the variable measuring agglomeration but not correlated with the growth measure.

According to Ciccone (2002) the main problem with estimating agglomeration effects is that it is hard to differentiate between two competing hypotheses concerning the correlation between agglomeration and productivity. The first one being, productivity is high because of agglomeration effects, and the second one, agglomeration is a consequence of high productivity.

In this study we take a different route when tackling this problem. Instead of using cross-section regression techniques on regional or country data we employ a time series approach. We simply pose the question of which of the two variables growth and concentration (granger-) causes the other. In doing so we circumvent some of the problems inherent in cross-section studies, while on the other hand we encounter others. For instance, we do not try to model any micro-foundations for economies of agglomeration. Instead we only focus on the inter-temporal relationship between the two variables.

3 Agglomeration and Economic Growth

A point of departure for spatial analysis of economic activities is that they are not evenly distributed across regions (and space). Production and population are both agglomerated in cities and urban regions. This very simple observation indicates that economies of agglomeration are important to include in analysis of growth and development. The theory of new economic geography (NEG) contains a number of reasonable arguments that stipulate how agglomeration economies, which characterize urban areas, are fundamental for regional development and economic growth. The economy is in general more diversified, in terms of supply of goods and services, jobs and labor supply, in urban areas compared to rural areas. This in turn allows for economies of specialization and scale in individual firms. A large urban region can offer a great variety of inputs in a spatially limited market place, which also form a strong basis for attracting demand from both firms and households.

Fujita et al. (1999) show how increasing returns due to external economies of scale, transport costs and the demand for manufacturing goods can serve as explanations to why economic activities agglomerate in space. At the same time, localization economies that occur due to industrial specialization and clusters can become significant also in smaller regions. The advantage of urban areas is assumed

6 Regional Economic Concentration and Growth

to depend on the existence of increasing returns to scale in production, both related to production conditions within firms and from external factors in the region where the firm is located.

Also, urban areas offer advantages with respect to knowledge flows. This occurs because urban areas can combine clusters in different industries with industrial diversity, and the propensity and effects from knowledge spill-over effects can be assumed to be stimulated in urban areas. In particular, knowledge-intensive production can be assumed to benefit from urban agglomeration since it offers opportunities of taking advantage of increasing returns in knowledge production. It is reasonable to assume that fundamental resources for technological and entrepreneurial knowledge and innovations are stimulated and emerge from agglomerations because they are formed in the course of development and localized combinations of industries and clusters.

Accordingly, economies of agglomeration are assumed to be one of the most general factors that explain regional development and economic growth. Geographical advantages due to the size of regional and local markets, and cumulative growth processes of population, human capital (specialized labor) as well as physical capital over time are assumed to be key factors that contribute to explain growth and development. The size of the population and growth rate of the population is then endogenous features in a region that are influential for future development.

The geographical concentration of industries, economic activities and population can be seen as a reflection of how strong the agglomeration economies are in an economy. Such effects may be generated directly because of plant sizes, via spillovers in technology or due to human capital, etc. Such effects can also be expected to be present, and differ between urban and rural areas, even if transport costs are small (Henderson 1988; Fujita et al. 1999).

The significance of agglomeration and urbanization economies and how a cumulative process explains growth and development of regions is not a new notion. The link between geographical agglomeration and economic performance was stressed in a 1970 article by Kaldor, who was analyzing the industrial society. The transformation of economies into more service- and knowledge-based production can be assumed to have strengthened this perspective (because of the greater need for human interaction). Kaldor (1970) writes on page 340 that "the fact that in all historical cases the development of manufacturing industries was closely associated with urbanization must have deep-seated causes which are unlikely to be rendered inoperative by the invention of some technology or new source of power." Thereby, Kaldor (like Jane Jacobs 1984) emphasize the function of cities as innovative places.

In Jacobs' seminal book from 1984 she states that metropolitan regions and urban economies are the backbone and motor of the wealth of nations, not vice versa. Later, Glaeser et al. (1992) also makes the conclusion that urban diversification promotes regional economic growth. A common element in Jacobs and Glaeser et al. is how they tie together the location of people and economic development in space. The spatial dimension (density and variety) on markets for the supply of services and commodities in cities is assumed to attract households. At the same time the purchasing power of the households attracts firms. This interrelated dependency is a fundament for cumulative processes in cities that boost development.

Another scholar who also has pointed out the function of cities as motors for development is Robert Lucas (1988). Lucas' basic argument was based on the consideration of how information and knowledge spillovers are dependent on spatial locations, and tend to agglomerate in cities that attract people (labor) with high level of education. Romer (1994) analyzed endogenous growth and accumulation of human capital, where localized knowledge explains growth performance.

This means that there are a number of strong arguments for why it is reasonable to expect that the regional market size and the urbanization process influence the growth process, both on regional and national level. More recently, Fujita and Thisse (2002) developed a model that depicts the connection between agglomeration and economic growth. The model is based on a Krugman-type of core-periphery model and a so-called Grossman-Helpman Romer type of model for endogenous growth. The results presented by Fujita and Thisse support the arguments that have been claimed earlier of how urbanization can be assumed to have influence on economic growth performance. A lesson that can be learned from these studies is that economic progress should not be expected to occur in all types or regions at the same time with the same magnitude. This is the same result that Hirschman (1958) claimed almost 50 years earlier. Hirschman argued that once economic progress appears in one region it would be likely to stimulate spatial concentration of economic growth in the proximity of the regional core, which is consistent with the result presented in Fujita and Thisse's analysis.

As a reflection of the vast number of studies in this particular field of theoretical research a number of empirical studies have been made focusing on the question of how urban agglomeration can explain growth and development on both regional and national level. In Sweden such studies have been carried out by both scholars in the field and by national authorities that have a special focus on growth and development (for example the Swedish Institute for Growth Policy Studies, the National Rural Development Agency and the Swedish Agency for economic and Regional Growth). Also the empirical studies indicate that urbanization is important for growth. However, the difference between rurality and urbanity is an interesting perspective in relation to these studies, which so far have not been very much analyzed. There is not one standard general definition of rurality, and studies in this field are not focused very much on the rural regions.

4 Defining Types of Regions

There are two essential features that frequently are used as a basis for defining rurality: (1) population density, and (2) regional specialization with respect to the agricultural and forest sector (Labrianidis 2004). However, the traditional definitions have a number of shortcomings since they do not take into account a number of evolving aspects of rural regions, such as tourism, etc. (Ilbery et al. 1998). In an international perspective, Sweden is usually characterized as an economy that, to a large extent, is dominated by rural areas. There are three metropolitan areas in Sweden (Stockholm, Gothenburg and Malmo), and a number of medium sized cities with suburbs that constitutes urban agglomerations. However, 25–45 % of the population is usually defined as living in urban areas, depending on the definition of "urban area". The rural regions of Sweden are developing in a divergent way where some regions are expanding while others are losing population and economic activities.

In this study we use a definition of rural and urban areas in Sweden, which has been created by the Swedish Board of Agriculture. This definition has been used in other studies of the Swedish economy (SOU 2006:101; Johansson and Klaesson 2008; Jordbruksverket 2009 RA09:2). This definition utilizes and builds on data on built-up areas, population and commuting patterns for municipalities (290 in Sweden), which are classified into three different groups. Thus, the basic building block is the municipality so that no municipality is split:

Metropolitan regions: Includes municipalities where the whole population lives in urban agglomerations. In addition to these "core" municipalities another group is added. This group consist of municipalities where more than 50 % of the working population commute to the "core". Using this definition, there are three metropolitan areas in Sweden: Stockholm, Göteborg och Malmö, including surrounding municipalities.

City regions: Includes municipalities with a population of at least 30,000 inhabitants in the urban agglomeration. Also in this type of region the same kind of commuting-dependent municipalities is added, where more than 50 % of the working population commute to the central municipalities. This definition result in 26 such regions.

Rural regions: Includes municipalities that are not included in the metropolitan regions group or city regions.

In the figure below we show a map of the categorization of Swedish municipalities. As displayed in the map the majority of Sweden's surface is falls in the rural regions category.

In Table 6.1 below some descriptive statistics for the three types of regions are given. The figures are averages over the time period studied in the empirical analysis (1987–2006). The three types of regions are of comparable size when it comes to population size, with the rural regions having a population of a little more than three million each and the two other a little below. The average yearly percentage growth rates (in brackets) show a clear pattern where the metropolitan regions grow the fastest, the City regions grow less and the rural regions decline (Fig. 6.1).

The employment figures show a similar but more marked pattern. When looking at the population density figures we see that the differences are huge. The population density is five times as big in the Metropolitan regions compared with the City regions. Comparing the Metropolitan regions with the Rural regions the difference is more than 23-fold.

5 Development of Cities and Rural Regions in Sweden

In this study we analyze urbanization in terms of agglomeration of population in urban areas, and if this phenomenon cause economic growth. This means that we focus on the relationship between the spatial structure of the population and

Table 6.1 Descriptive statistics for the three types of regions (averages over the period 1987–2006)

	Population	Employment	Population density	Wage-sum	Average wage
Metropolitan regions	2,947 (0.87)	1,511 (0.39)	176.2	299 (2.52)	197 (2.12)
City regions	2,564 (0.58)	1,213 (0.01)	35.5	226 (2.17)	187 (2.17)
Rural regions	3,289 (−0.11)	1,369 (−0.59)	7.4	254 (1.68)	187 (2.30)
Total/average	8,800 (0.42)	4,093 (−0.05)	73.0	779 (2.14)	190 (2.19)

Numbers within *brackets* are average yearly growth rates in percent

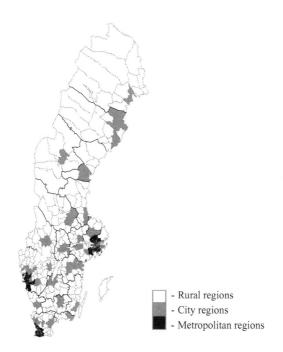

Fig. 6.1 Swedish municipalities classified into metropolitan regions, city regions and rural regions

economic growth (growth in GDP per capita). Therefore, it is relevant to describe some aspects of the spatial distribution of the population in Sweden, both long-term changes and the situation during the recent years.

In a historical perspective, cities increased in size during the era of industrialization and Sweden is not different from other countries in this respect. The industrialization era in Sweden was particularly strong between the years 1870 and 1970. From the 1970s and onward, around 85 % of the population in Sweden lives in cities and localities with a minimum agglomeration of 200 persons. However, there is still an ongoing process of structural population change taking place where the largest cities grow and smaller cities and localities (less than 10,000 inhabitants) tend to decline (Klaesson and Pettersson 2009). The long-term structural change

6 Regional Economic Concentration and Growth

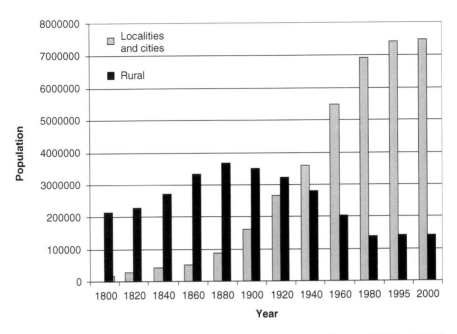

Fig. 6.2 Swedish population in cities and localities versus rural areas between 1,800 and 2,000 (Source: statistics Sweden (2007), and own calculation)

in population distribution between urban and rural areas is depicted in the figure below (using the definitions used by Statistics Sweden) (Fig. 6.2).

During the industrialization era, the growth of manufacturing jobs in the cities attracted people in rural areas to migrate into the cities. The increase in productivity in the agricultural sector also generated an excess of labor in rural areas, which was meet by an expanding demand for labor from the manufacturing plants in the cities (Schön 2000). During the nineteenth century the mortality rate also declined which contributed to a growth in the labor supply and a growth of the cities.

Evidently, the change in demographical structure depends the flows of migration. In addition, the rate of mortality and birth rates also contribute to the development of demographical change in a region. In order to receive a more complete understanding of the population dynamics, these three types of causes for population change have to be considered. In order to make an explorative description of the recent trends in population change in Sweden, we use the three types of regions presented above (Metropolitan regions, City regions and Rural regions) when we categorize our data. A first observation show that the population growth has been substantially stronger in Metropolitan and City regions compared to Rural regions (see the Figure below). During the years 1997–2006 the population growth in the Metropolitan regions in Sweden was twice as large as the average in Sweden. At the same time there was a significant decline of the population size in the rural regions.

The three largest Metropolitan regions experienced a net increase versus the Rural regions between 1997 and 2006 by around 350,000 individuals. This observation corresponds very well with the theoretical considerations presented above which states that the size of a region could be assumed to stimulate agglomeration of people, given that size does not create negative external economies.

In a next step we also compare the demographical composition of women and men in age cohorts, in the three types of regions. There are some differences between the regions that are worth to notice. The Metropolitan regions have a relatively larger number of "semi-young" and "middle-age" people. These age cohorts are the one from 25 to 44 years in the Figure below. The City regions have a relative strong attraction on young people in the age 10–19 years, and "old middle-age" people in the age of 44–64 years. In Rural regions, we find also a high share of youngsters in the age of 10–19 years, and a comparable high share of old people in the retirement age (65 years and older) (Figs. 6.3, 6.4, 6.5).

Considering the distribution of men and women we can observe two things. First, women dominates over men in the older age cohorts. Second, there are comparatively more women (or fewer men) in the age cohorts of 20–29 years in the Metropolitan regions compared to both City and Rural regions.

The migration flows revealed in the Fig. 6.6 below matches the figures presented above. Young people tend to migrate out from the Rural regions, and there is a relative strong inward flow of migration of these age cohorts into both Metropolitan and City regions. These differences in migration flows gets reduced in the older age cohorts (Fig. 6.6).

In a final step of the explorative analysis we acknowledge the ratio between birth and mortality in the three types of regions. The average of this ratio in the whole country is 1.16. Table 6.2 below reveals significant differences between the regions in this perspective. In the Metropolitan regions the ratio of birth divided by mortality is twice as large as in the Rural regions. Both the Metropolitan and City regions have higher values of the birth-mortality ratio compared to the country average.

From this descriptive and explorative analysis of the spatial differences of the population structure between the different areas we focus on in the study, we can make the following observations:

- The cities have grown in importance over time, and during the recent years the largest Metropolitan areas show the strongest growth performance in terms of population agglomeration
- During the recent years we find a decline in population size in the aggregate of the rural regions
- There are a number of differences in the demographical structure when we compare Metropolitan, City and Rural regions. In particular women in the ages of 20–29 years, and "semi-young" and "middle-age" cohorts (25–44 years) appears to be attracted to the Metropolitan regions
- According to the migration flows between the three types of regions we find that a high share of young people tend to move to the Metropolitan regions
- There are substantial differences in the birth-mortality ratio between the three types of regions. The birth-mortality ratio is twice as large in the Metropolitan regions compared to the Rural regions

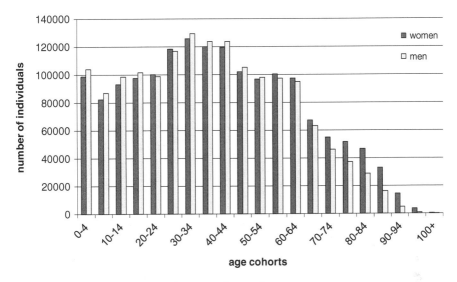

Fig. 6.3 Population structure 2006 in metropolitan regions

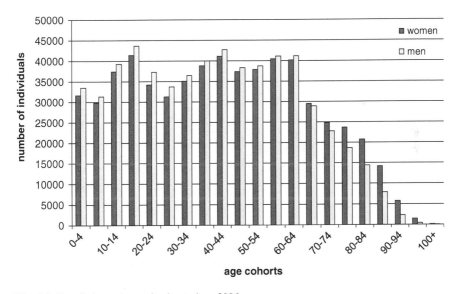

Fig. 6.4 Population structure in city regions 2006

6 Measuring Concentration and Economic Performance

There are many different measures that can be used in order to calculate the concentration of population. Some such measures are the Herfindahl index, the Gini coefficient or the slope of a zipf distribution. In this study, however, we have chosen the Shannon index. The Shannon index is derived from entropy theory dealing with order in a system. In this context the Shannon index takes on a maximum value

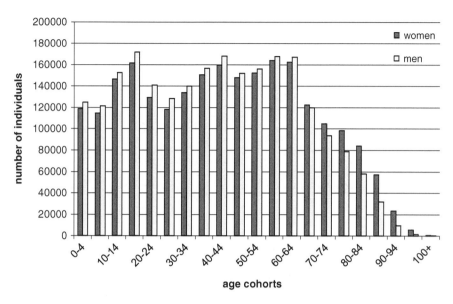

Fig. 6.5 Population structure in rural regions 2006

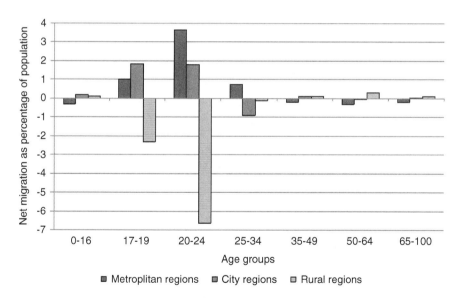

Fig. 6.6 Net migration as percentage of population by age groups

if population is spread out uniformly so that each region have the same population. The minimum value, zero, is attained if the whole population is concentrated in one region only. Thus, the calculated values will obviously fall in between these extremes. Over time when migration and other population changes occur the Shannon index will rise or decline depending on if these changes increases a more concentrated or even distribution of population.

6 Regional Economic Concentration and Growth

Table 6.2 Number of births divided by mortalities per region, 2006

	Births/mortalities
Metropolitan areas	1.62
Urban areas	1.21
Rural areas	0.80
Country average	1.16

The Shannon index is defined in the following way:

$$S = - \sum_{r=1}^{n} s_r \ln s_r$$

Where p_r is the population in region r and P is total population and $s_r = p_r/P$ is the share of population in region r.

As a measure of the economic performance in the three types of regions we use the ratio between total wage-sums and employment, that is, the average wage in each region.

Both of these measures, concentration and average wage is calculated for each type of region and for each year for the period 1987–2006. The interrelations between these two time-series for each region type is the topic of the analysis in the rest of this study.

7 The VAR Granger Causality Method

This thesis aims to utilize a vector autoregressive (VAR) Granger causality test to study the potential bidirectional relationship between regional concentration and productivity, where the former is approximated by the Shannon index (S) and the latter is approximated by average wages (W) aggregated over Swedish municipalities falling into three different categories of regions for 1987–2006. Granger causality analysis, the analytical method in this paper, utilizes the fact that past events may cause events to happen today while future events typically do not. Thus, we make use of the simple assumption that cause must precede effect. VAR Granger causality tests are applied to measure the chronological time-dependencies between S and W within each type of regions. For this specific paper, a Granger causality relationship can be defined as follows; S (the Shannon variable) does not Granger cause W (average wages), if and only if, prediction of W based on the universe U of predictors in the VAR model is no better than prediction based on $U - \{$lagged values of S$\}$, i.e. on the universe with the lagged values of S in the VAR model omitted, where $j = 1,2,3$.

In equivalence with time-series analysis in general, and also for the Granger causality test, the existence of nonstationary variables with deterministic or stochastic trends is very problematic, especially in finite samples (Hamilton 1994). Consequently, an important part of the Granger causality analysis is to determine whether the analyzed variables are cointegrated or not.

If the analyzed variables S ~ I(1) and W ~ I(1) are cointegrated (S,W) ~ CI(1,1), it is actually possible, at least in large samples, to conduct a VAR Granger causality test of I(1) variables in levels without taking first differences. This approach will not lead to spurious regressions (Doan 2007; Sims et al. 1990). However, if the variables S ~ I(1) and W ~ I(1) are *not* cointegrated, the Granger causality test must be specified in first differences (see Hamilton (1994) p. 553, Toda and Phillips (1994), or a general discussion in Enders (2004) p. 287). Under these circumstances, especially in small samples, it is clearly necessary to estimate the VAR-model in first differences (DVAR) despite the fact that Sims (1980) originally specified his VAR models in level.

Johansen's (1995) cointegration test is the standard approach to determine the crucial question whether the analyzed variables are cointegrated or not. However, notice that Johansen's cointegration test is only valid when working with series that are known to be integrated of the same order. Therefore, it is necessary to establish that the applied variables in the VAR model in fact are nonstationary. Thus, as is illustrated in the tables in the Appendix 1, Johansen cointegration tests are not valid unless it is confirmed that all variables are integrated of the same order (Enders 2004).

It is a stylized fact that one of the main challenges in time-series econometrics is the lack of power for unit root tests. Therefore an optimal choice of unit root test and, even more important, an optimal unit root testing *strategy* is crucial for the validity of the end result of the study. Therefore, *(e.g. in direct contrast to the strategies by Perron (1988), Dolado et al. (1990), Holden and Perman (1994), Ayat and Burridge (2000), or Enders (2004))*, the Elder and Kennedy (2001) unit root testing strategy is selected since it satisfies the following attractive properties; (1) a priori information regarding economic theory can be utilized, (2) implausible data generating processes are ruled out, and (3) mass significance is avoided. In Appendix 1, a more thorough motivation for the choice of unit root testing strategy is given.

Under the assumption that S and W are *not* cointegrated the VAR Granger causality test should be estimated in first differences. The existence or nonexistence of cointegration can be based on unit root tests if one concludes that the analyzed variables exhibit different integration orders. An equal integration order is a necessary, but not sufficient condition, for cointegration between two variables.

Consequently, if there is no confirmed cointegration relationship between S and W, the following general bivariate unrestricted DVAR(2)[1] model can for example (assuming the appropriate lag length is two) be applied to formulate a Granger causality test

---

[1] DVAR(2) is an abbreviation for differenced vector autoregressive model of order 2. Moreover, notice that even if there is only one single lag in a DVAR model this implies that the lag memory is infinite. For instance, the lag memory for an AR(1) parameter equal to β is equal to β^s after s time periods. According to Enders (2004) one should apply a lag length that is maximally $T^{1/3}$ where T is the number of observations, which implies that a maximum lag of $T^{1/3} = 20^{1/3} \approx 3$ lags should be applied. However, obviously, an information criteria (Schwarz-Bayes criteron) is applied to determine whether 1, 2 or 3 lags are appropriate.

6 Regional Economic Concentration and Growth

$$\begin{bmatrix} \Delta W_t \\ \Delta S_t \end{bmatrix} = \begin{bmatrix} \alpha_{10} \\ \alpha_{20} \end{bmatrix} + \begin{bmatrix} \beta_{11} & \beta_{12} \\ \beta_{21} & \beta_{22} \end{bmatrix} \begin{bmatrix} \Delta W_{t-1} \\ \Delta S_{t-1} \end{bmatrix} + \begin{bmatrix} \gamma_{11} & \gamma_{12} \\ \gamma_{21} & \gamma_{22} \end{bmatrix} \begin{bmatrix} \Delta W_{t-2} \\ \Delta S_{t-2} \end{bmatrix} + \begin{bmatrix} u_{1t} \\ u_{2t} \end{bmatrix} \quad (4.1)$$

where W represents the wage sum per capita, and S the Shannon index with Corr $(u_{1t}, u_{2t}) = 0$. For instance if the change in the Shannon-index variable (ΔS) is said to Granger cause the change in the average wage variable (ΔW) (i.e. β_{12} and γ_{12} are not both zero) this means that current values of W can be better predicted using past values of S, than if only past values of W are used to predict current values of W. For each pair of the equations this is tested by a joint F-test or a Wald test (due to better small-sample properties compared to the Lagrange multiplier (LM) or likelihood ratio (LRT) test).

The dynamic components that are included by the lags in the DVAR model circumvent some of the problems of omitted-variable bias; since the information in the lags is based on all relevant endogenous and exogenous variables, a potential omitted-variable problem may be reduced to a great extent. Moreover, in a (D)VAR framework we do not need to specify which variables are endogenous or exogenous – all variables are considered endogenous.

Beyond the previously stated arguments for VAR models in differences (DVAR), there are in fact other general reasons supporting this first-difference approach. According to Monte Carlo simulations in Clements and Hendry (1996), DVARs are more robust to structural breaks (less vulnerable to the intercept-shift problem which is a relevant aspect of the real world) than VAR models in levels. Moreover, according to Mizon (1995) and Clements and Hendry (1996), DVARs exhibit better forecasting capabilities. However, maybe the most important positive property of the DVAR method is it eliminates the risk of spurious regression relationships in small samples due to a stochastic trend.[2] This is supported by Hamilton (1994, p. 553) who states that "the small-sample distributions may well be improved by estimating the VAR in differences".

In summary, DVAR is a conservative approach since empirically it is common that unit root tests cannot distinguish stochastic trends (e.g. a random walk plus drift) from a deterministic time trend, especially in small samples. It is a stylized fact that stochastic trends are remedied by differencing while deterministic trends are remedied by detrending. However, if we (by mistake) detrend a stochastic trend this may lead to a spurious regression relationship. On the other hand, if we (by mistake) take the first difference (DVAR) of a deterministic-trend process this problem does not lead to a spurious regression relationship. One potential cost of specifying VAR model in first differences may be the worst-case scenario of potential inefficiency due to potential MA(1) errors in the residuals (if we, by mistake, cannot distinguish stochastic trends from deterministic trends). However, this worst-case scenario for DVAR models is far less severe, than the potential spurious regression relationships that may emerge from the use of simple VAR

---

[2] Sims, Stock, and Watson (1990) prove that these problems are eliminated asymptotically for VAR models. However, asymptotic results are not directly relevant in this paper since few observations are available.

models. Consequently, for all the above reasons, the DVAR approach can be considered a conservative approach since we will always avoid the risk of spurious regressions due to a misspecified trend. Therefore, it can quite straightforwardly be motivated that the risk of making a serious misjudgment regarding the trend is minimized if the VAR Granger test is conducted in first differences.

Another important question is one that cannot be formally answered solely by applying a Granger causality test – in which direction (positive or negative) does one variable affect another? In fact, in our case a Granger causality test can actually only determine whether S Granger causes W, and if W Granger causes S. It cannot determine whether for instance an increase in previous lags of S leads to a decrease or an increase in the current value of W. This is the reason why it is useful to consider impulse response functions. These functions are presented in Appendix 2.

8 Stationarity Analysis

It is well known that unit root tests (or cointegration tests) are not very reliable in small samples. Consequently, the modest sample size in this paper may be a reason for some of the conflicting conclusions from the unit root tests in Appendix 1. In fact, the unit root tests were consistent only in 1 out of the 12 tested processes, and it was never consistently concluded that $C(j)$ and $W(j)$, for $j = 1,\ldots,3$, exhibited the same integration order (at the 5 % level of significance).

The main conclusion from Appendix 1 is that there cannot be any cointegration relationship between $C(j)$ and $W(j)$ (for $j = 1,\ldots,3$) since the unit root tests indicates different integration orders for each pair of variables (in any given municipality category). However, since these test results are unreliable due to low power for unit root tests, it is very likely that some processes in fact follow unit root processes even though this is not always evident from the statistical test analysis. Integrated variables may cause spurious regression relationships in a Granger causality test. A conservative approach is therefore to study all the variables in first differences to avoid the problems of spurious regression and to reduce the effects of potential structural breaks. If some of the trends in fact are deterministic, instead of stochastic, this may lead to inefficiency due to moving-average errors, but this is most likely less problematic compared to the potential consequences of spurious regression relationships (which would be the risk if the GC test would be performed in levels). In summary, since it cannot be determined that the variables in fact are cointegrated, we specify the variables in first differences in the Granger causality analysis.

9 Granger Causality Analysis

A Granger causality test in an unrestricted DVAR model can be conducted by testing whether some parameters are jointly zero, usually by a standard Wald F-test. However, Granger causality analysis can be sensitive to the choice of lag order. Therefore, in order to determine the optimal lag length it is necessary

6 Regional Economic Concentration and Growth

Table 6.3 DVAR Granger causality test

Type of region	Null hypothesis	Granger causality Wald statistic	P-value (%)	Conclusion ($\alpha = 10\%$)
Metropolitan	H_0: ΔW does not Granger cause ΔS	1.73 [2]	21.81	H_0 is not rejected
	H_0: ΔS does not Granger cause ΔW	8.67*** [2]	0.47	H_0 is rejected $\Delta S \rightarrow \Delta W$
City	H_0: ΔW does not Granger cause ΔS	0.49 [2]	62.66	H_0 is not rejected
	H_0: ΔS does not Granger cause ΔW	3.73* [2]	5.48	H_0 is rejected $\Delta S \rightarrow \Delta W$
Rural	H_0: ΔW does not Granger cause ΔS	1.08 [2]	36.93	H_0 is not rejected
	H_0: ΔS does not Granger cause ΔW	1.26 [2]	31.98	H_0 is not rejected

The value within *brackets* in the second column is the applied number of lags in the Granger causality test. This value is based on the Schwarz information criterion (SIC) with a maximum lag 3 *(due to Enders, 2004, recommendation of $T^{1/3} \approx 3$)*
*** sign. at 1 % sign. level, ** sign. at 5 % sign. level, * sign. at 10 % sig. level

to apply an information criterion. In this paper the Schwarz-Bayes information criterion is applied since it is a standard consistent information criterion. The results from the Granger causality analysis are illustrated below in Table 6.3.

As is illustrated in Table 6.3, in the metropolitan regions there is a strong Granger causality in the direction from ΔS to ΔW, but no significant Granger causality is present in the reverse direction from ΔW to ΔS. The former relationship is significant at the 1 % significance level. A somewhat weaker, but still significant relationship, is also found for the corresponding variables in the City regions. In those regions, ΔS Granger causes ΔW, but there is no significant Granger causality relation in the opposite direction. In the rural regions no Granger causality relationships are found in either direction between the variables ΔS and ΔW.

Consequently, we can clearly observe that there is strong evidence supporting the hypothesis that geographical concentration in fact does Granger cause the average wages to grow in metropolitan- and in city regions, while these variables are dynamically independent in the rural regions. The strongest evidence that agglomeration Granger causes growth in economic activity can be found in the metropolitan regions. Likewise, there is a significant but weaker relationship indicating agglomeration of population Granger causes economic growth in the city regions. These results are fairly expected given the theoretical discussion above. Moreover, the independence between the Shannon index and the average wages in the rural regions can be motivated by considering that growth in low density circumstances can be explained by other factors such as industrial specialization (localization economies) and advantages derived from natural endowments.

A Granger causality relation indicates which of the variables in the VAR model that have chronological statistical significant impacts on the future values of each of the variables in the system. However, the F Wald test results will not, by construction, be able to exactly determine if the relationship is positive or negative. Therefore, to be completely accurate, it is actually necessary to consider an impulse response function (IRF) to determine if the Granger causality relationships are positive or negative. To be consistent with the hypothesis that agglomeration positively affects growth it is at least necessary that we do not find any significantly negative IRF-relationships between the studied variables and should instead tend to show positive IRF relationships. In summary, as can be seen Appendix 2, the impulse response functions for the analyzed relationships exhibit the expected patterns. This implies that the relationship in Table 6.3 is supported by logical and expected IRFs. More details are presented in association to the Appendix 2.

10 Conclusions

In this study we analyze the causality direction between urbanization and economic growth (which we define as growth of average wages) in different types of regions in the Swedish economy. In other words, the question if urbanization cause economic growth or vice versa. According to theoretical arguments from the research field of the new economic geography, it is reasonable to assume that agglomeration of people in cities, and growth of the size of cities, stimulate economic growth. In the analysis we also analyze if there is a difference between Metropolitan-, City- and Rural areas. This means that we also focus on the question of how urbanization may have different strength (with respect to fuel economic growth) in different types of areas. In the empirical analysis of the study, we use the Shannon-index of entropy based on spatial population distribution and average wages in Swedish municipalities.

Based on Swedish yearly data from 1987 to 2006, it is illustrated that the change in the Shannon index Granger causes the change in average wages in metropolitan regions and that the change in the Shannon index Granger causes changes in average wages in city regions, while there are no Granger causality relationships in the reverse direction for the metropolitan and for the city regions. However, for the rural regions no Granger causality is exhibited in either direction between the Shannon-index changes and the changes in average wages. The strongest relationship, at 1 % significance level, is found for the Shannon-index changes Granger causing changes in the average wages in the metropolitan regions, while a corresponding significant relationship, but not equally strong relationship, is found for the city regions. Geographical concentration has no affect on economic activity (per capita wages) in the rural regions. Based on the examined data set, geographical concentration which appears to be a driving force behind growing per capita wages in metropolitan and city regions but not in the rural regions.

Thus, we conclude that there are strong empirical indications that geographic agglomeration unidirectionally drives economic growth in metropolitan and city regions, while there is absolutely no empirical support for any corresponding causal relationship for these variables in the rural regions.

It is likely that these results originate from differences in industry structure with more knowledge-intensive sectors dominating in the urban regions. In rural regions it is reasonable to assume that growth can be explained by other factors such as

6 Regional Economic Concentration and Growth

Table 6.4 Conclusions for the five unit root tests (ADF, PP, DF-GLS, KPSS, and ERS)

This table summarizes the number of UR-tests that reject, or do not reject, unit roots for the variables in each respective municipality category. Consequently, these tests are fairly ambiguous, which is the reason why the, conservative, first-difference approach is applied in this study

Municipalities category	Variable	Unit root	No unit root
Metropolitan	S	2	3
	ΔS	2	3
City	S	4	1
	ΔS	4	1
Rural	S	3	2
	ΔS	4	1
Metropolitan	W	4	1
	ΔW	1	4
City	W	4	1
	ΔW	1	4
Rural	W	4	1
	ΔW	0	5

Applied unit root tests: augmented Dickey-Fuller test (ADF 1979), Phillips-Perron's test (Phillips and Perron 1988), generalized least squares detrended Dickey-Fuller test (DF-GLS 1996), Kwiatkowski-Schmidt-Perron-Shin (KPSS 1992), and Elliot, Rothenberg and Stock (ERS 1996)

industrial specialization (localization economies) and advantages derived from natural endowments.

Appendix 1: The Elder and Kennedy Unit Root Testing Strategy

Due to the fact that the applied unit root tests in this study (ADF, PP, ERS, KPSS and DF-GLS) can be specified with a constant, or a constant and a linear time trend, it is necessary to apply a unit root testing strategy. For instance, unit root testing strategies are proposed by Perron (1988), Dolado et al. (1990), Holden and Perman (1994), Ayat and Burridge (2000), Enders (2004), and Elder and Kennedy (2001). However, due to the subsequently mentioned reasons, the unit root testing strategy by Elder and Kennedy (2001) is applied in this paper. The main advantage of this strategy in comparison to the other strategies is that Elder and Kennedy utilize prior economic theoretical knowledge regarding certain variables, instead of applying sequential significance testing. Based on economic theory, we know that the Shannon index is a function of time and that the per capita wages in an industrialized country grows over time in the long run. Therefore, there is unnecessary to test whether the variables are trending or not. Another advantage of the Elder and Kennedy (2001) approach is that this strategy does not consider outcomes of a unit root test that are not realistic, for example the simultaneous existence of a unit root and a deterministic trend (see Perron 1988, p. 304 and Holden and Perman 1994, p. 63). A third important reason why the Elder and Kennedy approach is attractive is that it can avoid the mass significance that is the consequence of repeated sequential testing. Consequently, the

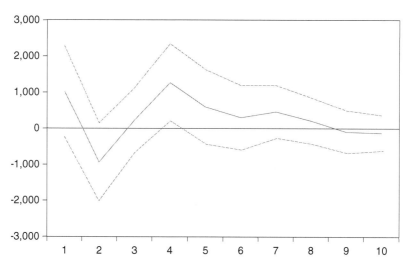

Fig. 6.7 Impulse response functions for the metropolitan regional model *(response to Cholesky one s.d. innovations ± 2 S.E, that is, response of ΔW to ΔS)*

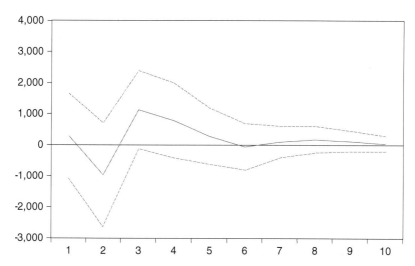

Fig. 6.8 Impulse response functions for the city regional model *(response to Cholesky one s.d. innovations ± 2 S.E, that is, response of ΔW to ΔS)*

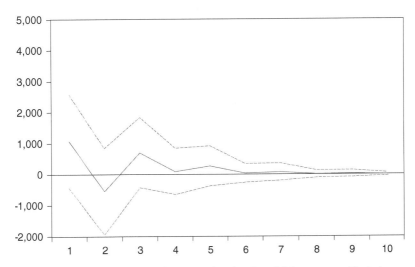

Fig. 6.9 Impulse response functions for the rural regional model *(response to Cholesky one s.d. innovations ± 2 S.E, that is, response of ΔW to ΔS)*

Elder and Kennedy (2001) approach is applied for this paper and the results are presented in the following Table (6.4) below.

Appendix 2: Impulse Response Functions

First of all, in the above graphs we can clearly observe that all shocks that these IRFs is exposed to, gradually dies away. This is an indication that the system is stable which is a necessary and important condition in Granger causality analysis. In the metropolitan regions, in Fig. 6.7 we can generally observe a positive response. Due to the fact that the significance is not equally strong in the city regions, as in the metropolitan regions, all responses on ΔW due to shocks in ΔS for the city regions are always within the error margin, and are thus not statistically significant. Consequently, we cannot draw any clear-cut conclusions from the graph in Fig. 6.8. However, the point estimates are almost all the time above zero, which is an indication that our theory may possibly be correct. In the last table, Fig. 6.9, the impulse response functions are continuously not significantly different from zero, which is what we expected based on our theory and on our prior analysis results.

References

Ayat L, Burridge P (2000) Unit root tests in the presence of uncertainty about the non-stochastic trend. J Econ 95(1):71–96

Bosker M (2007) Growth, agglomeration and convergence: a space-time analysis for European regions. Spat Econ Anal 2(1):91–110

Brulhart M, Mathys NA (2008) Sectoral agglomeration economies in a panel of European regions. Reg Sci Urban Econ 38:348–362

Ciccone A (2002) Agglomeration effects in Europe. Eur Econ Rev 46:213–227

Ciccone A, Hall RE (1996) Productivity and the density of economic activity. Am Econ Rev 86(1):54–70

Clements MP, Hendry DF (1996) Intercept corrections and structural change. J Appl Econ, Special issue: Econometric forecasting, 11(5):475–494

Dickey DA, Fuller WA (1979) Distribution of the estimators for autoregressive time series with a unit root. J Am Stat Assoc 74:427–431

Doan T (2007) RATS version 7, user's guide. Estima, Evanston

Dolado J, Jenkinson T, Sosvilla-Rivero S (1990) Cointegration and unit roots. J Econ Surv 4(3):249–273

Elder J, Kennedy PE (2001) Testing for unit roots: what should students be taught? J Econ Educ 32(2):137–146, Spring

Elliott G, Rothenberg TJ, Stock JH (1996) Efficient tests for an autoregressive unit root. Econometrica 64:813–836

Enders W (2004) Applied econometric times series, Wiley series in probability and statistics. Wiley, Hoboken

Fujita M, Thisse JF (2002) Economics of agglomeration: cities, industrial location, and regional growth. Cambridge University Press, Cambridge

Fujita M, Krugman P, Venables AJ (1999) The spatial economy. Cities, regions and international trade. The MIT Press, Cambridge, MA

Glaeser EL, Kallal HD, Scheinkman JA, Shleifer A (1992) Growth in cities. J Pol Econ 100(6):1126–1152

Hamilton JD (1994) Time series analysis. Princeton University Press, Princeton

Hanson GH (2001) Scale economies and the geographic concentration of industry. J Econ Geogr 1:255–276

Henderson JV (1988) Urban development: theory, fact, and illusion. Oxford Univ. Press, New York

Hirschman AO (1958) The strategy of economic development. Yale University Press, New Haven

Holden D, Perman R (1994) Unit roots and cointegration for the economist. In: Rao BB (ed) Cointegration for the applied economist. St. Martin's, New York, pp 47–112

Ilbery B, Bowler I, Clark G, Crockett A, Shaw A (1998) Farm-Based tourism as an alternative farm enterprise: a case study from the Northern Pennines, England. Reg Stud 32(4):355–364

Jacobs J (1984) Cities and the wealth of nations. Random House, New York

Johansen S (1995) Identifying restrictions of linear equations with applications to simultaneous equations and cointegration. J Econ 69:111–132

Johansson B, Klaesson J (2008) Landsbygdsföretagare måste fixa långa avstånd. In Ska hela Sverige leva? Formas Fokuserar

Jordbruksverket (2009) RA09:2, Nilsson, J., Petersson, M., and Petersson, L., Företagandet på Landsbygden. Stad eller land, gör det någon skillnad?

Kaldor N (1970) The case for regional policies. Scott J Pol Econ 17(3):337–348

Klaesson J, Pettersson L (2009) Urban–rural development in Sweden. In: Karlsson C, Andersson AE, Cheshire PC, Stough RR (eds) New directions in regional economic development. Springer, Berlin/Heidelberg

6 Regional Economic Concentration and Growth

Kwiatkowski D, Phillips PCB, Schmidt P, Shin Y (1992) Testing the null hypothesis of stationarity against the alternative of a unit root: how sure are we that economic time series have a unit root? J Econometrics 54:159–178

Labrianidis L (2004) The future of Europe's rural peripheries, Economic geography series. Ashgate, Aldershot

Lucas RE (1988) On the mechanics of economic development. J Monetary Econ 22:3–42

Mizon GE (1995) A simple message for autocorrelation correctors: don't. J Econ 69:267–288

Perron P (1988) Trends and random walks in macroeconomic time series. J Econ Dyn Control 12(12):297–332

Phillips PCB, Perron P (1988) Testing for a unit root in time series regression. Biometrika 75:335–346

Polese M (2005) Cities and national economic growth: a reappraisal. Urban Stud 42(8):1429–1451

Quigley JM (1998) Urban diversity and economic growth. J Econ Perspect 12:127–138

Romer P (1990) Endogenous technological change. J Pol Econ 98:71–102

Romer PM (1994) The origins of endogenous economic growth. J Econ Perspect 8(1):3–22

Sbergami F (2002) Agglomeration and economic growth. Some puzzles, HEI working paper, No: 02/2002

Schön L (2000) En modern svensk ekonomisk historia: tillväxt och omvandling under två sekel, SNS förlag

Sims C (1980) Macroeconomics and reality. Econometrica 48:1–48

Sims CA, Stock JH, Watson MW (1990) Inference in linear time series models with some unit roots. Econometrica 58(1):161–182

SOU 2006:106 Fakta – omvärld – inspiration

Toda HY, Phillips PCB (1994) Vector autoregression and causality: a theoretical overview and simulation study. Econo Rev 13:259–285

Varga A, Schalk HJ (2004) Knowledge spillovers, agglomeration and macroeconomic growth: an empirical approach. Reg Stud 38(8):977–989

Chapter 7
Metropolitan Labor Productivity and Urban Spatial Structure

A Comparison of U.S. Monocentric and Polycentric Metropolitan Areas

Evert J. Meijers

Abstract This paper questions the extent to which agglomeration economies can develop in a cluster of close-by cities, so-called polycentric metropolitan areas or polycentric urban regions (PURs). Theory suggests that agglomeration economies are nowadays increasingly associated with more dispersed spatial structures. Are polycentric metropolitan areas, despite their polycentric spatial layout, able to reap the advantages of urban size to a similar extent as monocentric metropolitan areas? By means of a novel method, the most monocentric metropolitan areas (a MSA or CSA dominated by a single city) and most polycentric metropolitan areas (MSAs or CSAs in which population is rather evenly distributed over their constituent cities) in the USA are identified. Polycentric metropolitan areas are furthermore divided into conurbations and polycentric metropolitan areas proper, which is based on the question of whether the cities in a polycentric metropolitan area are part of a contiguous urban area (conurbation) or not. Labor productivity serves as a proxy for agglomeration economies. Using 2006 data, strong evidence was found for metropolitan labor productivity, and hence agglomeration economies, being higher in polycentric metropolitan areas compared to monocentric ones. Referring to Alonso, this means that in polycentric metropolitan areas, cities are able to 'borrow size' from each other. The findings suggest that the location of a city nearby other relatively similar-sized cities results in a 'borrowed size' effect of 11 % in polycentric metropolitan areas. This borrowed size effects suggests that polycentric metropolitan areas on average outperform monocentric, single cities, controlling for the size of the urban population, urban density, human capital and the structure of the metropolitan economy. A similar result is found when explaining mean annual wages, with an elasticity of polycentricity of 5.7 %. Polycentric conurbations resemble monocentric metropolitan areas more than polycentric metro areas. Furthermore, it is demonstrated that while many sectors of economic activity have a

---

E.J. Meijers (✉)
OTB Research Institute for the Built Environment, Delft University of Technology,
P.O. Box 5030, Delft, GA 2600, The Netherlands
e-mail: e.j.meijers@tudelft.nl

J. Klaesson et al. (eds.), *Metropolitan Regions*, Advances in Spatial Science,
DOI 10.1007/978-3-642-32141-2_7, © Springer-Verlag Berlin Heidelberg 2013

142   E.J. Meijers

stronger presence in monocentric metropolitan areas, productivity in many sectors
tends to be higher in polycentric metropolitan areas. One explanation is that the
spatial range of agglomeration advantages has been regionalized, while agglomeration diseconomies remain relatively more limited to the local level.

Keywords Metropolitan labor productivity • Urban spatial structure •
Polycentricity

1 Introduction

In many countries and regions, sets of distinct but proximally-located and well-connected cities have become the object of regional development policies and strategic spatial planning policies. Policy practice often refers to such sets of cities as 'city networks' or 'urban networks' (Meijers 2005), though in the literature such regions are often referred to as polycentric or polynuclear urban regions (PURs). Polycentric urban regions are defined as collections of historically distinct and both administratively and politically independent cities located in close proximity, well connected through infrastructure and lacking one dominating city (Kloosterman and Lambregts 2001). Classic examples include large metropolitan areas as the Dutch Randstad region, the German Rhine-Ruhr region, the Kansai region in Japan or the San Francisco Bay Area. However, PURs of a more modest size are increasingly often being identified, for instance many of the '*Städtenetze*' in Germany, the '*réseaux de villes*' in France or the '*stedelijke netwerken*' in the Netherlands. Policy-makers assume that taking a set of small or medium-sized cities together opens up possibilities for regional economic growth. Taken individually, these cities fear being overlooked, but taken together, policy-makers feel that they would be able to 'play in the major leagues' (Priemus 1994) of national or international competition. The latter ambition can be considered the prime reason for the policy interest in such clusters of cities. In addition, another reason is increasing functional integration between the cities, possibly making such regional networks of cities the next stage in the expansion of urban living space. However, the functional rationality or economic reality of these policy concepts is often not uncontested (see for instance Lambooy 1998).

Precursors of the concept of PURs were discussed in the literature as early as the 1960s (Gottmann 1961; Burton 1963) or even earlier, such as Stein's Regional City (see Larsen 2005), but it is only in the past decade that the concept has gained substantial interest. Its inclusion in the European Spatial Development Perspective (CEC 1999), albeit in different terms, can be considered one of the accelerators of its spread across Europe (Davoudi 2003). In contrast, it appears that in the US this regional scale of polycentricity is not widely debated.[1] The changes in metropolitan

---

[1] Although there is an increased interest in mega-regions or 'megapolitan' regions on an even larger scale (see Carbonell and Yaro 2005; Lang and Dhavale 2005; Florida et al. 2008) and many ideas behind the PUR concept are likely to hold for such larger regions.

spatial structure have in recent decades predominantly been described at the scale of single metropolises rather than at the scale of a collection of close-by metropolises/cities (see Anas et al. 1998; Lee and Gordon 2007). While in Europe there seems to be no doubt that all post-industrial cities are becoming polycentric, this is not uncontested for US cities (Lee 2007) as many witness a general dispersion of employment locations (Gordon and Richardson 1996; Glaeser and Kahn 2001; Lang 2003) rather than a concentration in 'sub'-centers (Garreau 1991; Fujii and Hartshorn 1995). It is important to emphasise here that this paper addresses the higher spatial scale of a regional cluster of close-by cities, the constituent cities of which can often be considered polycentric in their own right.

Many of the recent contributions on polycentric urban regions have been primarily focused on establishing the concept of PURs in the academic and policy debate, on its defining characteristics and on research agenda-setting (see for instance Batten 1995; Dieleman and Faludi 1998; Kloosterman and Musterd 2001; Parr 2004), on its relevance for, or its potential application to specific PURs (Priemus 1994; Albrechts 1998; Bailey and Turok 2001; Turok and Bailey 2004; Meijers et al. 2008), whilst considerable attention has also been paid to capacity-building and governance in such regions (Albrechts 2001; Mueller 2001; Meijers and Romein 2003; Lambregts and Zonneveld 2004). As some of these authors argue, the focus in the discussion on PURs should now turn to empirically substantiating and validating the many claims that have been made for the PUR (Kloosterman and Musterd 2001; Parr 2004; Turok and Bailey 2004).

An important claim circulating addresses the economic significance of PURs, often in connection to their spatial-functional layout. The broad idea is that, taken together, PURs are able to develop new sources of competitive advantage and better market their city-regions. Due to their specific spatial structure, PURs would even have the potential to enjoy economies of scale, scope and complexity similar to their monocentric counterparts without, however, incurring the same costs or agglomeration diseconomies. Such claims have, however, so far remained unexplored. The aim of this paper is to establish whether agglomeration economies are as equally present in a cluster of nearby, but relatively small cities as in a single large city.

We will explore the question of to what extent agglomeration economies develop in a cluster of close-by cities in comparison to single, monocentric cities. More specifically, are PURs, despite their polycentric spatial layout, able to reap the advantages of urban size in a similar way to more monocentric urban areas? Put simply, is there a similar extent of agglomeration economies organised in two cities of, say, 200,000 inhabitants that are located close to each other as in one city of 400,000?

Agglomeration economies by definition result in productivity gains, which makes labor productivity an excellent proxy to study the development of agglomeration economies. Here, we will explore whether labor productivity in polycentric U.S. metropolitan areas is different from labor productivity in monocentric U.S.

metropolitan areas.[2] In Sect. 2, we will elaborate on recent discussions and insights in regional science related to network externalities between cities. For our analysis, we identify in Sect. 3 polycentric and monocentric U.S. metropolitan areas, applying a novel method to do so. Polycentric metropolitan areas are furthermore divided into 'polycentric conurbations' and 'polycentric metropolitan areas' proper, the distinguishing factor being the spatial separation between the cities. When the two largest cities in a polycentric metro area are part of the same built-up area, we refer to them as conurbations. In Sect. 4, following an initial comparison of basic data between monocentric metropolitan areas, polycentric conurbations and polycentric metropolitan areas, OLS estimates are presented explaining differences in labor productivity among these categories of metropolitan areas. To check for robustness, wages are also explained. Our attention is on the question as to whether the different urban shape (monocentric or polycentric) of a metropolitan area is significant in explaining labor productivity and wages. In Sect. 5, we analyse the relationship between urban spatial structure and metropolitan labor productivity in different sectors. Finally, the findings are discussed in the final section, Sect. 6. The most important finding is that urban spatial structure is a significant explanatory variable for both metropolitan labor productivity and wages. The more polycentric a metropolitan areas is, the higher labor productivity and wages are. While most sectors have a stronger presence in monocentric metropolitan areas, a considerable number of them seem to function better in polycentric metropolitan areas, as measured by their output per worker. As it is likely that localisation and most certainly urbanisation economies are less in polycentric metropolitan areas, it seems plausible that these deficits are more than compensated for by a relative lack of agglomeration diseconomies.

2 Externalities in a Cluster of Cities: Different Viewpoints

Economic growth theories are not very specific about the development of the urban spatial structure and the role that this structure plays in economic development (Meijers and Sandberg 2008). The study of agglomeration economies tends to be focused on single agglomerations and generally does not consider urban spatial structure except for a general indicator of density. This implies that the question addressed here, whether agglomeration economies may develop in a cluster of cities to a similar extent as in a metro area dominated by a single city, has not been extensively explored empirically, although several authors have addressed the issue in a more theoretical way. This section presents the various viewpoints found in the literature.

---

[2] As 'metropolitan area' is the common term for a city-region or urban region in the US, we will refer to PURs in the US context as 'polycentric metro area', its antonym obviously being 'monocentric metro area'.

To start with, several authors have questioned the use of the label 'agglomeration economies' in polycentric metropolitan areas. Given the physical spacing of cities, Parr (2002a) suggests using 'regional externalities', even though the label 'urban network externalities' (Capello 2000) may be more appropriate, although the latter applies not necessarily to networks between close-by cities, but also between more distant ones. Boix and Trullén (2007) differentiate between the agglomeration economies and 'network economies' between cities. Another label, 'borrowed size' was introduced several decades ago by Alonso (1973). This concept refers to the situation in which close-by and well-connected cities host urban functions normally found only in larger cities, because the support base is larger given the proximity to other people living in the nearby cities. Alonso used this to explain why smaller cities that are part of the megalopolitan urban complex on the Atlantic seaboard had much higher incomes than independent cities of similar size. The concept of borrowed size has not generated much research interest since it was coined by Alonso (1973). Phelps et al. (2001) can be considered an exception. They suggest that the concept of borrowed size is of value in understanding the geographical patterns of small firm formation and growth in the UK, especially in the South-East of England. Large cities were traditionally considered as offering the most appropriate environment for such firms as a result of localization economies (Hoover and Vernon 1959), a location in smaller, accessible rural villages located near to a large metropolis may now also allow these firms to access pecuniary and technological externalities as a result of the 'spatial externality fields' expanding over time.

This brings us to an unsolved debate in the literature, which is the spatial scale on which agglomeration economies occur (Moulaert and Djellal 1995; Richardson 1995; Parr 2002a; Brakman et al. 2005). Empirical evidence indicates that agglomeration economies attenuate with distance (Rosenthal and Strange 2004). For firms, the gains derived from a location in a metropolitan area are linked to different sources, e.g. localisation and urbanisation economies. Considering that for each firm different types of external economies play a role at different points in time, it is hard to generalise on the precise spatial scale of what Phelps (1992) termed 'spatial externality fields'. However, given the strong improvements in interurban and intraregional transportation and communication technologies, for some types of activities this spatial range might extend into close-by neighbouring cities, leading to a mutual borrowing of size. Agglomeration economies are then associated with a more dispersed regional spatial structure (Parr 2002a; Lambooy 2004; Capello and Camagni 2000).

It is not surprising that many local and regional policy-makers have embraced the idea of developing a regional city network, in particular in areas in which the cities are of a rather modest size when regarded from the international competitiveness perspective. After all, as Capello (2000, p. 1926) argues, 'the limit that the medium-sized cities come up against, and which often makes them succumb vis-à-vis the great metropolis, is the limit of critical mass and centrality'. Not surprisingly, the highest valued economic activities and the widest variety in economic and cultural functions are found within the largest agglomerations. Taken together, the cities in a polycentric metropolitan area could possibly enjoy more agglomeration economies. Such agglomeration economies, and urbanisation economies in particular, can be considered to be a function of the size, or scope (Parr 2002b) of a city: the larger the city, the higher productivity, innovation, the greater the variety of consumer products and producer inputs, and the higher the well-being of citizens (Quigley 1998; Catin 1995). A doubling of city size is typically associated with an increase in urbanisation economies of somewhere between 3 % and 10 % (Quigley 1998; Graham 2005; Strange 2005), and sometimes even 20 % (Kawashima 1975). Through a mutual process of borrowing size between medium-sized cities, they appear to be able to gain critical mass and hence agglomeration economies, for instance through forming 'club' type networks to exploit scale economies and 'web' type networks to profit from complementarities (Meijers 2005; Camagni 1993).

Another question is whether agglomeration diseconomies can also be 'borrowed' between close-by cities. Generally, agglomeration disadvantages such as traffic congestion, high property prices, residential segregation, crime and exposure to environmental pollution also increase with city-size. It appears that smaller cities have a greater endogenous capacity to keep these social, economic and environmental costs under control (Capello and Camagni 2000). Parr (2002a) states that while agglomeration economies can be accessed from more distant places, it appears that agglomeration diseconomies remain more spatially constrained in the larger cities.

Another positive view on the possibilities of 'borrowing size' in polycentric metropolitan areas can be found in Johansson and Quigley (2004, p. 175), who suggest that, in theory, networks may substitute for spatial proximity: 'for many transactions, an established network reduces the effective distance between nodes, reducing the transaction (or transport) costs that would otherwise be prohibitive. When co-location is infeasible, networks may substitute for agglomeration'. Technological advance should be considered the main driving force behind this substitution, although it remains unclear to what extent this substitution may take place (Johansson and Quigley 2004) and whether it also holds for networks between cities rather than between firms.

What this brief overview makes clear, is that there are theoretical grounds for policymakers to claim that the specific spatial structure of polycentric metropolitan areas is not necessarily a disadvantage when it comes to enjoying agglomeration economies. Doubts are, however, also raised. For instance, Bailey and Turok (2001) suggest that the idea that the integration of separate cities results in agglomeration advantages comparable to similar-sized monocentric cities is 'rather simplistic' (Bailey and Turok 2001). Parr (2004) points in this respect to the need for longer travel flows, longer commodity flows and less convenient flows of information in polycentric urban regions. Moreover, it should be reckoned that 'some of the advantages of urban size stem from the nature of the metropolitan environment, and are related to such factors as density, proximity, face-to-face contact, informal structures, unplanned interaction, etc.' (Parr 2004, p. 236), and consequently hold less for polycentric metropolitan areas. The finding that the more regions in the

Netherlands were polycentric regions, the less cultural, leisure and sports amenities were present is also relevant. Put another way, the more monocentric a region was, the more these amenities were present (Meijers 2008a).

To sum up, there are theoretical reasons to underline the hypothesis that cities in polycentric metropolitan areas may borrow size from each other, and at the same time reasons to assume that the extent to which this may take place is perhaps rather limited, although it is probably increasing. Given the lack of empirical work supporting these viewpoints, it remains to be seen whether, for instance, advanced specialised activities 'can also be realized in polynuclear urban structures, which lack the critical mass of large cities with agglomeration economies' (Lambooy 1998, p. 459). In the next sections we will empirically explore this strategic issue of whether a polycentric spatial lay-out influences the development of agglomeration economies. Evidence is gathered for the U.S. metropolitan areas.

3 Identifying Polycentric and Monocentric U.S. Metropolitan Areas

A first step in our analysis is to identify the U.S. metropolitan areas that are polycentric and those that are monocentric, an exercise that has not been carried out before. In the literature, one finds different interpretations of what makes a region polycentric (Meijers 2008b). Grossly speaking, there is an approach that defines polycentricity on the basis of urban morphology, while another approach adds relational aspects to it in the sense that a region can only be considered polycentric when the cities are strongly functionally linked, which is sometimes referred to as 'relational polycentricity' or 'functional polycentricity' (see for instance Nordregio et al. 2004; Green 2007). Champion (2001), who also identifies the previous approaches, adds a third, even more restrictive approach, which is that each city has a specialist function in the region (thus suggesting complementarity). Here, we adhere to the first and least restrictive vision for several reasons. In the first place, in its essence, 'polycentricity' refers to the plurality of centres in a given area. It therefore seems a priori a morphological concept (see also Kloosterman and Musterd 2001; Parr 2004). In the second place, we feel that it is advisable to use a different label for polycentric metro areas that are also strongly functionally interwoven. To avoid misunderstandings these could probably be better referred to as 'urban networks' or 'city networks' (see also Meijers 2007a, 2007b; IGEAT et al. 2007). We feel that the extent to which a polycentric metropolitan area has developed into such an urban network may constitute an important explanation of its performance in economic, social and environmental terms. Differentiating between these two concepts also allows for empirical research to underpin this.

According to the definition of PURs (Kloosterman and Lambregts 2001), one of their main characteristics is that no city dominates over other cities in economic, cultural and other respects. In other words, a polycentric urban system lacks strong

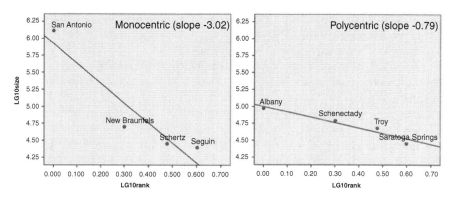

Fig. 7.1 Rank-size distributions to measure mono/polycentricity

hierarchy. The rank-size distribution of the regional urban system provides information on this hierarchy and is therefore an excellent indication of the extent of mono – or polycentricity (Nordregio et al. 2004). Parr (2004) also proposes the rather flat size distribution of cities in a metropolitan area as one of the defining characteristics. Figure 7.1 presents the four largest incorporated places in two metropolitan areas and also the regression line that best fits the distribution of their sizes. The argument now is that in a polycentric metropolitan area, with little hierarchy, this line will be flatter than in a monocentric metropolitan area. In this example, San Antonio is obviously monocentric, while Albany-Schenectady-Troy is a clear example of a polycentric metropolitan area.

Here we elaborate on the Nordregio et al. (2004) approach[3] and adopt it to the regional scale. When looking at the rank-size distribution of cities in a metropolitan area, a major issue is the question of how many cities should be included to base the regression line on. In general, sample size can be either a fixed number of towns, a fixed size threshold, or a size above which the sample accounts for some given proportion of a region's population (see also Cheshire 1999). The latter has disadvantages for this research, as it will turn out that the number of towns included in the analysis is large for polycentric areas and small for monocentric areas. Hence, the number of towns comprising a given proportion of the population is in itself an indicator of mono – or polycentricity and applying such a measure twice would distort the picture. A fixed size threshold is equally inappropriate as in large and more densely populated metropolitan areas a town of say 20,000 inhabitants may be insignificant, whereas it could be of great importance in a small or less populated metropolitan area. It could be argued that a town ranked for instance third in a metropolitan area is of importance in that area, despite its possible small size. Therefore, when measuring polycentricity, the sample size could best be based on a fixed number of towns. The question then is what this number should be. The answer seems arbitrary. Our tentative impression of the extent of polycentricity of a metropolitan area is often based on just a mere handful of places.

---

[3] Developed by Spiekermann and Wegener.

In this study we identified the extent to which a metropolitan area is monocentric or, on the contrary, polycentric by calculating the slope of the regression line of the rank-size distribution of incorporated places (cities)[4] in Combined Statistical Areas[5] (CSAs) as well as in those Metropolitan Statistical Areas (MSAs) not part of a CSA.[6] We did so for different numbers of incorporated places per CSA/MSA: Two, three and four. We then calculated the average of these three scores. This resulted in scoring each metropolitan area on a scale ranging from very mono-centric to very polycentric. In order to address our research question, to what extent polycentric metropolitan areas enjoy agglomeration economies compared to metropolitan areas in which the population is concentrated in a single city, we selected the most monocentric and most polycentric ones, thus those areas scoring at the extreme ends on the monocentricity-polycentricity scale. Two equally-sized groups were made, each one containing 33 metropolitan areas, which meant that Dallas-Fort Worth was the least polycentric area to be still considered polycentric, which seems justified given its metropolitan spatial structure. Table 7.1 presents the metropolitan areas selected and their score on the mono/polycentricity-scale.

The rank-size distribution does not provide information on the spread of cities over the metropolitan territory. This is, however, also of relevance. According to Parr (2004), a distinctive feature of a polycentric urban region is also a minimum spatial separation between the cities. Also the definition by Kloosterman and Lambregts (2001) refers to 'distinct cities'. Therefore, we need to filter out areas that are polycentric in terms of the rank-size distribution, but that are part of the same contiguous built-up area. In the latter case, the term conurbation is more appropriate. Table 7.1 further divides polycentric areas into 'polycentric conurbations' and 'polycentric metropolitan areas'. If the two largest cities belong to the same 'urban area', as delineated by the US Census Bureau to encompass densely settled territory, we labelled these 'polycentric conurbations'. Those

---

[4] Only considering incorporated places of at least 5,000 inhabitants in 2006. In those cases where the second incorporated place did not meet this threshold, we used its actual size in order to be able to calculate a slope.

[5] Metropolitan and micropolitan statistical areas (metro and micro areas; MSAs) are geographic entities defined by the U.S. Office of Management and Budget (OMB). A metro area contains a core urban area with a population of 50,000 or more, and a micro area contains an urban core with a population of at least 10,000 (but less than 50,000). Each metro or micro area consists of one or more counties and includes the counties containing the core urban area, as well as any adjacent counties that have a high degree of social and economic integration (as measured by commuting to work – 25 % of employed residents working in the core) with the urban core. MSAs that are adjacent may be joined in order to form a Combined Statistical Area if the employment interchange is at least 25. Adjacent MSAs that have an employment interchange measure of at least 15 and less than 25 will combine if local opinion favors combination.

[6] Note that this measurement method is basically scale-free. In stead of cities, one may prefer to look at the rank-size distribution of employment concentrations when studying polycentricity at the city-scale. Or, when studying the megaregions in the U.S., one may wish to consider the size distribution of metro areas within these megaregions. At the European scale, one would have to consider European equivalents of such mega-regions to describe the level of polycentricity. Therefore, the appropriate unit of analysis changes with the spatial resolution of the issue at stake.

Table 7.1 Monocentric and polycentric areas included in the analysis

Monocentric (33)		Polycentric (33)			
Monocentric metropolitan area (33)	Slope	Polycentric conurbation (18)	Slope	Polycentric metropolitan area (15)	Slope
Abilene, TX[a]	−4.95	Albany-Schenectady-Amsterdam, NY	−0.67	Appleton-Oshkosh-Neenah, WI	−0.67
Albuquerque, NM[a]	−3.09	Bloomington-normal, IL[a]	−0.49	El Centro, CA[a]	−0.47
Amarillo, TX[a]	−3.77	Charleston-North Charleston, SC[a]	−0.49	Greensboro-Winston-Salem-high point, NC	−0.80
Athens-Clarke County, GA[a]	−5.36	College Station-Bryan, TX[a]	−0.14	Greenville-Spartanburg-Anderson, SC	−0.65
Baton Rouge, LA	−3.06	Dallas-Fort Worth, TX	−1.04	Johnson City-Kingsport-Bristol (Tri-cities), TN-VA	−0.53
Billings, MT[a]	−3.96	Davenport-Moline-Rock Island, IA-IL[a]	−0.98	Killeen-Temple-Fort Hood, TX[a]	−1.03
Chicago, IL-IN-WI	−3.08	Fayetteville-Springdale-Rogers, AR-MO[a]	−0.28	Midland-Odessa, TX	−0.10
Colorado Springs, CO[a]	−3.76	Hartford-West Hartford-East Hartford, CT	−0.72	Portland-Lewiston-South Portland, ME	−0.82
Columbus, OH	−3.05	Kennewick-Richland-Pasco, WA[a]	−0.54	Raleigh-Durham-Cary, NC	−1.04
El Paso, TX[a]	−4.04	McAllen-Edinburg-Mission, TX[a]	−0.71	Salt Lake City-Ogden-Clearfield, UT	−0.55
Erie, PA[a]	−3.33	Miami-Fort Lauderdale-Miami Beach, FL[a]	−0.78	San Jose - San Francisco − Oakland, CA	−0.69
Fayetteville, NC[a]	−3.32	Minneapolis-St. Paul - St. Cloud, MN-WI	−1.00	Santa Barbara-Santa Maria, CA[a]	−0.47
Gainesville, FL[a]	−3.68	Palm Bay-Melbourne-Titusville, FL[a]	−0.66	South Bend-Elkhart-Mishawaka, IN-MI	−0.84
Houston, TX	−3.20	Provo-Orem, UT[a]	−0.76	Visalia-Porterville, CA[a]	−1.04
Jacksonville, FL[a]	−4.13	Sarasota-Bradenton-Punta Gorda, FL	−0.19	Washington-Baltimore-N. Virginia, DC-MD-VA-WV	−0.73
Laredo, TX[a]	−5.23	Scranton–Wilkes-Barre, PA[a]	−1.02		
Lincoln, NE[a]	−5.13	Tampa-St. Petersburg-Clearwater, FL[a]	−0.82		
Louisville/Jefferson County, KY-IN	−3.03	Virginia Beach-Norfolk-Newport N., VA-NC[a]	−0.73		
Lubbock, TX	−3.74				
Memphis, TN-MS-AR[a]	−2.91				
New York, NY-NJ-CT-PA	−3.70				
Philadelphia, PA-NJ-DE-MD	−3.09				
Pueblo, CO[a]	−8.28				
Rochester, MN[a]	−3.48				

7 Metropolitan Labor Productivity and Urban Spatial Structure

San Antonio, TX[a]	−3.80
Sioux Falls, SD[a]	−4.22
Springfield, IL[a]	−3.54
Tallahassee, FL[a]	−4.52
Topeka, KS[a]	−5.18
Tucson, AZ[a]	−3.03
Wichita Falls, TX[a]	−2.96
Wichita, KS	−3.16
Wilmington, NC[a]	−3.14

[a]Metropolitan statistical area; otherwise: combined statistical area

polycentric areas where the major cities were spatially separated are labelled 'polycentric metropolitan area'. It appears useful to make this distinction in our analysis, as it could be argued that conurbations resemble monocentric cities, except for the presence of administrative boundaries dividing the urban territory. Obviously, the main interest when considering regional externalities is in the polycentric metropolitan areas.

4 Labor Productivity and Urban Spatial Structure

Having identified three different types of metro areas from the spatial urban structure point of view, the first exercise is to compare them and to see to what extent they score differently on a number of basic variables relating to population, economy and income, see Table 7.2. On average, monocentric metropolitan areas have slightly more population, and what differs substantially is the size of the largest city, as we would expect. Monocentric metro areas also have a slightly higher employment rate and white/blue collar ratio, defined as the number of people in a management occupation divided by those in production. Polycentric metropolitan areas tend to do slightly better in terms of productivity and income. Perhaps surprisingly, urban densities are also higher. There are more people with a bachelor or higher degree in conurbations. However, none of these differences were significant in a one-way ANOVA (post Hoc test Bonferroni).

We consider labor productivity as a proxy for the extent to which agglomeration economies have developed. After all, agglomeration economies can be defined as productivity gains derived from the geographical clustering of firms and people.

While we have established that we cannot reject the hypothesis that the mean labor productivity in 2006 differed for metropolitan areas that are characterised by a different urban spatial structure, $F(66) = 0.577, p = 0.564$, this does not necessarily mean that the shape of the urban system in these areas is not of importance. In this section we analyse whether there is a difference between monocentric metropolitan areas, polycentric metropolitan areas and polycentric conurbations in labor productivity when controlling for other explanatory variables.

4.1 Models and Data

Here, labor productivity is defined as the GDP produced in a metropolitan area[7] divided by the total number of jobs[8] in that area. Data on GDP by metropolitan area

---

[7] Excluding the agriculture, fishing, hunting and mining sectors, as well as the public administration sector.

[8] Excluding self employment.

7 Metropolitan Labor Productivity and Urban Spatial Structure

Table 7.2 Comparison urban spatial structure and basic variables

Variable	Urban spatial structure	N	Mean	SD
Size urban population 2006	Monocentric metropolitan area	33	1007654	2287251
	Polycentric conurbation	18	853183	1497552
	Polycentric metropolitan area	15	791197	1306777
Population density urban area 2000	Monocentric metropolitan area	33	2932	2704
	Polycentric conurbation	18	2530	1192
	Polycentric metropolitan area	15	2982	1571
Size largest city 2006	Monocentric metropolitan area	33	720578	1481899
	Polycentric conurbation	18	219162	283892
	Polycentric metropolitan area	15	208837	252663
Educational attainment: % bachelor degree or higher 2006	Monocentric metropolitan area	33	26.7	5.5
	Polycentric conurbation	18	27.6	5.9
	Polycentric metropolitan area	15	25.4	9.4
Mean household income 2006	Monocentric metropolitan area	33	59213	8982
	Polycentric conurbation	18	61895	9048
	Polycentric metropolitan area	15	63984	13984
GDP per capita 2006	Monocentric metropolitan area	33	40389	9622
	Polycentric conurbation	18	39200	10835
	Polycentric metropolitan area	15	42673	12505
Employment rate 2006	Monocentric metropolitan area	33	0.888	0.076
	Polycentric conurbation	18	0.874	0.080
	Polycentric metropolitan area	15	0.872	0.099
White/blue collar ratio 2006	Monocentric metropolitan area	33	3.54	0.99
	Polycentric conurbation	18	3.44	1.06
	Polycentric metropolitan area	15	3.38	0.94
Labor productivity[a] 2006	Monocentric metropolitan area	33	77932	21042
	Polycentric conurbation	18	78998	18882
	Polycentric metropolitan area	15	84813	22766

Data sources: U.S. Census Bureau (American Community Survey [As the American Community Survey reports data at the level of MSAs (over 60,000 inhabitants), the values for CSAs were calculated as the weighted average of the findings for MSAs.]; Annual population estimates); U.S. Department of Commerce, BEA; U.S. Department of Labor, BLS

[a]Excludes government, agriculture and mining sectors

in the U.S. has been made available only recently by the U.S. Department of Commerce's Bureau of Economic Analysis (BEA). Data is available for the years 2001–2006, and we used the 2006 data. Data on the number of jobs were provided by the Bureau of Labor Statistics (BLS) of the U.S. Department of Labor. The BEA estimates enable a more direct measurement of labor productivity then previously possible, when many researchers used indirect proxies such as the mean annual wage, the reasoning being that higher productivity leads to higher wages. In order to check for the robustness of the findings, we developed models that explain labor productivity as well as the mean annual wage, and apply the same explanatory variables in both models. Like the productivity and wages data, all the data used for the explanatory variables was also collected at the scale of metropolitan areas (in case of CSAs, data for its constituent MSAs was summed up).

Labor productivity is linked to a variety of regional characteristics (OECD 2006). A first explanatory variable that is included in the analysis is the size of the urban population. Labor productivity tends to increase with the size of a city (Quigley 1998; Graham 2005; Strange 2005). Moreover, to study whether cities in polycentric metropolitan areas borrow size, it is necessary to control for different sizes of metropolitan areas. Here, we employ the variable size of the urban population, that is the population of all the places incorporated in the metropolitan area that have at least 25,000 inhabitants, according to the 2006 population estimates of the U.S. Census Bureau. A second explanatory variable that is somewhat related to the size of the urban population, but not to such an extent that it causes multicollinearity ($r = 0.5$), is density. Previous studies found that a doubling of densities tends to increase labor productivity by some 4 to 6 % (Ciccone and Hall 1996; Ciccone 2002). In the model we included the population density in urban areas (land area). As these urban areas were defined on the basis of the 2000 census, this variable concerns the year 2000. A more skilled labor force also influences productivity positively (OECD 2006). A proxy for this is the educational attainment of the metropolitan population, and we include the share of the population of 25 years and over that has a bachelor's degree or higher as a third explanatory variable. This data was derived from the 2006 American Community Survey. A fourth explanatory variable reflects differences between metropolitan areas in terms of their economy. High value-added activities contribute more to GDP than others. In order to control for this, we developed a 'white collar/blue collar'-ratio, which is calculated as the number of employed persons of over 16 years old with a management, professional or related occupation divided by the number of employed persons of 16 years and over with a production and transportation occupation. Finally, the focus in this analysis is on the question of whether agglomeration economies develop differently in metropolitan areas that have a different urban spatial structure. Analyses were run for each pair of metropolitan areas, making use of dummy variables. Models 1 and 4 compare monocentric metropolitan areas to polycentric metropolitan areas (dummy = 1). Models 2 and 5 compare monocentric metropolitan areas with polycentric conurbations (dummy = 1). Finally, models 3 and 6 confronts polycentric conurbations with polycentric metropolitan areas (dummy = 1).

4.2 Results

The OLS estimation results to explain metropolitan labor productivity are presented in Table 7.3, while Table 7.4 presents the results for the mean annual wage by metropolitan area.

All six models have substantial explanatory power. Models explaining the mean annual wage have a larger explanatory power than those explaining labor productivity. Also, the models provide for a better explanation of productivity and wage differentials for the metropolitan areas that have a truly opposite urban spatial structure, namely monocentric versus polycentric metropolitan areas. This is what we would have expected, as the urban spatial structure of polycentric conurbations is somewhere in between those of the monocentric and polycentric metropolitan areas.

As regards these selections of U.S. metropolitan areas, we found a positive and significant effect of population size in the range of 10 % for labor productivity and of about 3 % when explaining wages. Density also has a positive effect, with a significant elasticity in the range of 5–12 % in models 1, 2 and 4, but does not add significantly to explaining the labor differentials in the other models. Both findings are in line with the literature on these effects, as mentioned before. Educational attainment has a positive and significant effect of between 16 % and 36 %, depending on which types of metro areas are included the analysis. The metropolitan economic structure, as proxied by the white-blue collar ratio, also adds to the explanations, with a negative effect when explaining labor productivity and positive for explaining wages.

However, our prime concern in this paper is with urban spatial structure. Models 1 and 4 answer our question of whether cities that are proximally located are able to borrow size. The answer is yes. In comparison to a single large city, we find agglomeration effects to be not less in a cluster of smaller cities of the same size (when taken together). In fact, both labor productivity and wages are even significantly higher in polycentric metropolitan areas when other explanatory variables are controlled for. Labor productivity tends to be $\exp(b\text{-}V(b)/2)\text{-}1 = 11$ % higher and, along the same lines (Kennedy 1981), wages 5.7 % higher in polycentric metropolitan areas, compared to metropolitan areas where the population is concentrated in a single city. In other words, three cities of say 250,000 inhabitants located together are characterised by a higher labor productivity than one single city of 750,000, controlling for human capital, density and the structure of the metropolitan economy. This is, at the very least, a remarkable finding and perhaps even revolutionary. We will elaborate on its explanation in the concluding section. As regards the other comparison of different types of metro areas, we found that mean annual wages in polycentric conurbations are significantly higher, +3.8 % to be precise, compared to monocentric metropolitan areas. However, there is no effect of urban spatial structure on labor productivity between monocentric metro areas and conurbations. The different urban spatial structure of conurbations vis-à-vis polycentric metropolitan areas, thus whether or not cities are spatially separate, does not

Table 7.3 OLS estimation results; dependent: labor productivity (ln)

Regressors	(1) Monocentric versus polycentric			(2) Monocentric versus conurbation			(3) Conurbation versus polycentric		
	B	t	SE	B	t	SE	B	t	SE
Constant	8.131	16.44**	0.495	8.857	35.10**	0.252	8.756	10.13**	0.865
Size urban population (ln)	0.103	4.154**	0.025	0.103	8.507**	0.012	0.078	2.238*	0.035
Urban density (ln)	0.128	2.079*	0.062	0.065	2.476*	0.026	0.084	0.790	0.106
Educational attainment: % bachelor degree or higher (ln)	0.361	2.564*	0.141	0.223	3.158**	0.071	0.235	1.082	0.217
Ratio white/blue collar workers (ln)	−0.316	−2.241*	0.141	−0.140	−2.104*	0.066	0.058	0.221	0.262
Polycentric metropolitan area (dummy)	0.106	2.051*	0.052						
Polycentric conurbation (dummy)				0.000	1.472	0.000			
Polycentric metropolitan area (dummy)							0.112	1.541	0.073
N	48			51			33		
F	14,036**			29,673**			4,759**		
R^2	0.631			0.516			0.478		
Adjusted R^2	0.586			0.499			0.377		

* significant at the one per cent level
** significant at the five per cent level

7 Metropolitan Labor Productivity and Urban Spatial Structure

Table 7.4 OLS estimation results; dependent: mean annual wage (ln)

Regressors	(4) Monocentric versus polycentric			(5) Monocentric versus conurbation			(6) Conurbation versus polycentric		
	B	t	SE	B	t	SE	B	t	SE
Constant	8.794	54.30**	0.162	8.967	44.62**	0.201	9.129	30.87	0.296
Size urban population (ln)	0.033	4.019**	0.008	0.028	3.248**	0.009	0.025	2.131*	0.012
Urban density (ln)	0.052	2.593*	0.020	0.034	1.566	0.022	0.028	0.783	0.036
Educational attainment: % bachelor degree or higher (ln)	0.223	4.34**	0.046	0.212	3.732**	0.057	0.166	2.241*	0.074
Ratio white/blue collar workers (ln)	0.105	2.282*	0.046	0.156	3.025**	0.051	0.244	2.725*	0.090
Polycentric metropolitan area (dummy)	0.056	3.327**	0.017						
Polycentric conurbation (dummy)				0.038	2.020*	0.019			
Polycentric metropolitan area (dummy)							0.018	0.741	0.025
N	48			51			33		
F	51,180**			28,169**			22,324**		
R^2	0.862			0.758			0.811		
Adjusted R^2	0.845			0.731			0.775		

* significant at the one per cent level
** significant at the five per cent level

158 E.J. Meijers

influence either labor productivity or wages to a significant level. However the suggestion is that polycentric metropolitan areas also outperform conurbations. Before elaborating on these findings, we will examine the relationship between urban spatial structure and productivity in more detail, by exploring sectoral labor productivity.

5 Sectoral Labor Productivity and Urban Spatial Structure

The Bureau of Economic Analysis also publishes GDP per main sector of economic activity by metropolitan area. This allows an evaluation of whether certain types of economic activity perform better in a metro area with a specific urban spatial structure. We found that urban spatial structure plays a significant role in explaining productivity and wage differentials only when comparing the most extreme cases, thus monocentric metropolitan areas vis-à-vis polycentric metropolitan areas. As comparing these areas was also the prime focus in this paper, we will neglect the role of conurbations in this more detailed analysis of sectoral labor productivity.

Table 7.5 compares the presence of sectors in both metropolitan areas, as well as the output per worker in each of these sectors. An independent samples T-Test was run to flag significant differentials in the means for presence of sectors and in the means of output per worker between monocentric metropolitan areas and polycentric metropolitan areas.

The data on the presence of sectors was taken from the American Community Survey 2006[9]. Presented in Table 7.5 is the total share of employment in the sector in a metropolitan area divided by total employment in that metropolitan area. We used this employment data also to calculate output per worker per sector by metropolitan area. As sectoral GDP data is not always available for each sector of a metropolitan area due to issues of reliability, the number of cases is somewhat less for the sectoral labor productivity column.

Table 7.5 sheds light on the question of which sectors function better in a specific urban spatial structure. Companies in a specific sector may prefer one urban spatial structure over another one as it is likely that they yield different externalities for them. For instance, when proximity is of great importance, it would seem that

---

[9] Ideally the number of jobs is measured at the workplace rather than the place of residence. However, such job counts, provided through the Current Employment Statistics program, are not satisfactorily available at the level of metropolitan areas. We therefore rely on the American Community Survey estimates of the number of jobs in the main sectors of the economy (applying the NAICS definitions), in which respondents are registered at their place of residence. This seems, however, justified by the fact that we analyse CSAs and, if not applicable, MSAs, which are both defined on the basis of commuting patterns amongst others, in such a way that they represent large travel-to-work areas. In other words, the number of people working outside of the MSA or CSA in which they live is likely to be very limited.

Table 7.5 Results *T*-test of sectoral labor productivity versus urban spatial structure

Sector	Urban spatial structure	N	Mean share sector in total employment (%)	t	df	Sig. (2-tailed)	N	Mean labor productivity in sector (output per worker)	t	df	Sig. (2-tailed)
Agriculture, forestry, fishing and hunting, mining	Monocentric	33	1.46	−1.736[a]	46	0.104	20	119,503	0.633	28	0.532
	Polycentric	15	3.81				10	96,979			
Construction	Monocentric	33	7.69	0.693	46	0.492	28	51,412	−1.079	39	0.287
	Polycentric	15	7.33				13	56,003			
Manufacturing	Monocentric	33	9.15	−1.858[a]	46	0.079	29	102,272	0.446	41	0.658
	Polycentric	15	13.07				14	94,930			
Wholesale trade	Monocentric	33	3.27	−0.348	46	0.730	21	125,994	−0.724	26	0.476
	Polycentric	15	3.37				7	139,779			
Retail trade	Monocentric	33	11.63	0.830	46	0.411	33	50,398	−1.279	45	0.207
	Polycentric	15	11.33				14	53,491			
Transportation, warehousing, utilities	Monocentric	33	5.30	1.704	46	0.095	23	84,687	2.346[a]	29	0.026
	Polycentric	15	4.34				8	68,833			
Information	Monocentric	33	2.30	1.157	46	0.253	21	126,822	−0.515	30	0.610
	Polycentric	15	2.04				11	136,138			
Finance and insurance, real estate and rental, leasing	Monocentric	33	7.15	1.481	46	0.145	32	205,850	−0.395	42	0.695
	Polycentric	15	6.24				12	218,063			
Professional, scientific, management, administrative and waste management	Monocentric	33	9.13	−0.470[a]	46	0.644	23	81,559	−0.516	32	0.610
	Polycentric	15	9.64				11	86,818			
Educational services, health care, social assistance	Monocentric	33	23.30	1.874	46	0.067	27	35,469	1.303	40	0.200
	Polycentric	15	20.90				15	30,776			
Arts, entertainment, recreation, accommodation, food services	Monocentric	33	8.64	1.800	46	0.078	28	34,375	0.708	40	0.483
	Polycentric	15	7.93				14	32,096			
Other services	Monocentric	33	5.12	0.693	46	0.492	29	41,084	−0.093	40	0.926
	Polycentric	15	4.92				13	41,351			
Public administration	Monocentric	33	5.88	0.797	46	0.429	33	257,241	−0.374	46	0.710
	Polycentric	15	5.09				15	267,294			

[a]Equal variances not assumed

monocentric metropolitan areas have an advantage over polycentric metropolitan areas. When the availability of cheaper land is a critical factor, then this could well be the other way around.

A remarkable finding is that 10 out of 13 sectors have, on average, a stronger presence in monocentric metropolitan areas. For three sectors, this difference was statistically robust (at the 0.1 confidence level): transportation, education and health care, and the arts and leisure sectors. Financial services and the information sector also appear to be concentrated in monocentric metropolitan areas, although the result is less statistically robust. Conversely, we find that manufacturing has a significantly stronger presence in polycentric metropolitan areas, and the same seems to hold for agriculture and mining. These patterns follow conventional wisdom. Services that require propinquity in order to allow an easy exchange of information and the circulation of knowledge, such as financial services and information, are more present in monocentric metropolitan areas, which seem to provide a more metropolitan environment. The transportation sector might have a stronger presence in such metropolitan areas as a result of public transport having a larger share in the total movements in larger cities. Mass transit systems require a large concentration of people. Also, larger cities are more likely to have a significant airport than polycentric metropolitan areas (as was found in Southwest Europe, see Meijers et al. 2008). Path dependency is important here. Finally, the finding that arts and leisure are more present in U.S. monocentric metropolitan areas confirms a similar finding by Meijers (2008a) for the Netherlands.

However, while the presence of sectoral activity may indicate past locational preferences, a more up-to-date indicator of how well a sector functions in a particular urban-spatial structure is the 2006 labor productivity in these sectors (see Table 7.5). While 10 out of 13 sectors had a larger presence in monocentric metropolitan areas, only 5 out of 13 sectors record a higher output per worker in monocentric metropolitan areas. This is in line with the previous finding that labor productivity in total is significantly higher in polycentric metropolitan areas. While some care is needed in identifying the sectors that perform better in polycentric metropolitan areas given the t-values found, it appears that construction, retail trade, and to a lesser extent wholesale trade and financial and professional services function better in a polycentric metropolitan area. Activities that perform better in a monocentric metropolitan area are transportation, education and health care, arts and leisure, agriculture and manufacturing. While manufacturing is less present in a monocentric metropolitan area, it has indeed been established that manufacturing industries in larger metropolitan areas are more likely to be associated with higher-added-value activities such as R&D (Henderson 1997). While Table 7.5 provides a first indication of the relation between urban-spatial structure and sectoral labor productivity, more detailed analysis is needed in which sector-specific explanatory variables for output per worker are included, such as education of workers and co-location of firms in such sectors.

6 Conclusions

This paper questioned the extent to which agglomeration economies can develop in polycentric metropolitan areas. By polycentric metropolitan area, reference is made to the presence of several rather similar-sized cities within a metropolitan area. In order to analyse this, we compared polycentric metropolitan areas with monocentric metropolitan areas, which are metropolitan areas dominated by a single large city. Evidence was gathered for U.S. metropolitan areas. All CSAs and MSAs not included in a CSA that reach a population threshold set at a minimum of 100,000 inhabitants (taking the three largest places together), were scored on a scale ranging from very monocentric to very polycentric. In this paper, the 33 most monocentric and 33 most polycentric metropolitan areas were compared. These polycentric areas were further divided into conurbations, thus metropolitan areas in which the main cities are part of the same built-up urban area, and polycentric metropolitan areas in which cities are spatially separated. The development of agglomeration effects, proxied by labor productivity, has been compared between these different types of areas.

It was found that a polycentric metropolitan lay-out does not negatively influence productivity, as some expected because of the expected longer travel flows, commodity flows, less convenient flows of information and a lack of a metropolitan environment. In contrast, it would appear that the opposite is even true. Labor productivity and wages tend to be 11 % and 5.7 % higher respectively in polycentric metropolitan areas compared to monocentric metropolitan areas, when a range of other explanatory factors are controlled for. This supports the view that the spatial range within which agglomeration effects occur is substantially extending beyond the city limits and that, as a consequence, agglomeration effects are indeed associated with a more dispersed regional spatial structure.

One question that deserves further exploration is to what extent different types of agglomeration economies develop in polycentric metropolitan areas. Traditionally a distinction is made in the literature between industry-specific 'localisation'-economies, also called MAR scale economies (Marshall, Arrow, Romer), on the one hand, and more broadly based 'urbanisation' economies on the other. Localisation economies lead to productivity gains resulting from the concentration in space of similar industries. Urbanisation economies refer to gains derived from location in a larger and more diversified urban area (Jacobs 1969). Also competition (Porter 1990) enhances externalities, as it requires firms to be more innovative. It is unclear whether the urban spatial structure of metropolitan areas enhances or diminishes competition for firms, even though it is more evident that competition between cities is larger in polycentric metropolitan areas.

There are signs that localisation economies are less strong in polycentric metropolitan areas. Funderburg and Boarnet (2008) found that many industrial clusters operate at a rather limited spatial scale, although the exact scale may differ for different types of industries. A particular constraint to the spatial scale of competitive clusters is the costs of time and travel. Kloosterman and Lambregts (2001) argue that as localisation economies are strongly rooted in the local supply of highly specialised labor, and as the daily journey to work represents a particularly expensive kind of transaction (Scott 1998), the upper limit of the spatial scale of clusters seems to be set by travel to work areas (see also Phelps et al. 2001). As U.S. metropolitan areas are delimited on the basis of travel to work areas, they may provide the upper limit of spatial clustering. Also the circulation of non-standardised knowledge and ideas, which requires frequent, and often costly face to face contacts, is facilitated better in a 'metropolitan environment' (Glaeser 1998). Proximity, while not a guarantee for such externalities, seems to enable easier circulation of such non-standardised knowledge and ideas. Given its spatially dispersed urban structure, externalities relying on proximity do appear to be less present in a polycentric metropolitan area compared to a monocentric metropolitan area that is similar, except for its urban spatial structure.

Next to localisation economies, there also appear to be reasons to assume that urbanisation economies are relatively less present in polycentric metropolitan areas. As the economy is shifting from the production of physical goods to the production and diffusion of information, knowledge and innovation (Lambooy 1998a; Van Oort 2004), the attractiveness of cities for 'knowledge workers' and the 'creative class' (Florida 2002) is of particular significance. Important assets of cities include for instance the diversity of available consumption goods (Quigley 1998; Glaeser et al. 2001) and the presence of other residential amenities (Gottlieb 1995; Brueckner et al. 1999). Previously, I found that, in the Netherlands, the more polycentric a region, the less cultural, leisure and sports amenities were present. Conversely, the more monocentric a region was, the more these amenities were present (Meijers 2008a). Part of the explanation is that larger cities tend to get a disproportionately larger share of national tax revenues and central government spending, which obviously favours the financial base of monocentric metropolitan areas over polycentric ones. Another important explanation for the reason why urbanisation economies seem to be less present in polycentric metropolitan areas is that they are probably characterised by a less diversified economic structure. Polycentric metropolitan areas differ from monocentric ones in that they are characterised by less people living in urban areas, and that the largest city in the metro area is much smaller (see Table 7.2 before). However, urban size and diversity are strongly positively linked (Henderson 1997). For polycentric metropolitan areas in North-West Europe it was found that complementarities between the cities in such areas are rather low (Meijers 2007a), which does not foster diversity. Diversity is also not enhanced by the simple fact that different cities within a polycentric metropolitan area tend to share a long history of rivalry and competition. It has been suggested that interurban competition leads to duplication rather than complementarity: "The most oft-noted drawback of inter-territorial competition is serial reproduction, the imitation and replication of the same ideas from place to place" (Malecki 2004, p. 1112). Cities tend to market the same kind of images (Holcomb 1994) and copy each others successes as regards urban redevelopment projects, innovations and investments (Harvey 1989). Consequently, polycentric metropolitan areas appear to be less diversified.

So, only in the best-case scenario can we find localisation economies at the scale of polycentric metropolitan areas, and it is highly likely that urbanisation economies are less present in polycentric metropolitan areas compared to monocentric ones. It seems that this leaves only one explanation for the – from a theoretical perspective perhaps surprising – finding that productivity and wages are higher in a polycentric metropolitan area. This explanation is that there are less agglomeration diseconomies in polycentric metropolitan areas. Our findings suggest that smaller cities are better capable of limiting agglomeration disadvantages such as congestion, social problems, environmental concerns and crime. A more precise comparison of how typical agglomeration economies and agglomeration diseconomies develop in polycentric metropolitan areas is needed to certify this assumption. For the moment being, we may assume that the balance between agglomeration economies and agglomeration diseconomies is better in polycentric metro areas, leading to 'borrowed size' effects of an 11 % increase in labor productivity and an 5.7 % increase in wages. Our findings therefore support recent hints in the literature to conceptualize external economies in relational terms: external economies are 'not merely the exclusive properties of single bounded localities but shared increasingly among a number of places' (Phelps and Ozawa, 2003, p. 584).

Acknowledgement The paper has benefited from comments received during the workshop on 'Metropolitan Regions: Preconditions and Strategies for Growth and Development in the Global Economy', held in April 2008 in Linköping, Sweden, as well as from valuable comments by Martijn Burger and Erik Louw. The usual disclaimer applies. Financial support from the Netherlands Organisation for Scientific Research (NWO) is gratefully acknowledged.

References

Albrechts L (1998) The Flemish diamond: precious gem and virgin area. Eur Plann Stud 6:411–424
Albrechts L (2001) How to proceed from image and discourse to action: as applied to the Flemish diamond. Urban Stud 38:733–745
Alonso W (1973) Urban zero population growth. Daedalus 109:191–206
Anas A, Arnott R, Small KA (1998) Urban spatial structure. J Econ Lit 36:1426–1464
Bailey N, Turok I (2001) Central Scotland as a polycentric urban region: useful planning concept or chimera? Urban Stud 38:697–715
Batten DF (1995) Network cities: creative urban agglomerations for the twenty-first century. Urban Stud 32:313–327
Boix R, Trullén J (2007) Knowledge, networks of cities and growth in regional urban systems. Pap Reg Sci 86:551–574
Brakman S, Garretsen H, Gorter J, van der Horst A, Schramm M (2005) New economic geography, empirics, and regional policy. Special publication 56. Centraal Planbureau, The Hague
Brueckner JK, Thisse J-F, Zenou Y (1999) Why is central Paris rich and downtown Detroit poor? An amenity-based theory. Eur Econ Rev 43:91–107
Burton I (1963) A restatement of the dispersed city hypothesis. Ann Assoc Am Geogr 63:285–289

Camagni R (1993) From city hierarchy to city networks: reflections about an emerging paradigm. In: Lakshmanan TR, Nijkamp P (eds) Structure and change in the space economy: festschrift in honour of Martin Beckmann. Springer Verlag, Berlin, pp 66–87

Capello R (2000) The city network paradigm: measuring urban network externalities. Urban Stud 37:1925–1945

Capello R, Camagni R (2000) Beyond optimal city size: an evaluation of alternative urban growth patterns. Urban Stud 37:1479–1496

Carbonell A, Yaro RD (2005) American spatial development and the new megalopolis. Land Lines: Newsletter of the Lincoln Institute of Land Policy 17(2):1–4

Catin M (1995) Economies d'agglomération. Revue d'Economie Régionale et Urbaine 4:1–20

CEC, Commission of the European Communities (1999) European spatial development perspective: towards balanced and sustainable development of the territory of the EU. Office for Official Publications of the European Communities, Luxembourg

Champion AG (2001) A changing demographic regime and evolving polycentric urban regions: consequences for the size composition and distribution of city populations. Urban Stud 38: 657–677

Cheshire P (1999) Trends in sizes and structures of urban areas. In: Cheshire P, Mills ES (eds) Handbook of regional and urban economics, vol 3. Elsevier Science, Amsterdam, pp 1339–1372

Ciccone A (2002) Agglomeration effects in Europe. Eur Econ Rev 46:213–227

Ciccone A, Hall RE (1996) Productivity and the density of economic activity. Am Econ Rev 86: 54–70

Davoudi S (2003) Polycentricity in European spatial planning: from an analytical tool to a normative agenda. Eur Plann Stud 11:979–999

Dieleman FM, Faludi A (1998) Polynucleated metropolitan regions in Northwest Europe: theme of the special issue. Eur Plann Stud 6:365–377

IGEAT (Institut de Gestion de l'Environnement et d'Aménagement du Territoire, ULB) et al (2007) ESPON 1.4.3 Study on urban functions, project report. ULB/ESPON monitoring committee, Brussels/Luxembourg. See www.espon.eu

Florida R (2002) The rise of the creative class; and how it's transforming work, leisure, community & everyday life. Basic Books, New York

Florida R, Gulden T, Mellander C (2008) The rise of the mega-region. Camb J Reg Econ Soc 1:459–476

Fujii T, Hartshorn TA (1995) The changing metropolitan structure of Atlanta Georgia: locations of functions and regional structure in a multinucleated urban area. Urban Geogr 16:680–707

Funderburg RG, Boarnet MG (2008) Agglomeration potential: the spatial scale of industry linkages in the Southern California economy. Growth Change 39:24–57

Garreau J (1991) Edge city: life on the new frontier. Doubleday, New York

Glaeser EL (1998) Are cities dying? J Econ Perspect 12:139–160

Glaeser EL, Kahn ME (2001) Decentralized employment and the transformation of the American city. Working paper 8117, National Bureau of Economic Research

Glaeser E, Kolko J, Saiz A (2001) Consumer city. J Econ Geogr 1:27–50

Gordon P, Richardson HW (1996) Beyond polycentricity: the dispersed metropolis, Los Angeles, 1970–1990. J Am Plann Assoc 62:289–295

Gottlieb PD (1995) Residential amenities firm location and economic development. Urban Stud 32:1413–1436

Gottmann J (1961) Megalopolis, the urbanized northeastern seaboard of the United States. The Twentieth Century Fund, New York

Graham DJ (2005) Wide economic benefits of transport improvements: link between agglomeration and productivity. Imperial College London, London

Green N (2007) Functional polycentricity: a formal definition in terms of social network analysis. Urban Stud 44:2077–2103

7 Metropolitan Labor Productivity and Urban Spatial Structure

Harvey D (1989) From managerialism to entrepreneurialism: the transformation of urban governance in late capitalism. Geogr Ann 71B:3–17

Henderson V (1997) Medium size cities. Reg Sci Urban Econ 27:583–612

Holcomb B (1994) City make-overs: marketing the post-industrial city. In: Gold JR, Ward SV (eds) Place promotion: the use of publicity and marketing to sell towns and regions. Wiley, Chichester, pp 115–131

Hoover E, Vernon R (1959) Anatomy of a metropolis. Harvard University Press, Boston

Jacobs J (1969) The economy of cities. Random House, New York

Johansson B, Quigley JM (2004) Agglomeration and networks in spatial economies. Pap Reg Sci 83:165–176

Kawashima T (1975) Urban agglomeration economies in manufacturing industries. Pap Reg Sci Assoc 34:157–175

Kennedy PE (1981) Estimation with correctly interpreted dummy variables in semilogarithmic equations. Am Econ Rev 71:801

Kloosterman RC, Lambregts B (2001) Clustering of economic activities in polycentric urban regions: the case of the Randstad. Urban Stud 38:717–732

Kloosterman RC, Musterd S (2001) The polycentric urban region: towards a research agenda. Urban Stud 38:623–633

Lambooy JG (1998a) Polynucleation and economic development: the Randstad. Eur Plann Stud 6:457–466

Lambooy JG (2004) Geschakelde metropolen en de tussengebieden. Essay t.b.v. VROM-raad advies 043: Nederlandse steden in internationaal perspectief: profileren en verbinden. See www.vromraad.nl

Lambregts L, Zonneveld W (2004) From Randstad to Deltametropolis: changing attitudes towards the scattered metropolis. Eur Plann Stud 12:299–321

Lang RE (2003) Edgeless cities: exploring the elusive metropolis. Brookings Institution Press, Washington

Lang RE, Dhavale D (2005) America's megalopolitan areas. Land Lines: Newsletter of the Lincoln Institute of Land Policy 17(3):1–4

Larsen K (2005) Cities to come: Clarence Stein's postwar regionalism. J Plann Hist 4:33–51

Lee B (2007) "Edge" or "Edgeless" cities? Urban spatial structure in U.S. metropolitan areas, 1980 to 2000. J Reg Sci 47:479–515

Lee B, Gordon P (2007) Urban spatial structure and economic growth in US metropolitan areas. Paper presented at the 46th annual meeting of the Western Regional Science Association, Newport Beach

Malecki EJ (2004) Jockeying for position: what it means and why it matters to regional development policy when places compete. Reg Stud 38:1101–1120

Meijers E (2005) Polycentric urban regions and the quest for synergy: is a network of cities more than the sum of the parts? Urban Stud 42(4):765–781

Meijers E (2007a) Clones or complements? The division of labour between the main cities of the Randstad, the Flemish diamond and the RheinRuhr area. Reg Stud 41:889–900

Meijers E (2007b) From central place to network model: theory and evidence of a paradigm change. Tijdschrift voor Economische en Sociale Geografie 98:245–259

Meijers E (2008a) Summing small cities does not make a large city: polycentric urban regions and the provision of cultural, leisure and sports amenities. Urban Stud 45(11):2323–2342

Meijers E (2008b) Measuring polycentricity and its promises. Eur Plann Stud 16(9):1313–1323

Meijers E, Romein A (2003) Realizing potential: building regional organizing capacity in polycentric urban regions. Eur Urban Reg Stud 10:173–186

Meijers E, Sandberg K (2008) Reducing regional disparities by means of polycentric development: panacea or placebo? Scienze Regionali Italian J Reg Sci 7(2):71–96

Meijers E, Hoekstra J, Aguado R (2008) Strategic planning for city networks: the emergence of a Basque global city? Int Plann Stud 13(3):239–259

Moulaert F, Djellal F (1995) Information technology consultancy firms: economies of agglomeration from a wide-area perspective. Urban Stud 32:105–122

Mueller B (2001) Urban networks and polycentric spatial development in Europe – the case of Germany. EUREG 9:40–46

Nordregio et al (2004) ESPON 1.1.1: potentials for polycentric development in Europe, project report. Nordregio/ESPON Monitoring Committee, Stockholm/Luxembourg

Organisation for Economic Co-operation and Development (OECD) (2006) Competitive cities in the global economy, OECD territorial reviews. OECD, Paris

Parr JB (2002a) Agglomeration economies: ambiguities and confusions. Environ Plann A 34:717–731

Parr JB (2002b) Missing elements in the analysis of agglomeration economies. Int Reg Sci Rev 25: 151–168

Parr JB (2004) The polycentric urban region: a closer inspection. Reg Stud 38:231–240

Phelps NA (1992) External economies, agglomeration and flexible production. Trans Inst Brit Geogr NS 17:35–46

Phelps NA, Fallon RJ, Williams CL (2001) Small firms, borrowed size and the urban–rural shift. Reg Stud 35:613–624

Phelps NA, Ozawa T (2003) Contrasts in agglomeration: proto-industrial, industrial and post-industrial forms compared. Prog Human Geogr 27:583–604

Porter ME (1990) The competitive advantage of nations. The Free Press, New York

Priemus H (1994) Planning the Randstad: between economic growth and sustainability. Urban Stud 31:509–534

Quigley JM (1998) Urban diversity and economic growth. J Econ Perspect 12:127–138

Richardson HW (1995) Economies and diseconomies of agglomeration. In: Giersch H (ed) Urban agglomeration and economic growth. Springer, Berlin, pp 123–155

Rosenthal SS, Strange WC (2004) Evidence on the nature and sources of agglomeration economies. In: Henderson JV, Thisse J-F (eds) Handbook of regional and urban economics, vol 4, Cities and geography. Elsevier, Amsterdam, pp 2119–2171

Scott AJ (1998) Regions and the world economy: the coming shape of global production, competition, and political order. Oxford University Press, Oxford

Strange W (2005) Urban agglomeration. Forthcoming in Durlauf S, Blume L (eds) New Palgrave dictionary of economics (2nd edn). Macmillan, London

Turok I, Bailey N (2004) The theory of polynuclear urban regions and its application to central Scotland. Eur Plann Stud 12:371–389

van Oort FG (2004) Urban growth and innovation, spatially bounded externalities in the Netherlands. Ashgate, Aldershot

Chapter 8
Wages, Productivity and Industry Composition

Agglomeration Economies in Swedish Regions

Johan Klaesson and Hanna Larsson

Abstract It is a well known fact that wages have a tendency to be higher in larger regions. The source of the regional difference in wages between larger and smaller areas can be broadly divided into two parts. The first part can be attributed to the fact that regions have different industrial compositions. The second part is due to the fact that average regional productivity differs between regions. Using a decomposition method, akin to shift-share, we are able to separate regional wage disparities into an industrial composition component and productivity component. According to theory it is expected that productivity is higher in larger regions due to different kinds of economies of agglomeration. Also, larger regions are able to host a wider array of sectors compared to smaller regions. Output from sectors demanding a large local or regional market can only locate in larger regions. Examples of such sectors are e.g. various types of advanced services with high average wages. The purpose of the paper is to explain regional differences in wages and the productivity and composition components, respectively.

The paper tests the dependence of wages, productivity and industrial composition effects on regional size (using a market potential measure). In the estimation we control for regional differences in education, employment shares, average firm size and self-employment. Swedish regional data from 2004 are used. The results verify that larger regions on average have higher wages, originating from higher productivity and more favorable industry composition.

Keywords Agglomeration economies • Regions • Wages • Productivity • Industrial composition • Sweden

---

J. Klaesson (✉) • H. Larsson
Jönköping International Business School, Jönköping University, PO Box 1026, Jönköping 551 11, Sweden
e-mail: johan.klaesson@jibs.hj.se; hanna.larsson@jibs.hj.se

J. Klaesson et al. (eds.), *Metropolitan Regions*, Advances in Spatial Science,
DOI 10.1007/978-3-642-32141-2_8, © Springer-Verlag Berlin Heidelberg 2013

1 Introduction

In many places in the literature it is emphasized that concentration is a prevalent and ubiquitous feature of the geographical distribution of economic activity. This is true at all geographic levels (regional, national, international) and at all levels of industrial aggregation; with the possible exception of some primary industries. This general observation is a strong indication that there are economies connected to concentration of activities, were larger regions are premiered over smaller. There are many studies that are concerned with the sources of these economies and the effects that they have on efficiency and growth. One such effect is the translation of efficiency to wage levels. Research connected to the prevailing wage differences within nations is important for a better understanding of regional development, which in turn will have an effect on national welfare.

The regional difference in wages between larger and smaller regions can be broadly attributed to two sources. The first source is the fact that average regional productivity differs between regions. The second source is that the industrial composition differs between regions.

According to economic theory it is expected that productivity is higher in larger regions due to different kinds of economies of agglomeration. The conventional macroeconomic view is that productivity growth in turn drives wage growth. Also, larger regions are able to host a larger array of sectors compared to smaller regions. Output from sectors demanding a large local or regional market can only locate in larger regions.

Given the above discussion it is clear that there exist a basic link between market-size and diversity. The extent of diversity is limited to an upper level due to the presence of fixed costs in the individual intermediate input-producing firms. This relationship implies that the size of a region will decide the degree of diversification in intermediaries. This has an impact on the productivity of all firms in the region. Thus, agglomeration provides a large market and thereby enabling the support of a wide variety of differentiated inputs. As a result of economies of scale and increasing returns, the productivity of firms in the larger agglomerations can be expected to be higher. This gives a rationale for why many firms tend to locate in agglomerations.

This leads us to the purpose of this paper were the aim is to explain the regional differences in wages, productivity and industrial composition. The paper tests the dependence of wages, productivity and industrial composition effects on regional size which in turn is measured with a market potential measure. In addition, in the estimation we control for regional differences in education, employment shares, average firm size and self-employment.

There exists a large and expanding literature concerning the regional differences in productivity and wage rates. Ciccone and Hall (1996) was not the first study that examined the relationship between productivity and economies of agglomeration, but surely one of the most influential. In this seminal study agglomeration was approximated by economic density, calculated as employment per acre.

Since then several studies have deepened and broadened the literature in these matters. Glaeser and Mare (2001) for example used wage data to investigate the wage premium paid to workers in larger cities.

More recent studies by Ciccone (2002); Rice et al. (2006) and Combes et al. (2008) argue that spatial differences in income can be ascribed to productivity differences. Higher or lower productivity is in turn assumed to be reflected in value added per unit of labor, or in earnings. Their analyses have focused on three main explanations for spatial differences in wages and productivity: (1) agglomeration economies (2) skill or industry composition and (3) exogenous regional characteristics. This paper adheres to this literature, but extends it by introducing accessibility to Gross Regional Product (GRP) as a measure for regional market potential.

The paper is structured as follows. It continues in Sect. 2 with a more in-depth discussion on the relationship between agglomeration, productivity and industry composition. The relationship of the paper to the existing literature is discussed. Also, the selection of the control variables is discussed. In Sect. 3 the data used is presented in conjunction with a descriptive analysis. Section 4 present the empirical results from the estimated models. Section 5 offers some additional tests of the robustness of the results. The closing section summarizes the conclusions and gives suggestions for interesting future research.

2 Regional Differences in Wages

As has been briefly discussed in the introduction, regions with larger market size on average can be expected to have a higher average wage level, due to different forms of scale economies. This section will continue the arguments as well as motivate the various control variables used in the present study. Furthermore, a short description of the features of the Swedish labor market is also offered.

2.1 Agglomeration Economies

Economies of agglomeration means that cost reductions occur because economic activities are located in proximity to each other. The concept itself goes back to Weber ([1909] 1929) and Marshall (1920). Economies of agglomeration are also sometimes referred to as external economies of scale. That is, the agglomeration economies are external to the individual firms. Consequently, over time an abundance of concepts and elaborations of the general concept of agglomeration economies have evolved. (see McDonald 1997)

Ohlin (1933), categorized economies of agglomeration into four types: (1) economies of scale within the firm, (2) localization economies, which are external to the individual firm and arise from the size of the local industry to which the firm belongs, (3) urbanization economies, which are more general in that it refers to cost reductions that are external to the local industry and arise from the size of the local economy as a whole and (4) inter-industry linkages, which arise from transportation cost savings in purchases of intermediate inputs.

Before Ohlin's categorization, Marshall (1920) had already suggested three reasons for cost reductions to occur in an agglomeration. The first reason is due to knowledge spillovers, i.e. the spread of advances/innovations in production is assumed to be influenced by distance. The second explanation is the existence of a broad market for specialized skills. Specialized employees gain from having nearby access to many jobs that match their specialty. The benefits also go in the other direction. Firms benefit from having accessibility to a large pool of specialized employees matching their requirements. The third reason is the existence of backward and forward linkages between firms that are located in proximity to each other. The proximity means that the transport of inputs and outputs will be relatively inexpensive.

Hoover (1937), later made use of Ohlin's second and third categories, localization economies and urbanization economies, as he elaborated and popularized the two concepts. Hoover's definitions are the ones most often used to this present day. Localization economies can be captured by independent and similar small businesses in the form of positive external economies by locating in proximity of each other. This proximity between similar firms creates a market for specialized services, which can be provided by other independent firms as long as the total demand is great enough. In addition, it is possible to build up a local pool of labor with specialized skills. In this way, the businesses can take advantage of scale economies in production without resorting to large plants. The actual advantage over large-scale plants is that independence and flexibility are retained. Urbanization economies can bring about scale advantages that benefit a wider group of businesses. If, for example, general manufacturing increases in a particular area, the business services and workforce improve in size and variety. These advantages do not only relate to one sector of industry but to all. If educational standards improve, or if trucking companies expand their route network, every business will benefit.

Further, agglomeration economies can be differentiated as being predominantly static or dynamic in nature. In general a static economy of agglomeration is associated with a onetime shift in costs or productivity whereas a dynamic economy of agglomeration influences costs and productivity through time. Dynamic agglomeration economies are usually connected to the production and use of knowledge. This is at the heart of the endogenous growth theory (Romer 1986; Lucas 1988). Knowledge spillovers are an essential ingredient in this theory and since spillovers are facilitated by proximity between people and firms concentration and agglomeration are key concepts.

The empirical literature that aims to identify the sources of economies of agglomeration is reviewed in Rosenthal and Strange (2004).

2.2 Wages and Regional Characteristics

As hinted above some sources of regional wage differences work through scale economies. But there are several different ways for those to manifest themselves. For instance, differences in wages across regions could directly reflect spatial differences in the skill level and composition of the workforce. Theory argues that the division of labor, which leads to productivity gains, is limited by the extent of the market. Then naturally, workers in larger markets may enjoy higher wages because of greater possibilities for the division of labor.

According to Combes et al. (2008) there are reasons to believe that workers may spread across employment areas so that the measured and un-measured productive abilities of the local labor force may vary. Industries are not uniformly spread across regions and they require different combinations of labor skills. Accordingly, one should expect a higher mean wage in areas specialized in more skill-intensive industries. This brings us into the discussion on industry composition and wages.

Different industries or sectors differ in their ability to pay high wages. The difference in this ability may come from the competitive situation in that particular industry or the availability of factor inputs. Since regions differ in their industry structure, it is likely that some of the regional wage differences can be explained by these structural differences. Thereby some part of the wage differences across areas reflects spatial differences in industry structure. These differences may not be directly connected to regional productivity differences.

Combes and Overman (2004) argues that failure to control for heterogeneous skill composition between regions may significantly limit the interpretation that can be given to regional differences in labor productivity or wages. Hence, higher wages or productivity might not reflect real externalities if not taking labor skill composition into account.

Non-market interactions such as technological externalities, and in particular those originating from human capital, may also play an important role in explaining wage differences between regions (Rauch 1993). Sianesi and van Reenen (2003) presents a detailed literature review which provide strong evidence in favor of the view that the amount of human capital is positively correlated to productivity. Rauch (1993) argues that the level of human capital is a local public good, hence, regions or cities with higher levels of education attainment should consequently have higher wages. Rauch base this argument on 1980 US cross-sectional data on a regional level. Glaeser and Mare (2001) suggest that urban workers are more productive because cities enable workers to accumulate more human capital. This accumulation can work through more effective knowledge spillovers, proximity between skilled workers and between knowledge-intensive firms, in regions where knowledge are abundant and dense. These spillovers rely on face-to-face contacts that are more likely to occur in such knowledge-intensive regions. Knowledge can be transmitted either as a by-product that is non-intentional or in more formal types of collaborations.

Previous studies point to yet another regional characteristic that have a positive effect on productivity and wage levels. This characteristic is firm size. The size of a firm influences the possibility to exploit internal economies of scale, and as a consequence, positively influence labor productivity. Extensive research in the field confirms that larger firms tend to pay higher wages than smaller ones; see Moore (1911), later confirmed by Mellow (1982); Brown and Medoff (1989); Troske (1999) among several others. Average firm size in a region is, hence, an important component when explaining regional wage variation. According to Glaeser et al. (1992) firm size may also affect the level of productivity if it is related to market power, where the effect itself is ambiguous a priori. A large monopolistic firm may have higher incentive to conduct R&D due to a higher probability of retrieving the returns (Romer 1990) while at the same time small firms may experience a higher market pressure to innovate in order to stay competitive (Porter 1990).

Wages should logically also be influenced by the level of (un-)employment in the region. If the scarcity of labor increases wages go up, while if it decreases they will fall. In 1994 Blanchflower and Oswald presented their book "The Wage Curve", where they established a negative relation between unemployment and wages across regions over time.[1] Blanchflower and Oswald (1994) found that the employment elasticity of wages is, for most countries, approximately −0.1, with the US and UK being the main focus of the study. Since then several studies have been presented with mixed conclusions. A study by Albæk et al. (2000), analyzing pooled data on regional wage formation in the Nordic countries during the 1990s, systematically deviate from the results presented by Blanchflower and Oswald (1994). Even though Albæk et al. (2000) found a significant negative relationship between real wages and unemployment at the regional level, this relationship becomes unstable once accounting for regional fixed effects. The authors explain these results by the historically strong labor unions that negotiate wages at the national level in the Nordic countries. This negotiating model implies that there is only a small local wage drift influenced by the regional labor market conditions. According to Nijkamp and Poot (2005) the variation in findings within this field is a response to heterogeneity among the studies in terms of the type of data used and differences in model specification. In order to verify this Nijkamp & Poot performed a meta-analysis revealing that the wage curve is a robust empirical phenomenon. However, they also found clear evidence of a publication bias and when correcting for this bias the elasticity becomes less than −0.07.

Some emphasis should also be put on the rate of self-employment when explaining regional variations in wages. According to research, self-employment can work in dual ways when influencing regional wages. On the one hand high unemployment rates in a region may cause entrepreneurial activities, such as self-employment, to increase. This is referred to as a so called refugee effect, since the

---

[1] Blanchflower and Oswald (1990). . Refer to 16 previous studies in this topic between 1985 and 1990. The earliest study is by Bils 1985, who also supported an unemployment – wage elasticity of − 0.1.

8 Wages, Productivity and Industry Composition 173

prospect of other forms of employment is small. The relationship between wage rates and unemployment is expected to be negative. On the other hand, higher levels of self-employment may be a sign of true entrepreneurial ventures, referred to as a entrepreneurial effect, which, in the long-run, will reduce unemployment Thurik et al. (2007) and hence have positive effect on the regional wage level. There exists considerable theoretical and empirical support for both of these views.

While Oxenfeldt (1943) argues that low prospects for wage-employment will cause a higher self-employment level, Audretsch and Fritsch (1994) on the contrary found that this relation is negative. In a recent study Thurik et al. (2007) tested this ambiguity by using a two-equation vector autoregression model, for a panel of 23 OECD countries over the period 1974–2002. The result reveal that changes in unemployment have a positive impact on changes in self-employment rates, while simultaneously changes in self-employment rates have a negative impact on unemployment. However, the latter effect is stronger than the first one.

In addition, due to the assumption of total labor mobility the role of amenities will according to Roback (1982) also influences regional wage differences. In Roback's model, worker utility depends on the wage level, the price of land, and a vector of potential lifestyle or amenity characteristics. Wages and rents must adjust to equalize utility in all occupied locations. Otherwise some workers would have an incentive to move. Roback (1982) and more recent studies such as Graves et al. (1999) have included variables such as: education levels, crime rates, number of people living under the poverty line, congestion levels, local unemployment, weather conditions, population density and size etc., as proxies for the role played by amenities when investigating regional wage differences.

Criticism towards the "city size wage premium" has also been raised since it is plausible to imagine that workers with above average ability and motivation have a "lifestyle" preference for living in larger regions. Glaeser and Mare (2001) however, reject the argument that such omitted ability bias explains the city wage premium. They do so because including direct measures of ability (the AFQT test), instrumenting for place of birth, and then studying wages all fails to eliminate this wage premium.

There is also ample evidence of inter-industry wage differences that are related to institutional features such as unionization and not to productivity (Wheaton and Lewis, 2002) or industry composition.

2.3 The Functioning of the Swedish Labor Market

To enable us to fully interpret the results it is of some importance to take a closer look at the Swedish labor market and its dynamics. At the heart of "the Swedish model" is a system of collective bargaining between trade unions and employers' associations. Sweden distinguishes itself from most other countries in that the level of membership unions and other labor markets organizations is extremely high. Due to historical traditions the Swedish labor market has become centralized.

Central wage agreements are set by the labor unions and representatives from the employers to obtain low levels of income differences compared to most other countries.

Calmfors (1993a, b) argues that a highly centralized wage setting system causes wage levels to increase considerably slower compared to not so centralized systems. This leads to higher employment levels, which is at the heart of the Swedish model.

Calmfors (1993a, b) further states that the highest level of real wage increases is obtained in a system which lies in-between decentralization and centralization, i.e. wage agreements at the industry level. Up until 1983 the Swedish wage setting system was a text-book example of a highly centralized negotiation scheme (Lindgren 2006). Since then Sweden has moved towards a more decentralized system. At present, once framework agreements are set centrally for the corresponding employment sectors, individual collective agreements can be negotiated between employers and trade unions at a local level. A standard collective agreement is therefore not automatically applicable to all regions or to an entire industrial sector. The system is thus more flexible than before.

3 Data and Descriptive Analysis

As stated in the theoretical background, we assume that variation in average earnings mainly comes from two sources; (1) differences in the wage rates paid to workers in a given sector arising from productivity deviations across regions, (2) and differences in the industrial composition between regions. To be able to discriminate between these sources we use a method applied in Rice et al. (2006). Analogous to that study we decompose regional wages into two components, referred to as the productivity and industry composition indices. We do this in order to assess the impacts on these indices by agglomeration effects as well as the different control variables presented in the previous section. Swedish regional data from 2004 are used for this study, were the definition of a region is municipalities with local governments. There are 290 such regions in Sweden.

The decomposition is described in the following seven equations.

We start with four definitions (Eqs. 8.1, 8.2, 8.3, and 8.4).

$$w_r^s = \text{wage in sector } s \text{ in region } r \tag{8.1}$$

$$e_r^s = \text{employment in sector } s \text{ in region } r \tag{8.2}$$

$$E_r = \sum_s e_r^s = \text{total employment in region } r \tag{8.3}$$

$$\sigma_r^s = \frac{e_r^s}{E_r} = \text{employment share in sector } s \text{ in region } r \tag{8.4}$$

8 Wages, Productivity and Industry Composition

Next, using the definitions in Eqs. 8.1 and 8.2 we construct a measure for the average wage level in sector s.

$$\bar{w}^s = \frac{\sum_r e_r^s w_r^s}{\sum_r e_r^s} = \text{average wage in sector } s \tag{8.5}$$

Using 8.2 and 8.3 we form the total employment share in sector s.

$$\bar{\sigma}^s = \frac{\sum_r e_r^s}{\sum_i E_r} = \text{share of total employment in sector } s \tag{8.6}$$

Combining Eqs. 8.5 and 8.6 gives us the decomposed wage identity.

$$\bar{w}_r = \sum_s w_r^s \sigma_r^s = \sum_s w_r^s \bar{\sigma}^s + \sum_s \bar{w}^s \sigma_r^s + \sum_s \left(w_r^s - \bar{w}^s \right)\left(\sigma_r^s - \bar{\sigma}^s \right) - \sum_k \bar{w}^s \bar{\sigma}^s \tag{8.7}$$

where $\bar{w}_r$ is the average wage in region r. $\sum_s w_r^s \bar{\sigma}^s$ denotes the productivity index, where the industrial composition is assumed fixed at the average national level across regions. Thus, the variation in this index reflects the regional productivity differences. $\sum_s \bar{w}^s \sigma_r^s$ is the industrial composition index in which regional differences is attributed to differences in the composition of sectors in different regions. In this index the wages across sectors are assumed to be fixed at the average national level. The variation in this index represents the variation of the regional industry composition. The remaining terms in Eq. 8.7 represents the covariances between the industry employment shares and wages in region r.

Table 8.1 below presents the variables that we are using in the empirical analysis.

In Figs. 8.5, 8.6, and 8.7 found in Appendix 1 the correlation between the three variables wage, productivity index, and industrial composition index and our measure of market potential is displayed. The three figures all reveal a weak but positive relation to market potential.

The correlation matrix presented in Table 8.5 naturally show strong correlations between the three dependent variables, since the indices are derived from average wage. The correlation coefficients between the dependent variables and the market potential variable, accessibility to GRP, vary between 0.559 and 0.331. Two of the control variables, average firm size and self employment have a strong correlation vis-à-vis the three dependent variables. The self employment variable is the only variable that shows a negative relationship. This seems to indicate a "refugee" effect in terms of entrepreneurial activities. Education also presents high correlation values.

Furthermore, the descriptive statistics presented in Table 8.6 in Appendix 1 show that there is a large variation in the variables across Swedish regions. This is especially true for the control variables accessibility to GRP and education, but also

Table 8.1 Description of variables used

	Variable	Description	Expected sign
Dependent variables	Regional wage level (wage $= \overline{w}_r$)	The total wage sum in region r divided by the number of employees	
	Productivity index (Prod $= \sum_s w_r^s \bar{\sigma}^s$)	Weighted sum of the average earnings for each industry group in region r with the weights equal to average country share of the industry group in relation to total employment. The industry groups are divided into a two digit level	
	Industrial composition index (Comp $= \sum_s \bar{w}^s \sigma_r^s$)	Weighted sum of the shares of each industry group in region r. The weight is the average country earnings in terms of the industry groups	
Independent variables	Market potential (AccGRP)[a]	Accessibility to GRP (gross regional product) in region r discounted from other regions by travel time distances using a distance decay function	+
	Education (Edu)	Population in working age (20–64) with more than 3 years of university education divided by working age population without university education in region r	+
	Firm size (Fsize)	Number of employees divided by number of business establishments in region r	+
	Employment share (Empshare)	Number of employees as a share of people in working age (20–64) in region r	+
	Self-employment (Semp)	Number of self-employed persons as a share of the population in working age (20–64) in region r	+/−

[a]Agglomeration is measured as accessibility to GRP. The measure is obtained through the following formula; $AccGRP_r = \sum_k GRP_k \exp(-\lambda d_{rk})$ were Accessibility to GRP for municipality r is equal to the sum of the GRP in all other municipalities k discounted by the distance between municipality r and all other municipalities k, d_{rk}. λ is a distance decay parameter estimated using commuting patterns (see Johansson, Klaesson and Olsson 2001)

in terms of the average wage level itself. This supports the idea that Sweden is characterized by substantial income disparities; wages in the lowest earning region is 55 % lower than the level earned in the highest wage region.[2]

---

[2] Calculations based on figures from Statistics Sweden, 2004

8 Wages, Productivity and Industry Composition

Fig. 8.1 Average wage

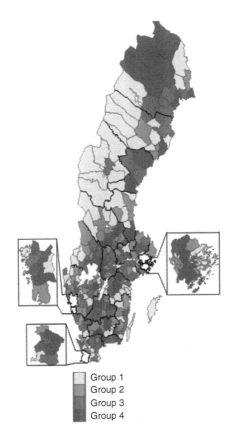

On the following two pages four different maps are provided in order to show the geographic distribution of the dependent variables. All the 289 included Swedish regions have been divided into four groups depending on their performance. High performing regions are marked in darker colors, group 3 and 4 respectively The real values and level of the intervals for the four different groups can be seen in Fig. 8.8 in Appendix 2.

Figure 8.1 displays the national variation in terms of average wages. One can see that it is especially areas in the three large city regions Stockholm, Gothenburg and Malmo which are marked as top-ranking. The map suggests that agglomeration in general has a substantial correlation with earnings since all dark areas are regions where Sweden's larger cities can be found; such as Linkoping/Norrkoping, Jonkoping and Karlstad etc. In terms of the lowest earning regions one can say that they often are rural, low populated regions with tendency to be located in the northern parts of Sweden. The fact that some of the northern regions are placed

Fig. 8.2 Productivity index

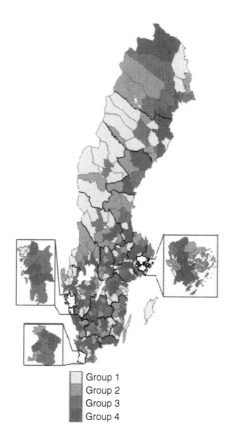

within group 3 and 4 can be explained by the high proportion of employed within the high-technology mining industry were wages traditionally has been very high.

When it comes to productivity, Fig. 8.2 reveals that it is once again predominately the regions within the large city areas that on average have a higher productivity index compared to the rest of Sweden. Once more the smaller regions far from a large market show the lowest levels of productivity. One can also observe that some of the "mining-municipalities" has a lower productivity level compared to wage, which can support the idea that there is a wage-premium in these areas to enable them to attract labor.

Figure 8.3 illustrates the geographical variation in terms of industry composition were more or less the same pattern is found as in terms of the wage and productivity distribution.

Fig. 8.3 Industry composition index

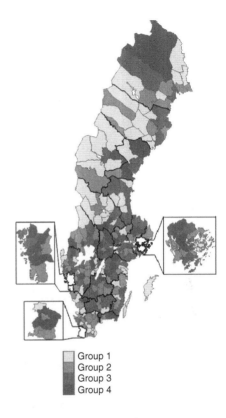

Finally, in Fig. 8.4 the accessibility to GRP clearly show that southern Sweden has a higher market potential than the south, this is most pronounced for regions situated in proximity to either Stockholm, Gothenburg or Malmo. All of the regions within these city areas belong to the highest rated group. The further away you get from these areas you will experience a fall in accessibility and market potential. Spikes in accessibility is then found in those regions that host medium-sized cities; e.g. Linkoping/Norrkoping, Jonkoping and Karlstad.

4 Empirical Results

Next let us turn to the empirical analysis of regional wages, productivity and industry composition. In the empirical models the estimated parameters are expressed as elasticities since all variables are logged.

The regression models to be estimated are:

$$ln\ wage = \beta_0 + \beta_1 \ln Fsize + \beta_2 \ln Semp + \beta_3 \ln Edu + \beta_4 \ln Empshare \\ + \beta_5 \ln AccGRP + \varepsilon \quad (8.8)$$

Fig. 8.4 Accessibility to GRP

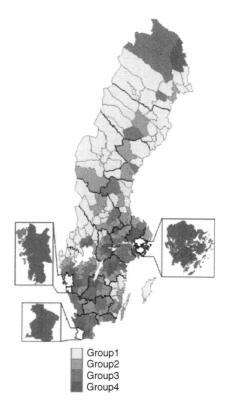

$$\ln prod = \beta_0 + \beta_1 \ln Fsize + \beta_2 \ln Semp + \beta_3 \ln Edu + \beta_4 \ln Empshare \\ + \beta_5 \ln AccGRP + \varepsilon \qquad (8.9)$$

$$\ln comp = \beta_0 + \beta_1 \ln Fsize + \beta_2 \ln Semp + \beta_3 \ln Edu + \beta_4 \ln Empshare \\ + \beta_5 \ln AccGRP + \varepsilon \qquad (8.10)$$

In order to check the robustness of the findings, the regression models are tested using three different methods. First a standard OLS approach is applied followed by spatial lag (SL) and spatial error (SE) models, adjusting for possible spatial autocorrelation. The SL and SE results can be found in Appendix 3. Additionally, instrumental variable (IV) estimation is applied to test for possible endogeneity problems.

4.1 Ordinary Least Squares

Table 8.2 below presents the OLS results for all the three regression models.

8 Wages, Productivity and Industry Composition

Table 8.2 Estimation results using OLS

	Wage	Prod.	Comp.
Market potential	0.017	0.018	0.009
	$(4.21)^{***}$	$(3.69)^{***}$	$(4.09)^{***}$
Education	0.046	0.105	−0.004
	$(5.06)^{***}$	$(8.42)^{***}$	(0.62)
Average firm size	0.057	0.059	0.022
	$(3.96)^{***}$	$(3.01)^{***}$	$(2.12)^{**}$
Employment	0.094	0.112	0.033
	$(4.84)^{***}$	$(4.89)^{***}$	$(2.83)^{***}$
Self-employment	−0.086	−0.046	−0.041
	$(6.10)^{***}$	$(2.48)^{**}$	$(3.92)^{***}$
Constant	11.962	12.099	12.177
	$(199.54)^{***}$	$(154.99)^{***}$	$(295.75)^{***}$
No. obs.	289	289	289
R^2	0.74	0.71	0.44

Robust t statistics in *parentheses*. *** significant at 1 % and ** significant at 5 % level

In Table 8.2, the OLS regression estimates are presented. The results clearly show that the three dependent variables, average wage, productivity and industry composition indices are significantly linked to the regional attributes.

The table displays that market potential, which is measured as accessibility to GRP, affects both productivity and industrial composition, and hence, the regional variation in average wages. The estimated elasticities reveals that a twice as large market potential is expected to have approximately 1.7 % higher wages. The productivity index is expected to be 1.8 % higher, and the industrial composition index is expected to be 0.9 % higher.

When comparing these results to earlier studies made in other countries, the elasticities seem to be lower in the case of Sweden. Factors that can explain this is (1) the use of accessibility to GRP as a measure of market potential, and (2) the functioning of the Swedish labor market, were wage differences traditionally has been comparatively low.

Table 8.2 also reveals how the control variables influence the regional variation in the dependent variables. As can been observed, all of the variables, with the exception of industry composition in relation to education, turn out to have a significant effect on wages, productivity and industry composition, respectively.

The results show that educational level in municipalities influence wages. It is, however, the productivity index which is most influenced by a high share of educated people in the region with an elasticity of 10.5 %, while there is no influence on the industrial composition index.

The second explanatory variable is average firm size in each municipality, which also turns out to have a significantly positive effect on all three dependent variables. Yet as in the case of education, the effect is found to be smallest for the industrial composition index. The results points to that there are significant effects from scale economies which are internal to the firms.

When it comes to the share of employed persons within the municipality the results are similar to that of the firm size variable. Higher competition among the employers to attract labor seems to increase wages.

The final control variable is the share of self-employed persons in a municipality. For all three dependent variables the effect is negative and significant. In particular, the negative influence is found to be the largest in terms of average wages. This supports the so called "refugee effect" discussed in earlier sections. Another explanation for the negative relation can also be the structure of the data set, were one cannot separate between incomes from self-employment or regular employment. For example an individual running his/her own business can withdraw or withhold money in irregular intervals, which implies that 1 year the dividend might be very high while being very low in a second period. If many self-employed chose to use the firm dividend to take out a small proportion as income during our reference year, this could then affect the outcome.

The explanatory powers of the regressions are very high for average wage and productivity where the R^2 is 71 % or higher. The weaker relationship for industry composition is confirmed by a lower R^2.

4.2 Testing for Endogeneity: IV Results

A problem connected to an analysis of the role played by agglomeration for productivity and income, relates to the fact that it is very hard to differentiate between two possible explanations for a positive correlation between productivity and agglomeration. Productivity and income may be high because of agglomeration effects; which is the underlying idea in this paper. However, there is also a possibility that agglomeration arises due to the fact that wages and productivity are high due to for example a positive regional specific shock which in turn attracts labor and firms. A recent study by Fu and Ross (2007) tests the above stated endogeneity problem; if wage premiums in clusters are caused by agglomeration economies or of regional characteristics, such as labor heterogeneity. Their result show that the causality runs from agglomeration to wage, and not the other way around.

However, if any of our local characteristics is endogenous in relation to the dependent variables, our models might omit unobserved abilities that will influence the results. If such omitted variables are also correlated with any right hand side variables, then a bias can result. Reverse-causality is hence potentially still a problem which must be tested for.

Furthermore, due to the model set-up another possible bias might arise. The reason is that we do not fully control for the type of labor or firms that are located in the agglomerations, hence there may be a selection bias present. Since some people and firms are more productive than others, this can result in varying levels of productivity and wages. This could explain the wage premium found in larger regions if we assume that more high-performing firms and individuals are located

8 Wages, Productivity and Industry Composition   183

Table 8.3 IV Estimation results for the wage equation

	Wage	Prod.	Comp.
Market potential	0.021	0.015	0.014
	(4.65)[***]	(3.14)[***]	(5.65)[***]
Education	0.042	0.111	-0.010
	(4.88)[***]	(8.94)[***]	(1.77)[*]
Average firm size	0.049	0.064	0.011
	(3.43)[***]	(3.12)[***]	(1.13)
Employment	0.096	0.100	0.041
	(5.15)[***]	(4.45)[***]	(3.80)[***]
Self-employment	−0.098	−0.049	-0.052
	(6.98)[***]	(2.50)[**]	(5.07)[***]
Constant	11.884	12.112	12.091
	(183.94)[***]	(143.08)[***]	(268.73)[***]
No. obs.	289	289	289
R^2	0.75	0.71	0.47

Dependent variable: wage
Robust t statistics in *parentheses*. [*] significant at 10 %, [**] significant at 5 % and [***] significant at 1 %

there. A study by Combes et al. (2009) however, confirms that productivity differences, and thus wage differences, predominantly can be explained by the presence of agglomeration economies.

The choice of the instruments is based on the assumption that the instrumental variables represents an exogenous regional characteristic that has lasting influence on localization decisions, and thus on agglomeration, but not on the present level of productivity and income. The instruments chosen are therefore: (1) municipal 1950 population, (2) population 1950 within 1 h driving distance, (3) municipal land area, (4) land area within 1 h driving distance, (5) dummies for municipalities belonging to Stockholm, Gothenburg and Malmo regions. The validity of these instruments refers to that they all in some way reflect the potential market size of a region. See Table 8.3 below for the IV results.

The IV estimates corroborates the findings from the OLS regressions presented in Table 8.2. However, when comparing the results to the OLS estimates there are some deviations in the elasticities for the control variables. In a majority of the cases the deviations among the elasticities are within the +/− 0.2 to 0.8 percentage bound. Especially it is for the self-employment, employment share and average firm size were the largest variations in comparison to the OLS results occur. The negative effect of self employment on average wages is 1.2 % higher than when estimating without instruments.

As stated earlier we have also used different spatial estimation techniques for both the OLS and IV regressions. Even though tests have indicated that there may be some problems with spatial regimes the results from these regressions do not differ in any significant way from the OLS estimations. (see Appendix 3, Table 8.7, 8.8, 8.9, 8.10, 8.11, and 8.12). This confirms the robustness of the results.

In summary we confirm earlier research by concluding that denser, larger firm dominating, more educated, and high employment areas are characterized by a higher wage on average.

5 Conclusion

The focus of this study has been to estimate regional agglomeration effects in Sweden. We have investigated how concentration and agglomeration influence regional wage levels. In addition, the regional average wage level has been decomposed into a regional productivity index and a regional industrial composition index.

In the productivity index the industrial composition are held constant and the average wage in a region is only influenced by the regional wage level per sector. The industrial composition index on the other hand, is calculated holding industrial sector wages constant across regions. The index is thus only influenced by industry composition. Using these indices we control for the fact that regions have different industry compositions and that the average regional productivity differs between regions.

In the empirical estimations we use the average regional wage level and the two indices as dependent variables. The major explanatory variable is our measure of agglomeration. As a proxy for agglomeration we use accessibility to gross regional product (GRP). This accessibility is calculated using municipal GRP for all regions and discounting them in space according to the driving time distance. Therefore, the measure takes into account both size effects and the spatial layout of the municipalities.

Also, in the regression analysis we control for other factors that may influence wage, productivity and industrial composition effects. These control variables are the education level in each municipality, the share of the working age population that holds a job, average firm size and the degree of self-employment.

The general result of the analysis is that economies of agglomeration are a prevalent feature across regions in Sweden. The results indicate that regional size (as measured by accessibility to GRP) influences productivity as well as industrial composition, and hence, the regional variation in average wages. The estimated elasticities show that a twice as large region is expected to have approximately 1.7 % higher wages. The productivity index is expected to be 1.8 % higher, and the industrial composition index is expected to be 0.9 % higher.

With reference to similar studies in other countries our estimated elasticities appear small. There are at least two factors that can potentially explain this result. The first is dependent on how agglomeration itself is measured. We use an accessibility measure while in the literature it is more common to use variables measuring regional size or density. The other factor has to do with the distribution of wages in Sweden. It is a well known fact that wage disparities are relatively small in Sweden. Wages are set in a collective bargaining between different unions and employer organizations.

Turning to the control variables, the education level in municipalities influence wages and, in particular, the productivity index (about twice as large effect), while there is no influence on the industrial composition index.

The share of employed people has a significant effect on all three dependent variables, but the size of effect on the industrial composition is about one third of the size compared to the other two.

The average size of the firms in each municipality has a significantly positive effect on all three dependent variables, but once again, the effect is the smallest for the industrial composition index. This points to that there are significant effects from scale economies that are internal to the firms.

The last explanatory variable is the share of self-employed people. For all three dependent variables the effect is negative and significant. In particular, the negative influence is the largest on the average wages.

In the estimation we have used some different spatial estimation techniques. Even though tests have indicated that there may be some problems with spatial regimes the results from these regressions do not differ in any significant way from the OLS estimations.

In addition, in the empirical analysis we have also used an instrumental variable approach to investigate possible bias from reverse causality from the dependent variables to the independent ones. Results indicate that this bias is probably small.

In this study, we have estimated relationships for the aggregate economy. Of course, it is quite possible that agglomeration effects differ between industries. Therefore, one way forward is to perform this kind of analysis on industrial aggregates. Especially, it should be interesting to compare different kinds of service sectors since it can be argued that they are more dependent on proximity to larger markets. Also, sectors with a high knowledge or R&D intensity may have more to gain from agglomerations, where knowledge spillovers can be expected to be more important.

One other possible way to continue and broaden the analysis is make use of the fact that our agglomeration proxy has the form of an accessibility variable. Since this variable is calculated using the time distance of the road network between municipalities it is possible to assess effects on wages, productivity and industrial composition from changes in the quality of the road infrastructure.

Appendix 1: Descriptive Statistics

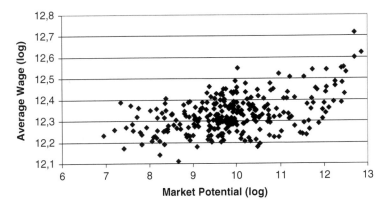

Fig. 8.5 Relationship between market potential and regional average wage

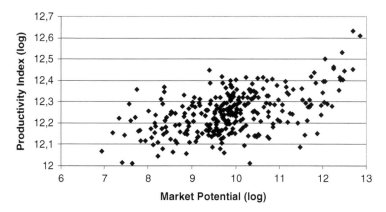

Fig. 8.6 Relationship between market potential and regional productivity index

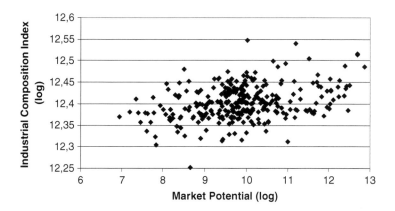

Fig. 8.7 Relationship between market potential and regional industrial composition index

In Table 8.4 the relationships between the three variables are presented.

Table 8.4 Relationship between productivity index, industrial composition index and average wages

Prod.index	0.680		0.496
	(21.88)***		(21.36)***
Comp.index		1.582	1.059
		(18.98)***	(18.48)***
Constant	4.007	−7.293	−6.886
	(10.53)***	(7.05)***	(10.70)***
Observations	289	289	289
R^2	0.63	0.56	0.83

*** significant at one per cent

8 Wages, Productivity and Industry Composition

Table 8.5 Correlation matrix

	Wage	Prod	Comp	AccGRP	Edu.	Empshare	Fsize	Selfem
Wage	1							
Prod.index	0.798	1						
Comp.index	0.747	0.433	1					
Acc. GRP	0.559	0.568	0.331	1				
Education	0.591	0.667	0.333	0.677	1			
Employ.share	0.430	0.374	0.336	−0.021	0.116	1		
Firm.size	0.750	0.635	0.613	0.246	0.318	0.542	1	
Selfemploy	−0.678	−0.572	−0.567	−0.264	−0.358	−0.187	−0.680	1

Table 8.6 Descriptive statistics

	Minimum	Maximum	Mean	Median	Std. deviation	Skewness
Wage	182074.56	333467.57	228062.34	227168.5	20322.98	1.12
Prod.index	164539.71	306625.15	209822.38	211247.0	21535.01	0.81
Comp.index	209460.61	281583.11	243793.33	244140.6	9945.66	0.41
Acc. GRP	1036.26	386378.32	39693.93	21279.5	59561.42	2.98
Education	0.09	0.85	0.19	0.17	.10	2.72
Employ.share	0.30	1.61	0.68	0.68	.14	0.70
Firm.size	1.52	9.29	3.43	3.38	1.32	1.061
Selfemploy	0.02	0.14	0.05	0.50	.01	0.94

Appendix 2: Regional Descriptive Statistics

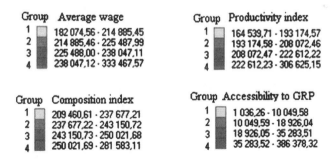

* Values measured in number of SEK

Fig. 8.8 Values corresponding to map groups

Appendix 3: Testing for Spatial Errors

SE = Spatial error model
SL = Spatial lag model

Table 8.7 Estimation results for the wage equation

	OLS	SL	SE
Ln Fsize	0.057	0.047	0.057
	$(3.96)^{***}$	$(3.31)^{***}$	$(3.60)^{***}$
Ln Semp	−0.086	−0.087	−0.079
	$(6.10)^{***}$	$(6.24)^{***}$	$(5.11)^{***}$
Ln Edu	0.046	0.044	0.040
	$(5.06)^{***}$	$(5.57)^{***}$	$(4.44)^{***}$
Ln Empshare	0.094	0.118	0.104
	$(4.84)^{***}$	$(6.50)^{***}$	$(5.28)^{***}$
Ln AccGRP	0.017	0.011	0.016
	$(4.21)^{***}$	$(2.99)^{***}$	$(3.28)^{***}$
Constant	11.962	6.244	11.987
	$(199.54)^{***}$	$(5.38)^{***}$	$(183.98)^{***}$
Obs.	289	289	289
R^2	0.74	0.77^a	0.74^a

Dependent variable: wage
Robust t statistics in *parentheses*. ***significant at 1 %
[a]Pseudo R-squared = ratio of the variance of the predicted values over the variance of the observed values for the dependent variable

Table 8.8 Estimation results for the productivity index equation

	OLS	SL	SE
Ln Fsize	0.059	0.056	0.058
	$(3.01)^{***}$	$(2.92)^{***}$	$(2.99)^{***}$
Ln Semp.	−0.046	−0.048	−0.047
	$(2.48)^{**}$	$(2.60)^{***}$	$(2.53)^{**}$
Ln Edu	0.105	0.105	0.106
	$(8.42)^{***}$	$(8.55)^{***}$	$(8.64)^{***}$
Ln Empshare	0.112	0.118	0.113
	$(4.89)^{***}$	$(5.24)^{***}$	$(4.98)^{***}$
Ln AccGRP	0.018	0.016	0.018
	$(3.69)^{***}$	$(2.80)^{***}$	$(3.80)^{***}$
Constant	12.099	10.791	12.097
	$(154.99)^{***}$	$(7.58)^{***}$	$(155.81)^{***}$
Obs.	289	289	289
R^2	0.71	0.72^a	0.71^a

Dependent variable: productivity index
Robust t statistics in *parentheses*. ** significant at 5 %; *** significant at 1 %
[a]Pseudo R-squared = ratio of the variance of the predicted values over the variance of the observed values for the dependent variable

8 Wages, Productivity and Industry Composition

Table 8.9 Estimation results for the industrial composition index equation

	OLS	SL	SE
Ln Fsize	0.022	0.015	0.016
	(2.12)[**]	(1.52)	(1.35)
Ln Semp	−0.041	−0.044	−0.045
	(3.92)[***]	(4.34)[***]	(3.90)[***]
Ln Edu	−0.004	−0.002	−0.004
	(0.62)	(0.31)	(0.67)
Ln Empshare	0.033	0.043	0.040
	(2.83)[***]	(3.86)[***]	(3.10)[***]
Ln AccGRP	0.009	0.006	0.007
	(4.09)[***]	(2.81)[***]	(2.17)[**]
Constant	12.177	6.077	12.194
	(295.75)[***]	(3.79)[***]	(272.40)[***]
Obs.	289	289	289
R^2	0.44	0.47[a]	0.43[a]

Dependent variable: industry composition index

Robust t statistics in *parentheses.* [**] significant at 5 %; [***] significant at 1 %

[a]Pseudo R-squared = ratio of the variance of the predicted values over the variance of the observed values for the dependent variable

Table 8.10 IV Estimation results for the wage equation

	OLS	SL	SE
Ln Acc. GRP	0.021	0.014	0.023
	(4.65)[***]	(3.03)[***]	(4.23)[***]
Ln education	0.042	0.043	0.037
	(4.88)[***]	(5.43)[***]	(4.35)[***]
Ln Employ.share	0.096	0.116	0.103
	(5.15)[***]	(6.51)[***]	(5.65)[***]
Ln Firm.size	0.049	0.044	0.051
	(3.43)[***]	(3.10)[***]	(3.38)[***]
Ln Selfemploy.	−0.098	−0.094	−0.088
	(6.98)[***]	(6.67)[***]	(5.80)[***]
Constant	11.884	6.662	11.893
	(183.94)[***]	(5.42)[***]	(174.67)[***]
Obs.	289	289	289
R^2	0.75	0.77[a]	0.75[a]

Dependent variable: wage

Robust t statistics in parentheses. [***] significant at 1 %

[a]Pseudo R-squared = ratio of the variance of the predicted values over the variance of the observed values for the dependent variable

Instruments: (1) municipal 1950 population, (2) population 1950 within 1 h driving distance, (3) municipal land area, (4) land area within 1 h driving distance, (5) dummies for municipalities belonging to Stockholm, Gothenburg and Malmo regions

Table 8.11 IV Estimation results for the productivity index equation

	OLS	SL	SE
Ln Acc. GRP	0.015	0.012	0.015
	$(3.14)^{***}$	$(2.07)^{**}$	$(3.03)^{***}$
Ln Education	0.111	0.111	0.111
	$(8.94)^{***}$	$(9.07)^{***}$	$(9.01)^{***}$
Ln Employ.share	0.100	0.107	0.100
	$(4.45)^{***}$	$(4.75)^{***}$	$(4.46)^{***}$
Ln Firm.size	0.064	0.062	0.064
	$(3.12)^{***}$	$(3.07)^{***}$	$(3.10)^{***}$
Ln Selfemploy.	−0.049	−0.049	−0.049
	$(2.50)^{**}$	$(2.54)^{**}$	$(2.47)^{**}$
Constant	12.112	10.388	12.112
	$(143.08)^{***}$	$(7.49)^{***}$	$(140.95)^{***}$
Obs.	289	289	289
R^2	0.71	0.71^a	0.71^a

Dependent variable: productivity index

Robust t statistics in *parentheses*. ** significant at 5 %; *** significant at 1 %

[a]Pseudo R-squared = ratio of the variance of the predicted values over the variance of the observed values for the dependent variable

Instruments: (1) municipal 1950 population, (2) population 1950 within 1 h driving distance, (3) municipal land area, (4) land area within 1 h driving distance, (5) dummies for municipalities belonging to Stockholm, Gothenburg and Malmo regions

Table 8.12 IV Estimation results for the industrial composition index equation

	OLS	SL	SE
Ln Acc. GRP	0.014	0.011	0.014
	$(5.65)^{***}$	$(3.98)^{***}$	$(4.69)^{***}$
Ln Education	−0.010	−0.008	−0.010
	$(1.77)^{*}$	(1.35)	$(1.72)^{*}$
Ln Employ.share	0.041	0.048	0.044
	$(3.80)^{***}$	$(4.39)^{***}$	$(3.92)^{***}$
Ln Firm.size	0.011	0.008	0.010
	(1.13)	(0.81)	(0.92)
Ln Selfemploy.	−0.052	−0.052	−0.051
	$(5.07)^{***}$	$(5.21)^{***}$	$(4.96)^{***}$
Constant	12.091	7.522	12.097
	$(268.73)^{***}$	$(4.10)^{***}$	$(249.08)^{***}$
Obs.	289	289	289
R^2	0.47	0.48^a	0.47^a

Dependent variable: Industry composition index

Robust t statistics in parentheses. * significant at 10 %; ** significant at 5 %; *** significant at 1 %

[a]Pseudo R-squared = ratio of the variance of the predicted values over the variance of the observed values for the dependent variable

Instruments: (1) municipal 1950 population, (2) population 1950 within 1 h driving distance, (3) municipal land area, (4) land area within 1 h driving distance, (5) dummies for municipalities belonging to Stockholm, Gothenburg and Malmo regions

Appendix 4: Regression Results Omitting the Control Variables

Table 8.13 Regression results for regional market size

	Wage	Prod.index	Comp.index
Acc. GRP	0.036	0.046	0.012
	$(7.72)^{***}$	$(9.13)^{***}$	$(6.23)^{***}$
Constant	11.977	11.796	12.283
	$(265.57)^{***}$	$(240.47)^{***}$	$(636.85)^{***}$
Obs.	289	289	289
R^2	0.24	0.28	0.12

Robust t statistics in *parentheses.* *** significant at 1 %

References

Albæk K, Asplund R et al (2000) Dimensions of the wage-unemployment relationship in the Nordic countries: wage flexibility without wage curves. Labour Market Committee, Nordic Council of Ministers

Audretsch DB, Fritsch M (1994) The geography of firm births in Germany. Reg Stud 28(4):359–365

Blanchflower DG, Oswald AJ (1990) The wage curve. Scand J Econ 92(2):215–235

Blanchflower DG, Oswald AJ (1994) The wage curve. MIT Press, Cambridge

Brown C, Medoff J (1989) The employer size-wage effect. J Polit Econ 97:1027–1059

Calmfors L (1993a) Centralisation of wage bargaining and macroeconomic performance. OECD Economic Studies No. 21

Calmfors L (1993b) Lessons from the macroeconomic experience of Sweden. Eur J Polit Econ 9:25–72

Ciccone A (2002) Agglomeration effects in Europe. Eur Econ Rev 46:213–227

Ciccone A, Hall RE (1996) Productivity and the density of economic activity. Am Econ Rev 86(1):54–70

Combes P-P, Overman HG (2004) Chapter 64. The spatial distribution of economic activities in the European Union. In: Henderson JV, Jacques-François T (eds) Handbook of regional and urban economics. Elsevier, Amsterdam

Combes P-P, Duranton G, Gobillon L (2008) Spatial wage disparities: sorting matters! J Urban Econ 63:723–742

Combes P-P, Duranton G, Puga D, Roux S (2009) The productivity advantages of large cities: distinguishing agglomeration from firm selection, WP. Centre for Economic Policy Research, London

Fu S, Ross SL (2007) Wage premia in employment clusters: agglomeration economies or worker heterogeneity? University of Connecticut, Department of economics working paper series. 26R

Glaeser EL, Mare DC (2001) Cities and skills. J Labor Econ 19(2):316–342

Glaeser EL, Kallal H, Sheinkman J, Schleifer A (1992) Growth in cities. J Polit Econ 100:1126–1152

Graves PE, Arthur MM, Sexton RL (1999) Amenities and the labor earnings function. J Labor Res XX(3):367–376

Hoover EM (1937) Spatial price discrimination. Rev Econ Stud 4:182–191

Lindgren K-O (2006) Roads from unemployment, institutional complementarities in product and labour market. Statsvetenskapliga institutionen, Uppsala

Lucas RE (1988) On the mechanics of economic development. J Monetary Econ 22:3–22

Marshall A (1920) Principles of economics, 8th edn. Macmillan, London

McDonald JF (1997) Fundamentals of urban economics. Prentice-Hall, New Jersey

Mellow W (1982) Employer size and wages. Rev Econ Stat 64:495–501

Moore HL (1911) Laws of wages an essay in statistical economics. Augustus M Kelly, New York

Nijkamp P, Poot J (2005) The last word on the wage curve? J Econ Surv 19(3):421–450

Ohlin B (1933) Interregional and international trade. Harvard University Press, Cambridge

Oxenfeldt A (1943) New firms and free enterprise. American Council on Public Affairs, Washington

Porter ME (1990) The competitive advantage of nations. The Free Press, New York

Rauch JE (1993) Productivity gains from geographic concentration of human capital: evidence from the cities. J Urban Econ 34:380–400

Rice P, Venables AJ, Patacchini E (2006) Spatial determinants of productivity: analysis for the regions of Great Britain. Reg Sci Urban Econ 36:727–752

Roback J (1982) Wages, rents and the quality of life. J Polit Econ 90(6):1257–1278

Romer P (1986) Increasing returns and long-run growth. J Polit Econ 94:1002–1037

Romer P (1990) Endogenous technological change. J Polit Econ 98:S71–S101

Rosenthal SS, Strange WC (2004) Evidence on the nature and sources of agglomeration economies. In: Henderson JV, Thisse JF (eds) Handbook in economics 7. Handbook of regional and urban economics, vol 4, Cities and geography. Elsevier, Amsterdam, pp 2119–2167

Sianesi B, Van Reenen J (2003) The returns to education: macroeconomics. J Econ Surv 17(2):157–200

Thurik AR, Carree MA et al (2007) Does self-employment reduce unemployment? Accepted for publication in J Bus Ventur (2008)

Troske KR (1999) Evidence on the employer size-wage premium for worker-establishment matched data. Rev Econ Stat 81(1):15–26

Wheaton WC, Lewis MJ (2002) Urban wages and labor market agglomerations. J Urban Econ 51:542–562. doi:10.1006/juec.2001.2257

Weber A (1909) Über den Standort der Industrien. Tübingen: J C B Mohr (English trans: The theory of the location industries. Chicago University Press, Chicago, 1929)

Part II
Policies and Institutions of Urban Change

Chapter 9
Scenarios for European Metropolitan Regions: Winners and Losers in a Globalized World

Roberta Capello and Ugo Fratesi

Abstract Cities are highlighted in traditional theories to be the most efficient drivers of economic growth. Considered as sort of collective agents, implicitly or explicitly defining specific development trajectories, cities compete in the global economy for their attractiveness, building on their historical strengths and identifying opportunities for diversification and enlargement of their specializations by strengthening their know-how and knowledge base. Therefore, cities pro-act, and react, to economic volatility, by anticipating expectations on future economic trends and by absorbing the economic effects once they take place. This is true for both virtuous as well as declining cycles of development. The reasons for their static and dynamic efficiency lie in three main elements: the physical size, source of economies of scale; the functional specialisation in advanced value-added functions, source of creativity, learning, and knowledge; the urban system (or the network of cities) in which cities lie, where advantages of scale can easily be exploited avoiding hyper-concentration of production and residential activities. In the age of globalisation like the one we are going through nowadays, cities are areas able to grasp advantages of international competition from outside Europe, and they are expected to be the drivers of growth. In this paper, the aim is to analyse – with a prospective approach – the economic performance that European cities will manifest under different assumptions on the globalisation patterns that may develop in the future. With respect to the present literature, this paper contributes in two new directions: firstly, the aim is to highlight empirically the different actions and reactions that cities of different size, different functional specialisation and located in regions with different settlement structures have in front of a world economic integration; secondly, the aim is to analyse how cities act and react to alternative globalisation patterns, to different quality of competition from outside Europe, which may be sources of different opportunities and threats for different urban areas.

R. Capello (✉) • U. Fratesi
Department of Building, Environment, Science and Technology (BEST), Politecnico di Milano, Milan, Italy
e-mail: Roberta.Capello@polimi.it

J. Klaesson et al. (eds.), *Metropolitan Regions*, Advances in Spatial Science,
DOI 10.1007/978-3-642-32141-2_9, © Springer-Verlag Berlin Heidelberg 2013

Keywords European metropolitan regions • Globalization scenarios • Urban systems • MASST model

1 Sources of Urban Efficiency and Growth[1]

Cities are the drivers of economic activities in a country. This is a well known statement in Urban Economics, rooted in the efficiency characterising an agglomerated organisation of production vis-à-vis a dispersed one. Productivity and performance are in fact raised by urban concentration. A city is a spatial cluster of productive and residential activities. The concentration of activities allows a density of contacts among economic agents, an easy access to advanced information and knowledge, a wide market for input and output; these are typical advantages springing from an urban location, that add to productivity and innovation capacities of firms.[2] A broad and diversified labour market, the availability of typically central and urban services (advanced, financial, insurance, managerial, etc.), a supply of managerial and executive skills, communication and information structures, characterize an urban location, and they affect the factor productivity of the firms situated therein.

But the importance of the city as the engine of development also resides in its ability to generate dynamic economies and to become the preferred location for new high-tech companies, and, in general, for innovative functions. This is due to the fact that urban concentration intensifies learning, innovation and creativity *à la* Florida (Florida 2004). Besides the well-known role attributed in the 1950s and 1960s to cities as 'incubators' of the new – or as the 'nurseries' of small firms – and supported by empirical data,[3] a new interpretative factor has recently been adduced in explanation of the dynamic efficiency of cities. The city and its urban system reduce uncertainty and generate processes of the socialization of knowledge and collective learning (Camagni 1999).

---

[1] A previous version of the paper was presented at the workshop on "Metropolitan regions: Preconditions and strategies for Growth and Development in the Global Economy", Linköping, Sweden, April 24–26, 2008. The paper has greatly benefited from comments and suggestions of an anonymous referee. Usual disclaims apply.

[2] As early as 1961, Chinitz stressed that cities with more competitive and diversified structures furnishing externalities for small firms have greater growth potential than cities with oligopolized and specialized structures in which the 'internalizing' of service functions by large firms impoverishes the urban environment. See Chinitz 1961. A vast literature exists on the measurement of urbanisation economies. Among others, see, Alonso 1971; Carlino 1980; Fujita 1985; Fujita et al. 1999; Henderson 1985, 1986; Mills 1993; Richardson 1972. For a review, Capello 2004.

[3] The pioneering studies by Vernon and Hoover and Vernon in the USA on the concentration of small and medium-sized firms in the heart of cities provided clear evidence of the 'incubator role' performed by cities. See Vernon 1960; Hoover and Vernon 1962.

Moreover, the role of urban functions on urban efficiency has been emphasised in the literature. In the well-known SOUDY (Supply-Oriented Urban Dynamic) model (Camagni et al. 1986), the presence of advanced urban functions allows a city to achieve efficiency thresholds for a larger urban size; an aggregate (urban) benefit curve is supposed to increase for higher order functions, due to: (1) growing entry barriers, (2) decreasing elasticity of demand which allows extra profits to be gained in all market conditions, and (3) increasing possibility of obtaining monopolistic revenues due to the use of scarce and qualified factors. Adding a typical Alonso's increasing aggregate (urban) location cost curve (Alonso 1960) to the benefit curve, the model demonstrates that efficient city sizes (i.e. city sizes for which benefits overweight costs) are achieved for higher city size in those cities where higher order functions are present.

It is not solely in the efficiency of the individual city that one grasps the effect of cities on regional economic development. As shown by the first theorists of general spatial equilibrium and the structure of city systems, Christaller (1933) and Lösch (1954), a well-balanced urban system with an even mix of large, medium and small cities and towns, endowed with efficient transport networks, is the ideal territorial system in terms of efficiency and well-being. A city system of this kind, in fact, makes it possible to exploit the geographical, historical and cultural specificities of each individual city, to provide a broad and diversified range of possible locations for firms and households, and to avoid the hyper-concentration of production and residential activities in a few large-sized cities, where the advantages of scale economies are easily eroded by the high social and environmental costs associated with large urban size.

Again in regard to city systems, an important theoretical step forward to the understanding of their dynamic efficiency has been made by the concept of city networks (Camagni 1993; Boix and Trullén 2007). A network organization of urban centres, hierarchically ordered or of similar size, gives rise to evident advantages associated inter alia with the innovative cooperation necessary for the undertaking of innovative projects (infrastructures, or service provision, or even large-scale urban planning).

Cities are therefore highlighted in well structured theories to be the most efficient drivers of economic growth. If this is the case, cities and regions – considered as sort of collective agents, implicitly or explicitly defining specific development trajectories – compete in the global economy for their attractiveness, building on their historical strengths and identifying opportunities for diversification and enlargement of their specializations by strengthening their know-how and knowledge base.

Regional and local governments have to commit themselves to the issue of external competitiveness and attractiveness of external firms: in fact, firms and industries choose – and create – cities, but also cities and regions attract and develop economic activities thanks to their factor endowment. In the case of advanced countries, these factors may be labelled as "the new territorial capital", i.e. the set of localized assets – natural, human, artificial, organizational, relational and cognitive – that constitute the competitive potential of a given territory: accessibility to large markets, agglomeration economies, presence of knowledge, creativity and entrepreneurial spirit, flexibility of the labour markets (rather than cost), presence of relational and social capital (Camagni 2007; Camagni and Capello 2010). These elements are expected to be present and to be more efficiently exploited in cities of larger size, of higher value added functional specialization, and more efficient spatial organization of the whole urban system in which the city lies.

Through the commitment of regional and local governments for local attractiveness and competitiveness, cities pro-act and/or react to economic volatility, by anticipating expectations on future economic trends and by absorbing the economic effects once they take place. This is true for both virtuous as well as declining cycles of development. In the age of globalisation like the one we are going through nowadays, cities are expected to be those territories able to grasp advantages of international competition from outside Europe, and they are expected to be the drivers of growth.

In this paper, the aim is to describe – with a prospective approach – the economic performance that European cities might achieve under different assumptions on globalization patterns. The purpose of this paper is therefore not to provide alternative images of the European territory in the future; the general aim is to understand how European cities, differentiated in terms of size, functional specialization and inserted in different urban systems, perform in an integrated world, and how this performance changes if a different, less open, globalization pattern is developed in the future.

The role of cities in the globalisation era is not certainly a new debate; on the contrary, it is a high topic in the scientific arena (e.g. Scott 2001; Taylor et al. 2007). With respect to the present literature, this paper contributes in two new directions: firstly, the aim is to highlight empirically the performance that cities of different size, different functional specialisation and located in regions with different settlement structures show in front of a decisive world economic integration; secondly, the aim is to analyse how cities perform if alternative globalisation patterns arise. This second aspect allows to measure a sensitivity of urban economies to open vs. protective global economies.

The paper is structured as follows. We first introduce a definition of cities applied in the empirical analysis of this paper, and the structural features on which the typology of cities is based (Sect. 2). We then present the scenario methodology and results of different globalisation patterns (Sect. 3). Section 4 presents the results by highlighting winners and losers, patterns of growth, and sensitivity to globalisation of the European metropolitan regions. Sect. 5 analyses the determinants of metropolitan regions' sensitivity to the process of economic integration. Sect. 6 presents some concluding remarks.

2 Metropolitan Regions: A Definition

One of the most debated issues in Urban Economics is the definition of cities. The problem of definition is also related to the fact that cities are complex and diverse, and present multifaceted aspects around which they can differ one another.

Many labels have been invented to identify different kinds of cities: the label 'world cities', in the words of Friedmann (1986), refers to those cities at the top of a world city hierarchy; the name 'global cities' of Saskia Sassen (1991) identifies major cities that are strategically global in their function; 'global-city regions' are, according to Allen Scott (2001), those cities whose economic (and social) development is linked to a global rather than to a national growth pattern, giving rise to a new regionalism; 'metropolitan cities' is a general term to identify large and densely populated cities.

Despite the precise meaning, from all definitions previously provided there is clear evidence that two major features are usually identified as key elements to create a typology of cities, as suggested from theory: from one side, their size, and from the other their functional role. A third rather important feature which is worth adding while dealing with the efficiency of cities relates to whether cities are part of a local urban system, or whether they are located in a rather non populated area.

The purpose of our analysis is to highlight the different growth trajectories that cities differentiated in terms of size, functional specialisation and spatial organization of the urban system show in front of an economic world integration process . This purpose therefore calls for a definition of cities that allows to differentiate them on the basis of these three features, two of them belonging to the city, one to their urban system. On the basis of data at NUTS2 level, we distinguish among three categories of metropolitan regions, on the basis of a classification developed in the ESPON project[4]:

- Regions characterised by the presence of cities characterised by high-value functions, called *MEGAs* (Metropolitan European Growth Areas) in the ESPON project, selected on the basis of five functional specialisation indicators: population, accessibility, degree of knowledge and distribution of headquarters of top European firms, as a measure of potential competitiveness. All these variables were collected at FUA (Functional Urban Area) level and then combined to yield an overall ranking of FUAs; the 76 FUAs with the highest average scores were labelled *MEGAs*. *MEGA* regions are the NUTS2 level administrative areas with at least one of the 76 FUAs located in them;
- Regions characterised by large cities, i.e. NUTS2 level administrative areas with at least one city of > 300,000 inhabitants and a population density > 150 inhabitants/km sq. We label them *'Metropolitan Urban Systems'*;
- Regions characterised by both a mega and with at least one city of > 300,000 inhabitants and a population density > 150 inhabitants/km sq. We label them *'Megas within a Metropolitan Urban System'*

This typology allows us to highlight the three main sources of urban efficiency on their own, or in combination. "Mega regions" highlight the importance of high level functions, easily identifiable in large cities; "metropolitan urban systems" underline the role of city systems; "Megas within a Metropolitan Urban System"

---

[4] See ESPON project 1.1.1. for technical details: available at the Espon website www.espon.eu.

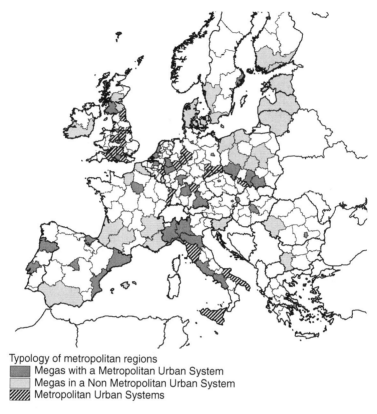

Map 9.1 Typology of metropolitan regions

measure a combined effect of an advanced and dynamic (large) city and a city system.

Map 9.1 provides the location of these three types of metropolitan regions; the classification ends up with 27 'Metropolitan Urban Systems', 27 'Megas' and 40 'Megas within an Urban System'. In Appendix of this chapter you find the list of NUTS 2 that pertain to different categories; in the last category mentioned, one can find, as expected, Paris and London, the two global cities of our database, and other important European cities like Milan, Amsterdam, Rotterdam, Lisbon, Porto, Rome, Naples, Krakow, Athens, most of them capital cities. In the 'Megas' category, important cities are present, like Marseille, Lyon, Bordeaux, Seville, Helsinki, Dublin. Finally, as part of the 'Metropolitan Urban Systems', one finds cities like Florence, Strasburg, Palermo, Bari, Newcastle-up-on Tyne, cities that are located in a densely populated region.

As one can see from Table 9.1, metropolitan regions are a relative minority among European regions, representing only 94 out of 259 Nuts-2 regions.[5] Within

---

[5] All the analysis and data of this paper are based on Nuts-2 1999 definition.

9 Scenarios for European Metropolitan Regions: Winners and Losers in a Globalized... 201

Table 9.1 Typology of metropolitan regions

	EU27	Old 15	New 12
Number of regions			
Megas with a Metropolitan Urban System	40	33	7
Megas in Non Metropolitan Urban Systems	27	16	11
Metropolitan Urban Systems	27	26	1
Non metropolitan regions	165	131	34
All regions	259	206	53
Percentage of GDP within the group of countries (year 2002)			
Megas with a Metropolitan Urban System	36.7	37.2	24.7
Megas in Non Metropolitan Urban Systems	13.8	13.0	31.6
Metropolitan Urban Systems	12.1	12.5	1.5
Non metropolitan regions	37.4	37.2	42.2
All regions	100	100	100
Percentage of EU27 GDP (year 2002)			
Megas with a Metropolitan Urban System	36.7	35.7	1.0
Megas in Non Metropolitan Urban Systems	13.8	12.5	1.3
Metropolitan Urban Systems	12.1	12.0	0.1
Non metropolitan regions	37.4	35.6	1.8
All regions	100	95.8	4.2

metropolitan regions, Megas with a Metropolitan Urban System prevail in Old 15 member countries and overall, whereas in the New 12 member countries Megas in Non Metropolitan Urban Systems are the most numerous group. Interestingly, there are 26 Metropolitan Urban Systems in Old 15 countries and only one (namely Moravskoslezko) in the New 12 countries.

Despite being a minority in number, metropolitan regions are a very important part of the European Economy, representing a significant majority of total European GDP in 2002 (Table 9.1). The share of total GDP accounted for by metropolitan regions is slightly larger among Old 15 countries, where Megas with a Metropolitan Urban System alone account for more than one third of total GDP. Among New 12 member countries, Megas with a Metropolitan Urban System account for around one quarter of total GDP, whereas almost one third is produced by Megas in Non Metropolitan Urban Systems.

Being total GDP in 2002 significantly unbalanced westwards, the weight of the three types of metropolitan systems in the EU27 are extremely similar to the ones of the Old 15 countries, and it is hence interesting to observe that, in 2002, more than one third of European GDP was produced by 33 Western Megas with a Metropolitan Urban System.

Having remarked the importance of metropolitan systems and their classification, the aim of the empirical analysis in the paper is to highlight which of these metropolitan regions are winners or losers in front of an economic world integration process. It is in fact true that – although these regions are expected to be the ones that probably gain the most from a globalisation process, with respect to other rural and less metropolitan regions – there will be among these categories some metropolitan regions which will lose or gain more than others. Winners or losers can be measured in terms of either per capita GDP, or patterns of growth, or speed of adjustment to global trends.

Before entering the empirical analysis, in the next section we present the two scenarios of different global strategies on which our empirical analysis rests.

3 Scenarios for European Metropolitan Regions

3.1 Scenario Methodology

The intention with our scenarios is not to provide precise estimates of future GDP levels, but rather to highlight the main tendencies, major adjustments to change, relative behavioural paths that will be at work, given some conditional assumptions about the influence of the main driving forces. To achieve such a goal, our methodology is neither that of a pure forecast nor that of a pure foresight. Our approach can be defined as a *quantitative foresight* in that it is the result of three major steps. The first involves scenario building whereby an image of the future is constructed on the assumption that a discontinuity will emerge in the main elements or driving forces that influence and regulate the system. The second step is to insert these changes into a model of structural relationships which in traditional manner links conditional (explanatory) variables and the dependent variables. The third step involves a simulation procedure leading to a 'conditional' forecast of the dependent variables.

The econometric model estimating the system of cause-effect relationships is termed the MASST (MAcroeconomic, Sectoral, Social and Territorial) model (Capello 2007; Capello et al. 2008); it is a new one conceptually defined for the purpose of investigating regional growth, its determinants and its territorial evolution. It draws on the most advanced theories of regional growth, without denying the importance of the achievements accomplished by the traditional theories. MASST explains relative regional growth through territorial and spatial factors such as agglomeration economies, territorial capital and spatial spillovers (i.e. the influence of each region on the growth trajectories of neighbouring regions). These factors determine the cumulative nature of regional growth patterns, as widely emphasised by the new endogenous growth theories (Romer 1986b; Lucas 1988b) and the 'new economic geography' (Krugman 1991; Krugman and Venables 1996) rooted in Myrdal's (1957) and Kaldor's (1970) cumulative causation theory.

The MASST model is structured as follows. It comprises two blocks of equations, one explaining national growth, and the other explaining regional differential growth. The sum of the two provides, by definition, total or absolute regional growth. This structure differs substantially from the existing econometric regional growth models, which in general move towards a direct interpretation of absolute regional growth either by replicating national macroeconomic models, or by constructing complex systems of equations for each region linking the region to both the national aggregate economy and to the other regional economies through input–output technical coefficients.

The advantage of the MASST model's structure is that a strong interconnection between regional and national growth is established: national macroeconomic trends and policies generate an effect on both national and regional growth, but at the same time regional structures and policies affect both regional and national performance in an *interactive national-regional* manner. This structure allows account to be taken of complex vertical feedbacks between the regional and national economy without imposing a complex system of interlinked equations.

The most innovative aspect of MASST is that, thanks to its simulation algorithm, it can be considered a 'generative' model of regional growth in the sense defined by Richardson (1969), even if it encompasses also macroeconomic and institutional aspects, which are typically national and top-down. In MASST, regional growth has a role in determining national performance. The model thus supersedes the limiting and erroneous role given in general to the regional side of growth models: that of simply distributing national growth among regions in a typical top-down approach, nor it is a simply generative model in which regions are the only actors and nations are just the sum of them.[6]

3.2 Scenario Description

The scenarios we present hereafter are built on different assumptions on globalisation patterns that may arise in the future. In fact, the interest for our analysis is hence to explore the performance of European cities if two extreme and opposite trajectories are identified as plausible; one is a more courageous, more risky and probably more expansive strategy put in place by BRIC (Brazil, Russia, India and China) countries, based on the willingness to compete at world scale by putting in place strong and decisive internal restructuring, reconverting and modernising processes. The second is a more protective strategy of BRIC countries reinforcing the present tendencies. The two trajectories have significantly different consequences for European cities, since competition hits different sectors, different functions, and with different intensity. Al this will be described in this paper.

These assumptions are associated with a clear division of labour in Europe that leads to an industrial East and a tertiary West: the Old 15 member countries put in place a reactive strategy to globalisation, i.e. a courageous and aggressive strategy which views external countries as potential markets for European goods and is based on the lifting of barriers against trade and migration flows. On the other hand, our scenarios envisage the New 12 countries to develop a cost-competitive strategy based mostly on FDI attraction thanks to the low cost of local resources. This

---

[6] For further specifications on the region-nation interaction in the MASST model the reader may refer to Capello (2007), Capello et al. (2008), Capello and Fratesi (2009 and 2010).

'exogenous' growth is expected, in the long run, to lead to a modern industrial culture and the acquisition of new technical knowledge, thus reinforcing local production activities.

In the first scenario, BRIC countries pursue a courageous, modernising strategy based on enhancing product quality, technological innovation in production processes, industrial specialisation, and on strengthening tertiary activities. The main idea is that future competitiveness of these countries will be based not on price but on product and process innovation. In the second scenario, which we labelled a *dual Europe in an integrated world*, the strategy of BRIC is an opposite one, i.e. a price-competitive strategy based on the continuous exploitation of a wide availability of cheap labour and land resources, postponing any strategy for reconversion of the present economic structure.

The driving forces of this scenario are a clear specialisation within Europe between the two blocks of countries. Western countries show a marked increase in tertiary activities as they transfer part of their industrial potential to Eastern European countries. The capacity of the EU 15 to operate on international markets depends closely on investment in R&D activity: the Lisbon strategy is resolutely pursued in these countries, and the quality of human capital increases. The modernising strategy of BRIC countries and the aggressive strategy of the Old 15 member countries require private investments which generate an increase in world demand for private financial capital. Real interest rates increase as a consequence. In Eastern countries the cost-competitive strategy leads to a currency devaluation, with a consequent rise in inflation rates; private investment growth rates are low and the limited demand for financial capital generates a low decrease in interest rates. Public investments are devoted to increasing the attractiveness of the countries to direct foreign investments with a consequent higher increase in public expenditure and in the share of FDI on private investments. This scenario assumes the introduction of renewable resources and efficient energy technologies in the Old 15, while the New 12 continue to be more directly dependent on traditional energy technologies. The price of energy on the world market is expected to increase due to the increasing oil demand by BRIC countries.[7]

The second scenario depicts a *dual Europe in a price-competitive world*. The profile of the Eastern and Western European countries is the one suggested in the previous scenario. However, this profile changes once the interactions with the external world are taken into account. Global cost-competition changes the assumption of the existence of a wide market for European products owing to a lower purchasing power growth in emerging countries. Eastern European countries encounter tougher competitive conditions in this scenario because similar strategies are undertaken by BRICs both in trade and in attracting foreign investment.

In qualitative terms the different strategy put in place in the external world entails a number of different assumptions. Firstly, it means greater and more direct competition between Eastern European countries and emerging countries as regards

---

[7] For detailed results at the regional level in the two scenarios, see Capello and Fratesi 2010.

both manufacturing products on the international market and FDI attraction. Secondly, the purchasing power in BRIC countries cannot be expected to increase, so that the capacity of European products to penetrate the international market diminishes. Thirdly, there will be a lower increase in energy prices than in the previous scenario because of lower demand in BRIC countries, for both production and household uses.

The choice of these two scenarios is not casual, but driven by our interest in interpreting the difference in growth rates of metropolitan regions due to a higher openness of emerging countries, and new market opportunities. This can be measured by the difference between growth rates of metropolitan regions achieved in the first and in the second scenario. We expect metropolitan areas to react differently to the different globalisation patterns according to their functional specialisation. We expect tertiary metropolitan areas to measure a lower dependence in growth rates due to new market opportunities; in the case of industrial metropolitan regions – on the contrary – growth opportunities are expected to be more subject to the emergence of new markets.

4 European Metropolitan Regions and Globalisation: Evidence from the MASST Model

4.1 Aggregate Simulation Results

The scenario of a Dual Europe in an Integrated World (Scenario I) is characterized by weak regional convergence at EU 27 level, since the growth rate of the poorer New 12 member states is considerably higher than the one of the Old 15 members (Table 9.2). Most Western regions lose some ground with respect to the average. Almost all regions of New 12 members, instead, are above the average, i.e. receive a converging push by the assumptions of a dual Europe in an integrated world.

Interestingly enough, in both scenarios, Megas within a metropolitan urban system or Megas in non- urbanised regions register a higher average growth rate with respect to the aggregate results. This is a first empirical evidence of the role of high-value functions for an efficient economic performance. Moreover, the results underline that metropolitan urban systems grow relatively less than the average, and in general less than metropolitan urban systems with a dynamic city: the inefficiencies arising from physical congestion out-weight the traditional advantages of agglomeration.

This last remark finds empirical roots in the fact that in our results the difference in aggregate growth rates is made by the presence of a city specialised in advanced functions, the so called megas in our typology. This is true for both the old 15 EU member countries and the new 12 countries of Eastern Europe. However, an interesting difference emerges between Eastern and Western metropolitan regions: in the latter, the congestion effects of metropolitan regions emerges quite clearly,

Table 9.2 Aggregate scenario results 2002–2015

	Average annual GDP growth rate			% of additional GDP generated			
	Scenario I	Scenario II	Difference I – II	Scenario I	Scenario II	Difference I – II	Percentage of GDP in 2002
EU27	3.15	2.78	0.37	100	100		
Old 15	3.12	2.74	0.38	94.8	94.4	0.41	95.8
New 12	3.75	3.53	0.22	5.2	5.6	−0.41	4.2
EU27				100	100		
Megas with a Metropolitan Urban System	3.43	3.11	0.31	40.6	42.0	−1.39	36.7
Megas in Non Metropolitan Urban Systems	3.66	3.26	0.40	16.6	16.7	−0.17	13.8
Metropolitan Urban Systems	2.53	2.20	0.33	9.3	9.2	0.10	12.1
Non metropolitan regions	2.87	2.43	0.44	33.5	32.0	1.45	37.4
Old 15				100	100		
Megas with a Metropolitan Urban System	3.41	3.09	0.32	41.3	42.8	−1.51	37.2
Megas in Non Metropolitan Urban Systems	3.62	3.20	0.42	15.6	15.7	−0.09	13.0
Metropolitan Urban Systems	2.53	2.20	0.33	9.8	9.7	0.07	12.5
Non metropolitan regions	2.84	2.39	0.45	33.3	31.8	1.52	37.2
New 12				100	100		
Megas with a Metropolitan Urban System	4.14	3.94	0.20	27.9	28.3	−0.31	24.7
Megas in Non Metropolitan Urban Systems	4.00	3.78	0.22	34.2	34.3	−0.12	31.6
Metropolitan Urban Systems	3.09	2.88	0.21	1.2	1.1	0.01	1.5
Non metropolitan regions	3.35	3.12	0.23	36.7	36.3	0.42	42.2

witnessed by a higher growth rate in both scenarios of Megas in non-metropolitan urban regions. In Eastern metropolitan regions, this is not the case: Megas within metropolitan urban systems register the highest growth rates, probably because of the availability of land for growth opportunities that characterise the Eastern countries with respect to the Western ones.

In this scenario, New 12 countries generate a share (5.2 %) of additional GDP which is larger than their share in 2002 (which was 4.2 %) but still remains far below the one of the more populated and richer Old 15 countries.

Metropolitan regions account for most of the growth, representing around two thirds of the total additional GDP both in the East and in the West. Of this additional GDP, most is generated by Western Megas with a Metropolitan Urban System (over 40 % of the total) and smaller quotas by the other metropolitan regions.

In New 12 countries, the additional GDP is almost equally divided between Megas with a Metropolitan Urban System, Megas in Non Metropolitan Urban Systems and non metropolitan regions, despite of the fact that the latter accounted by a far larger quota of GDP in 2002.

A world economic integration scenario (scenario I) is for all areas a more expansive scenario. The metropolitan regions achieving higher advantages in this scenario are the ones with a dynamic city (a 3.66 percentage point growth), probably able to increase their economic performance without paying for the congestion effects of metropolitan urban systems, as in the case of dynamic regions in a metropolitan urban system, registering a slightly lower annual average growth rate (3.43 %, Table 9.2).

The difference in growth opportunities in front of new markets (measured by the difference in the two scenarios) is higher for Megas in a non-metropolitan urban region. This is true for both Eastern and Western metropolitan regions, but more pronounced in Western countries (0.42 percentage point growth difference between the two scenarios with respect to 0.22 percentage difference in Eastern metropolitan regions) (Table 9.2).

Consistently with the results of average GDP growth rate, when one looks at the difference in the share of additional GDP, the share generated by urban regions is lower in scenario I. Statistical effects also arise, because total generated GDP is different in the two scenarios, explaining why the share of Megas with a Metropolitan Urban System is decreasing more than the one of Megas in Non Metropolitan Urban Systems (Table 9.2).

Results show how metropolitan regions generally outperform the rest of the EU in both scenarios, but this might be a country effect rather than the result of the fact that these areas are pulling the growth within their countries. To analyze this important aspect we calculate in Table 9.3 the annual average differential GDP growth rates between the metropolitan regions and their respective countries, in the past and in the two scenarios.

In the past, Megas with a Metropolitan Urban System and Megas in Non Metropolitan Urban Systems have significantly outperformed the rest of their countries, especially the former in New 12 and especially the latter in Old 15. This is probably due to the fact that Western Megas with a Metropolitan Urban

Table 9.3 GDP growth differentials of metropolitan regions with respect to their countries

	EU27	Old 15	New 12
Average annual differential of growth in the past (1998–2002)			
Megas with a Metropolitan Urban System	0.44	0.08	2.14
Megas in Non Metropolitan Urban Systems	0.19	0.26	0.11
Metropolitan Urban Systems	−0.59	−0.56	−1.26
All metropolitan regions	0.07	−0.11	0.78
Average annual differential of growth in scenario C			
Megas with a Metropolitan Urban System	0.29	0.21	0.68
Megas in Non Metropolitan Urban Systems	0.23	0.26	0.18
Metropolitan Urban Systems	−0.50	−0.52	−0.03
All metropolitan regions	0.05	−0.03	0.36
Average annual differential of growth in scenario D			
Megas with a Metropolitan Urban System	0.30	0.22	0.69
Megas in Non Metropolitan Urban Systems	0.17	0.17	0.17
Metropolitan Urban Systems	−0.53	−0.54	−0.02
All metropolitan regions	0.03	−0.06	0.35

System have already exploited most of their potential economies of agglomeration, whereas in Eastern countries there are still opportunities. Differently from the previous ones, Metropolitan Urban Systems have been systematically below the average, making us think that agglomeration, without dynamism and innovativeness, leads to congestion.

Due to the large number of Metropolitan Urban Systems, Western metropolitan regions have been outperformed by their respective countries, though not significantly, whereas in Easter countries metropolitan regions were significantly above the rest of their respective countries.

The two scenarios are quite similar to the past for what concerns the differential performance of metropolitan regions, though the performances of Megas with a Metropolitan Urban System and Megas in Non Metropolitan Urban Systems are more similar and the differences between East and West decrease as expected.

From these aggregate results two important messages come out, that need further investigation in the empirical analyses that follow: (1) metropolitan regions grow more than the rest of the countries especially when higher order functions are present; (2) the presence of metropolitan urban systems in Western countries seems to be of detriment to the overall metropolitan region's growth, probably due to the high physical congestion effects that limits growth locally.

A more territorially disaggregated analysis is necessary to strengthen and enlarge these first aggregate results. This is the subject matter of the next sections.

4.2 Winners and Losers Among Metropolitan Regions

A first area of analysis is the identification of winners and losers in front of globalisation patterns. The results we provide in this section relate to the first

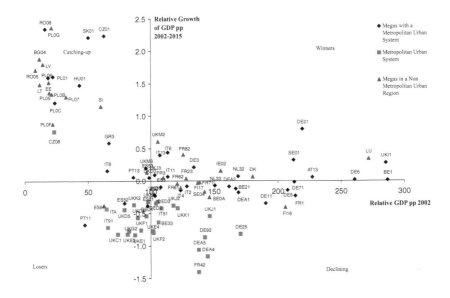

Fig. 9.1 Winners and losers in a scenario of globalization

scenario, in which globalisation is characterised by new market opportunities for Europe, and stronger competition. We can easily demonstrate that the main trends do not change for the second scenario.

As it can be observed from Fig. 9.1, the growth patterns of EU metropolitan regions are very differentiated and the general averages hide many features that characterize them individually.

In this figure, plotted are the growth rates of GDP per capita in the period 2002–2015 against the GDP per capita at the beginning of the period (year 2002), on a relative basis, taking the average of EU 27 GDP per capita (normalized to 100) and the average annual percentage growth rate of EU 27 (normalized to 0 in order to detect deviations).

The first general outcome that one could detect with a simple correlation analysis is that, overall, some convergence is expected to take place between EU27 metropolitan regions. However, as one can observe from the fact that all metropolitan regions belonging to New 12 member countries are in the upper left quadrant, this is mainly due to a country effect. In particular, the patterns of western and eastern metropolitan regions are almost separated in two sets.

Even more remarkable, though, is the fact that metropolitan regions belonging to different categories show differentiated situations. In particular, it is evident that the metropolitan urban systems without a Mega will lose ground with respect to the others in front of market opportunities. These areas, almost all belonging to the Old 15 member states of Europe, all fall within the two lower quadrants of the graph, i.e. they are declining (i.e. starting above the EU average but growing less than the average) or losers (i.e. starting below the EU average and also growing less than the

Table 9.4 Winners and losers in a scenario of globalization

	1	2	3	4	
Quadrant	Winners	Catching-up	Losers	Declining	All
Number of metropolitan regions					
Megas with a Metropolitan Urban System	12	12	3	13	40
Megas in a Non Metropolitan Urban Region	7	12	1	7	27
Metropolitan Urban System	0	1	12	14	27
All metropolitan regions	19	25	16	34	94
% of metropolitan regions					
Megas with a Metropolitan Urban System	30.0	30.0	7.5	32.5	100
Megas in a Non Metropolitan Urban Region	25.9	44.4	3.7	25.9	100
Metropolitan Urban System	0.0	3.7	44.4	51.9	100
All metropolitan regions	20.2	26.6	17.0	36.2	100

average). The only exception is the only Eastern region belonging to this category, Moravskoslezko (CZ08), which is catching up but less rapidly than the rest of Eastern metropolitan regions.

As one can observe from Table 9.4, only 3 Megas with a Metropolitan Urban System and only 1 Megas in a Non Metropolitan Urban Region fall in the "Losers" quadrant, representing 7.5 % and 3.7 % of the respective totals. On the contrary, 12 out of 16 regions in the Losers quadrant belong to Metropolitan Urban Systems, which suffer from not having the Mega. Megas with a Metropolitan Urban System are equally divided between the Winners, Catching-up ad declining quadrants, with the first group being mostly composed by Eastern regions and the two latter by Western ones. Megas in a Non Metropolitan Urban Region are over-represented in the Catching-up quadrant, due to the large number of New 12 regions in this category. Finally, Metropolitan Urban Systems, which are all in the Old 15 countries as mentioned above, are equally spread between the two low-growth quadrants, namely the Losers and the Declining ones.

The worst performers in front of globalisation trends belong to central countries such as France and Germany (e.g. Detmold, DEA4; Arnsberg, DEA5; Alsace, FR42) however also those belonging to UK, Italy and Spain are clustered with initial GDP per person around the EU average and less than average growth rates.

One can observe that already in 2002 the richest metropolitan regions were characterised by a Mega, a clear signal of the importance of high level urban functions. The MASST model supports that this pattern will even be reinforced in the future. In fact, almost all Megas with a Metropolitan Urban System and Megas in a Non Metropolitan Urban Region will have higher performance with respect to Metropolitan Urban Systems.

Generally speaking, megas in non-metropolitan urban systems are, with some exceptions, the winning areas in front of global market opportunities. The presence of a high level function, coupled with the lack of physical congestion of activities at the regional level, probably represents the most fruitful combination of metropolitan structural characteristics to grasp growth opportunities. Among the metropolitan regions without a Mega but with very high income per capita in 2002, the

Luxembourg (LU) is expected to emerge as a winner, whereas Helsinki (FI16) is expected not to grow as fast as in the past. The clearest winner among the Old 15 Megas in a Non Metropolitan Urban Region is in any case Edinburgh (UKM2), whose starting values were only slightly above the average in 2002.

For what concerns metropolitan urban systems with Megas, their future growth patterns are, with some exceptions, very much on the EU average; they do not lose or win much from new market opportunities. Most of them rich in 2002, these are forecasted to be by the model either average performers (e.g. Brussels, BE1; Hamburg, DE6; Wien, AT13; Frankfurt, DE71) or very slightly declining in relative terms (e.g. Paris, FR1; Bremen, DE5; Stuttgart, DE11). Only a few exceptions are clear winners, e.g. Munich (DE21), the clearest winners in the EU 15; Inner London (UKI1); Stockholm (SE01).

Among the poorest Old 15 metropolitan regions, some are expected to be catching up (e.g. GR3, Athens) whereas others are losers (e.g. PT11, Porto) but probably the presence of a capital is important in this case since Lisbon (PT13) is catching up.

As already mentioned, all metropolitan areas belonging to the New 12 member states are expected to be catching up, but with different intensities and with no clear convergence or divergence pattern within the group. Two Megas with a Metropolitan Urban System, Bratislava (SK01) and Prague (CZ01) were already the most advanced in the East and are among the fastest growing, together with two metropolitan areas whose starting values were lower: Bucharest (RO08) and Szczecin (PL0G), a Mega in a Non Metropolitan Urban Region.

4.3 Patterns of Growth in Metropolitan Regions

To better detect what the patterns of growth will be among European metropolitan regions in a scenario of globalization we disentangle the economic and demographic components that are behind GDP per capita growth; in this way we are sure that higher GDP per capita growth rates are associated to real positive economic dynamics rather than to statistical effects, capturing demographic dynamics.

Figure 9.2 helps us in this respect. It plots growth of GDP per capita and of population in the period 2002–2015, relatively to the European average growth. A 45° negative line passing through the origin approximates a condition of regional GDP growth rate equal to the European one; above this 45° negative line GDP growth at regional level is higher than the European average, while below this line are all situations of regional GDP growth lower than the EU average.

Six possible patterns of metropolitan GDP per capita growth emerge in Fig. 9.2, each as a result of a combination of statistical and economic effects. Quadrants 3 and 6 display false economic growth conditions; quadrant 3 depicts a situation of higher than average per capita GDP growth, when in reality GDP growth is below the average and this is the result of a lower than average population growth which

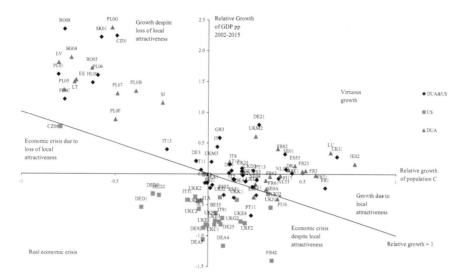

Fig. 9.2 Growth patterns of metropolitan areas in a scenario of globalization

more than counterbalances lower than average GDP growth. Quadrant 6, on the contrary, highlights an opposite situation, where relative GDP per capita declines while GDP growth in reality is above the EU average but the metropolitan area is attractive and there is higher than average population growth.

Quadrants 1 and 4 display the most straightforward economic conditions. In quadrant 1, metropolitan regions are above the average in total GDP growth, population growth and per capita GDP growth, thanks to the strong GDP growth which more than counterbalances the attractiveness of population. On the opposite side, metropolitan regions of quadrant 4 are in real economic crisis, being lower than the average in total GDP growth, population growth and also per capita GDP growth.

Finally, quadrants 2 and 5 depict situations which are less easy to interpret. In quadrant 2, there is an high per capita GDP growth which is due to two reinforcing effects: a higher than average GDP growth and a lower than average population growth. In quadrant 5, metropolitan regions experience a low per capita GDP growth, but this is associated to a higher than average population growth, which reinforces relative per capita GDP decline due to a lower than average total GDP growth.

Figure 9.2 shows interesting results. First of all, no metropolitan regions lie in quadrant 3, except one, Moravskoslezko (CZ08), which however enters in this area of the diagram not neatly. This means that no false economic growth conditions are hidden behind a relative GDP per capita growth in our metropolitan regions.

On the contrary, many metropolitan regions fall in quadrant 6, where a lower than average per capita growth is in reality caused by a higher than average increase in population; regions in this quadrant all belong to the Old 15 member states and all have a mega. This group includes metropolitan regions with a Mega and an

9 Scenarios for European Metropolitan Regions: Winners and Losers in a Globalized... 213

urban system (e.g. Paris, FR1; Rotterdam, NL33; Malmoe, SE04; Koln, DEA2; Birmingham, UKG3; Milan, IT2) as well as Megas in Non Metropolitan Urban Regions, such as Bordeaux (FR61), Lion (FR71), Stuttgart (DE11), Goteborg (SE0A). In these areas, the attractiveness of a Mega seems to compensate for a low increase of GDP per capita.

Interestingly enough, most of metropolitan regions belonging to Eastern countries fall into quadrant 2; their increase in wealth more than the average is certainly the result of both their capacity to grasp new market opportunities coupled with, unexpectedly, higher than average loss in population. All these areas have a mega and no clear differentiation emerges between those having also a Metropolitan System (e.g. Bucharest, RO08; Bratislava, SK01, Prague, CZ01; Krakow, PL06) and those which do not have it (e.g. Szczecin, PL0G; Sofia, BG04; Riga, LV; Ljubljana, SI; Warsaw, PL07; Poznan, PL0F). To this group, but with less remarkable absolute values, also belong a few Western Megas with a Metropolitan Urban System characterized by relatively decreasing population but also forecasted higher than average growth, such as Genoa (IT13) and Berlin (DE3).

The most virtuous metropolitan regions are located in quadrant 1. Within this group there are no Eastern regions, no Metropolitan Urban systems without a mega, but western regions with a Mega, either with or without an urban system. For example, among the first ones, we find London (UKI1), Stockholm (SE01), Munich (DE21), Athens (GR3), Rome (IT6), Wien (AT13). Among the second ones, we encounter Dublin (IE02), the Luxembourg (LU), Edinburgh (UKM2), Marseille (FR82). These cities are expected to experience the best possible situation: they will attract population and, at the same time, will be able to have gains of productivity or employment growth so that the income per person will be growing fast.

Metropolitan regions that will register relative economic decline in front of new market opportunities fall in quadrant 4. These Metropolitan Urban Systems are, for example, Chemnitz (DED1), Dresden (DED2), Leipzig (DED3), Tuscany (IT51) and Northumberland (UKC2).

Finally, metropolitan regions registering a real lower than average per capita GDP growth, worsened by statistical effects, are plotted in quadrant 5. These areas are again all belonging to the Old 15 EU member states and are predominantly Urban Systems without a Mega. Among these the Alsace (FR42), Leicestershire (UKF2), West Yorkshire (UKE4), Mittelfranken (DE25), Puglia (IT91), Gloucestershire (UKK1). Also some regions with a Mega belong to this group, but with total GDP growth only little below the average. These are for example the areas of Porto (PT11), Seville (ES61), Barcelona (ES51) and Valencia (ES52), all characterized by the fact that they are relatively peripheral at EU level and without the capital functions.

To summarize the results of Fig. 9.3 for the various types of metropolitan regions, the frequencies of cities in the various quadrants are depicted in Table 9.5. The Megas with a Metropolitan Urban System are predominantly (80 %) present in the quadrants 1, 2 and 6, the ones with larger than average GDP growth rate. Only a few of them are in this scenario in economic crisis despite local attractiveness and only two in real economic crisis (and with very little intensity). Megas in a Non

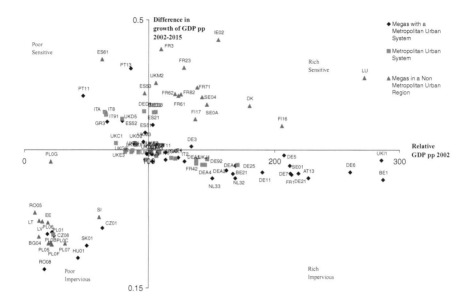

Fig. 9.3 Sensitivity of metropolitan regions to new market opportunities

Metropolitan Urban Region are even more characterized by their presence in the three high-growth quadrants, especially in quadrant 2, where Eastern Megas with a Metropolitan Urban System concentrate. Metropolitan Urban Systems, finally, are all but one concentrated in the fourth and fifth quadrant, where GDP growth rate is below the average, with slightly more than half of them being in crisis despite attractiveness of population.

4.4 Sensitivity of Metropolitan Regions to New Market Opportunities

All the analysis of Sect. 4.2 has been conducted in a scenario of globalization and BRIC countries increasingly integrating in the international markets beyond their present niche of low quality low price products. More interesting, however, it is to know which metropolitan regions are more sensitive to the quality of globalization processes, i.e. which regions are likely to be more affected by the behaviour of BRICs.

Sensitivity to new market opportunities is meant in this paper as a high volatility of cities to different world integration processes: in particular, sensitivity is the ability of metropolitan regions to get greater advantages from a scenario of strong integration with respect to a one in which new market opportunities are very limited, because the low purchasing power in BRIC countries remains very low. Sensitivity is therefore measured as the difference of average annual GDP per

Table 9.5 Growth patterns of metropolitan areas in a scenario of globalization

Quadrant	1 Virtuous growth	2 Growth despite loss of local attractiveness	3 Economic crisis due to loss of local attractiveness	4 Real economic crisis	5 Economic crisis despite local attractiveness	6 Growth due to local attractiveness	All
Number of metropolitan regions							
Megas with a Metropolitan Urban System	14	10	0	2	6	8	40
Megas in a Non Metropolitan Urban Region	8	11	0	0	2	6	27
Metropolitan Urban System	0	0	1	12	14	0	27
All metropolitan regions	22	21	1	14	22	14	94
% of metropolitan regions							
Megas with a Metropolitan Urban System	35.0	25.0	0	5.0	15.0	20.0	100
Megas in a Non Metropolitan Urban Region	29.6	40.7	0	0	7.4	22.2	100
Metropolitan Urban System	0	0	3.7	44.4	51.9	0	100
All metropolitan regions	23.4	22.3	1.1	14.9	23.4	14.9	100

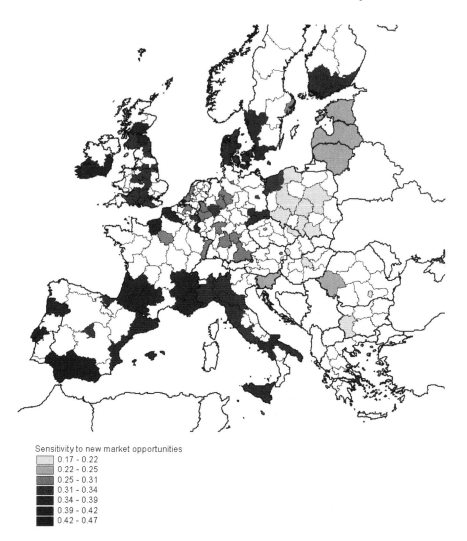

Map 9.2 Sensitivity of metropolitan regions to new market opportunities

person growth rate between 2002 and 2015 in the two scenarios, a measure which provides, more than pure GDP growth, a measure of the wealth created by the metropolitan area to its inhabitants. This variable will also be the one used for the regressions in Sect. 5.

The variable is mapped in Map 9.2, where it is evident that it is not distributed uniformly across Europe but is significantly lower in Eastern Europe. By looking at the numbers, it turns out that all metropolitan regions belonging to the New 12 member states are less sensitive to the possible different patterns of globalization. This obviously depends on the fact that both scenarios involve a dual Europe, in which the East behaves as the manufacturing belt to the West and hence the growth

9 Scenarios for European Metropolitan Regions: Winners and Losers in a Globalized... 217

Table 9.6 Sensitivity of metropolitan regions to new market opportunities

| | 1 | 2 | 3 | 4 | |
| | Rich | Poor | Poor | Rich | All |
Quadrant	sensitive	sensitive	impervious	impervious	quadrants
Number of metropolitan regions					
Megas with a Metropolitan Urban System	2	7	8	23	40
Megas in a Non Metropolitan Urban Region	2	6	7	12	27
Metropolitan Urban System	14	2	11	0	27
All metropolitan regions	18	15	26	35	94
% of metropolitan regions					
Megas with a Metropolitan Urban System	5.0	17.5	20.0	57.5	100
Megas in a Non Metropolitan Urban Region	7.4	22.2	25.9	44.4	100
Metropolitan Urban System	51.9	7.4	40.7	0	100
All metropolitan regions	19.1	16.0	27.7	37.2	100

of the East depends heavily on what happens in the West, whereas it is affected by external forces mainly indirectly, through the changes that these imply for the West.

To study the relationship between sensitivity and the initial situation of regions, Fig. 9.3 plots sensitivity (i.e. the difference in GDP per person growth in the period 2002–2015 between the two scenarios against) the initial relative GDP per person. This allows to distinguish four quadrants belonging to four different possible situations, according to the fact that regions are either sensitive or impervious to external globalization processes (vertical axis) and either rich or poor (horizontal axis). The data from the Figure are also synthesised in Table 9.6.

Among Eastern regions, there is not a clear relationship between initial GDP and sensitivity to world economic integration. It does appear, however, that metropolitan regions with a Mega but without a Metropolitan Urban System are more affected by the behaviour of BRICs than the others (e.g. Szczecin, PL0G; Ljubljana, SI; Timisoara, RO05).

Metropolitan regions of the Old 15 member states show a relatively less homogeneous behaviour. They belong to all four quadrants, although, due to the scenario hypothesis and the low sensitivity of the East, only a few of them result as poor and impervious.

Three clear patterns emerge among Western metropolitan areas: first Megas in Non Metropolitan Urban Systems are normally more sensitive than the other metropolitan regions. The second pattern is that regions with a Metropolitan Urban Systems are less affected despite of the fact that they have a Mega or not. The third one is that, among these Metropolitan Urban Systems, it appears that the poorest (in 2002) are more sensible to the shape of globalization forces than the richest.

These three patterns result in the fact that Western Megas in Non Metropolitan Urban Regions are almost all belonging to the quadrant of rich and sensitive regions

(Table 9.6). For example Dublin (IE02), the Luxembourg (LU), Lille (FR3), Le Havre (FR23), Lyon (FR71), Copenhagen (DK), Helsinki (FI16), Turku (FI17). The growth rate of these regions, despite of the fact that they are rich, is highly influenced by the behaviour of BRIC countries. These are not normally Megas of the first order and their specialization is often in advanced manufacturing instead of services.

A number of Old 15 metropolitan regions belong to the quadrant of the poor and sensitive. These are obviously the same peripheral areas which are less developed than those of the core of Europe. Interesting enough is to observe that the poorest metropolitan regions of Western Europe are also those which are more sensible to the type of globalization processes. They are in fact generally more manufacturing regions than the others and hence their products are at the same time more in competition with those of BRICs and more likely to be sold in the BRICs should these countries also become markets for European products. Apart from Seville (ES61) and, partially, Palma de Mallorca (ES53), all these regions hold a Metropolitan Urban System: Porto (PT11) and Lisbon (PT13), Athens (GR3), Naples (IT8), Puglia (IT91) and Sicilia (ITA), Merseyside (UKD5), Valencia (ES52), Chemnitz (DED1).

The final group of metropolitan regions is the one of the rich and impervious. This group includes most of the richest European regions (37 % of the total EU), which are also those where the presence of an important Mega is coupled with the presence of a Metropolitan Urban Systems. These are areas such as London (UKI1), Brussels (BE1), Hamburg (DE6), Wien (AT13), Stockholm (SE01), Munich (DE21), Frankfurt (DE71), Bremen (DE5), Paris (FR1), Stuttgart (DE11). These areas, being specialized in the most advanced qualifications and services, are among those which are more impervious to new market opportunities. This is at the same time a strength, since their growth rate is more than for the others endogenously determined, and a weakness since, due to their specialization, they are expected to be less able to take advantage of the possible opening of the BRIC markets. Also relatively less rich areas, having or not having a mega, are expected to be less affected by the type of globalization processes, e.g. Rotterdam (NL33), Antwerp (BE21), Milan (IT2), the Alsace (FR42) and Hannover (DE92).

5 Determinants of Metropolitan Regions' Sensitivity to New Market Opportunities

5.1 Characterizing the Behaviours of Metropolitan Regions: A Cluster Analysis

The previous analysis has scattered different behaviours of metropolitan regions in front of different globalisation patterns. We have also found out that there are some common behavioural patterns within the three main typologies of metropolitan regions we envisaged, but this is true at a general level.

It sounds rather interesting to go more in-depth in the descriptive analysis, trying to detect which are the main features that at present can characterise different behavioural patterns in front of different globalisation patterns in the future. In order to achieve this goal, a cluster analysis of metropolitan regions is run based on their characteristics as detected by their statistical values in the past (year 2002 or 2000 when only this data was available). The choice of past values is explained by two main reasons: (1) our interest lies in the present structural and endogenous features that can influence different behavioural growth patterns; (2) the risk of a tautological reasoning between the variables outcome of the model and the results of the cluster analysis.

Due to the fact that Eastern and Western metropolitan regions showed so far very differentiated patterns and that their values were almost separated sets in each single variable, we chose to run a cluster analysis by separating the metropolitan regions belonging to the Old 15 and the New 12 member states.[8]

The list of the variables on which the clusters were defined were hence the following ones, mainly measuring endogenous structural features of our metropolitan regions:

- Transport infrastructure endowment, calculated relative to the respective countries average, as a proxy for the whole infrastructure endowment of metropolitan regions;
- Share of employment in tertiary activities as a measure of the type of economic activities in the metropolitan region;
- Share of self-employees, as a proxy for entrepreneurship;
- Unemployment rate, as a measure for the functioning of the labour market in the area;
- Share of human resources in science and technology (HRST) as a measure of the innovative content of the economic activities;
- GDP per person in 2002 of the metropolitan region to capture all other economic features of the area which were not previously captured by any other regional variable.

With these variables it turned out in the dendogram that the best number of clusters to be analyzed was 4 for the West and 2 for the East. The metropolitan regions belonging to each cluster are represented in Map 9.3. Once created, clusters have been depicted also on the basis of their economic performance and territorial structure (Table 9.7).

First we study the situation of the West. The average population of metropolitan regions in each of the four clusters is almost identical, the average area is very similar in three out of four clusters, whereas it is much smaller in Cluster 1 (which

---

[8] Notice that, if one runs a cluster analysis with all 94 metropolitan regions, Eastern ones almost always form one cluster by themselves with no intersection with western ones.

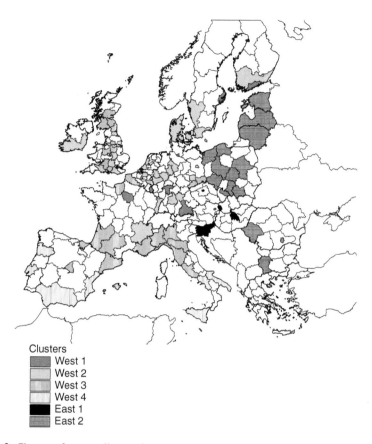

Map 9.3 Clusters of metropolitan regions

includes some 'inner areas') so that this cluster appears to be much denser in terms of population per square kilometer.

Two clusters, namely 1 and 2, appear to characterize regions which are richer, northern and more belonging to the Pentagon. Clusters 3 and 4, instead, are generally composed by areas out of the pentagon and hence more peripheral in EU terms. Clusters 1 and 2 are also characterized by higher income per capita than the other two, as well as higher infrastructure endowment and human resources in science and technology.

Cluster 1 is the smallest one and only includes 11 metropolitan regions, all of which with a Mega. 8 out of 11 regions are in the Pentagon and 9 out of 11 are Megas with a Metropolitan Urban System. The main structural features of this cluster are the following. It is a cluster characterised by the richest regions (237 % of EU average income per capita), by a significantly higher share of tertiary activities and a lower share of primary and secondary activities, by the highest share of science and technology activities. This is also the one with highest infrastructural endowment, highest accessibility and the lowest share of

Table 9.7 Characteristics of clusters of metropolitan regions

	West 1	West 2	West 3	West 4	Mean west	East 1	East 2	Mean east	All metropolitan regions
Observations	11	19	29	16	**75**	4	15	**19**	**94**
Pentagon regions	8	12	7	0	**27**	0	0	**0**	**27**
Megas with a Metropolitan Urban System	9	7	12	5	**33**	3	4	**7**	**40**
Metropolitan Urban System	0	6	10	10	**26**	0	1	**1**	**27**
Megas in a Non Metropolitan Urban Region	2	6	7	1	**16**	1	10	**11**	**27**
Average area	5,203	15,638	13,550	14,864	**13,135**	7,435	27,135	**22,988**	**15,127**
Average population (thousands)	2,729	2,982	2,992	2,930	**2,938**	1,657	2,723	**2,499**	**2,849**
Average population density	525	191	221	197	**224**	223	100	**109**	**188**
GDP as % of EU27	237	154	109	76	**132**	54	19	**26**	**111**
% primary employment	1.1	2.5	2.4	4.6	**2.7**	3.5	13.2	**11.2**	**4.4**
% secondary employment	20.7	29.5	28.2	28.6	**27.5**	28.5	32.6	**31.7**	**28.3**
% tertiary employment	78.2	68.0	69.4	66.8	**69.8**	68.0	54.2	**57.1**	**67.2**
Unemployment rate	3.4	3.0	3.9	4.7	**3.8**	2.6	6.5	**5.7**	**4.2**
HRST	23.0	19.6	15.7	12.1	**17.0**	20.0	13.1	**14.6**	**16.5**
Absolute infrastructure	0.28	0.12	0.09	0.06	**0.12**	0.14	0.05	**0.07**	**0.11**
Relative infrastructure	4.46	1.79	1.84	1.51	**2.14**	3.43	1.21	**1.68**	**2.05**
Self employees	8.61	9.93	13.59	15.87	**12.49**	13.70	15.26	**14.90**	**12.94**
Past DIF	0.68	−0.36	−0.22	−0.14	**−0.11**	1.48	0.60	**0.78**	**0.07**
Future DIF	0.22	−0.20	0.09	−0.22	**−0.03**	0.73	0.26	**0.36**	**0.05**
Future country growth	2.95	2.93	2.86	2.85	**2.9**	4.12	4.37	**4.3**	**3.2**
Growth scenario I	3.16	2.72	2.94	2.63	**2.9**	4.85	4.62	**4.7**	**3.2**
Growth scenario II	2.85	2.38	2.59	2.26	**2.5**	4.63	4.40	**4.4**	**2.9**
Sensitivity	0.3197	0.3393	0.3546	0.3652	**0.3478**	0.2160	0.2248	**0.2230**	**0.3226**
Past spillovers	0.011	0.011	0.010	0.008	**0.010**	0.010	0.009	**0.009**	**0.010**
Future spillovers	1.300	1.326	1.149	0.918	**1.167**	1.290	1.038	**1.091**	**1.152**

self-employees, signalling a small role for small entrepreneurial initiatives in these regions which are instead characterized by many headquarters of large firms. Cluster 1 can hence be labelled as a cluster of *advanced metropolitan regions specialized in tertiary activities.*

Linked to these structural features, an outperforming behaviour is measured: cluster 1 shows the highest growth rate in both scenarios, but, more interesting, as shown by the differentials, and as it was also in the period 1995–2002, regions belonging to this cluster are systematically outperforming their respective countries' growth rates, signalling that they are engines of their countries' growth. In line with this tendency, the metropolitan regions of this cluster are also those less sensitive to the type of competition put in place by the BRIC countries, probably due to their specialisation in value added tertiary activities, less vulnerable in terms of external competition.

Cluster 2 includes 19 metropolitan regions and is the second richest in terms of GDP per capita (154 % of EU27 average). As for cluster 1, its regions are generally core areas, 12 out of 19 are in the Pentagon. Cluster 2 is instead not characterized in terms of which type of metropolitan areas it is composed of, having the same number of the three types. As cluster 1, but less sizeably, this cluster is characterized by an high share of tertiary activities and a small share of primary activities. Share of self employment is also very limited, signalling that the high share of manufacturing activities (the largest, at 29.5 %), is mainly due to large enterprises. Infrastructural endowment is good in absolute terms but less than in cluster 1 and this is even more true in relative terms. Human resources in science and technology are diffused, since those of cluster 2 are advanced regions, but less than in cluster 1. These regions show patterns of potentially endogenous growth, having at present a lower than national average growth rates, that in the future will lower. Cluster 2 can be labelled a cluster of *advanced metropolitan regions with large and manufacturing firms.*

Associated to the structural features of Cluster 2 is a relatively contained performance. For instance, the differentials of growth with respect to the country were negative in the estimation period 1995–2002 and are forecasted to improve in the future, remaining however negative. This is confirmed by the fact that these metropolitan areas, the most manufacturing ones, are more sensitive than those of cluster 1 to the type of globalization processes taking place. In general these areas (Dublin and Copenhagen are probably an exception) belong to strong countries, but tend to be areas which are pulled by the growth of the rest of their country, i.e. are probably more sensitive than those of cluster 1 to demand factors. Growth in both scenarios is lower than for Clusters 1 (and also for cluster 3). In the cluster analysis, as a general rule and similarly to what was observed in Fig. 9.3, the sensitivity of metropolitan regions to globalization decreases with income per capita in 2002. This holds true also for the two other clusters, which are on average those comprising the less rich and less core metropolitan areas of Western Europe.

Cluster 3 comprises 29 metropolitan areas, of which only 7 in the Pentagon. As the previous one, this cluster is not very characterized in terms of what type of metropolitan regions it is composed of. This cluster still has on average a GDP per person in 2002 above the EU 27 mean, though slightly, and low primary and high tertiary employment. Human resources in science and technology are lower than in the two previous clusters, but self-employment is more diffused, signalling an economy more keen on SMEs; this characterize this cluster together with the presence of a relatively higher share of science and technology employment share with respect to cluster 4. Infrastructure is less developed than in the two previous clusters in absolute terms but high relatively to the countries to which these regions belong. Cluster 3 can be labelled *dynamic metropolitan regions with small firms*.

These structural features are linked to a relatively good performance. Metropolitan areas in this cluster are more endowed than their respective countries in most features; they are therefore expected to become among the puller of their respective countries, as detected by a growth differential which passes from negative to slightly positive. Being characterized by SMEs and relatively low tech activities, this cluster will likely be sensitive to the type of globalization process, implying that its firms will probably gain more than others should the BRICs become important markets, but also will need this in order to maintain a sustained growth. This is confirmed by the model simulations.

The poorest cluster in western Europe, being on average only at 76 % of EU 27 average GDP per person, is cluster 4. This cluster is composed by 16 metropolitan areas, of which only 6 having a Mega. This is the cluster with the most important role for primary activities, the less important presence of tertiary employment and the higher unemployment rate. Human resources in science and technology are at their lowest level among Western metropolitan regions as are infrastructure, both in absolute and in country relative terms. We chose to label Cluster 4 *poor metropolitan regions with small firms*.

All these weaknesses reflect in a forecasted performance which is the lowest in both scenarios. These metropolitan regions used to have a negative growth differential with respect with their countries and are expected to remain as such in the future. Being the most characterized by SMEs and low tech activities, these metropolitan regions are expected to be those whose growth patterns will be more dependent from what takes place at an international level, so that they could get an advantage if new markets open, but will also need this in order to contrast a growth which is endogenously weak.

Due to the scarcer number of metropolitan regions in the Eastern countries of Europe, two clusters resulted to be enough to characterize Eastern metropolitan regions.

The first Eastern cluster only comprises 4 regions, 3 of which Megas with a Metropolitan Urban System and 1 Mega in a Non Metropolitan Urban Region. These 4 regions are all capital ones, are the most densely populated and also the richest in Eastern countries. They have far less employment in agriculture and manufacturing, and more employment in services. Human resources in science and technology are more diffused, and infrastructure endowment is higher, both in absolute and in relative terms. Self employment is lower than in the rest of the New 12 member states, signalling less reliance on SMEs, and lower is also unemployment. The stronger structure of metropolitan regions of Eastern cluster 1 implies a performance which is higher in both scenarios. Moreover, the growth differential with respect to their countries used to be and is expected to remain higher than in Eastern cluster 2.[9]

In terms of sensitivity, remembering that the East is generally less sensitive than the West because of the scenario assumption of a dual Europe, the strongest, less reliant on manufacturing and SMEs, cluster 1 is expected to be the least sensitive to what will be the behaviours of BRIC countries in the future.

5.2 The Determinants of the Sensitivity to the Globalization Processes

To confirm through an interpretative approach the hints of the cluster analysis, we run an econometric analysis of the determinants of the sensitivity of metropolitan regions to the type of globalization which is taking place. The measure of sensitivity is the same which was exposed in Sect. 4.4, namely the difference of average annual GDP per person growth rate between 2002 and 2015 in a scenario of world integration with respect to another of price-competitiveness.

Notice that, apart from the Old 15 – New 12 member states differentiation, which is at the basis of the hypothesis of a 'dual' Europe, our results as far as metropolitan regions are concerned depend on the complex internal mechanisms of the MASST model, and not on our scenario assumptions.

The database is composed of 94 observations (one for each metropolitan region of the EU27), where the difference of performance between scenario I and scenario II is the dependent variable to be explained. As regressors, we use variables which are unrelated with the values used to design scenario hypotheses, and in particular variables which are related to the economic structure of the metropolitan regions:

– A dummy for Megas in a Non Metropolitan Urban Systems, since we have seen in Sect. 4 that these are generally more affected than the others by globalisation processes;
– The share of self-employment, a variable which, measuring the presence of individual entrepreneurs in a metropolitan region, is a proxy for entrepreneurship and reliance on small businesses. We expect this variable to be positively correlated with the sensitivity to the type of globalization, since entrepreneurial regions ought be more able to capture new market opportunities and also because, in general, small businesses are more influenced by any variation in demand;
– The unemployment rate (calculated in our case as % of unemployment on total population), as a good measure of the well functioning of the labour market in

---

[9] Notice that, due to the fact that development in the East used to be very centripetal in recent years and this is not expected to change in the next years, the growth differentials with respect to their countries are much higher for metropolitan regions in the East than for their Western counterparts.

9 Scenarios for European Metropolitan Regions: Winners and Losers in a Globalized...

the metropolitan region. We expect that metropolitan regions with higher unemployment rates, being less dynamic, are more influenced by external factors and by any change in the demand conditions;

- The share of employment in tertiary activities, a rough but significant measure of the specialization of the metropolitan region. We expect that metropolitan regions with higher incidence of tertiary activities are less affected by what type of globalization strategy is put in place by BRIC countries for two regions: first the demand for services is more local than the demand for manufacturing and agriculture; second, the opportunities entailed by the development of new markets in emerging countries will especially affect manufactured products, whereas the highest level service activities will not be as much affected by the patterns of emerging countries;
- The share of human resources in science and technology. Being a proxy for the level of advancement of the production system of metropolitan regions, these ought be negatively correlated with the changing patterns of the BRIC countries: at a first stage, the import by emerging countries will not involve the highest level of technology. Moreover, the demand for highest level products will continue to predominantly come from the internal market and, internationally, from advanced countries;
- The size of metropolitan region, measured by its absolute population. We expect this variable to be negatively correlated with the sensitivity of metropolitan regions to external globalization processes because larger geographical units are normally more diversified and less open, hence more depending on internal demand.

In addition to these explanatory variables, we also take into account two regional situations which can affect the sensitivity of metropolitan regions to the patterns of world economic integration: the first one depends on the scenario assumptions and is related to the fact that an area belongs to Old 15 or New 12 member states. As we already stated, both scenarios assume a dual Europe and that hence Eastern countries are developing essentially as the manufacturing belt of Europe. Being the demand for Eastern products essentially coming from the West, the effects of international changes on New 12 member states would be mediated and lower than in Old 15 member states (see Sect. 4.1).

The second element resides in the fact that a metropolitan region is or not in the Pentagon[10]. Being in the core of Europe ought be an element which assures more spillovers. However, we included the Pentagon because the regions of the core of Europe, performance being equal, are generally more endowed in many statistics such as research and innovation.

Regressions (shown in Table 9.8) are were run in cross-section for all European metropolitan regions and for the Western sub-set to account for the differences between Old 15 and New 12 member states. These differences are also evidenced

---

[10] Regions located within the pentagon delineated by the five European cities of London, Paris, Milan, Munich, Hamburg are called the Pentagon area.

Table 9.8 Regression results

Regression number	1		2		3		4		5		6	
Sample includes	All metropolitan regions		All metropolitan regions		Western metropolitan regions		Western metropolitan regions		Western metropolitan regions		Western metropolitan regions	
Variable	Coef. (*100)	Sig	Coef. (*100)	Sig	Coef. (*100)	Sig	Coef. (*100)	Sig	Coef. (*100)	Sig	Coef. (*100)	Sig
Megas in a Non Metropolitan Urban System (dummy)	6.258	***	6.295	***	8.135	***	8.205	***	8.088	***	8.179	***
Unemployment	0.297	*	0.328	*	0.504	***	0.551	***	0.530	***	0.578	***
Human resources in science and technology	−0.182	**	−0.182	**	−0.205	***	−0.201	**				
Pentagon area (dummy)	−1.642	**	−1.466	*	−0.920		−0.704					
Human resources in science and technology in the pentagon									−0.070	***	−0.057	**
Share of self employment	0.050		0.068		0.081		0.106		0.138	**	0.162	**
Share of tertiary activities	0.019		0.016		−0.035		−0.039		−0.070	*	−0.074	**
Size of metropolitan region (population)			0.000				0.000				0.000	
New member states (dummy)	−17.290	***	−17.446	***								
Constant	34.234	***	34.472	***	36.563	***	36.670	***	34.843	***	35.062	***
Obs	90		90		73		73		73		73	
F	57.05		48.22		46.64		42.59		38.04		32.41	
Prob > F	0		0		0		0		0		0	
R-squared	0.8416		0.8432		0.7641		0.7688		0.7371		0.742	

Dependent variable: sensitivity of metropolitan regions to the patterns of world integration, calculated as the difference of average annual growth of GDP per person between Scenarios I and II

*** significant at 1 per cent, ** significant at 5 per cent, *** significant at 10 per cent

by the very high and significant value of the New 12 dummy in regressions 1 and 2. Due to the limited number of observations, were not able to run regressions for Eastern metropolitan regions alone.

The results of the regressions confirm our expectations: the sensitivity to world economic integration is mostly explained by the structural variables previously mentioned, with the expected sign, with the exception of size.

First of all, as expected having read Sect. 4.4, the control variable of Megas in Non-Metropolitan Urban Systems is positive and highly significant in all regressions. The unemployment rate is highly significant and positive in all regressions, with a sensibly higher coefficient when the sample is reduced to Old 15 metropolitan regions. This means that, as expected, the regions where the labour market works worse are those which suffer more from the external challenges, especially in Western countries. Human resources in science and technology are negatively associated with high sensitivity, witnessing that areas with limited innovative capability are less able to produce endogenously their patterns of growth dynamics and hence have higher sensitivity to world economic integration. The dummy for Pentagon areas, a proxy for accessibility, is negative and significant among all metropolitan regions, but is not significant when only Western countries are considered. Since human resources in science and technology are higher among Pentagon areas and the two variables turned out to be collinear, we also run regressions in which the two variables are replaced by their product (regressions 5 and 6), confirming the negative and significant coefficient.

The results for the share of self-employment and the share of tertiary activities are less straightforward. The share of self-employment is positive in all regressions, but is detected as significant only in regressions 5 and 6 where no collinearity is present; the result is any case in favour of the hypothesis that more entrepreneurial metropolitan regions are more sensible to opportunities and also that small enterprises are generally more sensible to external conditions.

Also the share of tertiary activities turns out as insignificant in the first regressions until the collinearity issue is solved and it ends up being significant and having the expected negative sign, as we supposed based on the fact that service activities are normally less traded and also less likely to take advantage of external opportunities.

Finally, contrary to the hypothesis, the size of metropolitan regions, which should have affected the sensibility through the supposed greater openness of small regions, in instead insignificant in all regressions, both including and excluding the New 12 member countries.

6 Conclusions

In this paper we have analyzed the effects of new market opportunities on the European metropolitan regions in a framework of globalization. With the use of the MASST model, the performance of these regions in the future has been simulated to show that the patterns are differentiated for each individual area and also by three typologies of metropolitan regions.

Our results indicate that, first, the performance of metropolitan regions facing globalization highly depends on their economic structure. In particular, the strongest metropolitan regions, characterised by high-value functions, are expected to grow more, not only in absolute terms but also with respect to their respective countries, so that they assume a role of puller of national growth and gateway of new opportunities.

Second, we analysed the sensitivity to the patterns of new market opportunities and evidenced that, ceteris paribus, metropolitan regions with a high-value and tertiary functions are less sensitive than the others; at the same time, the most dynamic metropolitan regions are also those which are more able to capture new opportunities.

Our analysis, in conclusion, supports that a strong endogenous structure, made of high level functions, in both a tertiary and industrial context, is not only the key for growing more but also that it allows metropolitan regions to maintain sustained growth rates even under less favourable external economic conditions. Growth in metropolitan regions with a strong structure is hence mainly endogenous, depending on innovation, supply and internal factors and less on production, demand and external pulling factors.

Appendix: List of Regions and Their Typologies

Table 9.9 Regional names, codes and names of megas within

Code (Nuts2)	Name of region	Name of mega within	Typology
AT13	Wien	Wien	Megas with a Metropolitan Urban System
BE1	Région Bruxelles-capitale/Brussels hoofdstad gewest	Bruxelles/ Brussel	Megas with a Metropolitan Urban System
BE21	Antwerpen	Antwerpen	Megas with a Metropolitan Urban System
BE33	Liège	–	Metropolitan Urban System
BG04	Yugozapaden	Sofia	Megas in a Non Metropolitan Urban Region
CZ01	Praha	Praha	Megas with a Metropolitan Urban System
CZ08	Moravskoslezko	–	Metropolitan Urban System
DE11	Stuttgart	Stuttgart	Megas with a Metropolitan Urban System
DE21	Oberbayern	Muenchen	Megas with a Metropolitan Urban System
DE25	Mittelfranken	–	Metropolitan Urban System
DE3	Berlin	Berlin	Megas with a Metropolitan Urban System

(continued)

9 Scenarios for European Metropolitan Regions: Winners and Losers in a Globalized... 229

Table 9.9 (continued)

Code (Nuts2)	Name of region	Name of mega within	Typology
DE5	Bremen	Bremen	Megas with a Metropolitan Urban System
DE6	Hamburg	Hamburg	Megas with a Metropolitan Urban System
DE71	Darmstadt	Frankfurt Am Main	Megas with a Metropolitan Urban System
DE92	Hannover	–	Metropolitan Urban System
DEA1	Düsseldorf	Duesseldorf	Megas with a Metropolitan Urban System
DEA2	Köln	Koeln	Megas with a Metropolitan Urban System
DEA4	Detmold	–	Metropolitan Urban System
DEA5	Arnsberg	–	Metropolitan Urban System
DED1	Chemnitz	–	Metropolitan Urban System
DED2	Dresden	–	Metropolitan Urban System
DED3	Leipzig	–	Metropolitan Urban System
DK	Danmark	Koebenhavn	Megas in a Non Metropolitan Urban Region
EE	Eesti	Tallinn	Megas in a Non Metropolitan Urban Region
ES21	Pais Vasco	Bilbao	Megas with a Metropolitan Urban System
ES3	Comunidad de Madrid	Madrid	Megas with a Metropolitan Urban System
ES51	Cataluña	Barcelona	Megas with a Metropolitan Urban System
ES52	Comunidad Valenciana	Valencia	Megas with a Metropolitan Urban System
ES53	Islas Baleares	Palma De Mallorca	Megas in a Non Metropolitan Urban Region
ES61	Andalucia	Sevilla	Megas in a Non Metropolitan Urban Region
FI16	Uusimaa (suuralue)	Helsinki	Megas in a Non Metropolitan Urban Region
FI17	Etelä-Suomi	Turku	Megas in a Non Metropolitan Urban Region
FR1	Île de France	Paris	Megas with a Metropolitan Urban System
FR23	Haute-Normandie	Le Havre	Megas in a Non Metropolitan Urban Region
FR3	Nord – Pas-de-Calais	Lille	Megas in a Non Metropolitan Urban Region
FR42	Alsace	–	Metropolitan Urban System
FR61	Aquitaine	Bordeaux	Megas in a Non Metropolitan Urban Region
FR62	Midi-Pyrénées	Toulouse	Megas in a Non Metropolitan Urban Region
FR71	Rhône-Alpes	Lyon	Megas in a Non Metropolitan Urban Region

(continued)

Table 9.9 (continued)

Code (Nuts2)	Name of region	Name of mega within	Typology
FR82	Provence-Alpes-Côte d'Azur	Marseille-Aix-En-Pro	Megas in a Non Metropolitan Urban Region
GR3	Attiki	Athinai	Megas with a Metropolitan Urban System
HU01	Közép-Magyarország	Budapest	Megas with a Metropolitan Urban System
IE02	Southern and Eastern	Dublin	Megas in a Non Metropolitan Urban Region
IT11	Piemonte	Torino	Megas with a Metropolitan Urban System
IT13	Liguria	Genova	Megas with a Metropolitan Urban System
IT2	Lombardia	Milano	Megas with a Metropolitan Urban System
IT4	Emilia-Romagna	Bologna	Megas with a Metropolitan Urban System
IT51	Toscana	–	Metropolitan Urban System
IT6	Lazio	Roma	Megas with a Metropolitan Urban System
IT8	Campania	Napoli	Megas with a Metropolitan Urban System
IT91	Puglia	–	Metropolitan Urban System
ITA	Sicilia	–	Metropolitan Urban System
LT	Lietuva	Vilnius	Megas in a Non Metropolitan Urban Region
LU	Luxembourg	Luxembourg	Megas in a Non Metropolitan Urban Region
LV	Latvija	Riga	Megas in a Non Metropolitan Urban Region
NL32	Noord-Holland	Amsterdam	Megas with a Metropolitan Urban System
NL33	Zuid-Holland	Rotterdam	Megas with a Metropolitan Urban System
PL01	Dolnoslaskie	Wroclaw	Megas with a Metropolitan Urban System
PL05	Lódzkie	Lodz	Megas in a Non Metropolitan Urban Region
PL06	Malopolskie	Krakow	Megas with a Metropolitan Urban System
PL07	Mazowieckie	Warszawa	Megas in a Non Metropolitan Urban Region
PL0B	Pomorskie	Gdansk	Megas in a Non Metropolitan Urban Region
PL0C	Slaskie	Katowice	Megas with a Metropolitan Urban System
PL0F	Wielkopolskie	Poznan	Megas in a Non Metropolitan Urban Region
PL0G	Zachodniopomorskie	Szczecin	Megas in a Non Metropolitan Urban Region

(continued)

9 Scenarios for European Metropolitan Regions: Winners and Losers in a Globalized... 231

Table 9.9 (continued)

Code (Nuts2)	Name of region	Name of mega within	Typology
PT11	Norte	Porto	Megas with a Metropolitan Urban System
PT13	Lisboa e Vale do Tejo	Lisboa	Megas with a Metropolitan Urban System
RO05	Vest	Timisoara	Megas in a Non Metropolitan Urban Region
RO08	Bucuresti	Bucuresti	Megas with a Metropolitan Urban System
SE01	Stockholm	Stockholm	Megas with a Metropolitan Urban System
SE04	Sydsverige	Malmoe	Megas in a Non Metropolitan Urban Region
SE0A	Västsverige	Goeteborg	Megas in a Non Metropolitan Urban Region
SI	Slovenija	Ljubljana	Megas in a Non Metropolitan Urban Region
SK01	Bratislavský	Bratislava	Megas with a Metropolitan Urban System
UKC1	Tees Valley and Durham	–	Metropolitan Urban System
UKC2	Northumberland, Tyne and Wear	–	Metropolitan Urban System
UKD3	Greater Manchester	Greater Manchester	Megas with a Metropolitan Urban System
UKD5	Merseyside	–	Metropolitan Urban System
UKE1	East Riding and North Lincolnshire	–	Metropolitan Urban System
UKE3	South Yorkshire	–	Metropolitan Urban System
UKE4	West Yorkshire	–	Metropolitan Urban System
UKF1	Derbyshire and Nottinghamshire	–	Metropolitan Urban System
UKF2	Leicestershire, Rutland and Northants	–	Metropolitan Urban System
UKG2	Shropshire and Staffordshire	–	Metropolitan Urban System
UKG3	West Midlands	Birmingham	Megas with a Metropolitan Urban System
UKI1	Inner London	London	Megas with a Metropolitan Urban System
UKI2	Outer London	–	Metropolitan Urban System
UKJ1	Berkshire, Bucks and Oxfordshire	–	Metropolitan Urban System
UKJ2	Surrey, East and West Sussex	–	Metropolitan Urban System
UKJ3	Hampshire and Isle of Wight	Southampton/ Eastleig	Megas with a Metropolitan Urban System
UKK1	Gloucestershire, Wiltshire and North Somerset	–	Metropolitan Urban System
UKK2	Dorset and Somerset	–	Metropolitan Urban System
UKM2	Eastern Scotland	Edinburgh	Megas in a Non Metropolitan Urban Region
UKM3	South Western Scotland	Glasgow	Megas with a Metropolitan Urban System

References

Alonso (1960) A theory of the urban land market. Papers and proceedings of the regional science association 6:149–157

Alonso W (1971) The economics of urban size. Papers and proceedings of the regional science association 67–83

Boix R, Trullén J (2007) Knowledge, networks of cities and growth in regional urban systems. Pap Reg Sci 86(4):551–574

Camagni R (1993) From city hierarchy to city network: reflections about an emerging paradigm. In: Laschmanan T, Nijkamp P (eds) Structure and change in the space economy. Springer Verlag, Berlin, pp 66–90

Camagni R (1999) The city as a *milieu*: applying GREMI's approach to urban evolution. Revue d'Economie Régionale et Urbaine 3:591–606

Camagni R, Capello R (2010) Macroeconomic and territorial policies for regional competitiveness: an EU perspective. Reg Sci Policy Pract 2:1–19.

Camagni R, Diappi L, Leonardi G (1986) Urban growth and decline in a hierarchical system: a supply-oriented dynamic approach. Reg Sci Urban Econ 16:145–160

Capello R (2004) Beyond optimal city size: theory and evidence reconsidered. In: Capello R, Nijkamp P (eds) Urban dynamics and growth: advances in urban economics. Elsevier, Amsterdam, pp 57–86

Capello R (2007) A forecasting territorial model of regional growth: the MASST model. Ann Reg Sci 41(4):753–787

Capello R, Fratesi U (2009) Modelling European regional scenarios: aggressive versus defensive competitive strategies. Environ Plann A 41(2):481–504

Capello R, Fratesi U (2010) Globalization and a dual Europe: future alternative growth trajectories. Ann Reg Sci. doi:10.1007/s00168-009-0295-6

Capello R, Camagni R, Chizzolini B, Fratesi U (2008) Modelling regional scenarios for the enlarged Europe: European competitiveness and global strategies. Springer, Berlin

Carlino G (1980) Contrasts in agglomeration: New York and Pittsburgh reconsidered. Urban Stud 17:343–351

Chinitz B (1961) Contrasts in agglomeration: New York and Pittsburgh. Am Econ Rev Pap 51:279–289

Christaller W (1933) Die Zentralen Orte in Suddeuschland. Gustav Fischer Verlag, Jena

Florida R (2004) The flight of the creative class: the new global competition for talent. Harper Business, New York

Friedmann J (1986) The world city hypothesis. Dev Change 17:69–83

Fujita M (1985) Urban economic theory: land use and city size. Cambridge University Press, Cambridge, MA

Fujita M, Krugman P, Mori T (1999) On the evolution of hierarchical urban systems. European Econ Rev 43:209–251

Henderson J (1985) Economic theory and the cities. Academic, Orlando

Hoover EM, Vernon R (1962) Anatomy of a metropolis. Harvard University Press, Cambridge, MA

Kaldor N (1970) The case of regional policies. Scottish J Polit Econ 3:337–348

Krugman P (1991) Geography and trade. MIT Press, Cambridge, MA

Krugman P, Venables AJ (1996) Integration specialisation and adjustment. Eur Econ Rev 40:959–967

Lucas RE (1988b) On the mechanics of economic development. J Monetary Econ 22:3–42

Lösch A (1954) The economics of location. Yale University Press, New Haven (orig. edn (1940) Die Räumliche Ordnung der Wirtschaft. Gustav Fischer, Jena)

Mills E (1993) What makes metropolitan areas grow? In: Summers A, Cheshire P, Senn L (eds) Urban change in the United States and Western Europe. The Urban Institute, Washington, pp 193–216

Myrdal G (1957) Economic theory of under-developed regions. General Duckworth, London

Richardson HW (1969) Regional economics. World University, Redwood Press, Trowbridge

Richardson HW (1972) Optimality in city size, systems of cities and urban policy: a sceptic's view. Urban Stud 9:29–47

Romer PM (1986b) Increasing returns and long-run growth. J Pol Econ 94:1002–1037

Sassen S (1991) The global city. Princeton University Press, Princeton

Scott A (2001) Global city-regions. Oxford University Press, Oxford

Taylor P, Derubber B, Saey P, Witlox F (eds) (2007) Cities in globalisation. Routledge, London

Chapter 10
Metropolitan Regions and Export Renewal

Lina Bjerke and Charlie Karlsson

Abstract Metropolitan regions are advantageous location for new export products due to factors such as external economies, diversified industry environment and a large share of skilled labour. This is the main assumption of this paper. What happens to these products when the technology becomes common knowledge? Using empirical data on exports, we find that products with a high specialisation in the metropolitan region have a tendency to be successful in the non-metropolitan regions subsequent years. Also, this export product diffusion does not seem to be related to a location in the immediate proximity to the metropolitan region. Instead, the recipient regions are mainly characterised as being centrally located in its labour market region, having a high share of highly educated individuals. Features related product standardisation such as a large manufacturing sector and low labour costs cannot be distinguished as prominent features.

Keywords Metropolitan regions • Exports • Product innovation • Networks • Diffusion

1 Introduction

Our model intertwines two standard ingredients. The first of these emphasizes the impact of urban agglomerations. Metropolitan regions are large urban agglomerations that act as breeding places for innovations. The conventional

---

L. Bjerke (✉)
Jönköping International Business School, Box 1026, Jönköping 551 11, Sweden

CESIS, Royal Institute of Technology, Stockholm, Sweden
e-mail: lina.bjerke@jibs.hj.se

C. Karlsson
CESIS, Royal Institute of Technology, Stockholm, Sweden
e-mail: charlie.karlsson@jibs.hj.se

J. Klaesson et al. (eds.), *Metropolitan Regions*, Advances in Spatial Science,
DOI 10.1007/978-3-642-32141-2_10, © Springer-Verlag Berlin Heidelberg 2013

product life cycle model states that the need for skilled labor is the highest during the scientific phase. If the production of these products initially involves a relatively high share of skilled labor we assume that these are high value products. However, the speed of the technological change slows down along the product cycle, why the value of being located in a metropolitan region declines. The second relationship stresses the role of non-metropolitan regions in the product cycle. The non-metropolitan regions are biased towards process innovation rather than product innovation. Increasing competition as product ages raises incentives to relocate the production from metropolitan regions to non-metropolitan regions since the factor prices for land and labor are lower in these regions (Norton and Rees 1979; Vernon 1960). From this, we raise three main questions which we attempt to answer. First, what role does the Stockholm metropolitan region (henceforth Stockholm) play for the renewal of the export base in the non-metropolitan regions in Sweden between 1997 and 2003? Second, what type of regions gain from the renewal of their export base? Third, what factors can explain the spatial distribution of these gains?

We find that export products that are highly specialised in Stockholm are those products that successfully are imitated and/or diffused to the rest of Sweden in the following years. This relocation is mainly affected by the location factors in the recipient region rather than by geographical proximity to the metropolitan region. The framework of the classical product cycle theory does not seem to be appropriate to apply for these products which are highly specialised in Stockholm and have a high speed of diffusion. Regions characterised as low-wage regions cannot be distinguished favoured locations compared to regions with higher costs of labour. Instead, our results show that the recipient regions are self-sufficient geographical units which are not dependent upon a location near the metropolitan region. This finding has implications for understanding the dynamics between metropolitan regions and non-metropolitan regions.

Sweden is a small country and only Stockholm can be considered a real metropolitan region. Still, Stockholm is small compared to other European regions such as Paris and London or American regions such as New York. However, Stockholm is a very important region in Sweden and is the location for a majority of the large governmental, financial, and corporate headquarters in Sweden. It is also Sweden's largest global trade market whit nearly 30 % of the total export value and 16 % of the total import value in 2003. Also, Stockholm has a strategically good location in northern Europe as an important node for trade.

1.1 Issues and Background Literature

In recent decades, the world has experienced a new wave of economic globalisation. This has been facilitated by decreasing costs for transportation of goods, people, and information, deregulation, liberalisation, and lowered barriers for international trade and foreign direct investments. To a substantial extent globalisation has been orchestrated by large multinational firms in the old industrialised countries, who have used the emerging new economic arena to on the one hand out-source and off-shore production to lower production costs, and on the other locate production close to customers. In a parallel process, it has been possible to observe the emergence of a large number of new economic actors in a number of countries in particular in Asia with ambitions to penetrate the traditional export markets of the old industrialised countries. These developments have changed the rules of the game on the global economic arena and many regions have had to witness how their traditional export products have been out-competed by the new sources of products and the new actors, while other regions with a more favourable export specialisation have been able to keep or even improve their export position.

This raises fundamental questions about how regions renew their export base over time. The analysis of such renewal processes falls within the field of spatial industrial dynamics, which focuses on processes such as the evolution of technologies, firms, and industries within functional regions as well as within the system of functional regions (Karlsson 1999). During the last 50 years, much has been written within this field about the relationship in open economies between the economic milieu offered by different nations and functional regions and the location behaviour of firms and industries. It is generally assumed that for regions in richer countries to compete on the new global arena they must engage in product competition, i.e. specialise in products with unique characteristics that are difficult for the newer actors in the world economy to compete with. However, it is also generally assumed that the development of new products in the richer countries to a high extent is confined to the large metropolitan regions in these countries. The hypothesis that large urban agglomerations are particularly favourable breeding places for innovations is known as the urban hierarchy hypothesis[1] (Thompson 1965).[2] If these assumptions are correct, it is a major research issue to find out how the export base in non-metropolitan functional regions is renewed.

Metropolitan regions in developed countries are characterised by a concentration of human capital, research universities, private R&D, head-offices of large multinational companies, technology import firms, specialised business services, advanced customers, national government administration. These factors mutually create a complex and unique environment. With their high density of a large variety of economic actors in geographical proximity, they allow for intense face-to-face interaction, which stimulates knowledge exchange and knowledge creation

---

[1] This hypothesis has been criticised on theoretical grounds by, for example, Taylor (1986) and on empirical grounds by Howells (1983) and Kleinklencht and Poot (1992).

[2] The role of metropolitan regions for the development of new products was stressed already by Hoover and Vernon (1959).

(Saxenian 1994).[3] They also normally host one or several international airport(s), which make them well connected internationally. The characteristics of metropolitan regions generate specific agglomeration advantages, which make them superior as breeding places for innovations and new products (Ewers and Wettman 1980; Perrin 1988; Suarrez-Villa and Karlsson 1996). In particular, Glaeser (1999) emphasizes the role played by agglomeration economies for innovative activities by fostering localised learning processes. According to theory (Cantwell 1995), there are three major reasons why innovative activities concentrate in metropolitan regions: (1) there are economies of scale in the R&D function, and if they are strong enough, R&D will concentrate to a high extent in metropolitan regions, (2) there are location and urbanisation economies in R&D and innovation, and (3) innovation is seen as a demand-led process stimulated by the demand of high-income consumers and skill-intensive downstream production in metropolitan regions (Burenstam-Linder 1961; Schmookler 1966).

The general shift of economic activities between nations and between regions has been analysed within the framework of the spatial product life cycle theory (Norton and Rees 1979; Vernon 1966).[4] The decentralisation of economic activities within countries has also been analysed within the framework of the "filtering-down" theory (Erickson 1976; Thompson 1965). These theories have inspired the development of the "lead-lag"-model, which has been successfully applied on data for Sweden and Norway (Forslund and Johansson 1995). To the extent that new products survive long enough to mature, there will be a shift from product to process development and from product to price competition, which makes production less dependent upon the economic milieu in metropolitan regions and more sensitive to lower production costs.[5] In particular, Markusen (1985) has explored the spatial implications of qualitatively changed conditions of production and demand during the course of the product cycle, emphasizing the particular role of agglomeration economies during the innovative phases of an industry's product cycle. These factors will induce a diffusion of production from the metropolitan regions to the non-metropolitan regions, a pattern, which has been confirmed in several empirical studies (Brouwer et al. 1999; Erickson 1976; Ewers and Wettman 1980; Martin 1979; Oakey et al. 1980). Thus, we can understand how metropolitan regions play a critical role for the renewal of the export base in the rest of the country.

While larger countries such as the US, Japan and Great Britain have several metropolitan regions, smaller countries like Sweden, Denmark and Austria are dependent upon a single metropolitan region i.e., Stockholm, Copenhagen and Vienna. In the latter case, it is reasonable to assume that the renewal of the export

---

[3] However, results for the London conurbation reported by Gordon and McCann (2005) indicate that the importance of specifically local informal information spillovers is much more limited than has been suggested.

[4] The product life cycle theory can be seen as an extension of spatial theories of industrial dynamics developed by Marshall (1890), Kuznets (1929, 1930), Burns (1934), Schumpeter (1939), Clark (1940), and others.

[5] Duranton and Puga (2001) present a model where new products are developed in diversified cities, and relocated to specialised cities, when firms have found their ideal production process.

base in the remaining non-metropolitan regions to a substantial degree is dependent, on the one hand, on the characteristics and dynamics of the metropolitan region and, on the other hand, on the non-metropolitan regions' accessibility to the metropolitan region.

In smaller countries, the non-metropolitan regions to a substantial degree are linked up with the metropolitan region through various networks. The national infrastructure and transport networks are often organised with the metropolitan region as the central hub. The metropolitan region also plays a central role in many business networks. The large multinational companies normally have both their head offices and major R&D facilities in the metropolitan region, while their production and distribution facilities are located in many different non-metropolitan regions. Most of the firms that are specialised in the import of new technologies as well as many of the specialised business service firms are located in the metropolitan region. This obviously creates a number of dependencies between the metropolitan region and the non-metropolitan regions in a small country.

2 Spatial Product Shifts and Metropolitan Regions

The main point for our theoretical analysis is that metropolitan regions have advantageous such as external economies, diversified industry environment and a relatively large share of skilled labour. This makes these regions favourable locations for developing and exporting new products (Andersson and Johansson 1984). Their monopoly in such products generates a monopoly rent, which explains their higher wages. If we follow Krugman (1979a) we assume that the ability to exploit *new* technology place certain regions in advantageous positions in terms of development. A number of constraints sketch out the basic model of trade between the metropolitan region and the non-metropolitan regions. First, labour is the only production factor and this is immobile between the two regions. Second, all products are produced with the same production function. Third, the labour productivity for all products are the same in both regions and one need one unit of labour to produce one unit of old or new products. Finally, there are no costs of transportation and there are only two types of products: old products and new products. Old products have been developed earlier and the related technology is known to all. New products arise in the metropolitan region and are also produced there.

This two-region system presented in Krugman (1979a) tends to move toward a steady state where relative wages are constant and where the metropolitan region has a fixed mark-up to its advantage, which is an increasing function of the rate of new product development and a decreasing function of the speed with which new products become old products. The metropolitan region develops and exports new products and the non-metropolitan region exports old products. The non-metropolitan region increases its number of export products by imitating new products developed in the metropolitan region or if producers in the metropolitan region relocate their production to the non-metropolitan region when their products become old. Old and new products enter demand symmetrically and all individuals have the same utility function (Krugman 1979b):

$$U = \left\{ \sum_{i=1}^{n} c(i)^{\theta} \right\}^{\frac{1}{\theta}}, \quad 0 < \theta < 1 \tag{10.1}$$

where $c(i)$ is the consumption of the ith product and n is the total number of old and new products. Furthermore, there is a latent demand for not yet developed new products. If Δn new products are developed the consumers will now maximize

$U = \left\{ \sum_{i=1}^{n+\Delta n} c(i)^{\theta} \right\}^{\frac{1}{\theta}}$ under their budget restriction.

This implies that utility increases with an increased variety of available products for given incomes and prices. On the production side, all products are assumed to be produced under perfect competition with zero profits. That is, the prices of any products produced in a region equal the regional wage rates, $P_M = w_m$ and $P_{NM} = w_{NM}$.

All new products will be produced in the metropolitan region and whether the metropolitan will produce any old products at all depend on the relative wages. If $w_M/w_{NM} > 1$, the metropolitan region will specialize in new products.

Now consider what happens if some new products mature and become old products, so that they also can be produced in the non-metropolitan region. We study the relative demand for a product produced in the metropolitan region and one produced in the non-metropolitan region. The relative demand will according to Eq. 10.1 only depend on the relative prices:

$$\frac{C_M}{C_{NM}} = \left(\frac{P_M}{P_{NM}} \right)^{-(1/1-\theta)} = \left(\frac{w_M}{w_{NM}} \right)^{-(1/1-\theta)} \tag{10.2}$$

where c_M is the consumption of the metropolitan product and c_{NM} is the consumption of the non-metropolitan product. Labour demand in each region will be equal to the demand for each product times the number of products. By rearrangement, the relative wages can be expressed as a function of new to old products and relative labour forces. The relative wage rate in the metropolitan region is dependent on the relative importance of new products. An increase in the rate of new product development in the metropolitan region will increase its relative wage;

$$\frac{w_M}{w_{NM}} = \left(\frac{n_M}{n_{NM}} \right)^{1-\theta} \left(\frac{L_M}{L_{NM}} \right)^{-(1-\theta)} \tag{10.3}$$

What determines then the rate of new product development in metropolitan regions? In line with Krugman (1979b) we assume that the number of new products developed is proportional to the number of existing products $\dot{n} = in$. However, over time new products become old products, which in the same tradition can be expressed as $\dot{n}_{NM} = tn_M$ which implies that new products will become old products and can be produced in non-metropolitan regions with a time lag equal to $1/t$. The rate of change of the number of new products is equal to the difference between Eqs. 8 and 9, i.e., $= \dot{n}_M = in_M$.

The above described system is not stable but the stock of pro ducts will tend toward a stable mix. Defining the share of new products as $\sigma = n_M/n$ we have that;

$$\dot{\sigma} = \frac{\dot{n}_M}{n} - \frac{\sigma \dot{n}}{n} = i - (i + t)\sigma \qquad (10.4)$$

Hence, the system described will tend towards equilibrium at $\sigma = i/(i + t)$. The ratio of new to old products determines relative wages, implying that we in equilibrium have

$$\frac{n_M}{n_{NM}} = \frac{\sigma}{1 - \sigma} = \frac{i}{t} \qquad (10.5)$$

Although this framework is more spatially specific it follows the general assumptions of the product cycle theory as presented by Vernon (1966), Norton and Rees (1979), and Andersson and Johansson (1984). The metropolitan region can improve its relative situation by increasing the rate or new product development, while the non-metropolitan region can improve its situation by speeding up imitation of new products so that they age rapidly.

2.1 Urban Agglomeration

Metropolitan and non-metropolitan regions differ in many respects. The advantages of urban specialisation can be traced back to Marshall's (1890) type of localisation economies and Jacob's (1969) urbanisation economies. The congestion costs of being located in a highly diversified metropolitan region are outweighed by the reduced search costs for the ideal production process. The localisation economies are only created by those firms that are involved in the same type of production. Duranton and Puga (2001) suggest that these diversified cities with internal localisation economies act as nursery cities. The diversified regions are more suitable for the early innovative stages of the product cycle. When the best production process found in the diversified environment becomes less important, the production is relocated to a specialised region where mass production is profitable.

One significant difference between metropolitan and non-metropolitan regions is that the former have a higher concentration of skilled labour than the latter. We now assume that there are two types of labour: skilled labour and unskilled labour.

Skilled labour is characterised by being more mobile than unskilled, so we make the extreme assumption that skilled labour of which the total supply is fixed can move without frictions between the two regions, while unskilled labour is totally immobile. All products will be produced with unskilled and skilled labour. If new and old products enter demand symmetrically the metropolitan region, with a larger concentration of skilled labour specialises in new products. The same is true for the processes determining the rate of new product development and of product ageing.[6]

In the given setting new and old products as product groups can be looked upon as composite commodities since the relative prices within the groups are given. The relative prices on new and old products will determine the relative demand of the two commodities. To investigate the short-run equilibrium one now must observe that the relative supply of the two commodities no longer is fixed, since the fixed total supply of skilled labour can be relocated between the two regions. A rise in the relative price of new products, which increases the value of the marginal product of skilled labour, will induce skilled labour to move from the non-metropolitan to the metropolitan region until they earn the same wage in both regions. As a result, the output of new products will increase and that of old products decrease.

New product development in the metropolitan region, which increases the number of new products, increases the demand for new products, i.e. metropolitan products, at any given relative price. This will induce a rise in the price of new products, which will induce skilled labour to move to the metropolitan region. As a result, the wages of unskilled labour in the non-metropolitan region will decline. On the other hand, if the non-metropolitan region can speed up the imitation of new products and transform them into old products, production of old products will increase, skilled workers will start to move to the non-metropolitan region and the wages of unskilled workers in this region will increase. Interpreting the results, we can say that it is the region, which most rapidly can increase its product portfolio that will experience an inflow of skilled labour. It is important to notice the direction of the causation. It runs from new product development and product imitation, respectively, to skilled labour mobility, and not the other way around.

2.2 Mobility and Imitating Regions

The link between urban agglomeration and the mobility across locations can take many forms. If we assume that metropolitan regions are particularly good breeding places for innovations the imitation/diffusion of products from these regions to non-metropolitan regions can vary in the procedures (Johansson and Karlsson 2003):

1. Firms in the metropolitan region decentralise part or all of their activities, either to lower their production costs or because they are growing or because they intend to grow

---

[6] For further discussion on this discussion on old and new products in a setting of north–south trade please see Krugman (1979).

2. Firms can change their internal division of labour when they have production units in several different regions.
3. Firms in the metropolitan region outsource part or all of their production to independent firms (suppliers) in non-metropolitan regions
4. Firms in the metropolitan region make it possible for firms in non-metropolitan region to use their business concept via licensing, franchising, etc.
5. Firms in non-metropolitan regions imitate products produced by firms in the metropolitan region
6. Firms in the metropolitan region, which has developed new products based upon new knowledge and/or imitation of imported products, locate the production of these products to non-metropolitan regions.

Skilled labour not only plays a role in the production of new and old products but also in the development of new products and in the imitation of new products. Here we are, in particular, interested in the imitation process, i.e. in the factors, which determine the rate of diffusion of aging products from the metropolitan region to non-metropolitan regions. An inherent assumption in the product cycle theory is that products as they age demand less and less skilled labour for their production. An implication of this assumption is that it is those non-metropolitan regions with the largest accessible supply of skilled labour that will adopt aging products early, while non-metropolitan regions less well supplied with skilled labour have to wait until a later stage.

Johansson and Karlsson (1991) highlight three factors, which are resource and system conditions for both innovation and imitation activities: (1) relevant competence for development work, (2) information about customer preferences and willingness to pay for various product characteristics and (3) information about new technical solutions.

From the perspective of the non-metropolitan regions, their competence for development work is determined on the one hand by their accessible supply of skilled labour and on the other hand by their accessible supply of company R&D, university R&D and specialised R&D institutes and firms. Information about customers is a function of a region's accessibility to different markets and presence of firms with information and knowledge about different markets. Information about new technical solutions in non-metropolitan regions is a function among other things of their accessibility to the metropolitan region, since that region is the major hub for the import of new ideas, new knowledge, new innovations, new technologies, etc. from abroad as well as a major hub for knowledge creation due to a strong concentration of company and university R&D. To summarize, we expect non-metropolitan regions to differ in their capabilities to absorb export products from the metropolitan region and to transform them to their own export products depending on the institutional infrastructure, education, geography, and resources devoted to R&D (c.f., Maurseth and Verspagen 1999).

Johansson and Karlsson (2001) present a framework within which a non-metropolitan region's capacity to absorb new export products from a metropolitan region is dependent on technology and scale effects together with influences from durable regional characteristics. The technology and scale effects are dependent on the potential to realise internal economies of scale in firms and the extent of external economies of scale in terms of location and urbanisation economies. The potential to realise internal economies of scale are among things depending on the production technology in existing plants in the region and their degree of flexibility to produce varieties of existing products as well as products that are totally new to the region.

The durable regional characteristics consist of on the one hand accessibility to local and external market potentials for different types of products and on the other hand of the supply of durable capacities. The durable capacities represent regionally trapped resources, such as material and non-material infrastructure, the sector composition of the economy, i.e. its specialisation, and the labour force with its skill-distribution, which at least in the short-run is a trapped resource. The material infrastructure of regions is important in several respects. The intra-regional transport infrastructure determines the accessibility of economic actors within a region and thus the conditions for face-to-face interaction, which are critical for knowledge generation and knowledge diffusion and exchange (Lucas 1993).[7] In particular, we assume that the accessibility to human capital to be a critical factor for the capacity of non-metropolitan regions to adopt new export products from the metropolitan region (Andersson et al. 2007; Gråsjö 2006).

2.3 Hypotheses

New export products appear in the Stockholm metropolitan region and will thereafter diffuse to the non-metropolitan regions in Sweden. These are more favourable locations when the products are reaching a mature phase. We build the hypotheses on the main arguments in Johansson and Karlsson (2001, 2003) and formulate three main hypotheses:

Hypothesis 1. *Export products with a high specialisation in the metropolitan region in a given year have a strong export value growth in non metropolitan regions in the following years.*

This follows the theories of product cycles and the urban hierarchy/filtering down theories. Products follow a path of development and the optimal location change when the product goes from the stage of innovation towards standardisation. An export product emerges in the metropolitan region as a new innovation or a new import good. The diffusion to a location outside the metropolitan region occurs in order to reach e.g., lower factor costs or a specific business milieu.

Hypothesis 2. *The non-metropolitan accessibility to the metropolitan increases the probability of a high export value growth in the highly specialized export products in the metropolitan region.*

Links between the metropolitan region and other regions facilitate the diffusion of products. These links can be of physical infrastructural character but can also be industry specific such as knowledge networks. Built up competence and agglomeration of knowledge create externalities in the innovative metropolitan region. These

---

[7] Ciccone and Hall (1996) emphasize the importance of density for productivity.

10 Metropolitan Regions and Export Renewal

externalities are advantageous for the non metropolitan region in order to strengthen their export position. Producer services are distance sensitive and are largely dependent on face-to-face interactions and act as complement to manufacture (Gaspar and Glaeser 1998). The bivariate correlation between the distance to Stockholm and accessibility to producer services has the largest negative value. The further away you are from the metropolitan region the lower is your potential access to producer services. Two general hypotheses are specified regarding regional conditions for creating new export products.

Hypothesis 3. *Regional diversity of economic activities stimulates the adoption of new export products in non-metropolitan regions.*

This follows theory on diversity as those presented by Jacobs (1969). Hence, the emergence of new exports is dependent upon a rich and varied supply of production factors. Also, product cycle theories and the Dixit-Stiglitz-type of modelling suggest that the metropolitan regions, being the driving force of product and process development have higher wages than the regions where the products are relocated into per se. Mature products tend to locate in where there are low labour costs and favourable business milieus (Norton and Rees 1979).

Hypothesis 4. *Export products, which diffuse from metropolitan regions, will mainly be produced in non-metropolitan regions with a specialisation in the sector to which the product belong.*

This reasoning is developed in congruence with arguments of Marshall (1890), Arrow (1962) and Romer (1986), who contend that knowledge is largely sector-specific. This implies that export products, which diffuse from metropolitan regions, mainly will be produced in non-metropolitan regions with a specialisation in the sector to which the product belongs. If we assume that the export product has been relocated from the metropolitan region and adopted in a non-metropolitan region the success rate is most comparatively calculated as the export growth in the subsequent period. A high export value growth region has to possess advantageous factors such as compatible labour force, natural resources, educated labour, etc.

3 Data and Estimations

The data on exported products is provided by Statistics Sweden and covers the years between 1997 and 2003 and uses the 8-digit CN classification of products.[8] The data set is constructed in such a way that the export value, export volume and the number of firms can be calculated for every combination of urban area, 8-digit product and firm identification. Hence, the raw material consists of more than

---

[8] CN = Combined Nomenclature based on the Harmonized Commodity Description and Codifying System. Exports of services are not included and the agriculture, fishery and forestry are excluded when the sample is extracted.

246 L. Bjerke and C. Karlsson

600,000 observations. We are only interested in the products exported from Stockholm that are also represented in at least one of the other functional regions. Thus, those products that did not exist in any of the regions but Stockholm in 2003 have been removed. The export specialisation of the metropolitan region of Stockholm (henceforth, Stockholm) is calculated for the year 1997. The export value growth is calculated for the remaining 80 functional regions in Sweden between the years 1997 and 2003.

3.1 Descriptives, Sample Extraction and Model Estimation

In Sweden, there are 81 functional regions based on commuting patterns where the Stockholm region is numbered as 1. A functional region is constituted by one or several urban areas. In total, there are 289 urban areas in Sweden and 30 of these are within Stockholm. Consequently, 259 urban areas belong to any of the functional regions numbered 2–81. One urban area in each functional region can be considered the central urban area (hosting local government offices) and has a positive net migration of commuters.

Table 10.1 is a contingency table of the split sample. Rows represent the degree of export product specialisation of different products in Stockholm in 1997.[9] The 8-digit products are then divided according to their respective degree of specialisation. The specialisation, calculated as the location quotient has been divided into four groups: high, medium high, medium low and low export specialisation. Columns represent the export value growth between 1997 and 2003 of these products in the functional regions 2–81. This has been divided into five groups: high, medium high, medium low, low and negative export value growth. As indicated by the χ^2 value the data is not equally distributed over the cells. There are 580 export products with a high export specialisation in Stockholm in 1997 that also have had a high export value growth in the following 6-year period in the rest of Sweden. We are interested to learn what regions benefit and what characteristics spur the regional absorption of these highly specialised products in Stockholm so this group of products is the focus of the empirical analysis.[10] Henceforth, this group of export is called H^{++}. And the analysis is hereafter performed on the 259 urban areas in the functional regions 2–81.[11]

---

[9] Specialisation is calculated with a location quotient: $\sigma = \left[(EV^k_{Sthlm})/(\Sigma_{SthlmEV}) \right] / \left[EV^k_{Sweden}/\Sigma_{SwedenEV} \right]$, where EV is the export value, k is the 8-digit product. $\sigma > 1$: The product's share of Stockholm's export is larger than the product's share of Sweden's total export, i.e. the product is over represented. $\sigma < 1$: The product's share of Stockholm's exports is smaller than the product's share of Sweden's total exports, i.e. the product is under represented.

[10] 741 of the export products with a low export specialization in Stockholm in 1997 also had a negative growth in all other regions in Sweden between 1997 and 2003.

[11] No distinction is made with respect to novelty. That is, this group also comprises products that were not exported in 1997 but exported in 2003 in regions 2–81.

10 Metropolitan Regions and Export Renewal

Table 10.1 Contingency table of number of export products in each category i.e., export specialization (location quotient) in Stockholm in 1997 and export value growth in the remaining regions between 1997 and 2003

Export specialisation in Stockholm[b]	Export value growth in regions 2–81 between 1997 and 2003[a]					
	High (>4.22)	Medium High (4.21–1.30)	Medium Low (1.30–0.45)	Low (0.44–0)	Neg	Total
High (>2.34)	**580**	244	161	127	366	1,478
Medium high (>0.58)	212	249	220	238	561	1,480
Medium low (0.08)	158	205	256	225	634	1,478
Low (<0.08)	94	161	221	262	741	1,479
Total	1,044	859	858	852	2,302	5,915

Pearson Chi-Square 771,7 (*sig. 0.000*)
Likelihood ratio 726,3 (*sig. 0.000*)
Linear-by-linear association 531.2 (*sig. 0.000*)
[a]$(EV_{03} - EV_{97})/EV_{97}$
[b]Divided into quartiles of export specialization in Stockholm (LA 1) in 1997

The export value of H^{++} urban areas in the functional regions 2–81 serve as the observations for each urban area respectively. Thus, the export values for these particular products are the observations for each urban area respectively.

As many as 78 out of the 80 functional regions outside Stockholm had export in the group called H^{++} in 1997. In 2003 the number had decreased to 76. For those urban areas within these functional regions, 237 were represented as exporters of H^{++} in 1997. This increased to 246 by the year 2003. Table 10.2 presents the export value growth (in percent) for all categories in Table 10.1. The highest export value growth appears for the product group H^{++} in the upper left corner.

Table 10.3 describes the independent variables in the empirical analysis and presents the motivation of their importance in the analysis and also the expected impact on the dependent variable.

The descriptive statistics for all variables and their natural logs are presented in Table 10.4. Only 13 (22) of the 258 urban areas outside Stockholm had no exports in 2003 (1997) in the product group H^{++}.

Table 10.7 in Appendix 1 provides the rank of the export value growth in H^{++}, the share of employees in the manufacturing sector, density, share of highly educated labour and distance to Stockholm are presented. The ten regions with the highest export value growth in H^{++} have a relatively high share of employees within the manufacturing industry and a high share of highly educated labour. Figures 10.1, 10.2 and 10.3 in Appendix 1 shows the geographical distribution of the export value in H^{++} in 1997 and 2003, the unit value for H^{++} for both years respectively, and the export value growth during this time period. A darker shade in the maps indicates a higher value. An ocular inspection indicates a similar geographical distribution of the export value in both 1997 and 2003. The map of the absolute export value growth indicates a spread into regions further away from Stockholm. It is interesting to note that the unit value for the sum of all products in H^{++} is lower in 2003 (19.31) than in the year 1997 (31.24). This follows the

Table 10.2 Growth of export value between 1997 and 2003 in LA regions 2–81

Export specialisation in LA 1	Percentage change in export value per category				
	High	Medium high	Medium low	Low	Neg
High (>2.34)	25.5	1.83	0.84	0.34	−0.75
Medium high (>0.58)	20.21	1.7	0.77	0.27	−0.45
Medium low (0.08)	8.26	2.1	0.7	0.22	−0.76
Low (<0.08)	9.52	1.99	0.6	0.21	−0.45

Table 10.3 Explanatory variables explaining export product diffusion

Variable	Description[a]	Motivation	Effect
$Dist_i^{97}$	Distance between centre region i and centre of Stockholm (kilometres)	Proximity to diversity of sectors and variety of knowledge sources	−/+
$Manuf_i^{97}$	Share of employees in the manufacturing sector	Indicate favourable locations for old export products	+
Edu_i^{97}	Share of highly educated labour in region i with at least 3 years of university education	Knowledge and absorptive capacity of the regional workforce	+
$AccServ_i^{97}$	Access to producer services expressed as an exponentially decreasing function[a]	Indicate the distance sensitivity related to producer services	+
$Wage_i^{98}$	Annual wage per employee in the manufacturing sector in 1,000 SEK	Knowledge intensive metropolitan regions have higher wage levels	−
$D_{i,PubSec}^{97}$	D_1: 1 = large public sector; 0 otherwise	Control for a large employment share in the public sector	−
$D_{i,AgricSec}^{97}$	D_1: 1 = large agricultural sector; 0 otherwise	Control for a large employment share in the agricultural sector	−
$D_{i,Central}^{97}$	D_2: 1 = central urban area; 0 otherwise	Control for central urban areas in the functional region	+
$D_{i,Periph}^{97}$	D_3: 1 = peripheral urban area in large functional region; 0 otherwise	Control for peripheral urban areas in the functional region	−

All variables are figures of year 1997 except wage (1998)
[a]For further readings see (Andersson and Johansson 1995; Gråsjö 2005; Johansson et al. 2003; Weibull 1976)

arguments in product life cycle theories, urban agglomeration and filtering down. The products have a higher unit value in an earlier stage of the product cycle. They spread geographically along the phase of maturation and standardisation.

Building on the discussion above, the following model is estimated;

$$\ln EV_i^t = \ln EV_i^{t-1} + \ln Dist_{is}^{t-1} + \ln Manuf_i^{t-1} + \ln Edu_i^{t-1} + \ln AccServ_i^{t-1}$$
$$+ \ln Wage_i^{t-1} + D_i^{t-1} \qquad (10.6)$$

where $\ln EV_i^t$ is the export value of H^{++} in region i in the year 2003. By taking the bivariate correlations between all variables, the highest correlation appears between

10 Metropolitan Regions and Export Renewal

Table 10.4 Descriptive statistics non transformed variables the natural logarithm values in *italics*[a]

Variable	Mean	Median	Std. dev	Min	Max
EV_i^{03}	80.15 *(14.34)*	3.72 *(15.12)*	340.97 *(4.28)*	0.00 *(0.00)*	3,863.18 *(22.07)*
EV_i^{97}	3.01 *(11.33)*	0.20 *(12.23)*	16.60 *(4.25)*	0.00 *(0.00)*	249.21
$Dist_i^{97}$	417.84 *(5.91)*	401.10 *(5.99)*	206.47 *(0.52)*	71.94 *(4.28)*	1,227.02 *(7.11)*
$Manuf_i^{97}$	0.26 *(−1.45)*	0.25 *(−1.39)*	0.12 *(0.50)*	0.03 *(−3.44)*	0.69 *(−0.38)*
Edu_i^{97}	0.13 *(−2.09)*	0.12 *(−2.14)*	0.04 *(0.28)*	0.07 *(−2.61)*	0.38 *(−0.97)*
$AccServ_i^{97}$	$1.10e^5$ *(11.31)*	$1.17e^5$ *(11.67)*	$6.49e^4$ *(0.95)*	$2.50e^3$ *(7.83)*	$3.46e^5$ *(12.75)*
$Wage_i^{98}$	209.61 *(12.25)*	207.15 *(12.24)*	23.04 *(0.11)*	156.43 *(11.96)*	287.71 *(12.57)*
$D_{i,PubSec}^{97}$	0.11	0.00	0.31	0.00	1.00
$D_{i,AgricSec}^{97}$	0.33	0.00	0.47	0.00	1.00
$D_{i,Central}^{97}$	0.31	0.00	0.46	0.00	1.00
$D_{i,Periph}^{97}$	0.68	1.00	0.47	0.00	1.00

N is 258 and no missing values for all variables

A Breusch-Pagan/Cook-Weisberg test indicates that the linear regression (without the dummy variables) may suffer from heteroscedasticity

[a]13 urban areas have no export value in H++ 2003

the export value in H++ in region i in the year 2003, $\ln EV_i^t$ and the same value for the year 1997, $\ln EV_i^{t-1}$. This primary result indicates regional path dependency. Regions with a high export value have a tendency to attract the same type of products during the subsequent years.

The dummy variables indicating a large public sector, a large agricultural sector and peripheral regions in large functional regions are expected to have a negative impact on the export value growth in H++. The dummy indicating an urban area to be central in a functional region should exert an opposite effect. The regional share of employees within the manufacturing sector should have a positive impact from a product cycle perspective. Also, the regional share of highly educated labour may also impact positively from a product renewal perspective. Also, this holds for total access to producer services. The distance from region i to Stockholm do not necessarily have to be of major importance. Reduced costs of transportation also reduce the importance of a near location to the metropolitan region. So, for certain products to diffuse from the Stockholm metropolitan region the location may be of more importance than the distance per se.

The model estimations are presented in Table 10.5. Looking first at the export value in beginning of the time period, we see that it is stable cross all estimations. This result was anticipated and suggests rigidity in regional export patterns. Regions with a strong position in these high value export products are likely to continue on this path.

The distance to Stockholm is also positive throughout the models. The diffusion of these high value products does not seem to be distance sensitive in the sense of a

Table 10.5 Regression results, estimation method: OLS, dependent variable $= lnEV_i^{03}$ i.e. export value in H^{++} in 2003 in urban areas, inclusion of independent variable $lnEVi97$

	Models N = 258				
Variable	I	II	III	IV	V
$\ln EV_i^{97}$	0.42	0.42	0.40	0.39	0.39
	$(7.85)^{***}$	$(7.82)^{***}$	$(7.51)^{***}$	$(7.29)^{***}$	$(7.09)^{***}$
$\ln Dist_i^{97}$	0.88	0.90	0.84	1.06	1.22
	$(1.75)^{*}$	$(1.78)^{*}$	$(1.68)^{*}$	$(2.08)^{**}$	$(2.27)^{**}$
$\ln Manuf_i^{97}$	0.42	0.43	0.22	0.48	0.40
	(0.67)	(0.69)	(0.36)	(0.77)	(0.63)
$\ln Edu_i^{97}$	2.52	2.27	2.19	2.19	2.54
	$(2.24)^{**}$	$(1.96)^{*}$	$(1.94)^{*}$	$(1.95)^{*}$	$(2.23)^{**}$
$\ln AccServ_i^{97}$	1.35	1.40	1.40	1.57	1.65
	$(4.21)^{***}$	$(4.30)^{***}$	$(4.36)^{***}$	$(4.69)^{***}$	$(4.64)^{***}$
$\ln Wage_i^{98}$	3.55	3.61	2.55	3.49	3.75
	(1.39)	(1.41)	(0.99)	(1.38)	(1.46)
$D_{i,PubSec}^{97}$		0.64			
		(0.93)			
$D_{i,AgricSec}^{97}$			-0.97		
			$(-2.08)^{**}$		
$D_{i,Central}^{97}$				1.02	
				$(2.17)^{**}$	
$D_{i,Periph}^{97}$					-0.92
					$(-2.18)^{**}$
Adj R^2	0.46	0.46	0.46	0.47	0.47

*Significant at the 0.1 level, **significant at the 0.05 level, ***significant at the 0.01 level

geographical closeness to Stockholm. If these products follow the classical product cycle, they would have reached a phase of maturation and standardisation at the time of the relocation. Then, lower land rents and lower labour costs are more attractive than being close to the diverse metropolitan region. One may therefore also expect that a high access to producer services only plays a minor role in the relocation process of these products. This turns out to be true for all models. This argumentation is supported by the bivariate correlations which show that regional access to producer services and distance to Stockholm are negatively correlated.

The regional employment share of highly educated labour $\ln Edu_i^{-1}$ is positive. These high value export products need to be supported by human capital even though they have reached a phase where it is profitable to relocate or increase the number of production sites.

Neither coefficients nor significance are largely affected by the introduction of the dummy variables. Regions with a relatively large agricultural sector tend to be less attractive locations for the high value export products. These products are still dependent upon agglomeration to some extent and regions with peripheral locations are not surprisingly also less attractive. The opposite is true for regions defined as central urban areas. These results are showing the importance of the structure of the functional regions. Central urban areas often function as nodes of infrastructure and

10 Metropolitan Regions and Export Renewal

Table 10.6 Spatial lag model, estimations with spatial autocorrelation: dependent variable, EV_i^{03}

	Spatial lag (z-value) N = 258				
	I	II	III	IV	V
$\ln EV_i^{97}$	0.42	0.42	0.40	0.40	0.40
	$(8.08)^{***}$	$(8.08)^{***}$	$(7.71)^{***}$	$(7.55)^{***}$	$(7.61)^{***}$
$\ln Manuf_i^{97}$	0.53	0.55	0.29	0.61	0.64
	(0.86)	(0.90)	(0.47)	(1.00)	(1.04)
$\ln Edu_i^{97}$	2.81	2.55	2.39	2.50	2.97
	$(2.57)^{***}$	$(2.28)^{**}$	$(2.18)^{**}$	$(2.30)^{**}$	$(2.73)^{***}$
$\ln AccServ_i^{97}$	0.75	0.76	0.81	0.79	0.75
	$(2.24)^{**}$	$(2.31)^{**}$	$(2.44)^{**}$	$(2.46)^{**}$	$(2.33)^{**}$
$\ln Wage_i^{98}$	3.31	3.38	2.37	3.31	3.06
	(1.31)	(1.34)	(0.94)	(1.33)	(1.22)
$D_{i,PubSec}^{97}$		0.70			
		(1.01)			
$D_{i,AgricSec}^{97}$			-1.04		
			$(-2.26)^{**}$		
$D_{i,Central}^{97}$				1.08	
				$(2.30)^{**}$	
$D_{i,Periph}^{97}$					-0.85
					$(-2.03)^{**}$

*Significant at the 0.1 level, **significant at the 0.05 level, ***significant at the 0.01 level

local government offices which all are important factors. This structure is more lucid in the large functional regions than in small ones. Also, it is likely to believe that infrastructural links to the metropolitan region of Stockholm increase with the population size of the functional region (Johansson 1993).

The fact that the wage level is insignificant throughout the models is a striking result. No distinction can be made between low-wage regions and high-wage regions.

In addition to the OLS estimations we test for spatial autocorrelation. Table 10.8 in the Appendix 2 presents the Morans I's test under H_0: *independent observations*, for spatial dependence in export value in H^{++} across regions in Sweden. The tests are based on the spatial weight matrix with travel time distance by car measured in minutes. The weight matrix is standardized and all time distances w_{ij} exceeding 180 min are removed.[12] The null hypothesis of independent observations can be rejected and the sample suffers from spatial autocorrelation. OLS estimations rest on the assumption that observations are independent of one another. In the presence of spatial dependence, estimates are inefficient with incorrect standard errors and may create biased results.

---

[12] For a discussion on distance friction parameters (Hugosson and Johansson 2001).

Table 10.6 presents the spatial autoregressive model i.e., the spatial lag model. [13] A comparison between the OLS results and the spatial estimations in Table 10.6 indicates robustness in parameters and significant levels.

4 Summary and Discussion

It is well recognized that many new products arise in metropolitan regions. Depending on the type of products and the phase of product development, products change geographical location. Conventional product life cycle theory says that products follow innovation, growth, maturity and obsolescence. When the product reaches maturity and standardisation, the input of human capital is lower and products locate in the periphery where there are low prices of land and labour.

On a number of points, we find important deviations from these arguments. First, the wage level in the non-metropolitan regions are of no significance in the models. The relocation of these export products is not driven by the search for low-wage regions. Instead, firms search for regions with a relatively high share of educated individuals which can support the production of these export products. Second, the distance to Stockholm is positively related to the non-metropolitan export growth. Consequently, these products are not dependent upon a metropolitan industry environment. If we believe that products relocate in a phase of standardisation this would not be a surprising result. However, in a classical product cycle setting this is inconsistent with the fact that the wage level and whether or not it is a manufacturing region are insignificant in all models. This paper suggests instead a more diversified explanation with a number of arguments. First, the metropolitan region hamper these products to grow and in order to do grow they need to relocate some, or the entire part of their production to a non-metropolitan region. Second, the non-metropolitan regions seem to function as independent locations which mean that they are not affected by the geographical distance to Stockholm. This suggests that the non-metropolitan regions absorbing these export products have self sufficient production units. Third, the non-metropolitan regions with a prominently high export growth are not typical agricultural regions and they seem to be centrally located in each specific labour market region.

Much is yet to be explored in this area of research. The fact that the unit value of the H^{++} products went down during this 7 year period is not further investigated in this paper and needs a deeper analysis to explain. Also, a further decomposition of the product group H^{++} would be valuable in order to understand industry, or even product differences of diffusion between metropolitan regions and non metropolitan regions.

---

[13] The number of observations is 257. That is, the island Gotland has been removed from the spatial estimation since it creates bias in the distance matrix. An OLS estimation has been performed without Gotland but the results did not diverge from prior results. An estimation of a spatial error model has also been executed and the results are highly robust. The spatial error model considers the error process and not the model itself. The spatial lag model affects the dependent variable by values of the variables in the nearby locations (Anselin 1990).

10 Metropolitan Regions and Export Renewal 253

Appendix 1

Table 10.7 Absolute value growth of products in H^{++} in functional regions 2–81, share of highly educated labor, distance to Stockholm, share of employees within the manufacturing (In ascending order w.r.t export value growth in H^{++})

Functional region	No.	ΔH^{++}	Rank of share 2003[a]	Education share 1997	Distance Stockholm	Manuf.share 1997
Skövde	34	1,302.17	3	0.13	327	0.25
Jönköping	9	1,020.95	5	0.16	328	0.19
Örnsköldsvik	60	944.89	6	0.14	555	0.24
Hudiksvall	57	652.99	17	0.12	303	0.21
Haparanda	80	455.37	47	0.11	1,022	0.14
Gällivare	78	353.45	68	0.11	1,110	0.21
Fagersta	45	310.89	25	0.09	175	0.31
Ljungby	13	189.78	21	0.09	434	0.29
Arvika	40	178.1	39	0.1	376	0.29
Bengtsfors	31	164.66	52	0.08	407	0.19
Örebro	42	153.48	4	0.16	193	0.31
Nyköping	3	115.51	14	0.14	103	0.2
Lidköping	33	96.54	18	0.11	346	0.28
Hagfors	39	95.8	49	0.09	334	0.13
Malmö	25	86.86	1	0.22	602	0.24
Sundsvall	58	78.96	16	0.15	384	0.15
Gävle	53	72.04	23	0.14	177	0.23
Kalmar	16	53.71	15	0.14	388	0.22
Ljusdal	54	48.74	54	0.07	333	0.18
Norrköping	7	46.52	9	0.15	163	0.18
Vilhelmina	67	42.02	57	0.1	692	0.13
Uppsala	2	40.68	11	0.24	72	0.19
Växjö	14	36.39	22	0.15	411	0.15
Sunne	35	31.94	48	0.1	360	0.2
Eskilstuna	5	30.51	24	0.14	114	0.15
Västerås	44	30.05	13	0.17	110	0.18
Göteborg	28	29.01	2	0.21	469	0.2
Simrishamn	22	27.5	42	0.12	595	0.18
Hultsfred	15	26.43	19	0.08	306	0.29
Linköping	6	25.73	8	0.2	200	0.19
Falkenberg	27	20.62	31	0.12	491	0.2
Arvidsjaur	71	20.56	65	0.13	865	0.18
Storuman	65	20.49	75	0.1	760	0.12
Årjäng	37	20.19	51	0.07	401	0.17
Karlstad	36	18.65	38	0.17	302	0.2
Karlskrona	21	18.29	30	0.18	467	0.24
Eksjö	10	17.15	28	0.1	317	0.17
Malung	48	16.2	35	0.07	353	0.2
Halmstad	26	16	26	0.14	489	0.22

(continued)

Table 10.7 (continued)

Functional region	No.	ΔH^{++}	Rank of share 2003[a]	Education share 1997	Distance Stockholm	Manuf.share 1997
Uddevalla	29	15.92	10	0.14	430	0.17
Kristianstad	24	14.74	32	0.14	528	0.23
Ludvika	52	11.99	50	0.12	222	0.22
Borås	32	9.29	12	0.13	410	0.21
Avesta	51	8.84	72	0.1	157	0.2
Strömstad	30	8.1	37	0.1	497	0.28
Helsingborg	23	7.93	7	0.15	562	0.19
Östersund	64	7.82	33	0.17	542	0.13
Arboga	46	7.66	45	0.1	153	0.28
Tranås	11	6.4	43	0.1	269	0.27
Gnosjö	8	6.23	27	0.09	389	0.34
Karlskoga	43	5.84	34	0.13	243	0.18
Falun	50	5.68	36	0.15	224	0.24
Skellefteå	70	4.91	20	0.14	772	0.21
Vansbro	47	4.04	71	0.07	308	0.28
Luleå	79	2.74	53	0.18	905	0.16
Bollnäs	56	2.37	66	0.09	270	0.22
Åre	62	2.29	63	0.12	588	0.14
Älmhult	12	1.82	41	0.12	465	0.21
Kiruna	81	1.54	61	0.12	1,227	0.22
Karlshamn	20	1.35	46	0.11	494	0.18
Kalix	75	1.26	73	0.14	972	0.28
Filipstad	38	1.22	44	0.08	284	0.31
Lycksele	69	0.98	64	0.13	713	0.18
Härjedalen	63	0.71	70	0.07	435	0.14
Strömsund	61	0.47	69	0.09	606	0.19
Sollefteå	59	0.11	40	0.12	500	0.2
Sorsele	66	0	79	0.1	830	0.14
Arjeplog	72	0	76	0.1	909	0.17
Jokkmokk	73	0	77	0.11	1,022	0.27
Överkalix	74	0	80	0.09	997	0.22
Pajala	77	0	78	0.11	1,109	0.15
Mora	49	−0.03	60	0.11	308	0.23
Gotland	19	−0.05	67	0.14	201	0.13
Oskarshamn	17	−0.1	55	0.1	318	0.24
Västervik	18	−0.16	59	0.12	263	0.2
Katrineholm	4	−0.7	29	0.11	141	0.17
Umeå	68	−0.7	56	0.25	643	0.13
Övertorneå	76	−0.83	74	0.11	1,045	0.17
Åmål	41	−0.86	58	0.1	378	0.1
Söderhamn	55	−0.93	62	0.1	252	0.17

[a]The regional share H^{++} of the region's total export

Appendix 2

Table 10.8 Moran's I test for spatial dependence for all models in Table 10.4 for year 2003 model

Variable	Moran's I (p-$value$)[a, b]				
$lnEV_i^{03}$	0.078				
	(0.00)				
$lnEV_i^{97}$	0.035				
	(0.00)				
$lnManuf_i^{97}$	0.094				
	(0.00)				
$lnEdu_i^{97}$	0.062				
	(0.00)				
$lnAccServ_i^{97}$	0.336				
	(0.00)				
$lnWage_i^{98}$	0.067				
	(0.00)				
Dummy (1997)	**I**	**II**	**III**	**IV**	**V**
$D_{i,PubSec}^{97}$		0.017			
		(0.00)			
$D_{i,AgricSec}^{97}$			0.017		
			(0.00)		
$D_{i,Central}^{97}$				0.021	
				(0.00)	
$D_{i,Periph}^{97}$					0.060
					(0.00)

[a]Tests are based on 258*258 row-standardized symmetric weight matrix
[b]"-Tail test

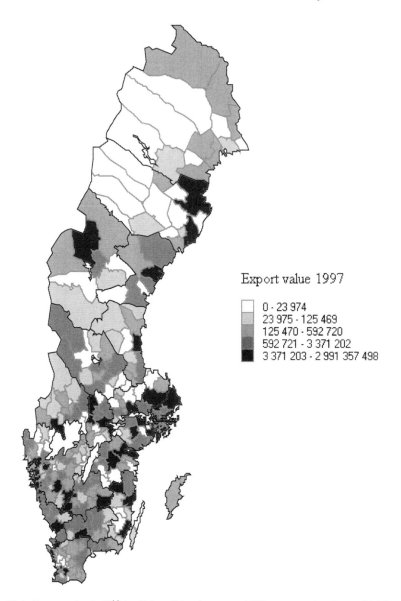

Fig. 10.1 Export value in H^{++} in all Swedish urban areas 1997, export unit value = 31.24

10 Metropolitan Regions and Export Renewal

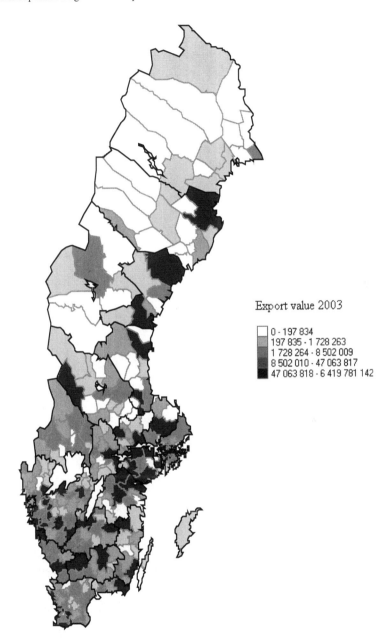

Fig. 10.2 Export value in H^{++} in all Swedish urban areas 2003, export unit value $= 19.31$

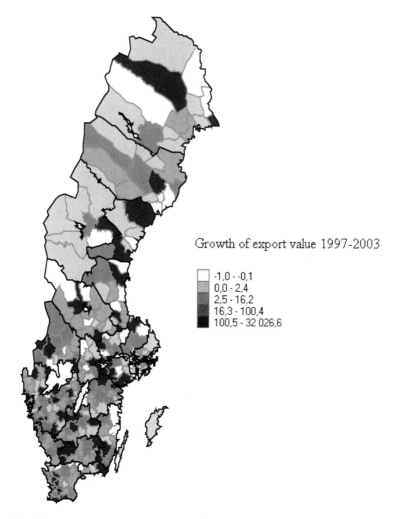

Fig. 10.3 Absolute growth of export value in H^{++} in all Swedish urban areas 1997–2003

References

Andersson ÅE, Johansson B (1984) Knowledge intensity and product cycles in metropolitan regions. Unpublished IIASA WP, International institute for applied systems analysis, Laxenburg

Andersson ÅE, Johansson B (1995) Förnyelse av Västsveriges Regioner: Borås en Framtida Marknadsplats i Norden (No. 92), Swedish Institute for Regional Research

Andersson M, Gråsjö U, Karlsson C (2007) Human capital and productivity in a spatial economic system. Ann Econ Stat/Annales d'Économie et de Statistique 87–88:125–143

Anselin L (1990) Spatial dependence and spatial structural instability in applied regression analysis. J Reg Sci 30(2):185

Arrow KJ (1962) The economic implications of learning by doing. Rev Econ Stud 29:155–173

10 Metropolitan Regions and Export Renewal

Brouwer E, Budil-Nadvornikova H, Kleinknecht A (1999) Are urban agglomerations a better breeding place for product innovation? An analysis of new product announcements. Reg Stud 33(6):541–549

Burenstam-Linder S (1961) An essay on trade and transformation. Wiley, New York

Burns AF (1934) Production trends in the United States since 1870. National Bureau of Economic Research, New York

Cantwell J (1995) The globalisation of technology: what remains of the product cycle model? Camb J Econ 19(1):155–174

Ciccone A, Hall RE (1996) Productivity and the density of economic activity. National Bureau of Economic Research working paper series, No 4313

Clark C (1940) The conditions of economic progress. Macmillan, London

Duranton G, Puga D (2001) Nursery cities: urban diversity, process innovation, and the life cycle of products. Am Econ Rev 91(5):1454–1477

Erickson RA (1976) The filtering-down process: industrial location in a nonmetropolitan area. Prof Geogr 28(3):254–260

Ewers H-J, Wettman RW (1980) Innovation-oriented regional policy. Reg Stud 14(3):161–179

Forslund U, Johansson B (1995) The Mälardalen: a leading region in Scandinavia. In: Cheshire LP, Gordon TI (eds) Territorial competition in an integrating Europe. Avebury, Aldershot, pp 3–27

Gaspar J, Glaeser EL (1998) Information technology and the future of cities. J Urban Econ 43(1):136–156

Glaeser E (1999) Learning in cities. J Urban Econ 46:254–277

Gordon IR, McCann P (2005) Innovation, agglomeration, and regional development. J Econ Geogr 5(5):523–543

Gråsjö U (2005) The importance of accessibility to R&D on patent production in Swedish municipalities

Gråsjö U (2006) Spatial spillovers of knowledge production: an accessibility approach. Jönköping International Business School (Internationella handelshögsk. i Jönköping), Jönköping

Hoover EM, Vernon R (1959) Anatomy of a metropolis. Harvard University Press, Cambridge, MA

Howells JRL (1983) Filter-down theory: location and technology in the UK pharmaceutical industry. Environ Plann 15:147–164

Hugosson P, Johansson B (2001) Business trips between functional regions. In: Hugosson P (ed) Interregional business travel and the economics of business interaction. Jönköping International Business School, Jönköping

Jacobs J (1969) The economy of cities. Random House, New York

Johansson B (1993) Ekonomisk dynamik i Europa : nätverk för handel, kunskapsimport och innovationer (1. uppl. ed.). Liber-Hermod i samarbete med Institutet för framtidsstudier, Malmö

Johansson B, Karlsson C (1991) Från brukssamhällets exportnät till kunskapssamhällets importnät, Karlstad

Johansson B, Karlsson C (2001) Geographic transaction costs and specialisation opportunities of small and medium-sized regions. In: Johansson B, Karlsson C, Stough RR (eds) Theories of endogenous regional growth lessons for regional policies. Springer, Berlin, pp 150–180

Johansson B, Karlsson C (2003) Växande branscher-om Stockholmsregionens samspel med övriga landet. Stockholms läns landsting, Regionplane och trafikkontoret, Stockholm

Johansson B, Klaesson J, Olsson M (2003) Commuters non-linear response to time distance. J Geogr Syst 5:315–329

Karlsson C (1999) Spatial industrial dynamics in Sweden: urban growth industries. Growth Change 30:184–212

Kleinknecht A, Poot T (1992) Do regions matter for R&D? Reg Stud J Reg Stud Assoc 26:221–232

Krugman P (1979a) A model of innovation, technology transfers, and the world distribution of income. J Polit Econ 87:253–266

Krugman PR (1979b) Increasing returns, monopolistic competition, and international trade. J Int Econ 9(4):469–479

Kuznets SS (1929) Retardation in economic growth. J Econ Bus Hist 1:534–560

Kuznets SS (1930) Secular movements in production and prices: their nature and their bearing upon cyclical fluctuations. Houghton Mifflin, Boston

Lucas RE Jr (1993) Making a miracle. Econometrica 61:251–272

Markusen JR (1985) Profit cycles, oligopoly and regional development. The MIT Press, Cambridge, MA

Marshall A (1890) Principles of economics, 8th edn. Macmillan, London

Martin F et al (1979) The interregional diffusion of innovations in Canada (Report to the Ministry of Supply and Services). Ottawa and Hull, Quebec

Maurseth PB, Verspagen B (1999) Europe: one or several systems of innovation? An analysis based upon patent citations. In: Fagerberg J, Guerrieri P, Verspagen B (eds) The economic challenge for Europe. Edward Elgar, Cheltenham, pp 18–43

Norton RD, Rees J (1979) The product cycle and the spatial decentralization of American manufacturing. Reg Stud 13(2):141–151

Oakey RP, Thwaites AT, Nash PA (1980) The regional distribution of innovative manufacturing establishments in Britain. Reg Stud J Reg Stud Assoc 14:235–253

Perrin J-C (1988) New technologies, local synergies and regional policies in Europe. In: Aydalot P, Keeble D (eds) High technology industry and innovative environments: the European experience. Routledge, London, pp 139–162

Romer PM (1986) Increasing returns and long-rung growth. J Polit Econ 94:1002–1037

Saxenian A (1994) Regional advantage: culture and competition in Silicon Valley and Route 128. Harvard University Press, Cambridge, MA

Schmookler J (1966) Invention and economic growth. Harvard University Press, Cambridge, MA

Schumpeter J (1939) Business cycles. McGraw Hill, New York

Suarrez-Villa L, Karlsson C (1996) The development of Sweden's R&D-intensive electronics industries: exports, outsourcing and territorial dispersion. Environ Plann A 28:783–817

Taylor M (1986) The product cycle model: a critique. Environ Plann A 18:751–761

Thompson WR (1965) A preface to urban economics. The John Hopkins University Press, Baltimore

Vernon R (1960) Metropolis 1985. Harvard University Press, Cambridge, MA

Vernon R (1966) International investment and international trade in the product cycle. Quart J Econ 80(2):190–207

Weibull JW (1976) An axiomatic approach to the measurement of accessibility. Reg Sci Urban Econ 6(4):357–379

Chapter 11
Market-Size and Employment

Separating Scale and Diversity Effects

Martin Andersson and Johan Klaesson

Abstract What drives the relation between market-size and employment? There is a relationship between the size of an agglomeration and its diversity; in terms of number of sectors present and in terms of number of firms within each sector. There is also a relationship between the size of different agglomerations and the average size of firms located in them. Total employment in a region may be expressed as the product of number of sectors, number of firms in each sector and average firm size in each sector.

In the literature it is emphasized that diversity may be important for aggregate productivity and growth. The scale of operations in individual firms may also be important for productivity. Thus, the productivity in a region depends on both external and internal economies of scale. Looking at the relationship between regional size and employment it is possible to reveal the relative importance of each of the three factors.

The applied technique allows us to untangle the overall elasticity of employment with respect to market-size and estimate the contribution of each component to the overall elasticity. Using data on Swedish regions over the time period 1990–2004 we show that there are marked differences between manufacturing and service sectors in terms of the contribution of the different components to the overall elasticity. The contribution of the respective component is also different for regional and extra-regional market-size.

Keywords Market potential • Market size • Scale economies • Employment • Diversity

---

M. Andersson (⊠) • J. Klaesson
Economics, Jönköping International Business School (JIBS), P.O. Box 1026, SE-551 11 Jönköping, Sweden
e-mail: Martin.Andersson@jibs.hj.se; Johan.Klaesson@jibs.hj.se

J. Klaesson et al. (eds.), *Metropolitan Regions*, Advances in Spatial Science, DOI 10.1007/978-3-642-32141-2_11, © Springer-Verlag Berlin Heidelberg 2013

1 Introduction

It is an empirical fact that regions with high market potential are associated with a large amount of employment. This pattern holds across both manufacturing and service sectors. The present paper analyzes the sources of this relationship and asks what drives a larger employment in regions with larger market-size. We focus on two types of effects. The first is a 'diversity-effect' that occurs because larger markets can host a richer set of firms and sectors. The second is a 'scale-effect' at the level of individual firms and establishments and refer to the tendency of firms and establishments to be larger in larger markets.

We estimate the relative importance of each type of effect based on data across Swedish municipalities over a 15-year period (1990–2004). We decompose total employment in each municipality and sector into three components reflecting (1) diversity in terms of branches of business in each sector, (2) diversity in terms of the number of establishments per branch and (3) internal scale of establishments in terms of the average size of the establishments. Each establishment is assumed to produce a distinct product or service, but establishments within a given branch of business are assumed to be more related than establishments in different branches. The applied methodology allows us to untangle the overall elasticity of employment with respect to market-size and estimate the contribution of each component to the overall elasticity.

1.1 Background and Motivation

The relationship between market-size and location of economic activity and the subsequent employment belongs to the classic research issues in regional science and urban economics. Market-size and distance to markets are essential ingredients in central place theory (Christaller 1933; Lösch 1954; Palander 1935), urban land-use models (von Thünen 1826; Alonso 1964) as well as in the basic firm-location models (Weber 1909; Moses 1958). This is also part of the major theme in new economic geography models (Krugman 1991; Fujita et al. 1999; Fujita and Thisse 2002).[1]

It can be perceived as obvious that larger markets are associated with larger employment. The elasticity of employment with respect to market-size is definitely expected to be positive. But this overall elasticity is a reflection of an underlying structure that can take different forms. Larger markets can for example be associated with a larger set of sectors and a larger set of firms. In this case, the relationship

---

[1] A major contribution of NEG models is their ability to explain spatial agglomeration as a self-reinforcing process involving backward and forward linkages (Krugman 1991): scale economies in production and trade costs make it advantageous to locate in locations with high access to suppliers (forward linkage) and large market-size (backward linkage). Access to markets and suppliers is highest in those locations where producers have already concentrated.

between employment and market-size can be attributed to a 'diversity-effect'. On the other hand, there are arguments in favor of that firms tend to be larger in locations with high market access. From this viewpoint, part of the observed overall relationship between market-size and employment can be attributed to 'scale-effect', originating from larger average establishment size in larger markets. Below we go through arguments for the different effects.

Two basic reasons why large markets are associated with larger employment are proximity to markets and access to inputs. The former is more often than not referred to as backward linkages and the latter to forward linkages (cf. Hirschman 1958). Regarding the market-access argument, most sectors (both manufacturing and services) are characterized by scale economies in production. Combined with positive trade costs this means that locations with better market access are advantageous. Larger markets can be expected to be associated with larger establishments. This suggests that the overall relationship between market-size and employment can partly be attributed to a 'scale-effect'. Such a hypothesis is supported by recent research which introduces heterogeneous firms in standard NEG-models (see e.g. Baldwin and Okubo 2006). In this case, the most productive firms have lower prices and thus sell more. Because of this they have the strongest incentive to locate in proximity to large markets, such that larger firms locate in larger markets. In standard NEG models, on the other hand, larger employment in larger market areas is due to the 'diversity-effect'. All firms are of equal size, but there is a larger set of firms (and products) in larger markets (see e.g. Matsuyama 1995).[2] In the literature on international trade the interpretation has been that larger markets foster specialization (Either 1982).

In general, the extent to which proximity to markets, as regards both inputs and outputs, matters for location depends on the distance-sensitivity of pertinent activities. Services are generally classified as distance-sensitive activities, involving face-to-face interaction in delivery and design processes. This is particularly pronounced in knowledge intensive business services (KIBS) characterized by high knowledge content and customization, and to a lesser extent in retail and wholesale activities involving standardized goods. However, proximity to customers is in general more important for the majority of services compared to manufacturing.

However, not only large firms with distance-sensitive transactions on the input and output side can benefit from locating in regions with high market-access. Arguments that go back to Marshall (1920), Ohlin (1933) and Chinitz (1961) state that scale economies that are external to the individual firms can materialize in large and dense regions. These external scale economies are usually termed localization or urbanization economies and are attributed to the size of the relevant local industry (localization economies) or the overall magnitude of economic activities in the region (urbanization economies). Reasons for external scale economies include (1) information spillovers, (2) labor pooling and (3) access to specialized input

---

[2] This originates from the special property of CES functions, and does not hold in models with variable substitution of elasticity.

suppliers (cf. Marshall 1920). Scale economies of this type can certainly be important for small firms. Actually, arguments can be made that external economies are particularly important for small firms since they may lack certain internal resources. Moreover, scholars frequently maintain that external economies of scale arising from the concentration of economic activity, cities in particular, are most important for knowledge intensive industries for innovations and novel ideas. Based on arguments pertaining to external scale economies, one would expect that small firms in particular in knowledge-intensive sectors to locate in large and dense regions, further motivating a diversity-effect in the relationship between market-size and employment.

In summary, there are various arguments of the location structure generating the overall relationship between market-size and employment. The analysis in this paper contributes to the knowledge of this structure and introduces a simple methodology to untangle the overall elasticity of market-size with respect to employment. We untangle this elasticity for two manufacturing sectors and two service sectors, respectively.

2 Empirical Strategy

2.1 Decomposing Total Employment

As stated in the introduction, the starting point for our analysis is that the magnitude of the total employment in a sector and location can be attributed to several different components. Employment can for instance be large due to many small establishments in a specific branch of business within a sector, a few large establishments or scattered establishments in several different branches of business in a given sector.

In the current analysis we focus the sources of larger employment in larger market areas and consider two types of effects: (1) a 'diversity-effect' which occurs because larger markets can host a richer set of firms and sectors and (2) a 'scale-effect' at the level of individual firms and establishments and refer to the tendency of larger firms and establishments in larger markets. In view of this we decompose total employment, S, in each sector and location into three components:

1. Branches of business within the sector (B)
2. Establishments per branch of business (E)
3. Establishments size (ES)

The first two components measure the diversity in a sector at two different aggregation levels. Branches of business pertain to the overall breadth of a sector. Establishments per branch refer to a finer aggregation level and measure the average breadth or scope of each such branch. Each establishment is assumed to produce a distinct product or service, but establishments within a given branch of business are assumed to be more related than establishments in different branches. Establishment size captures the scale-effect internal to the firm.

11 Market-Size and Employment

To empirically implement this decomposition we make use of a Swedish employment database, maintained by Statistics Sweden (SCB), that for each municipality and year (1990–2004) reports the total number of employees, establishments and branches of business (5-digit SIC codes). With this information we implement the described decomposition as follows. Starting with the identity:

$$S = Branches \cdot \frac{Establishments}{Branches} \cdot \frac{Employees}{Establishments} = B \cdot E \cdot ES \qquad (11.1)$$

In the above identity S denotes total employment. The number of branches of business is the number of SIC codes at the 5-digit level. As is evident from Eq. 11.1 the total employment in a location is expressed as the product of the number of branches of business (B), establishments per branch of business (E) and employment per establishments (ES).

The described decomposition methodology allows us to untangle the overall elasticity of employment w.r.t. employment and estimate the contribution of each respective component to the overall elasticity. To see this, consider the following empirical equation:

$$\ln S_m = \alpha + \beta \ln MS_m \qquad (11.2)$$

where MS denotes market-size and the subscript m denote a given municipality. In Eq. 11.2, β is the overall elasticity of employment w.r.t. market-size. As a next step we can relate each component of employment to the same measure of market-size:

$$\ln B_m = \alpha_1 + \beta_1 \ln MS_m \qquad (11.3a)$$

$$\ln E_m = \alpha_2 + \beta_2 \ln MS_m \qquad (11.3b)$$

$$\ln ES_m = \alpha_3 + \beta_3 \ln MS_m \qquad (11.3c)$$

The β's in the above equations is the elasticity of each of the respective components of total employment w.r.t. market-size. Since $\ln S_m = \ln B_m + \ln E_m + \ln ES_m$ from Eq. 11.1 the three elasticities associated with the three components of total employment sum to the overall elasticity in Eq. 11.2, i.e. $\beta = \beta_1 + \beta_2 + \beta_3$, such that:

$$\ln S_m = (\alpha_1 + \alpha_2 + \alpha_3) + (\beta_1 + \beta_2 + \beta_3) \ln MS_m \qquad (11.4)$$

This relationship follows directly from the construction of the employment components. By estimating Eqs. 11.2 and 11.3a, 11.3b and 11.3c we obtain an estimate of the contribution of each employment component to the overall elasticity of employment w.r.t market-size. The ratio β_1/β, for instance, express how much of the relationship between total employment and market-size that can be attributed to the fact that locations with larger market-size have a richer set of branches of business.

Table 11.1 Sector aggregates used in the empirical analysis

	Name	2-digit SIC	Description
Manufacturing	Food and clothing	15–19	Food and beverages, textiles and clothing (low-tech)
	Telecom, medical and vehicles	29–35	Machinery, electronics, telecommunications, medical instruments, vehicles (high-tech)
Services	Retail, wholesale and logistics	50, 51, 52, 55, 60–64	Retail and wholesale trade, transport and logistics services (low-end)
	Finance, R&D, marketing and management	65–67,70–74	Financial services, real estate, computer programming, R&D, managerial and marketing services (high-end)

In the empirical implementation we estimate Eqs. 11.2 and 11.3a, 11.3b and 11.3c on a yearly basis 1990–2004 across Swedish municipalities and obtain average elasticities over the 15-year time period. We make use of these to determine the overall structure.

2.2 Descriptives

The described methodology is applied on four sector aggregates, of which two are manufacturing and two are services. Table 11.1 present the four sector aggregates as well as their definition.

The manufacturing sectors comprise food and clothing and telecom, medical and vehicles. Food and clothing manufacturing is generally classified as less advanced than manufacturing in telecom, medical and vehicles. The two services sectors comprise classic consumer and producer services such as retail, wholesale and logistics, as well as branches of business that are more often than not classified as knowledge intensive business services (KIBS): finance, R&D, marketing and management.

Manufactures are in general less distance-sensitive and more export oriented than service sectors. Because of this, demand-side aspects are likely to play a more important role for the location pattern of services compared to manufacturing. Furthermore, internal scale economies are more pervasive in manufacturing than in services. These characteristics make it interesting to compare manufacturing and services as regards employment dependent on market-size.

Table 11.2 presents the total employment and total number of establishments in the four sector aggregates and each sector aggregate's share of the total employment in Sweden. These data are for the year 2000 and provide an overall picture of the size of the sector aggregates under study. The four sector aggregates roughly constitute about 50 % of Sweden's total employment and total number of establishments.[3] The

---

[3] A significant share of the remaining Swedish employment is found in the public sector.

11 Market-Size and Employment

Table 11.2 Employment and establishments in year 2000 in the sector aggregates

Name	Employment	Employment share (%)	Establishments	Establishment share (%)
Food and clothing	122,674	3	8,465	2
Telecom, medical and vehicles	303,823	8	8,764	2
Retail, wholesale and logistics	849,322	22	126,928	30
Finance, R&D, marketing and management	552,682	14	86,328	20
Sum	1,828,501	47	230,485	54

Table 11.3 Employment components in the sector aggregates, year 2000

Name	Branches of business (max)	Establishments per sector	Establishment size	Product (employment)
Food and clothing	84	101	14	122 674
Telecom, medical and vehicles	54	162	35	303 823
Retail, wholesale and logistics	176	721	7	849 322
Finance, R&D, marketing and management	79	1 093	6	552 682

manufacturing sectors are naturally the smallest ones in terms of both establishments and employment. Together they amount to 4 % of the total number of establishments and about 11 % of the employment. The largest service sector is retail, wholesale and logistics constituting about 22 % of the total employment in Sweden. The employment shares in all sector aggregates roughly correspond to their establishment share. It is however evident that manufacturing establishments are in general larger (in terms of employment) than services establishments.

The number of branches of business in each sector aggregate is defined as the number of 5-digit SIC codes which is comprised by the sector aggregate. The figures report the number of branches of business in Sweden for each sector aggregate. This means that they represent the maximum number of branches of business that a Swedish municipality can attain. This is largest in retail, wholesale and logistics and smallest in telecom, medical and vehicles. A municipality's actual number of branches is interpreted as reflecting the overall breadth of a sector group in a municipality. Establishments per sector represent the average breadth or scope of each branch in the sector aggregate. From Table 11.3 it is evident that there is marked difference between manufacturing and services for both establishments per branch of business and establishment size. Services are on the whole characterized by many smaller establishments within each branch of business, whereas manufacturing is characterized by larger establishments.

3 The Relationship Between Market-Size and Employment

3.1 Empirical Model

The model applied to estimate the elasticities of employment w.r.t market-size and its components described in Sect. 3 is presented in Eq. 11.5. As shown in the equation, the market-size of a municipality, m, is measured by (1) its regional market and (2) its extra-regional market accessibility. Each type of market-size is associated with a distinct parameter to be estimated, β and θ respectively. Regional accessibility pertains to the access to income originating in the local labor market region (LLM) the municipality belongs to. Such local labor market regions are defined by commuting patterns across municipality borders. In Eq. 11.5 the set $R = \{1, \ldots k, m, \ldots, n\}$ encompasses all municipalities belonging to the same LLM as municipality m. The extra-regional accessibility accounts for access to income from outside the region and is in essence the accessibility to income from the rest of the country.

$$\ln S_m = \alpha + \beta \ln\left(\underbrace{\sum_{k \in R} W_k e^{\{-\lambda t_{km}\}}}_{Regional\ market}\right) + \theta \ln\left(\underbrace{\sum_{s \notin R} W_s e^{\{-\lambda t_{sm}\}}}_{Extra\text{-}regional\ market}\right) + \sigma D_m^{Central} + \delta D_m^{Nc} + \varepsilon_m$$

$$(11.5)$$

For each municipality the regional accessibility to income, W, is the exponential distance-weighted sum of the incomes in all municipalities in the region.[4] The extra-regional accessibility accounts for income in municipalities outside the region the municipality belongs to. λ is a distance-friction parameter and t_{km} denotes the travel-time distance by car between municipality m and k. In our calculations of the accessibilities we apply the estimated values of λ obtained by Johansson et al. (2003) on Swedish commuting data. These estimated values represent the best available information. $D_m^{Central}$ is a dummy variable which is 1 of municipality m is the central (largest) municipality in the LLM-region and 0 otherwise. D_m^{Nc} is a dummy variable which is 1 if municipality m is a non-central municipality in a large ($\geq 100\ 000$ inhabitants) LLM.

The inclusion of accessibility variables means that the model captures characteristics in terms of market-size in each municipality as well as its surroundings. It is very likely that the relevant market for e.g. a supplier of services is not only the municipal market, but also the potential market in surrounding municipalities within a pertinent time-distance interval. Such a pattern implies the presence of spatial dependence in the sense that location (and consequently employment) is

---

[4] As shown by Weibull (1976 and 1980) accessibility measures based in exponential distance-decay functions satisfy criteria of consistency and meaningfulness.

11 Market-Size and Employment 269

partly a function of characteristics outside each municipality. From an econometric viewpoint the model in Eq. 11.5 account for such spatial dependence by means of spatially lagged independent variables (cf. Andersson and Gråsjö 2008), and is thus a form of a spatial cross-regressive model (cf. Rey and Montouri 1999). Thus, possible spatial interdependencies are modeled in the construction of the independent variables.

In the sequel, we estimate Eq. 11.5 by means of Ordinary Least Squares (OLS) on pooled yearly data for Swedish municipalities 1990-2004 and include time dummies. For each sector aggregate, the model is estimated with four different dependent variables: (1) total employment, (2) number of branches of business, (3) number of establishments per branch of business and (4) establishment size. By the estimations we obtain elasticities of employment and the three components of employment w.r.t both types of market-size.

3.2 Diversity, Scale and Employment Elasticities w.r.t. Market-Size

Table 11.4 presents the estimated elasticities w.r.t market-size: the number of branches of business within each sector aggregate, the number of establishments in each branch of business and the employment in each establishment (establishment size). The total employment elasticity can either be found by estimating it directly or simply calculate the sum of the three elasticities associated with the different components of employment.

Starting with the big picture we look at the employment elasticities. The elasticity for the food and clothing manufacturing industry sector is 0.43, for the telecom, medical and vehicle manufacturing sector it is 0.97, for the retail, wholesale and logistics sector it is 0.69 and finally for the finance, R&D, marketing and management the elasticity is 0.82. At first glance it may seem surprising that the largest elasticity relate to telecom, medical and vehicles manufacturing. But, if one looks at the two components of the elasticity we see that 0.38 relates to extra-regional accessibility. This means that this industry is located in places proximate to large markets. Thus, they are not located within these large markets, but next to them. It is also evident that the estimated elasticity between manufacturing employment and extra-regional accessibility can be ascribed to that larger establishments tend to be located in locations with high extra-regional accessibility.

If we concentrate on the regional part of the elasticities a clearer and perhaps more intuitive pattern emerges. The elasticity for the food and clothing manufacturing industry sector is 0.30, for the telecom, medical and vehicle manufacturing sector it is 0.59, for the retail, wholesale and logistics sector it is 0.68 and finally for the finance, R&D, marketing and management the elasticity is 0.81. These elasticities illustrate that for all four sectors, employment is larger in regions with larger regional market-size. The largest elasticities pertain to the two service sectors, to the extent

Table 11.4 Elasticities of employment with respect to market-size

	Market accessibility		
	Regional	*Extra-regional*	**Total**
Food and clothing			
Branches of business	0.18	0.01	**0.19**
Establishments per branch of business	0.12	−0.01	**0.11**
Employment per establishment	−0.01	0.12	**0.11**
Employment within sector	**0.30**	**0.13**	0.43
Telecom, medical and vehicles			
Branches of business	0.36	0.09	**0.45**
Establishments per branch of business	0.21	0.01	**0.22**
Employment per establishment	0.02	0.28	**0.30**
Employment within sector	**0.59**	**0.38**	0.97
Retail, wholesale and logistics			
Branches of business	0.25	0.03	**0.28**
Establishments per branch of business	0.29	−0.02	**0.27**
Employment per establishment	0.14	0.00	**0.14**
Employment within sector	**0.68**	**0.01**	0.69
Finance, R&D, marketing and management			
Branches of business	0.29	0.01	**0.30**
Establishments per branch of business	0.47	−0.02	**0.45**
Employment per establishment	0.05	0.02	**0.07**
Employment within sector	**0.81**	**0.01**	0.82

Note: The elasticities presented in the table are obtained from estimating Eq. 11.5 with ordinary least squares

that these sectors serve the regional market this is an expected result. The importance of a large regional market for the two manufacturing sectors can probably best be understood in terms of the input markets. These sectors are dependent on inputs in the form of labor, services and material (and capital) inputs. The two first types of inputs can be expected to be more readily available in larger regions.

Turning to the extra-regional component of market size there is a very distinct pattern. Employment elasticities w.r.t extra-regional market size in the two manufacturing sectors is much larger compared to the service sectors. As stated previously, this is driven by establishment size. For the two service sectors the employment elasticity w.r.t. the size of the extra-regional market is practically zero.

Now, we are turning to the decomposition of the employment effects into its three components. The employment elasticity is the sum of the elasticities for number of branches, establishments per branch and employment per establishment respectively. In Fig. 11.1a and b we express the elasticity of market-size w.r.t to the three components as a fraction of the overall elasticity of market-size w.r.t employment. In this manner, the contribution of the respective component to the overall elasticity is clearly observable, and we can compare across the sectors. Figure 11.1a presents the results for total market-size and Fig. 11.1b presents in a similar fashion the results for regional market-size.

From Fig. 11.1a it is clear that for the manufacturing sectors, the elasticity of employment w.r.t total market-size can mainly attributed to that branches of business

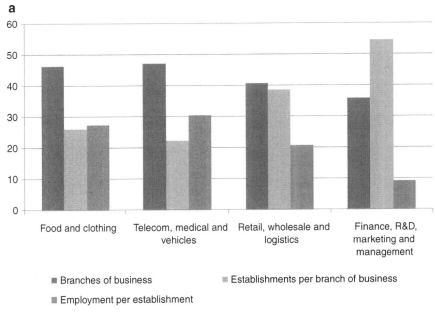

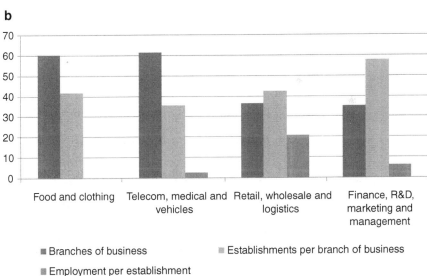

Fig. 11.1 (a) The contribution of different components of employment to the overall elasticity of total market-size with respect to employment. (b) The contribution of different components of employment to the overall elasticity of regional market-size with respect to employment

tend to increase with market-size. This component accounts for about 45 % of the overall relationship between market-size and employment in the two manufacturing sectors. Between 20 % and 30 % of the relationship can be attributed to that establishment per branch of business and employment per establishment, respectively are increasing in total market-size.

If we look at the two service sectors we see that for retail, wholesale and logistics the components branches per business and establishments per branch business account for an equal share of the overall relationship. The relative contribution of employment per establishment is small. For Finance, R&D, marketing and management the largest share (over 50 %) of the relationship between employment and market-size is due to that establishment per branch of business is increasing in market-size. More branches of business account for about 35 % of the overall relationship and a minor share is due to employment per establishment.

Figure 11.1b complements Fig. 11.1a and presents a similar calculation but is based on the estimated parameters associated with regional market-size.

In general Fig. 11.1b confirms the overall pattern in Fig. 11.1a. The main difference is that the Fig. 11.1b clearly illustrates that there is virtually no relationship between employment per establishment in the two manufacturing sectors and market-size. This can be explained by the tendency of large manufacturing establishments to be located outside larger regions. Other than this, we find a similar difference between manufacturing and services with regard to the regional market as we find for the total market-size.

4 Summary and Conclusions

In this paper we have asked the fundamental question: what drives the relationship between market-size and employment? In order to shed light on this question we introduced a simple but illustrative and intuitive decomposition methodology, which allows us to estimate the relative contribution of different components of total employment to the overall elasticity of employment with respect to market-size. We distinguished between three components: (1) branches of business, (2) establishments per branch of business and (3) employment per establishment. We applied our model to two manufacturing sectors and two services sectors. Our main findings can be summarized as follows:

- The overall elasticity of employment w.r.t market-size can be attributed to that all three components of employment vary with total market-size. This holds for services as well as for manufacturing sectors.
- For manufacturing sectors, we find that the elasticity of employment w.r.t total market-size can mainly be attributed to that branches of business tend to increase with market-size.
- For service sectors, the number of establishments per branch account for the largest fraction of the overall relationship between market-size and employment

These results suggest that larger service employment in larger markets is primarily driven by larger diversity in each branch. In larger markets, we see a wider set of establishments in each branch of business in the service sectors. For manufacturing sectors, it is driven by diversity in terms of branches of business.

11 Market-Size and Employment

This can partly be explained by that many branches of business in services are indeed present in most regions, whereas manufacturing sectors are more specialized across regions. The high share of establishments per branch of business in knowledge intensive services, such as finance, R&D, marketing and management, is consistent with that small and medium-sized knowledge-intensive business are attracted to externality-rich environments.

References

Alonso W (1964) Location and land use. Harvard University Press, Cambridge, MA

Andersson Gråsjö (2008) Andersson M and Gråsjö U (2008) Spatial dependence and the representation of space. Annal Reg Sci (forthcoming)

Baldwin RE, Okubo T (2006) Heterogeneous firms, agglomeration and economic geography: spatial selection and sorting. J Econ Geogr 6:323–346

Chinitz B (1961) Contrasts in agglomeration: New York and Pittsburgh. Am Econ Rev 51:279–289

Christaller W (1933) Die Zentralen Orte in Süddeutschland. Prentice-Hall, Englewood Cliffs. Baskin CW (1966) Central places in southern Germany (trans: Baskin CW)

Either WJ (1982) National and international returns to scale in the modern theory of international trade. Am Econ Rev 72(3):389–405

Fujita M, Thisse J-F (2002) Economics of agglomeration. Cities, industrial location, and regional growth. Cambridge University Press, Cambridge, UK

Fujita M, Krugman P, Venables AJ (1999) The spatial economy: cities, regions and international trade. MIT Press, Cambridge, MA

Hirschman A (1958) The strategy of economic development. Yale University Press, New Haven

Johansson B, Klaesson J, Olsson M (2003) Commuters' non-linear response to time distances. J Geogr Syst 5(3):315–329

Krugman P (1991) Geography and trade. MIT Press, Cambridge, MA

Lösch A (1954) The economics of location. Yale University Press, New Haven

Marshall A (1920) Principles of economics. Macmillan, London

Matsuyama K (1995) Complementarities and cumulative processes in models of monopolistic competition. J Econ Lit 33:701–729

Moses L (1958) Location and the theory of production. Q J Econ 78:259–272

Ohlin B (1933) Interregional and international trade. Harvard University Press, Cambridge, MA

Palander T (1935) Beiträge zur Standortstheorie. Almqvist and Wicksell, Uppsala

Rey S, Montouri BD (1999) U.S. regional income convergence: a spatial econometric perspective. Reg Stud 33:143–156

von Thunen JH (1826) Der isolierte Staat in Beziehung auf Landwirtschaft und Nationaloekonomie, Hamburg

Weber A (1909) Uber den Standort der Industrien. Friedrich CJ (1929) Alfred Weber's theory of the location of industries (trans: Friedrich CJ). University of Chicago Press, Chicago

Chapter 12
Do Planning Policies Limit the Expansion of Cities?

Stephen Sheppard

Abstract ... it is essential ... that the town should be planned as a whole, and not left to grow up in a chaotic manner as has been the case with all English towns, and more or less with the towns of all countries. A town, like a flower, or a tree, or an animal, should, at each stage of its growth, possess unity, symmetry, completeness, and the effect of growth should never be to destroy that unity, but to give it greater purpose. ...
— Ebenezer Howard, *Garden Cities of Tomorrow, 1898*

This paper considers whether planning policies, as practiced in the world's cities, have the potential for controlling or limiting the expansion of urban land use. The question is certainly relevant for design of policies to respond to urban sprawl. The analysis does not establish that these constraints are necessarily desirable, but does find some evidence that some aspects of planning regulations can be effective in limiting urban expansion.[1]

Keywords Land use • Remote sensing • Urban planning • Urban sprawl

---

[1] The assistance of Alison Kraley in organizing and preparing the data, and the support of the World Bank Research Committee and the US National Science Foundation grant SES-0433278 was indispensible in this research. Any errors in the text are the responsibility of the author.

S. Sheppard (✉)
Department of Economics, Williams College, 24 Hopkins Hall Drive, Williamstown, MA 01267, USA
e-mail: stephen.c.sheppard@williams.edu

J. Klaesson et al. (eds.), *Metropolitan Regions*, Advances in Spatial Science, DOI 10.1007/978-3-642-32141-2_12, © Springer-Verlag Berlin Heidelberg 2013

1 Introduction

Concern about urban "sprawl" has been present among the popular, policy and academic communities at least since the 1950s.[2] Concern about the levels of urban expansion continues. Urban expansion has become the object of more intense academic investigation as well as a search among policy makers for approaches that will eliminate or reduce the worst external costs associated with urban expansion, while at the same time permitting the economy to experience the improved productivity and other benefits that appear to be associated with urbanization.

While there is debate about the exact levels of external costs associated with urban expansion, the urgency of the concern is not misplaced. Having just passed the watershed mark of having over half of the world's population reside in urban places, the annual rate of growth of the global urban population is about 2 % and about 4 % in the poorest countries. If urban land per person remains constant, this implies a doubling of the "urban footprint" within the next 35 years. In actual fact the growth of incomes will accelerate this process, so that within the next three decades the countries of the world will be called upon to double the population accommodated within the built urban environment. Given that the present stock of structures and other capital that constitutes the built environment required about 3,000 years to accumulate, this is a daunting task. Of particular concern is the prospect that urbanization and urban expansion will proceed with insufficient plans to accommodate the growth and inadequate policies to contain it.

The purpose of this paper is to investigate whether planning policies, as practiced in the world's cities, offer any hope of controlling or limiting the expansion of urban land use associated with cities. The question is certainly relevant for design of policies to respond to urban expansion. If there are no policies that are capable of restricting total urban land use, then the most sensible alternative would seem to be to make ambitious preparations for the doubling of total urban land use within the next 30 years.

This paper is not concerned with whether restriction of total urban land use, if achievable, is desirable. There have been many other papers that considered this question. Cheshire and Sheppard 2002, for example, measure both the costs and benefits of land use regulation in the context of specific British cities. They conclude in that context that, on the margin, constraints appear to be too restrictive so that a modest relaxation of planning constraints would appear to be welfare-improving. Their estimates of the positive value of open space preservation and

---

[2] The first use of the term to describe urban expansion identified in the Oxford English Dictionary is in August of 1955, when a writer in the *Times* asserted that it was ". . . sad to think that London's great sprawl will inevitably engulf us sooner or later, no matter how many green belts are interposed in the meantime between the colossus and ourselves." Thus apparently from the very beginning there were doubts about the efficacy of planning policy in limiting urban expansion. Earlier usages of the term include that by Frederic Osborn (1946), a disciple of Ebenezer Howard, who attributed suburban sprawl to improved transportation available through "electric traction . . . and the petrol or gasoline motor. . . ." Black (1996) attributes the first use to Earle Draper, an urban planner active in several southeastern US cities.

limits on industrial land use suggest that, at least in some contexts, a complete absence of constraint on urban land use would also not be optimal. The paper does not consider all of the many different contexts in which planning policies **might** be effective in limiting urban land use. We simply ask whether, as practiced around the world, they are effective in reducing urban land use.

If planning policies are not effective in limiting total urban land use, it does not follow that planning itself is of no value to cities. Planning departments and "land use planning" policies (however conceived and practiced) can help improve the coherence of urban expansion and make the most effective use possible of public capital investment. These policies might reduce uncertainty about availability and location of roadways and other infrastructure and improve the efficiency of cities. To review the academic literature on this subject, however, is to be confronted repeatedly with assertions that the problem of urban expansion arises because of "inadequate planning" that, if corrected, will lead to denser and more compact cities. Our aim is to simply inquire whether, and to what extent, this is true.

2 The Impacts of Planning Policy

While many popular writers and some academics regard being "unplanned" as the *sine qua non* of urban sprawl, the evidence is at best mixed concerning whether formal planning policies have the effect of constraining the level of urban land use in cities. Studies on the subject tend to fall into (at least) three conceptual categories. There are studies that derive the impact of planning regulations using primarily theoretical arguments or simulation exercises. Second, there are studies whose primary focus is to use theoretical and empirical arguments to evaluate the potential benefits of planning regulations or to explore the interactions between other policies (such as those regarding taxation or public transportation) and land use planning policies. Finally, there are a limited number of empirical studies of the apparent effects of planning policies. It is with this latter group that this paper belongs.

Examples of the first group of studies would include Sheppard (1988), which derives the qualitative impacts on land use and land prices that result from changes in the availability of land for development, including the impact of urban growth boundaries. Turner (2007) provides a model in which the equilibrium density of development may diverge from (be less than) the efficient density and in this way captures a situation that could be properly be called "sprawl". He identifies circumstances when taxes on low density development may be welfare improving.

Burchfield et al. (2006) present an ambitious empirical examination of the causes of urban expansion. While their data are limited to the United States, their approach to analysis is otherwise similar to the one followed in this paper. Unfortunately, they do not directly look at the impact of planning policies. Nechyba and Walsh (2004) present a useful survey of some of the literature on urban sprawl, but unfortunately divert attention from the essential elements of urban sprawl – expanding use of land for urban purposes – and concentrate attention on sorting of different household types within the city. This emphasis on Tiebout sorting is of course interesting in other contexts but has little to do with increased total or per-capita use of land.

One difficulty with understanding and modeling the expected impacts of planning on total urban land use is that "planning" is a complex public function that incorporates aspects of civil engineering and provision of infrastructure, coordination of development activity, provision of public goods, and regulation of development. When a city makes provision for urban growth by obtaining rights-of-way for water and sewer lines or road construction, these activities might be called "planning" and even in some cities undertaken by a planning department, but they do not act to constrain urban land use. Development of "strategic plans" undertaken by planning departments in many countries may help coordinate development patterns and make for more efficient provision of infrastructure, but they don't necessarily limit total urban land use. To better understand this process, we require an abstract framework within which to characterize and present how planning might operate to regulate the expansion of cities.

Cheshire and Sheppard (2002) consider the impacts of specific types of land use planning in the context of specific small cities in England. The results are derived in the context of a relatively straightforward model of urban land use, which is adapted here to identify expected impacts. There are N households with identical preferences over residential land and a vector q of other goods. A household living distance x from the city center at angle (or direction) θ faces annual transportation costs given by $t(\tau, x, \theta)$. The variable τ represents the cost of inputs to transport production (such as the cost of fuel. We assume that $\frac{\partial t}{\partial \tau} > 0$ and $\frac{\partial t}{\partial x} > 0$. Each household has annual income M from employment in the city and thus has $M - t(\tau, x, \theta)$ to allocate between residential land and other goods.

Let $h(u, r, p)$ be the compensated demand for residential land, which depends on the utility level u, the price of land r and the vector of other goods prices p. Let $r(u, x, \theta, \tau, p, M)$ be the "bid rent" function defined as the price of residential land at each location (x, θ) that allows the household to achieve utility level u given that it has income M, faces prices of other goods p and must pay commuting costs $t(\tau, x, \theta)$. The value of agricultural land is given by R_a. In the absence of planning constraints, urban residential land use extends to a distance of $x_a(\theta)$, defined implicitly by the equality:

$$r(u, x_a(\theta), \theta, \tau, p, M) = R_a \tag{12.1}$$

Clearly, $x_a(\theta)$ depends upon u, τ, p, M and R_a as well as θ. To simplify notation we suppress these additional arguments except where confusion would result.

Planning constraints are represented in a stylized fashion. Policies such as urban growth boundaries and to some extent greenbelts attempt to constrain urban development from taking place beyond a particular distance from the center of the city. Suppose that for every direction θ there is a distance $\chi_2(\rho, \theta)$ that is the maximum distance where consumption of land for residential purposes is permitted. Here ρ is a planning policy parameter, and we assume that $\frac{\partial \chi_2}{\partial \rho} < 0$. This represents urban containment policy. Actual urban residential land use will extend to the distance min $(x_a(\theta), \chi_2(\rho, \theta))$.

Planning policies also might attempt to defend open spaces that are interior to the built-up area of the city. These may be parks, greenways, or even farm land that is not

12 Do Planning Policies Limit the Expansion of Cities?

allowed to be developed. To represent such policies, suppose that there is a parameter $0 < \omega \leq 1$ that specifies the share of land that may be privately consumed. If planners want to set aside land for parks, open space or some other form of shared land consumption within the built-up area, they may do so by setting ω to a value less than one. There is also a distance $\chi_1(\theta)$ that represents the innermost extent of residential land use, which depends on the level of commercial activity in the urban center and the land requirements for these non-residential activities.

Equilibrium is determined by a utility level $\hat{u}$ shared by all households having the property that:

$$N = \int_0^{2\pi} \int_{\chi_1(\theta)}^{\min(x_a(\theta),\chi_2(\rho,\theta))} \frac{\omega \cdot x}{h(\hat{u}, r(\hat{u}, x, \theta, \tau, p, M), p)} dxd\theta \qquad (12.2)$$

The intuition behind Eq. 12.2 is straightforward. The numerator is the density of land availability at distance x given planning policy ω. The denominator is the local density of land consumption by utility maximizing households. The ratio is the number of households accommodated at location (x, θ). Zero excess demand for land requires that integrating the number of households accommodated at each location over all urban locations must equal the total number of households to be accommodated.

In equilibrium, with each household achieving utility $\hat{u}$ the total amount of land consumed for private residential purposes in the urban area is obviously:

$$T = \int_0^{2\pi} \int_{\chi_1(\theta)}^{\min(x_a(\theta),\chi_2(\rho,\theta))} \omega \cdot x \, dxd\theta \qquad (12.3)$$

If $\omega = 1$, $\chi_1(\theta) = \bar{\chi}_1$ and $\min(x_a(\theta), \chi_2(\rho, \theta)) = \bar{\chi}_2$ then Eq. 12.3 reduces to $\pi \cdot \bar{\chi}_2^2 - \pi \cdot \bar{\chi}_1^2$. In the absence of these restrictions, Eq. 12.3 is used to give a general expression of total urban area.

Within the context of this model, several comparative static properties of the equilibrium are easily established. They are summarized as follows:

	Results	Description
1.	$\frac{\partial T}{\partial N} \geq 0$	Increasing population increases total urban land
2.	$\frac{\partial T}{\partial M} \geq 0$	Increasing household income increases total urban land
3.	$\frac{\partial T}{\partial \tau} \leq 0$	Increasing transport costs decreases total urban land
4.	$\frac{\partial T}{\partial R_a} \leq 0$	Increasing agricultural land value decreases total urban land
5.	$\frac{\partial T}{\partial \rho} \leq 0$	A stricter containment planning policies decreases total urban land
6.	$\frac{\partial T}{\partial \omega} \leq 0$	Increasing internal open space will decrease total urban land

Cheshire and Sheppard did not test whether some observed characteristic or activity of the UK planning system was actually associated with a change in ρ or ω (viewed through the lens of this model). Rather, they assumed that the planning system operated to set *some* level of these constraints. They used the estimated parameters from an almost ideal demand system to simulate the land value outcomes resulting from different values of the parameters, selecting the values $\hat{\omega}$ and $\hat{\rho}$ that provided the best fit to the observed data (pattern of land values and maximum extent of urban development). Using these values they were then able to consider and simulate counter-factual scenarios such as the impact of removing these planning constraints.

In this paper we consider a different question: is there some observable characteristic of planning practice or planning policies that is empirically associated with impacts on total urban land use of the sort suggested in the simple model described above? At the same time, and as a general test of the simple modeling approach itself, it is possible to see if the other predictions of the model concerning the impacts of population, income, transport costs and agricultural land values are supported empirically. If these predictions are generally supported then it might be reasonable to conclude that the model provides a useful framework within which to think about urban land use and land use regulation. We can then inquire what aspects, if any, of planning policies have an impact on the expansion of cities.

Before proceeding to describe the data used and the results obtained, one thing must be noted. It is clear that to test the model described here, we would need either a long and sufficiently varied time series of data for a single city, or a cross section of data from a variety of cities so that we can observe the variation in population, income, planning policies, and other variables that permit us to estimate the impacts. Ideally we would have a well designed panel of observations for a diverse and representative sample of cities. For the most part, such data do not exist. We make use of a unique data resource that provides measurements of total urban land cover obtained using consistent methodologies applied in a sample of cities around the world.

3 The Data

The data we analyze provide a measure of the total urban land cover in 120 cities around the world, at two points in time about a decade apart. The cities included in our sample represent a random sample of all urban places in the planet having metro area population in excess of 100,000 persons. The sample is stratified to ensure representation of cities by broad income group, size class, and global region. Thus we have a representative sample in the sense that the proportion of the global urban population that lives in small cities in low-income countries in Latin America (for example) is similar to the proportion of population in our total sample who lives in small cities in low-income Latin American cities. The location of cities, along with indicators of size and income category, is illustrated in Fig. 12.1.

For each of these cities, we bring together three types of data: satellite images that were analyzed to measure the total urban land cover in each city, detailed local data collected by field researchers who visited each city, mostly in 2005–2006, and national level data for the country in which each city is located collected from World Development Indicators and from other global data sources.

12 Do Planning Policies Limit the Expansion of Cities?

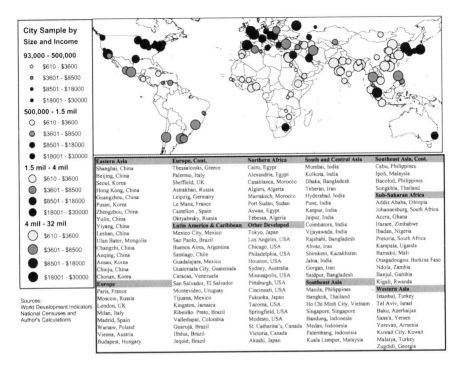

Fig. 12.1 Distribution of global urban sample

We obtained Landsat TM or ETM[3] satellite images for two points in time, approximately 10 years apart. The earliest images are from 1984, and on average the first images are from autumn of 1989. The latest images are from late 2002, and on average the second images are from fall of 1990. Thus on average, the two images are about 11 years apart. These satellite images are divided into pixels that correspond to an area on the surface that is 28.5 m^2. For each pixel the image provides 6 or 7 brightness levels of light, three in the visual spectrum and three in the infrared region. These brightness levels are used to "classify" the image. This means that an analytical procedure is used to sort pixels into categories corresponding to an estimate of conditions on the surface. The classification scheme used was simple and sorted pixels into three categories: urban cover, non-urban cover, and water. A supervised, three-pass cluster analysis procedure was used for each image. Pixel-level analysis and comparison with ground photographs taken by the field researchers indicates that pixels are correctly classified in between 85 % and 90 % of the cases. The concern in this analysis is with the aggregate urban land cover for the entire urban area. In a typical city, there will be well over a million pixels so that on average we expect the accuracy of measurement of total urban land use to be very high.

---

[3] The TM or Thematic Mapper instrument was included in Landsats 4 and 5 and so potentially provide data from late 1982 through 2007. The ETM or Enhanced Thematic Mapper instrument is on Landsat 7 and so provides data beginning in late 1999.

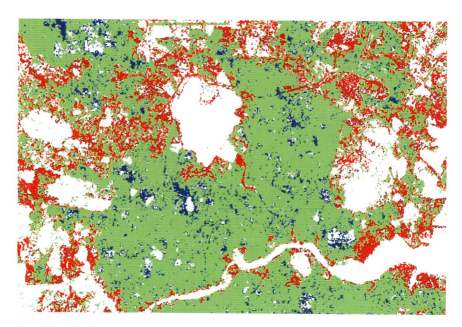

Fig. 12.2 Classification of urban land cover in Hyderabad, India

The final outcome is an image similar to that presented in Fig. 12.2. This image actually combines two classifications. One for November 1989, shown in green, and one for October 2001, combining all colors. The areas marked in red are represent new urban development at the periphery, while the areas in blue represent new urban development that is surrounded by areas that were developed in 1989. The area of each type of land use is recorded and this provides our measure of total urban land cover for each city and each date.

For every city, field researchers were hired to collect data on local population and housing conditions, the nature of local planning systems and planning institutions, local house prices and conditions, the extent and conditions of housing located in informal or squatter settlements, local housing finance, and local transportation and travel conditions. Each field researcher was provided with survey forms to complete and instructions, and were selected based on familiarity with the local city and conditions. For our analysis, we rely on the data collected concerning the nature of local planning and land use regulation. These data include information on the total staff employed in the planning department, the amount of time expected to obtain permission to convert land from rural to urban use. The amount of time expected to obtain permission to subdivide land already approved for urban use, and the number of compulsory demolitions of structures within the past year due to non-compliance with planning regulations. Field researchers met with varying degrees of cooperation from local planning authorities, and some data were not available for some cities.

Data on income, cost of motor fuel, prices, exchange rates, and other national level variables available in World Development Indicators are combined. These include, where required, estimates of real value added per hectare of land under cultivation (as a proxy for the value of agricultural land). We make use of the indices of

12 Do Planning Policies Limit the Expansion of Cities?

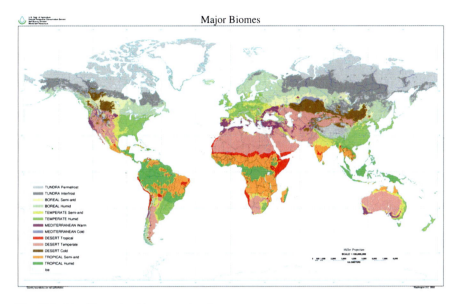

Fig. 12.3 Map illustrating biomes used as instruments

ethnic, religious and linguistic "fractionalization" discussed in Alesina et al. (2003). The location of the center of each urban area was determined (the centroid of the measured urban land cover) and used to determine latitude and longitude. These locations were combined with data on "biomes" – a classification of soil type and prevailing climate conditions – and these agri-climate indicators were used in the analysis. The global distribution of biomes is illustrated in Fig. 12.3.

Population data from national censuses was used for subareas within each city. These varied in size, and for some cities (Paris, Johannesburg, all US cities) the areas were small (similar to census tracts) but for other cities (for example, Accra and Cairo) the subareas for which population data were available were relatively large, and often extended well outside the built up area of the city. When the jurisdictions were completely covered by the available satellite imagery, we included the entire jurisdiction. If the image did not cover the entire jurisdiction, we estimated the population that would be expected to be within the image area by assuming an exponential population density function. We also assumed constant rates of change in population between the two censuses nearest our image dates, and interpolated (or extrapolated) the population to the date of the satellite image.[4] Table 12.1 presents descriptive statistics for all of the variables used in the analysis.

---

[4] This explains why the smallest city in our sample is listed as having a population in the earlier time period of less than 100,000. While all of our urban areas had 1990 populations of 100,000 for the metropolitan region, this was not quite true once we had truncated some sub areas to account for portions not covered by the satellite image and adjusted for the satellite image date.

Table 12.1 Descriptive statistics

Variable	μ	σ	Min	Max	Obs
Total urban land (KM^2)	402.81	635.11	8.92	4,268	240
Total population	3,363,025	4,459,765	93,040.91	27,200,000	240
Per capita income (2000 USD)	9,914.08	9,916.7	609.88	35,354	240
Agricultural land rent	3,347.65	12,569.78	68.84	150,542.9	240
Cost of motor fuel	0.62	0.36	0.02	1.56	240
Demolition orders	193.74	1,180.94	0	10,000	154
Planning staff	128.89	284.69	0	1,600	178
Planning staff per 100K	4.61	8.05	0	63.72	178
Delay convert rural to urban	13.8	44.48	1	416	182
Delay to subdivide land	5.68	8.78	0.08	75	206
Regional indicators					
East Asia	0.13	0.34	0	1	240
Europe	0.13	0.34	0	1	240
Latin America	0.13	0.34	0	1	240
North Africa	0.07	0.25	0	1	240
South-central Asia	0.13	0.34	0	1	240
Southeast Asia	0.1	0.3	0	1	240
Subsaharan Africa	0.1	0.3	0	1	240
West Asia	0.07	0.25	0	1	240
Other developed (excluded)	0.13	0.34	0	1	240
Instrumental variables					
Shallow groundwater	0.24	0.43	0	1	240
Boreal semi-arid	0.01	0.09	0	1	240
Boreal humid	0.02	0.13	0	1	240
Temperate semi-arid	0.16	0.37	0	1	240
Temperate humid	0.26	0.44	0	1	240
Mediterranean warm	0.11	0.31	0	1	240
Desert tropical	0.03	0.16	0	1	240
Desert temperate	0.08	0.28	0	1	240
Desert cold	0.02	0.13	0	1	240
Tropical semi-arid	0.19	0.39	0	1	240
Tropical humid	0.12	0.32	0	1	240
Latitude	22.98	21.85	-34.89	55.75	240
Longitude	30	73.61	-122.44	151.21	240
Maximum slope	25.96	14.96	4.16	78	240
Ethnic fractionalize	0.38	0.23	0	0.93	240
Language fractionalize	0.35	0.3	0	0.92	240
Religion fractionalize	0.46	0.25	0	0.86	240
Other variables					
Change in area	115.21	126.09	3.19	549.66	240
Change in pop	584,872.9	964,112	$-898,817.5$	4,916,813	240
Pct change in percap GDP	0.02	0.03	-0.08	0.09	240

4 Results

All models reported in this paper have been estimated using all available observations as a cross section data set with standard errors clustered for each city. In addition to population, income, transportation input cost, agricultural land values, and several measures of the level of land use planning, regional fixed effects are included to capture systematic influences of a cultural, economic, or technological nature that might cause all cities in a region to be similarly large or compact. In all cases, we estimate a model that is linear in the logarithms so that the equation to be estimated is:

$$
\begin{aligned}
\ln(UrbanArea) = {} & \beta_0 + \beta_1 \ln Pop + \beta_2 \ln Income + \beta_3 \ln AgriRent \\
& + \beta_4 \ln FuelCost + \beta_5 \ln Planning + \beta_6 EastAsia + \ldots \quad (12.4) \\
& + \beta_1 3WestAsia + \in
\end{aligned}
$$

A central econometric difficulty for analysis of these data concerns the endogeneity of several of the variables that are used to explain total urban land area. Consider income, for example. Suppose that a city has drawn a large positive ε for urban area so that it has a large amount of urban land cover. This urban land cover consists of built structures, roadways, and other types of physical capital so what we are really saying is that the city has an unusually large stock of physical capital. If this capital is productive, then it might work to increase incomes in the city so that measured income in the urban area will not be fixed, nor random but independent of the model error ε.

Whether failing to account for endogeneity of land use regulation biases the resulting analysis towards finding policies to be effective or finding them to be ineffective depends on the mechanism of endogeneity that is thought to hold. Formally, of course, the direction and magnitude of the bias depends on the structure of the covariance between the error in total urban footprint and the independent variables. An intuitive understanding of the difficulty can be developed by considering a couple of alternative cases. Cities that face high levels of population and income growth will, as a result of these factors, tend to experience high rates of urban expansion. If, in response to this, such cities adopt land use regulation in an effort to constrain urban expansion, the regulations might be partly effective but not fully. As a result cities with a higher probability of adopting growth controls will also exhibit urban expansion and the analysis may be biased towards finding anti-sprawl policies ineffective. Alternatively, it might be that land use regulation emerges primarily to serve the economic interests of existing land owners who seek, for example, to block construction of new housing so as to increase the value of their own property. Cities that are experiencing limited population growth or economic stagnation would tend to have stagnating or declining property values as well. If property owners control land use regulatory authorities in such cities, they might push for even more stringent controls as a way of defending property values against countervailing market forces. In this case we would be biased towards finding exaggerated impacts of land use controls.

We consider five different indicators of the level of planning activity. The number of compulsory demolitions of structures within the past year due to non-compliance with planning regulations, the total number of staff in the planning department, the total number of staff per 100,000 persons in the urban area, the delay (in months) to get permission to subdivide a parcel of urban land, and the delay to convert land from rural to urban use. There are other more conventional measures of the restrictiveness of planning regulations in cities, but some of these are rarely if ever applied in developing country cities (urban growth boundaries) or are difficult to measure (although work to complete these measures is in progress). The five variables considered in this paper have the advantage of being readily understood and reported by a relatively large share of planning offices in the sample of cities.

We endeavor to deal with the endogeneity problem using an instrumental variables approach. Before presenting those estimates it is worth examining, if only for comparison, the results estimated using a conventional OLS approach. Tables 12.2 and 12.3 present these results. In the first column of results estimates are presented for a model with no planning variables, followed by a model that includes compulsory demolitions, then planning staff, then planning staff per 100,000 population, then both delay variables, and finally the delay in converting rural to urban land. This last variable is of obvious relevance to urban expansion, since it is such conversion that is the very essence of urban sprawl. On the other hand, increasing or decreasing the delay might do little to affect the total urban land use in a city.

Table 12.2 presents several results that are of interest. First, note that the impacts of population, income, agricultural land value and transport costs are all of the correct sign and except in two cases all are statistically significant. They are also of magnitudes that are generally plausible. For example the impact of population is consistently slightly larger than 0.8 implying that doubling the population of the urban area increases total urban land use by slightly more than 80 %. This implies that as cities grow, the get larger but also get more dense. Other impacts are also of reasonable magnitudes.

The impact of planning variables is consistently small and never significant. Either planning has minimal impact on urban land use, or these variables are not good proxies for planning restrictiveness, or endogeneity of the sort discussed above is making it difficult to detect.

Before moving to consider the instrumental variables estimates, we note from Table 12.3 that the regional fixed effects are rarely significant. The excluded case is "Other Developed" country cities, which includes cities in the United States, Australia, Canada and Japan. It is not surprising that relative to these the European or South-central Asian cities tend to be smaller, although the effect is not always significant. It is worth noting that sub-Saharan African or West Asian cities tend to be larger (or not significantly different from) cities in the default category.

We need the instruments to be uncorrelated with random error in the total urban land use variable, but capable (as a group) of providing reasonable estimates of the endogenous variables. The instrumental variable strategy we employ uses four broad groups of variables as instruments for the potentially endogenous variables in the model. These are the biome in which the city is located (a rough indicator of the soil type, rainfall and climate factors), the location and topography (latitude,

Table 12.2 OLS estimates

Variable	No plan	Demolition orders	Planning staff	Plan staff per 100 K	Rural and subdiv delay	Rural delay
Population	0.8126***	0.8535***	0.8629***	0.8489***	0.8264***	0.8310***
σ	0.031	0.036	0.037	0.035	0.040	0.038
Income	0.5204***	0.7521***	0.6898***	0.6522***	0.6167***	0.6261***
σ	0.064	0.088	0.092	0.092	0.072	0.065
Agri-rent	−0.2268***	−0.2367***	−0.2903***	−0.2974***	−0.2479***	−0.2550***
σ	0.041	0.044	0.041	0.044	0.037	0.037
Fuel cost	−0.1453**	−0.1473**	−0.0516	−0.0496	−0.1750***	−0.1729***
σ	0.065	0.069	0.092	0.091	0.060	0.062
Rural-urban delay					−0.0155	−0.0209
σ					0.044	0.042
Subdivide delay					−0.0306	
σ					0.043	
Planning staff				−0.0079		
σ				0.026		
Planning staff per 100k			−0.0102			
σ			0.028			
Demolition orders		−0.0147				
σ		0.042				
Constant	−9.1926***	−12.1353***	−11.1391***	−10.5339	−10.1804***	−10.3290***
σ	0.740	0.987	0.959	1.050	0.958	0.873
F	88.8400***	84.3300***	101.2800***	101.1300***	72.2400***	83.8400***
R^2	0.839	0.873	0.875	0.873	0.862	0.870
Root MSE	0.52	0.49	0.49	0.48	0.48	0.48
Observations	240	154	178	174	176	182

*significant at 10 per cent, ** significant at 5 per cent, *** significant at 1 per cent

Table 12.3 OLS estimates of regional fixed effects

Variable	No plan	Demolition orders	Planning staff	Plan staff per 100 K	Rural and subdiv delay	Rural delay
East Asia	−0.1384	0.7348**	0.2995	0.2249	−0.0277	0.0251
σ	0.208	0.323	0.282	0.277	0.248	0.226
Europe	−0.3305**	−0.2024	−0.2508	−0.2726*	−0.3134*	−0.3210**
σ	0.137	0.156	0.155	0.157	0.160	0.158
Latin America	−0.3618**	−0.0680	−0.1146	−0.1668	−0.1263	−0.1013
σ	0.180	0.249	0.164	0.167	0.170	0.160
North Africa	−0.4464	−0.0552	0.1384	0.0570	−0.3153	−0.3001
σ	0.293	0.392	0.358	0.355	0.238	0.227
South Central Asia	−0.6620***	−0.0018	−0.1846	−0.2361	−0.4196**	−0.4210**
σ	0.208	0.298	0.265	0.260	0.210	0.190
Southeast Asia	−0.4608*	−0.2504	−0.2492	−0.3624	−0.3733*	−0.3346*
σ	0.240	0.229	0.237	0.244	0.192	0.187
Subsaharan Africa	0.0999	0.7644***	0.4964	0.3669	0.2634	0.2934
σ	0.199	0.285	0.300	0.316	0.242	0.209
West Asia	0.0646	0.5369***	0.5454**	0.4780*	0.2629	0.2989
σ	0.211	0.197	0.258	0.263	0.264	0.259

*significant at 10 per cent, ** significant at 5 per cent, *** significant at 1 per cent

longitude, presence of a shallow groundwater aquifer and slope of the steepest area developed in the earlier of our two image dates), and measures of the ethnic, linguistic and religious diversity of the national population using the same measures of "fractionalization" that were used in Alesina et al. (2003). These latter measures are included because of their plausible exogeneity to the process of urban land use, and their likely usefulness in capturing aspects of land use regulation and policy. Finally, the regional indicator variables that are included in the model are taken as exogenous and can therefore also serve as instruments for the endogenous (or potentially endogenous) variables.

Initially, consider the success of the instruments in the first stage equations. These are presented in Table 12.4. While a great many of the individual variables are not statistically significant, this is of minimal concern. Each equation has a set of variables that do seem to play a role and permit a reasonable forecast of the main variables.

It is worth noting that the biome variables play an important role in the Agricultural Rent model, as expected. The fractionalization variables play important roles for several variables, particularly the model for rural land conversion delays. This model also performs generally well with one of the higher levels of explanatory power and lower mean square errors.

Tables 12.5 and 12.6 present the instrumental variables estimates using these instruments and estimating the model described above. All IV estimates were obtained using the GMM procedure that is part of STATA's **ivreg2** procedure. Table 12.5 shows again that the estimated impact of population, income, agricultural land values, and transport costs are of the expected sign, a reasonable magnitude, and generally statistically significant, although in these estimates there is a bit less stability across various forms of the models. The impact of fuel

Table 12.4 First stage estimates

	Pop	Income	Agrent	Fuel	Demolish	Plan staff	Staff per C	Sub delay	Rur delay
East Asia	0.1703	-1.4938***	-0.4812	-0.2824*	1.5827**	-1.1344	-0.000070**	-0.9963**	-1.2744**
σ	0.738	0.131	0.409	0.168	0.702	1.046	0.00003	0.490	0.644
Europe	0.2375	0.1789	-0.1043	0.7133***	-1.0115*	1.6665*	0.000094***	0.4842	0.7347
σ	0.626	0.151	0.341	0.151	0.600	0.876	0.00003	0.527	0.658
Latin America	-0.0742	-1.1633***	1.4175***	-0.1227	1.5192	2.3477	0.000154**	0.3382	-0.7498
σ	0.848	0.308	0.438	0.298	1.157	1.538	0.00008	0.711	0.654
North Africa	-0.0527	-1.2682***	1.4921**	0.0631	4.8075***	1.3697	0.000052	0.5217	0.3503
σ	0.884	0.329	0.606	0.402	1.215	1.315	0.00005	0.862	0.694
S-Central Asia	0.0809	-1.2850***	0.4415	-0.2536	2.2873***	0.0062	0.000019	-0.3923	-0.0180
σ	0.753	0.246	0.446	0.330	0.850	1.199	0.00004	0.605	0.559
SE Asia	0.3088	-0.3635	1.7179***	-0.5940*	0.9770	0.2048	0.000039	0.0094	0.5019
σ	0.918	0.344	0.651	0.315	1.178	1.643	0.00004	0.659	0.719
Subsaharan Africa	-0.7685	-1.7587***	0.4633	-0.0910	2.1676**	2.3021	0.000202*	-0.0785	-0.8684*
σ	0.769	0.328	0.412	0.346	0.916	1.437	0.00012	0.559	0.452
West Asia	0.3525	-0.7246	1.8457**	0.5143*	-1.7522	0.9895	0.000013	-0.9983	0.6208
σ	0.844	0.438	0.713	0.274	1.267	1.524	0.00005	0.835	0.720
Shallow GWater	-0.2788	-0.0745	0.0115	0.0265	-0.7381**	-0.9342*	-0.000040	0.2671	-0.3082
σ	0.289	0.118	0.220	0.120	0.324	0.481	0.00003	0.243	0.233
Boreal humid	0.4243	-0.0496	-0.1725	-0.1620	0.6613***	-1.5319***	0.000025	-1.2183	1.0206
σ	1.864	0.360	0.508	0.371	0.187	0.428	0.00002	1.530	0.626
Temp semi-arid	0.8021	0.2968	1.7117***	0.3453	0.9636	0.2606	0.000025	0.1720	0.7542
σ	0.665	0.356	0.544	0.312	0.725	1.273	0.00005	1.039	0.711
Temp humid	1.2577*	0.7664*	1.9244***	0.3426	-0.0627	2.2475	0.000091*	0.5633	1.7837**
σ	0.661	0.389	0.593	0.316	0.652	1.399	0.00005	1.068	0.850
Medit warm	0.9587	0.5445	2.0557***	0.2406	-0.2138	1.9765	0.000081*	0.7407	2.3643***
σ	0.688	0.392	0.573	0.324	0.556	1.287	0.00005	1.029	0.814
Desert tropical	-0.8095	-0.1946	1.4797***	0.5435	-0.7943	0.5087	0.000065	-1.0810	-0.0080

(continued)

Table 12.4 (continued)

	Pop	Income	Agrent	Fuel	Demolish	Plan staff	Staff per C	Sub delay	Rur delay
σ	0.807	0.561	0.649	0.421	1.127	1.293	0.00005	1.204	1.073
Desert temperate	0.5416	0.2901	1.2933*	−0.1430	1.2253**	0.1029	0.000035	−0.1711	0.2088
σ	0.681	0.412	0.706	0.371	0.598	0.904	0.00003	0.995	0.630
Desert cold	1.1485	1.1533***	0.6288	−0.2629	−0.1890	1.3508	−0.000002	0.0411	1.4549
σ	1.205	0.395	1.266	0.797	1.476	1.605	0.00005	1.029	0.934
Trop. Semi-arid	1.1280	−0.1581	1.6571***	0.4457	−0.3052	0.6773	0.000023	−0.3780	1.1722
σ	0.698	0.420	0.568	0.354	0.706	1.361	0.00005	1.081	0.759
Trop. humid	0.3076	0.2360	2.0796***	0.7686**	−2.0399**	1.0218	0.000045	−0.5374	−0.5628
σ	0.884	0.454	0.648	0.349	0.967	1.452	0.00005	1.114	0.880
Latitude	−0.0093	−0.0052	0.0233***	−0.0065	0.0036	0.0234	0.000002**	0.0089	−0.0197**
σ	0.011	0.004	0.007	0.004	0.012	0.020	0.00000	0.008	0.008
Longitude	0.0015	−0.0062***	0.0032	−0.0016	0.0102*	0.0126*	0.000001*	0.0014	0.0034
σ	0.005	0.001	0.002	0.001	0.006	0.007	0.00000	0.003	0.003
Slope	−0.0474	0.2522***	0.2008	−0.0455	1.1745***	0.0827	0.000018	0.0094	−0.2460
σ	0.205	0.093	0.133	0.097	0.390	0.369	0.00002	0.211	0.192
Ethnic frac.	0.0625	−0.3021***	−0.3817***	−0.4465***	1.1057***	0.4051	0.000014	0.1511	0.6184***
σ	0.229	0.101	0.136	0.094	0.384	0.392	0.000001	0.245	0.196
Language frac.	−0.0890	0.0727	−0.1560	0.2011**	−0.6573**	−0.1517	0.000001	0.0088	−0.4490**
σ	0.190	0.088	0.130	0.077	0.302	0.372	0.00001	0.226	0.187
Religion frac.	−0.0244	0.0583	0.3036***	−0.0025	−0.0463	0.2046	0.000015	−0.1561	−0.3527*
σ	0.120	0.069	0.100	0.065	0.250	0.217	0.00001	0.132	0.112
Constant	13.0244***	8.4599***	2.92066***	−0.09455*	−2.9319**	1.1559	−0.000122	0.9239	1.6519
σ	0.973	0.482	0.766	0.520	1.329	2.019	0.00010	1.248	1.045
R^2	0.145	0.809	0.637	0.388	0.692	0.238	0.35620	0.392	0.592
Obs	240	240	240	240	178	178	178	206	182

****significant at 1 %,* ** *significant at 5 %,* **significant at 10 %*

12 Do Planning Policies Limit the Expansion of Cities?

Table 12.5 Instrumental variable estimates

Variable	No plan	Demolition orders	Planning staff	Plan staff per 100 K	Rural and subdiv delay	Rural delay
Population	0.6495***	0.7598***	0.8133***	0.7468***	0.9212***	0.8865***
σ	1.35	0.070	0.088	0.109	0.111	0.100
Income	0.5505***	0.6121***	0.3330**	0.4297***	0.5499***	0.6041***
σ	0.125	0.124	0.150	0.162	0.139	0.107
Agri-rent	−0.2755***	−0.2043***	−0.3149***	−0.2950***	−0.4309***	−0.3558***
σ	0.083	0.080	0.108	0.104	0.129	0.103
Fuel cost	−0.2813	−0.3985**	−0.2966	−0.3431	−0.0782	−0.2822
σ	0.188	0.168	0.233	0.230	0.271	0.194
Rural–urban delay					−0.2852**	−0.1335**
σ					0.116	0.067
Subdivide delay					0.3117*	
σ					0.175	
Planning staff			0.0476			
σ			0.076			
Planning staff per 100k				0.0127		
σ				0.081		
Demolition orders		0.0006				
σ		0.058				
Constant	−6.8255***	−9.7041***	−6.7306***	−6.9815***	−9.4717***	−10.0035***
σ	1.839	1.291	1.652	1.952	2.284	1.937
Anderson LR statistic	25.06**	27.34***	19.37*	23.73**	13.43	24.77**
Hansen J	14.46	14.77	11.67	10.58	9.39	11.36
x^2 Endogeneity test	20.13***	3.69	11.32**	11.2**	16.72**	15.5***
F-statistic	16.92***	29.18***	32.52***	22.56***	29.87***	33.2***
Centered R^2	0.8	0.85	0.83	0.83	0.77	0.85
Uncentered R^2	0.99	0.99	0.99	0.99	0.99	0.99
Root MSE	0.56	0.51	0.53	0.54	0.59	0.5
Observations	240	154	174	178	176	182

*significant at 10 per cent, ** significant at 5 per cent, *** significant at 1 per cent

Table 12.6 Regional fixed effects for IV models

Variable	No plan	Demolition orders	Planning staff	Plan staff per 100 K	Rural and subdiv delay	Rural delay
East Asia	−0.1473	0.1972	−0.4921	−0.3033	−0.1239	−0.2176
σ	0.360	0.473	0.422	0.453	0.377	0.305
Europe	−0.3369	−0.0868	−0.3827	−0.2605	−0.4910[*]	−0.2748
σ	0.213	0.159	0.268	0.276	0.284	0.222
Latin America	−0.4015	−0.2162	−0.6659[***]	−0.5147[*]	−0.2107	−0.1945
σ	0.265	0.255	0.244	0.275	0.281	0.235
North Africa	−0.6444	−0.6575	−1.0012[**]	−0.7975	−0.3032	−0.3625
σ	0.398	0.584	0.502	0.531	0.508	0.406
South Central Asia	−0.8055[**]	−0.6267	−1.2529[***]	−1.0841[**]	−0.5737	−0.7493[**]
σ	0.353	0.428	0.386	0.423	0.410	0.294
Southeast Asia	−0.4239	−0.4929	−1.1610[***]	−0.8579[*]	−0.2158	−0.4443
σ	0.396	0.379	0.419	0.465	0.529	0.378
Subsaharan Africa	−0.0266	0.2546	−0.7759	−0.4320	−0.0243	0.0765
σ	0.356	0.370	0.491	0.530	0.421	0.313
West Asia	−0.0595	0.1946	−0.1565	−0.0129	0.3226	0.2502
σ	0.324	0.308	0.357	0.404	0.385	0.354

*significant at 10 per cent, ** significant at 5 per cent, * significant at 1 per cent

cost is estimated with considerably less precision, and it may be that we need a broader measure of the costs of travel than the cost of gasoline, or that our instruments are just weak for this variable.

Is it really necessary to estimate these relationships using an instrumental variables approach? While income, population and planning policies all might be endogenous in principle, perhaps in practice the relationships are so weak that a more standard estimation procedure would be acceptable (and produce lower variance parameter estimates). We test this possibility using a statistic described more fully in Baum et al. (2007). The test is presented in the row in Table 12.5 labeled "χ^2 Endogeneity test." This test statistic is distributed χ^2 under the null that the variables representing population, income, agricultural rent, fuel costs and the planning variables are exogenous. As can be seen from the table this is rejected at the 95 % level or better for all cases except the case of using demolition orders as the measure of planning restrictiveness. It seems reasonable to conclude from this that there is an endogeneity problem in these data that must be addressed.

If an IV approach is required, one might be concerned that the instruments we have chosen are relevant to the task of modeling the endogenous variables. Even though the first stage estimates, presented in Table 12.4, appeared to perform reasonably well, the canonical correlation between the instrumental variables and the endogenous variables might generally be very low. The Anderson likelihood ratio statistic is designed to test exactly this concern. This statistic is based on a null hypothesis that the smallest canonical correlation between the instruments and endogenous covariates is zero and that the regressors are normally distributed. Failure to reject the null suggests concern about the relevance of the instruments. Table 12.5 indicates that all of the models reject the null at the 90 % level or better except the model that includes both the time delay in subdivision and the time delay in obtaining permission to develop rural land.

Finally, we might have established that an IV approach is necessary due to endogeneity, and identified a set of instrumental variables that are sufficiently closely correlated with the endogenous variables to be judged relevant, but we could still face the difficulty that the instruments themselves are not independent of the error term in the model. To provide a test of this concern we consider Hansen's J statistic test. This statistic is asymptotically distributed χ^2 under the null hypothesis of validity of the overidentifying restrictions in the model. These will fail if the instruments are endogenous or belong in the model directly. While the power of this test may be somewhat low in our modest sized samples (the distributional properties are established asymptotically), examination of the row in Table 12.5 that contains the Hansen J statistic shows that none of the tests reject the null hypothesis. To this extent, we suggest at least provisional acceptance of the proposition that there is endogeneity present that must be dealt with, that the instruments we use are relevant, and that they are sufficiently independent of the model error to provide a valid estimate. This is particularly true for the models that use total planning staff, planning staff per capita, and the delay in getting permission to develop rural land.

The demolition and staffing variables to indicate land use planning activities are again not statistically significant nor correctly signed. The situation is different for the indicators of planning delay, and in particular for the time delay in converting rural to urban land. This variable is significant (at the 95 % level) and correctly signed. This might provide a reasonable indicator of planning restrictiveness that can be collected and compared across cities globally. The estimates presented here indicate that a doubling of the delay (say from 6 to 12 months) would be associated in the data with about a 13 % reduction in total urban land use, *ceteris paribus*.

5 Conclusion

We conclude by drawing attention to three central points. First the simple model presented above generates comparative static predictions that are generally supported in the data. The impacts of population, income, and agricultural land values are clearly supported. The impact of transport cost (as represented by the price of motor fuel) is a bit less clear, but is generally supported. The impacts of those planning activities that result in delays in the conversion of land from rural to urban uses is associated with an impact that is statistically significant and correctly signed. The impact of internal open space preservation is possibly supported, although our measure of delay in conversion of rural to urban land is perhaps less clearly capturing this aspect of planning policy.

A second point to make is that our results seem to support the suggestion that some, if not all, aspects of planning are capable of constraining expanding land use in cities. It is impossible to say in general whether such constraint is welfare improving or reducing. Other investigations suggest it can be either.

Table 12.7 Impact of a one standard deviation change

	One σ %	% Urban land
Population	132.61 %	111.09 %
Income	100.03 %	59.32 %
Ag land value	375.48 %	−142.42 %
Fuel cost	57.63 %	−16.44 %
Rural to urban	322.38 %	−47.03 %

Finally, what about the relative power of these policies? They might be capable of constraining urban land use but so weak relative to the forces that are causing cities to expand that they are of little consequences. Table 12.7 presents some information on this issue by considering the percentage impact on total urban land use of a one standard deviation increase in the variable (measuring the standard deviation across our sample of cities).

	Result	Description	Confirmed
1.	$\frac{\partial T}{\partial N} \geq 0$	Increasing population increases total urban land	Yes
2.	$\frac{\partial T}{\partial M} \geq 0$	Increasing household income increases total urban land	Yes
3.	$\frac{\partial T}{\partial \tau} \leq 0$	Increasing transport costs decreases total urban land	Yes, weakly
4.	$\frac{\partial T}{\partial R_a} \leq 0$	Increasing agricultural land value decreases total urban land	Yes
5.	$\frac{\partial T}{\partial \rho} \leq 0$	A stricter containment planning policies decreases total urban land	Yes, for delay
6.	$\frac{\partial T}{\partial \omega} \leq 0$	Increasing internal open space will decrease total urban land	Possibly

The analysis suggests that while planning policies, and delay in land conversion in particular, are not the most powerful of impacts (that role is reserved, perhaps surprisingly, for the value of agricultural land, followed by population increase itself) it is of a comparable order of magnitude as the impact of income, and it might be reasonable to expect that some form of land use regulation policies could play a role in limiting urban expansion if it is determined that such constraint is desirable.

References

Alesina A, Devleeschauwer A, Easterly W, Kurlat S, Wacziarg R (2003) Fractionalization. J Econ Growth 8(2):155–194

Baum CF, Schaffer ME, Stillman S (2007) Enhanced routines for instrumental variables/gmm estimation and testing. Centre for Economic Reform and Transformation (working paper)

Black JT (1996) The economics of sprawl. Urban Land 55(3):52–53

Burchfield M, Overman HG, Puga D, Turner MA (2006) Causes of sprawl: a portrait from space. Quart J Econ 121(2):587–633

Cheshire P, Sheppard S (2002) The welfare economics of land use planning. J Urban Econ 52(2):242–269

Nechyba TJ, Walsh RP (2004) Urban sprawl. J Econ Perspect 18(4):177–200

Osborn F (1946) Garden cities of tomorrow, preface. MIT Press, Cambridge, MA, pp 9–28

Sheppard S (1988) The qualitative economics of development control. J Urban Econ 24(3):310–330

Turner MA (2007) A simple theory of smart growth and sprawl. J Urban Econ 61(1):21–44

Chapter 13
The Importance of ICT for Cities: e-Governance and Cyber Perceptions

Peter Nijkamp and Galit Cohen-Blankshtain

Abstract This paper offers a critical review of current debates on the importance and the potential of ICT for modern cities. Much attention is given to the opportunities offered by local e-governance, as a systematic strategy to exploit the potential of ICT for the public domain in European cities. Since the views of many experts and elected policy-makers in cities (so-called 'urban frontliners') is coloured by subjective expectations and perceptions, we examine in particular the extent to which the expected influences of ICT, as perceived by urban frontliners, affect their perceptions of the relevance of ICT to mitigate contemporary urban challenges. The final (empirical) part of the paper addresses the issue of the systematic study of cyber perceptions of cities in Europe.

PN290GCB

Keywords Urban policy • Perceptions • E-governance • ICT

1 ICT and e-Governance

The digital revolution – as a fruit of ICT usage – has not only exerted a profound impact on modern business life or on our daily ways of working or living, but begins to enter also increasingly the public domain. Governance and administrative institutions – ranging from local to national – are gradually adjusted to the new potential offered by modern cyberspace (mainly Internet-based). Cities in particular, where the interaction between citizens and government is rather direct, have recognized the efficiency gains of the electronic age. Consequently, in recent years

---

P. Nijkamp (✉)
Dept. of Spatial Economics, VU University, Amsterdam, The Netherlands
e-mail: pnijkamp@feweb.vu.nl

G. Cohen-Blankshtain
Dept. of Geography and School of Public Policy, Hebrew University, Jerusalem, Israel

J. Klaesson et al. (eds.), *Metropolitan Regions*, Advances in Spatial Science,
DOI 10.1007/978-3-642-32141-2_13, © Springer-Verlag Berlin Heidelberg 2013

the social science literature has been enriched with new terms like 'digital government', 'cyber government', 'virtual government' and 'e-government'. Clearly, the pace of acceptance of such concepts differs per country and per city, but there is an undeniable trend that the modern ICT is gradually imposing its footprints on the domain of public governance. It is clearly recognised in the modern digital research community that in an networked world – be it global or local – ICT offers many opportunities and venues for the public domain to realize many efficiency gains and to enhance the democratic interaction with citizens. In this paper we address in particular e-governance, as a modern usage of ICT opportunities – in particular the Internet – in order to judge the opportunities for better government. In addition to a review of these new opportunities, we will also study empirically the perceived importance of ICT in cities by investigating in more detail the 'cyber image' of cities in Europe.

Research on e-governance is nowadays booming and addresses many challenging topics such as information intelligibility and accessibility of information in a democratic society, digital democracy through ICT use, open source and privacy issues in an e-society, digital divide and democratic access, computer software and digital archives in a local democracy, data security and anonymity, awareness creation and public watchdog systems in an e-society, local process organizations of e-democracy and so forth (see e.g., Berra 2003; Chadwick and May 2003; Fountain 2001). The challenges are indeed numerous and cover all domains of public policy, such as security, socio-economic policy, health care, education, transportation, technology transfer, market governance, contingency management, environmental monitoring or resource management. The e-society has just entered its initial stages and its evolution will certainly be governed by many learning experiments, when technological, socio-political, legal and psychological determinants will influence its pathway (Docherty et al. 2001; Hood and Lodge 2004).

The growing importance of ICT in everyday life, business activities and governance prompts the need to incorporate it also in local democracy. Clearly, ICT policies at the local level are still in an early stage (Servon and Horrigan 1997; Cohen and Nijkamp 2004). Urban administrations are just beginning to wrestle with the wider economic and societal implications of the information revolution (Evans 2002). There is much talking about e.g. e-administration, but this is often more a wishful concept than a reality.

In several countries new research initiatives are planned to explore and exploit the benefits of e-governance, such as NSF's Cyberinfrastructure Program (see Arens et al. 2005) or the EU Intelcities program (see Curwell et al. 2005). The Cyberinfrastructure Program aims to address the potential of electronic infrastructure to enable more ubiquitous, comprehensive knowledge environments that provide complete functionality for the science engineering research community (in terms of people, data, information, tools and instruments) using modern ICT opportunities. The Intelcities Program is an EU program in the domain of networked businesses and governments and aims to explore and create a new and innovative set of e-government services to meet the needs of both citizens and businesses by providing interactive local on-line applications and services to citizens from the perspective of social inclusion and broad access.

The European Commission (2005a) has argued that Europe needs efficient, effective, inclusive and open governments in order to offer high quality services for citizens and business. It is foreseen that the introduction of e-governance will generate significant or even massive benefits. For example: the economic impact of moving towards electronic public procurement is generally assessed to be considerable, in terms of increasing efficiencies and reducing procurement costs, so that – given the size of public procurement (some 16 % of GDP on average in EU countries) and even assuming that only half of the saving would be realized – this saving would represent over 40 billion per annum in the EU. The expected revenues of e-governance[1] are indeed sky-rocketing and this expectation prompts research issues of various nature (Staples et al. 2002).

After the avalanche of new e-services in the private sector in Europe, we witness nowadays a formidable rise in e-governance services. At present, 90 % of public service providers in Europe offer already an on-line presence, while approximately one half of all basic public services (e.g., social security benefits, tax revenue services, elections, car registration, enrollment in educations) are fully interactive (see European Commission 2005b). It is expected that all these new e-services will generate high benefits for citizens and businesses in Europe and that e-governance will enhance the quality and efficiency of public services in Europe from local to European level. Of course, for such benefits to be realized it is necessary that the European 'information space' is open and efficiently organized, is ensuring an enhancement of the innovative and socio-economic potential in Europe and is favouring sustainable development in a participatory society (cf. Lash 2003).

The public sector itself will only be a major beneficiary of e-governance, if the interaction with citizens is improved, if governments use e-services as an enabling technology for enhancing the quality of public services, if governments are pro-active partners in socio-technological innovation (e.g., as a launching customer) and if they develop new concepts from the perspective of a knowledge-based innovation society OECD (2005). Consequently, there is a need for a systematic e-governance architecture which would ensure productivity and quality rise in the public sector on the basis of solid benchmark analysis, shared good experiences and lessons, and an efficient and non-bureaucratic organization of e-services.

Generally speaking, the benefits of e-governance – as a result of technical performance and organizational improvement – may be assessed on the basis of an improvement in efficiency (e.g., cost reduction or costs avoided), in effectiveness (e.g., higher client gains and opportunities) and in good governance (e.g., gain in trust of citizens due to de-bureaucratization). But the value analysis of each of these three items is a complicated matter characterized by an abundance of uncertainty, where the feasibility, the necessity, the risk-orientation and the acceptability by the public

---

[1] In the sequel of this paper we will use the term e-governance, which will be interpreted as the use of ICT, combined with organizational change and new skills to improve public services, increase democratic participation and enhance public policy-making, sometimes in combination with private sector initiatives.

play together a major role (cf. Graham and Marvin 1996). Since public authorities operate normally under strict budget constraints – and less under revenues constraints – it is difficult to judge the social and financial viability of e-governance projects. Unfortunately, the field is full of unjustified rhetoric, as witnessed by the following quotation: "78% of Information Systems projects failed to realise even 50% of the originally identified benefits" (*Management Today* 2001).

Admittedly, the high expectations on the public benefits of ICT are often based on vision, expectations and sometimes irrealistic assumptions. Views on ICT and its impact on urban and everyday lives may sometimes create a biased perspective affecting the willingness of urban frontliners to promote ICT policies. Against this background, the present paper aims to test the extent to which the local leadership's perception of ICT impacts affects their views of the relevance of ICT policy. The study is based on extensive data collection at local levels in Europe. After an overview of various issues related to e-governance in Europe and to cities in Europe, we will address more specifically the expectations on the 'cyber' potential of cities in Europe and test statistically the above hypothesis. The paper will be concluded with some policy lessons.

2   e-Governance in European Cities

ICT is an enabling technology that is – like any other technology – subjected to a normal life cycle, with one exception: in the public domain it is often linked to principles like democracy or equity. This may cause a hype in the initial stages of the technology, followed often by a period of disillusionment on the actual performance of ICT-services in the public domain, with at the end a collapse or an incorporation in existing mature markets in the domain concerned. e-Governance presupposes open and interactive communication channels, leading to deliberative democracy. If this condition is not met, it will end up with a misinformed democracy with information overload, loss of trust and quality of official information sources and media, and emerging trends towards new forms of e-bureaucracy. There is a major challenge for governments – from local to global levels – to ensure a balanced and efficient set of e-mechanisms that stimulate the trust and accountability of the public sector (see also Abramson and Morin 2003; Van der Meer and Van Winden 2003). As Salomon (1998) stresses, technology, in general – and ICT in particular – is not merely a collection of hardware. Technology is a socially perceived construct. Moreover, ICT is not neutral and may, depending on specific contextual and image factors, accommodate either dispersion or concentration trends Nijkamp and Salomon (1989). Moreover, the use of the technology is regulated, on the one hand, by the expected value it provides to the potential user and, on the other hand, by various rules and norms, and these uses and regulations determine the impacts of ICT on society and their spatial structure. This policy may have two forms. The ICT sector is either viewed as a final goal in itself, which has to be achieved through the implementation of proper policy incentives (e.g. fiscal policy, land use policy or educational policy as instruments to achieve ICT goals). Or it views ICT as a vehicle to achieve higher-order goals for the public domain (such as a strong international recognition or a recognized local democracy).

Since the mid 1990s we witness an avalanche of publications on the barriers and benefits of the digital revolution. It was suggested that we were all going to live in cyberspace, mainly Internet-based. These visions were sometimes based on irrealistic expectations or subjective images. This cyber revolution would not take place everywhere on the globe, but would have its origin in the modern city. Such cities were called digital cities. Clearly, in a virtual world many cities would have to seek for a new competitive position by exploiting the potential of new communication technologies. Such cities would have to orient themselves towards new telecommunication infrastructures, new modes of working, living and interacting, and new forms of policy-making (see also Boyer 1996). This development may lead to the emergence of various groups of citizens (see Graham and Aurigi 1997), viz. the information users, the information used, and the non-plugged population. This would also have a great impact on the public domain and the functioning of democracy at local level. In any case, the digital city is not yet reality; it is largely based on visions and beliefs.

There are many metaphors trying to capture the futuristic and far reaching consequences of ICT for the city and society at large (Graham and Marvin 1996). Urban planners and decision-makers may agree or disagree on these varied visionary thoughts, but surely cannot ignore them when policies for the future have to be developed. Expectations and concerns on ICT expressed in many respects (economic growth, social segregation, environmental issues and so on) may motivate decision-makers to employ different policies related to ICT. Thus, the intensive ICT debate raises the question on how urban decision-makers assess the opportunities from ICT policies and the relevance of such policies for their city, while recognizing that many views are based on unjustified perceptions or expectations.

Urban e-governance had been given much attention in recent policy debates in the EU, in particular in the context of the so-called Intelcities programme referred to above. Its aim was to develop an urban e-governance model, that would specify the benefits and the objectives for the users, address the challenges of delivery and success, highlights the special concerns of cities in Europe and map out policies that guide implementations. The final goal would be to foster a better city government, to offer better urban (e-)services, to enhance local democracy and to improve urban decision- and policy-making from a participatory perspective (see e.g., Conroy and Evans-Cowley 2006; Di Maria et al. 2004; Di Maria and Micelli 2004). The analysis of e-governance opportunities and limitations was based on field work in various European cities, where a systematically designed questionnaire was used to obtain a comprehensive view of local e-governance by various key groups such as citizens, businesses, governmental officers and professionals.

General research findings on the potential of e-governance for cities are:

– Presence of alternative approaches to e-governance, with quite opposite trends between northern (bottom-up) and southern (top-down) countries of Europe;

- Evolutionary trends in the adoption of technologies by governments from back-office reorganizations (focus on efficiency) to effective and interactive relationships with citizens and businesses (focus on communication);
- Existence of a primary interest of (local) governments in improving existing services through ICT and then enlarging the scope of the on-line services provided, ranked among the most important priorities (before e-democracy);
- Significant efforts made by all the European countries towards developing common policy frameworks, through *ad hoc* legislation, in the domain of e-governance, within the European general Information Society framework;
- Existence of a digital divide between European countries (and cities) in terms of ability and capacity to exploit information and communication technologies to achieve policy goals, with strong differences between northern and southern countries, although with some exceptions.

The specific results from the Intelcities research in the form of policy lessons and recommendations from and for the cities concerned were the following:

- Involve citizens and local communities on a stable basis in the use of ICTs through distributed points of access, easy-to-use technologies and services, social programs of inclusion and effective/efficient service responses (increased community value);
- Promote public-private partnerships with national and, most importantly, local IT operators to increase efficiency and also achieve tailor-made solutions as well (on a competitive basis, as in the case of re-use of solutions and knowledge developed – local markets for ICT solutions);
- Invest in networking (specially among cities and local authorities) to spread and re-use positive solutions and best practices as well as to pool resources for experimentation (sustainability);
- Foster qualified knowledge management strategies within governments – and between governments, business and communities – in terms of ICT-based content creation and management, information and process transparency.

Clearly, there is an enormous variety in the type and quality of e-services provided, to both citizens and businesses. Examples of such services offered to citizens are: civil registration systems, health system, social insurance systems, pensions (retirement provision systems), civil benefit systems, on-line applications, on-line service requests, on-line consultation possibilities, access to local politicians, and so forth. Next, promising and illustrative examples of e-services for businesses are: customer relationship management systems, funds systems, business budget systems, employer development systems, managing resources systems, business accountancy systems, customer declaration systems etc. Thus, there is a great variety of new challenges for governance systems to better serve a client and to create an added value to society.

We may conclude that nowadays a growing public interest in e-governance is arising which leads to policies and strategies to induce ICT development and mobilise it in order to achieve a variety of desired public goals (i.e. national ICT policies, improved local democracy, better public service provision or intervention and deregulation in the IT sector). Several publications on this subject have painted a picture of a future society in optimistic colours, but have failed to provide clear evidence of how to get from here to there and what will be the consequences of the adoption of these technologies on other constituents of society (Melody 1996). Alongside the expectation that the private sector will play a major role in the ICT field, the expected benefits from ICT are encouraging policy-makers and planners to formulate public policies, which favour the development and adoption of ICT in the public domain (Gibbs and Keite 1997; Graham 1997; Graham and Dominy 1991).

ICT is expected to have significant influences on the city, its shape and its metabolism. Therefore, one would expect that urban planners and urban decision makers are likely to be major players in the ICT field. Some scholars are urging and hurrying urban decision makers to act in that field (e.g. Caves and Walshok 1999). However, as Graham and Marvin (2000) argue, despite the central importance of the 'urban' in cyberspace debates, issues of urban policy and planning have often been absent within both the popular and academic sides of the discussion. There are however, several types of urban ICT policies that can be found in cities (Graham and Marvin 2000; Gibbs and Tanner 1997):

- Integrated transport and ICT policies (e.g., teleworking programmes, communication corridors);
- City-level new media and IT strategies (city networks, local services, infrastructure);
- Information districts and urban "televillages" (enabling advanced IT infrastructure to attract firms);
- Integration of marginal groups in the city through ICT initiatives and better access.

A specific area that has attracted a great deal of attention is the provision of municipal information and services through ICT applications (mainly via the Internet). The first goal is the improvement of services to the citizens, and the supply of more efficient services. A second goal is supplying information about the city to potential investors, inhabitants or tourists (unfortunately many municipal web-sites in Europe are available just to native-language speakers). A third goal is to increase public participation in local processes by better information and possibilities to react, on-line, to proposals in the city agenda (e-governance). Rouillard (1999) explores the possibilities of ICT as a tool for public participation and concludes that e-governance can make the policy-making process both transparent and vague, so it is not a guarantee for an informed public.

Pratchett (1999) stresses that ICT have the potential to fulfil three complementary roles of local authorities: local democracy; public policy making; and direct services delivery. However, as Pratchett claims, there is a systematic bias which favours service delivery applications and overlooks applications regarding the other two roles. The reason for the bias, according to Pratchett, is that the decision-makers who initiate the ICT policy are not active in the other policy areas.

Another important initiative is to increase access to the Internet in public places as part of the overall strategy to increase access to the Internet. Other cities have built community tele-centres, which are supposed to deliver public access to marginalised populations. In these centres (which also can be schools), in addition to access to Internet and other ICT services, there are often also training and support services. Clearly, without the appropriate skills, the availability of equipment and infrastructure is worthless.

Other tele-activities that are stimulated by the municipality aim to serve the disabled or other disadvantaged groups in order to help them overcome physical barriers. In some cities (e.g., Berlin), there are tele-video services to pensioners, to enable them to get help and guidance through the videophones. ICT may thus be a tool to enhance e-governance on the one hand and to reinforce the cyber image of cities on the other hand. In the next section we will pay more attention to the formation and perception of cyber images by cities.

In conclusion, information and knowledge have become critical success conditions of cities and regions in a modern economy (Oakey 1996). It is no surprise that many cities have started to acquire a new ICT-oriented profile in a globalizing and competitive economy (Drennan 2002). Urban administrations were keen on this new development and started to design city images which would emphasize the ICT potential of their cities.

The process of policy-making has an uncertain nature, both with regard to the future and the effectiveness of the policies that are implemented (Dror 1986). Moreover, the assessment of future situations is based on the way decision-makers evaluate the current situation and the picture that they have in mind. Thus, both expectations on the future and the assessment of reality serve as an important input for the policy-making process. Especially in the case of ICT, which is, as been said earlier, full of metaphors, it is important to include visions (values) as explanatory factor in the assessment of different policies.

It is thus critical to understand the extent to which urban policy makers perceive and assess the relevance of ICT for coping with contemporary urban challenges. Consequently, one should study their beliefs about the ability of ICT to affect both urban trends and their expectations about ICT influences on urban administration and urban governance. In our empirical part we will now test the relationships between the expected influences of ICT and the perceptions of the relevance of ICT policies.

3 Cyber Perceptions: Database and Methodology

As part of the European project TeleCityVision,[2] an extensive survey has been held targeting urban decision-makers (both politicians and responsible administrative staff) in more than 200 cities in seven European countries. The survey was conducted between May and September 1999. The questionnaires were sent to

---

[2] The survey was part of the European research project "TeleCityVision", funded by the European Commission. The partners are: BIS (Germany), COMTEC (Ireland), CTS (Norway), ESI (The Netherlands), FHC (Spain), ICCR (Austria), THEMA (France) and ZTG (Germany).

Table 13.1 The extent to which ICT is expected to affect urban trends (%)

	High	Medium	Low	None	No opinion
The importance of our city	54.6	34.5	10.1	0.7	0
The importance of *small cities*	28.3	43.7	23.4	1.6	3.1
The importance of large *cities*	58.5	31.4	7.4	0.6	2.1
Competition between our and other cities	44.4	39.0	14.5	2.2	0
The potential of our city to attract service companies	56.8	33.9	8.3	1.0	0
The potential of our city to attract *industrial enterprises*	23.7	38.6	31.9	5.8	0
The potential of our city to attract new residents	17.4	40.3	33.4	9.0	0
The importance of the central business district in our city	20.4	34.7	36.4	8.5	0
Suburbanisation	7.7	27.4	42.5	15.5	6.9
Socio-spatial segregation in our city	4.0	20.6	45.4	22.4	7.6
Traffic in our city	13.3	36.5	41.1	9.1	0
The flow of goods	16.2	34.7	38.0	9.2	0
The flow of people	13.1	39.1	37.8	9.1	0.9
The *effectiveness of environmental protection* in our city	13.2	40.5	34.7	11.6	0

N = 1391

various departments in the municipality that were supposed to have a direct or indirect influence on ICT related activities in the city, as well as to elected officials of the city (politicians). The effort to include various municipality department members in our sample was due to the fact that ICT policies and strategies do not have one recognized responsible body. In contrast to fields like transportation or education, where there is a clear address that is responsible for policies in the field, ICT tends to be a fragmented activity and there is no single clear address in the municipality responsible for all relevant information. A full analysis of the Dutch survey can be found in Cohen (2004).

The respondents were asked to evaluate extensively a variety of attributes and aspects related to their city, the urban policies and their opinions about ICT, as well as their personal use and satisfaction concerning ICT applications. Most of the answers to these questions are given on an ordinal scale, measuring the relative degree of agreement or disagreement with different statements, or the relevance of different issues for the city. Table 13.1 presents the distribution of respondent's views on the expected influences of ICT on various urban aspects. Table 13.2 present their views about the effect of ICT on urban governance.

As Table 13.1 indicates, most of the respondents view ICT as having considerable influence on the importance of their city and the competitive position of the city. They also attach high influence to ICT in attracting service companies to their

Table 13.2 The extent to which ICT affects urban governance aspects (%)

	Strongly agree	Agree	Disagree	Strongly disagree	No opinion
ICT changes the policy making process in our municipality	22.9	50.0	22.8	4.4	0
ICT makes the political decision-making process more efficient	21.7	45.3	25.9	7.1	0
The implementation of policies is more efficient with ICT	21.1	52.8	21.2	4.8	0
ICT improve communication within our city administration	53.8	40.8	4.5	0.8	0
ICT improves the ability of our city administration to serve the citizens	54.9	41.0	3.7	0.4	0
ICT improves citizen access to *useful* information	61.7	35.5	2.4	0.4	0
ICT gives the administration better access to public opinion	31.0	48.7	18.0	2.3	0
ICT leads the administration to take greater account of public opinion in forming policy	14.2	42.2	32.4	6.0	5.2
ICT increases citizen participation in the policy process	15.6	52.5	26.9	5.0	0

N = 1391

city and in enhancing the business attraction to their city. There are more sceptical opinions about the ability of ICT to affect spatial trends (such as suburbanization) or social aspects (e.g., social segregation).

Table 13.2 indicates the suspicious attitude of a large part of the respondents with regard to ICT-instigated improvements in urban governance. Most of the respondents believe that ICT improves citizens' access to useful information and will improve services given to citizen, but are more sceptical about the ability of these technologies to solve social problems or to improve the urban decision-making process.

Finally, Table 13.3 presents the distribution of the respondents' views about the relevance of ICT to various urban challenges. It shows that economic goals (such as general economic development, business attraction and competitiveness) are perceived as more relevant challenges to ICT compared with governance challenges.

Next, we will use the respondents' expectations on the nature and direction of ICT impacts on urban trends and urban governance to detect their beliefs about the ability of ICT measures to solve urban problems and promote urban development.

Table 13.3 The perceived relevance of ICT for urban challenges (%)

	Strongly agree	Agree	Disagree	Strongly disagree
Economic development is a very important area for the deployment of ICT	42.1	51.2	6.0	0.7
Attracting new enterprises is a very important area for the deployment of ICT	38.6	48.2	12.1	1.0
The application of ICT is intended to render the political/administrative process more transparent for citizens	25.5	52.2	20.1	2.2
Improving citizen-municipality relations is a very important rationale for the municipality's deployment of ICT	24.6	54.1	18.1	3.2
ICT is deployed in urban planning to improve planner-citizen communications	17.2	55.6	22.7	4.5
ICT enables better networking with other cities	36.7	55.2	6.5	1.6
ICT can make our municipality more competitive vis-à-vis other cities	43.2	48.0	8.1	0.7

4 Cyber Perceptions on Urban ICT Policies

As shown in Sect. 3, urban frontliners assess differently the influence of ICT on various aspects of urban future trends and urban governance. Now we will test the hypothesis that the more an urban frontliner believes in ICT influences on different urban features, the more he/she considers a variety of ICT policies as relevant to his/her city. In order to test this hypothesis, three aggregated variables were constructed on the base of the data discussed previously.

1. The dependent variable, the perceived relevance of ICT to meet urban challenges (ICT goals), is the sum of all variables presented in Table 13.3. The minimum value of ICT goals is 7 (none of the seven goals mentioned in Table 13.3 is relevant) and the maximum value is 28. Figure 13.1 shows the distribution of this ICT variable.
2. The independent variables, i.e., the views about the influence of ICT on urban trends (Table 13.1) and urban governance (Table 13.2), were also computed as the sum of all indicators shown in the mentioned tables. Table 13.4 presents descriptive statistics of these variables.

Table 13.5 then presents the results of a linear regression that was performed to test the above hypothesis about the impact of views about ICT impacts and views about the relevance of ICT as a policy tool to meet urban challenges.

Our model results that are presented in Table 13.5 show that there are positive and significant relationships between the perceived effects of ICT on the city and

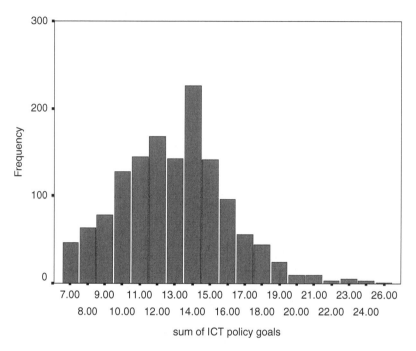

Fig. 13.1 Distribution of perceived ICT policy goals

Table 13.4 Descriptive statistics of the independent variables

	Minimum	Maximum	Mean	SDV
Influence of ICT on urban trends	14.0	56.0	30.6	6.5
Influence of ICT on urban governance	9.0	34.0	17.3	4.6

Table 13.5 Model results from regression analysis

Dependent variable: perceived ICT policy goals	BETA (standardized)	t value
The influence of ICT on urban trends	0.156	5.724
The influence of ICT on urban governance	0.510	18.774

$R^2 = 0.36$
$N = 1126$

the extent to which ICT is considered as a relevant policy tool for various urban challenges. Perceived influences of ICT on urban governance have greater impact on the perceptions of ICT policies, meaning that when an urban frontliner views ICT as having a significant impact on various administrative and decision making aspects, he/she tends to consider ICT as a suitable policy tool for various urban challenges. When ICT is not perceived as having an impact on urban development and urban governance, it is neither perceived as a relevant policy tool.

5 Concluding Remarks

Living in the 'Information Age' is a rather confusing experience. On the one hand, a growing share of our everyday life relies on electronic streams and invisible bits. On the other hand, the 'real' world exists and it demands physical and visible inputs; face-to-face meetings are still irreplaceable and there is still a growing demand for physical movements of people and goods. Using ICT to promote economic and social goals is therefore based on visions on the one hand, and critical judgment of the ICT potential on the other hand.

This paper has demonstrated that decision makers have different views on the potential and limitation of ICT effects on the urban environment. Such differences are also reflected in their views on the relevance of ICT in promoting urban goals. Therefore, anticipating ICT initiatives in European cities should be done not only by examining pan-European ICT initiatives, but also by studying beliefs and perceptions of local decision-makers and their perspectives. As demonstrated in this paper, local initiatives are likely to take place in cities that are led by front-liners who strongly believe in the abilities of ICT to affect their city in a positive and visible manner.

References

Abramson MA, Morin TL (eds) (2003) E government. Rowman & Littlefield, Lanham

Arens Y, Callen J, Dawes S, Fountain JE, Hovy E, Marchionini G (2005) Cyberinfrastructure and digital government. White paper submitted to national science foundation, Washington, DC. http://macaroni.isi.edu/~arens/CIandDG.pdf

Berra M (2003) Information communications technology and local development. Telematics Inform 20(3):215–234

Boyer K (1996) An assessment of managerial commitment to lean production. Int J Oper Prod Manage 16(9):48–59

Caves RW, Walshok MG (1999) Adopting innovations in information technology: the California municipal experience. Cities 16(1):3–12

Chadwick A, May C (2003) Interaction between states and citizens in the age of the internet. Governance 16(2):271–300

Cohen G, Nijkamp P (2004) City, ICT and policy. Investigaciones Regionales 4(1):29–51

Conroy MM, Evans-Cowley J (2006) E-participation in planning. Environ Plann C Gov Policy 24:371–384

Curwell S, Deakin M, Cooper I, Paskaleva-Shapira K, Ravetz J, Babicki D (2005) Citizens' expectations of information cities: implications for urban planning and design. Build Res Inform 33(1):55–66

Drennan MP (2002) Information economy and American cities. Johns Hopkins University Press, Baltimore

Di Maria E, Micelli S (eds) (2004) On line citizenship. Kluwer, Dordrecht/New York

Di Maria E, Vergani S, Paskaleva K (2004) E-Governance practices, strategies and policies of European cities. State-of-the-art, report, Intelcities programme, deliverable 11.1.2. European Commission, Brussels

Docherty I, Goodlad R, Paddison R (2001) Civic culture community and citizen participation in contrasting neighborhoods. Urban Stud 38(12):2225–2250

Dror Y (1986) Policymaking under adversity. Transaction Books, New Brunswick

European Commission (2005a) Signposts towards e-Government 2010. DG Information Society and Media, Brussels, Communication

European Commission (2005b) Fifth annual survey of online government services in Europe. DG Information Society and Media, Brussels, Communication

Evans R (2002) E-commerce, competitiveness and local and regional governance in greater Manchester and Merseyide: a preliminary assessment. Urban Stud 39(5–6):947–975

Fountain JE (2001) Building the virtual state. The Brookings Institution, Washington

Gibbs D, Keite T (1997) Information and communication technologies and local economy development polities: the British case. Reg Stud 3l(8):765–774

Gibbs D, Tanner K (1997) Information and communication technologies and local economic developments policies: the British case. Reg Stud 31(8):765–774

Graham S (1997) Telecommunications and the future of cities: debunking the myths. Cities 14(1):21–29

Graham S, Dominy GR (1991) Planning for the information city the UK case. Prog Plann 35(3):169–247

Graham S, Aurigi A (1997) Virtual cities, social polarization, and the crisis in urban public space. J Urban Technol 4:19–52

Graham S, Marvin S (1996) Tele-communications and the city. Routledge, London

Graham S, Marvin S (2000) Urban planning and the technological future of cities. In: Weeler JM, Ayoama Y, Warf B (eds) Cities in the telecommunications age. Routledge, New York, pp 71–96

Hood C, Lodge M (2004) Competency bureaucracy, and public management reform. Governance 17(3):313–333

Lash S (2003) Critique of information. Sage, London

Melody WH (1996) Towards a framework for designing information society policies. Telecommun Policy 20(4):243–259

Nijkamp P, Salomon I (1989) Future spatial impacts of telecommunications. Transport Plann Technol 13:275–287

Oakey R (ed) (1996) New technology-based firms in the 1990s. Paul Chapman, London

OECD (2005) e-Government for better government, Paris

Pratchett L (1999) New technologies and the modernization of local government: an analysis of biases and constraints. Public Admin 77(4):731–750

Rouillard L (1999) Technology and stimulation: for participative democracy in the area of new public management. Int Rev Admin Sci 65(3):371–380

Salomon I (1998) Technological change and social forecasting: the case of telecommuting as a travel substitute. Transport Res C 6:17–45

Servon LJ, Horrigan JB (1997) Urban poverty and access to information technology: a role for local government. J Urban Technol 4(3):61–81

Staples DS, Wong I, Seddon PB (2002) Having expectations of information systems benefits that match received benefits: does it really matter? Inf Manage 40(2):115–131

van der Meer A, van Winden W (2003) E-Governance in cities. Reg Stud 37(4):407–419

Chapter 14
Interlocking Firm Networks and Emerging Mega-City Regions in the Knowledge Economy

Alain Thierstein and Stefan Lüthi

Abstract The main objective of this contribution lies in the exploration of a new metropolitan form in the context of the knowledge economy: polycentric Mega-City Regions. In the first part, we focus on the theoretical building blocks of Mega-City Regions by considering these polycentric urban structures as an emerging spatial phenomenon based on re-scaling processes of agglomeration economies as well as network economies. By using the two inter-related concepts, we secondly analyse large-scale interlocking networks and functional urban hierarchies in nine Mega-City Regions in North West Europe: Munich, Northern Switzerland, the Dutch Randstad Region, South East England, Rhine-Ruhr, Rhine-Main, the Paris Region, Central Belgium and Greater Dublin. The main conclusion of the paper is that polycentric Mega-City Regions are becoming a more general phenomenon in advanced economies. The inter-urban functional linkages are found to be extending and intensifying while, at the same time, global functions are clustering and centralising. These apparently contradictory processes are intersecting on the Mega-City Region scale, which emerges as a new strategic location for activities of the knowledge economy.

Keywords Mega-city region • Knowledge economy • Interlocking firm networks • Advanced producer services firms • Agglomeration economies • North Western Europe

---

A. Thierstein (✉) • S. Lüthi (✉)
Chair for Territorial and Spatial Development, Munich University of Technology, Arcisstrasse 21, Munich 80333, Germany
e-mail: luethi@tum.de; thierstein@tum.de

J. Klaesson et al. (eds.), *Metropolitan Regions*, Advances in Spatial Science, DOI 10.1007/978-3-642-32141-2_14, © Springer-Verlag Berlin Heidelberg 2013

1 Introduction

Globalisation has entailed a reorganisation of spatial development processes on a global, European, national and regional scale. New forms of hierarchical and network development and functional differentiation between cities can be observed (Friedmann 1986; Sassen 2001). Scott (2001) and, recently, Hall and Pain (2006) argue that cities cannot be separated from their regional hinterlands as they often compose a functional division of labour in terms of different kinds of services and value chains among firms (Hall and Pain 2006; Scott 2001). Hence, the traditional hierarchical model of a core city dominating its urban hinterland is becoming increasingly obsolete. Instead, a process of selective decentralisation of particular urban functions, and the simultaneous re-concentration of others, has led to the emergence of polycentric Mega-City Regions (Kloosterman and Musterd 2001; Thierstein et al. 2008; Lüthi et al. 2008). This emerging urban form is spread out over a large area containing a number of cities more or less within commuting distance, and one or more international airports that link the region with other parts of the world (Hoyler et al. 2008b). Different attempts have been made to handle these extended urban regions analytically, and a variety of research projects and publications concerned with polycentricity on a city-regional scale has been produced (ESPON 2004; Hall and Pain 2006; Thierstein et al. 2006; Built Environment, 32.2, 2006; Regional Studies, 42.8, 2008). Furthermore, a number of labels have been used to denote the identified new metropolitan form (Hoyler et al. 2008b): for instance, polycentric urban regions (Kloosterman and Musterd 2001), global city-regions (Scott 2001) or Mega-City Regions (Hall and Pain 2006). The main objective of this contribution lies in the exploration of the Mega-City Region hypothesis. It is structured in four main sections. The first section focuses on the theoretical building blocks of the Mega-City Region concept. Based on these findings, the second section explains the Mega-City Region hypothesis that identifies polycentric Mega-City Regions as an emerging spatial phenomenon based on re-scaling processes of agglomeration and network economies. In the third section, we are looking at several Mega-City Regions in North West Europe by referring to two recent empirical research projects: the INTERREG IIIB study POLYNET (Hall and Pain 2006) and a case study about the emerging Mega-City Region of Munich Thierstein et al. (2007). The fourth section concludes by synthesising the main findings and putting them into the theoretical context.

2 Theoretical Background

In this section, the theoretical building blocks of the Mega-City Region hypothesis are discussed. Generally speaking, they can be divided into two bodies of literature stemming from different approaches to interpret global trends in spatial development: agglomeration economies and network economies.

2.1 Agglomeration Economies

'Agglomeration economies' is a generic concept, referring to a number of different theories: Traditional Agglomeration Models, New Industrial Geographies and Innovation Systems. The following section provides an overview of these theoretical concepts.

2.1.1 Traditional Agglomeration Models

Early theories on agglomeration economies are strongly inspired by Joseph Schumpeter (1926) and Alfred Marshall (1920). Schumpeter (1926) initially focused on the roles of entrepreneurs and their small companies in recognizing the importance of particular inventions and assembling the resources needed to turn them into marketable products (Schumpeter 1926). This process is well known as the Schumpeter I model. Alfred Marshall (1920), on the other hand, argued that spatial concentration could confer external economies on firms as they concentrated in particular cities. These external economies mainly take the form of increasing returns to scale as firms are able to take advantage of large pools of skilled labour, local markets and the easy transmission of new ideas (Marshall 1920). Marshall's concept has been taken up by Edgar M. Hoover (1937, 1948), who grouped the sources of agglomeration advantages into internal returns of scale, localisation and urbanisation economies. Localisation economies, on the one hand, arise as a particular industry concentrates in a given location leading to the development of local expertise, special skills and advantages that are specifically related to the industry in question. Urbanisation economies, on the other hand, arise from the diversity and the more general characteristics of a city; for instance the multiplicity of specialised business services, infrastructure and cultural and leisure functions that may be used by any firm in the city rather than only a single economic sector (Hoover 1937, 1948).

2.1.2 New Industrial Geographies

Based on these early agglomeration theories, a second wave of agglomeration models was developed in the 1980s onwards to explain why local space was still important for newly-developing forms of production. The most influential among these theories was Michel J. Piore's and Charles F. Sable's concept of flexible specialisation, which identified the breakdown and deverticalisation of large firms as a key characteristic in modern economies (Piore and Sable 1984). In the face of international competition and changing customer demands, this process is driven by the need for firms to be both more specialised and more flexible in the ways in which they organise their production. The result is a networked form of production that leads to a reconnection of economic activities to local space because of the need for proximity between the numerous specialists involved in any given value chain (Simmie 2005).

The flexible specialisation thesis inspired several new concepts dealing with innovation, knowledge and regional development. Influential among these were the Innovative Milieus and the New Industrial Districts and the New Industrial Spaces approach.

In the approach of the Innovative Milieu developed by the GREMI (Groupe de Recherche Européen sur les Milieux Innovateurs), firms are seen as part of a milieu with an innovative capacity. These milieus include a set of collective and dynamic processes incorporating many actors within a given region that lead to networks of synergy producing interrelationships and learning (Bramanti and Maggioni 1997; Maillat et al. 1993). In addition, the authors of the GREMI underline not only the importance of links within but also with the world outside the milieu. This is a critical extension to the local supply-side-focused networks of the traditional industrial districts approach (Simmie 2005).

The theory of the New Industrial District, first identified by Giacomo Becattini in the so-called Third Italy, emphasises the innovative capacity of small and medium-sized enterprises (SMEs) belonging to the same industry and local space. Commonly, industrial districts are defined as localised production systems, based on a strong local division of labour between small and specialised firms, which are integrated in the production and value chain of an industrial sector (Becattini 1989). Newer approaches, however, highlight that such networks also connect large firms and their suppliers and enable the introduction of flexible specialisation by facilitating subcontracting. As a consequence, the manufacturing depth of large companies is reduced and a smooth diffusion of innovation throughout the whole regional economy is facilitated (Grabher 1991).

A third influential approach inspired by the flexible specialisation thesis is the concept of New Industrial Spaces. Especially, the Californian School, led by Allen J. Scott, launched the notion of New Industrial Spaces by combining insights from different literatures such as industrial districts, flexible production systems, transaction economies and others (Storper and Walker 1988; Scott 1985). The authors argue that in flexible production systems, the tendency to agglomeration was reinforced not only by externalisation but also by intensified re-transacting, just-in-time processing, variable forms of inter-unit transacting and the proliferation of many small-scale linkages with low unit costs. Scott argues that the economic process of vertical disintegration into extended and specialised divisions of labour is leading to spatial forces that encourage small firms to concentrate in space (Scott 1985).

2.1.3 Innovation Systems

The multi-faceted character of agglomeration economies has also been discussed quite openly in evolutionary economics (Edquist and Johnson 1997). The key concepts of contemporary evolutionary theory stem from the Schumpeter II model (1942). In contrast to the Schumpeter I model, the Schumpeter II model recognises the significance of Research and Development (R&D) within large firms, where increased R&D activities are setting up a self-reinforcing circle leading to renewed impulses and finally to increased market concentrations. From a spatial point of view, this argument is interesting in regards to the establishment and persistence of R&D activities in particular Mega-City Regions. Schumpeter's ideas were taken up and further developed, for example by Richard Nelson and Sidney Winter in their work on the evolutionary theory of economic change (Nelson and Winter 1982). According to modern evolutionary theory, intra-firm networks of large multinational corporations (MNCs) are important driving forces in the global knowledge economy, concentrating and centralising their power in their headquarters that are often located in core metropolitan areas. The decisions of these MNCs about where they conduct their activities along the value chain play a major role in where innovation and knowledge are located. They can split its activities into units and localise and disperse these units in the most favourable places in terms of local knowledge resources and industrial culture (Massey 1985).

In the last 20 years, the literature on spatial innovation systems has shifted from the national (Edquist 1997; Nelson 1993; Lundvall 1988, 1992) to the regional (Asheim and Isaksen 1997; Cooke et al. 1998) and local dimension (Muscio 2006; Carrincazeaux et al. 2008). National Innovation Systems (NIS) can be defined as the elements and relationships which interact in the production, diffusion and use of new knowledge and are located within the borders of a nation state (Lundvall 1992). According to the Regional Innovation System (RIS) theory, on the other hand, it is the region that plays a central role in economic coordination, especially with respect to innovation, evolving into a "nexus of learning processes" (Cooke et al. 1998). RISs are complex systems with strong interactions between regional actors systematically engaged in interactive learning (Morgan 1997). The relevance of the local dimension of governance has finally led to the creation of a new strand of research in regional studies, stressing how local policies can play a key role in fostering learning processes. Accordingly, Local Innovation Systems (LIS) are based on the generation of localised learning systems where some local innovation policies are activated to transfer technologies, to enforce technological cooperation and to provide support and incentives to innovative networks. The strategic response of local actors to the challenge of increasing competition is the mechanism through which structural change and the economic dynamics at the local level are stimulated (Muscio 2006).

The interdependence between agglomeration and evolutionary economics are of great importance for the understanding of spatial development processes and the dynamics of polycentric Mega-City Regions. Morgan (1997) as well as Moulaert and Sekia (2003) refer especially to Michael Storper's work as the fullest attempt to marry these two disciplines (Morgan 1997; Moulaert and Sekia 2003). Michael Storper (1995) recognizes the principal dilemma of economic geography between the resurgence of regional economics and globalisation (Storper 1995). By combining insights from institutional, agglomeration and evolutionary economics, he explains this phenomenon by the association between organisational and technological learning within agglomerations, based on traded (input–output relations) and untraded interdependencies (regional conventions, norms and values, public institutions etc.).

An intermediate position between agglomeration economies and network economies is taken up by the French School of Proximity Dynamics, which made key contributions to the literature on Mega-City Regions in the 1990s, proposing that proximity covers a number of different dimensions (Torre and Rallet 2005). Therein a distinction is made between the relational and local aspects of proximity. Local proximity is defined as spatial distance between actors. Relational proximity, on the other hand, is associated with the closeness of actors in organizational terms, meaning that actors share the same relational space, for example the way interaction and coordination between actors is organized (Boschma 2005). However, as Boschma and Iammarino (2009) show, regional growth is not affected by simply being well connected to the outside world or having a high variety of knowledge flowing into the region. Rather they found evidence for the 'related variety concept': the highest learning opportunities are present when cognitive proximity between the extra-regional knowledge and the knowledge base of a region is neither too small nor too large (Boschma and Iammarino 2009).

2.2 Network Economies

Most observations on how external economies influence spatial development have focused on agglomeration economies. However, many of these investigations have failed to consider the contribution of global network economies. As argued by Cabus and Vanhaverbeke (2006), network economies need to be acknowledged as complementary to agglomeration economies (Cabus and Vanhaverbeke 2006). Simmie (2003) for example has observed that most innovative firms operate from rather than within localities (Simmie 2003). Therefore, in the following section, we will discuss some of the most important approaches relating to urban network economies. Generally speaking, they can be divided into two groups: World City Network models and Value Chain models.

2.2.1 World City Network Models

Much of world city research has been related to the emergence of a globally networked knowledge economy in which Advanced Producer Services (APS) firms play a predominant role. In this respect, Saskia Sassen's global city approach is an important contribution (Sassen 2001). It discovers a new geography of centrality in which the city centres or the central business districts form the heart of the global urban network. The functional centrality of these global cities leads to an increasing disconnection of the city centres from their broader hinterlands or adjacent metropolitan region. The reason for this disconnecting process lies, according to Sassen, in the location strategies of Advanced Producer Services (APS) firms as spearheads

14 Interlocking Firm Networks and Emerging Mega-City Regions in the Knowledge... 315

of the rising global knowledge economy. These enterprises are increasingly located just within the city centres of economic regions and connect these places directly with other city centres in the world (Sassen 2001).

In contrast to Saskia Sassen's global city approach, John Friedmann's world city concept argues that the territorial basis of world cities comprises not only the central city but also the whole economic space of the surrounding region. Therefore, world cities are often polycentric urban regions containing a number of historically distinct cities that are located in more or less close proximity. Furthermore, John Friedmann describes the rise of a transnational urban network, referring to a major geographical transformation of the capitalist world economy whose production systems are increasingly internationalised. This reconfiguration results in a new international division of labour whose main agents are multinational enterprises with complex spatial organisational structures. It is the presence of these multinational enterprises that makes world cities into geographical places of great economic power (Friedmann 1986).

Another heuristic framework about network cities is provided by Manuel Castells' highly influential concept of a space of flows (Castells 2000). He argues that the new spatial logic is determined by the pre-eminence of the space of flows over the space of places. By space of flows he refers to the system of exchange of information, capital and power that structures the basic processes of societies, economies and states between different localities, regardless of localisation. Furthermore, Castells (1989) argues that the "space of flows" and the creation of "multinuclear spatial structures" is not an undifferentiated process. Rather, it follows a hierarchical and functional logic. Higher-level functions tend to be concentrated in certain privileged locations, while assembly functions are scattered over more and varied locations. He argues that the more information-based an industry is, the clearer is the trend toward a hierarchical pattern of segmented location (Castells 1989).

While Friedmann (1986) and Castells (2000) offer a heuristic and theoretical framework as to why globalisation requires a networked conception of cities, Peter Taylor (2004) provides with his world city network approach an empirical instrument for analysing inter-city relations in terms of the organisational structure of the global economy (Taylor 2004). With his team – the Globalisation and World Cities Study Group (GaWC) at Loughborough University – he analyses the inter-city relations using a specific methodology, in which relationships between cities are not measured directly. Instead, the method uses a proxy by analysing the internal structures of large APS firms and revealing the relationships between head offices and other branches located all over the world.

2.2.2 Value Chain Models

Another starting point for understanding the changing nature of international trade and industrial organisation is contained in the notion of a value-added chain, as developed by international business scholars who have focused on the strategies of firms in the global economy. In its most basic form, a value-added chain is "...the process by which technology is combined with material and labour inputs, and then processed inputs are assembled, marketed, and distributed. A single firm may consist of only one link in this process, or it may be extensively vertically integrated..." (Kogut 1985:15). The key questions in this literature are which activities and technologies a firm keeps in-house and which should be outsourced to other firms, and where the various activities should be located Gereffi et al. (2005).

A rich literature has evolved in order to explain how global industries are organised and governed Coe et al. (2008). Three sets of terminology have become especially prominent. An early but still very active body of research exists on Global Commodity Chains (GCC), a term popularised by Gary Gereffi in a large number of publications since 1994. The GCC framework pays particular attention to the powerful role that large retailers and highly successful branded merchandisers have come to play in the governance of global production and distribution.

In the last decade, however, transnational giants have changed quite dramatically, outsourcing many activities and developing strategic alliances with competitors. They have become less vertically integrated and more network-orientated (Wildemann 2003). As a consequence of these structural changes, researchers at the Institute of Development Studies in Sussex have developed a second approach: the Global Value Chain (GVC) framework. In contrast to the GCC framework, the GVC approach attempts to delineate the varying governance structures both within and between different sectors (Coe et al. 2008:267). Thereby, the value chain is understood as providing the full range of activities that firms and workers engage in to bring a product or a service from its conception to its end-use and even beyond Gereffi et al. (2005).

Finally, the third approach is the Global Production Network (GPN) framework, initially developed by researchers in Manchester (Henderson et al. 2002). GPNs can be defined as the globally organised nexus of interconnected functions and operations through which goods and services are produced, distributed and consumed (Coe et al. 2004). Thereby, the process of embeddedness, both territorially and within business networks, is of great importance. Henderson et al. (2002) argue that the mode of territorial embeddedness or the degree of a GPN firm's commitment to a particular location is an important factor for value creation, enhancement and capture (Henderson et al. 2002).

3 The Mega-City Region Hypothesis

At the intersection of agglomeration economies, world city networks and global value chains, a new metropolitan form – so called polycentric Mega-City Regions – is emerging in advanced economies. However, Mega-City regions are not a completely new phenomenon. Jean Gottmann originally made similar observations as long ago as 1961 in his pioneering study "Megalopolis: The Urbanized North-eastern Seaboard of the United States" (Gottmann 1961). Few years later, Peter Hall (1966) observed that next to the traditional "highly centralised giant city" there exists a "polycentric type of metropolis". This polycentric metropolis consists of "a number of smaller, specialised, closely-related centres" and should be understood as "a perfectly natural form, which has evolved over a period of history quite as long as the single metropolitan centre" (Hall 1966). However, the most recent rediscovery of the concept has been in Eastern Asia, in areas like the Pearl River Delta and Yangtze River Delta regions in China, the Tokaido (Tokyo-Osaka) corridor in Japan, and Greater Jakarta (Hall 1999; Scott 2001).

Lately, Peter Hall and Kathy Pain (2006) emphasise its large-scale nature and developing polycentric structure by defining Mega-City Regions as "...a series of anything between 10 and 50 cities and towns physically separated but functionally networked, clustered around one or more larger central cities, and drawing enormous economic strength from a new functional division of labour. These places exist both as separate entities, in which most residents work locally and most workers are local residents, and as parts of a wider functional urban region connected by dense flows of people and information carried along motorways, high-speed rail lines and telecommunications cables" (Hall and Pain 2006:3). The key point of this definition is that Mega-City Regions are not solely characterised by simple attributes such as demographic size or physical settlement structures but as socio-economic relational processes linking regions to other cities and towns on different geographical scales. Thus, Mega-City Regions are defined by their linkages among its constituent functional parts and without any predefined territorial boundaries.

Referring to the Mega-City Region definition as suggested by Peter Hall and Kathy Pain (2006), we argue that the emergence of polycentric Mega-City Regions is the result of two interdependent processes: agglomeration economies as well as network economies. Agglomeration economies result from the clustering of knowledge-intensive firms in certain areas enabling them to benefit from spatial proximity and local knowledge spillovers. By local knowledge spillovers we understand both, intended flows of knowledge, such as input–output relations along the value chain, and unintended flows of knowledge, based on regional conventions, norms and values. Network economies, however, result from global sourcing strategies of knowledge-intensive firms leading to relational proximity and international knowledge exchange. Based on this functional logic, we argue that polycentric Mega-City Regions are the outcome of a spatial up-scaling of agglomeration economies and a spatial re-concentration process of network economies. Figure 14.1 depicts schematically the inter-relationships between the knowledge economy that basically follows a functional logic and the emergence of Mega-City Regions, which basically are the effect of spatial logic at work.

On the one hand, the up-scaling process of agglomeration economies is determined by the achievements realised in transportation and telecommunications technologies. The costs of several modes of transport and communication have drastically declined and, in some cases, speed and reliability have significantly improved. As a consequence, polycentric Mega-City Regions are increasingly enabled to achieve agglomeration economies of comparable magnitude to those of large mono-centric cities.

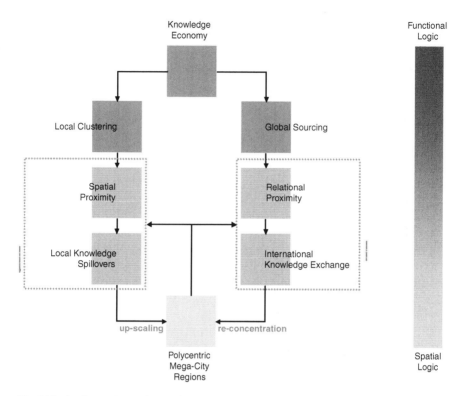

Fig. 14.1 Agglomeration and network economies in the context of Mega-City Region development (own illustration)

On the other hand, the spatial re-concentration of network economies is determined by the location behaviour of the knowledge economy. In order to improve their added value, knowledge-intensive firms need several local business conditions such as proximity to international gateway infrastructures like airports and high-speed train nodes. Many international knowledge-intensive enterprises have already recognised the advantage of being located around airports and within the corridors between the airport and the city. Furthermore, knowledge-intensive firms are looking for high quality infrastructures such as universities with a good reputation or large settlements of leading global companies, as well as for the availability of specialised knowledge, the presence of competitors, business partners and customers as well as qualified manpower.

All in all, the interplay between the up-scaling process of agglomeration economies and the re-concentration of network-economies is strongly subject to increasing returns leading to polycentric Mega-City Regions as essential spatial nodes and engines of today's global economy. In a similar way, but with regard to new information technologies, Manuel Castells (1989) argues that "...alongside the centralisation and metropolitanisation of information industries, there is also a process of decentralisation of service activities over regions, urban areas and locations within the major metropolitan areas; and this decentralisation is being helped, and sometimes even stimulated, by new information technologies" (Castells 1989:151). It is this two-fold process of simultaneous re-concentration and decentralisation, both elements associated with the same dynamics of the knowledge economy, which explains the complexity of Mega-City Region development.

4 Emerging Mega-City Regions in North West Europe

Different attempts have been made until now to analyse the polycentric structure of emerging Mega-City Regions in Europe (Hall and Pain 2006; Thierstein et al. 2007; and others). One of the most recent empirical research activities is the INTERREG IIIB Study POLYNET – Sustainable Management of European Polycentric Mega-City Regions (a comprehensive illustration of the POLYNET results is provided by Hall and Pain 2006). POLYNET aimed to investigate the polycentricity of eight Mega-City Regions in North West Europe and their current state of functional division of labour: South East England, the Paris Region, Central Belgium, the Dutch Randstad, Rhine-Main, Rhine-Ruhr, Northern Switzerland and Greater Dublin (Hall 2007). Based on the methodology of POLYNET, a second attempt to handle the Mega-City Region hypothesis analytically is the case study of Thierstein et al. (2007) about the emerging Mega-City Region of Munich Thierstein et al. (2007). This section presents the methodology and some empirical results of both research projects.

4.1 The Interlocking Network Model

With its seminal research, POLYNET introduced a new way of looking at polycentric urban structures and hierarchies, adopting Peter Taylor's world city network approach on the Mega-City Region scale (Taylor et al. 2008). Both Thierstein et al. (2007) as well as the POLYNET study started from the premise that intra-firm networks of Advanced Producer Services (APS) firms offer a strategic lens to examine intercity relations within and beyond larger urban regions, building theoretically on Saskia Sassen's (2001) identification of Advanced Producer Services (APS) as crucial actors and outcomes of globalisation and localisation processes and Manuel Castell's (2000) notion of a "space of flows". Thereby, the following business lines are considered: accounting, insurance, banking and finance, management- and IT-consulting, law, third- and fourth-party logistics, design and architecture as well as advertising and media. The analysis of the intra-firm networks of these business lines is based on the methodology of the Globalisation and World Cities Study Group (GaWC) (Taylor et al. 2008). This approach estimates city connectivities from the office networks of multi-location multi-branch enterprises. The basic premise of this method is that the more important the office, the greater its flow of information will be to other office locations. Thereby, the empirical work comprises two steps.

In a first step, a so-called 'service activity matrix' is developed. This matrix is defined by cities in the lines and knowledge-intensive firms in the columns. Each cell in the matrix shows a service value (v) that indicates the importance of a city to a firm. The importance is defined by the size of an office location and its function. By analysing the firms' websites, all office locations are rated on a scale of 0 to 3. The standard value for a cell in the matrix is 0 (no presence) or 2 (presence). If there is a clear indication that a location has a special relevance within the firm's network (e.g. headquarters, supra-office functions), its value is upgraded to 3. If the overall importance of a location in the firm's network is very low (e.g. small agency), the value is downgraded to 1.

In the second step, the interlocking network model established by Peter Taylor (2004) is used to estimate connectivities between cities within and beyond emerging Mega-City Regions (Taylor 2004). The primary outputs of this interlocking network analysis are network connectivities, a measure that estimates how well-connected a city is within the overall intra-firm network of knowledge-intensive enterprises.

There are different kinds of connectivity values that are calculated. The connectivity between two cities (a, b) of a certain firm (j) is analysed by multiplying their service values (v) representing the so-called *elemental interlock* (r_{abj}) between two cities for one firm:

$$r_{abj} = v_{aj} * v_{bj} \tag{14.1}$$

To calculate the total connectivity between two cities, one has to summarise the elemental interlocks for all firms located in these two cities. This leads to the so-called *city interlock* (r_{ab}):

$$r_{ab} = \sum r_{abj} \tag{14.2}$$

Aggregating the city interlocks for a single city produces the *interlock connectivity* (N_a). This measure describes the importance of a city within the intra-firm network of all knowledge-intensive enterprises that have been analysed.

$$N_a = \sum r_{ai} \quad (a \neq i) \tag{14.3}$$

Finally, if we relate the interlock connectivity for a given city to the city with the highest interlock connectivity, we gain an idea of its relative importance in respect to all other cities that have been considered.

The main limitation of this model is that it does not consider extra-firm networks in its conceptualisation. However both, intra-firm and extra-firm networks are important in analysing the patterns of the changing value chain of the knowledge economy. Intra-firm networks are of interest because of the growing prevalence of multinational and multi-location firms providing important vehicles for transferring results of research and development as well as knowledge. Extra-firm networks in addition are interesting because they generate possibilities for increased economies of scale through flexible, networked production complexes.

14 Interlocking Firm Networks and Emerging Mega-City Regions in the Knowledge...

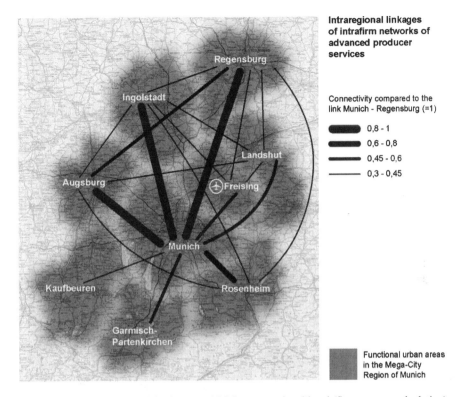

Fig. 14.2 Intra-firm connectivity between APS firms at regional level (Source: own calculation)

4.2 The Wider Munich Area as a Hierarchically Organized Mega-City Region

Based on the calculations of the interlocking network model, Thierstein et al. (2007) show that the wider Munich area can be regarded as an emerging functional region where sub-centres have different functional and hierarchical roles. In Fig. 14.2, they show the spatial patterns of the intra-firm connectivity between Advanced Producer Services (APS) firms in the wider Munich area. The analytical building blocks are built by nine Functional Urban Areas (FUAs): München, Kaufbeuren, Garmisch-Partenkirchen, Rosenheim, Landshut, Freising, Regensburg, Ingolstadt and Augsburg. All of them can be reached within a 1 h car journey from the city centre of Munich. Furthermore, they are defined as having an urban core of at least 15,000 inhabitants and over 50,000 in total population. The thickness of the lines illustrates the total connectivity between two FUAs. These connectivity values are related to the highest interlock connectivity of the study area, which is the connection between Munich and Regensburg. This high value is due to the fact that many Advanced Producer Services (APS) firms have relatively important and therefore highly-rated locations in both cities. The most important finding of this figure is that

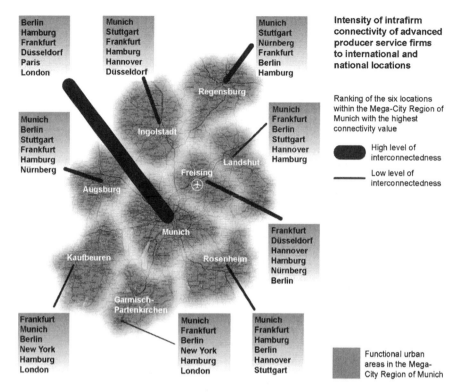

Fig. 14.3 Intensity and ranking of connectivity values created by intra-firm networks of APS companies (Source: own calculation)

the predominant part of intra-firm networks is located within the wider Munich area, defining it as a functionally polycentric Mega-City Region. In other words, since the FUAs within the study area are more closely linked with each other than with outlying FUAs, they begin to form a conglomerate of functionally linked cities that merits being labelled as an emerging Mega-City Region Thierstein et al. (2007).

In their case study, Thierstein et al. (2007) do not only identify the wider Munich area as a highly interconnected space of flows, but they also identify it as a hierarchically organized urban system. They show that there is a distinct functional urban hierarchy within the Mega-City Region, with Munich as primary city especially in respect to international intra-firm connectivity. Figure 14.3 shows this fact for international intra-firm networks of Advanced Producer Services (APS) firms. For each FUA, the six mostly connected locations are listed. The thickness of the lines reflects the total international connectivity for each FUA. The Figure shows that Munich is most strongly linked with four big national cities (Berlin, Hamburg, Frankfurt and Düsseldorf) followed by Paris and London as the first European destinations. This is a surprising finding because it could be assumed that – in an increasingly globalised world – international linkages would be more important for the APS sector in Munich. Another interesting feature concerns the connectivities

14 Interlocking Firm Networks and Emerging Mega-City Regions in the Knowledge... 323

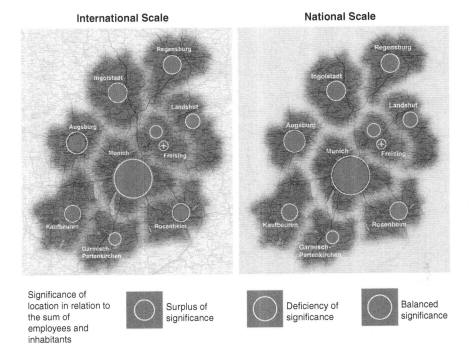

Fig. 14.4 Significance of Functional Urban Areas (FUAs) in the Mega-City Region of Munich for APS firms (Source: own calculation)

in the secondary cities around Munich. Most of them are primarily connected to Munich, generally followed by further German locations. This means that APS firms in these locations mainly have offices in Munich or other national urban centres, whereas offices in European or even international locations are quite rare. Hence, in the case of APS interlocking networks, medium-sized and small urban centres in the wider Munich area are not directly integrated into international networks of knowledge-intensive economic activities. Instead, they are well-integrated into large-scale regional networks of knowledge exchange. The city of Munich, however, is a central node and international gateway for smaller centres in the emerging Mega-City Region and acts as an important international knowledge-hub Thierstein et al. (2007).

In order to show the relative significance of the FUAs within the wider Munich area, Thierstein et al. (2007) put the interlock connectivity for each FUA in relation to the sum of its inhabitants and jobs. In Fig. 14.4, this relative significance is illustrated in the following way: the pink circle illustrates the connectivity value for the FUA and the white ring shows its sum total of inhabitants and jobs. Hence, an outer pink ring indicates a higher connectivity as expected in terms of inhabitants and jobs. This represents a surplus of significance. A smaller pink circle, in contrast, indicates a lower connectivity than expected, which represents a deficiency of significance. If one compares international and national connectivity values in this way, an interesting spatial pattern is revealed. Figure 14.4 confirms that Munich acts as an important hub for international connectivities, whereas the surrounding FUAs are particularly of national importance. The latter seem to have a crucial role as regional centres, supplying regional markets with services and products. In this sense, smaller FUAs have to be viewed as complementary centres taking over functions which cannot be provided by Munich itself. A special case within the study area is Freising, a small town that is quite close to Munich and immediately next to the international hub-airport. Freising shows a clear surplus of significance for both national and international connectivities. Obviously, despite its small size, Freising seems to benefit from a dense network of global companies owning branch offices in several international locations. As a consequence, Thierstein et al. (2007) conclude that Freising and Munich are not complementary but substitutive locations within the emerging Mega-City Region of Munich, which means that international firms hardly choose an office location at both sites.

4.3 Looking at Eight Emerging Mega-City Regions in North West Europe

In order to compare the functional polycentricity of different Mega-City Regions in North West Europe and the relative significance of its cities and towns, Thierstein et al. (2006) related the interlock connectivities for all FUAs in the POLYNET study to the sum of its inhabitants and jobs (Thierstein et al. 2006). In this section, we will take you on an analytical tour of the eight Mega-City Regions that have been under investigation in the POLYNET project.

4.3.1 The Mega-City Region of Northern Switzerland

A first case study of POLYNET is the European Metropolitan Region (EMR) of Northern Switzerland, an incipient Mega-City Region extending in discontinuous linear pattern from Zurich and its region westwards towards Basel. Figure 14.5 shows the significance of the most important FUAs in the Mega-City Region of Northern Switzerland for national and international connectivities. For international connectivities Zurich shows a quite balanced significance level. Important reasons for this international significance are Zurich's special role among top-ranking financial firms with international presence and its gateway function because of its international airport and the universities with their reputation, in particular the Swiss Federal Institute of Technology (ETH) (Thierstein et al. 2008). For national connectivities, however, Zurich's position seems to turn into a deficiency of significance, whereas other secondary centres gain in importance. A rather interesting example is Zug, a small agglomeration with about 95,000 inhabitants. From a relative perspective, it has comparatively strong connections with national and international locations.

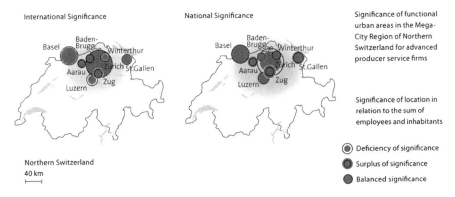

Fig. 14.5 Significance of Functional Urban Areas in the Mega-City Region of Northern Switzerland for APS firms (Thierstein et al. 2006)

The reason for Zug's relative importance lies, on the one hand, in its proximity to the international hub of Zurich and, on the other hand, in its attractive tax policy. Despite its small size, Zug seems to benefit from a dense network of global companies owning branch offices in several national and international locations giving it a special position within the emerging Mega-City Region of Northern Switzerland. It seems that the internationalisation of companies in a specific location has a greater effect on the degree of connectivity than the mere size of an agglomeration or a core city (Thierstein et al. 2008).

4.3.2 The Randstad Region

A second POLYNET case study is the Randstad in the Netherlands, encompassing the cities of Amsterdam, The Hague, Rotterdam and Utrecht, but now extending outwards to include cities such as Arnhem, Amersfoort and Breda. The area measures about 70 by 75 km and contains about 6.6 million people. They live in a large number of mainly medium-sized cities and in an even larger number of smaller towns and villages. This co-presence of many individual smaller and larger cities in a relatively small area gives the Randstad its archetypical polycentric appearance (Lambregts 2008). As Fig. 14.6 shows, for international APS enterprises, Amsterdam with its international airport is by far the most important location within the entire Mega-City Region. On the national scale, however, the other agglomerations such as Utrecht and Breda clearly gain in importance.

4.3.3 The Mega-City Region of South East England

A particularly interesting case within the POLYNET study is the Mega-City Region of South East England, where London is the centre of a system of some 30–40 cities and towns within a 150 km radius (Hall 2007). Ironically, although South East England appears relatively monocentric in terms of the size and distribution of its

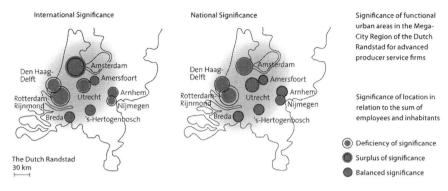

Fig. 14.6 Significance of Functional Urban Areas in the Mega-City Region of the Randstad Holland for APS firms (Thierstein et al. 2006)

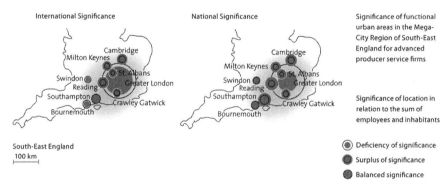

Fig. 14.7 Significance of Functional Urban Areas in the Mega-City Region of South East England for APS firms (Thierstein et al. 2006)

towns and cities, it proves the most functionally polycentric region in the POLYNET study (Pain 2008). Figure 14.7 shows clearly that the mere size of an agglomeration such as London does not automatically increase its functional significance. In absolute terms, London is clearly the most important location for international APS firms within the Mega-City Region of South East England. In relative terms, however, the smaller agglomerations such as Reading and Cambridge show relatively high international connectivities.

According to Pain (2008) the eight APS centres outside London do not show a notable sectoral specialisation. Financial services are well represented in Bournemouth and logistics in Milton Keynes, Reading and Crawley are seen as important emerging service clusters for accountancy and law, whereas Cambridge has a large representation of design and information technology firms. But in general, a wide variety of other sectors is also represented in these centres providing a great potential for urbanisation economies. Interestingly, this finding is in contrast to the results for more morphologically polycentric Mega-City Regions, such as the Randstad and the Rhine-Ruhr, which have a stronger sectoral specialisation between different agglomerations (Pain 2008).

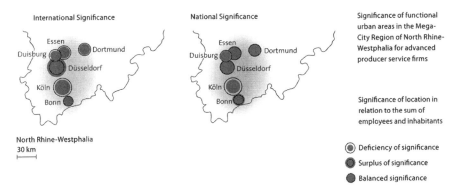

Fig. 14.8 Significance of Functional Urban Areas in the Mega-City Region of Rhine-Ruhr for APS firms (Thierstein et al. 2006)

4.3.4 The Rhine-Ruhr Region

A fourth POLYNET case study is Rhine-Ruhr, one of the world's largest polycentric Mega-City Regions, embracing 30–40 towns and cities with a total population of some 10 million people, and with no obvious 'core city'. Although the Rhine-Ruhr still has a relatively strong industrial base, de-industrialisation is taking place all across the region. However, some cities have been able to offset job losses in the Ruhr's industrial sector with new jobs in the tertiary sector. Due to several agglomeration advantages, the cities of Düsseldorf and Bonn have done much better in this respect. In the second half of the twentieth century, Düsseldorf profited enormously from the tertiary sector. Today it is one of the leading centres of the German advertising and fashion industry (Knapp and Schmitt 2008). The relative importance of both Düsseldorf and Bonn can also be seen in Fig. 14.8. On the national scale, the metropolitan cores of Rhine-Ruhr have – with the exception of Köln – quite balanced connectivity patterns. This means that these regional centres are interconnected almost to the same extent by nationally-orientated APS firms. On the international scale, however, the relative importance of Düsseldorf within Rhine-Ruhr increases, which underlines its important function as an international knowledge gateway connecting the Mega-City Region to a wider space of flows. In contrast to Düsseldorf and Bonn, the agglomeration of Köln – the fourth biggest city in Germany – is clearly less integrated in national and international APS networks. This shows, as with many other POLYNET case studies, that the mere size of an FUA does not automatically correlate with its significance in terms of international connectivity.

4.3.5 The Rhine-Main Region

The second German case study within the POLYNET project analyses the multi-scalar polycentricity in the Mega-City Region of Rhine-Main, which encompasses the cities of Frankfurt am Main, Wiesbaden and Mainz, but extending widely outwards as

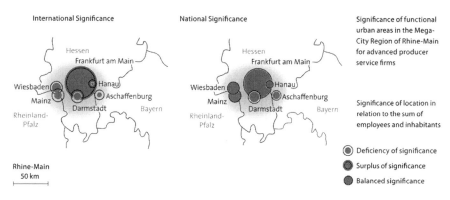

Fig. 14.9 Significance of Functional Urban Areas in the Mega-City Region of Rhine-Main for APS firms (Thierstein et al. 2006)

far as Hanau and Aschaffenburg in the east and Darmstadt in the south. Rhine-Main, Germany's second biggest metropolitan region after Rhine-Ruhr, has long been identified as the country's most globalised urban agglomeration, not least due to its core city Frankfurt am Main, Germany's undisputed financial centre (Grote 2004) and leading international logistics hub (Schamp 2001).

The analysis of network connectivities confirms Frankfurt's dominant position as the major hub of knowledge-intensive business services on both national and international scales (see Fig. 14.9). Note, however, that the relative significance of Frankfurt increases with geographical scale. On the national scale, Frankfurt is part of the 'urban circuit' of those German cities (Frankfurt, Hamburg, Munich, Düsseldorf, Berlin, Stuttgart and Cologne) that have long constituted the apex of a polycentric national configuration of cities and metropolitan regions, characterised by complementary functional and sectoral specialisation (Blotevogel 2000). Wiesbaden and Mainz, respective capitals of the states of Hessen and Rhineland-Palatinate, also show quite balanced interlock connectivities on the national scale. The national linkages of Darmstadt (a city with a strong information technology sector and technical university) as well as Aschaffenburg and Hanau (two smaller FUAs in eastern Rhine-Main that have retained a higher percentage of their industrial workforce) are clearly smaller than expected in terms of their inhabitant- and employment-size. This finding is even more pronounced on the international scale. Frankfurt clearly acts as 'first city' for internationally-orientated APS firms and therefore constitutes a key gateway to the other major cities and towns in Germany and the world (Hoyler et al. 2008a).

4.3.6 The Paris Region

The Paris region is an interesting POLYNET case study for testing the emergence of a polycentric Mega-City Region for two reasons. On the one hand, the Paris FUA is highly affected by globalisation processes, being with London one of the most

14 Interlocking Firm Networks and Emerging Mega-City Regions in the Knowledge... 329

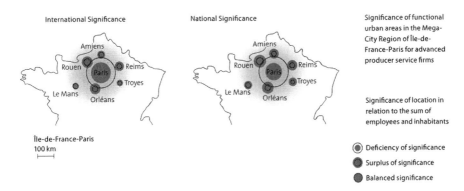

Fig. 14.10 Significance of Functional Urban Areas in the Paris Region for APS firms (Thierstein et al. 2006)

prominent global metropolises in Europe. On the other hand, the natural geological basin that surrounds the Paris region (Bassin parisien) contains a series of medium and small cities and towns of reasonable size constituting a demographic reserve almost equivalent to the Ile-de-France region's own population. From a morphological point of view, the urban structure in the Bassin parisien follows a relatively polycentric pattern. A series of middle-sized cities circle Paris linked by what is known as the Route of Cathedrals (Orléans, Rouen, Amiens, Reims) organising the Bassin parisien's demographic pattern (Halbert 2008).

In absolute terms, APS firms are still predominantly concentrated in the Paris FUA; more specifically, in the central part of its agglomeration, known as the 'Golden Triangle' linked by the city's western arrondissements, La Défense and the suburbs of Boulogne-Billancourt and Issy-les-Moulineux. However, when putting the connectivity value of the different FUAs in relation to inhabitants and employment, the secondary centres around Paris are clearly more networked on both national and the international scales (see Fig. 14.10). The FUA of Paris, on the other hand, does not achieve the degree of connectivity as expected in terms of its inhabitants and employment figures. One explanation for this astonishing finding is the pronounced functional division of labour within the Bassin parisien's urban system (Halbert 2004) giving the secondary cities more socio-economic weight in relative terms. Whereas Paris is specialised in research and development, management consulting, marketing, culture and the arts, secondary cities are focused on public services and some basic production activities such as manufacturing or logistics. As a consequence, spillovers from the Paris agglomeration affect positively these secondary cities that benefit from hosting deconcentrated functions which, in turn, develop local service economies and generate new revenues spent locally. Some of these secondary cities have been more successful than others, like Orléans for instance, which has found sectoral and functional specialisation that complements the economic profile of the whole Paris region (Halbert 2008).

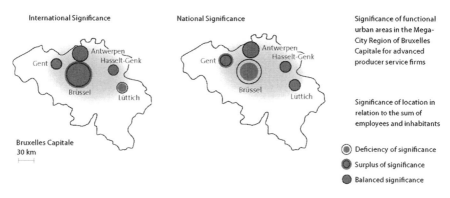

Fig. 14.11 Significance of Functional Urban Areas in the Mega-City Region of Central Belgium for APS firms (Thierstein et al. 2006)

4.3.7 Central Belgium

A seventh POLYNET case study is Central Belgium, comprising Brussels and a surrounding ring of large- and medium-sized cities, with a high degree of interdependence and a total population of ca. seven million (Hall 2007). The Belgian urban system is dominated by Brussels with almost twice as many inhabitants as Antwerp and six times more than Ghent (Vandermotten et al. 2006a). In terms of international APS connectivities, Fig. 14.11 shows for Brussels a clear surplus of significance. This position is intrinsically related to the location of European institutions in the city and to the resulting presence of international consulting, lawyers and other lobbyist offices (Vandermotten et al. 2006b). In addition to the presence of 'classic' subsidiaries of numerous multi-national companies (MNCs) Brussels is sometimes chosen by the latter for their European headquarters, while Belgian firms of international scope mostly choose Brussels as their decision-making centre (e.g. Dexia Group). Many internationally-orientated APS firms setting up in Belgium – especially advertising or law firms offering specialised services to international organisations and knowledge intensive logistics enterprises based around Brussels airport – opt for a location in Brussels itself without trying to establish subsidiaries in other Belgian cities. Due to the small size of Belgium, these firms have no difficulty in serving the whole of the national market from their Brussels base (Vandermotten et al. 2006a).

4.3.8 Greater Dublin

The last POLYNET case study is concerned with the functioning of Greater Dublin, an emerging Mega-City Region within a 50–60 km radius around the city of Dublin, developing particularly northwards along the Dublin-Belfast corridor. For the purpose of the POLYNET study, the Greater Dublin region is defined as a functional urban region comprising the Dublin metropolitan area and four surrounding

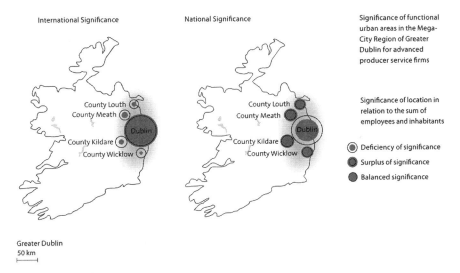

Fig. 14.12 Significance of Functional Urban Areas in Greater Dublin for APS firms (Thierstein et al. 2006)

local authorities in its hinterland: County Louth, County Meath, County Kildare and County Wicklow. In its urban settlement and employment structure, Greater Dublin is the most distinctive of all the eight POLYNET Mega-City Regions: it is completely dominated by the city of Dublin and its suburbs. However, while still relatively small, the major urban centres outside Dublin city have experienced dramatic population growth in the last decade Sokol et al. (2008). Figure 14.12 confirms this tendency where the four secondary centres possess a slight surplus of significance at the national level. In terms of international knowledge-intensive business services, however, the city of Dublin clearly acts as first city and therefore constitutes a key gateway for the entire Mega-City Region. One reason for this is the fact that for large international financial services players, the city of Dublin itself is a 'decentralised' location within a much larger corporate network. In other words, Dublin is often chosen as the off-shoring location of multi-national companies (MNCs) that relocate certain business functions from other, even higher cost locations such as London or Paris Sokol et al. (2008).

5 Conclusion

Comparing the different case studies presented above, three groups of FUAs stand out.

A first group is characterised by a strong deficiency of significance of the primary FUA on both scales, national and international. Surprisingly, Paris and London are the two only FUAs belonging to this group. In absolute terms, both cities are clearly the most important locations for international APS firms within their Mega-City

Regions. In relative terms, however, they do not achieve the degree of connectivity as expected in terms of their inhabitant and employment figures. This clearly shows that the mere size of an agglomeration does not automatically increase its functional significance. The interpretation of this finding in relation to the Mega-City Region hypothesis in Fig. 14.1 is that the up-scaling process of agglomeration economies is also present in big cities such as London and Paris, leading to distinct positive spillovers from the primary to the secondary FUAs. Hence, although South East England and the Paris region appear to be relatively mono-centric in physical terms, they prove the most functionally polycentric regions of all case studies.

A second group of FUAs is characterised by a strong surplus of significance of secondary FUA on both scales, national and international. The most typical examples of this group are the secondary cities around London and Paris, such as Cambridge and Reading or Rouen and Orléans respectively. In fact, this group seems to belong to the winners of spatial restructuring processes going on in London and Paris. These cities benefit from the up-scaling process of agglomeration economies by hosting deconcentrated functions, which develop local service economies and generate new revenues spent locally.

And finally, a third group of FUAs is characterised by a slight surplus of significance on the international scale. For Dublin, Brussels and to some extent Zurich, the differences between the international and the national scale are remarkably high. This means that many internationally oriented APS firms setting up in these cities hardly try to establish subsidiaries in the wider region. Hence, these primary cities can be interpreted as central nodes and international gateways with a high concentration of global network economies. The secondary cities in these emerging Mega-City Regions are not directly integrated into international networks of knowledge-intensive economic activities. Instead, they are well integrated into large-scale regional networks based on the increasing up-scaling process of agglomeration economies. For Amsterdam, Düsseldorf and Frankfurt, the differences between the international and the national scale are less pronounced. Especially for the Mega-City Regions of Amsterdam and Düsseldorf, this may be the consequence of their archetypical polycentric structure, leading to a fast intra-regional diffusion of international knowledge thanks to well-established agglomeration economies.

Over the last decades, Europe has experienced the reorganisation of functional-territorial division of labour in the knowledge economy. The increasing importance of network economies has introduced new thinking about space, place and scale that interprets regions as unbounded, relational spaces. From a relational point of view, regions can be defined by their linkages and relations within and beyond their territorial boundaries (Pike 2007). The increasing complexity of network economies leads to a kind of paradox associated with the emergence of Mega-City Regions. The inter-urban functional linkages are found to be extending and intensifying while, at the same time, global functions are clustering and centralising. Evidence from Thierstein et al. (2007) as well as POLYNET suggests that these apparently contradictory processes are intersecting on the Mega-City Region scale. While specialised global functions are concentrating in 'first cities', proximate regional centres are gaining complementary service functions across a wide geographical area. Because of the various requirements for competing in the world economy, it is not possible for a first city to act without the smaller agglomerations in its vicinity. Smaller cities fulfil an important role as complementary economic spaces. Interlocking networks of knowledge-intensive firms link these different agglomerations together, thus defining emerging Mega-City Regions as physically separated but functionally networked socio-economic spaces. As POLYNET shows, the clearest example of this phenomenon is South East England where secondary towns and cities around London are found to have synergistic roles with each other as well as with London itself – a phenomenon referred to in the POLYNET study as "functional polycentricity", which is caused by an extension of APS network relations through a Mega-City Region process (Hall and Pain 2006). The main conclusion of this paper is that polycentric Mega-City Regions emerge as a scale-dependent phenomenon based on the coming together of various interlocking firm networks of different organizational structures and scalar reach. Mega-City Regions are becoming a more general phenomenon in advanced economies based on re-scaling processes of agglomeration and network economies.

References

Asheim B, Isaksen A (1997) Location, agglomeration and innovation: towards regional innovation systems in Norway? Eur Plann Stud 5(3):299–310
Becattini G (1989) Sectors and/or districts: some remarks on the conceptual foundations of industrial economics. In: Goodman E, Bamford J (eds) Small firms and industrial districts in Italy. Routledge, London
Blotevogel HH (2000) Gibt es in Deutschland Metropolen? In: Matejovski D (ed) Metropolen: Laboratorien der Moderne. Campus, Frankfurt am Main
Boschma R (2005) Proximity and innovation: a critical assessment. Reg Stud 39(1):61–74
Boschma R, Iammarino S (2009) Related variety, trade linkages, and regional growth in Italy. Econ Geogr 85(3):289–311
Bramanti A, Maggioni MA (eds) (1997) The dynamics of milieux: the network analysis approach. Ashgate, Aldershot
Cabus P, Vanhaverbeke W (2006) The territoriality of the network economy and urban networks: evidence from Flanders. Entrep Reg Dev 18:25–53
Carrincazeaux C, Lung Y, Vicente J (2008) The scientific trajectory of the French school of proximity: interaction- and institution-based approaches to regional innovation systems. Eur Plann Stud 16(5):617–628
Castells M (1989) The informational city information technology, economic restructuring, urban-regional process. Blackwell, Oxford
Castells M (2000) The rise of the network society. The information age: economy, society and culture. Blackwell, Malden
Coe N, Hess M, Yeung H, Dicken P, Henderson J (2004) 'Globalising' regional development: a global production networks perspective. Trans Inst Br Geogr 29(4):468–484
Coe N, Dicken P, Hess M (2008) Introduction: global production networks—debates and challenges. J Econ Geogr 8:267–269
Cooke P, Uranga MG, Etxebarria G (1998) Regional systems of innovation: an evolutionary perspective. Environ Plann A 30:1563–1584
Edquist C (1997) Systems of innovation approaches – their emergence and characteristics. In: Edquist C (ed) Systems of innovation: technologies, institutions and organisations. Pinter, London/Washington

Edquist C, Johnson B (eds) (1997) Institutions and organisations in systems of innovation. Edward Elgar, Cheltenham

ESPON (2004) ESPON Project 1.1.1. Potentials for polycentric development in Europe. Project report. European spatial planning observation network ESPON, Luxembourg

Friedmann J (1986) The world city hypothesis. Dev Change 17:69–83

Gereffi G, Humphrey J, Sturgeon T (2005) The governance of global value chains. Rev Int Polit Econ 12(1):78–104

Gottmann J (1961) Megalopolis. The urbanized northeastern seaboard of the United States. Twentieth Century Fund, New York

Grabher G (1991) The embedded firm: the socio-economics of industrial networks. Routledge, London

Grote MH (2004) Die Entwicklung des Finanzplatzes Frankfurt. Duncker & Humblot, Berlin

Halbert L (2004) The intrametropolitan decentralisation of business services in the Paris region: patterns, interpretation, consequences. Econ Geogr 80:381–405

Halbert L (2008) Examining the mega-city-region hypothesis: evidence from the Paris city-region/Bassin parisien. Reg Stud 42(8):1147–1160

Hall P (1966) The world cities. Weidenfeld and Nicolson, London

Hall P (1999) Planning for the mega-city: a new eastern Asian urban form? In: Brotchie JF (ed) East west perspectives on 21st century urban development: sustainable eastern and western cities in the new millennium. Ashgate, Aldershot

Hall P (2007) Delineating urban territories. Is this a relevant issue? In: Cattan N (ed) Cities and networks in Europe. A critical approach of polycentrism. John Libbey Eurotext, Paris

Hall P, Pain K (2006) The polycentric metropolis. Learning from mega-city regions in Europe. Earthscan, London

Henderson J, Dicken P, Hess M, Coe N, Yeung W (2002) Global production networks and the analysis of economic development. Rev Int Polit Econ 9(3):436–464

Hoover EM (1937) Location theory and the shoe and leather industries. Harvard University Press, Cambridge, MA

Hoover EM (1948) The location of economic activity. McGraw-Hill, New York

Hoyler M, Freytag T, Mager C (2008a) Connecting rhine-main: the production of multi-scalar polycentricities through knowledge-intensive business services. Reg Stud 42(8):1095–1111

Hoyler M, Kloosterman RC, Sokol M (2008b) Polycentric puzzles – emerging mega-city regions seen through the lens of advanced producer services. Reg Stud 42(8):1055–1064

Kloosterman RC, Musterd S (2001) The polycentric urban region: towards a research agenda. Urban Stud 38(4):623–633

Knapp W, Schmitt P (2008) Discourse on 'metropolitan driving forces' and 'uneven development': Germany and the Rhine-Rruhr conurbation. Reg Stud 42(8):1187–1204

Kogut B (1985) Designing global strategies: comparative and competitive value-added chains. Sloan Manage Rev 26(4):15–28

Lambregts B (2008) Geographies of knowledge formation in mega-city regions: some evidence from the Dutch Randstad. Reg Stud 42(8):1173–1186

Lundvall BÅ (ed) (1988) Innovation as an interactive process: from user-producer interaction to the national system of innovation. Edward Elgar, Cheltenham

Lundvall BÅ (ed) (1992) Introduction in: national systems of innovation: towards a theory of innovation and interactive learning. Edward Elgar, Cheltenham

Lüthi S, Thierstein A, Goebel V (2008) Intra-firm and extra-firm linkages of the knowledge economy – the case of the mega-city region of Munich. Paper presented at the annual meeting of the Association of American Geographers (AAG), Boston

Maillat D, Quévit M, Senn L (1993) Réseaux d'innovation et milieux innovateurs: Un pari pour le développement régional. EDES, Neuchâtel

Marshall A (1920) Principles of economics, chapter 10 – industrial organisation, continued. The concentration of specialised industries in particular localities. Macmillan, London

Massey D (1985) Spatial divisions of labour. Social structures and the geography of production (reprint). MacMillan, London

Morgan K (1997) The learning region: institutions innovation and regional renewal. Reg Stud 31(5):491–503

Moulaert F, Sekia F (2003) Territorial innovation models: a critical survey. Reg Stud 37(3):289–302

Muscio A (2006) From regional innovation systems to local innovation systems: evidence from Italian industrial districts. Eur Plann Stud 14(6):773–789

Nelson R (1993) National innovation systems. Oxford University Press, Oxford

Nelson R, Winter S (1982) An evolutionary theory of economic change. The Belknap Press of Harvard University Press, Cambridge/London

Pain K (2008) Examining 'core-periphery' relationships in a global city-region: the case of London and South East England. Reg Stud 42(8):1161–1172

Pike A (2007) Editorial: whither regional studies? Reg Stud 41(9):1143–1148

Piore MJ, Sable CF (1984) The second industrial divide: possibilities for prosperity. Basic, New York

Sassen S (2001) The global city: New York, London, Tokyo. Princeton University Press, Oxford

Schamp EW (2001) Der Aufstieg von Frankfurt/Rhein-Main zur europäischen Metropolregion. Geogr Helv 56(3):169–178

Schumpeter JA (1926) Theorie der wirtschaftlichen Entwicklung, 2nd edn. Duncker & Humblot, München/Leipzig

Scott AJ (1985) Location processes, urbanisation and territorial development: an exploratory essay. Environ Plann A 17:479–501

Scott AJ (2001) Global city-regions: trends, theory, policy. Oxford University Press, Oxford

Simmie J (2003) Innovation and urban regions as national and international nodes for the transfer and sharing of knowledge. Reg Stud 37(6):607–620

Simmie J (2005) Innovation and space: a critical review of the literature. Reg Stud 39(6):789–804

Sokol M, van Egeraat C, Williams B (2008) Revisiting the 'informational city': space of flows polycentricity and the geography of knowledge-intensive business services in the emerging global city-region of Dublin. Reg Stud 42(8):1133–1146

Storper M (1995) The resurgence of regional economies ten years later: the region as a nexus of untraded interdependencies. Eur Urban Reg Stud 2:119–221

Storper M, Walker R (1988) The geographical foundations and social regulations of flexible production complexes, London

Taylor PJ (2004) World city network: a global urban analysis. Routledge, London

Taylor PJ, Evans DM, Pain K (2008) Application of the interlocking network model to mega-city-regions: measuring polycentricity within and beyond city-regions. Reg Stud 42(8):1079–1093

Thierstein A, Kruse C, Glanzmann L, Gabi S, Grillon N (2006) Raumentwicklung im Verborgenen Untersuchungen und Handlungsfelder für die Entwicklung der Metropolregion Nordschweiz. NZZ Buchverlag, Zurich

Thierstein A, Goebel V, Lüthi S (2007) Standortverflechtungen der Metropolregion München. Über Konnektivität in der Wissensökonomie. Lehrstuhl für Raumentwicklung, TU München, München

Thierstein A, Lüthi S, Kruse C, Gabi S, Glanzmann L (2008) Changing value chain of the knowledge economy. Spatial impact of intra-firm and inter-firm networks within the emerging mega-city region of Northern Switzerland. Reg Stud 42(8):1113–1131

Torre A, Rallet A (2005) Proximity and localization. Reg Stud 39(1):47–59

Vandermotten C, Roelandts M, Aujean L, Castiau E (2006a) Central Belgium: polycentrism in a federal context. In: Hall P, Pain K (eds) The polycentric metropolis learning from mega-city regions in Europe. Earthscan, London

Vandermotten C, Roelandts M, Aujean L, Castiau E (2006b) Globalisation and social dualisation, under an institutional constraint: the Brussels-capital case. Built Environ 32(2):148–156

Wildemann H (2003) Supply Chain Management Effizienzsteigerung in der unternehmensübergreifenden Wertschöpfungskette. TCW Transfer-Centrum, München

Part III
Case Studies of Urban Growth

Chapter 15
Polycentric Urban Trajectories and Urban Cultural Economy

Cultural Industries in Dutch Cities Since 1900

Michaël Deinema and Robert Kloosterman

Abstract This chapter traces the urban employment trends in cultural industries in the Netherlands from 1899 onwards and argues that a historical approach is necessary to understand economic geographical patterns in this post-industrial growth sector. Longitudinal employment data for the country's four main cities, as well as case-study information on the spatial and institutional development of separate cultural industries in the Netherlands, reveal long-term intercity hierarchies of performance and historically-rooted local specializations. The effects of historical local trajectories on the inter-urban distribution of Dutch cultural production are weighed against more volatile factors such as creative class densities. Implications for the general outlook and development of these post-industrial urban economies are then explored, whereby the connectivity of the cities in international and regional networks is taken into account. The chapter concludes with identifying the evolutionary mechanisms at work in Dutch cultural industries and the value of a historical perspective *vis-à-vis* other geographical approaches to the urban cultural economy. As the four examined Dutch cities are all part of the Randstad megacity region, the dynamic Dutch urban cultural economy represents an unlikely case for stable inequalities between cities based on local trajectories. Consequently, strong implications may be inferred for cultural industry dynamics in other contexts.

Keywords Postindustrial urban economy • Cultural industries • Path dependency • Competitiveness • Megacity region • The Netherlands

---

M. Deinema (✉)
University of Amsterdam, Amsterdam, The Netherlands
e-mail: M.N.Deinema@uva.nl

R. Kloosterman
Amsterdam Institute of Metropolitan and International Development Studies (AMIDSt)
and University of Amsterdam, Amsterdam, The Netherlands

J. Klaesson et al. (eds.), *Metropolitan Regions*, Advances in Spatial Science,
DOI 10.1007/978-3-642-32141-2_15, © Springer-Verlag Berlin Heidelberg 2013

1 Introduction

Under pressure of globalization, urban economies have had to undergo processes of restructuring over the past few decades and cities in high-wage Western countries such as the Netherlands have had to reposition themselves in a globalizing economy. Failure to do so is often held responsible for local economic stagnation and the rise of urban social ills. In recent years, societal developments associated with globalization, such as immigration issues, European integration, neoliberalization, and a perceived loss of national identity and social cohesion, have become strongly politicized in European countries (see for example Scheffer 2007). In the Netherlands, a small country with a traditionally open economy, this has led to an increasing polarization between 'cosmopolitans' and new right-wing populist parties that have taken up a fervently nationalist and anti-immigration stance, echoing increasingly-vocalized popular discontent regarding the effects of globalization.

In this polarizing process, new geographical divisions have emerged within the Dutch political landscape. A divergence has occurred between the country's four largest cities in terms of prevalent political attitudes. Whereas voters in the capital Amsterdam and in Utrecht, the smallest of the four cities, have so far generally sided with the cosmopolitan camp, Rotterdam and The Hague have drifted into the potentially murkier waters of nationalistic sentiment and growing inter-ethnic tension. The political divergence between Amsterdam and Rotterdam, particularly, is striking, as these two cities, the largest in the Netherlands, were both considered traditionally as left-wing labor-party strongholds. Conversely, The Hague and Utrecht have historically upheld a more conservative profile. But these latter two cities as well seem currently to be diverging towards opposite ends of the political spectrum.

The ethnic composition of the urban population is fairly similar in these four cities. Commentators such as the political scientist Mark Bovens have therefore concluded that the political divergence between the cities, and their differing levels of cosmopolitanism, is related to other factors, namely local levels of education and, especially, the extent to which the different cities have been able to produce and attract 'winners' rather than 'losers' of globalization (Volkskrant 2008, 2009; Trouw 2009). Because 'success' in these cases is mostly defined in terms of economic opportunity, and economic prospects of different sectors vary widely in the context of globalization, the political divergence is ultimately being related to differences in the economic profiles of these cities and their orientation on different sectors of the economy.

Presently, the so-called 'cultural industries', the producers of aesthetic or symbolic commodities, are often assigned a pivotal role in aligning post-industrial urban societies with the new economic and social realities of globalization. For this reason, many national and city government try to stimulate cultural production, such as architectural design, publishing, or media broadcasting, in their cities. But much remains unclear about the social role and the economic and geographical dynamics of cultural industries. Does a thriving local cultural industries sector guarantee or even indicate healthy economic and social development of a city in a globalizing, post-industrial context, enhancing the city's prospects of sustainable economic growth and offering its urban underclasses (often consisting mainly of immigrant groups) the opportunities of social mobility? Or do these industries, as some commentators suggest, present cities with an illusionary and ephemeral economic basis (Peck 2005) and reflect the bankruptcy of local cultural authenticity and cohesion (Cf. Lampel and Shamsie 2006), or even the social ills and economic dead-endedness that are sometimes believed to inspire true art (Cf. Hall 1998; Scott 2007)?

There has also been debate about the ability of public interventions to effectively and positively stimulate the development of local cultural industries. It is sometimes claimed that cultural industries generally evolve incrementally according to long local historical trajectories. Long local histories in particular forms of cultural production enable the slow development of expertise and the build-up of valuable networks and reputations that may be required to compete successfully in these industries. It is therefore unclear to what extent competitive cultural production can be set up on a short-term basis in places where already well-established, pre-existing 'art worlds' (Becker 1982) are lacking. Some cities may simply be better historically conditioned than others to compete in cultural industries, so that little can be done to change, instantaneously, the 'cultural potential' of a city. It thus remains to be conclusively shown if cultural industries are as imminently desirable as they are often made out to be, and also whether or not the short-term creation of a vibrant cultural industries scene is feasible in every city.

This paper aims to provide insight into both these questions by examining the recent state of the cultural industries in the four largest cities of the Netherlands as well as the long-term historical dynamic of these industries in the Netherlands throughout the twentieth century. This will show whether or not the Dutch cities that currently enjoy a relatively good or improving position with regards to cultural production are the same as those that display greater levels of cosmopolitanism, economic optimism and social stability. It will also show whether these positions have remained fairly constant over the twentieth century, and are thus likely to be historically conditioned, or have been subject to major shifts, in which case the fortunes of a city's local cultural industries may perhaps change or be changed fairly easily.

The Dutch case is particularly interesting in this regard for two reasons. First, the political shift towards nationalism in the Netherlands has surprised Dutch and international commentators alike because this country was previously considered a champion of multiculturalism and cultural liberalism (Entzinger 2003). Secondly, the geographical dynamic of cultural industries in the Netherlands provides a good window unto the weight of local history in determining the strength of local cultural industries. Many cultural industries have century-long histories in the Netherlands. Furthermore, and more importantly, the Netherlands is a highly polycentric country which lacks a single, 'natural' metropolitan and cultural center. The four cities that are examined here, are in fact all part of the larger conurbation called 'the Randstad' that is often regarded by urban planners and geographers as a paradigmatic example of a multi-nuclear urban region (Hoyler et al. 2008; Lambregts 2008). The cities are thus all relatively close together and interconnected so that mobility between them is relatively easy, for producers as well as consumers of cultural industries. Nevertheless, each city has its own historically formed and distinct local character. This case thus enables an assessment of the importance of differences in local characteristics under conditions of strong interrelatedness that make the potential for inter-urban redistributions of activities relatively high.

2 The Promise of Cultural Industries and Their Geographical Dynamic

The transition to a post-industrial and globalizing economy during the last few decades of the twentieth century has had several main effects on Western cities. First of all, a general economic resurgence of cities seems to have taken place, with new service- and consumption-led activities concentrating mainly in metropolitan areas (Zukin 1995; Scott 1998). This resurgence has fueled processes of gentrification and a new flow of domestic as well as overseas immigrants into the prime urban areas of Western countries, largely reversing earlier trends of urban decay, rising unemployment and the flight of urban middle-classes to suburban areas. Secondly, new social tensions and forms of economic, social and political polarization have emerged. According to sociologist Saskia Sassen especially 'global cities', the central service nodes of the globalized economy, have seen their labor markets polarize to the extent that the increase in low-end unskilled service jobs, mostly filled by foreign immigrant groups, as well as in high-end positions in advanced producer services firms, has largely eliminated the availability and economic significance of intermediary forms of employment. This gradual disappearance of middle-of-the-road jobs has increased barriers to upward labor mobility, as entry into higher strata of the metropolitan labor force now requires a substantial 'leap' in terms of (especially) education, and the option of a gradual climb up the labor ladder is no longer available in many cases (Sassen 1991).

Despite the social dangers accompanying labor market polarization, policymakers and academics have generally aimed to stimulate post-industrial development in cities. One reason for this attitude has been that few alternatives exist for urban economies in high-wage countries, as standardized manufacturing activities have been increasingly off-shored. Cities that have not managed to adapt well to the new economic circumstances, especially former centers of manufacturing such as Detroit, have experienced stagnation and worse social ills than those associated with global cities. It is within this general political and economic context that countless city councils have been keen to accept as policy paradigms new theories of urban economic development revolving around the 'creative'. Richard Florida's notion of the economic importance of attracting the so-called 'creative class' and Charles Landry's concept of the 'creative city' have led to the formulation and implementation of generalized recipes for stimulating the local 'creative economy' of cities (Florida 2002; Landry 2000). These recipes seem to have been interpreted in many cases as a type of policy panacea (cf. Martin and Sunley 2003), although (needless to say) they have not proven their effectiveness in every urban setting (Peck 2005; Markusen 2006). Attempts to refine formulas for stimulating the urban creative economy (that has become something of an urban policy Holy Grail) have continued and have usually accorded a central role to cultural industries, fields of production that generate goods and services that derive their value mainly from their aesthetic and symbolic characteristics rather than from their use-value (Scott 2000; Kloosterman 2004).

Cultural industries have attracted much attention from policymakers and academics alike because employment in these industries has grown rapidly in recent decades. For this reason, they are considered (potentially) important pillars of post-industrial urban economies (Kloosterman 2004). As prime creators and conveyors of aesthetic and symbolic value, these industries are also valued for their potential positive spillover effects on other economic sectors that need to adapt their products to more general trends of a 'culturalizing economy' that places an increasing premium on the aesthetic appeal of goods and services, and on the consumer experiences products induce (Lash and Urry 1994). Furthermore, cultural industries are prized for more than their economic potential. The artistic element of cultural industries is considered instrumental in efforts to regenerate decrepit inner-city neighborhoods both socially and culturally (Scott 2007). With such reputed positive economic and social externalities associated with urban cultural industries, it is not surprising that this sector is deemed worthy of public investment and intervention.

Much recent research into the geographical dynamics of cultural industries, however, suggests that active policy-intervention aimed at stimulating competitive cultural production may not be sufficient to provide the preconditions that these industries need to flourish, especially not in cities where policymakers cannot build on an already well-developed and established cultural scene. Economic geographers such as Allen Scott and Andy Pratt have argued that cultural producers often depend on local 'art worlds' to perform competitively. Unlike Richard Florida, they regard 'creativity' as the outcome of complex social interactions involving many different actors engaged in related activities, rather than as an innate characteristic of a specific 'class' of individuals (Scott 2000; Pratt 2008). Complex specialized production systems of interdependent artists or designers, distributors, retailers, critics, trainers or teachers, specialized material suppliers and many types of industry-specific services underpin competitive cultural production. Such production systems are usually localized as they emerge from intense interactions that often require actors to be in close proximity to each other. Just as in high-technology industries such as computer software production therefore, cultural industries producers agglomerate in clusters, unusual spatial concentrations of related economic activity (Saxenian 1994). Hollywood (and Bollywood) film production, Broadway theater and Milan fashion are prime examples of the tendency of cultural industries to form their own industry-specific hotspots and 'Silicon Valleys' (Scott 2005; Wenting 2008).

The concentration of specialized firms, producers, artists, facilities and institutions, that make clusters such as Hollywood the 'place to be' for a specific cultural industry and enable competitive cultural production, has to evolve over time. Through collaboration as well as vigorous competition, different firms and institutions in a cluster provide each other with incentives for ongoing specialization. Furthermore, they need to adapt their expertise and practices to one another to reap the full benefits of being located close together, or simply to keep up. The different actors in clusters thus collectively form 'ecologies' that are not simply created but grow and develop interdependently (Grabher 2001). The cluster model implies that cultural industries become entwined with and rooted in specific cities. The success of a local cultural industry therefore often depends and builds on the historical development of that industry in the city in question. This means that some cities may be better suited than others to compete in specific fields of cultural production by virtue of the weight of history and the local presence of complex, 'organic' networks of producers supported by 'thick' webs of specialized institutions (Amin and Thrift 1995) that took a long time to develop and are hard to copy elsewhere in the short-term.

If cultural industries indeed develop primarily in clusters, strong historical continuity in the geographical distribution of particular types of cultural producers may be expected. Although the evolutionary cluster model is theoretically sound and empirically supported by a host of case studies (e.g. Rantisi 2004; Van der Groep 2008; Kloosterman and Stegmeijer 2005; Kloosterman 2008), studies that systematically map the long-term geographical dynamic of cultural industries growth are scarce (cf. Wenting 2008). To help this dynamic, this paper thus sets out in the following sections to empirically examine to what extent the distribution of employment in cultural industries between the four main cities in the Netherlands has changed since 1900. The long-term evolution of the relative positions of the four major cities in the Netherlands will be determined for the cultural sector as a whole, and for several different key cultural industries separately, with the use of both quantitative employment data and qualitative information concerning the development of Dutch cultural industries. Before these findings are presented, however, a short description of the four cities in question will be provided, as well as a preliminary analysis of the general fortunes of the cultural sector on the national scale from 1900 onwards.

3 The Four Largest Cities of the Netherlands

3.1 Amsterdam

Amsterdam is the largest city in the Netherlands and the country's capital, although it does not hold the seat of government. The city experienced strong growth during the country's Golden Age that started during the last decades of the sixteenth century, when the Dutch started a successful national revolt against their Spanish overlords, and lasted until the beginning of the eighteenth century. The city profited strongly from a naval blockade of the Schelde River that gave access to Spanish-held Antwerp, Northern Europe's largest and most prosperous port city at the start of the Dutch Revolt. Many Antwerp merchants, artist and intellectuals fled to

Amsterdam, contributing to a period of prolonged economic growth that turned the city into the center of an extended overseas trading empire. At the start of the seventeenth century, the world's first stock exchange and the first multinational corporation (the Dutch East India Company) were founded in this city that consequently became the heart of Europe's financial networks. During subsequent decades, Amsterdam expanded physically through the creation of a planned canal belt that is presently a candidate UNESCO World Heritage site and earned the city the reputation of being 'the Venice of the North'. Simultaneously, Amsterdam became an important European center of culture, with painters such as Rembrandt and philosophers such as Baruch Spinoza achieving long-lasting international fame. The city's art markets and book trade industry developed rapidly and its painters and publishers exported widely throughout Europe. The city also became very attractive to new groups of foreign immigrants. Foreign intellectuals such as Rene Descartes and John Locke spent part of their working lives in Amsterdam. Many skilled and unskilled temporary immigrants came from the German territories, Scandinavia, and France and were drawn to the city by its booming economy. Furthermore, two groups that were prosecuted on religious grounds in their home countries, French Protestant Huguenots and Iberian Jews, settled permanently in Amsterdam as this relatively tolerant city afforded them religious liberties and plentiful economic opportunities.

Presently, Amsterdam is the Netherland's financial and business center as well as the country's main tourist destination (Engelen and Grote 2009; Bontje and Sleutjes 2007). By virtue of its many internationally operating firms and cultural influence, Amsterdam is considered an 'incipient global city' of similar standing to Boston, Milan and Moscow (Taylor 2005). It is the eighth most popular tourist city in Europe (Bremner 2007) and its airport Schiphol is Europe's fifth largest (Airports Council International 2008). The city owes its world-wide cultural appeal partly to its Golden Age heritage, with the paintings of Rembrandt and other 'Dutch masters' as well as the city's renowned canal belt attracting many tourists. Another important aspect of Amsterdam that has shaped its international image, is the strong cultural permissiveness and liberalism that has come to the fore since the 1960s and manifests itself most clearly in the city's infamous Red Light District, its marihuana-selling coffeeshops, and its lively and open gay scene.

3.2 Rotterdam

Rotterdam is the country's second largest city. It is located at the mouth of the Maas river (a main artery of the river Rhine) and contains Europe's busiest port. Although the city was already home to the philosopher Erasmus around 1500, it long remained a relatively stagnant town. This changed in the nineteenth century when trade with England and German economic growth, concentrating especially in the Ruhr-Rhine region, stimulated much port activity. Rotterdam thus profited strongly from the industrialization of neighboring countries. The city quickly expanded and started to rival Amsterdam in terms of its size and population. The city and its surrounding region became a hotbed of (heavy) industrial activity and during the twentieth century Rotterdam became one of the country's strongholds of socialism and union organization.

In 1940, the city was targeted by German bombing raids in the Nazi's effort to subdue the Netherlands. Its historic city center was all but destroyed. Since then Rotterdam has been rebuilt and now possesses one of Europe's most modern inner cities, containing skyscrapers and an innovatively designed shopping area (Kloosterman and Stegmeijer 2005). Throughout its postwar physical transformation, Rotterdam's economy has remained oriented towards shipping and manufacturing. The city has therefore suffered from processes of deindustrialization which have produced rising unemployment and crime rates, as well as rising social tensions between its native-Dutch population and immigrant groups. Rotterdam is currently one of the major focal points in the country's increasing political polarization, with populist, nationalistic parties receiving much support in the city. In attempts to spur the city's economy and abate social tensions, successive national and local governments have invested heavily in Rotterdam's physical and cultural infrastructure over the last three decades. New museums, cultural institutions and festivals have been set up, and feats of iconic architecture have been financed, as a means to raise Rotterdam's cultural profile and to make the city more attractive to foreign investors and innovative entrepreneurs.

3.3 The Hague

While it is not the country's official capital, The Hague, the Netherlands' third largest city, holds the national seat of government. Due to the presence of the country's main royal palace The Hague is known as the 'court city'. It is the center of Dutch politics and houses the country's ministries and parliament as well as countless foreign embassies. It is consequently home to many civil servants, lobbyists and legal experts. At least since the The Hague Peace Conference of 1899 the city has been at the forefront of the evolving system of international law and arbitration and it has hosted the International Court of Justice from 1946 onwards. The Hague's position as political center has its roots in medieval times when the counts of Holland used the city as their administrative center and court. When, during the seventeenth century, this region became Northern Europe's most prominent economic powerhouse, the Province of Holland (which comprised the two present-day provinces of North and South Holland that include Amsterdam and Rotterdam respectively) became dominant in the country's affairs and its age-old administrative center attained a status similar to that of national capital.

Due to a geographical position, away from major rivers, that inhibited maritime access the city lagged strongly behind Amsterdam in terms of population growth and economic prowess. At the start of the nineteenth century, the former Dutch Republic became the Kingdom of the Netherlands and the monarch's court as well as a national parliament were established in The Hague. The city grew in tandem with the scope of the national administration and attracted wealthy (and particularly aristocratic) elites that drew in many types of servants in their wake. Henceforth The Hague's economy revolved mainly around the needs and leisure of the city's elites. An adjacent, poor fishermen's village (Scheveningen), for example, was turned into an elite beach resort. The city's economic orientation largely kept out heavy manufacturing industries, and generated one of the widest social-economic divides in the Netherlands. This division is still manifest today, as The Hague boasts some of the richest, as well as some of the poorest neighborhoods in the country (NRC 2006).

3.4 Utrecht

Utrecht is one of the oldest cities of the Netherlands and was founded by the Romans. It lies close to the geographical center of the country and along the main branch of the river Rhine. Since early medieval times, the city has held an archbishopric seat and has lain at the heart of the episcopal hierarchy in the Netherlands. This Catholic significance of Utrecht was interrupted when in the sixteenth century Protestants took control of the country, but was re-established in the nineteenth century when a new liberal constitution guaranteed religious liberty. Since then, the city has again become a main center for the country's Catholic clergy.

Due to its favorable geographical position, the city has become in the twentieth century the main hub of the country's busy railway system and road network. This hub-function has made Utrecht attractive to businesses, commuters, students and day trippers alike. The city has therefore gained strongly in terms of its population and economic significance over the course of the twentieth century. It has also attracted a large foreign immigrant population. Yet inter-ethnic and other social tensions have remained relatively mild. Utrecht is now considered, just like Amsterdam, to be one of the most 'cosmopolitan' cities of the Netherlands (Trouw 2009), and among its inhabitants one finds, more often than in many other cities, the 'winners' of globalization.

4 Just a Fad? The Growth of Cultural Industries in the Netherlands Since 1900

During the twentieth century the Dutch economy underwent fundamental economic transformations. Around 1900 agriculture still provided work to around 30 % of the Dutch labor force and traditional crafts still played a substantial role in terms of employment, next to trade-related activities and industrial manufacturing (Van Zanden 1997). At the start of the twenty-first century by contrast, agriculture and manufacturing taken together account for no more than around twenty percent of total employment (CBS 2007: 12). While the Dutch economy was never as outspokenly industrial as Belgium's, for example, the services sector dominates in present-day the Netherlands like never before. How have the cultural industries developed throughout this century that first saw the Netherlands increasingly industrialize and then, after 1960, deindustrialize.

The following three figures provide a rough indication of the twentieth-century growth of the Dutch cultural economy by comparing the development of employment in economic branches that include cultural industries professions with the growth of employment in the wider economy. In order to stress the relevance of urban as opposed to rural economic activity, employment in agriculture and fishing has been left out of the comparison.

The systems of industrial classification used by the Dutch Central Bureau of Statistics for its economic surveys and corporate censuses, do not always enable a firm handle on developments in the cultural industries. Especially between 1930 (when an extensive nation-wide occupational survey was held) and 1993 (when a renewed and extended system of classification was introduced) few specific data on these industries are available. The figures thus largely reflect a fairly rough estimate based on data concerning employment in several wider corporate categories such as 'the liberal professions' and 'business services' in which cultural industries were presumably best represented. Because of the changes in the systems of industrial classification used (as well as in the system of geographical subdivision that defined economic geographical units for administrative purposes), the comparison between general employment growth and employment growth in economic fields that may serve as proxies for the cultural industries has been subdivided into three distinct periods. More specific research into the growth of eight emblematic cultural industries in the Netherlands between 1993 and 2001 has produced results similar to those displayed in Fig. 15.1c, thereby confirming the relative accuracy of the proxies used here (Kloosterman 2004).

Despite the shortcomings of this initial overview, it is clear that the growth of cultural industries in the Netherlands is not exclusively a recent phenomenon. Insofar as conclusions may be drawn from these preliminary data, this analysis indicates that employment in cultural industries (or at least in related sectors) rose at higher rates than employment in the Dutch (urban) economy as a whole during most decades of the twentieth century, apart from the 1920s. The relatively fast rises during the periods 1899–1920, 1930–1950 and 1980–1988 are quite surprising as these were all relatively difficult periods for the Dutch economy, involving much political and economic restructuring. It seems therefore that, for a relatively long time already, cultural industries have formed an attractive alternative to other, failing forms of enterprise in the Netherlands. Employment in activities focusing on cultural production has thus become steadily more important for the Netherlands as a whole over the last 100 years, albeit in leaps and bounds.

15 Polycentric Urban Trajectories and Urban Cultural Economy

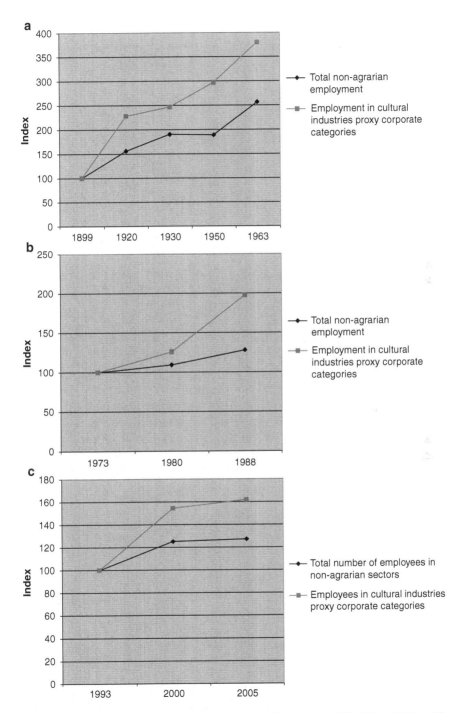

Fig. 15.1 (a) Development of employment in the Netherlands 1899–1963 (1899 = 100). (b) Development of employment in the Netherlands 1973–1988 (1973 = 100). (c) Growth in number of employees in the Netherlands 1993–2005 (1993 = 100)

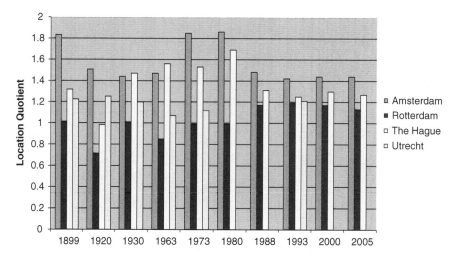

Fig. 15.2 Representation of cultural industries proxy corporate categories in urban employment 1899–2005 (1 = national average)

5 Urban Positions in the Dutch Cultural Economy

Did the growth of this steadily increasing cultural economy take place primarily in the country's four largest cities? And were different cities more prominent within the Dutch cultural industries at different times during the twentieth century, or was there continuity in the 'cultural hierarchy' between cities throughout this century in which the economy, society and culture all underwent great changes? In order to answer these questions, location quotients of employment in the cultural sector have been ascertained for the four cities for different years during the period studied. These location quotients (LQs) represent the share of the cultural sector in each city's local economy divided by the share of the cultural sector in the national (non-agrarian) economy as a whole. They are based on the same employment data analyzed above, only now this data has been differentiated per city. As such, these LQs allow us to see whether specific cities are disproportionally represented in these industries at different times by showing whether the share of their workforce that is employed in the cultural economy is above or below the national average.

Figure 15.2 shows that, by and large, this growing sector was concentrated disproportionally in the major cities, and particularly in Amsterdam, throughout the period 1899–2005. In 1899 and 1920, as well as from 1973 onwards, the creative sector was relatively better represented within the Amsterdam economy than within the economies of the three other cities. Only in 1930 and 1963 did The Hague's creative sector outperform Amsterdam's in terms of its prominence within the local urban economy. Rotterdam displayed a continuously mediocre orientation on this sector throughout the twentieth century, and only started to slightly outperform the national average in 1980. Improvement in Rotterdam coincided with relative decline

15 Polycentric Urban Trajectories and Urban Cultural Economy

in Amsterdam and The Hague. Furthermore, Rotterdam's fortunes improved at a time when a dynamic architectural scene started to emerge in Rotterdam, following the establishment the Office of Metropolitan Architecture (the design agency of the famous architect Rem Koolhaas) and the National Architecture Institute in the city (Kloosterman and Stegmeijer 2005; Kloosterman 2008). The data found on Utrecht unfortunately do not cover the entire period under study but do indicate a fairly continuous slight overrepresentation of the creative sector in the local economy.

The positioning of the four cities relative to each other in the creative sector has varied throughout the century, but only slightly so. The creative sectors in Amsterdam and The Hague outperformed those in Rotterdam and Utrecht in the past, and still do so in the present. Usually Amsterdam held top rank. There do not seem to have been many instances in which major redistributions between the four cities took place. In terms of their 'creative fortunes', the hierarchy between the four cities thus appears to have remained largely intact since 1900.

6 Separate Cultural Industries

The cultural industries include a wide array of fields of production, ranging from publishing and the graphic industry to theater to the clothing industry. What these industries have in common is that they dictate styles, need to innovate continually, and produce as commodities the beauty or symbolism that we refer to as cultural. In all cultural industries, value is created mainly through the appearance, presentation and aesthetic impact of products and services rather than through their functionality. However, when it comes to their geographical dynamics and relations to places (and place-specific historical trajectories), important differences exist between these industries and distinctions can be made between them along different dimensions.

The degree of product mobility, for example, differs per industry: books are more easily transported than theater performances. The content, as well as the form, of products determine their mobility as some products cross national or cultural boundaries more easily than others. Products bound to languages that are spoken in modest linguistic areas, such as Dutch, are unlikely to reach international markets, and may be expected to be less sensitive to global market developments and competition than products that travel more easily across linguistic boundaries. The height of entry barriers also differs per industry. Activities such as film production generally require relatively high initial investments whereas the production of paintings often does not.

Differences such as these may influence the degree to which production in a specific cultural industry is place-bound. Some branches of the cultural economy may therefore be less amenable to local policies, or vulnerable to local developments, than others. To gain a fuller understanding of the rootedness of cultural economic activity in particular Dutch cities, the geographical distribution and long-term geographical dynamics of separate cultural industries in the Netherlands will be compared here. This comparison may also contribute to discussions regarding breadth of economically-productive 'creativity', as it will show to what extent, within the Dutch context at least, local creative prowess spills over from one cultural industry to another. If all cultural industries concentrate equally in the same cities, then a general artistic atmosphere is a valuable asset in a city's economy and efforts should be made to enhance such an atmosphere and attract and retain 'creative' people. If, on the other hand, separate industries are distributed differently across cities and display fairly autonomous dynamics, that would indicate that cultural industries thrive on local specialization and on industry-specific practices, expertise and institutions that presumably take time to evolve.

A preliminary categorization of the field of cultural production will guide the following discussion of separate cultural industries. The cultural sector is sometimes divided into three categories: (1) Arts, (2) Media and entertainment, and (3) Creative business services. The first category includes literature, music and the visual and performing arts, the second contains broadcasting, film production, computer games and the publishing industry, while the third category refers to activities that add symbolic or aesthetic value to functional goods and services produced in other industries. Creative business services thus include architecture, advertising, design and fashion. These categories tend to correspond to different types of industry organization and market orientation (Pratt 2004; Bontje and Sleutjes 2007; Stam et al. 2008), a point which will be elaborated in the rest of this section. To these three existing categories, a fourth will be added here to better reflect historical diversity in this long-term overview of the production of cultural commodities. This fourth category, the *creative crafts*, covers industries that involve the manual production or manipulation of aesthetic objects and that have largely disappeared (in their traditional form) as significant sources of employment in the Netherlands.

7 The Creative Crafts: Diamond Cutting, Garment Industry, and Arts and Crafts

The creative crafts include industries such as jewelry making and diamond cutting, watch making, arts and crafts, and the garment industry insofar as it involves manual production and customized tailoring. In most of these industries, traditional forms of manual, short-run (or one-off) production were increasingly replaced by automated, standardized mass-production over the course of the twentieth century. As such they have lost many of their original creative qualities (Cf. Glasmeier 1991, 2000). By and large, craftsmanship is no longer required in these industries' productive processes, and in many cases production has been outsourced to low-wage countries (see for example Rantisi 2004). Consequently, these industries have lost nearly all of their significance for the Dutch economy and hardly retain a presence on Dutch urban labor markets. The aesthetic design of products is now usually separated from their physical production. Through processes of increasing

15 Polycentric Urban Trajectories and Urban Cultural Economy

division of labor, both in the organizational and geographical sense, product design and product realization have become separate tasks, often performed by different firms in different places.

During the first half of the twentieth century, however, these tasks were often still intimately related, which is why creative crafts are considered cultural industries in this overview (see also Scott 2000). An analysis of the spatial patterns of these creative crafts may contribute to more general insights about the geographical dynamics of cultural industries and the factors that support their growth in specific places. Furthermore, some of these industries may have left significant traces on the Dutch cultural economy, by stimulating local design activity for example. They may thus have played important formative roles in present-day cultural industries and may have influenced continuing historical trajectories of the cultural economy in certain cities.

7.1 Garment Industry

The textile industry was one of the main generators of nineteenth-century processes of industrialization and automation, but the manufacturing of clothes long remained a fairly craft-like activity. It often took place in small workshops rather than in large factories. Garments were produced in direct collaboration with retailers in order to cater to the specific demands of individual customers or to be able to respond to the latest fashions (Rantisi 2004; Breward and Gilbert 2008). Until the 1960s, when international competition put increasing pressure on Dutch garment producers, the garment industry formed a large and important sector in the Netherlands. In 1899 it accounted for around seven percent of total non-agrarian employment in the country, and in 1963 still accounted for nearly four percent. As can be seen in Fig. 15.3, the industry was of still greater importance for the Amsterdam economy; up until 1930 the industry was also overrepresented in Rotterdam and The Hague. The industry declined rapidly from the 1960s onwards and around 2000 hardly any meaningful (material) garment production still took place in the Netherlands, apart from small, niche-oriented series (Sanders 2002). An important part of larger-scale garment production in the Netherlands was moved away from major cities long before this time as factory production could easily take place elsewhere in the country where wages were generally lower. Nevertheless, Amsterdam was long able to retain its leading position within the Dutch garment industry, in part thanks to the workshops of Turkish immigrants that employed much informal labor (Raes et al. 2002).

Although the garment industry in Amsterdam still trailed behind its counterparts in The Hague and Utrecht at the turn of the twentieth century, by 1920 the capital city had taken the lead. Afterwards, it never surrendered that position. Jewish tailors fleeing Germany arrived as refugees in Amsterdam in the 1930s and added to the city's already sizeable multitude of garment producers. Partly due to the expertise that these refugees brought with them, the city remained at the heart of the Dutch

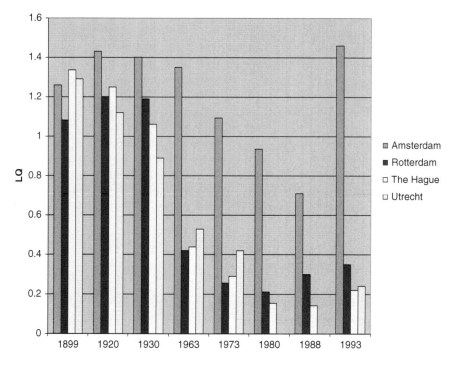

Fig. 15.3 Urban concentrations of employment in garment industry 1899–1993

garment industry during the postwar period. Ultimately, decline caused by a steadily worsening international competitive position could not be averted. Despite this fact, new immigrant groups provided the impulse for a modest revival during the early 1990s. In the meantime, Amsterdam had already become the center of an emerging Dutch fashion industry that focuses almost exclusively on design (Wenting 2008). It seems likely that the well-developed garment industry Amsterdam spurred the emergence of the local fashion industry, as it did in New York (Rantisi 2004).

It also appears that immigrant groups, especially Jewish and Turkish immigrants, played an important role in fueling the growth of this creative craft sector. This would not be the first time. The diamond cutting industry in Amsterdam, that was world famous before World War II, had been originally set up by Jewish immigrants during the eighteenth century. This industry, which incidentally was by far the most geographically concentrated of all cultural industries in the Netherlands (both in 1899 and in 1920 more than 99 % of the approximately 10,000 people employed in the Dutch diamond cutting industry worked in Amsterdam!), remained throughout its history almost exclusively in the hands of the local Jewish community. Sadly, this community was all but wiped out during the Holocaust and the Amsterdam diamond cutting industry was virtually destroyed. At present, a popular museum in Amsterdam devoted to this industry serves as the clearest remaining testimony to the city's century-long global prominence in the diamond trade that ended with World War II.

7.2 Arts and Crafts

Perhaps the purest form of creative craftsmanship could be found in the arts and crafts sector that focused on the (usually manual) production of elaborately adornments for functional objects, as in copper foil glasswork, calligraphy, lace and engraving. Arts and crafts declined quickly during the first decades of the twentieth century and by 1950 they were no longer considered a separate economic category and had ceased to play a significant role within the Dutch economy. Improved automated production of glasswork, table cloths, toys, small statues, musical instruments, and the like, had undermined these manual crafts. The knowledge and skills of craftsmen in this sector, however, were not completely lost. They evolved to form the basis for, on the one hand, specific styles within the visual arts, and on the other, for the commercial activities that today are known collectively as industrial design. In the same way as the garment industry, therefore, the arts and crafts have produced a strong legacy within the field of cultural production. Nowadays, industrial designers such as Marcel Wanders and Hella Jongerius create aesthetically designed functional objects, just like the craftsmen of the past. The great difference, however, lies in the fact that industrial designers usually create only prototypes while their actual products are mechanically (re)produced. Here as well, design and (re)production have become (spatially) separated. Industrial designers today are often employed by large corporations such as Philips (in Eindhoven) or are active in independent design agencies that constitute part of the creative business services sector.

Around 1900, arts and crafts in the Netherlands depended mainly on local markets and on a relatively well-to-do clientele. As such, they concentrated heavily in the major cities. Rotterdam formed an exception to this rule, perhaps because the city was too strongly oriented towards standardized industrial mass-production. In relative terms, Utrecht displayed the strongest concentration of arts and crafts at this time. This was possibly due to the presence of an archbishop's seat in the city and a local demand for catholic imagery. Such church patronage, however, proved insufficient for maintaining this local sector in the long run. In The Hague, the arts and crafts also started off from a strong position at the beginning of the twentieth century but were afterwards partly subsumed by the art world proper as *art nouveau*, which was inspired by the arts and crafts, gained a strong foothold (Cf. Becker 1982). In the visual arts, the 'The Hague School', of which Jan Toorop was the most important representative, formed the leading Dutch exponent of this new international art movement. This collection of painters based in The Hague built on both the local arts and crafts scene and the city's strong position within the Dutch visual arts world (Heij 2004). Amsterdam only became an important center for the Dutch arts and crafts industry during the 1920s when the industry as a whole was already experiencing stagnation and decline in the Netherlands. This temporary upsurge in the country's capital was probably due to the fact that in 1924 two arts and crafts schools in Amsterdam were combined to form the

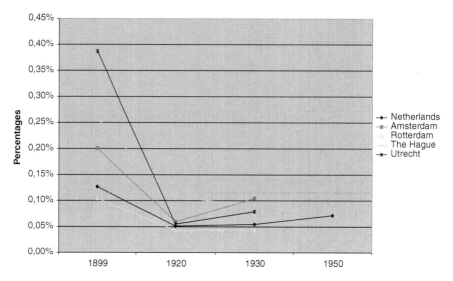

Fig. 15.4 Percentage of active non-agrarian labor force employed in arts and crafts per city

new Institute for Arts and Crafts Education, that would in later years become the prestigious Gerrit Rietveld Academy[1] for art and design (Fig. 15.4).

8 The Arts

The fine arts, meaning the visual arts and literature, together with the performing arts take up a special position within the cultural industries. They are often seen as the 'creative core' of the cultural sector, and considered the most experimental and authentic, as well as the least commercially-oriented, of the cultural industries (Pratt 2004; Throsby 2008). This is why the arts have been extensively subsidized by European national governments following World War II and why they take up a central position in Dutch cultural policy. During the postwar heyday of the Dutch welfare state, state subsidies for the arts were distributed through centrally-led national organizations. Only the theater world in Amsterdam, Rotterdam and The Hague was supported by local governments rather than by the national state. From the 1980s onwards, when neoliberalism gained momentum, national art policies became largely decentralized and market-driven (Department of Education, Culture

---

[1] Gerrit Rietveld (1888–1964) was a Dutch architect and designer linked to the 'De Stijl' art movement that included painter Piet Mondriaan. His experimental furniture designs earned him world-wide acclaim.

and Science 2006). Ever since then, the Dutch art sector has expanded rapidly, where growth in this sector had lagged behind total employment growth between 1930 and 1993. Financial emancipation and commercialization has clearly boosted the arts sector in the Netherlands. The number of persons employed in the arts and art-related activities grew 50 % more rapidly than total employment figures between 1993 and 2005. Despite this recent strong expansion, the arts' share in national non-agrarian employment was still slightly smaller in 2005 than it had been during the first decades of the twentieth century. Apparently, this cultural industry, which lacks easily reproducible products and is therefore prone to the so-called 'Baumol's cost disease' of relatively stagnant labor productivity (Pratt 2004), profited preciously little from strong postwar growth in mass-consumption and from a standardized national system of subsidies.

The arts' expansion over the past two decades has been accompanied by a growing role for Amsterdam. The Dutch world of theater, hardly regarded a true art form before World War II, has traditionally centered on Amsterdam, partly due to the presence there of prestigious theaters and music venues. Amsterdam's domination in this field especially has been retained and strengthened. In general, the arts and related services increasingly agglomerate here. Amsterdam is by far the country's most important center of the art trade and for museums, although further growth in these fields has lagged behind that in the three other cities since 1993. Especially the Utrecht art scene has slowly started to catch up since then. Rotterdam on the other hand was unable during the entire period under study to establish itself as an arts city and has even lost some ground since 1900. More striking than Rotterdam's continuous artistic mediocrity, is the strong decline of The Hague's position within the Dutch art world. The city holds the oldest arts academy in the Netherlands and in 1920 and 1930 The Hague was still the most artistic city of the country. Especially the visual arts flourished there. At the start of the twenty-first century, however, little more than half of this strong degree of arts concentration is left. The art scene in The Hague has not managed to profit from the recent commercialization of the arts sector, perhaps due to a slightly elitist mentality. Nevertheless, the city remains an important arts center and, just as in Amsterdam, artists on average earn more in The Hague than elsewhere in the country (Rengers 2002). Overall, it appears that the arts in particular, the most central core of cultural production, display high degrees of geographical concentration and are bound to specific cities on a long-term basis (Fig. 15.5).

9 Media and Entertainment

The media sector has certain characteristics that distinguish it from other cultural industries and from the arts especially. In the media sector, for example, production and consumption do not necessarily occur simultaneously and within the same

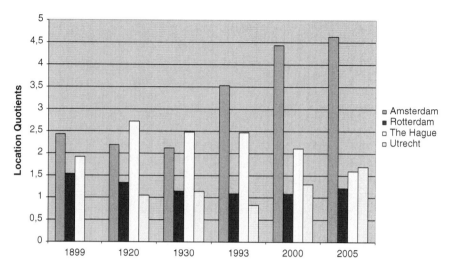

Fig. 15.5 Urban concentrations of employment in the arts and art venues

venue as is the case with the performing arts. Broadcasters and publishers more easily attain a national or even international market reach so that competition more often takes place on an extra-local level. Not only is their geographical market reach relatively wide, media also cater to all layers of society whereas the arts only rarely manage to do so. This favors a relatively business-like, rather than predominantly artistic attitude. Furthermore, the production processes of media companies often require large-scale investments, and the extensive use of technologies in this sector has made it sensitive to technological changes. These characteristics taken together have assured that in the course of the twentieth century the media sector has grown expansively and has become increasingly concentrated, now largely dominated by a limited number of large organizations on which many smaller specialized firms are dependent.

9.1 Broadcasting

Unlike most cultural industries in the Netherlands, broadcasters have historically been subject to extensive state regulation. After a short period of private experiments, several public radio stations developed around a Philips transmitter factory in the small town of Hilversum during the 1920s. While the first regular radio-broadcasting station in the world was operated by an engineer from a house in The Hague (Scientific Council for Government Policy 2006; see also Van der Groep 2008), the economies of scale created by the Philips-backed factory in Hilversum enabled cost cuts that allowed broadcasting companies there to survive, unlike the station of the

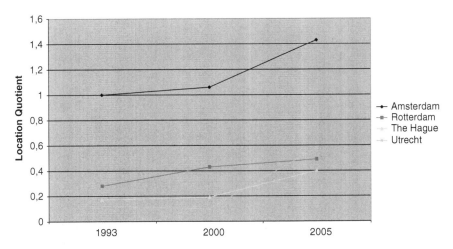

Fig. 15.6 Cities reinforcing their position in broadcasting employment

pioneer in The Hague that had to discontinue its broadcasts in 1924 for lack of funds. Because of their political significance and the influence of radio and television on public opinion, broadcasters were strictly regulated to conform to a Dutch political system that was strictly 'pillarized' (up until the 1960s) and divided according to the different *weltanschauungen* prevalent in Dutch society. Commercial stations were outlawed until the late 1980s and the state determined that all public broadcasters had to be based in Hilversum so that economies of scale would limit costs. Because of this history, at present 71 % of all people employed in broadcasting in the Netherlands work in Hilversum (Bontje and Sleutjes 2007: 66). The broadcasting industry now employs over 11,000 people and has become exceptionally rooted in a minor city due to (former) conditions of production and a long period of strict regulation.

Ever since government media policies have been liberalized and technological breakthroughs in telecommunication have lowered the costs of broadcasting, Amsterdam has been on the advance in this industry. At the start of the 1990s Amsterdam already possessed many film- and video-production companies as well as many advertising agencies, and these seem to have created a welcoming climate for new broadcasting companies setting up in Amsterdam (Kloosterman 2004). In fact, all four major cities have strengthened their positions in the broadcasting industry over the past 15 years, although Rotterdam, The Hague and Utrecht have not yet come close to challenging Amsterdam in this regard. The industry appears to be growing especially rapidly in Utrecht, a city in which also the film- and video-production industry is doing well. This confirms the impression engendered by the developments in Amsterdam that these related, but nominally separate cultural industries benefit strongly from each others presence in a city (Fig. 15.6).

9.2 Publishing

The age-old societal position and strength of the publishing industry in the Netherlands precluded the kind of twentieth-century regulation that newer broadcasting media were subject to. Already in the seventeenth century, Amsterdam was one of the hotspots of European book production and a cradle of journalism and the newspaper press. During the twentieth century, the city remained at the heart of the printed word in the Netherlands, although it faced stiff competition from especially The Hague for a long time. The graphic sector, including both publishing and printing companies, grew steadily until the turn of the millennium and more than kept up with general employment growth. Publishers, rather than printers, accounted for more than the lion's share of this increase. The number of people acting as publishers or working for publishing companies rose from 567 around 1900–37,500 a century later. This amounts to an increase of no less than 6,600 %, which is 12 times as high as the total growth of employment in the Netherlands over the twentieth century. This tremendous growth was mainly the result of skyrocketing demand for published works among a Dutch population that became ever better educated and richer. While the fortunes of publishers rose spectacularly, employment in printing firms stagnated and dropped due to increasing mechanization. A stricter division of labor emerged between publishers and printers. Competition between cities for production of the printed word thus revolved more around the establishment or expansion of publishing companies than around printers. During the first half of the twentieth century, The Hague slightly outperformed Amsterdam in this respect, although Amsterdam always housed more publishers in terms of absolute numbers. The Hague's prowess in this industry was due in part to the strong concentration of literary authors there and partly due to the city's publishers of legal works and official state documents. Throughout this time, Amsterdam did remain the unchallenged center of the Dutch newspaper press and of journalism.

In the 1930s, Amsterdam as well as The Hague attracted so-called *Exil* publishers: Jews and socialists fleeing Nazi Germany. In Amsterdam, this influx contributed to the development of academic publishers and the publishing of international academic books and journals. In the postwar period Amsterdam became a global leader in this field as the company Elsevier became the largest publisher of academic work in the world. Amsterdam publishers also started to outperform their colleagues in The Hague in the fields of fiction and literature, probably responding to the trend that saw authors and poets along with other artists move to Amsterdam (as described above) – although it is difficult to distinguish cause and effect in this case. Amsterdam was also the city where during the second half of the century the country's most important training facilities for publishers were established (the Frederik Muller Academy, founded in Amsterdam in the 1960s, was even the first academy for publishers in the world) and around the year 2000 some organizations related to the book trade moved their headquarters from The Hague to the capital (Deinema 2008). For these reasons among others, Amsterdam was elected UNESCO World Book Capital for the year 2008 (Fig. 15.7).

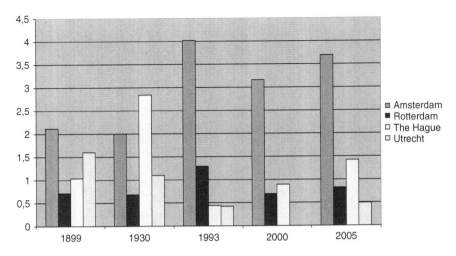

Fig. 15.7 Location quotients of major Dutch cities in publishing industry, 1899–2005

10 Creative Business Services

The professionalization of creative business services, by architects, fashion designers and advertising agencies, is mostly a twentieth-century phenomenon. Many of the services rendered by these professions were originally tasks performed by craftsmen or firms that produced the designed or advertised goods and services themselves. It was only over the course of the twentieth century that Dutch firms increasingly turned to external experts to fulfill these functions. Creative business services therefore generally cannot bow on such eminent long histories as some other cultural industries and cannot look back on centuries-long trajectories of development in specific cities, although they may have emerged from older established local industries. Consequently, creative business services achieved tempestuous growth rates with employment for architectural and technical design agencies increasing 20-fold since 1930 while employment in the advertising industry has multiplied by a factor 30 since that same year.

10.1 Architecture

Until several years ago, The Hague possessed the highest concentration of architects in the Netherlands. Amsterdam always trailed behind the court city in this respect and has even experienced a relative slump during the past 15 years. This mediocre performance comes in spite of the fact that the capital city was once a hotbed of architectural creativity; in the 1920s and 1930s 'Amsterdam School' architects were heralded internationally as innovators of architecture and urban

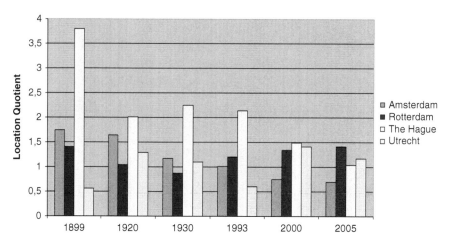

Fig. 15.8 Urban concentrations of employment in architectural and technical design 1899–2005

planning. The architectural sector in The Hague long benefited from a rich and elite local clientele and from commissions for public projects of great prestige such as new national government buildings. Presently, however, The Hague plays a much more modest role within the Dutch architectural scene. Since the 1990s, it has become an international trend that prestigious iconic projects are designed by global 'starchitects'. This trend robbed architects in The Hague of their formerly privileged position, but has stimulated the exponential growth of a new architecture cluster in Rotterdam containing globally renowned agencies such as Erick van Egeraat, MVRDV and Rem Koolhaas' OMA.

The growth of the number of architects in Rotterdam, their successes, and the emergence of related activities in the city such as two publishers (NAi and 010) that specialize in books on architecture for a global market, is the result of a fortunate coincidence. At the start of the 1980s, the national government sought to strengthen the city's cultural infrastructure by establishing the new National Architecture Institute and the (also architecture-related) Berlage Institute there. Almost simultaneously, the Dutch (but England-based) architect Rem Koolhaas, who had become well-known in international architectural circles with the publication of his influential book 'Delirious New York' in 1978, moved to Rotterdam in 1981 because he had just received several commissions in the Netherlands and was attracted to Rotterdam's cheap office space and 'empty' cultural environment (Kloosterman 2008). Partly due to Koolhaas, the Dutch architectural scene was reinvigorated and gained a strong international orientation. A local institutional infrastructure of specialized training facilities, funding agencies, meeting places, and publishers, combined with the charisma and international appeal of Koolhaas, spurred the emergence of an internationally competitive architectural cluster in Rotterdam. OMA still functions as an important breeding ground for architectural talent, with young Dutch and foreign designers gaining experience there for several years before starting their own independent agencies, often in Rotterdam (Fig. 15.8).

10.2 Advertising

While architectural design activities in the Netherlands are currently concentrated mainly in Rotterdam, advertising agencies generally prefer Amsterdam as their base of operations. This was already the case in 1930 and remains so today. The advertising industry is 2,5 times as important to Amsterdam's local labor market as it is on average in the country as a whole. Interestingly, Turkish immigrants have started to enter the advertising industry in Amsterdam and have contributed to its growth and diversity. The capital's advertising agencies are also held in high international regard and produce global advertising campaigns for large multinational companies. Generally speaking, however, the industry's focus is still largely confined to the national market and, during the first half of the twentieth century, even revolved mostly around local markets. This explains why Rotterdam and The Hague –together with Amsterdam the most sizeable and well-developed consumer markets in the Netherlands – still accounted for a substantial share of Dutch commercial advertising activity in 1930. Since then the industry has devolved and has become more spread out throughout the country. During the intervening period, consumer markets outside of the four major cities have grown and developed to a great extent. The devolution of an important share of advertising activity away from the major urban center has been further enabled by the increased market reach of advertising agencies that no longer need to be located in the same locality as their main customers, and can now cater to the national market as a whole rather than just to their own local market (Cf. Lambregts et al. 2005; Lambregts 2008). However, the fact that this market reach has expanded has had yet another effect. It made inter-urban competition possible in this industry, allowing Amsterdam's advertising industry to outcompete its smaller and less-developed counterparts in Rotterdam and The Hague even in their own local markets. Therefore, while the share of the four cities in the industry nationally has decreased, advertising in Amsterdam has become more important relative to that in Rotterdam and The Hague.

The ability of advertisers to reach large audiences, either locally or nationally, is partly dependent on collaborations with the media sector. Indeed, specialists in advertising can hardly do without a strong sense of media-affinity. As Amsterdam has traditionally formed the heart of the national daily press (and has recently attained a fairly strong position in broadcasting and film- and video-production as well) it is not surprising that the capital's advertising agencies have managed to hold on to their dominant position. The benefits of this relationship have been mutual, as advertisements are an important source of revenue for media-companies. A similar symbiosis has occurred in Utrecht. In that city, the rising fortunes of the advertising industry and of the broadcasting industry have gone hand in hand. Over recent years, both sectors grew in Utrecht to a similar extent (Fig. 15.9).

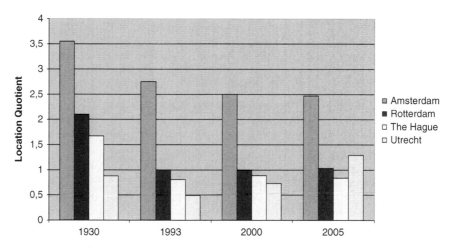

Fig. 15.9 Urban concentrations of employment in advertising industry 1930 and 1993–2005

11 The Four Cities Considered Separately

Although different types of producers in many Dutch cities play a role in the Dutch world of cultural industries, this historical survey has shown that, in the twentieth century at least, this type of activity has been a predominantly metropolitan affair. To the local economies of the major urban regions these industries have proven to be of greater importance than to the country as a whole. This seems to be especially true as this survey has focused almost exclusively on the primary producers of cultural goods and services. Derivative forms of economic activity, such as specialized art shops, employment agencies for designers, and all sorts of suppliers, are probably concentrated in the major cities as well. What has become equally clear is that Amsterdam, Rotterdam, The Hague and Utrecht differ to a significant extent in their ability -both past and present- to sustain specific cultural industries and have them flourish. Apart from specific local environments that nourish particular types of cultural enterprises, the ability of a city to attract talent from afar also appears to be of the utmost importance. While the different industries examined all display their own spatial dynamic, within cities they may also be interconnected. Furthermore, there may be a relation with the city's attractiveness to a broadly-defined 'creative class'. Not only artistic types are counted among this class but also a large proportion of the highly-educated population, including academics, managers and lawyers (Florida 2002). It is due to these possible relations with the wider urban context that the four main Dutch cities will each be treated separately now.

11.1 Utrecht

Unfortunately reliable data are not available for all cultural industries in Utrecht, the city that during the twentieth century grew the fastest of the main four in terms of its population and employment figures. The information that has been uncovered points to a difficult trajectory throughout the century, with, for example, a strong decline of the graphic sector and publishing industry. However, at the start of the twenty-first century, Utrecht has attained a strong position in the realms of advertising, architecture, the arts and broadcasting. Some of these reinforce each other through symbiotic connections. And in the case of broadcasting, Utrecht has perhaps profited – in the same way as Amsterdam – from its proximity to Hilversum.

Which conditions have enabled this upward march? Well, to start, Utrecht has finally attained a metropolitan character. Whereas around 1900 the city's number of inhabitants was less than a fifth of Amsterdam's (and a third of Rotterdam's), today Utrecht has grown to almost half of Amsterdam's size. Perhaps a more important advantage lies in the fact that Utrecht's university is the largest of the country. Its students refresh the city's population every year and form a large supply of highly-educated consumers, employees and entrepreneurs. The share of the creative class in the local labor market is higher here than in any other town or city in the Netherlands, and this has been the case since at least 1995 (Marlet and Van Woerkens 2007). These highly-educated inhabitants create greater demand for the arts as well as an atmosphere in which creative endeavors flourish. It cannot be a coincidence that the IT sector in Utrecht is almost as big as that in Amsterdam, twice as big as in Rotterdam, and four times the size of the sector in The Hague.[2] In an era in which production as well as distribution in cultural industries is increasingly digitized, a strong local specialization in IT can be very useful to a city's cultural entrepreneurs.

11.2 The Hague

After 1930, and especially during the last decades of the twentieth century, The Hague's share of Dutch cultural production has gone through an extended period of steady decline. While this city, which houses the royal court and holds the seat of government, formed an important centre for the arts, architecture and the printed word in the past, it seems now to have become a mediocre player in these fields – despite the fact that its publishing scene has exhibited a minor revival over recent years. The city may have a rich tradition in cultural industries, it has lost its grip on this sector. The art world in The Hague has been bled dry partly by Amsterdam's even greater power of attraction on artists. But one specific weakness in The Hague's own cultural tradition has rendered it especially vulnerable to stagnation: its cultural producers specialized historically in catering to the elites. In the past

---

[2] Data taken from www.statline.nl, the website of the Dutch Central Bureau of Statistics.

the city owed its position as prominent centre for the arts and architecture to the presence of a rich, partly aristocratic, clientele, and to the patronage of the national government.

The Hague's printers serviced the national government by printing official documents, while its publishers published the country's jurisprudence. Local architects designed the state buildings and foreign embassies in the city, and the many fine artists in The Hague appealed mainly to distinctly elite tastes. But cultural production aimed mainly at state commissions and a rich upper class has proven partly unsustainable in this case. When the consumption of culture – especially of the written word – became largely democratized after World War II, and the state started to liberalize after 1980, The Hague's traditions impeded the shift in focus required to take advantage of these developments. The contrast between the traditions of cultural production in The Hague and Amsterdam are telling in this respect. While The Hague has historically produced many prominent painters, such as Jan Toorop, Hendrik Mesdag and Isaac Israels who together formed the 'The Hague School', Amsterdam has always been the country's theatre Mecca. Although the latter cultural form was hardly counted among the arts prior to World War II, it drew larger audiences, and was more strongly bound to specific places and venues than the highly-mobile and lightly-packed visual artists were.

Besides the strong orientation on a (relatively small) elite consumer base, another factor may account for the declining trend that has threatened to eliminate, over the last 20 years especially, The Hague's prominence in cultural industries. As the sole exception among the four main cities, The Hague lacks a university. It therefore cannot boast a large group of young and highly-educated consumers with a penchant for innovative cultural forms. Despite the cultural heritage of the city, and the fact that The Hague remains the Netherlands' political centre, the share of the creative class in its population hardly exceeds the national average (Marlet and Van Woerkens 2007). Apparently, this exerts a fairly strong negative influence on The Hague's cultural industries.

11.3   Rotterdam

Throughout the twentieth century Rotterdam lagged behind when it came to cultural production. It is bound by an industrial character which underrates adornment and the arts, and places a premium on functionality. Nevertheless, Rotterdam's skyline forms the clearest indication that the city hardly lacks aesthetics or a sense of symbolism. Its lively architectural scene, shows clearly how a local cultural industry may emerge. A combination of physical emptiness (a result of World War II bombing raids on the city), an institutional infrastructure for architectural design that was partly planned and created by the national government, and the fairly incidental arrival of a practitioner of Rem Koolhaas' prominence, has resulted in an internationally renowned cluster.

It remains to be seen if these successes in the field of architecture will form the prelude to Rotterdam's advance along a broader cultural front. The architectural profession requires formal training and its designs can only be realized through large pecuniary investments. Barriers to entering the ranks of either producers or (formal) consumers of architecture are therefore quite high, limiting the prospects for easy spillover of the architects' skills. However, the architects beautify their own city as well which can create strong aesthetic impulses for Rotterdam's inhabitants. Furthermore, the architectural cluster may expand into several related cultural fields such as interior design, installation art and perhaps computer art as well as the use of digital design programming is widespread among architects.

11.4 Amsterdam

Without any doubt, Amsterdam should be seen as the Netherlands' cultural capital (Kloosterman 2004; Marlet and Van Woerkens 2004). Direct interaction between specific cultural industries and a general artistic atmosphere has turned the city into a source and catalyst of creativity, as well as a magnet for Dutch and foreign talent. Not only tourists are attracted to the countless cultural amenities in Amsterdam; it has been demonstrated, for example, that the city's theatre scene has a significant positive effect on Amsterdam's desirability as place of residence. No other city holds such appeal to people seeking to relocate within the Netherlands. This appeal has naturally led to an expansion of Amsterdam's already sizeable creative class that is the country's largest in absolute terms and third largest (After Utrecht and Delft) when considered as a percentage of the total local population (Marlet and Van Woerkens 2007: 14, 232 and 235). Several factors are at the root of this cultural prowess. The specific local trajectories of particular cultural industries have played a role in this respect, but so has the great degree of local tolerance shown historically toward immigrant groups. According to the local press, Amsterdam houses more different nationalities (177) than any other city in the world (*Trouw* 2007). In the same way that Jews built up Amsterdam's diamond industry, and Jewish refugees provided new impulses to the city's clothing and publishing industry[3] during the 1930s, so can other groups of newcomers play a decisive and innovative role in Amsterdam's present or future cultural industries.

The industries that are presently flourishing in the country's capital, did not all develop in the same way, nor did they all arise at the same time. Amsterdam's fashion design industry, for example, should be seen as a legacy of the old local clothing industry that has all but withered away. The internationally successful academic publishers operating out of Amsterdam have likewise profited from the institutional infrastructures and reputation that they inherited from their seventeenth century predecessors who had made the city into the early-modern 'bookstore of the world'

---

[3] In early modern times, Protestant refugees from Flanders and France similarly invigorated Amsterdam's publishing industry and book trade.

(Berkvens-Stevelinck et al. 1992; Deinema 2008). Combined with the impulses delivered by their colleagues who fled to Amsterdam from Nazi Germany, these legacies gave the city's publishers a strong head start in the newly emerging market for international academic journals. The plethora of visual artists and galleries also attests to the lingering effects of Amsterdam's early modern position as one of Europe's main centers for arts and culture. The city's theatre scene, on the other hand, is more likely to have originated in a similarly enduring aspect of Amsterdam's distinct traditions and local atmosphere. The same taste for frivolous entertainment that during the second half of the twentieth century produced the infamous Red Light District and coffeeshops that have come to symbolize the city, probably found its expression in the city's many theatre halls and performance venues during the first half of the century.

Amsterdam's early lead in the newer advertising industry was probably spurred by the size of its local consumer market, as well as by its well-developed printed media sector. The recent expansion of the broadcasting industry in Amsterdam is strengthened in turn by the city's advertising agencies. These rising fortunes can also be attributed in part to the concentration of film and video producers in the city that has developed around the national film academy. In general, most cultural industries in Amsterdam continually benefit from the city's two universities, its vocational colleges, art-related academies (including, among others, an Art and Design Academy, Theater School, Music Conservatory, and Multimedia College), and its many other training and knowledge facilities. Not only do these produce highly-skilled entrepreneurs and specialized labor pools in the city that enhance the industries' performance, they also serve to attract, retain and create a wide base of local consumers with a general taste for culture.

The symbiotic effects of all these industries, and the stimulants and incentives provided by the presence of such a wide range of culturally-engaged or culturally-interested inhabitants, appear to be so strong that rapid and ongoing processes of gentrification have not yet repelled artists and small entrepreneurs in the cultural sector. However, gentrification does represent a danger to this sector. In cities such as New York, for example, this process of city upgrading has often led to the displacement of artists from central city areas or from the city altogether (Ley 2003: 2540). While Amsterdam's cultural scenes have clearly contributed to its gentrification, the rising land rents associated with this process may eventually start to take their toll on the city's cultural industries. These threaten to undermine the ability of young artists and artistic start-ups in precarious financial situations to maintain a base in Amsterdam. Local authorities are well aware of the detrimental effect that such an artistic exodus could have on the city's economy and attractiveness. In order to assure the sustainability of Amsterdam's vibrant cultural atmosphere, and the ability of local enterprises to produce experimental and innovative, the city government has put in place a 'breeding place' program that aims to provide artists and new cultural enterprises with access to affordable workspace. However much the success of cultural industries in a city is affected by intangible local assets such as an artistic atmosphere, traditions, reputation and heritage, programs of this type recognize that material and economic preconditions are equally essential.

12 Conclusions and Discussion

The cultural industries in the Netherlands have obviously gained in economic importance since 1900 (especially since 1980, see Fig. 15.1a, b and c), and there seems to be a correspondence between the Dutch cities that are currently doing well in cultural industries and those in which cosmopolitan political attitudes are prevalent. Amsterdam is clearly the country's cultural capital and the champion among Dutch cities when it comes to prowess in the cultural industries, and Utrecht, another city that is counted among the winners of globalization, is steadily expanding its base of cultural production. Rotterdam, on the other hand, the city that has been at the heart of recent political polarization in the Netherlands, trails behind these cities where the cultural sector as a whole is concerned although it has achieved significant successes in the field of architectural design. And The Hague, while it remains a relatively important cultural center, has seen its fortunes decline rapidly across a gamut of cultural industries over the last few decades. Obviously, the process of globalization has hurt the cultural sector in The Hague, a development that reveals, just as growing social tensions in that city do, a mismatch between conditions in The Hague and the demands of a globalizing economy.

Although there appears to be a connection between the fortunes of these city's cultural industries and their present political orientation, the causal relations between these phenomena remain unclear. Do successful cultural industries make cities more socially and politically stable under present conditions or is success in cultural industries a manifestation of a city's cosmopolitanism? Answering this question has remained outside of the scope of this survey of cultural industries in the Netherlands, as it requires far more in-depth qualitative research into the workings of the cultural sector and its relations to specific urban social conditions. However, the emergence of a successful architecture cluster in Rotterdam and the growth of a broadcasting media cluster in the small town of Hilversum in any case suggest that cosmopolitanism of a place is not in every case a necessary precondition to the successful development of a local cultural industry.

The data presented reveal fairly strong historical continuities in the distribution of cultural industries activities among the four cities. It therefore seems that important local assets and infrastructures that support cultural production in a city are histori- cally formed. Such assets may therefore be difficult to create. This survey has also shown that cultural industries often thrive on industry-specific local specialization as the geographical distribution of different industries has followed different historical trajectories. In some cases, such as in the garment industry, the publishing industry and in advertising, immigrant groups have contributed significantly to local cultural industries providing innovative inputs. This confirms claims of the sector's openness to migrant entreprencurship. However, it seems that successes of migrants in the cultural sector in the Netherlands were achieved in the twentieth mainly when they were absorbed into specific, already well-functioning and sizeable, local cultural industries. The inclusion into existing local industry infrastructures seems to have been more prevalent than the creation of new local clusters by migrants.

Local specialization is thus important to particular cultural industries, but evidence has also been presented of symbiotic relations between some different forms of local cultural production. In some cases, successes in one cultural industry have stimulated, or gone hand in hand, with successes in another. The local fortunes of the advertising industry, for example, seem to be connected to that of the local media sector, and vice versa. The implied interdependence of some cultural industries on the one hand makes the dynamics of cultural industries more complex and 'intimidating' for policymakers and academics and begs the question: which industry stimulates which? If several industries form a large complex production system or 'ecology' and seem unable to thrive without one another, the problem of endogeneity presents itself. If one seeks to stimulate these industries, where should one start, with the proverbial chicken or with the egg? On the other hand, symbiotic relations between different industries imply potentially positive 'multiplier effects' to successful targeted interventions. The (albeit bounded) transferability of expertise, creativity, and success across (some) cultural industries also enables a dynamism in this sector that suggests that the 'cultural fortunes' of cities may shift, as cross-fertilization often produces innovations and new possibilities. New opportunities may develop at the intersections of different cultural fields, where new niches may emerge that require their own new institutions that are not yet rooted in a particular city.

It seems that especially with the development of local knowledge infrastructures, government intervention may influence the geographical dynamic of cultural industries. The presence of large universities has a seemingly positive effect on cultural industries in Amsterdam and Utrecht, while the lack thereof has handicapped The Hague's cultural sector. In two instances, government intervention has clearly played a role in the creation of a local cluster, shaping the further trajectory of a specific cultural industry. In Rotterdam, the establishment of institutions specialized in architecture have been instrumental in spurring the growth of Rotterdam's architecture industry, although it seems unlike that they would have had the same positive effect without the fortuitous arrival of Rem Koolhaas in the city. In the other case, that of the broadcasting cluster in Hilversum, strict long-term regulation and the restriction of broadcasting activities elsewhere assured that this cultural industry became rooted in a small town. It remains to be seen, however, if Hilversum can long retain its enviable position now that broadcasting has been liberalized and the major cities are already showing signs of strong growth in this industry. Despite the differences between architectural design and broadcasting they share a characteristic that perhaps makes their geographical distribution more amenable to policy manipulation than is the case in other cultural industries. Broadcasting and architectural design are both high-cost industries. In broadcasting costs are relatively high on the supply side. In architecture costs are relatively high on the demand side, so that architects are dependent on large commissions. Large organizations such as the state

15 Polycentric Urban Trajectories and Urban Cultural Economy

may therefore exert more influence on these industries than on video-production for example, either as supply-side investors, or as commissioning customers.

Increasingly, however, cultural industries depend on the breadth, rather than the wealth, of their consumer base. As the decline of The Hague's position within Dutch cultural production shows, complacency and elitism do not help local cultural industries. An elitist orientation of cultural producers may have provided a powerful stimulus to cultural industries in the past, but sustained economic growth in the Netherlands over the twentieth century has democratized cultural consumption. Demand for cultural products is income elastic, as these products do not belong to the prime necessities of life. Rising general incomes may quickly increase the cultural industries' potential pool of consumers, including poorer immigrant groups. The continued importance of elitist cultural centers is thus not assured and this may hold powerful implications for the future development of the cultural sector in rapidly growing, emerging economies like Brazil, as well as for the shape that the international distribution of cultural products industries may assume over the course of the twenty-first century.

References

Airports Council International (2008) http://www.aci-africa.aero/cda/aci_common/display/main/aci_content07_banners.jsp?zn=aci&cp=1_725_2__

Amin A, Thrift N (1995) Globalisation, institutional "thickness" and the local economy. In: Healey P et al (eds) Managing cities the new urban context. Wiley, Chichester, pp 91–109

Becker HS (1982) Art worlds. University of California Press, Berkeley

Berkvens-Stevelinck C, Bots H, Hoftijzer PG, Lankhorst OS (eds) (1992) Le Magasin de l'Univers, the Dutch Republic as the Centre of the European Book trade. E.J Brill, Leiden

Bontje M, en Sleutjes B (2007) Amsterdam: history meets modernity. Pathways to creative and knowledge-based regions (ACRE report 2.1). Amsterdam, s.n

Bremner C (2007) Top 150 city destinations: London leads the way. http://www.euromonitor.com/Top_150_City_Destinations_London_Leads_the_Way. Consulted 11 Aug 2009

Breward C, Gilbert D (2008) Anticipations of the new urban cultural economy: fashion and the transformation of London's west end, 1955–1975. In: Hessler M, Zimmermann C (eds) Creative urban milieus: historical perspectives on culture, economy, and the city. Campus Verlag, Frankfurt/New York, pp 159–178

CBS (2007) Statistisch Jaarboek 2007. CBS, Voorburg/Heerlen

Deinema M (2008) Amsterdam's re-emergence as a major publishing hub in a changing international context. Paper presented at the IXth international conference of the European Association for Urban History, Lyon, 29 Aug 2008

Department of Education, Culture and Science (2006) Cultural policy in the Netherlands, 2006 edn. Ministerie van OCW/Boekmanstudies, Den Haag/Amsterdam

Engelen E, Grote MH (2009) Stock exchange virtualisation and the decline of second-tier financial centres – the cases of Amsterdam and Frankfurt. J Econ Geogr, pp 1–18 (Advanced Access published online 10 June 2009)

Entzinger H (2003) The rise and fall of multiculturalism: the case of the Netherlands. In: Joppke C, Morawska E (eds) Toward assimilation and citizenship. Palgrave-Macmillan, Basingstoke

Florida R (2002) The rise of the creative class: and how it's transforming work, leisure, community and everyday life. Basic Books, New York

Glasmeier A (1991) Technological discontinuities and flexible production networks: the case of Switzerland and the world watch industry. Res Policy 20:469–485

Glasmeier A (2000) Manufacturing time: global competition in the watch industry, 1795–2000. Guildford Press, New York

Grabher G (2001) Ecologies of creativity: the village, the group, and the heterarchic organization of the British advertising industry. Environ Plann A 33:351–374

Hall P (1998) Cities and civilization. Pantheon Books, New York

Heij JJ (2004) Vernieuwing en Bezinning: Nederlandse Beeldende Kunst en Kunstnijverheid ca. 1885–1935 uit de Collectie van het Drents Museum. Waanders, Zwolle

Hoyler M, Kloosterman RC, Sokol M (2008) Polycentric puzzles – emerging mega-city regions seen through the lens of advanced producer services. Reg Stud 42(8):1055–1064

Kloosterman RC (2004) Recent employment trends in the cultural industries in Amsterdam, Rotterdam, The Hague and Utrecht: a first exploration. Tijdschrift voor Economische en Sociale Geografie 95(2):243–252

Kloosterman RC (2008) Walls and bridges: knowledge spillovers between 'superdutch' architectural firms. J Econ Geogr 8(4):545–563

Kloosterman RC, Stegmeijer E (2005) Delirious Rotterdam: the formation of an innovative cluster of architectural firms. In: Boschma RA, Kloosterman RC (eds) Learning from clusters; a critical assessment from an economic-geographical perspective. Springer, Berlin, pp 203–224

Lambregts B (2008) Geographies of knowledge formation in mega-city regions: some evidence from the Dutch Randstad. Reg Stud 42(8):1173–1186

Lambregts B, Röling R, van der Werff M (2005) De stad als décor voor kennisontwikkeling in de zakelijke dienstverlening, Agora, no 3, pp 24–27

Lampel J, Shamsie J (2006) Uncertain globalization: evolutionary scenarios for the future development of cultural industries. In: Lampel J, Shamsie J, Kant TK (eds) The business of culture: strategic perspectives on entertainment and media. Lawrence Erlbaum, Mahwah/New York

Landry C (2000) The creative city: a toolkit for urban innovators. Earthscan, London

Lash S, Urry J (1994) Economies of signs and space. Sage, London

Ley D (2003) Artists, aestheticisation and the field of gentrification. Urban Stud 40(12):2527–2544

Markusen A (2006) Urban development and the politics of a creative class: evidence from a study of artists. Environ Plann A 38:1921–1940

Marlet G, en van Woerkens C (2004) Atlas voor Nederlandse gemeenten. Stichting Atlas voor gemeenten, Utrecht

Marlet G, en van Woerkens C (2007) Atlas voor Nederlandse gemeenten. Stichting Atlas voor gemeenten, Utrecht

Martin R, Sunley P (2003) Deconstructing clusters: chaotic concept or policy panacea? J Econ Geogr 3:5–35

NRC (2006) Den Haag: een stad van extremen, 12 Jan 2006

Peck J (2005) Struggling with the creative class. Int J Urban Reg Res 29(4):740–770

Pratt A (2004) Creative clusters: towards the governance of the creative industries production system? Med Int Aust 112:50–66

Pratt A (2008) Creative cities: the cultural industries and the creative class. Geografiska Annal Ser B Hum Geogr 90(2):107–117

Raes S, Rath J, Dreef M, Kumcu A, Reil F, Zorlu A (2002) Amsterdam: stitched up. In: Rath J (ed) Unravelling the rag trade: immigrant entrepreneurship in seven world cities. Berg, Oxford, pp 89–112

Rantisi N (2004) The ascendance of New York fashion. Int J Urban Reg Res 28(1):86–106

Rengers M (2002) Economic lives of artists. Studies into careers and the labour market in the cultural sector. s.n, Utrecht

Sanders E (2002) Nederlandse haute couture, couture en prêt-à-porter in Amsterdam: culturele economie en concurrentie. Master's thesis, Department of Geography and Planning, University of Amsterdam

Sassen S (1991) The global city: New York, London, Tokyo. Princeton University Press, Princeton

Saxenian A (1994) Regional advantage, culture and competition in Silicon Valley and Route 128. Harvard University Press, Cambridge, MA

Scheffer P (2007) Het Land van Aankomst. Bezige Bij, Amsterdam

Scientific Council for Government Policy (2006) Media policy for the digital age. Amsterdam University Press, Amsterdam

Scott A (1998) Regions and the world economy: the coming shape of global production, competition, and political order. Oxford University Press, Oxford

Scott AJ (2000) The cultural economy of cities; essays on the geography of image-producing industries. Sage, London/Thousand Oaks/New Delhi

Scott A (2005) On Hollywood: the Place, the Industry. Princeton University Press, Princeton

Scott AJ (2007) Capitalism and urbanization in a new key? The cognitive-cultural dimension. Soc Forces 85(4):1465–1482

Stam E, de Jong JPJ, Marlet G (2008) Creative industries in the Netherlands: structure, development, innovativeness and effects on urban growth. Geografiska Annal Ser B Hum Geogr 90(2):119–132

Taylor PJ (2005) Leading world cities: empirical evaluations of urban nodes in multiple networks. Urban Stud 42(9):1593–1608

Throsby D (2008) Modelling the cultural industries. Int J Cult Pol 14(3):217–232

Trouw (2007) Amsterdam stad met meeste nationaliteiten (177) ter wereld, 22 augustus 2007

Trouw (2009) PVV en D66 verscheuren Randstad, 6 Jun 2009

Van der Groep R (2008) L'audiovisuel aux Pays-Bas, trajectories divergentes et flexibilité. In: Leriche F, Daviet S, Sibertin-Blanc M, en Zuliani J-M (red) Les industries culturelles et ses territoires. Presses Universitaires du Mirail, Toulouse, pp 159–172

van Zanden JL (1997) Een klein land in de 20e eeuw: economische geschiedenis van Nederland 1914–1995. Het Spectrum, Utrecht

Volkskrant (2008) Dicht de kloof met de verliezers, 28 Oct 2008

Volkskrant (2009) Wilders wint dankzij PvdA en VVD, 6 April 2009

Wenting R (2008) Spinoff dynamics and the spatial formation of the fashion design industry, 1858–2005. J Econ Geogr 8:593–614

Zukin S (1995) The cultures of cities. Blackwell, Chichester

Chapter 16
Analysing the Competitive Advantage of Cities in the Dutch Randstad by Urban Market Overlap

Martijn J. Burger, Frank G. van Oort, Ronald S. Wall, and Mark J.P.M. Thissen

Abstract In the modern economy, cities are assumed to be in fierce competition. In contrast with this, regional and national Dutch policymakers advocate the Randstad region as a single urban region in which economic complementarities are supposed to be numerous. Using insights from urban systems theory and urban ecology, we introduce an indicator to estimate the degree of revealed competition between cities based on patterns of inter-firm relations between these cities. Results indicate that urban competition is more the rule than the much-anticipated urban complementarities, as urban functional influences of the Randstad cities spatially overlap.

Keywords Urban competition • Urban complementarities • Randstad Holland

1 Introduction

At the present day and age, it has become widely acknowledged in urban studies and the planning literature that cities compete over product markets, inward investments, firm establishments, tourists, hallmark events and government funding (Lever and Turok 1999) and that this competition takes place at a local, regional, national, and even continental and global scales (Gordon 1999). In order to maintain their position within the urban system, cities have to work on their

M.J. Burger (✉)
Erasmus University Rotterdam and ERIM, Rotterdam, The Netherlands
e-mail: mburger@ese.eur.nl

F.G. van Oort
University Utrecht, Utrecht, The Netherlands

R.S. Wall
Erasmus University Rotterdam, Rotterdam, The Netherlands

M.J.P.M. Thissen
Netherlands Environmental Assessment Agency (PBL), The Hague, The Netherlands

J. Klaesson et al. (eds.), *Metropolitan Regions*, Advances in Spatial Science, 375
DOI 10.1007/978-3-642-32141-2_16, © Springer-Verlag Berlin Heidelberg 2013

competitiveness, or their ability to successfully compete with other cities. As a result, local authorities put ever more effort into enabling and maintaining their cities as attractive locations of residence and firm location.[1] In order to keep and attract firms, workers and tourists one should not only think of cost reductions such as tax credits and project financing, but also of investments in amenities, physical infrastructure, and public transportation networks (Begg 2002).

This increased interest in the concept of 'urban competitiveness' has resulted in a substantial number of urban ranking lists, in which cities are compared on their internal characteristics, such as their economic performance (Kresl and Singh 1999; Lever 1999), creativity and innovativeness (Florida 2005), and access and quality of services (Kaufmann et al. 2005). This benchmarking of cities has not only come to pass in academia and commercial research, but also engrained within public policy and popular culture. Nowadays, local authorities increasingly publicise their relative competitive stance with that of other places (Malecki 2002), while at the same time many newspapers and magazines (e.g., *Fortune Magazine*, *Forbes*, *Money*) seem to be obsessed with rankings of how cities compare to each other (McCann 2004).

Nevertheless, empirical evidence on urban competition remains limited. Although most studies on urban competitiveness assume that cities compete *vis-à-vis* one another, little attention is paid to measuring the intensity of competition between cities. Yet, in order to validate the urban competitiveness concept, it is important to understand to what extent cities compete and where this competition comes from. Shifting our focus from urban competitiveness to urban competition in terms of market overlap can enrich the literature on competitive cities by providing a method to identify the strongest competitors from the rest.

In this chapter we focus on the measurement of revealed competition between cities. We calculate the relative amount of market overlap that a certain city has with any other city within an urban system, identify clusters of competitive cities, and the determinants of this competition. Using insights from urban systems theory and urban ecology, we thus measure the intensity of competition between cities[2] in the Dutch Randstad on the basis of the functional linkages that these cities have with other cities. In this, we argue that cities are in competition to the extent that they serve the same market area for the same urban functions (see Berry et al. 1988). Although there are many dimensions upon which cities can compete (Lever and Turok 1999), we will focus on *economic competition* between cities in terms of providing similar products to the same market areas. In particular, attention is

---

[1] Cities compete over firms and households simultaneously, as often the employment-population interdependency is large and circular in cities (Carlino and Mills 1987). For the Dutch Randstad, recent studies show that "people follow jobs more than the other way around", but that this causality is scale, sector, regional and time dependent (De Graaff et al. 2010). Not surprisingly, especially non-basic jobs follow people in the Randstad region, and controlled for that the causality is not that clear. In this paper we focus on basic industries, and hence are little served by this earlier literature on employment-population dynamics.

[2] By contrast, economists usually define competition as a market or industry property.

16 Analysing the Competitive Advantage of Cities in the Dutch Randstad... 377

drawn to firms in basic sectors (manufacturing, wholesale and producer services), which have a non-local export market and are according to Economic Base Theory (Blumenfeld 1955) considered most important for local economic growth.[3]

Our main conclusion is that in the Dutch Randstad region, urban competition is more the rule than the much-anticipated urban complementarities, as urban functional influences – especially of the four largest cities - spatially overlap. This questions recent policy initiatives towards a functional unification of the Randstad striving for economic complementarities (OECD 2007). The prosperous co-evolution of the Randstad economy with growing urban competition even suggests a positive relationship that better should *not* be battled by policy.

The remainder of this chapter is organized as follows: In Sect. 2, we focus on the conceptualization of economic competition between cities using different dimensions of urban systems outlined by Gordon (1999). Section 3 is devoted to how economic competition between cities can be measured, using a measure of overlapping market areas derived from statistical ecology. Section 4 provides an application of this method to competition between cities in the Randstad Holland. Section 5 discusses the results in a policy perspective.

2 Urban Systems and Inter-urban Competition

2.1 Competition and Complementarities in Urban Systems

Recently, there has been increased interest in the role and nature of the dynamics of urban systems. In this literature, it is contended that the rise of the *network economy*– exemplified by recent advances in transport and communication technology, the ongoing globalization, the rise of common markets, growth of multinational firms, and the individualization of production – has had a significant impact on the spatial economic structure of cities and regions (Batten 1995). At the local level, the monocentric city is perishing and suburban areas are emerging into local centres that start competing with the original core. At the same time, economic processes are taking place at an ever larger geographical scale than those of the 'traditional' city itself (Kloosterman and Musterd 2001). Cities are no longer confined by territorial delineations, but by patterns of interaction (Pred 1977). In this, 'urban competitiveness' should be considered as a 'networked phenomenon', dependent on a 'society of cities', in which 'no city develops in isolation' (Storper 1997) - but forms part of a 'system of cities' (cf. Berry 1964). However, when the market areas of cities show an increasing amount of overlap, it is likely that the

---

[3] Although we only focus on economic competition between cities, the proposed indicator in this chapter is not particularly limited to competition between cities and can without any difficulties be applied to other dimensions of urban competition and other forms of territorial competition, such as competition between regions.

competition between these cities intensifies. When cities expand their market areas, it is therefore to be expected that their market areas will increasingly overlap with the market areas of other cities and the degree of competition between these cities increases. Cities then start to function as *substitutes* to each other.

This conceptualization of cities competing over overlapping market areas has a long-standing history in urban systems research in general, and in retail geography in particular (see e.g., Berry et al. 1988; Parr 1995). Early research by Galpin (1915) on urban–rural relations and by Reilly (1931) on retail location, already pointed out that centres compete as locations can be served from several centres. Firms and consumers usually choose between different locations to buy their goods and services. For example, in Reilly's *Law of Retail Gravitation* it is explicitly accounted for that the sales potential of a given retail centre is not only dependent on the size of this centre and the consumer expenditure in the surrounding area, but also on the extent to which a retail centre is surrounded by competing retail centres, which attract consumers from similar locations (see also Huff 1964; Lakshmanan and Hansen 1965). This argument can be extended to competition between cities in general in terms of market area overlap: cities are in competition to the extent that the goods and services produced in these cities are exported to similar locations. This can concern both trade in intermediate and final goods and services. The actors then are municipality and regional councils that take measures to improve the competitive position of their city-region, but also national authorities (e.g. responsible for infrastructure), large companies and real estate developers play a role in this process (Ho 2000).

However, market area overlap in different functions in itself does not necessarily constitute urban competition. On the contrary, if in an urban system the various cities specialize in different sectors, they in fact complement each other by fulfilling different economic roles (Van Oort et al. 2010). The situation of two cities within the same urban system that each produces different goods or services for which the other has an effective demand, can lead to an exchange between the two places. For example, a city specialized in financial services can provide these services to a city specialized in manufacturing, and vice versa. Hence, cities do not have to produce all different types of goods demanded in the city, but can benefit from specializations elsewhere in the urban network (Meijers 2005). Gordon (1999) mentions in this respect the delegation of routine administrative tasks of headquarters to places offering blue-collar labour at lower pay rates.

2.2 Defining Competition between Cities

Along these lines, two conditions for the existence of economic competition between cities can be identified, namely (1) geographic market overlap and (2) functional overlap.

2.2.1 Dimension 1: Geographical Market Overlap

Cities are in competition to the extent that they serve the same market area or have overlapping market areas. As outlined in the previous section, geographic market overlap does not necessarily have to be based on physical proximity. Cities are in competition to the extent they have exporting linkages (of goods, services and provisions) to the same other cities. Competition between cities can take place at various geographical scales, in which contending cities at a local scale do not necessarily have to be in competition at a national or international scale.[4] For example, the Dutch cities Amsterdam and Rotterdam may compete locally, sharing the same hinterland (Randstad Holland), but may differ in their functional linkages to the rest of the world. Likewise, London and Paris may compete on a global scale, but not on a local scale, serving different local hinterlands (the Greater South East and Ile-de-France respectively).

2.2.2 Dimension 2: Functional Overlap

Cities are in competition to the extent that they perform the same function within an urban system. In this sense, we can distinguish between (1) sectoral overlap and (2) organizational overlap. First, cities are in competition to the extent they are specialized in the same sectors or produce the same products. Competition is here conceptualized as the lack of inter-urban industrial differentiation, in which cities have overlapping product niches. In this respect, Markusen and Schrock (2006) explicitly point to the mimicking of the success of legendary cases such as Silicon Valley and the Cambridge cluster, as drivers behind this overlap. Nowadays, most cities endeavour to be clusters of high-tech or creative industries. As a result, cities become less distinctive and competition intensifies. Second, cities are in competition to the extent they perform the same organizational function (Gordon 1999). One can think of the traditional division between white-collar and blue-collar work, but also of a division between headquarter and subsidiary (production plant) functions. It is in the *absence* of functional differentiation of labour, that these cities are more likely to be in competition.

When both the geographic and functional niches of cities overlap, cities are in competition as they have to share the same 'part of the pie'. In sum, cities (that are not distinctive and) that serve the same hinterland for the same functions are expected to compete for the same market area in terms of the acquisition and retention of the same firms and customers.

---

[4] In other words, one can speak here of non-perfect aggregation across spatial scales.

Fig. 16.1 Functional linkages in a hypothetical urban system

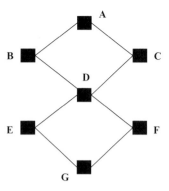

3 Measuring Urban Market Overlap

Although the existence of urban competition is widely recognized in urban geography and planning, few attempts have been made to explicitly measure the extent of competition between cities or within a sub-system of cities. By employing the two dimensions of urban market overlap discussed in the previous section, we will now turn to our measurement of urban competition.

We use a measure derived from statistical ecology that looks at niche overlap. The theoretical concept of niches dates back to the first half of the twentieth century and then mainly concerned descriptive biological studies on the overlap of the habitats of different species.[5] In its original connotation, a niche of species is defined as the set of environmental states in which a species thrives and typically consists of the resources on which a species depends for its survival. From the 1970s onwards, the concept of niche has become widespread in the social sciences, most notably in organization studies (Hannan and Freeman 1977; Podolny et al. 1996) and social network analysis (Burt and Talmud 1993; Sohn 2004). Analogous to its ecological and organizational counterpart, an urban niche can be regarded as the market area of a city in which it employs its economic activities, or in which it fulfills its activities. In this, overlapping market areas result in urban competition. Consider the following urban linkage structure for a *particular function* in Fig. 16.1.

In this urban system, for this particular urban function:

- Cities A and G are linked to different cities (to cities B and C and cities E and F respectively). For this reason, the similarity between their geographical markets is 0 %, meaning that there is no urban competition between cities A and G.
- Cities B and C have exactly the same linkage structure, as both cities are linked to city A and D. Hence, the similarity between their networks is 100 %, meaning that the geographical markets of cities B and C maximally overlap.

---

[5] An overview of the history of the niche concept in the ecological and social sciences can be found in Popielarz and Neal (2007).

16 Analysing the Competitive Advantage of Cities in the Dutch Randstad...

- Cities A and D have a partly overlapping linkage structure. Although cities A and D are both linked to cities B and C, city D is also linked to cities E and F. Hence, the intensity of competition between cities A and D is intermediate as their geographical markets only partly overlap.

In line with the theoretical concept of niche overlap, two cities are in competition to the extent they are linked to the same other cities for equal functions. In contrast to the artificial urban system above, real urban systems usually differ in size, while simultaneously the functional linkages between cities can differ in intensity. Hence, in order to facilitate comparisons of the degree of urban competition between cities, the strength of linkages between two cities should be expressed as the relative dependency of a city on another city. For example, if city A has two linkages with city B and one linkage with city C, the geographical market (niche) of city A for the urban function under consideration consists for 2/3 of city B and for 1/3 of city C. Hence, it is best to speak of 'revealed competition' between cities as it is based on the observed behavior of economic actors (firms, consumers) in these cities rather than their preferences (Berry et al. 1988). In addition, this provides a means to differentiate from more economic accounts of competition, in which the degree of competition is perceived as a property of an industry or market and not as a property of a relationship between two actors.

Over the years, several statistical approaches to formally measure overlap between members of a population have been developed. Amongst others, we find the alpha-coefficient, Euclidean distance, Manhattan distance, cosine, and standardized versions of these similarity indices (e.g., Bray-Curtis, Kulczynski, Gower metric).[6] Notwithstanding their computational differences, a central element of these measures is that they look at the *dissimilarity* or *ecological distance* between the members of a given population.

Based on comparative research in ecological statistics (e.g., McCune and Grace 2002) and our interest in compositional overlap (rather than absolute overlap),[7] we use in our study the relative Manhattan distance to measure ecological distance, or in our case the absence of overlap between the geographical markets of cities for a particular function. First, the relative Manhattan distance has the desired property that it uses value zero when there is a maximum niche overlap and a constant maximum value (e.g., 1) when there is no niche overlap (Beals 1984). Second, the relative Manhattan distance shows a low discrepancy between the predicted and observed similarity. Third, the relative Manhattan distance has a robust linear relationship with true ecological distance when tested with simulated data (Faith et al. 1987).

---

[6] See McCune and Grace (2002) for an overview of all basic measures of niche overlap.

[7] For this reason, we do not use the also recommended Bray-Curtis or Kulczynski coefficient to measure ecological distance. However, from a mathematical point of view, both the Bray-Curtis and the Kulczynski coefficient equal the Relative Manhattan distance when standardized to equal totals (see Faith et al. 1987).

The relative Manhattan distance measures the relative distance or *dissimilarity* in niche between two species i and j for a particular urban function k, here expressed in the non-overlapping of geographical markets between two cities i and j. More formally (16.1):

$$RDISTANCE_{ijk} = 1 - \left[\sum_{h=1}^{p} MIN \left(\frac{a_{ih,k}}{\sum\limits_{h=1}^{p} a_{ih,k}}, \frac{a_{jh,k}}{\sum\limits_{h=1}^{p} a_{jh,k}} \right) \right], i \neq j \neq h, \qquad (16.1)$$

which can be rewritten as (16.2),

$$RDISTANCE_{ijk} = \frac{1}{2} \sum_{h=1}^{p} \left| \frac{a_{ih,k}}{\sum\limits_{h=1}^{p} a_{ih,k}} - \frac{a_{jh,k}}{\sum\limits_{h=1}^{p} a_{jh,k}} \right|, i \neq j \neq h \qquad (16.2)$$

in which $a_{ih,k}$ is the strength of the urban linkage (e.g., the number of business interactions) between city i and a third city h for urban function k, and $a_{jh,k}$ the strength of the urban linkages between city j and city h for urban function k. When measuring the intensity of competition between cities i and j, linkages between city i and j are excluded, as well as linkages that remain within a city in order to measure genuine competition and not urban complementarities. The distance measure is relative because it gives the absolute difference between the cities divided by their absolute sum. In other words, by standardizing the absolute difference to sample totals, the total non-overlap of the geographical markets of the two cities i and j is converted into a percentage non-overlap of the geographical markets of two cities. This allows comparison of the cities by the relative distribution of urban linkages across space. The degree of similarity between two cities or the *competition coefficient* can then be expressed as (16.3):

$$COMPETITION_{ijk} = 1 - RDISTANCE_{ijk} \qquad (16.3)$$

The competition coefficient $COMPETITION_{ijk}$ typically ranges between 0 and 1. If the competition coefficient equals zero, the geographical markets of cities i and j are totally different and the intensity of competition between the two cities is at minimum. If the competition coefficient equals one, the geographical markets of cities i and j completely overlap and the intensity of competition between the two cities is at maximum.

Equations 16.1, 16.2, and 16.3 present a method to estimate the intensity of competition between cities for one particular urban function. This function can range from global command centers in the advanced producer services sector to the production site in the textiles and apparel commodity chain. The total intensity of competition between two cities for a number of urban functions can be estimated by

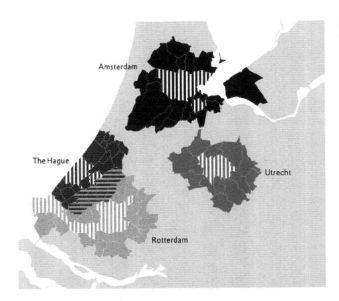

Fig. 16.2 The Dutch Randstad

weighting the competition coefficients for the different urban functions k with the overall importance of these urban functions in the two cities.

4 Urban Market Overlap in the Dutch Randstad

4.1 Urban Complementarities in the Randstad

In order to show how the described techniques in the previous section can be used, we show the case of economic competition in the Dutch Randstad. From a geographical point of view, the Randstad is known as the urban conurbation in the western part of the Netherlands, in which four major cities (Amsterdam, Rotterdam, Den Haag, and Utrecht) and a number of smaller towns (like Delft, Haarlem and Leiden) are located within close proximity of each other (see Fig. 16.2). The Randstad constitutes the heart of the Dutch economy, with 50 % of the gross national product being generated on approximately 25 % of the country's total land area. Having a population of six million inhabitants, the Randstad houses over one third of the Dutch population. However, in the debate on spatial planning and economic policy in the Netherlands, the 'Randstad' is more than just a collection of cities. The Randstad is seen as a single, contiguous urban region. This also follows from its name, since it includes the Dutch word for 'city'. Suggestions that the region functions as an integrated economic entity for basic industries, like manufacturing activities, distribution activities and business services, are numerous (Dieleman and

Musterd 1992; Sachar 1994; Kloosterman and Lambregts 2001; Lambregts 2008). Based on these suggestions, regional and national policymakers now more than ever aim at the concentrated location of (inter)national firms and businesses in this networked region in order to profit optimally from economic growth potentials.

Nevertheless, simply assigning a name, such as the Randstad, to a collection of towns and cities does not automatically meld them into a spatial and functional integrated city with economic complementarities. On the contrary – in the light of our analysis – instead of complementarities, competition and functional overlap between cities might exist. Earlier (and by now quite dated) research has hinted at this, but never quantified this accurately. Early centrality and hierarchy studies of industrial activities in the Randstad (Buursink 1971) suggested competition between cities, but did not use flow or network data to prove this. Location studies of firms (predominantly in business sectors) in the Randstad suggested that the employment structures of cities in the Randstad increasingly resemble each other over time, but do not take this further into the concepts of competition or complementarities (Atzema and De Smidt 1992; Hessels 1992).

Competition between cities is stressed in a recent discussion on the issuing of new industrial sites in the Randstad. Although the market for new real estate and industrial sites is stable and characterized by replacement more than expansion, all larger cities provide new space for new and moving firms (Van Oort et al. 2007). In this zero-sum game, places have to end up empty. This is generally regarded as a negative (spoiling) aspect of inter-urban competition (cf. Farell 1996). However, others suggest that urban competition is a good thing as it causes survivors and winners to be more vital and competitive (cf. Glaeser 2001). As for the Dutch Randstad, policymakers stress the complementarities view - partly out of wishful thinking and partly out of lack of knowledge about urban competition within the region due to a lack of reliable urban-economic interaction data.

4.2 Data

To analyze urban market overlap of cities in Randstad Holland, we use a dataset on inter-firm relationships including the purchasing and selling of products and services. The data stems from a 2005 survey among more than 20,000 firms in manufacturing, wholesale, and commercial services with more than one employee that are based in Randstad Holland (Van Oort et al. 2010). A random stratified sample, taking size and regions into account, was taken from the LISA database – an employment register of all Dutch establishments (see Van Oort 2007).[8]

---

[8] The survey focused on the ten most important selling and purchasing relations of firms. These can be with firms within or outside the own municipality. This restriction to ten relations leads to a potential bias in the network structure of large firms, but large firms are not over represented in cities in the Randstad (Van Oort et al. 2010). The 1676 establishments (8 %) that filled out the survey are representative in terms of the stratification by region and firm size. We are not able to differentiate results to various sectors.

Fig. 16.3 Inter-firm relations between 69 municipalities in the Dutch Randstad

Subsequently, the data were aggregated to the municipal level to analyze the overlap of urban networks. Figure 16.3 shows the network of inter-firm relationships for the entire Randstad. In this figure, the respondent population is not classified by sector. The lines represent the relationships between firms in different municipalities, where the thickness of the lines represent the number of business relations between two municipalities. On the basis of these business relationships, the market areas of the different municipalities can be demarcated. Nevertheless, it should be noted that about 50 % of the inter-firm relationships of firms that are located in the Randstad region are targeted at a location outside the Randstad. Hence, in the remaining of this empirical example we only analyze local competition between municipalities in the Dutch Randstad by looking at the overlap of local market areas.

4.3 Competition Coefficients of Cities in Randstad Holland

In measuring the intensity of competition between cities, we estimated the competition coefficients for manufacturing, wholesale and business services activities.

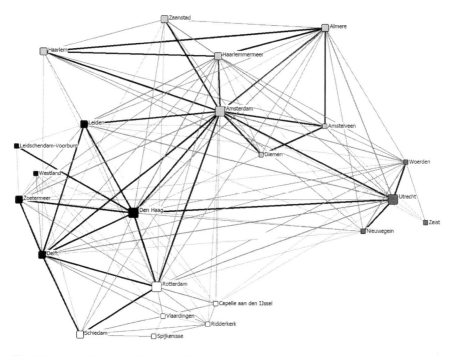

Fig. 16.4 Inter-city competition in the Randstad trade network

Subsequently, a composite measure of competition between any two cities in the region was created by weighting the competition coefficients for the different sectors by the overall importance of these sectors in the two cities (in terms of the total number of linkages); the resulting indicator represents the average degree of competition that firms in a certain city face from firms in the other city.

In our analysis, we focus on urban competition between the 23 largest and most prominent cities in the Dutch Randstad network,[9] by examining to what extent their linkage pattern of trade relations to *all* other municipalities in this network are similar. Overall, the competition coefficients of these municipality pairs typically range between 25 % (between smaller cities) and 75 % (between larger cities). Figure 16.4 provides a graphical representation of this matrix in terms of a network

---

[9] These are the cities with more than 40,000 inhabitants in the Dutch Randstad in 2006: Almere, Amstelveen, Amsterdam, Capelle aan den IJssel, Delft, Den Haag, Diemen, Haarlem, Haarlemmermeer (Schiphol), Leiden, Leidschendam-Voorburg, Nieuwegein, Ridderkerk, Rotterdam, Schiedam, Spijkenisse, Utrecht, Vlaardingen, Westland, Woerden, Zaanstad, Zeist en Zoetermeer.

diagram.[10] The network diagram consists of nodes (vertices) and linkages (edges). The nodes in the network represent the different municipalities, where the size of the nodes represents the position of a city in the corporate inter-city network of advanced producer services based on the total number of linkages a city has. This position can range from primary municipalities (Amsterdam, Rotterdam, Den Haag, and Utrecht) to secondary (e.g., Delft, Haarlem, Leiden) and tertiary centres of municipalities that have relatively few linkages with other municipalities. As indicated earlier, lower order centres (villages, hamlets) are excluded from this analysis. The colour of the node represent the region in which the city is situated (Amsterdam (light grey), Den Haag (black), Rotterdam (white), or Utrecht (dark grey)).

The linkages between the cities in the network diagram represent the nature of urban relationships, where the thickness of the linkages represent the intensity of competition between the different cities. If there is no linkage drawn between two cities, the competition coefficient is lower than 50 %. Both cities are then (relatively) linked to different cities in the Randstad trade network. A thin inter-city linkage indicates that the competition coefficient ranges between 50 % and 65 % (intermediate market overlap). Finally, a thick (black) inter-city linkage indicates that the degree of geographical market overlap between two cities is over 65 % (strong overlap), meaning that both cities are to a large extent linked to similar cities. For this reason, the intensity of market overlap between these cities is fiercest.

Looking at the overall pattern of competitive relations, a number of observations can be made. First, competition between cities has a strong geographical dimension. The intensity of competition between cities that are geographically proximate is stronger than competition between cities that are geographically distant. The intensity of competition between cities situated in different urban regions is low. Moreover, if there is a strong intensity of competition between cities situated in different regions, it concerns mostly competition between higher-order centres. In fact, the degree of market overlap between Amsterdam, Den Haag, Rotterdam and Utrecht is among the highest in the Randstad network. This is not surprising since these higher-order centres serve a more diverse geographical market with a larger geographical scope than the lower order centres (Berry et al. 1988).

In contrast, smaller centres face relatively little economic competition from the other centres in the Randstad. This can be explained by the fact that the trade relations of these lower-order centres have a primarily local scope. Applying a hierarchical cluster analysis on the competition coefficients (Johnson 1967) identifies that four major (local) clusters of competing cities can be identified (see Fig. 16.5), namely (1) the Amsterdam region, (2) the Utrecht region, (3) The The-Hague-Rotterdam region and the area surrounding the city of Rotterdam. These results confirm the

---

[10] The graphical representation was made using the UCINET software (Borgatti et al. 2002). This representation is not completely comparable to the geographical maps presented in Figs. 16.2 and 16.3, as the best UCINET network visualisation does not stick to geographical location.

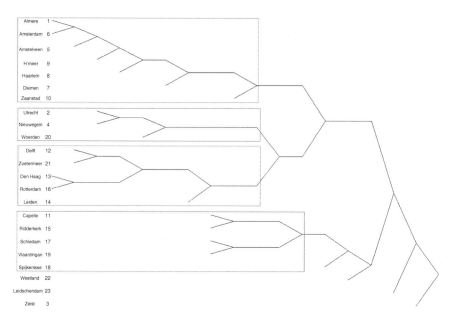

Fig. 16.5 Hierarchical cluster analysis of urban market overlap in the Dutch Randstad

rather local orientation of most cities within the Dutch Randstad. The market overlap between cities of different order that are geographically proximate, is very limited.

5 Discussion

In order to maintain their position within the urban system, cities have to work on their competitiveness, or their ability to successfully compete with other cities. As a result, local authorities put ever more effort into enabling and maintaining their cities as attractive locations of residence. In contrast with this, regional and national Dutch policymakers advocate the Randstad region as a single urban region in which economic complementarities are supposed to be numerous. The main policy conclusion of our research is that urban competition is more the rule than the much-anticipated urban complementarities, as urban functional influences spatially overlap. This is especially the case for the four largest cities (Amsterdam, Rotterdam, The Hague and Utrecht), which have the highest degree of market overlap in the Randstad network. The competitive climate between cities, leading to redundant supply of business estates, inefficient land-use patterns, rent losses and superfluous costs of acquisition, is usually seen as a negative thing (Farell 1996). But the competitive urban climate in the Randstad region coincides with particularly strong economic growth values in terms of employment and productivity growth (OECD 2007; Van Oort et al. 2010) – suggesting that competition might as well function as catalyst for vital urban development (compare similar arguments by Glaeser 2001 and Porter 1995).[11]

We introduced a measure for this, applied from comparative research in ecological statistics. Naturally, this is only a small amount of the competition that the cities in this network receive from all other cities: preferably the intensity of competition between cities should be measured across a full and more detailed spectrum of urban functions. Nonetheless, when urban niches are fully specified in terms of geography and functions, the resulting niche overlap measure can indicate the amount of market overlap a city has with other cities in the urban network. Further research should concentrate on relating aggregated competition coefficients in a regression framework to link market overlaps to urban performance. Accordingly, the focus then shifts from urban competition as an independent variable ("causes of urban competition") to urban competition as an independent variable ("consequence of urban competition").

References

Atzema O, De Smidt M (1992) Selection and duality in the employment structure of the Randstad. Tijdschrift voor Economische en Sociale Geografie 83:289–305

Batten DF (1995) Network cities: creative urban agglomerations for the 21st century. Urban Stud 32:313–327

Beals EW (1984) Bray-Curtis ordination: an effective strategy for analysis of multivariate ecological data. Adv Ecol Res 14:1–55

Begg I (2002) Urban competitiveness policies for dynamic cities. The Policy Press, Bristol

Berry BJL (1964) Cities as systems within systems of cities. Pap Reg Sci 13:147–163

Berry BJL, Parr J, Epstein G, Gosh A, Smith R (1988) Market centres and retail location: theory and applications. Prentice Hall, Englewood Cliffs

Blumenfeld H (1955) The economic base of the metropolis. J Am Inst Plann 21:114–132

Borgatti SP, Everett MG, Freeman LC (2002) UCINET for windows: software for social network analysis. Analytic Technologies, Harvard

Boston TD, Ross CL (2002) The inner city, urban poverty and economic development in the next century. Transaction Publishers, London

Burt RS, Talmud I (1993) Market niche. Soc Netw 15:133–149

Buursink J (1971) Centraliteit en Hiërarchie. De Theorie der Centrale plaatsen in Enkele Nederlandse Industriegebieden. Van Gorcum, Assen

Carlino GA, Mills ES (1987) The determinants of country growth. J Reg Sci 27:39–54

De Graaff T, Van Oort F, Florax R (2010) Sectoral heterogeneity, accessibility and population-employment dynamics in Dutch cities. Working paper, Free University Amsterdam

Dieleman FM, Musterd S (1992) The Randstad: a research and policy laboratory. Kluwer, Dordrecht

Faith DP, Minchin PR, Belbin L (1987) Compositional dissimilarity as a robust measure of ecological distance. Plant Ecol 69:57–68

Farell J (1996) Creating local competition. Fed Commun Law J 49:201–215

Florida R (2005) Cities and the creative class. Routledge, New York

---

[11] For an overview of arguments in favor and against competitiveness of cities, see the papers collected in Boston and Ross (2002).

Galpin J (1915) The social anatomy of an agricultural community, Research bulletin 34. Agricultural Experiment Station of University of Wisconsin, Madison

Glaeser EL (2001) The economics of location-based tax incentives, Harvard institute of economic research, discussion paper no. 1932. Harvard University, Cambridge, MA

Gordon IR (1999) Internationalisation and urban competition. Urban Stud 36:1001–1016

Hannan MT, Freeman JH (1977) The population ecology of organizations. Am J Sociol 82:929–964

Hessels M (1992) Locational dynamics of business services. An intrametropolitan study on the Randstad Holland. NGS 147, University of Utrecht

Ho KC (2000) Competing to be regional centres: a multi-agency, multi-locational perspective. Urban Stud 37:2337–2356

Huff DL (1964) Defining and estimating a trade area. J Market 28(3):34–38

Johnson SC (1967) Hierarchical clustering schemes. Psychometrika 32:241–253

Kaufmann D, Leautier FA, Mastruzzi M (2005) Globalization and urban performance. In: Leautier FA (ed) Cities in globalizing world: governance, performance and sustainability. World Bank, Washington, DC, pp 27–68

Kloosterman RC, Lambregts B (2001) Clustering of economic activities in polycentric urban regions: the case of the Randstad. Urban Stud 38:717–732

Kloosterman RC, Musterd S (2001) The polycentric urban region: towards a research agenda. Urban Stud 38:623–633

Kresl PK, Singh B (1999) Competitiveness and the urban economy: twenty-four large US metropolitan areas. Urban Stud 36:1017–1027

Lakshmanan JR, Hansen WG (1965) A retail market potential model. J Am Plann Assoc 31:134–143

Lambregts B (2008) Geographies of knowledge formation in mega-city regions: some evidence from the Dutch Randstad. Reg Stud 42:1173–1186

Lever WF (1999) Competitive cities in Europe. Urban Stud 36:935–948

Lever WF, Turok I (1999) Competitive cities: introduction to the review. Urban Stud 36:791–793

Malecki EJ (2002) Hard and soft networks for urban competitiveness. Urban Stud 39:929–945

Markusen A, Schrock G (2006) The distinctive city: divergent patterns in growth, hierarchy and specialization. Urban Stud 43:1301–1323

McCann EJ (2004) 'Best places': interurban competition, quality of life and popular media discourse. Urban Stud 41:1909–1929

McCune B, Grace JB (2002) Analysis of ecological communities. MjM Software Design, Gleneden Beach

Meijers E (2005) Polycentric urban networks and the quest for synergy: is a network of cities more than the sum of its parts? Urban Stud 42:765–781

OECD (2007) Territorial review of Randstad Holland, Netherlands. OECD, Paris

Parr JB (1995) Alternative approaches to market-area structure in the urban system. Urban Stud 32:1317–1329

Podolny JM, Stuart TE, Hannan MT (1996) Networks knowledge and niches competition in the worldwide semiconductor industry 1984–1991. Am J Sociol 102:659–689

Popielarz PA, Neal ZP (2007) The niche as theoretical tool. Annu Rev Sociol 33:65–84

Porter M (1995) The competitive advantage of the inner city. Harvard Business Review, Boston, pp 55–71

Pred A (1977) City systems in advanced economies: past growth, present processes and future development options. Hutchinson, London

Reilly WJ (1931) The law of retail gravitation. Knickerbocker, New York

Sachar A (1994) Randstad Holland: a world city? Urban Stud 31:381–400

Sohn M (2004) Distance and cosine measures of niche overlap. Soc Netw 23:141–165

Storper M (1997) The regional world: territorial development in a global economy. Guilford Press, New York

Van Oort FG (2007) Spatial and sectoral composition effects of agglomeration economies in the Netherlands. Pap Reg Sci 86:5–30

Van Oort FG, Ponds R, Van Vliet J, Van Amsterdam H, Declerk S, Knoben J, Pellenbarg P, Weltevreden J (2007) Verhuizingen van bedrijven en groei van werkgelegenheid. NaI Uitgevers and Ruimtelijk Planbureau, Rotterdam/Den Haag

Van Oort FG, Burger MJ, Raspe O (2010) On the economic foundation of the urban network paradigm: spatial integration, functional integration and economic complementarities with the Dutch Randstad. Urban Stud 47:725–748

Chapter 17
Capitalising on Institutional Diversity and Complementary Resources in Cross-Border Metropolitan Regions: The Case of Electronics Firms in Hong Kong and the Pearl River Delta

Javier Revilla Diez, Daniel Schiller, and Susanne Meyer

Abstract The opening of China during the last 30 years has resulted in tremendous cross-border economic activities of Hong Kong manufacturers in the Pearl River Delta (PRD). Economic activities in the Greater Pearl River Delta (GPRD) are embedded into global value chains and shaped by the specific 'front office-back factory' division of labour between Hong Kong and the Chinese mainland. This business model has facilitated the rapid industrialisation of the PRD and the transformation of the HK economy towards sophisticated manufacturing-related business services (FHKI 2003, 2007). More recently, the competitiveness of the business model has been put under strain by forceful challenges that change the business environment in the PRD: rising production costs, upgrading pressures, new regulations for export processing businesses, labour shortages, a more employee-friendly labour law, and environmental issues. Against this background, it is the purpose of this paper to present and discuss findings from two surveys of electronics firms in HK and the PRD conducted in 2007 and 2008. The research question is based on the agility hypothesis, that supposes that business in highly competitive environments depends on competencies and resources of firms to capitalise on formal and informal business practices alike to gain flexibility. The results of our analysis may help to better understand how the HK-PRD business model did develop and eventually may sustain its competitiveness in the face of new challenges. We began with the overview of our HK as well as PRD sample in order to figure out whether there are indeed strong needs embedded in the current business and political conditions for informal and flexible organisation of firms. After that, we focussed on "customer-producer relations" and "industrial innovation" on the other hand to clarify how firms operating in the GPRD transformed the needs for agility

---

J.R. Diez (✉) • D. Schiller
University of Hannover, Hannover, Germany
e-mail: diez@wigeo.uni-hannover.de

S. Meyer
Yamanashi University, Takeda, Kofu, Japan

J. Klaesson et al. (eds.), *Metropolitan Regions*, Advances in Spatial Science,
DOI 10.1007/978-3-642-32141-2_17, © Springer-Verlag Berlin Heidelberg 2013

into different kinds of means and actions in these two areas to sustain their competitiveness in the global market. With respect to agile firm organisation in general, the findings of our research confirm the hypothesis about the interaction of informal arrangements and flexible firm organisation. Informal institutions for doing business in the GPRD are not going to become less important with further development and improvement of the Chinese legal system. Adequate application of informal factors within given formal constellations enhances the capabilities of firms to more flexibly react to the fast changes in the political and business environment to sustain their competitiveness in the global market.

Keywords Institutions • Governance • Customer–producer relations • Proximity • Hong Kong • Electronics industry

1 Introduction

The opening of China during the last 30 years has resulted in tremendous cross-border economic activities of Hong Kong manufacturers in the Pearl River Delta (PRD). Economic activities in the Greater Pearl River Delta (GPRD) are embedded into global value chains and shaped by the specific 'front office-back factory' division of labour between Hong Kong and the Chinese mainland. This business model has facilitated the rapid industrialisation of the PRD and the transformation of the HK economy towards sophisticated manufacturing-related business services (FHKI 2003, 2007).

More recently, the competitiveness of the business model has been put under strain by forceful challenges that change the business environment in the PRD: rising production costs, upgrading pressures, new regulations for export processing businesses, labour shortages, a more employee-friendly labour law, and environmental issues. On the global scale the economic downswing in major customer markets, e.g. the US, and new competitors at other locations are major issues. A recent call of Guangdong's vice-governor Wan Qingliang suggests that the provincial government in Guangdong is going to adjust its policy towards HK manufacturers in the province. The new strategy seems to be in favour of encouraging upgrading of HK-owned low-value factories rather than trying to move these factories out of the province (SCMP 2008).

Against this background, it is the purpose of this paper to present and discuss findings from two surveys of electronics firms in HK and the PRD conducted in 2007 and 2008. The research question is based on the agility hypothesis, that supposes that business in highly competitive environments depends on competencies and resources of firms to capitalise on formal and informal business practices alike to gain flexibility. The results of our analysis may help to better understand how the HK-PRD business model did develop and eventually may sustain its competitiveness in the face of new challenges.

2 Conceptual Background: Agility and Regional Institutions

2.1 The Agility Hypothesis

In developing countries, economic activities of multinational and local companies are mostly located at the lower end of the value chain (Ernst and Kim 2002; Ernst 2002). Therefore, they do not require advanced technological capabilities but cost-efficiency. To be cost-efficient in highly competitive markets (e.g. consumer electronics, IT, food processing, textiles), companies need specific competencies to pool inputs (resources) into the production process that go beyond the concepts of flexible specialization and lean production. Hence, the notion of agility transcends the dichotomy of low-cost vs. high-tech capabilities in the mainstream of the literature by moving the focus towards the economic and social organisation of firms.

The underlying organisational principles of agile firm organisation have not yet been analysed sufficiently. Our paper is based on the assumption that cost- and time-sensitive production in the Greater Pearl River Delta (GPRD)[1] is embedded within fragmented global value chains and therefore largely benefits from informal dynamics (Cheng and Gereffi 1994; Sindzingre 2006). In tough competitive situations, agile firm organisation is an organisational innovation to achieve a sustained competitive advantage by seizing opportunities and coping with threats and uncertainty in volatile markets. Informal dynamics of agile firm organisation are most suitably analysed when its institutional foundations are taken into account. Institutions and governance aspects will be analysed within an informal/formal and spatial (global/national/urban) continuum rather than within a dichotomy that has proven to fall short in capturing the multiple facets of informality.

Business conditions for agile firm organisation are expected to be most suitable in mega-urban regions due to their thick and differentiated input markets. Strategies of agile companies both depend on the existence of regional markets and shape their economic and social development. Therefore, they are expected to have an immense impact on mega-urban economies. The effects of agile firm organisation can be felt in different areas such as labour and human capital, business finance, and technology transfer (Amin 2002; Carr and Chen 2002; Hussmanns 2004; Allen et al. 2006; Kim 2003). Above that, bridging organisations (e.g. knowledge-intensive business services, KIBS) and social institutions (e.g. guanxi networks, informal networks of transforming collectives, social capital) are playing a major role to stabilise the agile pooling of inputs (North 1990; Chen and Chen 2004; Williams and Zhang 2001; Woolcock and Narayan 2000; Chopra 2001; Durlauf and Fafchamps 2005). The building blocks to analyse agile firm organisation are summarized in Fig. 17.1. Each facet will be further elaborated in the following discussion.

---

[1] The Greater Pearl River Delta (GPRD) comprises nine mainland municipalities of Guangdong province (Dongguan, Foshan, Guangzhou, Huizhou, Jiangmen, Shenzhen, Zhaoqing, Zhongshan, and Zhuhai) and the Hong Kong and Macao Special Administrative Regions.

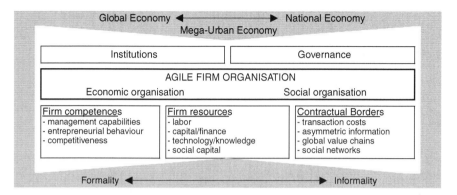

Fig. 17.1 Conceptual framework for global and informal dynamics of agile firm organisation in mega-urban regions (Source: by the authors)

2.2 Agile Firm Organisation and Sustained Competitive Advantage

An analysis of firm organisation has to start with a definition of where a firm starts and where it ends. Two different schools of thought have developed an explanation why firms exist by either a transaction cost or an asymmetric information approach. The existence of organisations of all kinds (e.g. firms, governments, universities, etc.) is justified by the fact that most economic decisions are shaped by uncertainty and a lack of information (Arrow 1974). Therefore, the challenging topic is not to explain why firms exist, but to develop a model that predicts the optimal mix of internal and external operations for a particular firm.

2.2.1 Contractual Borders of the Firm

Transaction cost economics (TCE) opened the "black box" of the firm by analysing internal mechanisms of firm organisation. TCE are related with Williamson (1998) who build on earlier writings by Coase (1937) on the "Nature of the Firm". The aim of TCE is to explain which parts of the production process are either vertically integrated within the hierarchy of the firm or acquired via the market. Transaction costs (TC) result from market imperfections due to the underlying assumptions of bounded rationality and opportunism of economic actors. Generally speaking, high transaction costs result to a high extent by imperfect formal (laws, regulations, etc.) and informal (trust etc.) institutions. So it might be very costly and difficult to take defecting contract partners to court. In Williamson's framework, TCs are determined by three variables: frequency, uncertainty, and asset specificity of transactions. The higher the TCs, the more likely a process will be integrated vertically.

Hence, TCE made essential contributions to the understanding of firm organisation, e.g. when applied to the question whether a firm should integrate parts of the value chain or outsource it to subcontractors (Grossman and Helpman 2002, 2005; Johansson and Quigley 2004; Johansson 2005). This model has also been applied to explain the division of foreign ownership and local control over inputs in outsourcing to China Feenstra et al. (2003). Nevertheless, it falls short in understanding informal institutions (e.g. trust, reputation) that are shaping the behaviour of economic actors.

The TCE perspective will be broadened by the asymmetric information (AI) approach that is closely connected with J.E. Stiglitz (e.g. Stiglitz 1984; Greenwald and Stiglitz 1986). Akerlof (1970) has been the first to analyse the effects of imperfect information in the used car market. Information about a product differs between market participants. Thus, transactions are prone to adverse selection and moral hazard. Different modes of signalling by the supplier and screening by the buyer can reduce this risk and are often combined with informality. Information asymmetries are expected to be highest in developing countries (Stiglitz 1986).

Both perspectives rest upon a dualistic understanding of organisations (markets vs. hierarchy), whereas more recent research stresses the existence of hybrid organisation (e.g. networks, informal contracts) as a distinctive way to coordinate economic activity (Powell 1990).

From the economic point of view, markets should be the most efficient governance mode to organise the production process and herewith relations to customers and producers. Markets are coordinated by prices. Therefore, they remain highly impersonal in comparison to hybrid forms or hierarchies (Menard 2005). The existence of a large number of potential trading partners provides an extensive choice on the one hand, but on the other hand also increases the cost of finding the right trading partner (Bickenbach et al. 1999). Customers and producers can be randomly paired and exchanged. Therefore, specific investments are rare on markets. Market transactions provide players with considerable autonomy and flexibility to exploit profit opportunities by adjusting their behaviour to unfolding events. But in the case of major events which require the adaptation of the entire value chain, market-based chains have difficulties adapting because of their anonymous organisation. Contracts constitute an important arrangement for organising market transactions, since firms do not have much else for the parties to rely upon. Different governance modes use distinct forms of contracts. The classical contracts characterised by legal rules, formal documents and self-liquidating transactions are typical for market transactions (Menard 2005). Therefore, effective third-party enforcement mechanisms (public ordering) are required, which are usually associated with a market-oriented institutional setting (Menard 2005). Markets rely heavily on a formal setting according to the definition of informality. The relationships are usually organised in impersonal ways, and contracts are therefore mostly written in detail and enforcement is organised by courts.

At the other end of the spectrum lies the hierarchical exchange. It characterises transactions that take place under the unified ownership and control of one firm (vertical integration). When investments are very specific, vertical integration is often the best way to protect investments against opportunistic behaviour.

The biggest disadvantage of hierarchies is their low-powered economic stimulation, which reduces their ability to adapt quickly to unpredictable market changes. Moreover, the limited external exchange of information and knowledge can lead to lock-in effects. In contrast, hierarchies provide relatively efficient mechanisms for responding to major market changes where coordinated adaptation of several units of a value chain is necessary (adaptation of entire units). As firms do not need proper contracts for internal firm organisation, managers can easily react to orders and have the right to reallocate tasks (Menard 2005; Klein 2005). It can be expected that HK firms opt more often for a hierarchical organisation when working in China, because it seems to be suitable even if environments are no longer so uncertain. Williamson (1998) refers to a third mode of organisation – the T-mode, where T indicates a temporary or transitional situation. This form can be observed in developing markets where technology and rivalry are undergoing rapid changes. According to Williamson (1998: 50) "Joint ventures [...] should sometimes be thought of as T-modes of organization that permit the parties to remain players in a fast-moving environment." Parties can pool resources to meet market demand for price and quality. Unsuccessful joint ventures (JVs) will transform to other governance modes later on, while successful JVs will remain in operation. In this work, T-modes are counted among hybrid forms of organisation. It can be expected that during economic transition in China, firms tend to rely more heavily on those intermediate forms to keep their exibility.

In between markets and hierarchies, the extreme modes of governance, there is a broad range of hybrid governance structures. Examples of hybrid modes include the exchange of shares with trading partners, a joint ownership arrangement, the issuing of a licence to another firm, long-term contracting (framework agreements), franchising, strategic alliances etc. (Shelanski and Klein 1995; Klein 2005; Menard 2004). Hybrids develop when markets shape up as being unable to adequately allocate the relevant resources and capabilities in situations where vertical integration would reduce flexibility, create irreversibility and weaken market stimulation. In choosing a specific form of hybrid, contracting parties attempt to retain the respective advantages and avoid the respective disadvantages of markets and hierarchies for transactions. According to Menard (2004), three regularities characterise hybrids: pooling of resources, contracting modes and competing. The capitalisation on pooled resources and capabilities requires inter-firm coordination and cooperation. This involves the risk of opportunistic behaviour. Therefore, the identity of partners is important. Hybrids involve joint planning and an exchange of codified and tacit knowledge, competencies and technologies. It can be expected that firms which produce complex products for the high-end market rely more often on hybrid firms than on hierarchies or markets (Wang and Nicholas 2007). They want to avoid opportunistic behaviour – a risk of markets. Additionally, they want to facilitate external knowledge transfer, which is difficult in hierarchies. Pooling resources does not make sense without some continuity in their relationship. This leads to different contracting modes – the second regularity. Classical contracts tend only to provide a relatively simple and uniform framework. They are less suitable for serving hybrids in long-term relationships. This assumes that hybrids rely much more on personal issues, because otherwise the risk of opportunistic behaviour is too high. Without a certain degree of informal constraints-trust, reputation, reciprocity – hybrids do not work efficiently (Bickenbach et al. 1999; Shelanski and Klein 1995; Menard 2005). Therefore, hybrid modes are taken as more informal modes of governance in this work. A third determinant is the role of competition and cooperation among partners. Although they cooperate on some issues, parties also compete against each other. The risk results from difficulties in changing trading partners and unforeseeable revisions regarding the cooperation. Moreover, despite the advantage of limited opportunistic behaviour in long-term cooperation, firms have to bear in mind that they sometimes miss out on good deals from other firms (McMillan 1995: 213). The traits of hybrids seem to be characterised by intimacy, privacy and interdependency of partners. As already discussed by Granovetter, too strong ties result in decreased flexibility and may lead to a lock-in. Additionally, it is not that easy to change the hybrid configuration. It is time consuming and costly to build up such a network of reliable partners. Therefore, firms are not willing to change these network relations too often because than they have to make new investment Karlsson et al. (2005).

Different forms provide firms with different opportunities for doing business. Networked forms of organisation are becoming more important in the economy due to large hierarchies' inability to respond flexibly to competitive changes in global markets and their resistance to innovations (lock-in). Within networks, communication and coordination takes place by relational, reciprocal, and reputational interdependence mainly based on informal dynamics. Hybrid forms of organisation are expected to have the highest potential to reduce uncertainties in economic interactions (Koppenjan and Klijn 2004).

2.2.2 Informal Foundations of Agile Firm Organisation

As outlined above, the paper aims at testing the hypothesis that a sustained competitive advantage (SCA) can be achieved through the use of agility and informal institutions. The informal foundations of agile firm organisations will be discussed from a resource-based viewpoint of firm organisation.

The resource-based view (RBV) of firm is concerned with resources (e.g. assets, capabilities, organisational processes, etc.) that enable a firm to produce their final products more efficiently and effectively. Barney (1991: 101) divides firm resources into three categories: physical capital, human capital, and organisational capital resources. According to Porter (1996), a firm strategy can use these resources to achieve a SCA against its competitors, i.e. a unique competitive position which cannot be imitated by competitors – a comprehensive review of SCA definitions can be found in Hoffman (2000). Hence, the uniqueness of firm strategies based on informal procedures (e.g. planning, controlling, and coordinating systems, relations within a firm and with its environment) are expected to be higher than those solely based on formal procedures.

Agile firm organisation is an organisational innovation that has an effect on the competitive position of the firm. It transcends popular concepts of competitiveness that have been shaped by cost competitiveness and product differentiation

Fig. 17.2 Impact of agile firm organisation on the competitive position (Source: by the authors)

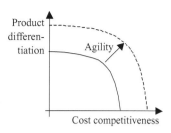

(see Fig. 17.2, Porter 1996). The notion of agility came into use with the publication of a report on enterprise strategies in the twenty-first century Iacocca Institute (1991). It has then been popularised by one of the authors of this report (Kidd 1994). On the basis of his work, agile firm organisation is defined as an "organisation's capacity to gain competitive advantage by intelligently, rapidly, and proactively seizing opportunities and reacting to threats" (Bessant et al. 2002: 487). It is closely connected with concepts like flexible or lean production (Gunasekaran and Yusuf 2002). However, these concepts are mainly concerned with restricting firm activities to its core competencies and speeding up production processes (Kidd 1994: 10). Agile firm organisation moves the focus towards the integration of organisational and management structures that enhances the capacities of the firm. Therefore, it is rather a pattern of behaviour than a specific response or outcome (Bessant et al. 2002: 488).

Agile firm organisation is closely connected with recent changes in production systems. Piore and Sabel (1984) have described newly emerging network structures in industrial production that offer competitive advantages for flexibly specialised small and medium-sized enterprises (SMEs). Within this production paradigm, ownership of resources is less important than knowledge about where to access them and how to manage them in relation to the production network (Hakansson and Snehota 1997). Know-who and know-where are becoming as important or even more important than know-how (Harryson 2002). If resources for the production and distribution process (e.g. labour, finance, market access) are governed by a network-structure external to the firm, an adoption of informal practices is usually required (Cheng and Gereffi 1994). Hence, the informal foundations of agility are based on a firm's organisational capability to pool physical and human capital resources by a flexible combination of formal and informal procedures that are exemplified in the next section (for a compact economic discussion of these trends in business organisation see the papers in Siebert 1995).

2.2.3 Resources and Competences for Agile Firm Organisation in Newly Industrialised Regions

In developing countries, a firm-centered perspective has to be based on the development of technological capabilities (Lall 1992) and the concept of the latecomer firm (Mathews 2002). Latecomer firms are mostly lacking essential resources to achieve sustained competitiveness. Therefore, they have to span links to other actors and generate opportunities to leverage resources. For example, an OEM subcontractor can leverage knowledge from customer linkages in developed countries. To internalise the knowledge, i.e. to learn (Viotti 2002), latecomer firms need a sufficient amount of absorptive capacity (Cohen and Levinthal 1990). Thus, latecomer firms can extend their technological capabilities and reach a sustained competitive advantage by leveraging external resources (Mathews 2002).

However, this development path is not an easy one. Amongst others, it depends on the management competences, the entrepreneurial behaviour, and the institutional framework to leverage resources (e.g. opportunity to establish links, access to and transferability of resources, formal and informal institutional barriers). The competence-based view of the firm – based on the ideas of Veblen (1898) – extends the analysis of resources needed for a firm's competitiveness. It specifies the kinds of competences a firm need to make use of these resources, i.e. how it may capitalise on them (Foss 1998). Therefore, it is closely related with concepts of bounded rationality and innovative learning.

Management competences are closely related with entrepreneurial behaviour, i.e. the alertness to changing economic conditions and the capacity to discover profit opportunities by either imitation or innovation (Kirzner 1988). Yu (2000) has elaborated that the dynamic entrepreneurship in Hong Kong and the GPRD differs markedly from other regions. Its uniqueness is based on the ability to seize opportunities by creative imitation. Latecomer firms from Hong Kong attack markets more flexibly than established companies (guerrilla entrepreneurship) and use the advantages that are offered by regional arbitrageurship and co-ordination between Hong Kong and mainland locations (Yu 2000). The cultural, economic, and political environment in the GPRD has been beneficial for entrepreneurial strategies that are conducive to informal dynamics of agile firm organisation.

Besides strategies and competences, agile firms are dependent on the institutional framework for leveraging labour, capital and technological resources. They are trying to pool inputs according to volatile market demands. Examples of institutions needed for agility are:

- Flexible or low regulations for labour conditions,
- Migration laws ensuring an abundant availability of workers with low payment,
- Incentive systems to improve retention and loyalty of high skilled employees,
- Access to different methods of financing,
- Flexible approval procedures,
- Weak enforcement of intellectual property rights,
- Lackadaisical execution of environmental requirements,
- Direct access to decision makers in favour of own requirements,
- Social capital (e.g. guanxi) to stabilise the volatility brought about by agility.

2.3 Greater Pearl River Delta: The World Factory in Perspective

Agile firm organization is closely related with the development of mega-urban regions. Their thick input markets and global–local interfaces are particularly suitable for this kind of firm organisation. Above that, highly flexible modes of production with intense interregional and intraregional interactions had an outstanding impact on the creation of mega-urban regions, particularly in East Asia. They are main drivers of settlement dynamics, contribute to the loss of planning control and governability, and constitute the complexity and dynamics of material and resource flows in these regions.

From precolonial times onwards, the GPRD has been among China's interfaces to global markets and first experiments introducing market-like elements to the Chinese economy have been made in the GPRD. The delta has been one of the fastest growing regions in the world since the economic co-operation between Hong Kong and Guangdong started with the establishment of Special Economic Zones (SEZs) in Shenzhen and Zhuhai in the 1970s. A recent survey estimates that about 60,000 companies with ten million employees in the mainland municipalities of the GPRD are linked with Hong Kong based companies. Industrial output and exports of the GPRD are higher than those of the Yangtze Delta Region surrounding Shanghai (Enright et al. 2005). Today, the GPRD promotes itself as the factory of the world (BrandHK 2005).

The relocation of industries has led to a complex system of megacities and suburban areas that has been described as a mega-urban region or a megalopolis (Castells 1996: 406; Lin 2001: 386). According to census data, the population of the GPRD climbed to about 50 million in 2002 even though the registered population is smaller since it does not include migrant workers. The largest cities are Guangzhou (9.9 million inhabitants), Shenzhen (7.0), Hong Kong (6.8), Dongguan (6.5), and Foshan (5.3) (Enright et al. 2005: 18, 48). In 2002, the GPRD (without Hong Kong and Macao) accounts for 3 % of the Chinese population, 9 % of its GDP, but 34 % of its trade and 22 % of its foreign investments (Enright et al. 2005: 11).

According to Enright et al. (2005), industrial output in the GPRD is mainly from light manufacturing (e.g. toys, textiles, and garments) and the electrical and electronics industry (e.g. consumer electronics, watches). The few heavy industries (e.g. chemicals or plastics) mainly serve as suppliers for these industries. Table 17.1 indicates regional differences between Hong Kong and four mainland municipalities of the GPRD with the highest GDP. Since the figures differ widely between sectors and sub-regions we will select a significant sample to analyse agility in different regions and sectors.

The accelerated development of the GPRD can only be fully understood if its informal dynamics are taken into account. Relocation of subcontracted manufacturing from Hong Kong and Taiwan has been accompanied by an inflow of production factors from other parts of China (e.g. migrant workers) and from all over the world (e.g. foreign direct investment) (Chen 1994). It has been mainly driven by market-forces and completely changed the face of the GPRD within a few

17 Capitalising on Institutional Diversity and Complementary Resources ... 403

Table 17.1 GDP and gross industrial output of selected industries in the GPRD, 2002

	Hong Kong	GPRD (mainland)	Guangzhou	Shenzhen	Foshan	Dongguan
Total GDP in billion USD	154.99	113.75	36.25	27.26	14.20	8.13
GDP in industry in billion USD	19.22	56.62	12.91	13.00	7.19	4.19
GDP in service in billion USD	135.46	51.52	20.18	12.11	5.77	3.29
Share of selected industries in total industrial output of these industries	100%	100%	100%	100%	100%	100%
Electronic/telecom equipment	11%	46%	17%	82%	15%	63%
Electric equipment/ machinery	8%	17%	13%	7%	48%	12%
Textiles and garments	52%	10%	14%	3%	16%	10%
Chemicals	8%	8%	20%	2%	5%	5%
Transport equipment	9%	7%	24%	2%	5%	1%
Plastic products	a	6%	7%	4%	10%	8%
Metal products	13%	6%	5%	0%	1%	1%

Source: own calculations based on Enright et al. 2005; Enright and Scott 2005
[a]Included in chemicals

decades. The 'one country, two systems' policy opens the opportunity to take advantage of the market-led system in Hong Kong and of regulations in the Chinese mainland by informal sidestepping.

Specific kinds of entrepreneurship and social capital add up to the importance of informality in the GPRD. Above that, Hong Kong has been ranked as the world's freest economy for the 12th consecutive year in the Index of Economic Freedom of the Heritage Foundation (2006). Its unique openness to exports and foreign investors is making agile firm organisation and informality more likely than in other parts of Asia. The development of the GPRD has been based on the paradoxical combination of mass production in SMEs, e.g. in electronic devices and toys (Augustin-Jean 2005). Hence, the GPRD is particularly suitable as a study region for our research question.

Intraregional linkages and a spatial division of labour between Hong Kong and the mainland municipalities of the GPRD have been one of the critical factors to the growth of the region as a whole (FHKI 2003). Input factors are complementary to a large extent, i.e. technology, finance, and management know-how are available in Hong Kong, labour and land are deployed in the mainland. This unique combination of low-cost and knowledge-based production has lead to the competitiveness of GPRD's companies (Meng et al. 2000; Enright et al. 2005). Recently, many mainland companies or manufacturing bases succeeded in upgrading their position in the value chain. Although most of the headquarter functions or knowledge-intensive business services (KIBS) are located in Hong Kong, intermediate capabilities (e.g. industrial engineering, design) have been developed in the mainland. Besides that, one should not forget about the big number of endogenous firms in Guangdong; some of them even established their own multinational production networks (e.g. Huawei, TCL). Walcott (2002) observes an endogenous Chinese development model in the Shenzhen Hi-Tech Industrial Park which she labels "bridge high technology". Chinese high-tech start-ups are producing in the GPRD, but still depend on interregional links with Chinese universities for knowledge and financial inputs.

Agile firm organisation and informality are expected to have specific spatial effects in mega-urban regions. On the one hand, these regions are most suitable for production of this kind due to their thick input markets. On the other hand, agile firms can sustain their competitive advantage by co-location and spatial monopolies. Hence, their existence initiates regional agility and volatility of input markets and locational decisions. As shown above, informal social networks can stabilise this process.

3 Data and Methods

The data for this paper has been collected by two surveys of electronics firms in HK and the PRD. The electronics industry has been selected because it is the most important manufacturing industry in the PRD and closely connected to HK via cross-border business models. Its sub-sectors electronic information and electrical machinery and special purpose equipment are two of the three emerging industries in PRD with very high average annual growth rates between 2001 and 2005 of 32.4 % and 26.4 % respectively (FHKI 2007: 36). Above that, the electronics industry covers a broad range of activities from household appliances and consumer electronics to semiconductors and integrated circuits. It consists of companies that are producing parts and components, and companies that assemble final goods. Therefore, it is possible to analyse developments at different phases of the value chains and in sub-sectors at different technological levels. Many of its sub-sectors offer potentials for upgrading and innovation activities. Electronics is also favoured by the provincial government of Guangdong as a future growth sector. If compared to the textile or toy industry, it is also not that much influenced by external regulations, e.g. the multi-fibre agreement, or distinct market dynamics like, e.g. seasonal cycles.

The HK survey has been conducted between August and December 2007. A database with 4,640 electronics SMEs in Hong Kong with production facilities in the PRD has been provided by the HKTDC. A random sample of 3,000 companies has been contacted and 104 firms have been interviewed face-to-face with a standardised questionnaire by interviewers of the Social Science Research Centre, Hong Kong University. The PRD survey was carried out by the Center for Urban and Regional Studies at Sun-Yat-Sen University, Guangzhou, between November 2007 and February 2008 with a focus on Dongguan and Guangzhou.

It is well known that Shenzhen and Dongguan are the most important production locations for HK firms in the PRD due to historic reasons. It is expected that business models connecting HK and Shenzhen/Dongguan are similar. Therefore, a comparison of applied business models connecting HK firms directly (Dongguan/ Shenzhen) and maybe more indirectly (Guangzhou) with firms in the PRD promised to be more interesting. Finally, Dongguan and Guangzhou were selected to conduct the PRD survey. Dongguan was preferred to Shenzhen due to accessibility to firms.

Firms in Dongguan were selected from the Guangdong Electronics Company Catalogue 2007. Firms in Guangzhou have been sampled from a list of the Statistical Bureau of Guangzhou in special industrial districts with a high density of electronics firms, i.e. Luogang, Tianhe, Baiyun, Panyu and Huadu. In total, 222 telephone interviews have been carried out based on a standardised questionnaire. 116 firms are located in Guangzhou, 89 in Dongguan, and 18 in adjacent districts. The sample structure will be described in more detail below. In addition to the surveys, our research team carried out ten in-depth interviews with large electronics companies in Hong Kong and more than 30 interviews with experts in HK and the PRD, e.g. bankers, lawyers, traders, politicians, and academics.

4 Customer Producer Relations in the GPRD

This section aims at providing an overview about the functionality of the HK firm's network in the GPRD. In times of permanently shortened production cycles in the electronics industry and high market volatility due to steady changing customer demand, efficient value chains are fragmented and spread worldwide. The GPRD hosts successfully one of the major production centres of the electronics industry. As firms cannot survive as single units in the globalised world, they are integrated into network structures. A major competitive advantage of the firms in GPRD is its excellent and well-functioned firm network. This section seeks to analyse and highlight the special structure of relations in the GPRD production network. First, the economic integration of the GPRD in the world economy will be focused on combined with a spatial analysis of the production network in the GPRD. Second, the governance of relations to customers and producers will be analysed and third, the way HK and PRD firms smooth their relations by informal modes will be highlighted in terms of customer and producer recruitment, orders dealing and dispute resolution.

4.1 GPRD's Integration in the World Economy

4.1.1 Main Markets

The integration in the world economy can be recognised by the analysis of markets. Firms were asked in the survey to indicate their final product markets. Thereby, they should focus on the end consumer market not the location where the firm sells

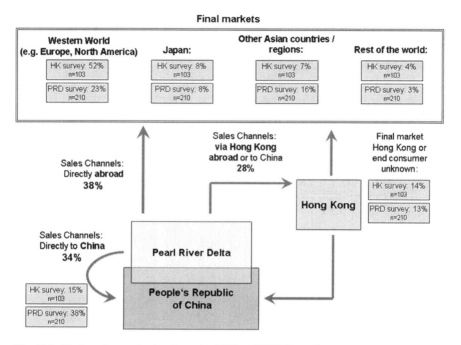

Fig. 17.3 Final markets and sales channels of HK and PRD firms (Source: own survey)

the products next to (e.g. when they sell products via trading companies). Fig. 17.3 compares the sales volume 2006 of firms in the HK and PRD survey. Whereas firms in the HK survey find their most important single markets in North America and Europe (each 26 %), products made in firms in the PRD survey mainly serve market in China (38 %). Surveyed PRD firms are much more oriented on the Chinese market, but they also play on the global platform. 23 % of their products are sold to North America and Europe. 13 % of the surveyed PRD firms and 14 % of the surveyed firms in HK indicated to have their main market in HK. But it is well known, that some firms engaged in component manufacturing do not know their final markets' share. It is expected that they indicated to sell to HK based firms without knowing the further sales' distribution of their HK customer. This explains why the share of firms reporting that HK is an important market is relatively high. The international orientation of HK firms is manifold. First, large international lead firms discovered HK manufacturers as reliable and price-competitive suppliers for production outsourcing. Second, Chinas opening and its processing trade policy, which encouraged HK firms to produce, but not to sell to the PRD in the past, forced HK firms to sell on the international instead on the Chinese market. By now, HK firms are discovering the Chinese market as well. 15 % of firms in the HK survey reported to find their final consumers in China. Whereas HK firms sell more goods on the Chinese market, firms in PRD become more internationally oriented. This sets the GPRD in a more powerful position as a global production centre.

4.1.2 Sales Channels

The analysis of sales channels concentrates on how firms organise to transfer their products to their final markets. In the 1980s HK firms provided sophisticated global sales and distribution channels. Surely, this contributed to the lead firms' decision to outsource to HK firms. Thus, nowadays parts of the PRD production is transferred to consumers via those channels as well. According to the survey in the PRD, 28 % of all PRD sales are organised via HK. They distribute as following: 13 % of all PRD sales are managed by a HK-based affiliates, 8 % via a HK based trading companies and 7 % via other HK based firms. Products sold via HK are either intended for the Chinese or international market. 38 % of the PRD sales go directly to international markets and another 34 % are sold directly to China. A differentiation according to the ownership structure reports, that HK-owned firms in the PRD are responsible for the biggest share of products sold via HK, whereas Chinese and Taiwanese owned firms in the PRD account for the high share of products sold directly to the Chinese market. For HK entrepreneurs in the PRD it is profitable to use their established sales and distribution network. Chinese owned firms in the PRD only partly refer to those channels. They tend to independently build up their own sales and distribution network.

4.1.3 Producer Network in the PRD

In the following section we will elaborate upon what our survey says about how production networks in the GPRD are organised. For an illustration of business networks in the GPRD, firms were asked about their customer and producer relations. HK firms' most important customers are mainly located in final markets, which mean North America (23 %), Europe (22 %) and HK (21 %) itself. Therefore it can be assumed that HK firms concentrated on manufacturing and exports of final electronics products. In contrary 40 % of all PRD firms have their most important customer in HK. The location of final markets of surveyed firms in the PRD differs substantially from the location of the location of their most important customer. This illustrates that firms in HK have an essential role as a customer for products manufactured in the PRD. HK and PRD firms work on different steps in the global value chain system. Only some PRD firms take on a position in the global value chain comparable to firms located in HK. Reversely, HK firms mainly indicated their most important producer to be located in the PRD. In the HK survey, firms indicated that Shenzhen and Dongguan host each 39 % of the main producers. In comparison, only 3 % of the surveyed HK firms' producers are located in Guangzhou.

As mentioned in the introduction, the business models connecting HK firms with Shenzhen and Dongguan are expected to be similar. Therefore, the PRD survey was conducted in Guangzhou and Dongguan to give a comparison. 41 % of the firms in the PRD survey are located in Dongguan and another 53 % are located in Guangzhou. In both cities, districts with a high density of electronics firms were

Table 17.2 Proximity of firms in the PRD survey and their most important producers

If firm is in Dongguan, then producers are in spatial proximity		If firm is in Guangzhou, then producers are in spatial proximity	
Location	Percentage	Location	Percentage
Same city	16	Same city	36
Guangzhou	2	Dongguan	5
Shenzhen	19	Shenzhen	7
Guangdong (elsewhere)	33	Guangdong (elsewhere)	24
China (elsewhere)	13	China (elsewhere)	10
Hong Kong	2	Hong Kong	8
Other Asian regions	11	Other Asian regions	6
North America/Europe	4	North America/Europe	4
Total	100	Total	100

Source: own survey

selected. In Guangzhou, the Tianhe, Panyu and Huadu District were most relevant, in Dongguan Changan, Dongcheng and Houjie District were selected.

It has been shown, that firms in the HK survey work closely with their producers in the PRD. They are expected to forward orders to the first tier producer in the PRD. Additionally, firms in the PRD survey were asked to indicate the spatial distribution of their producer network. This second tier producer network is also located in the PRD in proximity to the first tier producers (see Table 17.2). Firms in Dongguan reported to have their most important producers in Dongguan (16 %), Shenzhen (19 %) or elsewhere in Guangdong (33 %). Producers in Guangzhou indicated to have 36 % of their producers in Guangzhou and 24 % elsewhere in Guangdong. Firms in Dongguan and Shenzhen are less relevant for them. In Dongguan as well as in Guangzhou about 17 % of the main producers are located abroad. It can be assumed that high qualified products like semiconductors are supplied from abroad. Producer network in PRD seem to be locally concentrated in the cities without far reaching linkages. But firms in Guangzhou concentrate their producers in closer proximity then firms in Dongguan do. This is statistically significant. Both cities host firms which are mainly linked to HK, because their main customer is located in HK (firms in Guangzhou: 55 %, firms in Dongguan: 68 %). Additionally, firms in Guangzhou indicated to source and import a substantial part of their products in HK (firms in Guangzhou: 46 %, firms in Dongguan: 39 %).

The survey revealed that HK firms concentrate on final products' sales to end markets. PRD firms focus on both the Chinese and the international market. Despite HK is only of minor importance as final market, it takes its role as the important sales channel for PRD made goods. A detailed view on the production networks in PRD shows, that HK firms' producers are mainly located in Dongguan and Shenzhen. HK firms first moved their production into the PRD and concentrated on these two cities. Guangzhou as the core city in Guangdong province has a relatively low importance for HK firms as a location for production. But a comparative analysis of firms in Dongguan and Guangzhou shows that firms in Guangzhou also have strong connections to HK. The surveyed firms in Dongguan and

Guangzhou dominantly fall back on producers located in close proximity to them. Despite the extensive international distribution network of products made in PRD, one characteristic of production networks is their local concentration. This could be an essential characteristic for the agility of firms in the PRD.

4.2 Governance of Customers and Producers in the GPRD

4.2.1 Hong Kong's Impact on the PRD

As strong interaction could be found between HK based and PRD based firms, it seems of importance to look how those linkages are organised. Well known is that HK firms tend to set up their own production site in the PRD, but from the survey it can be seen, that cooperation with firms in the PRD are also of high importance (see Table 17.3). Out of 104 surveyed firms in HK, 35 firms indicated to have no own production plants in the PRD and another 60 firms reported to have no plants under cooperation agreement. 57 firms in HK indicated to have one wholly owned production site in the PRD and 12 firms even have two or more production sites. Moreover, 22 firms reported to control production plants under cooperation agreement and another 22 firms govern two or more of those plants. Firms could additionally indicate exactly how many production plants they manage entirely or partly. Out of 88 production plants which are wholly owned 78 (89 %) are located in the PRD. Out of another 163 production plants under cooperation 145 (89 %) are established in the PRD. This lets conclude, that 223 (89 %) firms in the PRD are directly managed and governed by 104 HK firms (proportion 1: 2.4). HK firms' impact in terms of management and governance in PRD seems to be very high. Since these data only refer to SMEs in the HK survey, the figure would be expected to rise if large HK conglomerates were included.

4.2.2 Governance Modes of Customer and Producer Relations

HK firms mainly organise their production in the PRD within their own company (hierarchy). Alternative modes to organise customer or producer relations are equity cooperation, non-equity cooperation and markets. When firms organise their production in joint ventures, they decide to cooperate with another firm and share the ownership of the production unit. When firms decide to cooperate without shared ownership (non-equity cooperation), they conclude an agreement which provides a rough framework about the collaboration without fixing the details. It requires the mutual understanding of partners. Cooperation of any type always implies a lot of understanding and reliability between managers. Thus, cooperation needs more informal modes to make it work successfully. When firms act on markets, they only have buying and selling agreements without any further cooperation or commitment.

Table 17.3 Organisation of HK managed production plants in the PRD

	100% own production plants				Plants under cooperation				Sum of all
	0	1	2+	Sum	0	1	2+	Sum	
No. of firms in the HK survey	35	57	12	104	60	22	22	104	–
No. of production plants, thereof	0	57 (100%)	31 (100%)	38 (100%)	0	22 (100%)	141 (100%)	163 (100%)	251 (100%)
In the PRD	0	54 (95%)	24 (77%)	78 (89%)	0	20 (91%)	125 (89%)	145 (89%)	223 (89%)
Elsewhere	0	3 (5%)	7 (23%)	10 (11%)	0	2 (9%)	16 (11%)	18 (11%)	28 (11%)

Source: own survey

As HK firms first moved their production to the PRD, they set up own production sites and adapted to the weak institutional environment in China. A lack of legal security and reliability and missing business and trade laws led to a cross border production pattern, where HK firms dominantly managed production in the PRD. Formal laws in China did not provide enough safeguard to protect trade. Despite HK managers started to smooth relations by the establishment of personal relations to Chinese partners in daily business, they did not decide to rely on Chinese firms for their production. Moreover, there was a shortage of suppliers in the PRD and a lack of capabilities to provide quality products. But especially in the beginning firms were hindered to set up own production sites, because the Chinese government forced HK firms to organise production processes within joint ventures with Chinese firm. Only HK firms which moved to the PRD in the end of the 1980s were allowed to establish own production sites.

In contrast, firms in the HK survey prefer market based relations (see Table 17.4) with their global customers. Customers usually place orders to firms in HK (66 %). Worldwide established institutions to regulate international trade provide sufficient safeguards for HK firms. 28 % of the firms in HK cooperate with their customers, only 6 % have any equity relations. However, HK firms organise their customer relations via markets, but cross border production of HK firms is organised via complete control (55 %). *In contrast*, electronics firms in the PRD survey mainly receive orders from customers in HK (65 %). Only 18 % of the surveyed firms are affiliates of HK based firms. Despite over half of all surveyed firms in HK have own affiliates in the PRD, they only account for a small part of all firms in the PRD. The PRD survey shows that it is typical for HK owned firms to have own production sites in the PRD. Firms in the PRD owned from Chinese, Taiwanese or other foreigners typically work on cooperation or market based relation with customers in HK. When firms in the PRD survey indicated how they organise their relation to their most important producer, 65 % indicated to buy supplies from independent producers. Another 20 % cooperate with their producers and only 15 % of the firms in the PRD survey receive their most important supplies from firms which they wholly or partially own. Comparing customer and producer relations of firms in the HK survey, large differences can be seen which are statistically significant. Firms in the HK sample have hierarchical relations with their producers and market like relations with their customers. Although firms in the PRD survey prefer market like relations with customers and producer, their distribution according to the organisational modes is significantly different.

Table 17.5 informs about which factors determine what governance modes firms in the HK and PRD survey prefer to organise their customer and producer relations. For firms in the HK and PRD survey it was found that the higher the profits made with one partner (*Dependence on customers and producers*), the more likely the relationship is to be organised in a hierarchical way. This seems to be natural, if firms have set up their own affiliates, then most of the production is run by that affiliate. Firms rarely begin subcontracting large shares of production to other firms. Using the market place means choosing the best partner and spreading risk, which usually results in a more diverse pool of customers and suppliers. As political

Table 17.4 Organisation of customer and producer relations of HK and PRD based firms

	To most important	n	Hierarchy (wholly owned affiliate) (%)	Equity cooperation (e.g. joint venture) (%)	Non-equity cooperation (%)	Market (just placing orders) (%)	Sum (%)
HK survey	Customer	104	2	4	28	66	100
	Producer in the PRD	104	55	16	16	13	100
PRD survey	Customers in HK	88	18	10	7	65	100
	Producer	215	9	6	20	65	100

Source: own survey

17 Capitalising on Institutional Diversity and Complementary Resources ... 413

Table 17.5 Factors determining which governance mode firms select to organise customer and producer relations

Determinants	Trend to hierarchical relations	Significance
HK firms		
Location of customers and producers (1)	When customers or producers are in China	++
Dependance on customers and producers (2)	The higher the volume of sales or products bought	++
Years of working experience (3)	The more working experience exists	++
PRD firms		
Dependence on customers and producers (2)	The higher the volume of sales or products bought	+
Working experience (3)	The more working experience exists	++
Ownership structure (4)	The more foreign capital is involved	+
Innovativeness (5)	The more innovative firms are	+

Source: own survey

+ significant (on $p < 0.05$), tested Cramer's V

++ highly significant (on $p < 0.01$), tested Cramer's V

Classification

(1) = China, abroad

(2) = 20 % or less, 21–50 %, 51–80 %, more than 80 % (data 2006)

(3) = 6 years or less, 7–10 years, 11–16 years, 17 years or more

(4) = PRD: 100 % CN owned, CN/foreign Joint Venture, 100 % foreign owned, floating shares

(5) = less than 50 points, 50–90 points, 90 points or more

changes can be sudden in the PRD, HK firms prefer to control and govern the maximum share of their production. Moreover, the years of working experience (*Working experience*) with customers and producers is significantly associated with certain governance modes. With an increasing number of years the likelihood that transactions are embedded in hierarchies rises. As markets ease the switch of partners, those relations are naturally shorter, but in the PRD the location-specific institutions act cumulatively on that pattern. Relations of HK firms to the PRD producers set up before China entered the WTO and CEPA was concluded (*working experience more than 6 years*) were difficult to manage on a market basis. Firms which established contracts after 2001 (*working experience 6 years or less*) could enjoy a much more stable situation in China, which encourages more HK firms to work within cooperation or market-like relations. This also explains why foreign owned firms (*Ownership structure*) in the PRD survey more often indicated to work with own affiliates instead of independent producers. Moreover, in the PRD survey, innovative firms more often indicated to work in hierarchies with their customers and producers (*Innovativeness*). This can be explained first by the ownership of firms. Foreign firms tend to be more knowledge-intensive as Chinese firms and as seen above foreign firms prefer to work in hierarchies with their customers and producers. Second, the more innovative a firm is, the more formal safeguards are needed to protect against imitation. Hierarchies provide the highest safeguards (e.g. full control) to ensure against knowledge flow to outsiders. In the HK sample governance modes highly depend on the *location of customers and producers*,

Table 17.6 Governance modes and years of working experience of surveyed firms in HK

| Governance mode | Years of working experience with most important producer | | | | |
	6 years or less (%)	7–10 years (%)	11–16 years (%)	17 years or more (%)	In total (%)
Hierarchy	40	47	69	100	55
Equity cooperation	17	16	23	0	16
Non-equity cooperation	26	21	4	0	16
Market	19	16	4	0	13
Total	100	100	100	100	100

Source: own survey

which indicates that the institutional environment in certain locations is highly influencing. Other factors like firm size (employees, sales) or age are insignificant for the choice of governance modes.

4.2.3 New Trends to Organise Relations in the PRD

As formal rules and safeguard provided by laws improved in the PRD, business uncertainty decreased. Our survey shows that HK firms obviously started to rethink about the organisational modes applied to producers in the PRD. 100 % of all firms in the HK survey which have worked with their producers for 17 years or more applied a hierarchical relation. But only 40 % of firms in the HK survey which have worked with their producers for 6 years or less indicated to have a hierarchical relation. It must be assumed, that some firms changed their governance modes over time (e.g. firms separated from their Chinese joint venture partner after they were allowed to establish a wholly foreign owned firm), but this is still an exception. Firms usually tend to stick to the originally chosen governance mode regarding a certain producer. Firms in the HK survey which indicated that they start to work with their main producer in the PRD 6 or less years ago, more often apply equity or non-equity cooperation (see Table 17.6). Firms in HK tend to concentrate on brand building, innovation, product development and marketing, instead the extension of their factories. Own factories are used to produce high-sophisticated innovative products. Qualified Chinese firms can take over the mass production process. They build up relations to new independent producers, which take over the role of the most important producer.

The cross border production pattern changes and successful firms in HK tend to look for appropriate partners to supply them. It could be shown that firms in the HK survey have changed their behaviour in the last 10 years significantly and preferred cooperation to Chinese firms instead of strongly organised hierarchies. Although they do not have full control and influence on producers, they have to manage fast changing orders and shorter delivery times. They must keep their flexibility. This is only manageable with a reliable relation to producers. The next section will focus on how firms select new producers, gain new customers and whether they keep their

17 Capitalising on Institutional Diversity and Complementary Resources ... 415

supply flexibility. Furthermore, it will be analysed how firms solve disputes with those producers. It will be examined how firms organise their cooperation relations and what impact informal arrangements have.

In summary, to reach flexibility, firms have different *options to organise their relations to customers and producers*. The most important producer of firms in the HK survey is mostly an own production site (hierarchy) in the PRD. However, the more recently a producer in the PRD has been chosen, the more often it is not organised as an own production site, but as a (non-equity) cooperation or a joint venture partner (equity cooperation). To be successful, cooperation requires additional safeguards based on informal and personal linkages. In contrary, the relation to the most important customer is organised via market-based buying and selling agreements, cooperation is rare. The differences in customer and producer relations can be explained partly by the weak-developed institutional environment in China which forced HK firms to control wholly-owned plants in the PRD. It did not provide enough stability for market-based transactions. Additionally, the quality of Chinese producers was low in the beginning. Recently, improvements of the Chinese institutional system and better qualified producers allow for a shift from wholly-owned production sites to cooperative partners. As a result, more informal governance modes are required to increase mutual understanding and reliability.

4.3 Competitive Advantages by Smoothing Relations

4.3.1 Customer Recruitment

When firms in HK look for new customers, they have different opportunities to contact and gain them. A very official and formal process would be to participate on bidding competitions. Furthermore firm can search actively for new customers. E.g. they can exhibit on fairs, they can work with sales agents or use member lists of business associations to contact new customers. More informal and personal is the use of business contacts, e.g. potential customers can be recommended by business partners. When firms rely on private contacts to gain new customers, it is even more informal. Surveyed firms in HK ranked the different channels to contact customer on a scale from (1) very important to (5) not important. Table 17.7 presents that *active searching* (2.65) is most important for firms in the HK survey to contact new customers. The use of *business contacts* was ranked second, *private contacts* and *bidding competition* is of lower importance. Informal channels which are based on business and private contacts are only of medium importance. A correlation analysis shows the connectivity between the data. If the figure (correlation coefficient) in the matrix in Table 17.7 is close to 1, firms which reported a high importance of one channel also reported a high importance of another contact channel. If the figure is close to 0 no correlation between the channels can be assumed. In Table 17.7 it is apparent, that firms which ranked active searching high, also significantly often emphasised the importance of private contacts (correlation 0.335). Firms which

Table 17.7 Importance of contact channels for HK firms and their correlation

Contact mode	Importance HK[a]	Correlation			
		(1)	(2)	(3)	(4)
(1) Active searching (fairs, agents, internet)	2.65	1	0.094	0.335[+]	0.124
(2) Business contacts (former workers, recommendations)	3.06		1	0.502[+]	0.355[+]
(3) Private contact to potential customers (e.g. family ties)	4.28			1	0.308[+]
(4) Bidding competition	3.99				1

Source: own survey
[+] = The correlation is significant on the level of 0.01
[++] = The correlation is significant on the level of 0.05
[a]Mean value, 1 = very important to 5 = not important

Table 17.8 Selection criteria for producers in the PRD since 1997 (HK survey)

	Equity-cooperation[a]	Non-equity cooperation[a]
Expertise	2.09	2.06
Good reputation	2.00	2.06
Good experiences in former business	1.81	2.13
Existence of personal relationships	2.00	2.81
Get along with local workers/suppliers well	2.91	3.13
Get along well with public officials	3.18	4.19
Required by CN law	3.91	4.63

Source: own survey
[a]Mean value, 1 = very important to 5 = not important

ranked formal bidding competition high also significantly often stressed the importance of business and private contacts (0.355 and 0.308). This leads to the conclusion that firms in the HK survey tend to combine formal and informal channels to recruit new customers. It cannot be confirmed that firms in HK use a more formal western style to manage their customer relations. They use the spectrum of formal and informal opportunities, which certainly contribute to their success to attract new business to HK.

4.3.2 Producer Selection

As firms in the HK survey indicated that cooperation partners in the PRD become more important, the selection criteria for producers in cooperation are analysed. Thus, equity and non-equity cooperation to producers are analysed which were established after 1997. This focus is set to show how firms nowadays select their producers (see Table 17.8). When firms look for joint venture partners good experiences in former business (1.81) is most important to select them. The second most important criteria is a good reputation and personal relations (both 2.00). Former motivations (like getting along well with public official, suppliers or

17 Capitalising on Institutional Diversity and Complementary Resources ...

Table 17.9 Days of negotiation with customers and producers according to their governance mode

	n=76 (%)	Days of negotiation with customers (mean value)	n=74 (%)	Days of negotiation with producers (mean value)
Hierarchy	2	nA	46	2
Equity cooperation	1	nA	19	6
Non-equity cooperation	36	7	22	4
Market	61	13	13	7
Total	100		100	

Source: own survey
nA = not available, sample to small

workers) to take on Chinese partners in form of joint venture have lost their importance nowadays. When firms in the HK survey decide to invest in a shared owned firm, they consider a smooth relation to their partner. They have to ensure mutual understanding when quick response is required and strategic agreements are concluded. When mutual understanding is missing, firm's risk to invest without returns is too high. If firms in HK search for partners on the basis of non-equity cooperation, they rank the expertise and reputation of partners highest (both 2.06). Non-equity cooperation is not as long term oriented as equity cooperation. Therefore firms in HK put less emphasis on mutual understanding but more on expertise of partners.

4.3.3 Flexibility in Relations

For firms in HK quick response to orders is most important for successful dealing with them. Thus, quality in customer and producer relations can be measured by the time they need to agree on order details, before the production process starts. As demand is changing quickly, western lead firms require a quick reaction of firms in HK to their orders. When customers decided to place an order to a HK electronics firm, they want to keep the time to negotiate contractual details low as it delays the start of the production process. From Table 17.9 can be seen, that firms in the HK survey which work in close cooperation with their customers (framework agreement is concluded in advance) need only half of the time (7 days) to work out contractual details. When customers' relations are market driven, firms need about 13 days to agree on details which need to be fixed before a final order can start the production process. After HK firms have received orders from international customers they have to negotiate with their producers as they need supplies from them. When firms in HK have own production sites in the PRD, only 2 days are necessary to pass on final product specifications or delivery schedules, before the production process can start. When firms in HK organise their production in a joint venture it already takes 6 days until final details are agreed with the management of the joint venture. Firms which have reliable cooperation partners in the PRD only

418   J.R. Diez et al.

Table 17.10 Modes of dispute resolution of firms in the HK and the PRD survey

Mode of dispute resolution	HK survey (%)	PRD survey (%)
Negotiation only	45	62
Negotiation and mediation	11	27
Negotiation, mediation, arbitration and letigation	44	11
Total	100	100

Source: own survey

need 4 days to pass on and finalise order details with their producers. When firms in the HK survey rely on market relations with their producers it takes them another 7 days to work out price, delivery time and product quantity and quality before the production process can start.

Cooperation with customers which is based on framework agreements concluded in advance provide a basement for quicker exchange than market relations although the majority of HK firms do not take advantage from cooperation. Cooperation requires more mutual understanding and personal effort to maintain, but it seems to enhance firms' flexibility. No doubt that own production sites minimise the time to pass on orders, but reliable producers in non-equity cooperation also shorten the time of negotiation. The advantage of own (sometimes expensive) production sites to keep flexibility is vanishing.

4.3.4 Dispute Resolution

Despite firms select their producers carefully and work out appropriate contracts to safeguard trade, it might happen that disputes occur. Dispute resolution can be very formally organised when firms go for litigation. But firms can also decide for alternative dispute settlement. They might negotiate, mediate or arbitrate with their producers. Negotiation is the most informal mode to solve disputes. When negotiation does not lead to a satisfying result, firms can go for mediation. A third person tries to support parties to solve their conflicts, but the third person is not allowed to judge. Mediation is more formal than negotiation, but still provides more informal elements than arbitration. Arbitration can follow mediation or negotiation when no solution is reached. Arbitration requires one or three arbitrators who have the right to give a judgement. Arbitration is a direct alternative for litigation, but it is confidential and not open for the public. It has a similar status to litigation, but it still ensures more privacy. Its character tends to be less formal than litigation. 45 % of the surveyed firms in HK indicated that until now they have used only negotiation to settle disputes with producers (see Table 17.10). 11 % used negotiations followed by mediation and 44 % reported that they also consider arbitration and litigation for dispute resolution. Nearly half of the firms in the HK survey only rely on informal dispute resolution processes. The other half uses the entire spectrum of opportunities to solve dispute. In contrary surveyed firms in the PRD significantly more often negotiate only with their producers (62 %). Another 27 % step on to

when disputes occur. Only a few firms go for arbitration and litigation with their producers. Firms in the PRD very strictly keep to negotiation only. This can be explained by the lacking quality and reliability of the Chinese court system. Firms are forced to solve conflicts informally among them. The survey in HK shows that a functional legal system encourages more firms to find the appropriate dispute resolution process. Although HK firms can use courts, most firms in HK still prefer negotiation as informal mode to solve disputes, because in many cases this is most appropriate one. Negotiation can take place quickly and often with relatively little expense in contrast to taking the dispute to court. It focuses on the parties' real commercial, emotional and psychological needs and not just on their legal rights. Negotiation gives the parties an opportunity to participate and control directly and informally in resolving their own dispute. Negotiation relies on the good will to reach an agreement confidentially. This increases the probability to stay with the reached agreement later on, even if it is not legally binding. Negotiation is confidential, nobody loses his face and reputation in the public. Privacy and confidentiality is a culturally embedded value of the Chinese society. When the situation requires it, firms in HK take their producers to court. This does not happen immediately, but follows a negotiation process. The results show again that firms in HK tend to use formal and informal modes of dispute resolution at the same time. This makes them flexible while having the chance to choose the appropriate mode to solve disputes, which contribute as an explanation for the competitiveness of firms in HK.

The results obtained clearly underline that agile firms make use of formal and informal business practices in order to gain flexibility:

- When firms in HK *are searching new customers or producers* they apply a combination of formal and informal modes. This mix provides an opportunity to choose flexibly the most appropriate option, e.g. quick identification by informal modes versus quality-driven but more time consuming identification by formal modes. Customers are most often gained by active searching (e.g. via sales agents, exhibitions and fairs) which is directed by business and personal contacts. Selection criteria for cooperation partners in the PRD are their expertise combined with a good reputation and experiences in the past.
- To compete on a global scale, firms need to *minimise negotiation time.* Our survey results indicate that response time of customer-producer relations of firms in the HK survey which are based on cooperation can compete with those organised in a hierarchical way. Thus, cooperation which requires more informal modes of understanding can guarantee a quick and flexible response to global markets at the same time.
- *Conflicts with producers* are solved by negotiations by half of the firms in the HK sample. Negotiations are also based on informality in order to keep privacy and confidentiality. But firms do not hesitate to go for arbitration or litigation when negotiations fail. An informal conflict solution is mostly the quicker alternative. Again, the use of informal modes increases the choice of options to solve disputes which enhances flexibility.

5 Conclusions

Since the open-door policies initiated in the special economic zones in the PRD in 1978, more and more HK firms have gradually relocated or expanded parts of their business operation from HK into the PRD, which has strongly contributed to the economic development and prosperity in this region. As results, more and more cross-border economic activities occurred and the economic integration within the GPRD has been intensified. With rapid changes in the global business environment and in the political arrangements towards innovation and upgrading, firms supposedly need to efficiently utilise available resources, inclusive their informal assets such as personal networks to increase their capability to flexibly and effectively cope with the new challenges.

HK-related firms are well-known in their capability to quickly adapt themselves to the new market conditions. To figure out whether and to what extent HK-related firms utilise informal assets and institutions available to increase their behavioural flexibility, we conducted HK survey on the electronics SMEs as well as PRD survey on electronics firms in 2007 and 2008. Several in-depth interviews with large electronics firms in HK and with experts from different areas in the GPRD were also carried out to complement our surveys. Our findings were summarised in this paper. We began with the overview of our HK as well as PRD sample in order to figure out whether there are indeed strong needs embedded in the current business and political conditions for informal and flexible organisation of firms. After that, we focussed on "customer-producer relations" and "industrial innovation" on the other hand to clarify how firms operating in the GPRD transformed the needs for agility into different kinds of means and actions in these two areas to sustain their competitiveness in the global market.

Regarding needs for agility, we find that about 66 % of firms from our HK sample and almost 60 % of those from our PRD sample faced strongly increasing competition in the last 5 years. Taking firms facing moderately increasing competition also into consideration, the corresponding figure for firms from both surveys amounted to more than 90 %. Despite intensifying competition, markets of major products of the responding firms were still characterised with growing trends in general, however, also with high-level volatility. This corresponds to our assumption about the current business conditions faced by firms in the GPRD. To rapidly response to the changing business environments and to quickly react to the new challenges, high predictability of firms with respect to changes in, for example, price, volume and political arrangements would be advantageous. In this regard, we find that government regulations in China have been the least predictable, while the required quality of products and delivery times are well predictable. Price and volume of orders are prone to quite unforeseeable changes. This result of relatively low predictability corresponds on the one hand with the fast changing conditions faced by firms operating in the GPRD. On the other hand, such low predictability implies that firms are forced to put more attention and give more efforts to make them be capable to cope with all possible emerging situations as quickly as possible.

With respect to transforming needs for agility into diversified actions and means to cope with new challenges, we find that firms have adapted their governance modes regarding to their relationships to their customers and produces, so that the modes can function compatibly with the up-to-date business environments. Long-term cooperation relationships with their producers and customers enabled them to more flexibly react to the changing requirements of the markets. Regarding to searching for new customers and selecting adequate production partners, informal channels were of slightly lower importance than formal ones. However, our analysis also shows that both types of channels were applied at the same time in reality, indicating the complementary character between informal and formal institutions. In addition, we also find the importance of informal ways for firms operating in the GPRD in dealing with business disputes. While firms in HK tended to use formal and informal modes of dispute resolution at the same time, firms in the PRD preferred informal negotiations than formal litigation.

With respect to agile firm organisation in general, the findings of our research confirm the hypothesis about the interaction of informal arrangements and flexible firm organisation. Informal institutions for doing business in the GPRD are not going to become less important with further development and improvement of the Chinese legal system. Adequate application of informal factors within given formal constellations enhances the capabilities of firms to more flexibly react to the fast changes in the political and business environment to sustain their competitiveness in the global market. However, future research is needed. This paper has focused on producer and customer relations. The research has to be expanded to investigate organisation and governance modes in other critical business areas such as innovation and finance. But in the long run, a crucial research question for the competitiveness of the GPRD is whether the detected business model, which has its roots in low-cost, high-volume production and a spatial division of labour between HK and the PRD, will be appropriate when firms are upgrading by improving either their innovation capabilities or their position in the value chain. The rapid restructuring has started to shape the PRD's economy: More and more firms are enhancing their technological and management capabilities setting the base for an upgrading of the overall economy, which is also complemented by education and training efforts.

References

Akerlof GA (1970) The market for 'lemons': quality uncertainty and the market mechanism. Q J Econ 84:488–500

Allen F, Qian J, Qian M (2006) Building China's financial system in the 21st century: banks, markets, and beyond. In: Brandt L, Rawski T (ed) China's economic transition: origins, outcomes, mechanisms, and consequences

Amin N (2002) The informal sector in Asia from the decent work perspective. Working paper on the informal economy 2002/4. ILO, Geneva

Arrow K (1974) The limits of organization. Norton, New York

Augustin-Jean L (2005) Urban planning in Hong Kong and integration with the Pearl River Delta: a historical account of local development. GeoJournal 62:1–13

Barney J (1991) Firm resources and sustained competitive advantage. J Manage 17:99–120

Bessant J, Knowles D, Briffa G, Francis D (2002) Developing the agile enterprise. Int J Technol Manage 24:484–497

Bickenbach F, Kumkar L, Soltwedel R (1999) The new institutional economics of antitrust and regulation. Tech rep No 961. Kiel Institute of World Economics, Kiel

Brand HK (2005) Pearl River Delta – factory of the world. Brand Hong Kong. Available online: http://www.brandhk.gov.hk/brandhk/e_pdf/efact12.pdf. Accessed 29 Jan 2006

Carr M, Chen M (2002) Globalization and the informal economy: how global trade and investment impact on the working poor. Working paper on the informal economy 2002/1. ILO, Geneva

Castells M (1996) The rise of the network society. Blackwell, Oxford

Chen X (1994) The new spatial division of labor and commodity chains in the greater South China economic region. In: Gereffi G, Korzeniewicz M (eds) Commodity chains and global capitalism. Praeger, Westport, pp 165–186

Chen X-P, Chen CC (2004) On the intricacies of the Chinese guanxi: a process model of guanxi development. Asia Pacific J Manage 21:305–324

Cheng L, Gereffi G (1994) The informal economy in East Asian development. Int J Urban Reg 18:194–219

Chopra K (2001) Social capital and development: the role of formal and informal institutions in a developing country. Paper presented at the workshop on poverty alleviation and sustainable development by the international institute for sustainable development, Ottawa

Coase R (1937) The nature of the firm. Economica 4:386–405

Cohen W, Levinthal D (1990) Absorptive capacity: a new perspective on learning and innovation. Adm Sci Q 35:128–152

Durlauf S, Fafchamps M (2005) Social Capital. In: Durlauf S, Aghion P (eds) Handbook of economic growth. Wiley, New York

Enright M, Scott E, Chang K (2005) Regional powerhouse: the greater Pearl river delta and the rise of China. Wiley, Singapore

Ernst D (2002) Global production networks and the changing geography of innovation systems Implications for developing countries. J Econ Innov New Technol 12:1–27

Ernst D, Kim L (2002) Global production networks, knowledge diffusion, and local capability formation. Res Policy 31:1417–1429

Feenstra RC, Hanson GH, Lin S (2003) The value of information in international trade: gains to outsourcing through Hong Kong. Tech Rep 9328. National Bureau of Economic Research, Cambridge

FHKI (2003) Made in PRD: the changing face of HK manufacturers. Tech Rep. Federation of Hong Kong Industries, Hong Kong

FHKI (2007) Made in PRD. Challenges and opportunities for HK industries. Federation of Hong Kong Industries, Hong Kong

Foss N (1998) The competence-based approach: Veblenian ideas in the modern theory of the firm. Cambridge J Econ 22:479–495

Greenwald B, Stiglitz JE (1986) Externalities in economies with imperfect information and incomplete markets. Q J Econ 101:229–264

Grossman G, Helpman E (2002) Integration vs. outsourcing in industry equilibrium. Q J Econ 117:85–120

Grossman G, Helpman E (2005) Outsourcing in a global economy. Rev Econ Stud 72:135–160

Gunasekaran A, Yusuf Y (2002) Agile manufacturing: a taxonomy of strategic and technological imperatives. Int J Prod Res 40:1357–1385

Hakansson H, Snehota I (1997) No business is an Island: the network concept of business strategy. In: Ford D (ed) Understanding business markets: interaction, relationships and networks, 2nd edn. Fort Worth, London, pp 136–150

Harryson S (2002) Why know-who trumps know-how. Strat + Bus 27(2):16–21

Heritage Foundation (2006) Index of economic freedom. www.heritage.org/Index. Accessed 10 Feb 2009

Hoffman N (2000) An examination of the "sustainable competitive advantage" concept: past, present, and future. Academy of marketing science review 4. http://www.amsreview.org/articles/hoffman04-2000.pdf. Accessed 18 Dec 2005

Hussmanns R (2004) Measuring the informal economy: from employment in the informal sector to informal employment. Policy Integration Department working paper No. 53. International labour office, Geneva

Iacocca Institute (1991) 21st century manufacturing enterprise strategy. An industry-led view, vol 1 & 2. Iacocca Institute, Bethlehem

Johansson B (2005) Parsing the menagerie of agglomeration and network externalities. In: Industrial clusters and inter-firm networks. Edward Elgar, Cheltenham, pp 107–147

Johansson B, Quigley J (2004) Agglomeration and networks in spatial economies. Pap Reg Sci 83(1):165–176

Karlsson C, Johansson B, Stough R (2005) Industrial clusters and inter-firm networks. Edward Elgar, Cheltenham

Kidd PT (1994) Agile manufacturing: forging new frontiers. Addison-Wesley, Wokingham

Kim L (2003) Technology transfer & intellectual property rights: the Korean experience. UNCTAD-ICTSD project on IPRs and sustainable development. UNCTAD, Geneva

Kirzner IM (1988) Unternehmer und Marktdynamik. Philosophia, München

Klein PG (2005) The make-or-buy decision: lessons from empirical studies. In: Menard C (ed) Handbook of new institutional economics. Springer, Dordrecht

Koppenjan J, Klijn E-H (2004) Managing uncertainties in networks: a network approach to problem solving and decision making. Routledge, London

Lall S (1992) Technological capabilities and industrialization. World Dev 20(2):165–186

Lin G (2001) Metropolitan development in a transitional socialist economy: spatial restructuring in the Pearl river delta, China. Urban Stud 38:383–406

Mathews JA (2002) Competitive advantages of the late-comer firms: a resources based account of industrial catch-up strategies. Asia Pacific J Manage 19(4):467–488

McMillan J (1995) Reorganizing vertical supply relationships. In: Siebert H (ed) Trends in business organization: do participation and cooperation increase competitiveness? J.C.B. Mohr, Tuebingen, pp 203–222

Menard C (2004) The economics of hybrid organizations. J Inst Theor Econ 160(3):345–376

Menard C (2005) A new institutional approach to organization. In: Menard C (ed) Handbook of new institutional economics. Springer, Dordrecht

Meng X, Wang M, Li G (2000) Case of the garment industry in Shenzhen City, China. Urban partnership background series 7. World Bank, Washington

North D (1990) Institutions, institutional change and economic performance. University Press, Cambridge

Piore M, Sabel C (1984) The second industrial divide: possibilities for prosperity. Basic Books, New York

Porter ME (1996) What is strategy? Harv Bus Rev 74:61–80

Powell WW (1990) Neither market nor hierarchy – network forms of organization. Res Organ Behav 12:295–336

SCMP (2008) Guangdong want HK plants to stay. South China morning post, 4 July 2008

Shelanski HA, Klein PG (1995) Empirical-research in transaction cost economics – a review and assessment. J Law Econ Organ 11(2):335–361

Sindzingre A (2006) The relevance of the concepts of formality and informality: a theoretical appraisal. In: Guha-Khasnobis B, Kanbur R, Ostrom E (eds) Linking the formal and informal economy: concepts and policies. Oxford University Press, Oxford, pp 58–74

Stiglitz J (1984) Information and economic analysis: a perspective. Conference papers of the Royal Economic Society. Oxford 21–44

Stiglitz JE (1986) The new development economics. World Dev 14:257–265

Veblen T (1898) Why is economics not an evolutionary science? Cambridge J Econ 22:403–414 (reprinted 1998)

Viotti E (2002) National learning systems: a new approach on technical change in late industrializing economies and evidences from the cases of Brazil and South Korea. Technol Forecast Soc 69(7):653–680

Walcott S (2002) Chinese industrial and science parks: bridging the gap. Prof Geogr 54(3):349–364

Wang Y, Nicholas S (2007) The formation and evolution of non-equity strategic alliances in China. Asia Pacific J Manage 24:131–150

Williams A, Zhang X (2001) Structural changes in Chinese industry with emphasis on product development. Paper presented at the fourth SMESME international conference, Aalborg

Williamson OE (1998) Transaction cost economics: how it works; where it is headed. De Econ 146(1):23–58

Woolcock M, Narayan D (2000) Social capital: implications for development theory, research, and policy. World Bank Res Obser 15:225–249

Yu TF-L (2000) Hong Kong's entrepreneurship: behaviours and determinants. Entrep Reg Dev 12:179–194

Chapter 18
Impacts of Transport Infrastructure Policies in Population-Declining Metropolitan Area

Business Productivity and Quality of Urban Life in Tokyo

Kiyoshi Yamasaki, Takayuki Ueda, and Shinichi Muto

Abstract In The Tokyo metropolitan area, population growth and economic growth have caused serious urban problems like sprawl at urban fringe, heavy congestion not only in road network but also in railway network, environmental emission and so on. Although there still now remain the difficult problems for us to tackle with, the transport infrastructure policies until today have succeeded in sustaining the high business productivity with high spatial agglomeration and quality of life in the population-growing trend.

Japan is however now at the down-slope of the population trend curve and Tokyo is predicted to begin a decade-long decline in population. The significant population decline in Tokyo metropolitan area is an inexperienced situation for the people and policy makers. They may be concerned that the population decline would reduce the great merit of spatial agglomeration in Tokyo. The question at the heart of policy discussion is how we can sustain the high level of business productivity and quality of life in the Tokyo metropolitan area by spatial restructuring. This paper has developed the Computable Urban Economic Model, which re-formalizes the conventional landuse-transport interaction model on the basis of microeconomic foundation, so as to answer the above question.

As a result, we found that the central Tokyo remains as the center of the economy in 2050 with high spatial agglomeration since the agglomeration is accelerated by the scale economy. On the other hand, population which is not affected by agglomeration, is decreasing at each zone with the same level.

K. Yamasaki (✉)
Value Management Institute, Tokyo, Takeda, Kofu, Japan
e-mail: kiyoshi_yamasaki@vmi.co.jp

T. Ueda
School of Engineering, The University of Tokyo, Tokyo, Takeda, Kofu, Japan

S. Muto
Department of Civil and Environmental Planning, Yamanashi University, Takeda, Kofu, Japan

J. Klaesson et al. (eds.), *Metropolitan Regions*, Advances in Spatial Science,
DOI 10.1007/978-3-642-32141-2_18, © Springer-Verlag Berlin Heidelberg 2013

The investment to the three Ring Roads is expected to contribute to developing more dispersive urban structure since the three Ring Roads increase the transportation convenience at the suburb and it induces to the entry of the firms and population as well. This does not, however, the central Tokyo loses its competitiveness but they still remain strong in terms of the spatial distribution of the firms. The reduction of population mitigates the congestion of the road network. It enables us to increase our convenience in terms of the trip by car. It induces to more trips to the households and business people, which bring about more communication, that is one of the keys for the productivity growth and the enhancement of households' utility. During this period, traffic density of car increase due to the enhancement of the transport convenience by car.

Keywords Spatial agglomeration • Productivity • Land use • Induced and development traffic • Network

1 Introduction

Tokyo has been the largest metropolitan area in the world and the growth pole which has led the Japanese national economy. Since the years of rapid economic growth after the War, Tokyo has attracted a huge amount of population from the country-sides to result in mono-centric spatial structure of Japan.

In Tokyo metropolitan area, the population growth and the economic growth have caused the serious urban problems like sprawl at urban fringe, heavy congestion not only in road network but also in rail network, environmental emission and so on. Transport infrastructure systems in the metropolitan area have been developed so as to solve these problems by expanding the coverage and capacity of the networks. Although there still now remain the difficult problems for us to tackle with, the transport infrastructure policies until today have succeeded in sustaining the high business productivity and quality of urban life in the population-growing trend. The spatial agglomeration in Tokyo metropolitan area has been functioning effectively with the transport infrastructures.

Japan is now at the down-slope of the population trend curve and Tokyo is predicted to soon lose its population in a decade. The significant population decline in Tokyo metropolitan area is an inexperienced situation for the people and policy makers. They may be afraid that the population decline would reduce the great merit of spatial agglomeration in Tokyo. The question at the heart of policy discussion is how we can sustain the high level of business productivity and quality of urban life including residential environment in the Tokyo metropolitan area by spatial restructuring. We should evaluate transport infrastructure policies so as to answer the question.

The population decline may make incentives for business sectors to relocate to more productive districts where they can enjoy the more advantage in the exchange of information and knowledge though business communication. In other words, the population decline may result in more extensive local agglomeration of business sectors. Some types of transport infrastructure policies can contribute to such spatial restructuring. The population decline will also greatly impact on housing market or residential land market. Transport infrastructure policies affect on the spatial distribution of residents and then the quality of their urban life. Since the impacts of the policies are so location-specific, we do need a well-designed tool for geographical analysis.

We employ the Computable Urban Economic (CUE) model as the tool for the policy analysis. The CUE model is developed in the tradition of Transport-Land Use Interaction (TLUI) model. We should remark on the merits of the CUE in contrast to the old TLUI models. First, the CUE model is fully based on the urban economic theory in Alonso tradition. The microeconomic foundation in urban economics enables us to evaluate policies consistently with standard methodologies of cost benefit analysis. The location choice behaviors of residents and business sectors are described b logit model in the Anas tradition Anas (1984) and the demand–supply in land markets should determine land price distribution in an urban economy. The transport demand for each type of transport service are derived from utility maximizing behavior or profit utility maximizing behavior and the user equilibrium of transport network in the Wardrop tradition is simulated.

This paper shows the impacts of transport infrastructure policies in the population-declining metropolitan area by applying the CUE model to the greater Tokyo Metropolitan Area. We examine whether or not the polices under discussions between policy makers can sustain business productivity and quality of urban life in Tokyo at a population declining trend.

2 Structure of the Computable Urban Economic Model

2.1 Sketch of the Model

2.1.1 Features of the Model

There are two advantages for the CUE, which introduces the microeconomic foundation into the conventional transportation/land-use model.

One is consistency of behavior hypothesis with a simulation result. The behaviors of the household and the firm are formalized on the basis of the micro-economics. Micro-econometrics including the discrete choice model has enables the utility-max or the profit-max behaviors to be statistically verified so that the microeconomic behavior hypothesis can work as an operational tool.

The other is that the model enables us to evaluate the benefit of a transport policy in the incidence form where the distribution of project benefits among stakeholders in spatial dimension. In contrast, a conventional transport/land-use model measures the project benefit only in the origin form where the benefit of transport users and supplies are accounted for. The project benefit in the incidence form can provide policy makers with information like "who is benefited?", "where and how much benefit is generated ?". This advantage contributes to consideration of the fair balance among the stakeholders on sharing the cost and benefit of a transport project.

In the CUE model, the land and the transport markets attain an equilibrium simultaneously. The equilibrium of the transport market is attained according to the first Wardrop principle. This is represented by the point where the inverse demand function intersects with the average cost function (link performance function, not the marginal cost function). We then assume that users in a road network only consider the information on the average cost and pay less attention to the marginal increase in the user cost that occurs from an additional user.

The traffic assignment is based on the average cost. The composite average cost, which denotes the transportation cost from the specific origin to the destination, is the horizontal summation of the link transportation costs, This inverse demand function indicating the number of OD trips changes its functional form according to the land-use at each zone and the trip generation. On the one hand, the composite average cost function shifts to the right horizontally if the number of links increases because of the further increase in the OD trips. The change in the transport cost causes the change in the land-use and then the state of the transport system shifts to a new equilibrium through the change in the inverse demand function.

The equilibrium of the land market is attained by adjusting the rent at each zone. The supply function for land is the marginal cost curve assumed not to shift endogenously. The demand for land is derived from multiplying the population at each zone with the per capita land demand or the individual land demand. The individual land demand is derived from the household's or resident's utility maximization.

The total population is distributed to each zone according to the utility values at each zone. Thus, the decrease in the transport cost due to a road network development would increase the net income (gross income minus commuting cost), the individual land demand and the population at the zone. The limited availability of the land at each zone makes the land rent higher and the price mechanism clears the market.

The CUE model attains the equilibrium if the transport market is cleared for each OD demand and the supply and demand of the land market are equalized for each zone. Since the CUE model adopts the stochastic approach, the logit model which assume the Gambel distribution in the error term, is used for both transport and location choice.

2.1.2 Major Assumptions in the Model

The CUE model in this paper has the following assumptions

- The Tokyo Metropolitan Area that is divided into 197 zones.
- There are households with an identical preference and firms with an identical production technology for the composite good and absentee landowners each of which representatively owns the land.

18 Impacts of Transport Infrastructure Policies in Population-Declining Metropolitan... 429

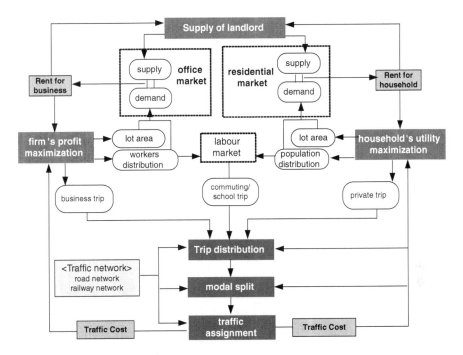

Fig. 18.1 Whole structure of CUE

- The land markets for the residential use and for business use are assumed to exist in each zone.
- The prices except land rents, such as the wage and the composite good price are assumed to be constant at the WITH/WITHOUT case.
- Total number of households and employees are also given.

The household maximizes the utility under the income constraint and chooses the residential zone to locate according to the attractiveness of each zone. The firm maximizes its profit by using land and business trip and sells the products to the households. The firm also chooses its location according to the profit. Finally, the absentee landlord provides with land available to the households and the firms in order to get the rent. The absentee landlord decides how much percentage of land available is supplied to the market.

As is already mentioned, the CUE model requires simultaneous equilibrium of land and transport markets, which is adjusted by the generalized transport cost and the rent of the land. The overall structure of the CUE model is shown in the Fig. 18.1.

2.2 Formulation of Each Agent's Behavior

2.2.1 The Model of the Household Behavior

The household earns the income by providing labor and consumes the composite good and land service so as to maximize his utility under his budget and time constraint. By incorporating the time constraint, consumptions of time resources for the trip or labor, can be considered in the model. In order to consume the composite good, the household need input the travel trips. These trips can be interpreted as the private trips. This utility maximizing behavior is formulated as follows.

$$V_i^H = \max_{z_i, a_i, x_i} \left[\alpha_Z \ln z_i + \alpha_a \ln a_i + \alpha_x \ln x_i^p \right] \tag{18.1}$$

$$\text{st. } z_i + r_i a_i + q_i^p x_i^p = w\left(T - q_i^w x_i^w - q_i^s x_i^s\right) \tag{18.2}$$

$V^H i$: utility level at zone i
Z_i: consumption level of composite good
a_i: land service
x^P_i: private trip
r_i: residential land rent
q^P_i: the average generalized price of private trip
T: total time available
x^w_i: number of the commuting trip (business)
x^s_i: number of the commuting trip (school)
q^w_i: commuting cost (business)
q^s_i: commuting cost (school)
α: distribution parameter

Price q of private trip is defined by the transport cost multiplied by the wage rate. Then, the constraint includes the notion of time as a part of household's income. The solution of the utility maximization problem defined by (18.1) and (18.2) gives demand functions as follows.

$$z_i = \alpha_Z I_i \quad a_i = \frac{\alpha_a}{r_i} I_i \quad x_i = \frac{\alpha_x}{q_i} I_i$$
$$I_i = w\left(T - q_i^w x_i^w - q_i^s x_i^s\right) \tag{18.3}$$

The induced traffic is considered at the generation stage, since the private trip increases as the private and commuting trip cost decreases. We can obtain the indirect utility function by substituting (18.3) into (18.1).

$$V_i^H = \ln I_i - \alpha_a \ln r_i - \alpha_x \ln q_i + C$$
$$where, C = \alpha_z \ln \alpha_z + \alpha_a \ln \alpha_a + \alpha_x \ln \alpha_x \tag{18.4}$$

18 Impacts of Transport Infrastructure Policies in Population-Declining Metropolitan... 431

The household chooses the zone to reside according to distribution of the attractive index for each zone which is given by (18.4). We assume the probability of the residential location choice is given by the following.

$$P_i^H = \frac{\exp \theta^H V_i^H}{\sum_i \exp \theta^H V_i^H} \tag{18.5}$$

P_i^H: probability that a household chooses zone i
V_i^H: utility level at zone i
θ_H: logit parameter

Equation 18.5 is deduced from the following problem.[1]

$$S^H = \max_{P_i^H} \sum_i \left[P_i^H V_i^H - \frac{1}{\theta^H} P_i^H \ln P_i^H \right] \tag{18.6}$$
$$st. \sum_i P_i^H = 1$$

Ueda (1992) shows that the utility level at each zone becomes identical if we only consider the deterministic where the entropy term in (18.6) can be omitted. When θ^H is large enough, we can ignore the entropy term.

$$S^H = \max_{P_i^H} \left[\sum_i P_i^H V_i^H \right]$$
$$st. \sum_i P_i^H = 1 \tag{18.7}$$

The Kuhn-Tucker condition for the problem is given as follows.

$$L = \sum_i P_i V_i - \lambda \left(1 - \sum_i P_i \right)$$
$$\frac{\partial L}{\partial P_i} = V_i - \lambda \qquad \frac{\partial L}{\partial \lambda} = 1 - \sum_i P_i \tag{18.8}$$

From the condition above, we have the relationship below.

$$V_i^H = \lambda \quad if \quad P_i^H \geq 0$$
$$V_i^H \leq \lambda \quad if \quad P_i^H = 0 \tag{18.9}$$

---

[1] This can be interpreted as the expected utility maximization behavior of the risk averter when the Gambel distribution is assumed for the uncertainty of the utility. See Ueda and Tsutsumi (1999).

432 K. Yamasaki et al.

Thus, (18.9) suggests that (18.6) includes the notion of the equalized utility in urban economics.

2.2.2 Firm's Behavior

The firm produces the composite goods by inputting land service, business trips so as to maximize its profit under the production technology constraint. This behavior is formulated by below.

$$\Pi_i^B = \max_{Z_i, A_i, X_i} [Z_i - R_i A_i - Q_i X_i] \tag{18.10}$$

$$\text{st. } Z_i = \eta_i E^\sigma A_i^{\beta_A} X_i^{\beta_x} \tag{18.11}$$

Π^B_i: profit at zone i
Z_i: output of the composite goods firm
A_i: land service
X: business trip input
R_i: business land rent
Q_i: the average generalized price of business trip
η: parameter regarding to production efficiency
σ, β: parameter
Ei: employees at zone i

As is shown in Fig. 18.2, the actual employee density at the central Tokyo is much higher than the population density. It means that there is high productivity as a result of frequent business communication, which has been enabled *by spatial agglomeration*.

In order to describe the mechanism of the spatial agglomeration, the positive externality has been introduced into the description of production technology. That is, the total factor productivity in a production function is dependent upon employee worker of each zone.

The solution of the profit maximizing problem in (18.10) and (18.11) yields factor demand functions of A and Xi respectively.

$$A_i = \frac{\beta_A}{R_i} Z_i \quad X_i = \frac{\beta_X}{Q_i} Z_i \tag{18.12}$$

$$Z_i = \left[\eta_i E^\sigma \left(\frac{\beta_A}{R_i} \right)^{\beta_A} \left(\frac{\beta_X}{Q_i} \right)^{\beta_X} \right]^{(\beta_A + \beta_X)} \tag{18.13}$$

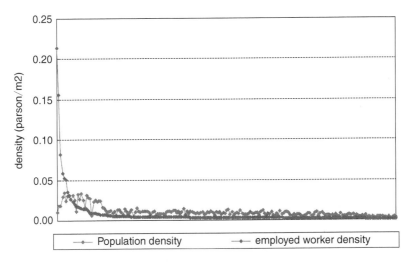

Fig. 18.2 Actual employee density and population density

The firm's location choice behavior is formulated as well as the household's one. As a result, the probability choosing zone i to locate is determined by the following logit type model.

$$P_i^B = \frac{\exp \theta^B \Pi_i^B}{\sum_i \exp \theta^B \Pi_i^B} \quad (18.14)$$

2.2.3 Land Supply by the Absentee Landlord

The absentee landowner supplies the land for the households and firms with the land supply function in (18.15). Note that the value in the parenthesis is assumed to take the range from zero to one.

$$y_i^H = \overline{y_i^H} \cdot \left(1 - \frac{\sigma_i^H}{r_i}\right) \quad (18.15)$$

$$y_i^B = \overline{y_i^B} \cdot \left(1 - \frac{\sigma_i^B}{R_i}\right) \quad (18.16)$$

y_i^H: land supply for residential use
y_i^B: land supply for business use
$\overline{y_i^H}, \overline{y_i^B}$: land area available to supply
σ: parameter

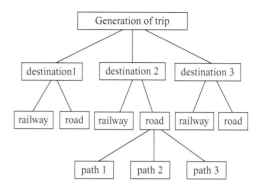

Fig. 18.3 Choice structure of nested logit model

2.3 Formulation of Transportation Behavior

The Fig. 18.3 shows the structure of the nested logit model we use in the CUE model. Although the structure could be changed[2] due to the reflection of the result of the parameter estimation, the present research adopted the structure which is the same as the conventional four step estimation. In addition, these structures are basically applied to the trip moving to the different zone. The ratio of this trip and the trip inside the zone never changes.

2.3.1 Model of Trip Generation

Since commuting trips (business and school) has less influenced by the change in the transportation services, we used linear regression model for the generation forecast. However, we assume that the demand function of the private and business trip does not include traffic fares.

2.3.2 Choice of Destination and Modal Split

We formulate destination choice and modal split of each reason to move (eq. private, business, etc.) by the nested logit model explained above. In order to decide the cost inherent to each zone, C_{ijm}, we follow the proceeding work by Yoshida and Harada (1999), which introduced the variable dependent upon the amount of the zone area. The Generalized transportation cost includes gasoline for automobiles and fare for railways.

---

[2] For example, Maruyama (2002) reversed the order of the destination choice and modal split.

18 Impacts of Transport Infrastructure Policies in Population-Declining Metropolitan... 435

$$P_{ijm} = \frac{\exp\left[-\theta_1\left(C_{ijm} + q_{ijm}\right)\right]}{\sum_m \exp\left[-\theta_1\left(C_{ijm} + q_{ijm}\right)\right]} \qquad (18.17)$$

$$P_{ij} = \frac{\exp\left[-\theta_2\left(C_{ij}^D + S_{ij}^D\right)\right]}{\sum_j \exp\left[-\theta_2\left(C_{ij}^D + S_{ij}^D\right)\right]} \qquad (18.18)$$

$$S_{ij}^D = -\frac{1}{\theta_1} \ln \sum_m \exp\left[-\theta_1\left\{q_{ijm} + C_{ij}^S\right\}\right] \qquad (18.19)$$

P_{ij}: probability of choosing zone j as destination by the trip generated at zone i
P_{ijm}: probability of choosing mode m at link ij

S^D_{ij}: expected minimum cost regarding to modal split
q_{ijm}: transportation cost of mode m at link ij
C_{ijm}: cost inherent to mode m at link ij(constant)
C^D_{ij}: cost inherent to ij (constant)
$\theta 1, \theta 2$: logit parameter

2.3.3 Traffic Assignment

The traffic assignment analysis is carried out by using the OD table and road network data. Here we apply the stochastic user equilibrium traffic assignment. By solving the problem, the probability where route k of transportation mode m between OD pair ij is determined by the following.

$$P_{ijmk} = \frac{\exp\left[-\theta_3\,q_{ijmk}\right]}{\sum_k \exp\left[-\theta_3\,q_{ijmk}\right]} \qquad (18.20)$$

The traffic cost of route k is the sum of the traffic cost of each link.

$$q_{ijmk} = \sum_a \delta^a_{ijmk}t(x_a) \qquad (18.21)$$

P_{ijmk}: probability of choosing route k of mode m in OD pair ij
q_{ijmk}: transportation cost of route k of mode m in OD pair ij
t: average transportation cost of link a

δ^a_{ijmk}: variable which takes 1 if route k of mode m in OD pair ij includes link a
 (0 otherwise)
$\theta 3$: logit parameter

3 Estimation of Parameters

3.1 Land-Use Section

3.1.1 Distribution Parameter of the Production Function

The distribution parameter of the firm is set based on "Annual report on prefectural accounts (2003 edition)". The land input is determined by the property income of the annual report and the gross regional product is used for the composite goods. The business trip input of the firm is calculated by using the total transportation cost based on the network distribution (Table 18.1).

3.1.2 Parameter on Utility Function

Parameter of utility function is estimated by using "Annual report on prefectural accounts (2003 edition)" Table 18.2 shows the result and the amount of the land demand is approximately 14.4 %.

3.2 Transport Section

The estimation result of the destination choice and the modal split in the transportation model are shown in Table 18.3 and 18.4.

4 Applications

4.1 Details of Assumptions and Settings

4.1.1 Coverage Area and Transport Infrastructures

The coverage area includes the southern part of Ibaraki prefecture in addition to Tokyo metropolitan area (Tokyo metropolitan, Kanagawa prefecture, Chiba prefecture and Saitama prefecture). The coverage area is divided into 197 zones. At the central Tokyo, the density of the employee is higher than that of population (Figs. 18.4, 18.5, and 18.6)

Figure 18.7 shows the road network considered. In this paper, we have excluded the local street. Figure 18.8 is the railway network and it has included only when a railway has been located in more than two zones.

18 Impacts of Transport Infrastructure Policies in Population-Declining Metropolitan... 437

Table 18.1 Distribution parameters of production function

	Parameters	t-statistic	R-squared
Input of land(B_A)	0.0062	11.0214	0.4558
Input of business trip(B_x)	0.0202	13.2672	0.8710

Table 18.2 Parameter on utility function of the household

	Parameters	t-statistic	R-squared
Consumption on private trip(α_X)	0.0295	22.8870	0.7287
Consumption on land(α_a)	0.1769	12.2045	0.2376

Table 18.3 The result of parameter estimation for modal split

	Commute		School		Private		Business	
	Parameter	t-statistic	Parameter	t-statistic	Parameter	t-statistic	Parameter	t-statistic
Transport cost	−0.070	−54.99	−0.026	−9.67	−0.061	−36.93	−0.036	−27.13
Density of stations	0.565	17.67	0.129	2.36	0.462	29.23	0.313	32.285
Egress	−0.790	−28.24	−0.311	−6.52	−0.914	−19.46	−1.038	−26.54
Constant	−0.858	−20.98	−1.910	−27.34	0.226	4.892	0.225	6.079
R-squared	0.801		0.752		0.700		0.660	
Sample	5,207		1,182		3,869		3,638	

Table 18.4 The result of parameter estimation for choice of destination

	Commute		School		Private		Business	
	Parameter	t-statistic	Parameter	t-statistic	Parameter	t-statistic	Parameter	t-statistic
Expected minimum cost	−0.030	−88.59	−0.021	−50.93	−0.022	−68.06	−0.018	−69.86
Density of employee	1.162	71.338	0.750	41.861	0.897	54.272	1.053	72.866
R-squared	0.69898		0.56896		0.70227		0.82461	
Sample	11,122		7,507		9,518		9,523	

4.1.2 Total Population and Employees in Metropolitan Area

The total population in the Tokyo metropolitan area has been predicted by using the growth rate of population at the Tokyo metropolitan area shown in *Population Projections by Prefecture* (2007) published by the National Institute of Population and Social Security Research. As a result, the total population in 2050 decreases 9 % compared to 2000. As for the forecast of the employee, there is little survey

Fig. 18.4 Coverage area (197 Zone)

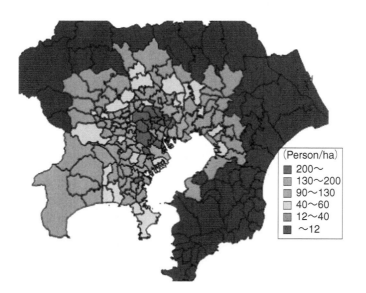

Fig. 18.5 Population density distribution

available than population. Although some other report set the growth rate of employee worker unchanged for next 25 or 30 years, we adopt the half of the growth rate of the population. Then population framework for the model is

18 Impacts of Transport Infrastructure Policies in Population-Declining Metropolitan... 439

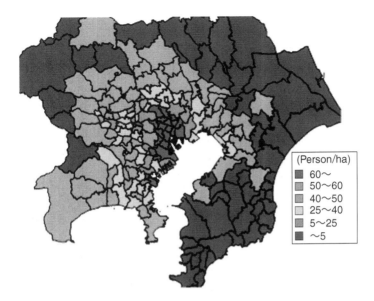

Fig. 18.6 Employee density distribution

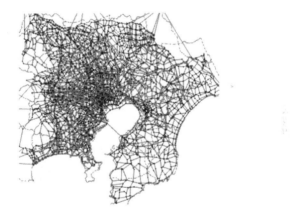

Fig. 18.7 Road network

summarized in Fig. 18.9. The population in Tokyo metropolitan area will become 31.6 million while the number of the employee worker will be 16.7 million in 2050.

4.1.3 Transport Infrastructure Policy

We will simulate the socio-economic impacts on Tokyo metropolitan area in 2050 between the cases with/without the three-Ring Road (Fig. 18.10).

Fig. 18.8 Railway network

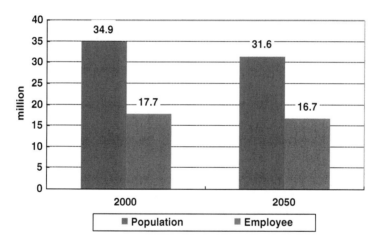

Fig. 18.9 Total population and employees in metropolitan area

4.1.4 Setting of Cases

We apply the CUE model to evaluate the effects of transport infrastructure in the Tokyo Metropolitan Area. In this paper, the following four cases are simulated. The first two cases combined are able to evaluate the effect of the three Ring road at year 2000. while the last two cases do the same for year 2050. By recombining the four cases we can compare the effect at 2000 with that of 2050 (Table 18.5).

18 Impacts of Transport Infrastructure Policies in Population-Declining Metropolitan... 441

Fig. 18.10 Plans for construction of three-ring road (Source: MLIT web page)

Table 18.5 The cases

	Year	Three-ring road
Case1	2000	Without
Case2		With
Case3	2050	Without
Case4		With

4.2 Impacts on Land Use

4.2.1 Changes in Population

The following two figures show the change in the population at each zone in 2050 compared to 2000 (without). Figure 18.11 says there is no difference among zones even though their population densities are quite diverse. In Fig. 18.12, however, the decrease of the population becomes smaller when the population density is small. This is because in the difference of Case 3 and Case 4 is "with or without" of the three Ring Road, which is surrounded by the less population density areas.

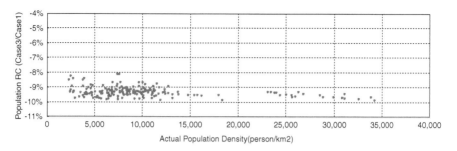

Fig. 18.11 Population change in 2050 (without three ring-road) (Case3/Case1)

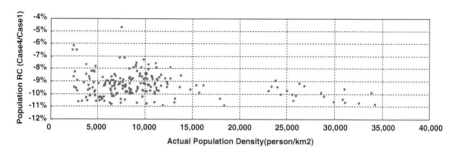

Fig. 18.12 Population change in 2050 (with three ring-road) (Case4/Case1)

4.2.2 Changes in Employee

Figure 18.13 shows the change of the employee worker density of each zone in Case 3. There is less decrease in Chiyoda-ku, Minato-ku and Chuo-ku while the zone with lower density located in the suburb has bigger decrease. This depends on our specification of the production function, which increases the productivity when the employee density becomes higher. The same figure for Case 4 is drawn in Fig. 18.14. There are some zones whose employee densities are low but the degree of decrease is not as much as Fig. 18.13. The main reason for this is because the existence of the three Ring Road increases the productivity of low employee worker density area through the additional entry of firms.

4.2.3 Passenger and Traffic Modal Split

The passenger trip in 2050 decreases about 8 % in each case. This decrease brings about the increase in transport share of car for 1 %. The construction of three Ring Road makes passenger trip increase about 3 % and the transport share of car about 0.5 %.

The heavily populated area like Tokyo metropolitan area tends to be short supply in terms of the road infrastructure and it leads to the higher share of the railway.

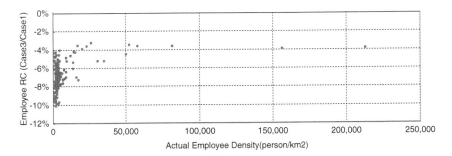

Fig. 18.13 Change of employee worker (without three ring-road) (Case3/Case1)

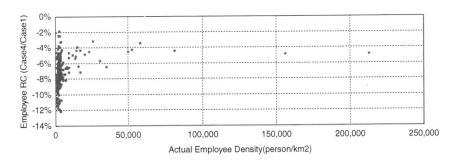

Fig. 18.14 Change of employee worker (with three ring-road) (Case4/Case1)

There is a possibility that the transport share by car would be increased when the heavy congestion is mitigated because of population decrease. In addition, construction of an arterial high-standard highway like three Ring Road might induce more car traffic since it enhances the convenience (ig. 18.15).

4.2.4 Evaluation Indices

Next we compare the Evaluation index of the road network between 2000 and 2050. The passenger trip by car decreases according to the population and employee worker's decrease in 2050. However, it is still higher than the total rate of population decrease, which is 8 % by 2050. As we pointed out before, it is because the decrease of the passenger trip by car mitigates the congestion and it results in increasing the transport share by car. If the three Ring Roads are completed, the rate of decrease becomes smaller as well.

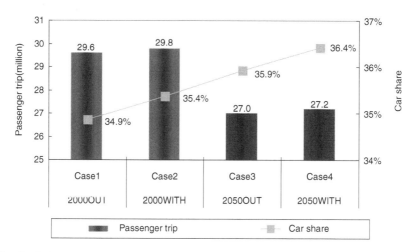

Fig. 18.15 Comparisons of passenger trip and car share

The average trip length by car in 2050 gets longer a little bit in Case 3 while it becomes longer buy 1.6 % in Case 4. The product of the average trip length by car and the passenger trip by car remains at an lower decrease rate of 2.8 %.

The total traffic cost, which is an index to measure the efficiency of the total road network, decreases 9.4 % in 2050 with Case 3 while it is 10 % in Case 4, both of which are much better than the one in 2000.

The average speed by car increases by 4 % even in Case 3. This is because of less congestion by population decrease and this effect is much higher in Case 4. The average speed increases 8.7 % if the 3 Ring Road is completed.

One of the distinguished features of the CUE model is that it can consider induced traffic and the developed traffic. In case 3 (without the induced and developed traffic) CO_2 emission in 2050 decreases by 7.1 % while in Case 4 (with the induced and developed traffic) 6.9 %. Thus considering the induced and developed traffic increases only 0.2 % of CO_2 emission(Figs. 18.16, 18.17, 18.18, 18.19, 18.20, and 18.21).

4.2.5 Traffic Volume Change in the Road Network

In this subsection, we analyze the traffic volume on the network in each case. Comparing Case 3 and Case 1, the traffic volume is significantly reduced due to reduction of passenger trip followed by population decrease. As a result, there is almost no link whose traffic volume is increased compared to 2000.

When we compare Case 1 with Case 4, there is huge increase around the three Ring Road while the links in the other area basically decrease the traffic volume.

18 Impacts of Transport Infrastructure Policies in Population-Declining Metropolitan... 445

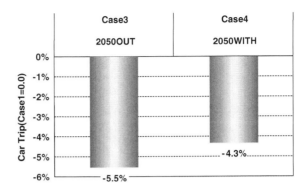

Fig. 18.16 Change in passenger trip by car

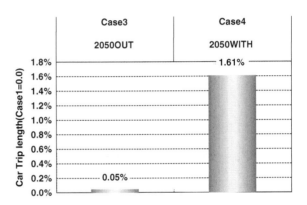

Fig. 18.17 Change in average trip length by car

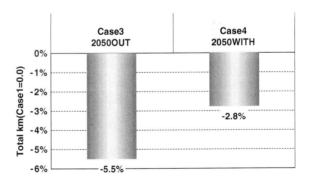

Fig. 18.18 Change in total km

The links which are directly connected with the three Ring Road, we observe the increase in terms of the traffic volume due to the induced traffic and the developed traffic. In order to visually check this situation, we compare Case 3 with case 4 as follows (Figs. 18.22, 18.23, and 18.24).

Fig. 18.19 Change in total traffic cost

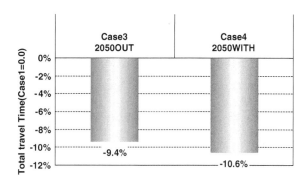

Fig. 18.20 Change in average speed by car

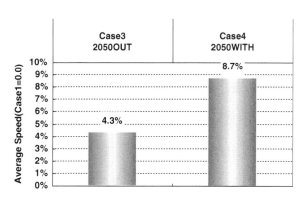

Fig. 18.21 Change in emission of CO2

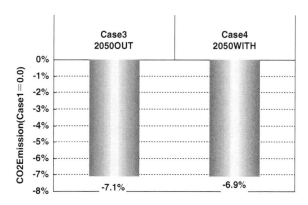

4.2.6 The Result of the Benefit Evaluation

Finally we analyze the total benefit of road construction when the population decrease. As is shown in Fig. 18.25, the benefit decreases about 7.8 % in 2050 compared to 2000. Since the change of the population is about 9 % and change in employee worker is 6 %, it seems that the change of the benefit depends upon population change.

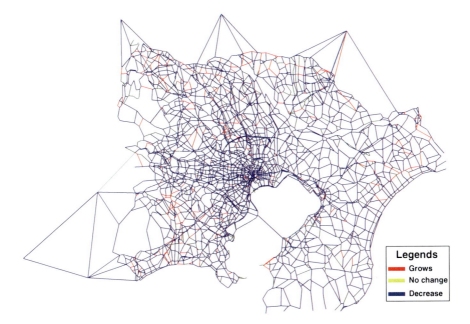

Fig. 18.22 Case3 2050/with -Case1 2000/without

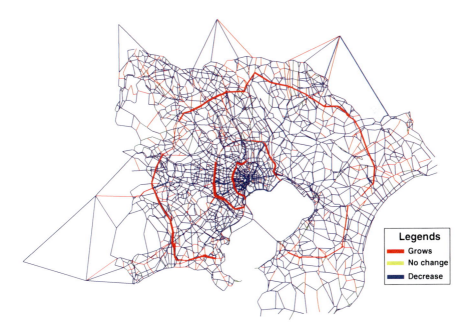

Fig. 18.23 Case4 2050/with -Case1 2000/without

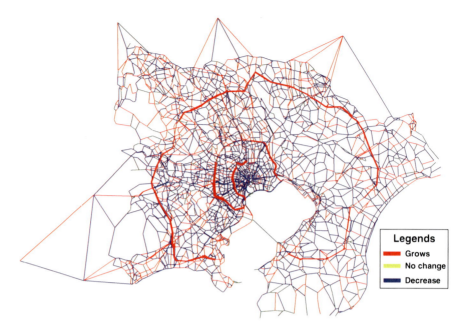

Fig. 18.24 Case4 2050/with -Case3 2050/without

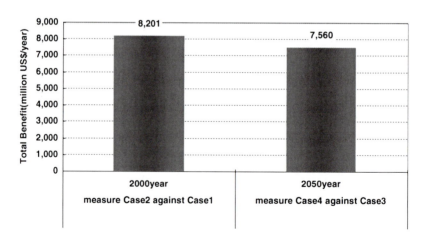

Fig. 18.25 Change of benefit

5 Conclusion

In this paper, we analyzed the effect of road construction at Tokyo metropolitan area when population is decreasing by using the CUE model. As a result, we found that the central Tokyo remains as the center of the economy in 2050 with high spatial agglomeration since the agglomeration is accelerated by the scale economy.

On the other hand, population which is not affected by agglomeration, is decreasing at each zone with the same level.

The investment to the three Ring Roads is expected to contribute to developing more dispersive urban structure since the three Ring Roads increase the transportation convenience at the suburb and it induces to the entry of the firms and population as well. This does not, however, the central Tokyo loses its competitiveness but they still remain strong in terms of the spatial distribution of the firms.

The reduction of population mitigates the congestion of the road network.. It enables us to increase our convenience in terms of the trip by car. It induces to more trips to the households and business people, which bring about more communication, that is one of the keys for the productivity growth and the enhancement of households' utility. During this period, motorization advances due to the enhancement of the transport convenience by car.

For other general indices, it is worthy of attention that CO_2 emission decreases significantly in2050. The better use by less congestion on the network enables us to curb the developed and induced traffic, which leads to less CO_2 emission(0.2 %).

In Japan, population has started decreasing and it is expected to decreasing in Tokyo metropolitan area as well after 2015. We have not had enough research results showing the effect of the currently on-going transport projects after the long population-decreasing period, which Japanese has never experienced. The analysis in this paper partly answered these questions by showing the urban structure of Tokyo metropolitan area after 50 years with consistency in terms of traffic status, firm location and household location due to the intrinsic feature of the CUE model. In order to make public decision-making efficient, we will continue to try to simulate far-distant future with various scenarios.

References

Anas A (1984) Discrete choice theory and the general equilibrium of employment, housing and travel networks in a Lowry-type model of the urban economy. Environ Plann 16(11):1489–1502

Maruyama T, Harata N, Ohta K (2002) Application of a combined network equilibrium model to mega metropolitan area. Infrastruct Plann Rev 19(3):551–560 (in Japanese)

Ueda T (1992) A general equilibrium model with re-defined location surplus. Infrastruct Plann Rev 10:183–190 (in Japanese)

Ueda T, Tsutsumi M (1999) A unified framework of land use models recently developed in Japan. In: Proceedings of the Japan society of civil engineers, no 625, pp 65–78

Yoshida A, Harada N (1999) Aggregate destination choice models incorporating probabilistic formation of a choice set. In: Proceedings of the Japan society of civil engineers, no 618, pp 1–13 (in Japanese)

Chapter 19
Innovation and Knowledge Links in Metropolitan Regions: The Case of Vienna

Franz Tödtling and Michaela Trippl

Abstract Metropolitan regions are often key centers of research, education and business services, and tend to have excellent preconditions for innovation and knowledge based sectors. They often have a highly qualified workforce and provide access to specialized resources and inputs for innovation. Consequently these centers are regarded to be important nodes in the knowledge-based economy. However, there is also evidence showing that metropolitan regions may suffer from innovation problems such as missing knowledge linkages between science and business, or a lack of innovation culture. The metropolitan region of Vienna is an interesting case of in this context since its regional innovation system (RIS) is well endowed with knowledge organizations such as universities, specialized schools and research institutes in many fields. It is also a central location for business services, and well connected via a good transport and telecommunication infrastructure within Europe and beyond. Still, Vienna seems to have faced innovation problems in the past such as missing venture capital and weak relations between science and business. The aim of this chapter is to examine whether these past deficiencies of Vienna's RIS are still characteristic features also of the new knowledge intensive industries such as ICT and biotech that have grown in the last few years in the region.

Keywords Metropolitan regions • Regional innovation systems • Knowledge links • R&D cooperations • ICT • Biotechnology • Vienna

---

F. Tödtling (✉) • M. Trippl
Institute for the Environment and Regional Development, Vienna University of Economics and Business, Vienna, Austria
e-mail: Franz.Tocdtling@wu.ac.at

J. Klaesson et al. (eds.), *Metropolitan Regions*, Advances in Spatial Science,
DOI 10.1007/978-3-642-32141-2_19, © Springer-Verlag Berlin Heidelberg 2013

1 Introduction

Metropolitan regions are usually regarded as locations with excellent preconditions for innovation and knowledge based sectors, since they tend to be the key centers of research, education, financial and business services and culture. They often have a highly qualified work force as well as good living conditions which attract further talent and skills. They also provide access to relevant resources, inputs and customers. Given the high density and large variety of knowledge generating organizations present in metropolitan regions and the good availability of expertise and skills, these areas are acknowledged to be important nodes in the knowledge-based economy (see, for instance, Brandt et al. 2009). It is still a matter of debate whether Marshallian externalities (i.e. advantages of specialization and of industrial clustering), Jacobian externalities (advantages of diversification and of urbanization) or advantages of related variety (see, for instance, Frenken et al. 2007) prevail in such locations and are most favorable for innovation. There is some agreement that "institutional thickness", i.e. a high density of economic activities, knowledge organizations and supporting institutions, and cognitive, spatial and other types of proximities are supporting and enhancing innovation (Brower et al. 1999; Simmie 2003; Boschma 2005).

There is, however, also empirical evidence showing that the positive relation between metropolitan regions and innovation may not be as clear as it seems to be at the first glance. In fact, many metropolitan regions suffer from various kinds of innovation problems and impediments to knowledge exchange which might produce other results than those stated above, such as the following:

- Metropolitan regions might lack particular elements of a regional innovation system (RIS), such as leading research organizations, international companies or knowledge intensive firms, innovation intermediaries and knowledge transfer organizations, innovation finance and venture capital (problem of "missing elements").
- The two RIS subsystems of knowledge generation and of knowledge application might be weakly connected and there might be a lack of networking between firms in the RIS and in relevant clusters. In the literature such a constellation is referred to as "fragmented" innovation system (Tödtling and Trippl 2005). Missing knowledge linkages (i.e., fragmentation) are regarded to constitute a major RIS deficiency (Lundvall and Borras 1999; Edquist 2005; Tödtling and Trippl 2005), because intensive flows and exchanges of knowledge, skills and human capital are seen to constitute a crucial building block of RIS, leading to systemic innovation activities (Autio 1998; Cooke et al. 2000).
- For historic reasons there might also be a specialization in low tech or non-innovative industries or a lack of innovative functions such as R&D and marketing (structural problem).
- Finally, the behavioral attitudes and routines of managers and of the labor force might hamper innovation, i.e. there might be a lack of innovation culture in a particular region (Saxenian 1994; Tödtling and Trippl 2008).

The case of the metropolitan region of Vienna is interesting in this context since it can be regarded as "institutionally thick" in regard to the general knowledge infrastructure and research organizations. Within Austria, the Vienna region is the prime centre of universities, schools and research institutes in many fields. It is also a central location for knowledge intensive services as well as for regional headquarters of multinational companies (for Austria and its neighboring Eastern European countries), and it is well connected via a good transport and telecommunication infrastructure. Still, at least until the mid 1990s, Vienna has faced several innovation problems:

- Vienna has suffered to some extent from the weaknesses of Austria's national innovation system, which has been characterized by a low R&D quota, weak patenting activities and a poor availability of venture capital (see Cooke et al. 2007). Although Vienna has performed better in these indicators than the rest of Austria it was not able to fully overcome some of those weaknesses.
- Vienna seems to have developed only few networks and knowledge interactions in the field of innovation in the past (Tödtling 2002; Fritsch 2003), thus reflecting features of a "fragmented metropolitan RIS" (Tödtling and Trippl 2005). Such a problem of fragmentation would be a particular problem for the development of knowledge intensive sectors in a region, since these sectors strongly depend on intensive interactions between research and industry, as well as on vivid knowledge exchange among companies (Saxenian 1994; Keeble and Wilkinson 2000.

The central purpose of this chapter is to examine whether or not the key deficiency of Vienna's RIS in the past, i.e. fragmentation (as pointed out in Sect. 2), is also a characteristic feature of new knowledge intensive industries, which have emerged and grown in the last few years in the region under investigation. Such sectors are regarded to be vital for the competitiveness of metropolitan regions. To observe fragmentation in these sectors would imply a serious problem for Vienna's future competitiveness in the knowledge economy.

The remainder of this chapter is organized as follows. Section 2 provides a short literature review on innovation activities and problems in metropolitan regions. In the empirical part (Sect. 3) we focus on two key knowledge-based industries, that is medical biotechnology and ICT, and investigate the nature of knowledge linkages of Viennese firms in those sectors. The notion of knowledge linkages will be used as generic term (see also Tödtling et al. 2006) that covers market relations (e.g. R&D contracts and licensing), formal co-operations (e.g. R&D partnerships), knowledge spillovers (e.g. monitoring of competitors) and informal networks. In addition, we look at the spatial levels (regional, national, international), as well as the key partners involved in those relationships. Finally, Sect. 4 summarizes the main results and draws some conclusions.

2 Metropolitan Regions and Innovation: The View from the Literature

In the past years a number of studies have investigated the geography of innovation and the role of metropolitan regions in the innovation process (Tödtling 1992, 1994; Feldman 1994; Audretsch 1998; Baptista and Swann 1998; Fritsch 2000, 2003; Fischer and Fröhlich 2001; Gehrke and Legler 2001, European Commission 2003). The following patterns were identified:

- R&D activities, patenting and major product innovations are usually highly concentrated in larger agglomerations (Brower et al. 1999; Feldman and Audretsch 1999; Breschi 2000; Paci and Usai 2000; Fischer et al. 2001; Gehrke and Legler 2001; Simmie 2003).
- Knowledge spillovers which can be observed in industrial clusters and agglomerations are often spatially bounded to a certain geographical distance from these centers (Jaffe et al. 1993; Audretsch and Feldman 1996; Anselin et al. 1997; Baptista and Swann 1998; Baptista 2003; Bottazzi and Peri 2003).
- There is still a debate in the literature whether specialized (Marshall/Arrow/Romer) or diversified (Jacobs) agglomerations are more conducive for innovation. While some authors (Baptista and Swann 1998; Porter 1998; Cooke 2002; Fritsch and Franke 2004) argue in accordance with Marshall for innovation advantages of specialization, others state in accordance with Jacobs that diversification is more favorable (Tichy 2001). Feldman and Audretsch (1999) argue more specifically that innovation is stimulated by the presence of complementary industries sharing a common knowledge base. Similarly, taking an evolutionary perspective, Frenken et al. (2007) have pointed out that "related variety" might be the most supportive industrial environment for innovation in the long run since it allows to combine synergetic advantages of specialization (within broader sectors) with the advantages of diversity and variety (among subsectors).

Peripheral regions are regarded as less innovative in comparison to agglomerations: In such areas companies have often a lower R&D intensity and fewer product innovations, and innovation is more focused on product modifications and new processes instead (Tödtling 1992; Feldman 1994; Fritsch 2000). Also old industrial areas were found to be less innovative with a focus on incremental and process innovation due to predominance of mature industries and externally controlled firms (Tödtling 1992; Cooke 1995; Tichy 2001). In general, thus, there is some indication that metropolitan regions are more innovative than other types of regions. The situation is more complex, however, as we also may find innovative clusters in rural areas (Fritsch 2003), innovative restructuring in old industrial areas (Trippl and Otto 2009), as well as innovation problems in metropolitan regions.

A number of studies have investigated regional innovation in the framework of innovation systems (De la Mothe and Paquet 1998; Tödtling and Kaufmann 1999; Cooke et al. 2000; Sternberg 2000; Asheim et al. 2003). These RIS based studies have related the innovation performance of firms with the character of their networks and to institutional factors (Thomi and Werner 2001; Doloreux 2002; Fornahl and Brenner 2003; Cooke et al. 2004). Departing from the main deficiencies of RIS, Tödtling and Trippl (2005) have drawn a distinction between "organizationally thin RIS", "RIS characterized by lock in" and "fragmented RIS". In particular the problem of fragmentation can often be assigned to metropolitan regions.

Summing up the view from the literature, we find that metropolitan regions are generally regarded as centers of innovation, benefiting from knowledge externalities and agglomeration economies. Leading research organizations and universities, business services, as well as headquarters of international firms and high-tech companies are often concentrated in metropolitan regions (Moulaert and Tödtling 1995; Keeble and Wilkinson 1999). As a consequence, R&D activities, patenting activities and major product innovations are usually above the country average (Brower et al. 1999; Feldman and Audretsch 1999; Fischer et al. 2001; Gehrke and Legler 2001; Simmie 2003). Given the good availability of crucial innovation inputs and the high density of knowledge generating and exploiting organizations, metropolitan regions are regarded as important nodes in the emerging knowledge-based economy (Brandt et al. 2009). However, not all metropolitan regions are such centers of innovation. Some are lacking dynamic clusters of innovative firms, despite the fact that individual technology companies, R&D activities and research organizations may be present. There may exist highly developed public research and educational institutions and a dense supply of knowledge intensive business services. The problem of fragmentation,, i.e. the lack of networks and of interactive learning, however, seems to represent an important innovation barrier in some metropolitan regions. The two RIS subsystems of knowledge generation and application then operate separately, as university-firm links are at a low level. Also, innovation networking among local companies may be weak in such contexts (Fritsch 2003), even if customer and supplier links among firms exist. As a consequence, the development of new technologies and the formation of new firms are often below expectations. Examples here could be the region of South East Brabant in Holland (Eindhoven: Cooke et al. 2000) and the metropolitan region of Frankfurt which also show some of the stated features. In an interesting case study for Frankfurt Schamp (2001) observed a weak regional networking and an erosion of innovative functions in particular for the more established and internationalized industries; chemicals and automobiles. Better developed innovation networks were identified for the new sectors biotechnology and financial services, however. Also for Vienna some previous studies have identified some innovation problems, in particular of fragmentation. There was a considerable gap in the interaction between a relatively well developed subsystem of knowledge generation (universities and research organizations) and the subsystem of knowledge application and commercialization (Tödtling 2002; Fritsch 2003). In the next section we are going to investigate to which extent this also applies for two selected knowledge intensive sectors, ICT and biotechnology which we have studied in greater detail. In particular for these kinds of sectors, both local and international knowledge interactions and networks are regarded to be of key importance for the innovation performance and

456 F. Tödtling and M. Trippl

competitiveness (Camagni 1991; Saxenian 1994; Keeble and Wilkinson 1999; Bathelt et al. 2004; Cooke et al. 2007).

3 Innovation and Knowledge Links in the Vienna Metropolitan Region

This section deals with the case of the metropolitan region of Vienna. After a brief overview of basic socio-economic features we are going to explore in more detail the knowledge generating capacity and innovation potential of the region. This is followed by an analysis of spatial pattern of innovation partnering and knowledge sourcing activities of firms in two key knowledge-based sectors: medical biotechnology and information and communication technologies (ICT). The key aim of this section is to explore whether these two sectors reflect a traditional key weakness of Vienna's RIS, that is, fragmentation. Indeed, in the past, several studies have shown that there is little innovation networking between companies and research organizations (Fröhlich and Gassler 1999; Rohn 2000), pointing to a serious system failure of the RIS Vienna. According to Rohn (2000) this RIS deficiency was partly the outcome of a certain mismatch of the research done at local universities and the needs of the firms present in the region.

3.1 Methodological Notes

We use data from the Austrian national statistic office and from Eurostat to explore the socio-economic characteristics and innovation capacity of the Vienna metropolitan region. The empirical analysis of knowledge networking in the ICT and biotech sector draws on data collected in the context of two research projects. The findings reported below for biotechnology stem from the project "Collective Learning in Knowledge Economies: Milieu or Market?" (2002–2004) which received financial support from the Austrian Science Fund. This analysis has been updated in a follow-up project on the Vienna Biotechnology Cluster in 2005–2006. The results are based on face-to-face interviews carried out for both projects. We conducted 41 interviews, using semi-standardized questionnaires. A number of 21 interviews have been taken with companies. This sample covers big pharma firms, young biotechnology companies and suppliers. Moreover, we have interviewed 11 representatives of knowledge providers (including university institutes and other public and private research organizations). Finally, nine interviews have been taken with representatives of the policy and supporting system, four of which have been with regional actors and five with national ones. The empirical results for the ICT sector draw on data gathered in the research project "Innovation and knowledge networks in the Vienna ICT cluster" (2006–2007), which has been financially supported by the Jubilee Fund of the

19 Innovation and Knowledge Links in Metropolitan Regions: The Case of Vienna

Table 19.1 Socio-economic characteristics of the Vienna metropolitan region

	Vienna	Austria
Area, km^{2a}	414.87	83,871.97
Population (2008)[a]	1,677867	8,331,930
Number of plants (2001)[a]	87.691	396.238
Number of employees (2001)[a]	821,458	3,420,788
Number of firms (2006)[b]	68,322	290,735
Number of employees (2006)[b]	614,938	2,308,789
Unemployment rate (2006)[a]	8.8 %	4.7 %
Gross domestic product per head (2005)[a]	41.100(138)	29.800(100)
Annual GDP growth (period: 1996–2005)[a]	3.2	3.5

Sources: [a]Statistik Austria (2009); [b]Statistik Austria (2008); own calculations

city of Vienna for the Vienna University of Economics and Business. In this project, a web-based survey has been carried out. We sampled 1084 Viennese ICT firms which were listed in the AURELIA database and invited them to fill in a questionnaire. A number of 73 firms responded, yielding a response rate of about 7 %. This rather low response rate is partly due to the fact that there were a large number of self-employed or free-lancers included in the sample with not more than one employee. The questionnaire did not really fit this type of firm, leading to a low number of responses from this group of companies. Larger firms, thus, are overrepresented to a certain extent among the respondents.

There are differences in the methodological approach (face-to-face interviews for studying biotechnology, web-based survey for analyzing the ICT sector). Furthermore, not all kinds of knowledge linkages can be explored in the same detail for both sectors. These differences in methodology and data constitute some limitations and drawbacks for our analysis, because we cannot directly compare biotech and ICT. Nevertheless, the information gathered for these two sectors enables us to explore how (from which sources and at which geographical levels) the companies in the two sectors are sourcing knowledge and whether or not the biotech and ICT industries in Vienna suffer from fragmentation.

3.2 Socio-economic Features and Innovation Potentials of the Vienna Metropolitan Region

Vienna is the federal capital of Austria and it constitutes one of the country's nine provinces. As shown in Table 19.1, it covers an area of 415 km^2 (0.5 % of Austria), hosting more than 1.6 million inhabitants in 2008 (20 % of the Austrian total). Vienna is by far the richest Austrian region. Its regional gross domestic product per head is clearly above the Austrian average. However, in the last 10 years annual GDP growth has been slightly below the national average. In 2006 Vienna had an unemployment rate of 8.8 %, whilst the Austrian average amounts to only 4.7 %.

Table 19.2 R&D personnel (2006) and R&D expenditures in % of GDP (2006)

	All sectors	Business sector	Higher education sector	Government sector	Private non-profit sector
R&D personnel (full time equivalent)					
Vienna	19,207	10,784	6,671	1,620	132
(%)	(100 %)	(56.1 %)	(34.7 %)	(8.4 %)	(0.7 %)
Austria	49,378	34,126	12,668	2,423	161
(%)	(100 %)	(69.1 %)	(25.7 %)	(4.9 %)	(0.3 %)
R&D expenditures in % of GDP					
Vienna	3.54	2.09	1.15	1.15	0.02
Austria	2.46	1.73	0.59	0.59	0.01

Source: Eurostat

In 2001 Vienna hosted about 88,000 plants (representing 22 % of the Austrian total), employing 821.458 persons (24 % of the Austrian total). Using the most recent data (which are, however, not available at the plant level but only at the firm level), we find almost 70,000 firms which provide jobs for more than 600,000 workers in 2006.

The metropolitan region of Vienna represents Austria's undisputed centre of knowledge production and innovation. Vienna is well endowed with knowledge generating organizations. It hosts not fewer than 25 public universities and art academies. Furthermore, there is a large number of non-university research organizations, technical colleges and innovation centers. The most important knowledge production organizations relevant for business innovation are the University of Vienna, the Technical University of Vienna, the Medical University of Vienna and the Vienna University of Natural Resources and Applied Life Sciences. Moreover, there are 50 research institutions of the Austrian Academy of Sciences, more than 100 institutes and research sites of the Ludwig Boltzmann Society (focus on human medicine), about 250 further non-university research institutions in different fields and several technical colleges.

In the Vienna metropolitan region we find more than 136,000 students or a share of 54 % of the Austrian total and about 19,000 R&D workers, representing 39 % of the Austrian total. Whilst the share of R&D workers in total employment amounts to 4.58 % in Vienna, the respective percentage for Austria as a whole is only 2.14 %. Although the majority of R&D personnel can be found in the business sector (56 %), this share is lower in Vienna than it is in Austria as a whole (69 %, Table 19.2). This implies that in Vienna the share of R&D personnel employed in the higher education sector is clearly above the national average. The distribution of R&D workers across sub-sectors points to strengths in the RIS subsystem of knowledge generation, whereas Vienna's subsystem of knowledge exploitation is somewhat weaker in comparison.

From the European Regional Innovation Scoreboard (Hollanders 2006, Table 19.3) we can observe that Vienna scores particularly well in public R&D

19 Innovation and Knowledge Links in Metropolitan Regions: The Case of Vienna 459

Table 19.3 Regional innovation scoreboard indicators 2006 (EU = 100)

	HRSTC	Life-long-learning	Med/hi-tech manuf.	Hi-tech services	Public R&D	Business R&D	Patents
Vienna	95	139	97	159	201	154	102
Austria	67	110	97	91	97	97	118

Source: Eurostat
HRSTC: Human resources in science and technology – core (% of population)
Life-long learning: Participation in life-long learning per 100 population aged 25–64
Med/hi-tech manuf.: Employment in medium-high and high-tech manufacturing (% of total workforce)
Hi-tech services: employment in high-tech services (% of workforce)
Public R&D: public R&D expenditures (% of GDP)
Business R&D: business R&D expenditures (% of GDP)
Patents: EPO patents per million population

Table 19.4 Patent indicators

	High-tech patents (2004)[a]	ICT patents (2004)[b]	Biotech patents (2004)[c]
Vienna	63.77	75.88	19.23
Austria	22.65	36.98	6.49

Source: Eurostat
[a]High-tech patent applications to the EPO per million of inhabitants
[b]ICT patent applications to the EPO per million of inhabitants
[c]Biotech patent applications to the EPO per million of inhabitants

(indicator of 201), as well as in business R&D (154) and in high tech services (159). A below average performance we find in the HRSTC (low share of academics) as well as in medium and high tech manufacturing. The overall patenting activity according to this data set is below the Austrian and the EU average. Table 19.4 reveals, however, that Vienna has a rather good performance in high tech patents which are clearly above the Austrian average. This holds true for high-tech patents in general, and is also observable for the fields of ICT and biotech in particular.

Table 19.5 provides a comparative overview on the economic structure of Vienna and Austria. Unsurprisingly, the service sector is clearly dominating in the Vienna metropolitan region. A particular high importance of knowledge intensive services could be found here. In accordance with Table 19.3 above, high tech and medium high tech manufacturing, in contrast, play a minor role. This is due to the strong losses of manufacturing jobs in Vienna in the past decades (Mayerhofer 2006).

Vienna, thus, constitutes the core centre of knowledge generation and – transmission within Austria with particular strengths in public R&D and knowledge intensive services. However, so far it is unclear to which extent the business sector is able to benefit from these knowledge organizations, e.g. through dense innovation interactions. In the past there were indications that the interaction between the companies present in the region and the knowledge generating organizations was low, resulting in a rather fragmented innovation system (Tödtling 2002; Fritsch 2003; Tödtling and Trippl 2005). Therefore, in the

Table 19.5 Shares of employment (2007) – NUTS 2 level

Sector (NACE codes)	Vienna	Austria
Agriculture, hunting, forestry, fishing mining and quarrying (A to C = 01–14)	**0.8**	**5.8**
Manufacturing (D)	**11.2**	**18.2**
High and medium high tech manufacturing	5.2	6.7
Low and medium low tech manufacturing	6.0	11.5
Electricity, gas, water supply and construction (E, F)	**7.9**	**8.6**
Services (G to Q = 50 to 99)	**80.1**	**67.1**
Knowledge intensive services	41.7	30.0
Less knowledge intensive services	38.4	37.1

Source: Eurostat

Table 19.6 Proportion of medical biotechnology companies in Austrian provinces (2006)

Region	Number of firms	*Proportion of firms (%)*
Vienna	77	*67*
Styria	10	*8.7*
Lower Austria	10	*8.7*
Tyrol	9	*7.8*
Upper Austria	4	*3.5*
Salzburg	4	*3.5*
Vorarlberg	1	*0.8*
Total	115	*100*

Source: BIT and LISA (2004), complemented and updated by our own inquiry

remaining part of this chapter we intend to explore, whether this phenomenon of fragmentation, is also a characteristic feature of new high tech and knowledge based sectors which have emerged and grown in the last few years in the Vienna metropolitan region. Such industries are acknowledged to play a central role for the current and future competitiveness and dynamics of metropolitan regions. To observe fragmentation in these sectors would imply a serious problem for Vienna's future competitiveness in the emerging knowledge-based economy.

3.3 Biotechnology

The metropolitan region of Vienna is by far the most important location for Austrian medical biotechnology firms. As revealed in Table 19.6, not fewer than 77 biotech companies (representing 67 % of all Austrian medical biotech firms) could be found in Vienna, pointing to a strong geographical concentration of this emerging knowledge based sector in the metropolitan region studied here.

Vienna's medical biotech industry hosts a few subsidiaries of big pharma companies such as Boehringer Ingelheim and Baxter, which perform as key actors in the local cluster. Boehringer Ingelheim's activities in Vienna comprise the company's centre for cancer research, a centre of competence in biopharmaceutical production, and its basic research subsidiary, the Institute of Molecular Pathology (IMP). Baxter Austria is the company's most important research operation outside the United States. The largest pharmaceutical producer in Austria is Novartis, a Swiss multinational company, employing more than 3,000 workers. However, in 2008, Novartis closed its research institute in Vienna to bundle these activities in its hometown Basel.

The Vienna region hosts about 25 dedicated biotech companies. Examples include Intercell (vaccines against oncological and infectious diseases), Igeneon (oncology), Austrianova (oncology, gene therapy) or Green Hills Biotechnology (oncology). About 40 % of the dedicated biotech firms were founded within the past few years and many of them employ fewer than ten workers. Then, there are about 20 specialized suppliers operating in the area. This segment mainly consists of producers of research agents (Nano-S, Bender Med Systems), bioinformatics providers (Emergentec, Insilico) and firms performing clinical trials services. Venture capital firms and business angels are a missing element in the cluster. The main reason for this is the bank-dominated landscape in Austria, which coincides with a preference for traditional credit instruments and a widespread adversity to risk taking. Consequently, successful companies like Intercell or Igeneon had to attract external financing from international venture capitalists and funds.

Despite the recent loss of the Novartis Research Institute (NRI), Vienna still has an excellent scientific base in medical biotechnology, comprising five universities, several hospitals and a range of other public and private research institutes. Key players are the Institute of Molecular Pathology (IMP) which is Boehringer Ingelheim's cancer research centre, and the Antibiotic Research institute Vienna (ABRI) which is owned by Biochemie Kundl (part of Sandoz R&D). A further strengthening of the local research base could be observed as the Austrian Academy of Sciences has established recently two new institutes, namely the Institute of Molecular Biotechnology (IMBA) and the Research Centre for Molecular Medicine (CeMM). Moreover, five co-operative research centers between university institutes and firms have been set up in the Vienna region. Finally, a technical college for biotechnology has also been created in order to improve the supply of specialized and highly skilled labor.

In a next step we explore the spatial dimension of knowledge circulation that underpins innovation in the Vienna medical biotech industry. In face-to-face interviews 21 firms (see methodological notes) were asked to indicate their most important knowledge sources and to specify their location as well as the type of knowledge exchange with these sources. We identified a number of 149 knowledge linkages. Knowledge links we understand in a broad way including all external relations of companies used for sourcing and acquiring relevant knowledge in the innovation process (see Tödtling et al. 2006). Such relations can be to other companies (such as suppliers or customers) or to universities and research organizations (e.g. R&D collaborations), and they may be of formal nature (e.g. based on contracts or written agreements) or of informal kind (e.g. not formalized relations at professional meetings or fairs etc.). As shown in Table 19.7,

Table 19.7 Number of knowledge links and their geography in the Vienna biotechnology cluster (2006)

	Total		Vienna			Austria			International		
	Number of links		With firms	With RO	*Total*	With firms	With RO	*Total*	With firms	With RO	*Total*
Market links	30	(20 %)	2	8	*10*	0	0	*0*	13	7	*20*
Formal co-operations	79	(53 %)	14	25	*39*	2	5	*7*	17	17	*33*
Informal links and spillovers	40	(27 %)	6	10	*16*	0	0	*0*	15	9	*24*
Total	**149**	**(100 %)**			*65*			*7*			*77*

RO research organization (universities, clinics)

formal co-operations and R&D partnerships constitute the most important single mode of knowledge acquisition and exchange for the studied Vienna biotechnology firms. Exploring the geography of co-operative linkages we found that almost 50 % of them are maintained with local partners. There is evidence for close local co-operation between academic institutions and firms (i.e. university-industry partnerships) and to a lesser extent for inter-firm collaborations. Given these results, one can hardly argue that the local biotech innovation system is suffering from fragmentation. Some of the formal linkages reflect conscious policy efforts to boost the level of interaction in the Austrian and Viennese biotech scene. In the past years, for example, several biotech related competence centers, jointly run by universities and firms, have been established in Vienna with financial support of local and national governments (for a more detailed discussion of this issue see Tödtling and Trippl 2007; Trippl and Tödtling 2007). Innovation networks and R&D collaborations established by Viennese biotech firms are not confined to the local level, however. The studied companies have forged co-operative relations with internationally renowned knowledge centers and are also inserted into various collaborative endeavors with multinational pharmaceutical companies located elsewhere.

Furthermore, our study has shown that Vienna biotech companies also make use of knowledge and expertise which can be 'bought in the market place', pointing to the significance of relations such as contract research, buying of licenses, buying of knowledge related services. Overall, these linkages seem to be less important than knowledge flows via co-operations which are considered to be more durable and interactive than market links. Table 19.7 illustrates that market links (i.e. the buying of knowledge or of technology) have been mainly found at the international level. However, also local interactions of this type play a role, amounting to 30 % of all market links. They include, amongst others, ties between local firms and university institutes and hospitals, being largely about contract research, the testing of assays and the buying of patents and licenses.

Apart from formal co-operation and market linkages there are also spillovers and informal links which give rise to knowledge flows in the Vienna biotechnology

19 Innovation and Knowledge Links in Metropolitan Regions: The Case of Vienna

Table 19.8 Characterization of spin-off companies in the sample (2006)

		Number of companies	Percentages
Age of firm	Not older than 10 years	13	87
	Older than 10 years	2	13
	Total	*15*	*100*
Firm size (number of employees)	1–10	8	53
	11–50	5	33
	More than 50	2	13
	Total	*15*	*100*
Location of parent organization	Local	14	93
	National	0	0
	International	1	7
	Total	*15*	*100*
Type of parent organization	Academic institution	11	73
	Firm	4	27
	Total	*15*	*100*

cluster (see Table 19.7). These result from regular professional meetings and talks, the reading of literature and also from the monitoring of competitors. The Vienna region is of crucial significance when it comes to analyze the spatial dimension of knowledge spillovers. The relevance of the local level, where 40 % of all spillovers and informal links could be observed (see Table 19.7), results partly from intensive informal networking between local companies and research organizations. Unsurprisingly, this phenomenon is most apparent between spin-offs and their academic parent organizations and tends to be particularly strong in those cases, where the start-up firm is located at the site of the university institute from which it emanated. Furthermore, about 25 % of the firms stated to have established people-based informal links with other local companies and there is also evidence of intense monitoring of competitors within the Vienna biotech industry. It is worth mentioning that the emergence of personal relationships among local actors has been supported by policy actions. Of key importance in this respect has been the organization of so called 'Life Science Circles' and other meetings which have brought local companies together, stimulating an informal exchange of ideas and experiences. Our study, however, also demonstrates that knowledge spillovers are only partially geographically bounded, as 60 % could be found at the international scale (Table 19.7). International knowledge spillovers are the outcome of gaining new knowledge by reading scientific literature and patent specifications, by monitoring the activities of international competitors and by establishing informal links to them and other distant firms. International congresses and fairs have been identified to play a key role in this respect.

In the next section we take a closer look at two specific core mechanisms of knowledge transmission, that is, spin-offs and recruitment of highly skilled labor.

Spin-off processes are a rather recent phenomenon in the Vienna biotechnology cluster. As shown in Table 19.8, most of spin-off companies included in our study are rather young and small. Like in other regions (Keeble and Wilkinson 2000) new firm creation in the Vienna biotech industry is a highly localized process. The overwhelming majority of all spin-out companies originated from parent organizations operating in the region. Looking at the type of incubators a clear dominance of local universities was found. These findings point to a strong localized use and transfer of academic knowledge to the industrial world, providing further evidence for the view that fragmentation is not a core problem in Vienna's emerging biotech sector.

Similar results were obtained from the analysis of labor market recruitment and labor mobility of highly-skilled employees. The local level turned out to be crucially significant in this regard. For the large majority of the surveyed companies the local universities are the essential source of highly qualified labor. This was confirmed in interviews both with firms and universities. However, only little evidence for movements of skilled workers between local biotech companies was found. Importantly, we could observe an inflow of international scientific and industrial expertise. The research organizations present in Vienna attract scientists from all over the world. Even more interesting is the employment of foreign top managers in some growing Viennese biotech companies. This is noteworthy, because local managerial competencies in the field of biotechnology are a missing ingredient in the Vienna biotech cluster. Vienna biotech firms deal with this deficiency of the local system by recruiting experienced managers from abroad.

3.4   Information and Communication Technologies (ICT) Sector

The metropolitan region of Vienna is not only the key centre of Austria's emerging biotechnology sector, but it is also the core region of the nation's ICT industry. The ICT sector is older and by far larger than the biotech industry. Adopting a broad definition of the ICT sector as it has been proposed by the OECD (2004), we find more than 5,500 ICT firms in Vienna (35 % of the Austrian ICT industry), providing employment opportunities for approximately 78,918 workers (61 % of all Austrian ICT employees, see Table 19.9).

In terms of number of firms, it is particularly the ICT subsector "NACE 72: Computers and related activities" which is dominating in Vienna. It contains almost 5,000 firms (88 % of all ICT firms located in Vienna). Due to the small size of many companies in that subsector, it "only" employs 20,250 workers, however (26 % of all ICT workers employed in Vienna). The largest ICT subsector in terms of employees present in Vienna is "NACE 64: Post and telecommunications" (44,000 workers employed by 205 companies), followed by "NACE 72: Computers and related activities" (see above), "NACE 32: Manufacture of radio, television and communication equipment and apparatus" (12,235 workers, 79 firms), and "NACE 33: Manufacture of medical, precision and optical instruments, watches and clocks" (353 companies employing 2,324 workers). The subsector "NACE 33: Manufacture of office machinery and computers" is almost negligible both in terms of number of firms and employees in comparison.

19 Innovation and Knowledge Links in Metropolitan Regions: The Case of Vienna

Table 19.9 Proportion of ICT companies in different Austrian provinces (2007)

Region	Number of firms	*Proportion of firms (%)*
Vienna	5575	*35*
Styria	1855	*12*
Lower Austria	2891	*18*
Tyrol	979	*6*
Upper Austria	2051	*13*
Salzburg	925	*6*
Vorarlberg	564	*4*
Carinthia	673	*4*
Burgenland	339	*2*
Total	15852	*100*

Source: Statistik Austria 2008 (own calculations)

The metropolitan region of Vienna is well endowed with knowledge generating organizations in the field of ICT. Key actors are the Technical University of Vienna (faculty of electrical engineering and information technology), University of Vienna (faculty of computer sciences), and Medical University of Vienna (Section of Medical Computer Vision, and excellence centre for telemedicine). Among the non-academic research institutes we find the Austrian Research Institute for Artificial Intelligence (OFAI) of the Austrian Society for Cybernetic Studies (OSGK) and Seibersdorf Research (medical informatics). Furthermore, there are several co-operative research institutes located in Vienna. In the field of ICT not fewer than four CD Labs and four competence centers could be found in the region.

Innovation is an important competitive strategy of the surveyed Vienna ICT companies. Not fewer than 71 % of the firms included in our sample reported having improved existing products in the 3 years prior to our study (incremental innovation). But there is also evidence for more radical forms of innovation. A share of 49 % of the sampled firms generated innovations which are new to the market (radical innovation) and another 55 % realized innovations which are at least new to the firm.

In the following we explore the geography of knowledge links maintained by innovative Vienna ICT firms to find out whether or not this knowledge based sector suffers from fragmentation. As already mentioned above (see methodological notes) our findings are based on a web-based survey of 73 ICT firms located in Vienna. We analyze knowledge linkages to various sources at different spatial scales and we explore the relative importance of different modes of knowledge exchange by calculating the share of Viennese ICT firms which perform such activities (and not, as done in the biotech study, by looking at the respective number of knowledge links).

As shown in Table 19.10, for the surveyed Vienna ICT companies the local level is highly relevant for knowledge sharing activities with multiple partners during the innovation process. For knowledge linkages to clients, service firms, technology centers and particularly universities in the Vienna region is the most important interaction space. The empirical findings, thus, suggest that in the Vienna ICT

Table 19.10 Knowledge sources and their geography in the Vienna ICT sector (% of all responding ICT firms; multiple answers possible) 2007

	Vienna	Rest Austria	Europe	USA and Canada	Asia	Rest of the world
Customers	39.1	36.2	33.3	4.3	2.9	4.3
Suppliers	18.8	23.2	23.1	26.1	10.1	5.8
Competitors	26.1	21.7	29.0	10.1	1.4	1.4
Service firms	27.5	15.9	7.2	4.3	1.4	1.4
Commercial R&D	15.9	11.6	5.8	1.4	0.0	2.9
Universities	31.9	15.9	10.1	4.3	1.4	0.0
Technical colleges	21.7	21.7	2.9	0.0	0.0	0.0
Non-profit R&D	5.8	7.2	4.3	0.0	0.0	0.0
Technology centers	15.9	8.7	2.9	0.0	0.0	0.0

Table 19.11 Mechanisms of knowledge transfer (% of all responding ICT firms, multiple answers possible) 2007

	% of firms
Market linkages	
Contract research	22
Consulting	20
Buying licenses	9
Buying machinery, software	20
Formal co-operations	
R&D collaborations	32
Joint use of R&D facilities	9
Spillovers and informal networks	
Recruiting specialists	41
Monitoring competitors	52
Reading scientific publications	55
Informal contacts	61
Participating in conferences/fairs	42

industry localized knowledge circulation is pivotal. Consequently, there are hardly any reasons for assuming that fragmentation is a dominating feature in this knowledge based sector. To be sure, there is also evidence of innovation networking with national and international partners such as clients, suppliers and other knowledge sources, pointing to a rather high degree of embeddedness of Viennese ICT firms into the national innovation system and European knowledge networks. The firms in this sector, thus, demonstrate both local and international knowledge links.

Concerning the modes of knowledge exchange we found a clear dominance of informal networks and spillovers (Table 19.11). Informal contacts, reading scientific publications, monitoring competitors, participating in conferences and fairs, as well as recruiting highly qualified people turned out to be the favorite knowledge sourcing activities performed by the surveyed companies. Except from R&D collaborations formal networks play a negligible role. The same holds true for market links. This is a clear difference to the biotechnology sector where knowledge flows show a more formalized nature.

19 Innovation and Knowledge Links in Metropolitan Regions: The Case of Vienna

Table 19.12 Recruiting highly qualified workers – sources and geography (% of all responding ICT firms, multiple answers possible) 2007

	Vienna	Austria	International
Universities	49	23	19
Technical colleges	38	29	7
Companies	33	25	9

Table 19.13 Spatial pattern of R&D co-operations (% of all responding ICT firms, multiple answers possible) 2007

	Vienna	Rest Austria	EU-EFTA	USA and Canada	Asia	Rest of the World
Customers	15	12	9	1	1	0
Suppliers	9	7	7	0	0	0
Competitors	15	6	6	0	0	0
Service firms	10	4	4	0	0	0
Commercial R&D	13	9	3	0	0	0
Universities	19	6	4	3	1	0
Technical colleges	10	10	0	0	0	0
Non-profit R&D	6	6	4	0	0	0
Technology centers	9	4	0	0	0	0

In the following section we have a closer look on two key channels of knowledge transmission, namely labor market recruitment and R&D collaborations, focusing particularly on the geography of these modes of knowledge exchange.

As it is shown in Table 19.12, the local labor market plays a crucial role for innovating Viennese ICT firms. Indeed, there is evidence of strong knowledge flows from universities, technical colleges and ICT companies to the surveyed firms via mobility of highly skilled labor. At the same time we could observe that also the national labor market and universities located in other countries are relevant when it comes to recruit specialists. In comparison, labor mobility among companies is a less important mechanism for knowledge transfer.

As noted above, about 40 % of the ICT firms included in the sample are involved in R&D co-operations. The analysis of the spatial dimension of these formal linkages reveals that R&D collaborations are highly localized in nature (Table 19.13). These findings differ from some other studies which have pointed to a highly international character of such formal R&D collaborations and knowledge "pipelines" (Hagedoorn 2002; Bathelt et al. 2004).

The surveyed ICT companies maintain such links with a variety of local partners. We could observe a particular strong role of local universities, local customers and local competitors. In the case of customers these could e.g. be the involvement of lead users in the development of particular hard- or software, drawing on their respective "user knowledge" (see, for instance, von Hippel 1988). To a lesser extent, R&D co-operations are also found with partners at the national and European levels, whereas other parts of the world (USA and Canada, Asia, other countries) are negligible.

3.5 The Role of Policy in Promoting the Local Embeddedness of Vienna's Biotechnology and ICT Sectors

The empirical findings reported above provide evidence for a high degree of embeddedness of Viennese biotech and ICT firms, brought about by rather vivid knowledge sharing activities and innovation partnering at the local level. Arguably, the intensity of local knowledge circulation found in the biotech and ICT sectors has – to some extent – been positively influenced by conscious policy efforts. In the past 10 years, stimulation of knowledge links has become a core strategy of innovation and technology policies, both at the national and the local levels. We find various national initiatives which explicitly aim at fostering knowledge interactions in biotechnology (such as the Genome Research Program and the initiative LISA-Life Science Austria) and in ICT (for example the FIT-IT program). Furthermore, the local biotech and ICT sector benefit from the so called "Competence Centre program" which promotes the establishment of new research centers, which are jointly run by universities and companies. In sharp contrast to the past, fostering knowledge linkages is also at the top of the local policy agenda today. For a long time, Vienna's economic policy was about providing subsidies to individual companies and attracting multinational companies. It was only by the end of the 1990s that issues of innovation and technology gained importance. Today, Vienna' strategic policy priorities are on life sciences, ICT, creative industries and the automotive sector. This reorientation has been accompanied by a process of institution building. At the beginning of the new millennium two new funding organizations (ZIT Center for Innovation and Technology, and Vienna Science and Technology Fund) have been created. They have special programs for biotechnology and ICT, organized as contests of proposals. Another new centre is "Inits", which has been founded in 2003. Its aim is to support technology-oriented spin-offs from the academic sector by offering counseling and assistance to scientists in the process of turning a good idea into a viable business. Overall, the local policy system has undergone a far reaching transformation. The new policy routines are strongly about promoting high tech industries and fostering local knowledge connections.

4 Summary and Conclusions

Metropolitan regions are often considered as centers of innovation and knowledge intensive activities, and they are regarded as key nodes of knowledge networks. They are usually well equipped with public and private research organizations, universities and higher educational institutions as well as with high ranking business services (Brower et al. 1999; Simmie 2003). Not all metropolitan regions are vibrant innovation systems, however. Some of these regions suffer from a problem of fragmentation in their respective RIS (Tödtling and Trippl 2005). They may lack sufficient interaction between the RIS subsystems of knowledge generation and knowledge exploitation. Also a certain level of knowledge exchange among firms might be missing.

Vienna seems to be a good example for this phenomenon. On the one hand it is clearly the key centre of research and higher education as well as of knowledge intensive sectors and business services within Austria. On the other hand its RIS has shown characteristics of fragmentation in some previous studies. In particular there was little interaction between the research sector (mainly made up by public universities) and the business sector. Our investigations of two growing knowledge intensive sectors in the region, the biotech industry and the ICT sector, have demonstrated that fragmentation within these industries may not be a prime innovation barrier. Both for the biotech sector and for the ICT sector we found quite intensive knowledge interactions at the regional level. Firms in both sectors were also linked to international partners in their innovation process. In addition we found a variety of knowledge interactions, both formal (market links and formal co-operations) and informal (knowledge spillovers and informal contacts) ones. Policies at the regional and national levels in the past decade might also have contributed to a rather high level of innovation networking.

Barriers for the development of these sectors, however, still exist. First, as other investigations have shown (Trippl et al. 2007) there are quite strong differences among companies in their level of innovation and innovation interaction. Such a segmented nature is clearly visible in the ICT sector where some large, partly international firms with a high level of R&D activities and some dynamic SMEs exist next to a large segment of very small firms which are not able to perform any R&D or to maintain relationships to research organizations. Then, in the biotech sector there seems to be a lack of critical mass. So far there are rather few dedicated biotech companies and spinoffs, partly due to missing entrepreneurial spirit among researchers and a lack of venture capital. Furthermore, Austria and Vienna do not have any home grown large pharmaceutical companies to act as leading firms in a local cluster. Consequently, the Vienna biotech sector, despite its recent growth, seems to still be in a rather vulnerable state.

Overall, we find that in some respects the metropolitan region of Vienna performs its function as a centre in the knowledge economy. At least for the two knowledge based sectors included in our studies, we could observe that Vienna's RIS has overcome its state of fragmentation found in earlier studies. For a dynamic and enduring development of knowledge intensive sectors, however, there are still barriers indicated above which should be targeted by regional innovation policy. What remains obscure, so far, is whether local knowledge sharing activities could also be found in other sectors than those investigated here. This would reflect a transformation of the whole RIS from a fragmented towards a more integrated one. More research considering a broader set of industries, thus, seems to be necessary to explore whether or not ICT and biotech constitute integrated islands in a fragmented RIS.

References

Anselin L, Varga A, Acs Z (1997) Local geographic spillovers between university research and high technology innovations. J Urban Econ 42:422–448

Asheim B, Isaksen A, Nauwelaers C, Tödtling F (eds) (2003) Regional innovation policy for small-medium enterprises. Edward Elgar, Cheltenham

Audretsch D (1998) Agglomeration and the location of innovative activity. Oxford Rev Econ Pol 14:18–29

Audretsch D, Feldman M (1996) Innovative clusters and the industry life cycle. Rev Ind Organ 11:253–273

Autio E (1998) Evaluation of RTD in regional systems of innovation. Eur Plan Stud 6:131–140

Baptista R (2003) Productivity and density of regional clusters. In: Bröcker J, Dohse D, Soltwedel R (eds) Innovation clusters and interregional competition. Springer, Berlin, pp 163–181

Baptista R, Swann P (1998) Do firms in clusters innovate more? Res Policy 27:525–540

Bathelt H, Malmberg A, Maskell P (2004) Clusters and knowledge: local buzz, global pipelines and the process of knowledge creation. Prog Hum Geog 28:31–56

BIT Bureau for International Research and Technology Cooperation and LISA Life Science Austria (2004) Bio-Tech in Austria. BIT/LISA, Vienna

Boschma R (2005) Proximity and innovation: a critical assessment. Reg Stud 39:61–74

Bottazzi L, Peri G (2003) Innovation and spillovers in regions: evidence from European patent data. Eur Econ Rev 47:687–710

Brandt A, Hahn C, Krätke S, Kiese M (2009) Metropolitan regions in the knowledge economy: network analysis as strategic information tool. Tijdschr Econ Soc Ge 100:236–249

Breschi S (2000) The geography of innovation: a cross-industry analysis. Reg Stud 34:213–229

Brower E, Budil-Nadvornikowa H, Kleinknecht A (1999) Are urban agglomerations a better breeding place for product innovation? An analysis of new product announcements. Reg Stud 33:541–549

Camagni R (1991) Local 'milieu', uncertainty and innovation networks: towards a new dynamic theory of economic space. In: Camagni R (ed) Innovation networks: spatial perspectives. Belhaven Press, London, pp 121–144

Cooke P (ed) (1995) The rise of the rustbelt. UCL Press, London

Cooke P (2002) Knowledge economies. Clusters, learning and cooperative advantage. Routledge, London

Cooke P, Boekholt P, Tödtling F (2000) The governance of innovation in Europe. Pinter, London

Cooke P, Heidenreich M, Braczyk H-J (eds) (2004) Regional Innovation Systems, 2nd edn. UCL Press, London

Cooke P, DeLaurentis C, Tödtling F, Trippl M (2007) Regional knowledge economies. Edward Elgar, Cheltenham

De la Mothe J, Paquet G (eds) (1998) Local and regional systems of innovation. Kluwer, Boston

Doloreux D (2002) What we should know about regional systems of innovation. Technol Soc 24:243–263

European Commission (2003) 2003 European innovation scoreboard: technical paper no 3 regional innovation performances. European commission, Brusseles

Feldman M (1994) The geography of innovation. Kluwer, Boston

Feldman M, Audretsch D (1999) Innovation in cities: science-based diversity, specialization and localized competition. Eur Econ Rev 43:409–429

Fischer M, Fröhlich J (eds) (2001) Knowledge, complexity, and innovation systems. Springer, Berlin

Fischer M, Fröhlich J, Gassler H, Varga A (2001) The role of space in the creation of knowledge in Austria – an exploratory spatial analysis. In: Fischer M, Fröhlich J (eds) Knowledge, complexity, and innovation systems. Springer, Berlin, pp 124–145

Fornahl D, Brenner T (eds) (2003) Cooperation, networks and institutions in regional innovation systems. Edward Elgar, Cheltenham

19 Innovation and Knowledge Links in Metropolitan Regions: The Case of Vienna 471

Frenken K, Van Oort F, Verburg T (2007) Related variety, unrelated variety and regional economic growth. Reg Stud 41:685–697

Fritsch M (2000) Interregional differences in R&D activities – an empirical investigation. Eur Plann Stud 8:409–427

Fritsch M (2003) Does R&D-Cooperation behaviour differ between regions? Ind Innov 10:25–39

Fritsch M, Franke G (2004) Innovation, regional knowledge spillovers and R&D cooperation. Res Policy 33:245–255

Fröhlich J, Gassler H (1999) Das Innovationssystem Wiens und Ansatzpunkte für technologie-politsche Strategien. In: Schmee J, Weigl A (eds) Wiener Wirtschaft 1945–1998. Peter Lang Verlag, Frankfurt

Gehrke B, Legler H (2001) Innovationspotenziale deutscher Regionen im europäischen Vergleich. Duncker & Humblot, Berlin

Hagedoorn J (2002) Inter-firm R&D partnerships: an overview of major trends and patterns since 1960. Res Policy 31:477–492

Jaffe AB, Trajtenberg M, Henderson R (1993) Geographic localization of knowledge spillovers as evidenced by patent citations. Q J Econ 79:577–598

Keeble D, Wilkinson F (eds) (1999) Special issue: regional networking, collective learning and innovation in high technology SMEs in Europe. Regional Studies, 33 (Special issue)

Keeble D, Wilkinson F (eds) (2000) High-technology clusters, networking and collective learning in Europe. Ashgate, Aldershot

Mayerhofer P (2006) Wien in einer erweiterten Union. Ökonomische Effekte der Ostintegration auf die Wiener Wirtschaft. LIT Verlag, Wien

Moulaert F, Tödtling F (eds) (1995) The geography of advanced producer services in Europe. Prog Plann, 43 (Special issue)

OECD (2004) Information technology outlook. OECD, Paris

Paci R, Usai S (2000) Technological enclaves and industrial districts: an analysis of the regional distribution of innovative activity in Europe. Reg Stud 34:97–114

Porter M (1998) On competition. Harvard Business School Press, Boston

Rohn W (2000) Forschungseinrichtungen in der Agglomeration Wien. Stellung im Innovation-sprozess und Einbindung in innovative Netzwerke. ISR-Forschungsberichte 21. Verlag der Österreichischen Akademie der Wissenschaften, Wien

Saxenian A (1994) Regional advantage: culture and competition in Silicon Valley and Route 128. Harvard University Press, Cambridge, MA

Schamp E (2001) Reorganisation metropolitaner Wissenssysteme im Spannungsfeld zwischen lokalen und nicht-lokalen Anstrengungen. Zeitschrift für Wirtschaftsgeographie 45:231–245

Simmie J (2003) Innovation and urban regions as national and international nodes for the transfer and sharing of knowledge. Reg Stud 37:607–620

Statistik Austria (2009) Statistisches jahrbuch 2008. Wien

Statistik Austria (2008) Leistungs- und Strukturstatistik. Produktion & Dienstleistungen, Wien

Sternberg R (2000) Innovation networks and regional development – evidence from the European Regional Innovation Survey (ERIS): theoretical concepts, methodological approach, empirical basis and introduction to the theme issue. Eur Plann Stud 8:389–407

Thomi W, Werner R (2001) Regionale Innovationssysteme. Zeitschrift für Wirtschaftsgeographie 45:202–218

Tichy G (2001) Regionale Kompetenzzyklen – Zur Bedeutung von Produktlebenszyklus- und Clusteransätzen im regionalen Kontext. Zeitschrift für Wirtschaftsgeographie 45:181–201

Tödtling F (1992) Technological change at the regional level: the role of location, firm structure, and strategy. Environ Plann A 24:1565–1584

Tödtling F (1994) The uneven landscape of innovation poles: local embeddedness and global networks. In: Amin A, Thrift N (eds) Globalization, institutions, and regional development in Europe. Oxford University Press, New York, pp 68–90

Tödtling F (2002) Die Region Wien aus einer Innovationssystem-Perspektive. In: Schmee J (ed) Dienstleistungsmetropole Wien. Arbeiterkammer Wien, Wien, pp 42–53

Tödtling F, Trippl M (2008) Regional innovation cultures. Paper prepared for the CURE workshop, Vienna, 26–27 Sept 2008

Tödtling F, Kaufmann A (1999) Innovation systems in regions of Europe – a comparative perspective. Eur Plann Stud 7:699–717

Tödtling F, Trippl M (2005) One size fits all? Towards a differentiated regional innovation policy approach. Res Policy 34:1203–1219

Tödtling F, Trippl M (2007) Knowledge links in high-technology industries: markets, networks or milieu? The case of the Vienna biotechnology cluster. Int J Entrep Innovat Manag 7:346–364

Tödtling F, Lehner P, Trippl M (2006) Innovation in knowledge intensive industries: the nature and geography of knowledge links. Eur Plann Stud 14:1035–1058

Trippl M, Otto A (2009) How to turn the fate of old industrial areas: a comparison of cluster-based renewal processes in Styria and the Saarland. Environ Plann A 41:1217–1233

Trippl M, Tödtling F (2007) Developing biotechnology clusters in non-high technology regions – the case of Austria. Ind Innov 14:27–47

Trippl M, Lengauer L, Tödtling F (2007) Innovation und Wissensnetze im Wiener Informations- und Kommunikationtechnologiecluster, Forschungsbericht, Institut für Regional- und Umweltwirtschaft, Wirtschaftsuniversität Wien

Von Hippel E (1988) The sources of innovation. Oxford University Press, New York

Chapter 20
Immigrant Location Patterns in a Southern European Metropolis: The Case of Athens

Paschalis A. Arvanitidis, George Petrakos, and Dimitrios Skouras

Abstract Over the last two decades, Greece has seen a substantial influx of economic immigrants giving rise to a number of studies examining the social, economic and spatial implications immigration has for the country. In terms of the spatial impact, the observed tendency is immigrants to move primarily into metropolitan areas, which offer employment opportunities and anonymity. However, very little is known with regard to the specific, intra-urban, locations immigrants choose for their residence and the factors that affect such decisions. The current study attempts to shed light on the above issues, analysing the spatial distribution of economic immigrants within the metropolitan area of Athens, their mobility patterns and the resultant metropolitan structure. Our findings indicate a slight preference for central areas, but, over the time, the general dispersion of such immigrants to peripheral locations. On these grounds, spatial segregation, to the formation of clear ethnic enclaves, seems less plausible.

Keywords Immigrants • Location • Segregation • Athens

Dedication: We like to dedicate this paper to the memory of our co-author, Dimitrios. Major Dimitrios Skouras was killed during a military exercise on the night of November 5th, 2008 when his Apache helicopter crashed.

P.A. Arvanitidis (✉)
Department of Economics, University of Thessaly, 43 Korai St, Volos 38333, Greece
e-mail: parvanit@uth.gr

G. Petrakos
Department of Planning and Regional Development, University of Thessaly, Pedion Areos, Volos 38334, Greece

D. Skouras
Hellenic Army Aviation Corps. & Department of Planning and Regional Development, University of Thessaly, Pedion Areos, Volos 38334, Greece

J. Klaesson et al. (eds.), *Metropolitan Regions*, Advances in Spatial Science, DOI 10.1007/978-3-642-32141-2_20, © Springer-Verlag Berlin Heidelberg 2013   473

1 Introduction

Over the last 20 years or so, Greece has seen a substantial influx of immigrant populations originating primarily from the countries of ex USSR, the Balkans and Eastern Europe, as well as from Asia and Africa. Currently, according to official estimates, people originating from such places make up about one million of Greece total population, compared to about 50,000 in 1991, of which the vast majority (over 60 %) are economic immigrants from Albania (Arvanitidis and Skouras 2008).

This phenomenon has attracted increasing attention in the literature, giving rise to a number of studies examining the economic, social and spatial implications immigration has for the country (see Lazaridis 1996; Psimmenos 1995, 1998; Lianos 2001; Cavounidis 2002; Lianos and Papakonstantinou 2003; Labrianidis et al. 2004; Baldwin-Edwards 2005; Arapoglou 2006; Rovolis and Tragaki 2006; Maloutas 2007; Arvanitidis and Skouras 2008; Cavounidis et al. 2008). As regards its spatial impact, the general trend reported is that new-comers move primarily into the metropolitan areas (Rovolis and Tragaki 2006), which offer anonymity and substantial employment opportunities. Within the urban frame, immigrants seems to show a preference for central locations (Maloutas 2007), where accessibility is high (due to transport networks) and low-cost housing is available (Arvanitidis and Skouras 2007).

In the light of these arguments the current study analyses the residential distribution of various immigrant groups within Athens' metropolitan area, to assess their locational preferences, the degree of their mobility and the pattern of their spatial development. In doing so, the paper utilizes data from the 2001 National Census, whereas the spatial unit of data collection and analysis is the Census Collection District (*apografikos tomeas*), which is the smallest available.

The paper is structured as follows. The next section outlines the theoretical models that have been developed to explain immigrants' spatial behaviour. On these grounds, Sects. 3 and 4 review the empirical literature to delineate the international and national experience respectively. These are followed by Sect. 5, which briefly outlines the research method employed, and Sect. 6, which discusses immigrants' intra-urban locational pattern and assesses the degree of segregation exhibited. Finally, Sect. 7 concludes the paper by summarising the key findings.

2 The Spatial Behaviour of Immigrants: Conceptual Considerations

The location preferences of immigrants, as well as any minority group in general, and the spatial patterns that result from their decisions have been discussed in the literature under the theme of *segregation*. Initial approaches to segregation, however, dealt with space implicitly, simply assuming that the social environment

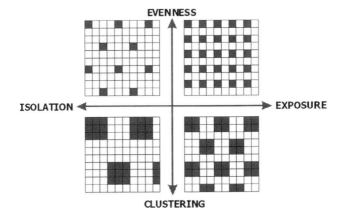

Fig. 20.1 Dimensions of spatial segregation (Source: based on Reardon and O'Sullivan 2004)

of different groups corresponds to some organisational unit that has a spatial substance. These treatments have been repeatedly criticised in the literature for their simplistic approach and their inability to properly project such social phenomena on space (see Openshaw and Taylor 1979; White 1983; Massey and Denton 1988; Morrill 1991; Wong 1993, 1997, 2002; Reardon and O'Sullivan 2004).

A notable attempt to put space into the forefront of the analysis of segregation is Massey and Denton (1988). Employing notions available from the economics literature, they identified five separate dimensions to the segregation of any one group: evenness, exposure, concentration, clustering, and centralization. *Evenness* refers to the differential distribution of the subject population, *exposure* denotes the likelihood of interaction between groups, *concentration* addresses the relative amount of physical space occupied, *centralization* indicates the degree to which a group is located near the urban centre, and *clustering* specifies the gathering of group members into one certain space.

More recently, other scholars (Reardon and O'Sullivan 2004) have elaborated on the above approach to develop more refined measures of spatial segregation that analyse patterning along two axes: one indicating spatial exposure or spatial isolation and the other indicating spatial evenness or spatial clustering (see Fig. 20.1). Spatial exposure/isolation refers to the extent that people belonging to one group are mixed with people of other groups or remain spatially isolated in their local spatial environments. Spatial evenness/clustering assesses the distribution of a group in the residential space, specifying the extent to which its members prefer to locate close to each other (i.e. to cluster together). The combination of the two analytical concepts gives four patterns of residential location, as shown in Fig. 20.1. The upper half of the diagram presents two patterns of evenly distributed ('black' and 'white') households, indicating low levels of spatial clustering (or high levels of spatial evenness). The difference between the two is on the degree of exposure they go through. People of the two groups in the upper-right pattern are equally mixed with each other, whereas in the upper-left quadrant 'black' households are more isolated. In turn, both patterns at the bottom half of the figure indicates high degrees of clustering: the right one presents a 'black' community with higher exposure, whereas at the left one higher degrees of isolation are evident.

Turning to the reasons behind the development of the various patterns of residential segregation, two major streams of explanation have been put forward: cultural and economic. Cultural explanations argue that minority group members tend to locate close to each other in order to take advantage of their closely-integrated social networks and to retain valued elements of their cultural heritage, such as language and religion (Boal 1976; Hugo 1996; Dunn 1998). Economic explanations draw attention to the functioning of both the labour and the housing markets, asserting that newcomers tend to concentrate in specific areas of the city (usually the least expensive ones) due to income and information limitations (Massey 1985; Bartel 1989; Boal 1996; Kempen and Ozuekren 1998). These arise, firstly, because immigrants are usually low-skilled, low-paid, unemployment-prone workers (Tripier 1990; Ulrich 1994), and, secondly, because they are faced with both restricted access to housing and other information regarding the institutional mechanisms of the host society (Yinger 1986; Kesteloot 1995; Petsimeris 1995; Pacione 1996). It is important to mention that economic explanations see intra-urban low-priced housing as the cause behind the spatial clustering of minority group members, whereas for cultural explanations low-priced houses is rather a side-effect caused by the decrease of desirability of the particular location to other groups of inhabitants.

In order to analyse the dynamics of spatial settlement of immigrants, three fully fledged explanatory models have been put forward (Freeman 2000). These are the *spatial assimilation* model, the *spatial stratification* model and the *residential preference* model, which are discussed next.

The spatial assimilation model, developed by the Chicago School of Human Ecology, argues for the time-progressive dispersal of initially spatial-concentrated immigrant groups (Dunn 1998). Concentration is rooted in the cultural character of immigration but is reinforced by economic considerations that affect the immigration process. It is expected that during the initial stages of immigration, newcomers would cluster together in order to take advantage of the social and kinship networks of their co-ethnics (Cutler et al. 1999). These networks provide social support and information as well as employment opportunities. However, as time goes by, the gradual acquisition of the language, values, and manners of the host society (a process called *acculturation*), achieved through prolonged contact with natives and through mass institutions such as schools and the media, would lead to the spatial assimilation of the immigrants (Freeman 2000). This is because, as the degree of acculturation increases and the socioeconomic status of the immigrants rises, the social distance between natives and immigrants diminishes, leading to a decrease in the spatial distances between them (Hawley 1950; Park 1926). Thus, immigrants move out of the poor inner-city areas to the outer suburbs, starting to integrate spatially with the natives (Massey 1985; Kempen and Ozuekren 1998).

Although the spatial assimilation model describes relatively well the progress of spatial settlement for most immigrant groups, e.g. the non-English speaking populations in Sydney and Melbourne in Australia (Grimes 1993; Hugo 1996) and the black Caribbean people in Greater London (Peach 1996), it encounters serious problems in explaining the spatial patterns of minorities with African heritage, namely African Americans and Puerto Ricans, in the USA (Freeman 2000). This has led to the development of the place stratification model.

The place stratification model considers urban space as a hierarchy of places ordered in terms of desirability and the quality of life they provide to urban dwellers (Logan 1978). Natives occupy the most desirable places, keeping immigrants, and generally ethic and racial minorities, at a distance (Cutler et al. 1999). This situation reflects the perception that the natives have of immigrants and their place in the society. Immigrants are attributed with a low social status and remain segregated, even if they are financially able to take up residence in areas occupied by natives (Alba and Logan 1993; Freeman 2000). The place hierarchy is maintained through institutional mechanisms (red-lining, exclusionary zoning, etc.) and/or discriminatory acts on the part of the host society, which can be explicit, such as violence against minorities (Cutler et al. 1999; Anas 2004), or implicit, such as discrimination on the housing and land market (Yinger 1986; Cutler et al. 1999; Ahmed and Hammarstedt 2008). In the case of hierarchy disturbance, natives are expected to depart from the 'invaded' area in a progressive manner, leaving immigrants to constitute, slowly but steadily, the majority population in the area.

While the place stratification model envisages spatial segregation being imposed on immigrants (by other urban groups), the residential preference model asserts that this is in fact a decision of the immigrants themselves. That is, members of the immigrant group 'prefer' to reside with their co-ethnics and to remain spatially segregated, even when they have the financial means or the social status that would enable them to move elsewhere (Freeman 2000; Anas 2004). There are many benefits to be gained from such spatial behaviour. To newcomers, the community's social network would provide not only emotional, social and cultural support, but also other vital 'resources', such as housing and valuable information (on the host institutional framework and the labour market) (Freeman 2000). To all other members, the community represents the stronghold of their own cultural identity (in a sense it constitutes a specific ethnic local public good). It enables them to sustain aspects of their pre-migration cultural practices (religion, language, etc.) while also facilitating their assimilation into wider society. This element constitutes the key difference between the residential preference model and the spatial assimilation model; that is, there is no acculturation process envisaged in the former.

3 Some International Evidence on the Spatial Behaviour of Immigrants

What becomes apparent from the above discussion is that the intra-urban location decisions of immigrants are determined by both cultural and economic factors. When cultural reasons prevail over economic ones, immigrant concentration is expected to be strong and sustained in the long-run. In contrast, dominance of economic considerations over cultural ones would lead, in the long-run, to smoother residential patterns characterised by greater evenness. A number of studies have attempted to explore these issues in empirical research and to assess the role played by, and significance attached to, each set of determinants with regard to the developed urban residential structure.

In a study examining patterns of residential location among immigrants in Oslo, Blom (1999) supported the view that the most significant factor in determining immigrant's locational behaviour is economic resources; though cultural reasons also appear to play an important causal role. This is interpreted as an assimilation tendency where immigrants, after a certain length of stay, start to conform to local residential patterns. On these grounds, dispersal of foreign-born inhabitants is observed after an initial period of concentrated immigrant housing. Djuve and Hagen (1995) come to a similar conclusion, drawing on survey research they conducted on a sample of 329 refugees in Oslo. They found that affordability of housing was the main reason behind the latter's decision to settle in a particular residential area within the city, rather than 'preferences for living close to countrymen'. Analogous evidence has also been provided by Zang and Hassan (1996); Lan-Hung and Jung-Chung (2005) and Burnley (2005), who explored the residential preferences of immigrants in Australian metropolises. These studies indicated that, while immigrant groups may prefer to settle in close proximity to their family and kin for practical and/or emotional reasons, their locational choice depends largely on income and housing affordability, availability of neighbourhood services and closeness to work, giving rise to more assimilated residential patterns.

In a recent study investigating immigration dynamics and resulting residential patterns in the four largest Dutch cities (i.e. Amsterdam, Rotterdam, The Hague and Utrecht), Bontje and Latten (2005) observe a strong exchange of population subgroups. Natives show an ongoing outflow from certain urban neighbourhoods, where foreign-born population is increasingly settling in. These neighbourhoods have formed the basis of immigrant communities that are growing fast through family reunification and family formation. In fact, in some areas the share of foreigners has reached "... levels above 70 per cent and even 80 per cent, in contrast to the national share of 10 per cent" (Bontje and Latten 2005: 450). This can be seen as an example of joint implementation of economic and cultural factors, where economic reasons account for the initial stages of immigrant concentration, and cultural reasons justify its enhancement and longevity. Similar conclusions are drawn by Bolt et al. (2002) who, on the basis of both income and ethnicity, predict further strengthening of segregation and concentration of immigrants in the Dutch cities. However, there are researchers (Deurloo and Musterd 1998; Musterd and Deurloo 2002) who assert that the observed patterns of immigrant residential concentration tend not to be stable and therefore spatial integration is to be seen.

The situation across the Atlantic appears to be more complex. Scholars, such as Freeman (2000), Johnston et al. (2003) and Myers and Liu (2005), report a process of immigrant clustering in the American Metropolises similar to the one described above (i.e. fuelled by a time-lagged implementation of economic and cultural factors), but only for certain ethnic groups. Thus, it is argued that initially Asian and Latino immigrants were located in the degraded inner-city areas due to economic reasons, whereas subsequent newcomers of the same ethnic groups settled in the same neighbourhoods on the basis of cultural reasons. However, as they climb up the socioeconomic ladder they tend to move out and to assimilate into 'white' neighbourhoods. In contrast to Asian and Latino groups, the form of residential patterning exhibited by African Americans is somewhat different, in both its character and intensity (Massey and Denton 1985, 1987; Denton and Massey 1988; Harrison and Weinberg 1992; Alba and Logan 1993; Logan et al. 1996; Clark and Ware 1997; Freeman 2000). This ethnic group seems to place greater emphasis on cultural factors and, on these grounds, to show more concentrated patterns of residential location.

A similar situation is also observed in some European cities, such as Lisbon. Malheiros (2000) and Malheiros and Vala (2004) distinguish between two groups of immigrants with different locational behaviour. African-origin immigrants are more 'consolidated' in their residential pattern, whereas all other groups (dominated by Eastern Europeans and Brazilians) temporarily settle within their co-ethnics, only to flee out when their socio-economic conditions improve. Malheiros (2000) argues that a significant factor behind this dual pattern of immigrant settlement is the housing market and the policies adopted by the local authorities (of freezing property rents, tight controls over evictions, and loose enforcement of legal procedures over illegal constructions) that have reinforced the concentration of the less-affluent African-origin immigrants.

Concluding this discussion, it becomes clear that is no common pattern of immigrant residential location evident in the majority of places. Stated differently, economic and cultural factors influence the locational choice and the residential patterns of immigrants to a different degree, depending on the local conditions, policies and institutions, the cultural and economic background of immigrants and the time that immigration takes place. It is on these grounds that Musterd et al. (1998), having analysed immigrant residential behaviour in nine European metropolises, identifies the establishment of four spatial patterns: (a) clustering of immigrants in inner-city locations, (b) concentrations of immigrants outside central areas, (c) scattered immigrants but with clustering in inner-city locations, and (d) scattered immigrants but with concentrations in locations outside the city centre.

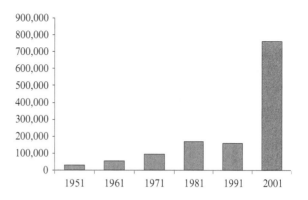

Fig. 20.2 Number of foreign citizens in Greece (population censuses 1951–2001) (Source: own elaboration [ESYE])

4 Immigrants in Greek Metropolises: A Review of the Literature

For many decades Greece has been a labour-exporting country. In fact, almost two million Greeks emigrated since the end of the nineteenth century to countries of North America (especially to the USA), Oceania and northern Europe (Kotzamanis 2008). The reversal of migratory balance started in the mid-1970s with the returning of the first waves of 'repatriates',[1] but it really took off in the early 1990s (see Fig. 20.2), fuelled by the border opening in East Europe and the subsequent adoption of restrictive policies by the traditional destination countries of northern Europe (King 2000; Rovolis and Tragaki 2006). During this period the vast majority of immigrants which entered the country were undocumented, whereas legal status was granted under the first, second and third regularisation programmes, took place in 1997–8, 2001–2 and 2005–6 respectively. Despite these regularisation campaigns and relevant legislative attempts aiming to deal with immigration in a more comprehensive way,[2] illegal immigration has remained an issue of concern and integration proved to be quite a challenge for both the Greek state and the Greek society in general (Cavounidis 2007).

Today, migrants constitute a significant part of Greece's population. According to the 2001 Census of the National Statistical Service (ESYE), which provides the most recent and reliable information, the estimated number of non-nationals living in the country was 762,191 people, amounting to approximately 7 % of the total

---

[1] Consisted of returning Greek guest workers, members of the Greek Diaspora from Egypt or elsewhere, as well as political exiles from the time of the Civil War of the 1940s.

[2] Laws 2910/2001, 3386/2005 and 3536/2007, and Presidential Decrees 358/1997, 359/1997, 131/2006 and 150/2006.

Table 20.1 Immigrants in Greece (2001)

Origin	Numbers	%	Sex ratio[a]
Europe	640,997	84.10	1.14
Southeastern	500,280	65.64	1.33
Central and East	74,682	9.80	0.60
EU-15	46,869	6.15	0.67
Rest of Europe[b]	19,166	2.51	0.86
Asia	68,361	8.97	2.07
America	27,293	3.58	0.88
Africa	15,620	2.05	1.99
Oceania	9,060	1.19	0.87
Albania	438,036	57.47	1.42
Bulgaria	35,104	4.61	0.66
Georgia	22,875	3.00	0.76
Romania	21,994	2.89	1.30
India and Pakistan	18,346	2.41	17.91
Russia	17,535	2.30	0.60
Ukraine	13,616	1.79	0.33
Poland	12,831	1.68	0.85
Egypt	7,448	0.98	3.24
Philippines	6,478	0.85	0.31
Total	762,191	100.00	1.20

Source: own elaboration (2001 population census, ESYE)
[a]Males to females
[b]Mainly Cypriots

population (as compared to 1.4 %, 10 years earlier). It is important to note that other studies have put this figure up to one million, when unregistered or Greek ethnic immigrants are taken into account (OECD 2001; Lianos et al. 2008). By 2003, there have been approximately 130,000 foreign children attending state schools (of which about 32,000 were ethnic Greeks), comprising 11 % of primary school registrations and the 8 % of secondary school registrations (Baldwin-Edwards 2005).

Contrary to the experience of other European countries, the majority of immigrants in Greece comes from a restricted number of countries, with few, if any, historic or cultural links (Rovolis and Tragaki 2006). Thus, only five countries of origin (out of more than 200 in total) count for about 70 % of all non-nationals, while ten countries represent more than 80 % of them (see Table 20.1). The majority of immigrants (eight out of ten) come from Europe, especially from Albania (57.5 %) and to a lesser extent from other Balkan countries, the Central-eastern Europe and the Republics of ex-USSR. Asians represent 9 % of the foreign population, Africans about 2 %, and those from America and Oceania, which are largely repatriates who have returned to their homeland with their families, amount to 4.8 %.

Table 20.2 Immigrants in Athens metropolitan region in 2001 (ranked by size)

	Nationality	Numbers	In percentage (%)	
			of total	cumulative
1	Albanians	209,333	62.06	
2	Poles	11,529	3.42	65.48
3	Russians	11,465	3.40	68.88
4	Bulgarians	11,141	3.30	72.18
5	Romanians	10,270	3.04	75.23
6	Pakistani	10,133	3.00	78.23
7	Ukrainians	9,996	2.96	81.20
8	Egyptians	7,187	2.13	83.33
9	Iraqis	6,618	1.96	85.29
10	Filipinos	6,484	1.92	87.21
11	Bangladeshi	4,767	1.41	88.62
12	Syrians	4,713	1.40	90.02

Source: own elaboration (EKKE-ESYE 2005)

Immigrants in Greece tend to be young (average age of about 29 years old), mostly men (about 55 %) that come to the country mainly for economic reasons (although women migrate for family reasons too) (Rovolis and Tragaki 2006). The majority of them work in construction, agriculture, manufacturing and various low and semi-skilled services in tourism, catering, domestic service, etc. (Lianos and Papakonstantinou 2003; Kanellopoulos 2008). Partly because of the exclusionary legal framework and partly due to the structural characteristics of the Greek labour market, the big bulk of immigrant labour has been absorbed by the underground economy and informal employment remains widespread for large shares of foreign workers, even after legal status is achieved (Kanellopoulos et al. 2006).

In terms of geographical location, the majority of immigrants found residence in the metropolitan areas of Athens and Thessaloniki (Rovolis and Tragaki 2006; Kotzamanis 2008). As regards the immigrant's intra-metropolitan location pattern, researchers (Lazaridis 1996; Psimmenos 1995, 1998; Baldwin-Edwards 2005; Maloutas 2007) have reported a tendency of the former to concentrate in the old city centre and other poor areas of Athens, which are characterised by low-quality housing and lack of public facilities. This literature identifies three reasons that inform such decisions. The main explanation is economic, where immigrants choose to take up residence in these areas simply because rents are low and there is housing stock available. This is supported by cultural issues. Co-ethnics already reside in these areas, and newcomers decide to settle there too, in order to take advantage of the social and kinship networks which offer social and emotional support and valuable information regarding the host institutions and opportunities.

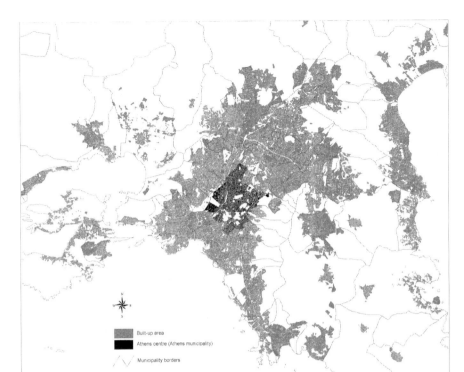

Map 20.1 Athens metropolitan region (Source: own elaboration [EKKE cartographic platform])

Interestingly, however, concentration seems to be fuelled by a third factor: the xenophobic intolerance of the natives. Greece has a history of high levels of xenophobia recorded in opinion polls, although rather less visible in reality. In support of this argument Baldwin-Edwards (2005) mentions the results of a survey conducted in 2002 amongst 2,100 households living in Athens metropolis: it was found that 44 % of respondents believed that immigrants should live separately from Greeks, in other areas.[3] Although high levels of racial intolerance are clearly linked with low educational and income levels, the point that clearly emerges is that

---

[3] Other incidents that could be interpreted along this line include the continuing public advertisements and notices in Athens refusing to rent property to foreigners. As Psimmenos (2001) clearly states, few natives would be willing to rent their property to a foreigner (especially of Albanian origins) if there are chances to rent it to someone else.

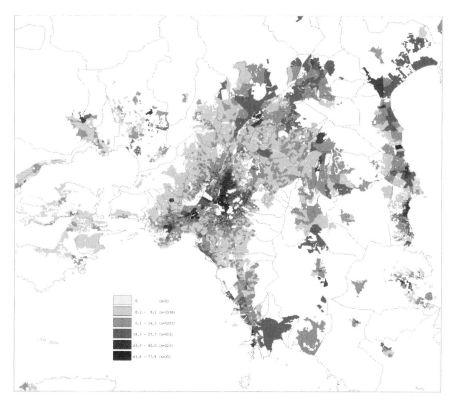

Map 20.2 Immigrants' spatial distribution within Athens metropolitan region (all nationalities) (Source: own elaboration [EKKE cartographic platform])

Greeks would not object to the creation of ethnic ghettos, presumably with little comprehension of their long-term implications.

This tendency of immigrants (a significant number of whom have been illegal) to locate in Athens inner-city over the 1990s worried the Greek government, who consequently intensified the policing of such areas.[4] Actually, this was so intense that in June 1998, migrants had held a rally for the first time in Athens demonstrating for their right to have a place to live[5] (Lazaridis and Psimmenos 2000). Under the

---

[4] Researchers such as Lazaridis and Psimmenos (2000) have linked those measures to an overall local-government strategy to regenerate the centre of Athens.

[5] Baldwin-Edwards (2005) argues that after intense criticism from leading academics, several state institutions and agencies dealing with immigrants on a regular basis have started to become more sensitised to issues relating to immigrants' rights and social integration. These agencies include various arms of the Ministry of Labour (OAED, IKA) and also the Greek police, to which clear instructions have been given in a circular from the Ministry of Public Order to respect immigrants' rights and prohibit police violence.

20 Immigrant Location Patterns in a Southern European Metropolis: The Case of... 485

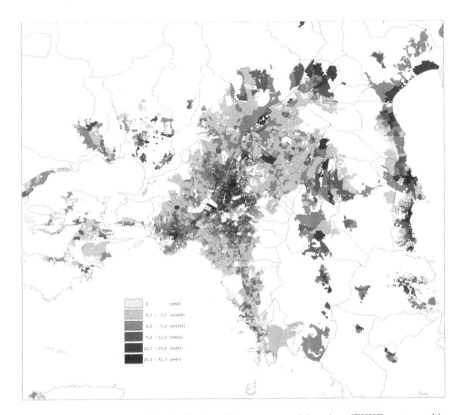

Map 20.3 Albanians spatial distribution (Source: own elaboration [EKKE cartographic platform])

weight of these pressures some immigrants had moved out of the city centre, finding residence in the surrounding municipalities. In spatial terms this gave rise to higher rates of integration between immigrants and natives and to a more dispersed residential pattern of the former.

Thessaloniki presents a very similar picture to the case of Athens. Economic reasons on the part of the immigrants, and a hesitancy to rent property to foreigners on the part of the natives, led the immigrant population to take up residence in both the inner-city and the western suburbs where housing is cheap, constructions are old and the residential quality is low (Velentzas et al. 1996; Hatziprokopiou 2003). However, there are no visible clusters of immigrants and the resulting patterns of residence do not seem to lead to any kind of excessive concentration in which ethnic ghettoes could be developed (Kokkali 2005).

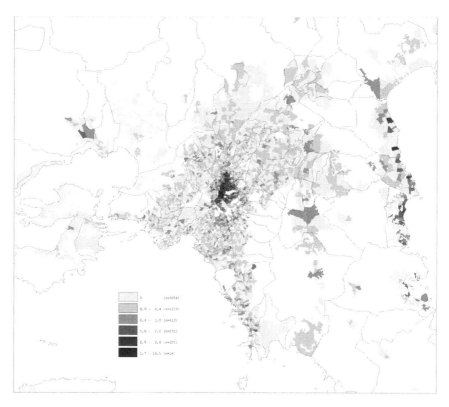

Map 20.4 Poles spatial distribution (Source: own elaboration [EKKE cartographic platform])

5 Exploring Immigrant Location in Athens Metropolitan Area: Methodological Issues

Having outlined some general trends in immigrants' locational behaviour, the rest of the paper analyses the residential distribution of various immigrant groups within Athens metropolitan region. The aim is to shed light on their locational preferences, exposing the pattern of their spatial arrangement over time and assessing the degree of their segregation. In doing so, data from the 2001 National Census were acquired at the smallest available spatial unit, which is the Census Collection District – CCD (*apografikos tomeas*).

The populations chosen for analysis are immigrants from Eastern Europe (postsocialist countries), Africa and Asia. These are largely economic immigrants[6]

---

[6] Although the majority of these people are economic (labour force) immigrants there is a small number of refugees and asylum seekers coming mostly from Iraq.

20 Immigrant Location Patterns in a Southern European Metropolis: The Case of... 487

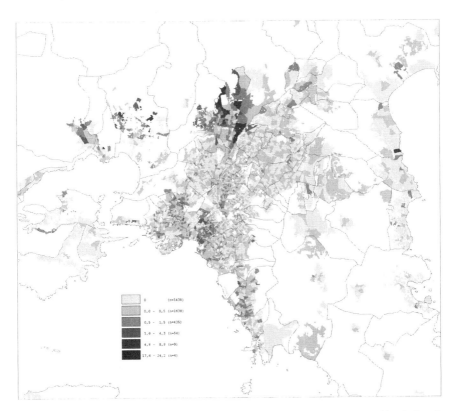

Map 20.5 Russians spatial distribution (Source: own elaboration [EKKE cartographic platform])

coming primarily from 12 countries: Albania, Poland, Russia, Bulgaria, Romania, Ukraine, Egypt, Iraq, Syria, Pakistan, Bangladesh, and Philippines. These populations as a whole exceed the 90 % of the total number of immigrants found residence in Athens metropolis (see Table 20.2).

Two methods of analysis have been employed. First we examined the degree of residential segregation exhibited within specific areas. In particular, we calculated the Dissimilarity Index[7] (D) in each one of the municipalities comprising the metropolitan region, in order to assess the relative dominance of each immigrant group in an area as compared to the native population (or the proportion of immigrants that would need to move out in order to achieve an even distribution). The basic formula for the Index is:

---

[7] This is the most widely-used measure of residential segregation developed by Duncan and Duncan (1955).

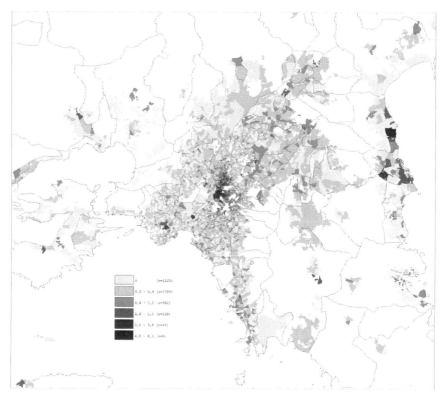

Map 20.6 Bulgarians spatial distribution (Source: own elaboration [EKKE cartographic platform])

$$D = \frac{1}{2} \sum \left| \frac{M_i}{M} - \frac{N_i}{N} \right|$$

where M_i is the population of immigrants that reside in a spatial unit i, M is the overall immigrant population living in the metropolitan region, and N_i and N are the populations of natives in unit i and the whole region respectively. The Dissimilarity Index varies from −1 to 1. Zero denotes an even distribution between the two groups (immigrants and natives), whereas the values of −1 and 1 indicate the dominance of natives and immigrants in the area respectively.

Analysis based on the Dissimilarity Index moved in two directions. We started by comparing the indices of the city centre (Athens municipality), for each immigrant group, with those of the periphery (that is all other municipalities) to investigate whether there is any immigrant population that is over-represented (that is,

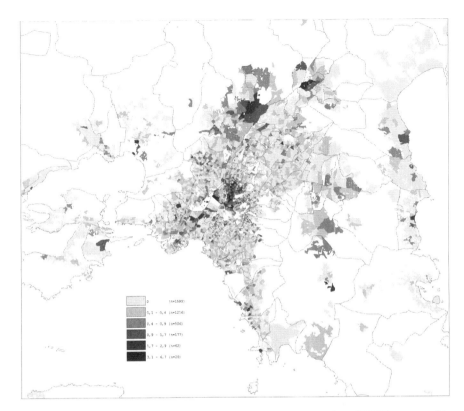

Map 20.7 Romanians spatial distribution(Source: own elaboration [EKKE cartographic platform])

concentrates) either in the city centre (*centralization*) or in the rest of the region. Next, we examine the dissimilarity indices of all municipalities to identify those areas where specific ethnic populations dominate.

Segregation analysis was complemented with cartographic presentations of the residential location of immigrants in order to expose the current pattern of spatial distribution (in 2001) and its changes over time. First, we started with a simple display of the relative distribution of immigrants (as a percentage of the total population) in order to identify patterns of clustering and isolation. Then, we looked into mobility patterns to assess changes in the locational preferences of immigrants over time. In particular, we examined whether immigrants had changed their residence either 1 or 6 years before 2001 (where the National Census took place), that is in 1995 or 2000 respectively. Since detailed information on the mobility pattern of each ethnic group of immigrants is not available (apart from Albanian

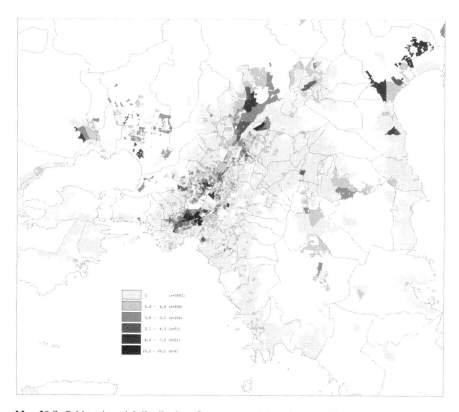

Map 20.8 Pakistani spatial distribution (Source: own elaboration [EKKE cartographic platform])

which comprise more than half of the immigrants in total), analysis at this stage was conducted on an aggregate level of immigrants' region of origin (i.e. Eastern Europe, North Africa, West Asia, Central-South Asia and South-East Asia).

6 Exploring Immigrant Location in Athens Metropolitan Area: Analysis and Discussion

Analysis starts by examining the degree of immigrant evenness/clustering (with the use of D) within each one of the municipalities comprising the metropolitan region. It then moves to consider the overall pattern of immigrant distribution across Athens region and to assess the extent of their clustering and isolation. Table 20.2

20 Immigrant Location Patterns in a Southern European Metropolis: The Case of... 491

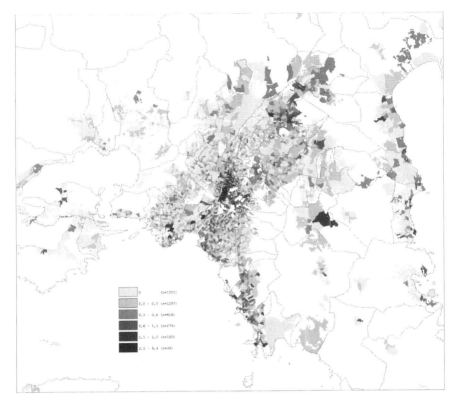

Map 20.9 Ukrainians spatial distribution (Source: own elaboration [EKKE cartographic platform])

provides the D values of each immigrant group for Athens centre and periphery, as well as such values for all municipalities in the region. Map 20.1 provides a picture of the built up areas in Athens region, whereas Maps 20.2, 20.3, 20.4, 20.5, 20.6, 20.7, 20.8, 20.9, 20.10, 20.11, 20.12, 20.13, and 20.14 depict the spatial distribution of each immigrant group (CDD is the unit of analysis). The darker the colour, the higher the proportion of immigrants in the area is.

As can be seen from Table 20.3 (see also Map 20.2), Athens central area seems to exert an attraction to the totality of immigrants that find residence in the Greek capital. This verifies the previously reported trend of immigrants to concentrate in the Athens inner-city (see Sect. 4 above). Out of the 12 nationalities that have been examined, only three groups, Russians, Pakistani and Iraqis, seems to be overshadowed by the native population in the city centre (negative D value).

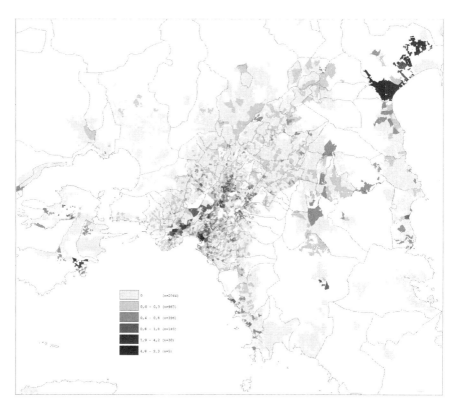

Map 20.10 Egyptians spatial distribution (Source: own elaboration [EKKE cartographic platform])

Of the rest, the greatest clustering is exhibited by Bangladeshi (D is close to 0.4), followed by Filipinos and Poles (both Ds are close to 0.2).

The Dissimilarity Indices on the second column of Table 20.3 make clear that apart from central Athens, immigrants as a whole are over-represented (at a minor degree) in 11 other municipalities. These are the areas of Ag Ioannis Rentis (0.002) and Dafni (0.002) both neighbouring Athens centre at the south, Voula (0.002), Vouliagmani (0.002) and Vari (0.001) which are on the south-east end of the city, Kropia (0.002), Artemida (0.002), Nea Makri (0.002) and Marathonas (0.002) which are on the east (the last three on the Aegean seaside), Ag Stefanos (0.002) on the north and Aspropyrgos (0.002) on the west of the metropolitan region.

For those municipalities dominated by immigrants, the degree of segregation of each immigrant group is as follows (see Table 20.3). In Ag. Ioannis Rentis seven

20 Immigrant Location Patterns in a Southern European Metropolis: The Case of...

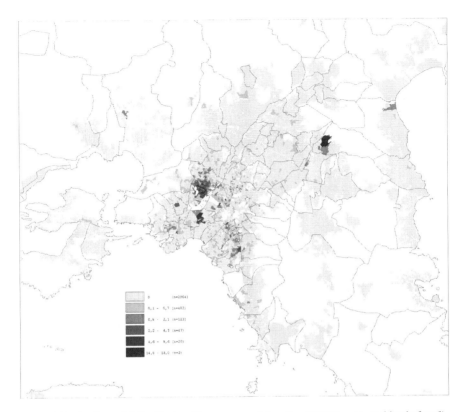

Map 20.11 Iraqis spatial distribution (Source: own elaboration [EKKE cartographic platform])

out of the 12 nationalities are over-represented, with Pakistani (0.034), Iraqis (0.008), Bangladeshi (0.006) and Egyptians (0.005) showing the highest segregation degree. Bangladeshi (0.020), Egyptians (0.011) and Pakistani (0.006) are also over-represented in Piraeus. In Acharnes segregation is high for immigrants of Russia (0.098), Pakistan (0.041), Romania (0.010) and Bangladesh (0.007), whereas in Metamorfosi over-representation is evident only in Pakistani (0.012). Filipinos, working primarily in domestic help, are found in excess in the high-class areas of Kifisia (0.007), Vouliagmeni (0.004) and Voula (0.002).

Other municipalities with relative dominance of immigrants are Peristeri and Aegaleo, both over-represented by Iraqis (Ds are 0.156 and 0.133 respectively). Of all areas examined, those which provide residence to five and above immigrant groups of high segregation are the following: Ag. Ioannis Rentis (seven groups),

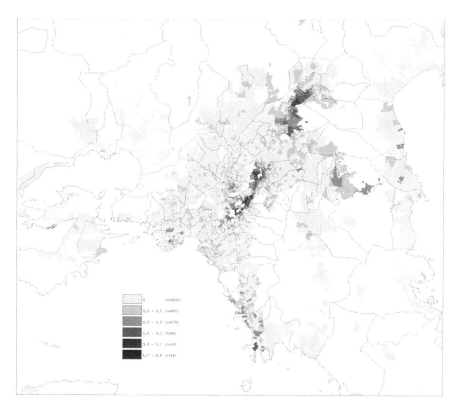

Map 20.12 Filipinos spatial distribution (Source: own elaboration [EKKE cartographic platform])

Avlona (five), Voula (five), Tavros (five) and Psychiko (five). In contrast, those municipalities where immigrants are under-represented (which means that natives dominate) are: Ag. Paraskevi, Amarousio, Ampelakia, Argyroupoli, Vrilissia, Vyronas, Galatsi, Gerakas, Glyka Nera, Ilioupoli, Iraklio, Melissia, Nea Smyrni, Neo Psychiko, Papagos, Perama, Pefki and Xolargos.

The overall pattern of immigrant distribution is displayed in Map 20.2. As can be seen immigrants as a whole are scattered all over the metropolitan region, indicating low levels of isolation. High clustering is evident in city centre, though it extends down to Piraeus through the neighbouring municipality of Ag. Ioannis Rentis. In the periphery, clustering is observed in Aspropyrgos on the west, in the areas of Metamorfosi, Acharnes and Kifisia on the north of the city, in Ag. Stefanos further up, in Penteli and Anthousa on the city east and in Voula, Vouliagmani and

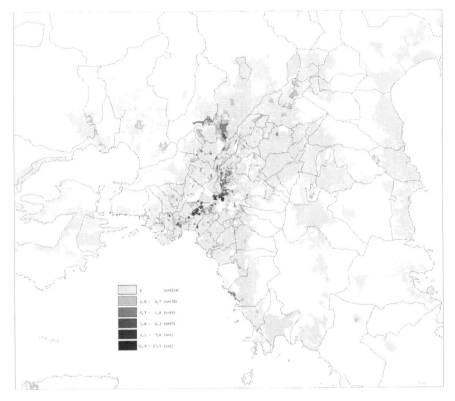

Map 20.13 Bangladeshi spatial distribution (Source: own elaboration [EKKE cartographic platform])

Vari on the city south-east. In addition, a considerable degree of immigrant concentration is apparent in the east side of the region, across the Aegean seaside (municipalities of Marathonas, Nea Makri, Rafina and Artemida).

Maps 20.3, 20.4, 20.5, 20.6, 20.7, 20.8, 20.9, 20.10, 20.11, 20.12, 20.13, and 20.14 provide a picture of the spatial distribution of each one of the immigrant group examined. Albanians, comprising the 62 % of the immigrants as a whole, deserve special attention. Observing the pattern of their distribution across the region (Map 20.3), it becomes evident that they exhibit the greatest dispersion, as compared to the other nationalities. They are over-represented in 28 municipalities of the metropolis, with central Athens receiving the majority of these people (D is 0.166). Around the city centre, areas with relatively high percentage in Albanian population are Dafni, Ag. Ioannis Rentis and Piraeus on the south, and Ag.

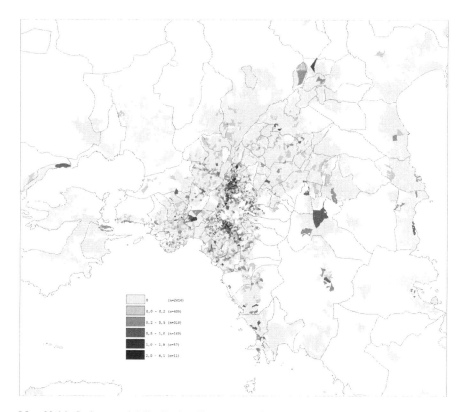

Map 20.14 Syrians spatial distribution (Source: own elaboration [EKKE cartographic platform])

Anargyroi, Nea Ionia and Amarousio on the north. In the periphery, clustering is evident in Aspropyrgos on the west, Metamorfosi, Kifisia, Acharnes and Ag. Stefanos on the north, in Penteli and Anthousa on the east as well as in a number of municipalities on the east seaside (Marathonas, Nea Makri, Rafina, Artemida and Markopoulos).

Although immigrants as a whole are dispersed all over the metropolitan region, the exposure/isolation pattern of each one of the nationalities under study differs. Two groups can be identified: one of relative exposure and one of isolation. As Maps 20.4, 20.5, 20.6, 20.7, 20.8, 20.9, 20.10, 20.11, 20.12, 20.13, and 20.14 indicate, people originating from Eastern European countries (Albania, Bulgaria, Poland, Romania, Russia and Ukraine) seems to follow a pattern of relative dispersion across the metropolitan region. In turn, those coming from North Africa and Asia (Egypt, Syria, Iraq, Pakistan, Bangladesh and Philippines) appear to live

Table 20.3 Dissimilarity index per area

Municipality	Total	Albanians	Poles	Russians	Bulgarians	Romanians	Pakistani	Ukrainians	Egyptians	Iraqis	Filipinos	Bangladeshi	Syrians
Athens inner-city (Athens municipality)	**0.18042**	**0.16554**	**0.19105**	−0.05754	**0.13976**	**0.12146**	−0.03138	**0.11134**	**0.10679**	−0.00026	**0.19732**	**0.39641**	**0.15785**
Periphery (all other municipalities)	−0.17806	−0.16554	−0.58756	−0.09188	−0.48543	−0.44903	−0.14410	−0.42885	−0.41998	−0.20625	−0.60071	**0.08655**	−0.52211
Acharnes	−0.00386	−0.00826	−0.01859	**0.09826**	−0.01736	**0.00971**	**0.04067**	−0.01292	−0.01937	−0.02011	−0.01981	**0.00699**	−0.01976
Aegaleo	−0.00668	−0.00708	−0.01825	−0.01164	−0.01560	−0.00784	**0.01621**	−0.01656	−0.01625	**0.13330**	−0.02014	**0.00247**	−0.01288
Ag. Anargyroi	−0.00094	**0.00288**	−0.00735	−0.00416	−0.00715	−0.00404	**0.00998**	−0.00507	−0.00746	−0.00778	−0.00848	**0.00840**	−0.00711
Ag. Dimitrios	−0.00655	−0.00529	−0.00962	−0.00808	−0.01308	−0.01359	−0.01257	−0.01161	−0.01183	**0.03576**	−0.01771	−0.00170	−0.00728
Ag. Ioannis Rentis	**0.00201**	**0.00104**	−0.00355	**0.00066**	−0.00261	**0.00329**	**0.03435**	−0.00271	**0.00525**	**0.00827**	−0.00352	**0.00596**	−0.00092
Ag. Paraskevi	−0.00506	−0.00882	−0.01213	−0.01253	−0.00869	−0.01330	−0.01350	−0.00924	−0.01127	−0.01547	−0.01451	−0.00146	−0.01489
Ag. Stefanos	**0.00234**	**0.00548**	−0.00219	−0.00232	−0.00104	−0.00127	−0.00068	−0.00199	−0.00162	−0.00262	−0.00233	−0.00026	−0.00031
Ag. Varbara	−0.00405	−0.00393	−0.00723	**0.01141**	−0.00669	−0.00561	−0.00134	−0.00590	−0.00631	**0.00383**	−0.00840	**0.00148**	−0.00768
Alimos	−0.00240	−0.00688	−0.00699	−0.00410	−0.00587	−0.00704	−0.01044	−0.00343	−0.00613	−0.00400	−0.00955	**0.00090**	−0.00531
Amarousio	−0.00709	−0.00934	−0.01586	−0.01486	−0.01225	−0.01341	−0.01897	−0.01314	−0.01568	−0.01883	−0.01669	−0.00133	−0.01551
Ampelakia	−0.00100	−0.00058	−0.00185	−0.00143	−0.00159	−0.00101	−0.00196	−0.00167	−0.00136	−0.00195	−0.00186	−0.00020	−0.00155
Ano Liosia	−0.00275	−0.00268	−0.00641	**0.01020**	−0.00591	−0.00299	−0.00163	−0.00483	−0.00478	−0.00686	−0.00507	**0.00674**	−0.00491
Argyroupoli	−0.00348	−0.00383	−0.00626	−0.00550	−0.00607	−0.00673	−0.00819	−0.00563	−0.00620	−0.00891	−0.00861	−0.00093	−0.00520
Artemida	**0.00215**	**0.00579**	**0.00156**	−0.00309	−0.00301	−0.00288	−0.00475	**0.00009**	−0.00284	−0.00483	−0.00435	−0.00036	−0.00388
Aspropyrgos	**0.00231**	**0.00514**	−0.00739	**0.02651**	−0.00595	−0.00132	**0.02194**	−0.00526	−0.00725	−0.00578	−0.00764	**0.00009**	−0.00750
Avlona	**0.00098**	**0.00173**	−0.00116	−0.00082	−0.00118	−0.00042	**0.00692**	−0.00114	**0.00017**	**0.00082**	−0.00133	**0.00047**	−0.00129
Dafni	**0.00201**	**0.00508**	−0.00325	−0.00463	−0.00186	−0.00350	−0.00390	−0.00407	−0.00411	**0.01383**	−0.00421	**0.00081**	**0.00671**
Drapetsona	−0.00164	−0.00132	−0.00290	**0.00254**	−0.00207	−0.00089	−0.00350	−0.00289	−0.00289	−0.00346	−0.00349	**0.00013**	−0.00277
Elefsina	−0.00066	−0.00085	−0.00613	**0.03383**	−0.00490	−0.00196	−0.00386	−0.00377	−0.00604	−0.00676	**0.00964**	**0.00063**	−0.00700
Elliniko	−0.00104	−0.00221	−0.00326	−0.00086	−0.00295	−0.00384	−0.00321	−0.00056	−0.00305	−0.00140	−0.00388	**0.00003**	−0.00301
Fili	−0.00020	**0.00021**	−0.00077	−0.00059	−0.00064	−0.00042	−0.00082	−0.00068	−0.00082	−0.00057	−0.00072	−0.00008	−0.00082
Filothei	**0.00003**	−0.00197	−0.00168	−0.00039	**0.00141**	−0.00179	−0.00206	**0.00294**	−0.00166	−0.00205	**0.00662**	−0.00008	−0.00165
Galatsi	−0.00670	−0.00358	−0.01034	−0.01143	−0.01012	−0.01168	−0.01577	−0.01028	−0.01320	−0.01518	−0.01560	−0.00100	−0.00803
Gerakas	−0.00143	−0.00037	−0.00286	−0.00282	−0.00266	−0.00347	−0.00371	−0.00310	−0.00357	−0.00350	−0.00387	−0.00039	−0.00333
Glyfada	**0.00024**	−0.00711	−0.01509	−0.00043	−0.01264	−0.01318	−0.02153	−0.00614	−0.01417	−0.01891	−0.01346	−0.00078	−0.01572
Glyka Nera	−0.00058	−0.00003	−0.00168	−0.00124	−0.00099	−0.00144	−0.00041	−0.00170	−0.00184	−0.00184	−0.00184	−0.00018	−0.00130
Ilio (Nea Liosia)	−0.00800	−0.00078	−0.01523	−0.01738	−0.01706	−0.00979	−0.00726	−0.01837	−0.02002	−0.01590	−0.02212	**0.00241**	−0.01516
Ilioupoli	−0.01067	−0.00898	−0.01695	−0.01319	−0.01374	−0.01669	−0.02036	−0.01607	−0.01622	−0.01757	−0.02023	−0.00175	−0.01127

(continued)

Table 20.3 (continued)

Municipality	Total	Albanians	Poles	Russians	Bulgarians	Romanians	Pakistani	Ukrainians	Egyptians	Iraqis	Filipinos	Bangladeshi	Syrians
Iraklio	−0.00655	−0.00538	−0.01069	−0.00949	−0.00881	−0.00884	−0.00565	−0.00895	−0.01141	−0.01268	−0.01223	−0.00091	−0.01022
Kaisariani	**0.00018**	**0.00097**	−0.00414	−0.00521	−0.00375	−0.00491	−0.00733	−0.00374	−0.00146	−0.00683	−0.00437	−0.00012	−0.00569
Kallithea	−0.00279	−0.00832	−0.02093	**0.05045**	−0.01405	−0.01374	−0.01533	−0.00314	**0.04741**	−0.02189	−0.02571	**0.00651**	−0.00102
Kalyvia Thorikou	**0.00056**	**0.00212**	−0.00284	−0.00217	−0.00253	−0.00250	−0.00262	−0.00126	−0.00228	−0.00312	−0.00271	−0.00021	−0.00296
Kamatero	−0.00343	−0.00247	−0.00470	−0.00158	−0.00553	−0.00491	−0.00468	−0.00464	−0.00569	−0.00594	−0.00609	**0.00943**	−0.00551
Keratea	−0.00110	**0.00038**	−0.00346	−0.00284	−0.00276	−0.00360	−0.00367	−0.00332	−0.00347	−0.00367	−0.00367	−0.00037	−0.00367
Keratsini	−0.01031	−0.00627	−0.01510	−0.00638	−0.01660	−0.01468	−0.01801	−0.01186	−0.01305	−0.02007	−0.01776	**0.00082**	−0.01603
Kifisia	−0.00015	−0.00711	−0.01043	−0.00742	−0.00609	−0.00844	−0.00863	**0.00032**	−0.00816	−0.01208	**0.00969**	−0.00062	−0.00839
Korydallos	−0.00806	−0.00658	−0.01585	**0.00399**	−0.01307	−0.00727	−0.01543	−0.01084	−0.01463	−0.00139	−0.01813	**0.00401**	−0.01435
Kropia	**0.00174**	**0.00461**	−0.00295	−0.00140	−0.00518	−0.00350	**0.00531**	−0.00369	−0.00530	−0.00699	−0.00642	−0.00070	−0.00319
Lavreotiki	−0.00140	−0.00220	−0.00289	−0.00067	−0.00252	−0.00234	−0.00294	−0.00266	−0.00165	**0.00366**	−0.00284	−0.00029	−0.00267
Lykovrysi	−0.00080	−0.00043	−0.00200	−0.00181	−0.00172	−0.00173	**0.00212**	−0.00191	−0.00226	−0.00226	−0.00286	−0.00023	−0.00226
Mandra	−0.00119	−0.00018	−0.00261	**0.00133**	−0.00279	−0.00223	−0.00031	−0.00295	−0.00301	−0.00339	−0.00332	−0.00035	−0.00351
Marathonas	**0.00160**	**0.00158**	−0.00211	−0.00187	−0.00126	−0.00248	**0.01126**	−0.00149	**0.01561**	−0.00248	−0.00248	**0.00025**	−0.00234
Markopoulos	−0.00058	**0.00156**	−0.00288	−0.00379	−0.00268	−0.00391	−0.00373	−0.00326	−0.00421	−0.00431	−0.00393	−0.00043	−0.00417
Megara	−0.00168	**0.00197**	−0.00719	−0.00770	−0.00687	−0.00623	**0.00647**	−0.00672	−0.00737	−0.00777	−0.00758	−0.00078	−0.00749
Melissia	−0.00118	−0.00226	−0.00506	−0.00427	−0.00354	−0.00373	−0.00531	−0.00330	−0.00448	−0.00535	−0.00490	−0.00055	−0.00398
Metamorfosi	−0.00256	−0.00137	−0.00494	−0.00429	−0.00466	−0.00382	**0.01183**	−0.00542	−0.00699	−0.00738	−0.00719	**0.00012**	−0.00684
Mosxato	−0.00256	−0.00280	−0.00354	**0.00035**	−0.00440	−0.00397	−0.00276	−0.00253	−0.00149	−0.00646	−0.00627	**0.00217**	−0.00578
Nea Chalkidona	**0.00022**	**0.00092**	−0.00091	−0.00124	−0.00137	−0.00148	**0.00594**	−0.00100	−0.00213	−0.00270	−0.00244	**0.00107**	−0.00133
Nea Erythraia	−0.00004	−0.00069	−0.00331	−0.00326	−0.00280	−0.00385	−0.00423	−0.00157	−0.00372	−0.00419	**0.00150**	**0.00067**	−0.00418
Nea Filadelfia	−0.00104	−0.00221	−0.00326	−0.00086	−0.00295	−0.00384	−0.00321	−0.00056	−0.00305	−0.00140	−0.00388	**0.00003**	−0.00301
Nea Ionia	−0.00262	**0.00493**	−0.01500	−0.01116	−0.01040	−0.01256	**0.02684**	−0.01251	−0.01516	−0.01697	−0.01729	**0.00233**	−0.01643
Nea Makri	**0.00175**	**0.00205**	**0.00325**	**0.00052**	**0.00027**	−0.00296	**0.01031**	−0.00143	−0.00092	−0.00123	−0.00324	−0.00041	−0.00369
Nea Peramos	−0.00053	**0.00015**	−0.00206	−0.00131	−0.00067	−0.00126	−0.00140	−0.00157	−0.00127	−0.00206	−0.00206	−0.00021	−0.00165
Nea Smyrni	−0.00427	−0.00940	−0.01397	−0.00358	−0.00823	−0.01442	−0.01994	−0.00464	−0.00997	−0.00964	−0.01640	−0.00145	−0.01000
Neo Psychiko	−0.00122	−0.00170	−0.00224	−0.00145	−0.00134	−0.00203	−0.00295	−0.00086	−0.00284	−0.00304	−0.00084	−0.00018	−0.00290
Nikaia	−0.00960	−0.00598	−0.02209	−0.00565	−0.01845	−0.01016	**0.01031**	−0.01861	−0.01988	−0.01973	−0.02498	−0.00087	−0.01619
Paiania	−0.00095	**0.00033**	−0.00270	−0.00315	−0.00220	−0.00239	−0.00352	−0.00191	−0.00270	−0.00360	−0.00324	−0.00036	−0.00183
Palaio Faliro	**0.00068**	−0.01011	−0.01278	−0.00036	−0.00782	−0.01087	−0.01747	−0.00119	−0.00124	−0.01577	−0.00341	−0.00132	−0.00523
Pallini	−0.00033	**0.00071**	−0.00365	−0.00375	−0.00266	−0.00230	−0.00365	−0.00361	−0.00247	−0.00466	−0.00974	−0.00034	−0.00425
Papagos	−0.00218	−0.00340	−0.00298	−0.00251	−0.00160	−0.00332	−0.00372	−0.00246	−0.00332	−0.00372	−0.00239	−0.00025	−0.00345

Pefki	−0.00317	−0.00354	−0.00470	−0.00366	−0.00385	−0.00528	−0.00530	−0.00379	−0.00455	−0.00529	−0.00497	−0.00055	−0.00541
Perama	−0.00323	−0.00203	−0.00494	−0.00134	−0.00547	−0.00441	−0.00523	−0.00126	−0.00369	−0.00717	−0.00488	−0.00072	−0.00486
Peristeri	−0.01114	−0.00871	−0.03197	−0.02235	−0.02737	−0.02281	**0.05898**	−0.02853	−0.02221	**0.15581**	−0.03658	**0.00966**	−0.02543
Petroupoli	−0.00911	−0.00861	−0.01035	−0.00933	−0.01130	−0.00230	−0.01298	−0.01159	−0.01298	−0.01260	−0.01319	**0.00037**	−0.01184
Piraeus	−0.00557	−0.00006	−0.03641	−0.01725	−0.02965	−0.02323	**0.00601**	−0.02194	**0.01079**	−0.02040	−0.03557	**0.02036**	−0.02800
Psychiko	**0.00126**	−0.00297	−0.00106	**0.00820**	**0.00245**	**0.00083**	−0.00291	**0.00037**	−0.00198	−0.00283	**0.01503**	−0.00006	−0.00294
Rafina	**0.00136**	**0.00323**	**0.00016**	−0.00232	**0.00199**	−0.00263	−0.00305	−0.00189	−0.00221	−0.00317	−0.00263	−0.00008	−0.00289
Spata-Loutsa	−0.00003	**0.00188**	−0.00267	−0.00253	−0.00192	−0.00243	−0.00224	−0.00199	−0.00134	−0.00283	−0.00283	−0.00028	−0.00283
Tavros	**0.00008**	**0.00007**	−0.00347	**0.00455**	−0.00282	−0.00140	**0.00739**	−0.00205	**0.00260**	−0.00391	−0.00387	**0.00804**	−0.00130
Vari	**0.00145**	**0.00157**	−0.00023	**0.00089**	−0.00220	−0.00217	−0.00305	**0.00160**	−0.00215	−0.00280	−0.00190	**0.00153**	−0.00006
Voula	**0.00220**	−0.00282	−0.00399	−0.00236	−0.00203	−0.00424	−0.00578	−0.00024	−0.00335	−0.00526	**0.00193**	**0.00002**	−0.00427
Vouliagmeni	**0.00244**	**0.00002**	−0.00073	−0.00006	−0.00034	−0.00079	−0.00070	**0.00137**	−0.00120	−0.00179	**0.00354**	**0.00092**	**0.00011**
Vrilissia	−0.00334	−0.00581	−0.00607	−0.00383	−0.00347	−0.00657	−0.00715	−0.00393	−0.00574	−0.00723	−0.00599	−0.00072	−0.00682
Vyronas	−0.00469	−0.00080	−0.01159	−0.00739	−0.00991	−0.00589	−0.01497	−0.01060	−0.01259	−0.01668	−0.01477	−0.00097	−0.01135
Xaidari	−0.00829	−0.00788	−0.01142	−0.00905	−0.01029	−0.00981	**0.00244**	−0.01065	−0.01101	−0.00891	−0.01261	−0.00068	−0.01194
Xalandri	−0.00555	−0.00678	−0.01727	−0.01401	−0.00830	−0.01320	−0.01812	−0.00663	−0.01575	−0.01701	−0.01249	**0.00608**	−0.01740
Xolargos	−0.00334	−0.00416	−0.00735	−0.00711	−0.00517	−0.00691	−0.00900	−0.00414	−0.00770	−0.00886	−0.00737	−0.00090	−0.00790
Ymittos	−0.00048	**0.00039**	−0.00236	−0.00197	−0.00134	−0.00216	−0.00311	−0.00198	−0.00281	−0.00086	−0.00282	−0.00031	−0.00120
Zefyrio	−0.00194	−0.00157	−0.00235	−0.00124	−0.00221	−0.00097	−0.00246	−0.00246	−0.00235	−0.00245	−0.00245	**0.00172**	−0.00232
Zografos	−0.00200	−0.00477	−0.01486	−0.01390	−0.00800	−0.01707	−0.02057	−0.01287	−0.01069	−0.01574	−0.01102	**0.00009**	−0.00344

Source: own elaboration (EKKE-ESYE 2005)

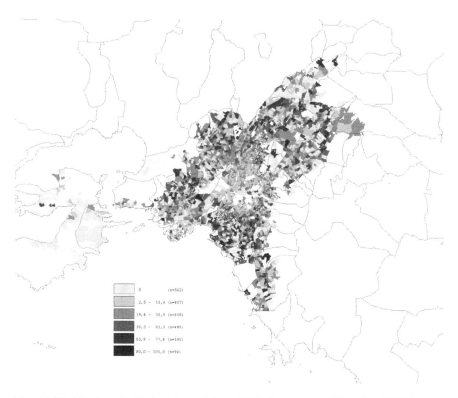

Map 20.15 Albanians destinations (moved in at 1995) (Source: own elaboration [EKKE cartographic platform])

in relative isolation. As discussed in Sect. 2, such behaviour is driven by cultural and/or economic factors. Religion might be an important parameter here since in five out of the six countries of the second group, i.e. Egypt, Syria, Iraq, Pakistan and Bangladesh, the official creed is Islam, whereas the Greek official religion is Christianity. As concerns Filipinos, the other nationality of the second group, economic reasons might be of primary importance, since these people (who are not in their majority Muslims) are employed largely in domestic help and reside with the wealthy families that employ them in specific parts of the city (Psychico, Ekali, Kifisia, Vouliagmeni).

As regards the clustering/evenness dimension, we observe eight nationalities of immigrants to exhibit a similar pattern, which is described by both high

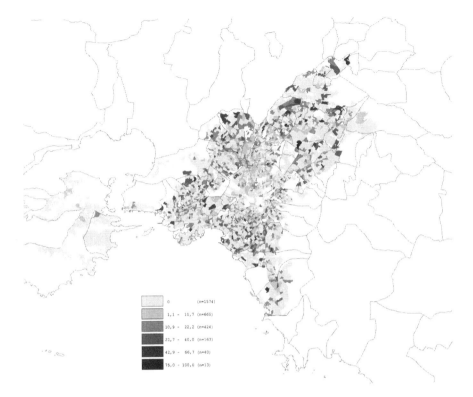

Map 20.16 Albanians destinations (moved in at 2000) (Source: own elaboration [EKKE cartographic platform])

concentration within the city centre (centralisation) and relatively lower concentrations in other parts of the metropolitan region. In particular, apart from central Athens, people originating from Poland and Bulgaria show a preference for residence in municipalities at the east coast (Marathonas, Nea Makri, Rafina, Artemida), Romanians in local concentrations in Ag. Ioannis Rentis and Acharnes, whereas Ukrainians are deployed in Mosxato and Piraeus at the south and Filothei and Psychiko at the north of the city centre, as well as in the adjacent areas of Kifisia, Acharnes, Nea Erythraia and Ekali (see Maps 20.4, 20.6, 20.7 and 20.9 respectively).

Syrians and Egyptians (Maps 20.14 and 20.10 respectively) are quite centralised, showing a preference for the inner-city and nearby municipalities at the south (Dafni, Kallithea, Tavros, Ag Ioannis Rentis and Piraeus). So do Bangladeshi (Map 20.13), who apart from the city centre, where their over-representation

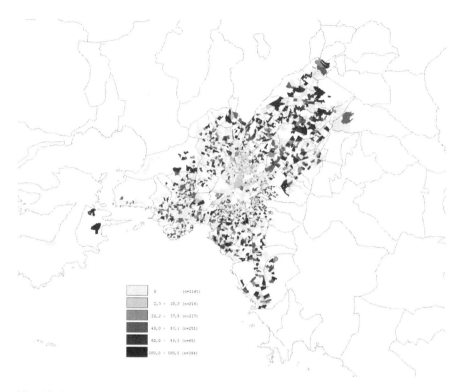

Map 20.17 East Europeans destinations (moved in at 1995) (Source: own elaboration [EKKE cartographic platform])

(measured by D) is almost double as compared to those of other immigrants groups, find residence in Ag Ioannis Rentis and Piraeus (southern at the city-centre), as well as in the adjacent area of northern municipalities of Kamatero, Acharnes, Zefyrio and Ano Liosia. In turn, Filipinos are seen to reside (Map 20.12) not only in central Athens but also in the high-income areas of Filothei and Psychico at the north of the city centre, Kifisia and Ekali further up, and Vouliagmeni at the south-east of the city, where they are employed in the domestic help.

The rest three nationalities of immigrants, i.e. Iraqis, Pakistani and Russians seems to follow a different location pattern, characterised by low centralisation. In particular, the vast majority of Iraqis, which exhibit the most isolated and clustering pattern of the three,[8] find home in the adjacent municipalities of Ag. Ioannis Rendis,

---

[8] This behaviour might be related to the fact that most Iraqis are in fact asylum-seekers and refugees rather than economic immigrants. We thank the anonymous referee for bringing this point to our attention.

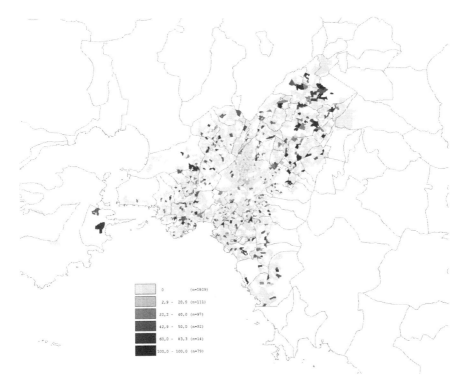

Map 20.18 East Europeans destinations (moved in at 2000) (Source: own elaboration [EKKE cartographic platform])

Aegaleo and Peristeri located on the west of central Athens (Map 20.11). In turn, Pakistani are deployed along a west-north corridor (across the Kifisou Avenue), taking up residence in the municipalities of Ag. Ioannis Rendis, Aegaleo, Peristeri, Ag. Anargyroi, Acharnes and Metamorfosi (Map 20.8). Finally, Russians, who in their majority are repatriated Greek-ethnic Pontians, exhibit a highly exposure pattern but with increased clustering in Acharnes and Ano Liosia (Map 20.5). These are areas where land had been made available (at low cost) by the Greek government aiming to assist Greek-Pontians' residency and integration.

Apart from determining the current distribution of immigrants across Athens metropolitan region, the study is also interested in its dynamics, which are reflected on the mobility pattern of the immigrants. On these grounds, the rest of the paper

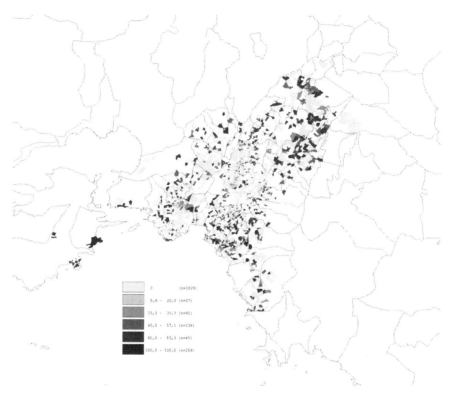

Map 20.19 West Asians destinations (moved in at 1995) (Source: own elaboration [EKKE cartographic platform])

looks at the changes in immigrant residential location took place in the years of 1995 and 2000, where data from the 2001 census are available. In particular, Maps 20.15, 20.16, 20.17, 20.18, 20.19, 20.20, 20.21, 20.22, 20.23, 20.24, 20.25, and 20.26 highlight those areas (at the CDD level) where immigrants have recently moved in, or more precisely, the areas where immigrant reside during the 2001 census but they have moved in there either a year or 6 years ago (that is in 2000 or in 1995, respectively).

What becomes evident from the cartographic representations below (Maps 20.15, 20.16, 20.17, 20.18, 20.19, 20.20, 20.21, 20.22, 20.23, and 20.24) is a clear tendency of immigrants to decentralise, that is, to move out of the central Athens and to take up residence in the peripheral municipalities of the city. This is the case both in 1995 and in 2000 time points. This exodus, however, is not uniform

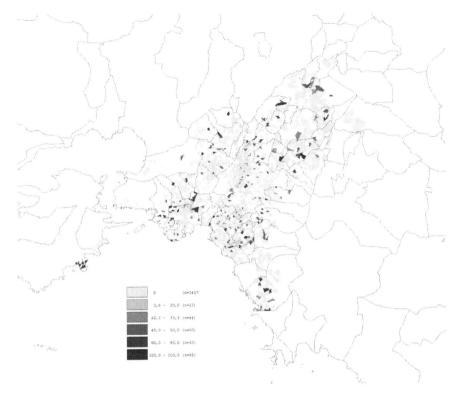

Map 20.20 West Asians destinations (moved in at 2000) (Source: own elaboration [EKKE cartographic platform])

either across time or across immigrant groups. As regards the former, the data indicate the gradual increase of immigrants' decentralisation over time. In particular, changes in residential location took place in 2000 constitute the 23 % of the totality of movements occurred since 1995. This means that one out of four immigrants who have changed area of residence within this 6 years time frame she did so over the last year.

The second point raised highlights the fact that mobility is not the same for all immigrant groups examined. In particular, people of East European countries, and especially Albanians, exhibit a much higher mobility degree as compared to Asians or Africans. Actually, about half (45 %) of the Albanians that live in Athens have, within the examined period, moved houses from the central area to

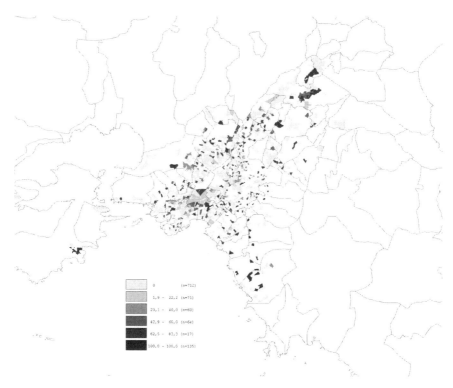

Map 20.21 Central-South Asians destinations (moved in at 1995) (Source: own elaboration [EKKE cartographic platform])

municipalities in the periphery, whereas the respective figure for Asian or Africans is below 10 %.

7 Conclusions

The current research has analysed the residential distribution of various immigrant groups within Athens metropolitan region. In particular, it has determine both the pattern of isolation, clustering and centralisation immigrants display and the degree of segregation exhibited within specific areas, and assessed the dynamics of the aforementioned configurations. Such analysis enables to shed light on the locational

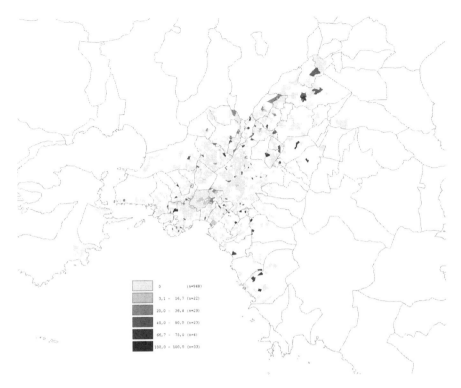

Map 20.22 Central-South Asians destinations (moved in at 2000) (Source: own elaboration [EKKE cartographic platform])

preferences of various immigrant groups, on possible changes of these preferences over time, and on the emerging form of their spatial arrangements.

Our findings indicate the preference of immigrants for central locations, where accessibility is high, due to transport networks, and low-cost housing is available. This trend has been also reported in other studies, such as Psimmenos (1995, 1998), Baldwin-Edwards (2005) and Maloutas (2007), but the current research adds four clarifications on the issue.

First, the emerging pattern of immigrants' residential location is described as one of increasing exposure and decentralisation. This is principally attributable to the locational behaviour of Eastern Europeans, and particularly of Albanians,[9] which is characterised by relative dispersion on the one hand, and increasing

---

[9] Note that Eastern Europeans comprise more than 78 % of the totality of immigrants, with Albanians being the 62 %.

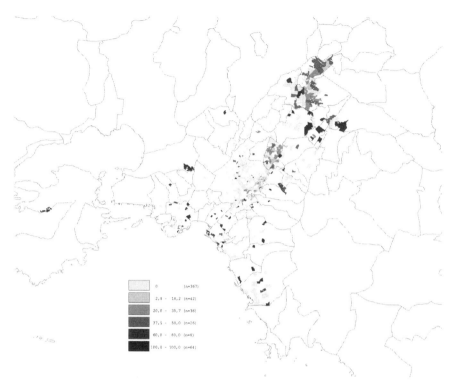

Map 20.23 South-East Asians destinations (moved in at 1995) (Source: own elaboration [EKKE cartographic platform])

mobility from central areas to the peripheral locations on the other. Along these lines it is of interest to note that an important role to the aforementioned distribution is played by Russians, which is the third, in terms of size, group of immigrants, exhibiting a highly exposure pattern with relative clustering in away-from-the-centre northern municipalities of the metropolis.

Second, the locational pattern and dynamics are not uniform to all groups of immigrants. Whereas Eastern Europeans (with possible exception this of Poles) show signs of dispersion, and perhaps integration with the local population, those who are coming from Asia and Africa are seen to exhibit a rather seclusive behaviour and a pattern of location characterised by relative isolation and low mobility. Given the present small size of the latter groups it can be argued that no

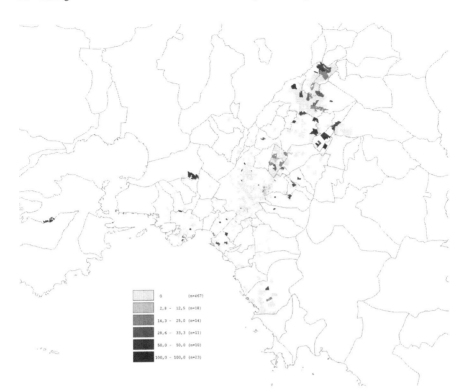

Map 20.24 South-East Asians destinations (moved in at 2000) (Source: own elaboration [EKKE cartographic platform])

specific ethnic ghettos are under formation, though there are no guarantees that this will be the case in the future.

Third, although economic factors are significant determinants of immigrants' locational decisions, it seems that cultural reasons play a key role too, especially for specific immigrant groups. Thus, for instance, one can easily attribute the initial location of newcomers from Philippines within the wealthy neighbourhoods of Ekali, Vouliagmeni, Psychico and Kifisia, to pure economic reasons, as these people were primarily employed in the domestic help of the high-income families residing in those areas. However, there are difficulties in explaining why people remained there, once the community increased its size with the arrival of further Filipinos, without reference to cultural reasons. Similarly, the initial location of Russian-Pontians in Acharnes may be due to economic reasons, and in particular

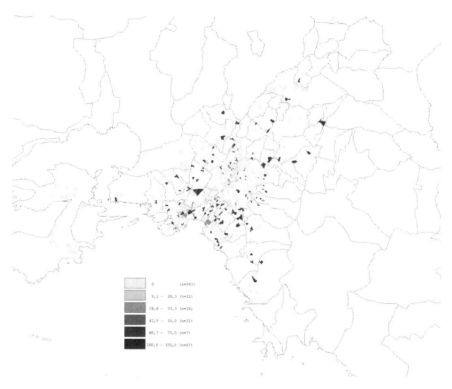

Map 20.25 North Africans destinations (moved in at 1995) (Source: own elaboration [EKKE cartographic platform])

to the policies of low-cost housing put forth by the Greek government over the 1990s, but the further enlargement of the community within the same area should be seen as a side-effect of the close-knit ethnic networks of support developed in the area.

Finally, it becomes evident that we know relatively little of the processes and factors determining the intra-urban locational decisions of immigrants. Perhaps this may be due to the too-short experience Greece has on the issue, and perhaps it might be necessary for patterns to establish before we could be able to draw firm conclusion on the subject. At the moment we can argue that both economic and cultural features affect the locational choices of immigrants, but further research needs to be put forward in order to shed light on these matters, investigating in more detail the specific qualities (which might be related to the housing stock, labour opportunities, local institutions, immigrants' nationality, religion, family structure, etc.) that define the locational behaviour of these people.

20 Immigrant Location Patterns in a Southern European Metropolis: The Case of... 511

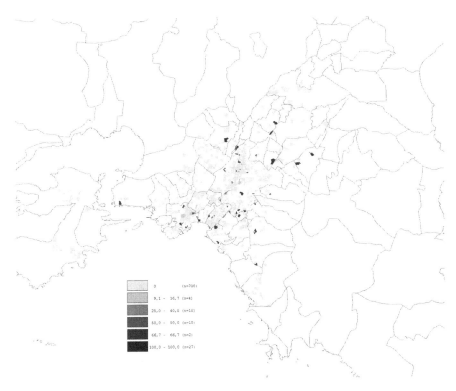

Map 20.26 North Africans destinations (moved in at 2000) (Source: own elaboration [EKKE cartographic platform])

References

Ahmed AM, Hammarstedt M (2008) Discrimination in the rental housing market: a field experiment on the internet. J Urban Econ 64(2):362–372
Alba RD, Logan JR (1993) Minority proximity to whites in suburbs: an individual-level analysis of segregation. Am J Sociol 98(13):88–1427
Anas A (2004) Ethnic segregation and ghettos. In: Arnott RJ, McMillen DP (eds) A companion to urban economics. Blackwell, London, pp 536–554
Arapoglou VP (2006) Immigration, segregation and urban development in Athens: the relevance of the LA debate for Southern European metropolises. Greek Rev Soc Res 121(C):11–38
Arvanitidis P, Skouras D (2007) Intra-urban patterns of immigrant location and the housing market: a preliminary investigation. Fondazione Eni Enrico Mattei working paper series, 42.2007
Arvanitidis P, Skouras D (2008) The residential characteristics of immigrants in the medium-sized city of Volos: a preliminary investigation. Department of planning and regional development, University of Thessaly, Discussion paper series, 14(10):177–198
Baldwin-Edwards M (2005) The integration of immigrants in Athens: developing indicators and statistical measures. Mediterranean Migration Observatory- UEHR and Panteion University, Athens

Bartel AP (1989) Where do the new U.S. immigrants live? J Labour Econ 7(4):371–391

Blom S (1999) Residential concentration among immigrants in Oslo. Int Migr 37(3):617–628

Boal FW (1976) Ethnic residential segregation. In: Herbert DT, Johnston RJ (eds) Social areas in cities, vol 1, Spatial processes and form. Wiley, London, pp 41–79

Boal FW (1996) Immigration and ethnicity in the urban Milieu. In: Roseman CC, Laux HD, Thieme G (eds) Ethnicity, geographic perspectives on ethnic change in modern cities. Rowman and Littlefield, Maryland, pp 283–304

Bolt G, Hooimeijer P, van Kempen R (2002) Ethnic segregation in the Netherlands: new patterns, new policies? Tijdschr Econ Soc Ge 93(2):214–220

Bontje M, Latten J (2005) Stable size, changing composition: recent migration dynamics of the Dutch large cities. Tijdschr Econ Soc Ge 96(4):444–451

Burnley I (2005) Immigration and housing in an emerging global city, Sydney, Australia. Urban Pol Res 23(3):329–345

Cavounidis J (2002) Migration in Southern Europe and the case of Greece. Int Migr 40(1):45–70

Cavounidis J (2007) New elements of Greek policies concerning irregular migrants: the policy of regulations of unauthorised migrants. IMEPO, Athens

Cavounidis J, Kontis A, Lianos T, Fakiolas R (eds) (2008) Immigration in Green: experiences, policies and prospects, vol 1. IMEPO, Athens (in Greek)

Clark WA, Ware J (1997) Trends in residential segregation by socioeconomic status in California. Urban Aff Rev 32:825–843

Cutler DM, Glaeser EL, Vigdor JL (1999) The rise and decline of the American Ghetto. J Pol Econ 107(3):455–506

Denton NA, Massey DS (1988) Residential segregation of blacks, Hispanics and Asians by socioeconomic status and generation. Soc Sci Quart 69:797–818

Deurloo MC, Musterd S (1998) Ethnic clusters in Amsterdam, 1994–96: a micro-area analysis. Urban Stud 35(3):385–396

Djuve AB, Hagen K (1995) "Find me a job! Living conditions among refugees in Oslo", Fafo Report 184. The Research Foundation Fafo, Oslo

Duncan OD, Duncan B (1955) A methodological analysis of segregation indexes. Am Sociol Rev 20:210–217

Dunn KM (1998) Rethinking ethnic concentration: the case of Cabramatta, Sydney. Urban Stud 35 (3):503–527

EKKE – ESYE (National Centre for Social Research – National Statistical Service of Greece) (2005) Panorama of Greek census data 1991–2001. Application under experimental and restricted use at the EKKE

Freeman L (2000) Minority housing segregation: a test of three perspectives. J Urban Aff 22 (1):15–35

Grimes S (1993) Residential segregation in Australian cities: a literature review. Int Migr Rev 27 (1):103–120

Harrison RJ, Weinberg DH (1992) Racial and ethnic segregation in 1990. Paper presented at the annual meeting of the Population Association of America, Denver

Hatziprokopiou P (2003) Albanian immigrants in Thessaloniki, Greece: processes of economic and social incorporation. J Ethnic Migration Stud 29:1033–1057

Hawley A (1950) Human ecology. Ronald, New York

Hugo GJ (1996) Diversity down under: the changing ethnic mosaic of Sydney and Melbourne. In: Roseman CC, Laux HD, Thieme G (eds) EthniCity: geographic perspectives on ethnic change in modern cities. Rowman and Littlefield, Maryland, pp 102–134

Johnston RJ, Poulsen MF, Forrest J (2003) And did the walls come tumbling down? Ethnic residential segregation in four US metropolitan areas, 1980–2000. Urban Geogr 24:560–581

Kanellopoulos K (2008) Attributes and contribution of immigrants in the labour market. In: Cavounidis J, Kontis A, Lianos T, Fakiolas R (eds) Immigration in green: experiences, policies and prospects, vol 1. IMEPO, Athens, pp 1542–173 (in Greek)

Kanellopoulos K, Gregou M, Petralias A (2006) Illegal immigrants in Greece: state approaches, their profile and social situation. BMN and Centre for Planning and Economic Research, Athens

Kesteloot C (1995) The creation of socio-spatial marginalization in Brussels: a tale of flexibility, geographical competition and guestworker neighbourhoods. In: Sadler D, Hadjimichalis C (eds) Europe at the margins: new mosaics of inequality. Wiley, Chichester, pp 82–99

King R (2000) Southern Europe in the changing global map of migration. In: King R, Lazaridis G, Tsardanidis C (eds) Eldorado or fortress? Migration in Southern Europe. Macmillan, London, pp 3–26

Kokkali IE (2005) Albanian immigration and urban transformations in Greece Albanian migrant strategies in Thessaloniki, Greece. Paper presented at the 2nd LSE Ph.D. symposium on modern Greece, London, 10 June 2005

Kotzamanis B (2008) Immigrants in Greece, primary analysis of their geographical dispersion and this contribution to population changes of the last decade. In: Cavounidis J, Kontis A, Lianos T, Fakiolas R (eds) Immigration in green: experiences, policies and prospects, vol 1. IMEPO, Athens, pp 12–37 (in Greek)

Labrianidis L, Lyberaki A, Tinios P, Hatziprokopiou P (2004) Inflow of migrants and outflow of investment: aspects of interdependence between Greece and the Balkans. J Ethnic Migr Stud 30(6):1183–1208

Lan-Hung C, Jung-Chung H (2005) Locational decisions and residential preferences of Taiwanese immigrants in Australia. GeoJ 64(1):75–89

Lazaridis G (1996) Immigration to Greece: a critical evaluation of Greek policy. New Comm 22 (2):335–348

Lazaridis G, Psimmenos I (2000) Migrant flows from Albania to Greece: economic, social and spatial exclusion. In: King R, Lazaridis G, Tsardanidis C (eds) Eldorado or fortress? Migration in Southern Europe. Macmillan, London, pp 170–185

Lianos T (2001) Illegal migrants to Greece and their choice of destination. Int Migr 39(2):4–28

Lianos T, Papakonstantinou P (2003) Modern migration in Greece: economic research. KEPE, Athens (in Greek)

Lianos T, Kanellopoulos K, Gregou M, Papakonstantinou P (2008) Estimation of the number of immigrants residing illegally in Greece. IMEPO, Athens (in Greek)

Logan JR (1978) Growth, politics and the stratification of places. Am J Sociol 84:404–416

Logan JR, Alba R, Leung S (1996) Minority access to white neighbourhoods: a multiregional comparison. Soc Forces 74:851–881

Malheiros J (2000) Urban restructuring and immigration in Lisbon. In: King R, Lazaridis G, Tsardanidis C (eds) Eldorado or fortress? Macmillan, London, pp 207–231

Malheiros JM, Vala F (2004) Immigration and city change: the Lisbon Metropolis at the turn of the twentieth century. J Ethnic Migr Stud 30(6):1065–1086

Maloutas T (2007) Segregation, social polarization and immigration in Athens during the 1990s: theoretical expectations and contextual difference. Int J Urban Reg Res 31(4):733–758

Massey DS (1985) Ethnic residential segregation: a theoretical synthesis and empirical review. Soc Soc Res 69(3):315–350

Massey DS, Denton NA (1985) Spatial assimilation as a socioeconomic outcome. Am Sociol Rev 50:94–106

Massey DS, Denton NA (1987) Trends in the residential segregation of Hispanics, blacks and Asians: 1970–1980. Am Sociol Rev 52:802–824

Massey DS, Denton NA (1988) The dimensions of residential segregation. Soc Forces 67:281–315

Morrill RL (1991) On the measure of spatial segregation. Geog Res Forum 11:25–36

Musterd S, Deurloo R (2002) Unstable immigrant concentrations in Amsterdam: spatial segregation and integration of newcomers. Housing Stud 17(3):487–503

Musterd S, Ostendorf W, Breebaart M (1998) Multi-ethnic metropolis: patterns and policies. Kluwer, London

Myers D, Liu CY (2005) The emerging dominance of immigrants in the US housing market 1970–2000. Urban Pol Res 23(3):347–365

OECD (2001) Trends in international migration. OECD, Paris

Openshaw S, Taylor P (1979) A million or so correlation coefficients: three experiments on the modifiable area unit problem. In: Wrigley N (ed) Statistical applications in the spatial sciences. Pion, London, pp 127–144

Pacione M (1996) Ethnic segregation in the European city. Geogr 81:120–132

Park RE (1926) The urban community as a spatial pattern and a moral order. In: Burgess EW (ed) The urban community. University of Chicago Press, Chicago, pp 21–31

Peach C (1996) Does Britain have ghettos? Trans Inst Br Geogr 21:216–235

Petsimeris P (1995) Une methode pour l' analyse de la division ethnique et sociale de l' espace intra-metropolitan du Grand Londres. L' Espace Geographique 1995-2:139–154

Psimmenos I (1995) Immigration from Balkans. Glorybook – Papazisis, Athens (in Greek)

Psimmenos I (1998) Creating places of social segregation: the case of unofficial Albanian immigrants in Athens city centre. In: Kasimati K (ed) Social segregation: the Greek experience. Gutenberg, Athens, pp 221–273 (in Greek)

Psimmenos I (2001) Immigration from the Balkans, social exclusion in Athens. Papazisis, Athens

Reardon FS, O' Sullivan D (2004) Measures of spatial segregation. Soc Methodol 34(1):121–162

Rovolis A, Tragaki A (2006) Ethnic characteristics and geographical distribution of immigrants in Greece. Eur Urban Reg Stud 13(2):99–111

Tripier M (1990) L'immigration dans la classe ouvriere en France. L' Harmattan, Paris

Ulrich R (1994) The impact of foreigners on the public purse. In: Spencer S (ed) Immigration as an economic asset: the German experience. Trentham Books, Stoke-on-Trent, pp 65–91

van Kempen R, Ozuekren AS (1998) Ethnic segregation in cities: new forms and explanations in a dynamic world. Urban Stud 35(10):1631–1656

Velentzas K, Kalogirou S, Karagianni H, Katsikas N, Papamichos M, Hatziprokopiou P, Chlomoudis K (1996) Housing market in Thessaloniki. Paratiritis, Thessaloniki

White MJ (1983) The measurement of spatial segregation. Am J Sociol 88:1008–1018

Wong WS (1993) Spatial indices of segregation. Urban Stud 30:559–572

Wong WS (1997) Spatial dependency of segregation indices. Can Geogr 41:128–136

Wong WS (2002) Spatial measures of segregation and GIS. Urban Geogr 23:85–92

Yinger J (1986) Measuring racial discrimination with fair housing audits: caught in the act. Am Econ Rev 76(5):881–893

Zang X, Hassan R (1996) Residential choices of immigrants in Australia. Int Migr 34(4):567–582

Printed by Publishers' Graphics LLC
MLSI130618.15.15.120